Machine Learning and Metaheuristic Computation

IEEE Press
445 Hoes Lane
Piscataway, NJ 08854

Machine Learning and Metaheuristic Computation

Erik Cuevas, Jorge Galvez, Omar Avalos, and Fernando Wario
University of Guadalajara, Mexico

IEEE Press
WILEY

Published by John Wiley & Sons, Inc., Hoboken, New Jersey.
Published simultaneously in Canada.

Library of Congress Cataloging-in-Publication Data Applied for:

Hardback ISBN: 9781394229642

Cover Design: Wiley
Cover Image: © Doris – Magic Artist/Shutterstock

Set in 9.5/12.5pt STIXTwoText by Straive, Chennai, India

Contents

About the Authors

Erik Cuevas is currently working as a professor in the Department of Electronics at the University of Guadalajara, Mexico. He completed his BE in electronics and communication from the University of Guadalajara in 1996, and his postgraduate degree ME in applied electronics from ITESO, Guadalajara, Mexico, in 1998. He received his PhD in artificial intelligence from Freie Universität Berlin, Germany, in 2007. Dr. Cuevas currently serves as an associate editor in *Applied Soft Computing, Applied Mathematical Modelling, Artificial Intelligence Review, International Journal of Machine Learning and Cybernetics, ISA Transactions, Neural Processing Letters,* and *Mathematics and Computers in Simulation*. His research interests include metaheuristics and evolutionary computation in a wide range of applications such as image processing and machine learning.

Jorge Galvez serves as a full-time professor within the Department of Innovation Based on Information and Knowledge at the University Center for Exact Sciences and Engineering (CUCEI) of the University of Guadalajara, Mexico. In 2011, he earned a Bachelor of Science degree in informatics. In 2015, he obtained a Master of Science degree in electronics and computing. In 2019, he completed his Doctor of Philosophy degree in electronics and computer science from Universidad de Guadalajara. Since 2019, he has been a member of the Mexican National Research System (SNII I). His research agenda includes machine learning, deep learning, evolutionary computation, computer vision, complex systems, and robotics. Additionally, he serves as an editor for the Computation and Informatics section of the journal *ReCIBE*, which is published by the University of Guadalajara.

Omar Avalos is a professor in the Department of Electronics at the University of Guadalajara, Mexico. In 2013, he completed the BS degree in Communications and Electronics, and the MSc and PhD degrees in electronics and computer science from the Universidad de Guadalajara in 2015 and 2019, respectively. During his formation, he participated in different projects such as the Autonomus-Mini in collaboration with the Freie Universität Berlin and the development of a humanoid robot, just to mention a few. He is a member of the Mexican National Research System (SNI I). His research interests include different applications of Artificial Intelligence in different engineering fields, such as biomedical applications, improvement of energy consumption, system identification, and image processing.

Fernando Wario is an associate professor at the University of Guadalajara, Mexico, and an associate researcher at the Institute for Cognitive Sciences and Technologies (ISTC) of the Italian National Research Council (CNR). Fernando earned his PhD in computer science from the Freie Universtität Berlin in 2018, funded by a German Academic Exchange Service (DAAD) scholarship. Previous to his PhD studies, Fernando earned an MSc in electronic and computer science engineering delivered by the Universidad de Guadalajara in 2010 and a Bachelor in electronic engineering from the same institution in 2005. The research interest of Fernando spans over computational ethology, computer vision, heuristic optimization, complex systems, and swarm intelligence.

Preface

Machine Learning and Metaheuristic Computation represent two rapidly expanding domains within the realm of artificial intelligence, each boasting a vast array of applications in computer science. Machine learning, on one hand, encompasses a variety of deterministic and statistical methodologies designed to extract and interpret information from data. This field primarily focuses on identifying and analyzing patterns, a process crucial for understanding complex datasets. Metaheuristic computation, conversely, deals with optimization techniques that leverage collective insights from multiple search agents. This approach is instrumental in enhancing the precision of locating optimal solutions for diverse problems. While machine learning and metaheuristic computation are traditionally associated with different scientific communities, they share a fundamental reliance on advanced computational paradigms. When integrated, these fields can effectively complement each other, mitigating their individual limitations and amplifying their strengths. This synergy not only bridges the gap between two distinct areas of study but also unlocks new potentials in artificial intelligence research and applications.

Metaheuristic schemes have increasingly been utilized to augment machine learning methods, capitalizing on the fact that many processes of machine learning can be considered as optimization problems. This synergy has catalyzed the rapid development of a variety of classifiers and data analysis techniques. The fusion of machine learning and metaheuristic approaches has led to significant advancements in the field, enabling more sophisticated and effective methods for data identification and analysis. Conversely, machine learning techniques have been instrumental in the design and enhancement of metaheuristic algorithms. During the execution of metaheuristic methods, a substantial amount of data, including agent positions and corresponding objective values, is generated. This data trove offers a wealth of information, often underutilized. However, the application of machine learning techniques to this data has opened new avenues. By analyzing and extracting latent insights from the operational data of metaheuristic methods, Machine learning can significantly enhance the efficiency and effectiveness of these algorithms. This interplay between machine learning and metaheuristic schemes exemplifies a virtuous cycle, where each field informs and improves the other, leading to more refined and powerful computational tools.

This book aims to serve as a vital bridge connecting the communities of machine learning and metaheuristic methods, addressing a significant knowledge gap between these two fields. For enthusiasts and practitioners in machine learning who may not be well-versed in metaheuristic computation, this book is an essential resource. It elucidates that metaheuristic techniques are not merely theoretical constructs but practical tools capable of addressing and solving substantial problems frequently encountered in the realm of machine learning. These insights are particularly beneficial for those looking to expand their toolkit beyond conventional machine learning methodologies. Conversely, for those immersed in the world of metaheuristic computation, the book offers a valuable perspective on how machine learning problems can be effectively reformulated as optimization tasks. This recontextualization is key for metaheuristic practitioners aiming to apply their expertise to the nuanced challenges of machine learning. Overall, the book strives to foster a mutual understanding and collaboration between these two communities, highlighting how their combined strengths can lead to groundbreaking advancements in the field of artificial intelligence.

This book stands out not only for its comprehensive coverage of the most pivotal methods and techniques in machine learning and metaheuristic approaches but also for its extensive inclusion of MATLAB code and practical implementations. This aspect is considered the cornerstone of the book's value. It acknowledges a crucial truth: even readers with a robust mathematical background may struggle to fully grasp a specific method or algorithm until they see it actualized in code. Implementations in the code serve to dissolve any ambiguities or uncertainties that might arise from theoretical descriptions alone, making the material significantly more accessible and clearer. This approach ensures that the learning process is not just theoretical, but also practical and intuitive. As readers progress through the book, moving from fundamental to more advanced methodologies, the computational focus – exemplified through the implemented code – aids in crystallizing their understanding of the different models. This not only reinforces their mathematical concepts but also provides a hands-on experience that is critical in comprehending and applying machine learning and metaheuristic strategies effectively.

This book uniquely positions itself not just as a reference text, but also as a comprehensive course, offering flexibility in how readers engage with its content. It is structured to allow random access, meaning readers can dive into specific chapters or themes as needed, without necessarily following a linear progression. Unlike other books that focus solely on theory and suggest that readers implement algorithms from scratch in exercises, this book takes a different approach. Drawing from our teaching experience, we've found that students learn more rapidly and effectively when they have access to existing code that they can modify and experiment with. This practical, hands-on methodology is central to our book's design.

Many books in the field of machine learning and metaheuristic optimization are crafted with an audience that has advanced training in mathematical sciences in mind. However, after a thorough review of several related texts, it became evident that there is a demand for a more inclusive approach that caters to a wider array of readers and students. Recognizing this gap, the proposed book aims to bridge it by offering a broader and less technically dense exploration of these subjects. While it covers many of the same topics found in other works, this book shifts the focus towards a more accessible presentation. Emphasis is placed on the description, implementation, and practical application of methods rather than delving deeply into the mathematical intricacies. This approach makes the book more approachable for those who may not have a strong background in mathematics, broadening its appeal and utility. It aims to demystify complex concepts and make the fascinating world of machine learning and metaheuristic optimization accessible to a more diverse readership, encouraging engagement and learning across a broader spectrum of individuals.

To start learning machine learning and metaheuristic methods can be overwhelming considering the great number of mathematical concepts and computational techniques. Some very practical books try to satisfy this question by providing chapters where they indicate how to use off-the-shelf recipes for toy problems. However, what happens if some assumptions of the black-box model are not fulfilled. Is it possible to trust its results? Under such conditions, it is necessary to modify or adapt the model. To do this, it is important that a book provides the conceptual tools to appreciate and identify the underlying mathematics. The objective of this book is to be in the middle point, which means to give a rigorous but accessible vision of most of the machine learning algorithms and the most popular approaches of metaheuristic optimization.

Despite the advanced mathematical concepts underpinning machine learning and metaheuristic methods, it is entirely feasible to optimize systems or train models without an in-depth understanding of matrix algebra and calculus. For numerous readers, engaging with machine learning and metaheuristic techniques through programming rather than through complex mathematical formulations presents a more achievable goal. This approach aligns precisely with one of the key objectives of this book: to utilize MATLAB as a means to inspire readers to seamlessly integrate machine learning and optimization systems into their work. The strategy is to introduce and incorporate mathematical concepts only as necessary, easing the reader into the theoretical aspects without overwhelming them from the outset. This methodology not only makes the subject matter more accessible but also demonstrates the practical application of these concepts, thereby demystifying the process and encouraging a broader audience to delve into the fascinating world of machine learning and metaheuristics with confidence and curiosity.

Written from a teaching perspective, this book is primarily designed to function as a comprehensive textbook for undergraduate and postgraduate students specializing in science, electrical engineering, or computational mathematics. Its content and structure make it highly suitable for a range of courses, including artificial intelligence, machine learning, electrical engineering, evolutionary computation, and metaheuristics. The book's utility extends beyond academic settings, as it also serves as a valuable reference for researchers in the machine learning and metaheuristic communities. The material, with its detailed yet accessible approach, is poised to enhance their knowledge and support their ongoing projects. Furthermore, the book is a significant resource for engineers and application developers. Recognizing the diverse needs and time constraints of professionals in these fields, the book is carefully structured to allow each chapter to be read independently. This feature enables readers to quickly access specific, relevant information, making it immensely practical for solving real-world industrial problems. Whether it is for academic purposes, research, or practical applications in various industries, this book offers a wealth of information that is easily navigable and highly applicable to a wide range of challenges and projects in the realms of machine learning and metaheuristics.

This book is organized into three distinct parts, each focusing on a crucial aspect of the interplay between machine learning and metaheuristic algorithms. The first part lays the foundation by discussing the main methods and algorithms that underpin both machine learning and metaheuristic approaches. This section serves as both an introduction and a deep dive into the fundamental concepts, providing readers with a solid understanding of the principles that guide these two areas of study. Moving forward, the second part shifts focus on machine learning techniques, specifically how they are applied within algorithms to enhance their search strategies. This part of the book is particularly insightful for those interested in how machine learning can be leveraged to optimize and refine the problem-solving processes inherent in algorithmic searches. Finally, the third section completes the circle by exploring the main algorithms and metaheuristic mechanisms that are employed to improve machine learning techniques. This includes a detailed examination of how metaheuristics can be tailored to improve the efficiency, accuracy, and overall performance of machine learning models. Together, these sections provide a comprehensive overview that not only demystifies complex concepts but also illustrates the synergistic potential of combining machine learning with metaheuristic algorithms to tackle a wide array of challenges in computational science and engineering.

The journey of writing this book was enriched and made possible by the invaluable contributions of numerous colleagues and students, each bringing forth a wealth of ideas and critical insights.

In these lines, we extend our deepest gratitude to our esteemed colleagues and the dedicated students at the University of Guadalajara. Their thorough evaluation and constructive criticism have been instrumental in shaping the content and direction of this work.

Erik Cuevas, Jorge Galvez, Omar Avalos, and Fernando Wario
University of Guadalajara, Mexico

23 June 2024

Acknowledgments

The journey of writing this book was enriched and made possible by the invaluable contributions of numerous colleagues and students, each bringing forth a wealth of ideas and critical insights. Their dedication and intellectual generosity have significantly enhanced the depth and quality of this work. In these lines, we extend our deepest gratitude to our esteemed colleagues and the dedicated students at the University of Guadalajara. Their rigorous evaluation and constructive criticism have been instrumental in shaping both the content and direction of this book. We are particularly grateful for their willingness to engage in meaningful dialogue, challenge assumptions, and provide diverse perspectives that have broadened our understanding and approach. We would also like to express our sincere appreciation to Nandhini Karuppiah, Victoria Bradshaw, and Aileen Storry for their exceptional efforts in the planning, development, and production of this book. Their hard work and commitment to excellence have been crucial in bringing this project to fruition.

Introduction

This book aims to serve as a significant link between the machine learning and metaheuristic methods communities, addressing the considerable knowledge gap between these two disciplines. Many books about machine learning and metaheuristic optimization have been written for readers with advanced mathematical backgrounds. However, the proposed book takes a different approach, providing a broader and less mathematically dense exploration of these topics. While this book covers many of the same subjects as other works, it focuses on a more accessible presentation. The emphasis is on describing, implementing, and applying methods in practical situations, rather than delving deeply into intricate mathematical concepts. This approach makes the book more suitable for individuals who may not have a strong background in mathematics, thus increasing its appeal and usefulness. The book aims to simplify complex ideas and make the fascinating world of machine learning and metaheuristic optimization accessible to a wide range of readers, encouraging engagement and learning across a diverse spectrum of individuals.

This book is distinguished not only by its comprehensive treatment of the most essential methods and techniques in machine learning and metaheuristic approaches but also by its extensive inclusion of MATLAB code and practical applications. This aspect is regarded as the cornerstone of the book's value proposition, acknowledging an important truth: even readers with a strong mathematical foundation may struggle to fully comprehend a specific method or algorithm until they witness its implementation in code. The inclusion of code serves to dispel any ambiguities or uncertainties that may arise from theoretical descriptions alone, making the material considerably more accessible and clearer.

This book, written from a teaching perspective, serves as an in-depth textbook for undergraduate and graduate students specializing in science, electrical engineering, or computational mathematics. Its content and structure make it suitable for a broad range of applications, such as artificial intelligence, machine learning, electrical engineering, evolutionary computation, and metaheuristics. The book's utility extends beyond academic settings, as it also serves as a valuable reference for researchers in machine learning and metaheuristic communities. The material, with its detailed yet accessible approach, is poised to enhance their knowledge and support ongoing projects. The book also serves as a significant resource for engineers and application developers, recognizing the diverse needs and time constraints of professionals in these fields. The book's structure allows each chapter to be read independently, enabling readers to quickly access specific relevant information, making it practical for solving real-world industrial problems. This book offers a wealth of information that is easily navigable and highly applicable to a wide range of challenges and projects in the realms of machine learning and metaheuristics, whether for academic purposes, research, or practical applications in various industries.

1

Fundamentals of Machine Learning

1.1 Introduction

In this chapter, we delve into the essential concepts of machine learning, aiming to offer a clear and detailed understanding of its key principles and approaches. We begin by exploring the basics, including data collection and preprocessing, and then advance to more complex topics such as choosing the right algorithms, training processes, and evaluating model performance. The chapter's structure methodically unpacks machine learning's complexities, ensuring that readers not only comprehend its theoretical foundations but also understand how to apply these concepts practically in diverse situations. This journey through machine learning will provide readers with a solid base of knowledge, encompassing critical areas like supervised and unsupervised learning, the importance of model optimization, and the pivotal role of data in creating precise and dependable models. This foundational understanding is crucial for anyone aspiring to explore machine learning more deeply or to effectively implement its techniques across various fields.

Machine learning (Alpaydin 2021) represents a fusion of disciplines, embodying the intersection and synergy of computer science, statistics, neurobiology, and control theory. This multidisciplinary field has emerged as a cornerstone in numerous domains, fundamentally altering the landscape of software programming. In the past, the pivotal question in computing was, "How to program a computer?" However, with the advent of machine learning, this query has evolved dramatically. Now, the question at the forefront is, "How will computers program themselves?" This shift signifies a profound change in our approach to computing, where the focus is on designing algorithms that enable machines to learn from and adapt to data, rather than just executing predefined instructions. This evolution not only expands the capabilities of computers but also reshapes our understanding of programming and problem-solving in the digital age.

Machine learning stands as a fundamental method that imparts computers with their own form of intelligence, mirroring the learning processes observed in humans. This field inherently interconnects with and draws parallels to the study and research of human learning. Just as the human brain and its complex network of neurons lay the groundwork for human insight and understanding, Artificial Neural Networks (ANNs) serve a similar role in the realm of computers. These ANNs form the crux of decision-making activities within machines, enabling them to process, analyze, and learn from data in a manner akin to human cognitive processes. This similarity underscores the deep, intrinsic relationship between machine learning and human learning, highlighting how machines are designed to emulate and learn from the intricate patterns of human intelligence and decision-making.

Machine Learning and Metaheuristic Computation, First Edition.
Erik Cuevas, Jorge Galvez, Omar Avalos, and Fernando Wario.

Machine learning enables us to discover models (Mahesh 2020) that describe a given set of data, essentially establishing a link between input variables and output variables within a system. This process often involves hypothesizing the presence of a mechanism responsible for the parametric generation of data. However, the precise values of these parameters are typically unknown and need to be inferred. To achieve this, machine learning utilizes a variety of statistical techniques, including Induction, Deduction, and Abduction. These methods collectively contribute to the process of understanding and interpreting the data. Induction allows for generalizing from specific instances to broader rules, Deduction involves applying general rules to specific instances, and Abduction aids in forming plausible hypotheses that explain the observed data. This interplay of techniques is crucial for developing accurate and reliable models that can effectively represent the underlying patterns and relationships within the data, as illustrated in Figure 1.1.

Induction, a key process in the realm of scientific inquiry, involves extracting general laws or principles from a specific set of observed data. This method stands in contrast to deduction, where the goal is to predict the value of specific variables based on pre-established general laws. Induction is foundational to the scientific method, serving as the primary mechanism through which general laws are derived. These laws, often articulated in mathematical language, are not assumed a priori but are instead developed through careful observation and analysis of phenomena. By observing patterns, trends, and relationships within the data, scientists use induction to formulate broad, overarching theories that can explain and predict a wide range of phenomena. This approach is central to the advancement of scientific knowledge, allowing for the conversion of discrete, individual observations into universally applicable laws and principles.

The process of observation in scientific and analytical contexts involves the measurement of various variables, leading to the acquisition of data that characterizes the observed phenomena. This data, rich in details and insights, forms the basis for developing models that can interpret and make sense of these observations. Once established, these models possess the capability to make predictions about new, unseen data. This entire procedure, where one starts with a collection of observations and progresses to making predictions for new scenarios, is known as inference. Inference is a fundamental component in many fields, particularly in statistics and machine learning, where it plays a crucial role in extrapolating from known data to predict future events, trends, or behaviors. It embodies the essence of learning from experience and applying that knowledge to new, often uncharted, situations.

Inductive learning, a fundamental approach in the realm of knowledge acquisition and machine learning, begins with observations derived from the surrounding environment. This method

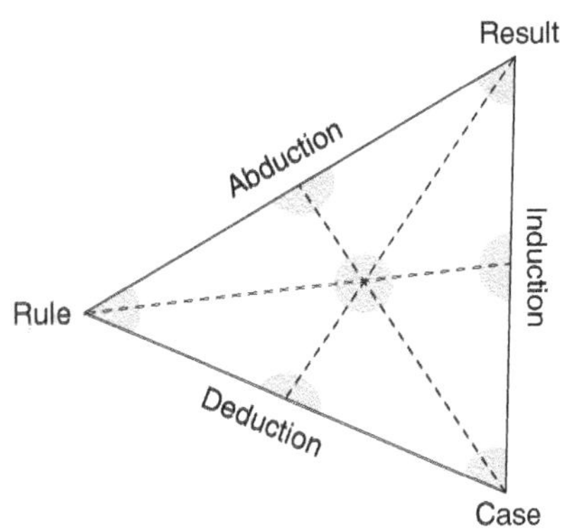

Figure 1.1 Peirce's triangle symbolizes a framework outlining the connections among various patterns of reasoning.

involves analyzing and understanding these observations to generalize and extract broader knowledge or patterns. The goal of inductive learning is to develop insights or models that are not only applicable to the initially observed cases but also hold validity for scenarios that have not yet been encountered. Essentially, it's a process of learning from specific instances and then applying that learning to make predictions or inferences about future, unseen situations. While there's an inherent uncertainty in assuming that these generalizations will always apply to new cases, the strength of inductive learning lies in its ability to adapt and learn from ongoing experiences, constantly refining its understanding and predictions. Thus, inductive learning represents a hopeful endeavor to extrapolate from known data to the unknown, continuously expanding the frontiers of knowledge and prediction.

Inductive learning, a key methodology in understanding and interpreting data, can be broadly categorized into two distinct types:

- **Learning by Example** (Menon et al. 2013): This approach is centered around gaining knowledge from a specific set of examples. It involves analyzing "positive examples," which are instances embodying the concept that needs to be learned, and "negative examples," which are instances that do not represent the concept. By examining these examples, the learning process discerns the defining characteristics of the concept, distinguishing what qualifies as an instance and what does not. This method is particularly prevalent in supervised learning scenarios in machine learning, where the model learns to classify or predict outcomes based on labeled training data.
- **Learning Regularity** (Gauci and Stanley 2008): Unlike learning by example, learning regularity does not focus on a specific concept. Instead, the objective here is to identify patterns, trends, or common characteristics within the provided instances. This type of learning looks for underlying regularities or consistencies in the data that might not be immediately apparent. It's more about uncovering hidden structures or relationships within the data rather than classifying or categorizing it. This form of inductive learning is often used in unsupervised learning scenarios, where the data does not come with predefined labels or categories.

Both types of inductive learning are crucial for understanding complex datasets and are widely applied in various fields, from artificial intelligence to statistical analysis, each serving different purposes but under the same structure of learning from and making inferences based on observed data.

Machine learning systems often outperform traditional algorithms in various complex scenarios, raising a natural question: Why is this the case? The reasons behind the limitations of traditional algorithms are multifaceted:

Difficulty in Problem Formalization: Traditional algorithms require explicit programming based on a well-defined set of rules. However, many real-world problems are not easily formalized into computational steps. For instance, most people can recognize a friend's voice but would struggle to describe the exact computational process to identify the speaker from a sound recording. This gap between human cognitive abilities and algorithmic description is where machine learning excels, as it learns to perform tasks without explicit programming.

High Number of Variables at Play: In problems like character recognition from documents, the sheer number of variables involved makes the task daunting for traditional algorithms. Specifying all potentially relevant parameters is not only complex but may also vary significantly

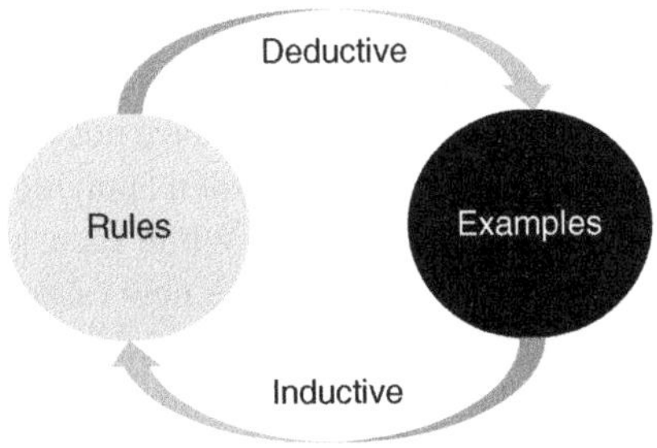

Figure 1.2 Representation of deductive and inductive learning in the context of machine learning.

across different contexts or languages. Machine learning, on the other hand, can handle high-dimensional data and learn from it, making it more adaptable to such complex scenarios.

Lack of Theory: Some domains, such as predicting financial market performance, lack precise mathematical laws or theories. Traditional algorithms often depend on established theories or models, which, when absent, can lead to their failure. Machine learning can work around this by identifying patterns and making predictions based on data, without relying on pre-existing theoretical frameworks.

Need for Customization: Traditional algorithms typically don't account for individual user preferences, which can vary widely. What is considered an important feature by one user might be irrelevant to another. Machine learning systems, particularly those involving personalization, can learn and adapt to individual user preferences, distinguishing between what is interesting and uninteresting for each user.

In summary, the flexibility, adaptability, and ability to learn from data make machine learning systems more effective in scenarios where traditional algorithms struggle due to complexity, lack of theory, and the need for customization.

In the context of machine learning, deductive and inductive learning represent two fundamental approaches to how algorithms process and learn from data. Deductive learning is a top-down approach, where learning begins with a general theory or set of rules and then applies these to specific instances. In this method, the algorithm uses pre-existing knowledge or hypotheses to make predictions or decisions, following a logical progression from the general to the specific. It's akin to applying a known formula to solve a new problem. Inductive learning, on the other hand, is a bottom-up approach. It starts with specific examples or data points and works to identify general patterns or rules. This approach does not begin with a preconceived theory but rather builds one based on the observation of individual instances. Machine learning models using inductive learning, like neural networks, are particularly adept at recognizing patterns in complex data sets and making predictions for new, unseen data. Both approaches are integral to the field of machine learning, each offering distinct ways of interpreting data and making decisions. Figure 1.2 shows a representation of deductive and inductive learning in the context of machine learning.

1.2 Different Types of Machine Learning Approaches

The effectiveness of machine learning largely hinges on the sophistication and continual evolution of its algorithms. These algorithms can be broadly categorized into different types based on the nature of the learning signal or the type of feedback the system uses. Understanding these categories is key to appreciating the versatility and power of machine learning:

- **Supervised Learning**: In supervised learning (Muhammad and Yan 2015), the algorithm is trained on a labeled dataset, where each input data point is paired with a corresponding output (or label). The primary objective is to generate a function that maps inputs to desired outputs. This approach is akin to learning with a teacher who provides examples of correct input-output pairs. The algorithm uses these examples to learn the underlying structure of the data and to make predictions or decisions for new, unseen data. Supervised learning is extensively used for tasks like classification and regression, where the goal is to construct predictive models.
- **Unsupervised Learning**: Unlike supervised learning, unsupervised learning (Celebi and Aydin 2016) algorithms deal with input data that is not labeled. The goal here is to explore the structure of the data and identify patterns or features that can describe the data's underlying characteristics. Since there are no specific output variables to predict or classify, unsupervised learning is more about discovering hidden structures in the data. This approach is fundamental for tasks like clustering, dimensionality reduction, and associative rule learning. A typical application of unsupervised learning can be seen in search engines, where algorithms work to organize and categorize vast amounts of data without explicit human intervention.
- **Reinforcement Learning**: Reinforcement learning (Sugiyama 2015) is a distinct paradigm where the learning process is driven by interactions with an environment. In this approach, an algorithm, typically referred to as an agent, learns to make decisions by performing actions and observing the results of these actions. The algorithm receives feedback in the form of rewards or penalties, which guide it towards the most effective strategies over time. The unique aspect of reinforcement learning is its focus on sequential decision-making, where the outcomes of previous actions influence future decisions. This method is widely used in dynamic environments, like game playing, robotics, and navigation, where the algorithm must continually adapt to changing conditions.

Each of these machine learning approaches offers a unique way of understanding and interacting with data, and they are chosen based on the specific requirements and constraints of the problem at hand. Their diversity and adaptability are what make machine learning a powerful and versatile tool across various domains.

Figure 1.3 illustrates a hierarchical classification of machine learning approaches, categorizing them into three primary types: supervised learning, unsupervised learning, and reinforcement learning. Each of these categories is further distinguished by their key methodologies or applications. Supervised learning, which involves training algorithms on labeled datasets to predict outcomes or classify data, is characterized mainly by techniques like regression and classification. These methods enable the algorithm to establish a relationship between input and output variables for predictive modeling or to categorize data into different classes based on learned patterns. Unsupervised learning, on the other hand, focuses on identifying patterns or structures in unlabeled data, primarily through clustering. Clustering algorithms group data based on similarities or patterns without prior knowledge of what these groups might represent. Finally, reinforcement learning, a distinct approach that emphasizes learning through interaction with an environment, is widely recognized for its application in deep learning. In this context, deep learning models, particularly those involving neural networks, are trained to make a series of

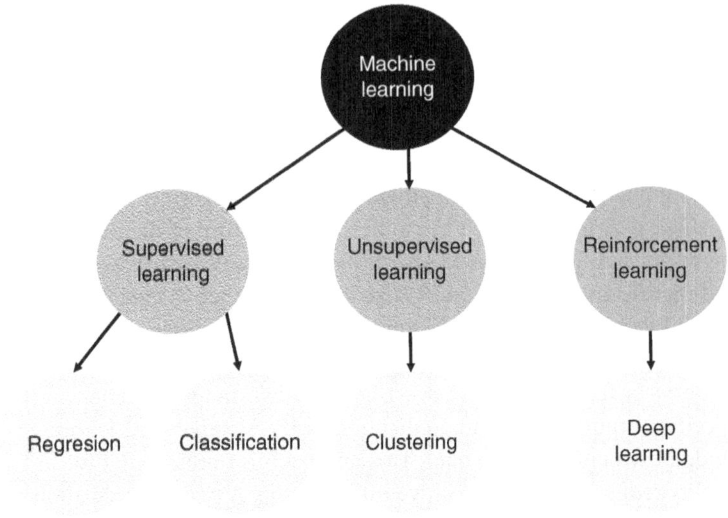

Figure 1.3 Hierarchical classification of machine learning approaches.

decisions, improving their performance based on the feedback received in the form of rewards or penalties. Each of these approaches represents a unique facet of machine learning, demonstrating the field's versatility and breadth in solving various types of problems.

1.3 Supervised Learning

Supervised learning (Muhammad and Yan 2015) is a pivotal technique in machine learning, designed to enable computer systems to automatically solve relevant tasks. The process begins by defining a set of input data, denoted as set I, which usually consists of vectors. This input data represents the information the system will learn from. Next, the set of desired output data is established, referred to as set O. These outputs are the correct answers or results that the system aims to predict or classify based on the inputs. The core of supervised learning involves defining a function f, which effectively maps each element of the input set I to its corresponding element in the output set O. This mapping is crucial as it forms the basis of the learning process. The combination of input data with their corresponding outputs constitutes what is known as a training set. This training set is used to "teach" the machine learning model, allowing it to learn the relationship between inputs and outputs. The model undergoes a training phase where it adjusts its parameters to minimize errors in its predictions or classifications. This entire workflow of supervised learning, from input data to the definition of the function and the creation of a training set, is succinctly illustrated in the subsequent Figure 1.4, providing a clear visual representation of how this process unfolds.

Supervised learning algorithms operate on a fundamental premise given a sufficient number of examples; they can develop a derived function f_B that closely approximates a target function f_A. This approximation is key to the success of these algorithms. If the derived function f_B accurately approximates the desired function f_A, it should be able to produce output responses that are similar to those generated by f_A when presented with new input data. The underlying concept here is that similar inputs will lead to similar outputs. This assumption, although not universally valid in the real world, holds true in most scenarios.

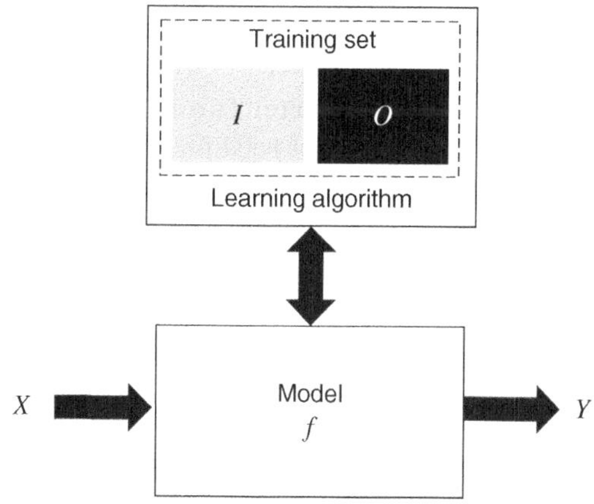

Figure 1.4 Structure for supervised learning.

However, the efficacy of supervised learning algorithms is heavily contingent on the quality and quantity of the input data they are trained on. If the training set is too small, the algorithm may not "experience" enough variety in the data to make accurate predictions or classifications for new, unseen inputs. This is akin to having an inadequate learning experience. On the other hand, an excessively large training set can lead to its own set of challenges. Processing a vast amount of inputs can slow down the algorithm, and the derived function B might become overly complex, potentially leading to issues like overfitting, where the model performs well on the training data but poorly on new data.

Therefore, the balance and quality of the input data are crucial. They determine not just the performance of the algorithm in terms of speed and efficiency but also its ability to generalize well from the training data to real-world situations. This delicate balance between the quantity of data and the complexity of the derived function is a critical aspect of designing and implementing effective supervised learning algorithms.

Experience with supervised learning algorithms reveals a significant sensitivity to noise in the data. Even a small amount of incorrect or misleading data can severely compromise the reliability of the entire system. This susceptibility means that the presence of anomalies or errors in the training set can lead the algorithm to make incorrect predictions or decisions, impacting its overall effectiveness. Supervised learning also allows for the categorization of problems based on the nature of the output data. When the output is categorical, such as determining whether a data point belongs or does not belong to a certain class, the task is known as a classification problem. This involves categorizing data into discrete groups or classes. On the other hand, if the output is a continuous real value within a certain range, the task is termed a regression problem. In regression, the algorithm predicts a continuous quantity, such as a price or a temperature. This distinction between classification and regression is fundamental in supervised learning, guiding the choice of algorithms and methods used to tackle different types of predictive modeling tasks. Understanding whether a problem is a classification or regression problem is crucial for applying the appropriate techniques and achieving accurate results.

Supervised learning, a branch of machine learning, can be innovatively applied to enhance metaheuristic methods. Metaheuristics are high-level problem-solving frameworks designed to guide underlying heuristics in exploring and exploiting the search space of complex optimization problems. Integrating supervised learning with metaheuristics creates a synergy that can significantly improve the performance and efficiency of these algorithms. Here's how supervised learning can be applied in this context:

- **Parameter Tuning**: Metaheuristic algorithms often come with several parameters that need fine-tuning for optimal performance. Supervised learning can be used to learn the best parameter settings for a given problem. By training a model on different instances of the problem with various parameter configurations and their respective performances, the algorithm can predict the most effective parameters for new instances.
- **Selection of Heuristics**: In many cases, a metaheuristic framework can use different heuristics or strategies at different stages of the search process. Supervised learning can help in dynamically selecting the most appropriate heuristic based on the current state of the search. This selection is done by training a model on historical data that maps states of the problem to the most effective heuristics.
- **Solution Improvement**: Supervised learning can be employed to refine the solutions generated by metaheuristics. For instance, a predictive model can be trained on high-quality solutions to learn their characteristics. This model can then guide the search process toward regions of the search space that are more likely to contain high-quality solutions.
- **Predictive Termination**: Often, it's challenging to determine when a metaheuristic algorithm should stop searching for a better solution. Supervised learning models can be trained to predict the likelihood of finding a significantly better solution based on the current state of the search, thereby optimizing the computational effort.
- **Learning Problem-Specific Characteristics**: For problems that have various instances with different characteristics, supervised learning can help in understanding these variations. This knowledge can then be used to adapt the metaheuristic strategy to be more effective for specific types of instances.

By combining the adaptive and predictive capabilities of supervised learning with the exploratory strength of metaheuristics, these methods can become more robust, efficient, and effective in solving a wide range of optimization problems. This integration marks a significant step towards creating intelligent systems that can learn from past experiences and adapt their strategies accordingly.

1.4 Unsupervised Learning

Unsupervised learning (Celebi and Aydin 2016), a distinct branch of machine learning, focuses on extracting information automatically from databases without prior knowledge or labels about the data. This process stands in contrast to supervised learning, where models are trained with data that is clearly labeled or categorized. In unsupervised learning, there's no predefined information about the classes to which the data points belong or any specific output associated with a given input. The primary objective is to explore the data and identify inherent structures or patterns. One common goal is to discover groups or clusters of data points that share similar characteristics, a process known as clustering. These algorithms work by identifying commonalities and differences within the data, grouping similar items together while separating dissimilar ones.

Unsupervised learning algorithms have a wide array of applications, with search engines being a notable example. In the context of search engines, these algorithms use one or more keywords

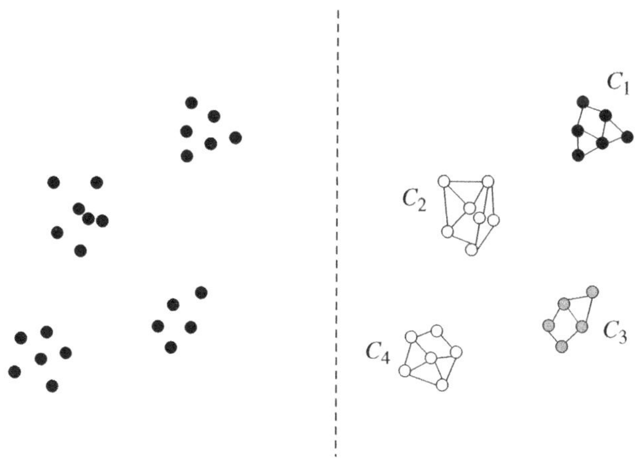

Figure 1.5 Effects of the clustering process under unsupervised learning.

to generate a relevant list of links or results. They analyze vast amounts of web data, understanding and categorizing content, to provide users with links that are most pertinent to their search queries. This capability to sift through and make sense of large, unstructured datasets without explicit guidance makes unsupervised learning an invaluable tool in areas where understanding complex patterns and relationships within data is crucial.

The effectiveness of unsupervised learning algorithms hinges on their ability to extract useful information from databases. The core principle of these algorithms is to analyze and compare data, searching for patterns in the form of similarities or differences among data points. Central to this process is the set of features that describe each example in the dataset. These features, which can vary widely depending on the nature of the data and the specific problem at hand, serve as the basis for the algorithms' analysis. By examining these features, unsupervised learning algorithms can group data points with similar characteristics or identify outliers that differ significantly from the rest. The value of these algorithms lies in their capacity to uncover hidden structures or groupings within the data, which might not be apparent without this analysis. The absence of pre-assigned labels or classifications means that the algorithms must rely entirely on the inherent properties of the data, making the choice and quality of features critical for the successful application of unsupervised learning techniques. This focus on feature-based analysis makes unsupervised learning particularly well suited for exploratory data analysis, pattern recognition, and anomaly detection.

Figure 1.5 effectively demonstrates the application and use case of clustering within the field of unsupervised learning. Clustering is a technique where data is sorted into various groups or clusters. The strategy here is to ensure that data points within the same group are as close or similar to each other as possible while maintaining a maximized distance or dissimilarity between different groups. In the context of Figure 1.5, the left portion of the image presents the input data as it is initially fed into the algorithm, likely appearing as a scattered, unstructured collection of data points. The right side of the figure, however, reveals the outcome post the application of the clustering algorithm. Here, the data is visibly segmented into four distinct groups. This visual comparison effectively illustrates the transformation from a disorganized set of data points to a structured arrangement where similar data are grouped together, highlighting the core functionality and efficacy of clustering in unsupervised learning. The before-and-after representation in Figure 1.5 not only clarifies the process of clustering but also underscores the value of unsupervised learning in discovering inherent patterns and relationships within a dataset.

Unsupervised learning, particularly clustering, can play a crucial role in enhancing metaheuristic methods. Metaheuristics are algorithms used for solving complex optimization problems where traditional methods may not be effective or feasible. The application of unsupervised learning and clustering in metaheuristics can lead to more efficient search strategies, better solution quality, and an improved understanding of the problem space. Here's how these techniques can be integrated:

- **Initial Solution Generation**: Clustering can be used to analyze the structure of the problem space and identify regions that are likely to contain high-quality solutions. By clustering similar solutions or problem instances, metaheuristic algorithms can focus their search on the most promising areas of the solution space, improving efficiency and effectiveness.
- **Adaptive Operator Selection**: In metaheuristics, different operators (like mutation, crossover, etc., in genetic algorithms) can be applied during the search process. Clustering can be used to group similar solutions and apply the most suitable operator for each cluster. This adaptive approach can enhance the search process by tailoring operations to specific characteristics of the solution space.
- **Diversity Maintenance**: One of the challenges in metaheuristics is to maintain diversity in the set of potential solutions to avoid premature convergence to suboptimal solutions. Clustering can help in identifying and maintaining diverse solutions by ensuring that different clusters of solutions are represented in the population.
- **Problem Decomposition**: For very complex problems, unsupervised learning can be used to decompose the problem into smaller, more manageable sub-problems. By clustering similar components or aspects of the problem, metaheuristics can solve each sub-problem separately or in a coordinated manner, improving overall solution quality and reducing computational complexity.
- **Performance Analysis**: After the metaheuristic has been run, unsupervised learning can be applied to the obtained solutions to understand the distribution of solutions and the characteristics of high-performing solutions. This analysis can provide insights for further refining the metaheuristic algorithm.
- **Hybrid Algorithms**: Unsupervised learning and clustering can be integrated into metaheuristic algorithms to create hybrid approaches. For example, a clustering algorithm can be used to analyze initial data and set parameters for a genetic algorithm, or to select between different metaheuristic strategies during the search process.

In summary, unsupervised learning, especially clustering, can be effectively applied in various stages of metaheuristic methods, from initial solution generation to post-optimization analysis. This integration can lead to more targeted searches, better handling of solution diversity, and deeper insights into the nature of the optimization problem, ultimately enhancing the performance of metaheuristic algorithms.

1.5 Reinforcement Learning

Reinforcement learning (Sugiyama 2015) is a type of machine learning that focuses on developing algorithms capable of learning and adapting to changes in their environment. This technique is grounded in the concept of learning through interaction, where the algorithm, often termed as an agent, makes choices and receives feedback from the environment in the form of stimuli. These stimuli are essentially rewards or penalties based on the actions taken by the algorithm. When the algorithm makes a correct or beneficial choice, it receives a reward (or premium), whereas an incorrect or undesirable choice results in a penalty. The overarching goal of a system employing reinforcement learning is to maximize the cumulative reward over time. This is achieved by the algorithm continuously refining its strategy or policy to make better decisions based on the outcomes of its past actions. Through this trial-and-error learning process, the algorithm gradually learns the optimal set of actions to take in various situations to achieve the best possible result. This method is particularly powerful in scenarios where the right course of action is not known a priori and must be discovered through interaction with the environment.

In supervised learning, the presence of a "teacher" is a defining characteristic, where the learning system is guided by clearly defined correct outputs for given inputs. This method, often described as "learning with a teacher," involves training the algorithm using a dataset where each input (or feature) is explicitly paired with the correct output (or label). However, this ideal scenario is not always feasible. In many real-world applications, the information available for training is only qualitative, and often binary in nature, representing simple dichotomies like right/wrong or success/failure. This kind of data provides a more basic form of guidance compared to detailed labels, posing a challenge in effectively training the system. The algorithm must learn from this limited feedback, which offers less granularity and specificity about the desired output. Consequently, the learning process in such situations relies heavily on the ability of the algorithm to interpret and learn from these binary or qualitative cues to make accurate predictions or decisions. This approach, while more challenging than learning with explicit labels, is crucial in situations where detailed labeled data is not available or practical to obtain.

The information used in the context of reinforcement learning is known as reinforcement signals. These signals are pivotal in guiding the learning process of the algorithm, or agent, but they differ significantly from the detailed feedback provided in supervised learning. In reinforcement learning, the system provides feedback in the form of rewards or penalties based on the actions taken by the agent. However, it does not offer explicit guidance on how the agent should update its behavior or internal parameters, such as weights, to improve its performance. This lack of direct instruction means that traditional methods like defining a cost function or calculating a gradient, commonly used in supervised learning, are not applicable.

The primary goal of the system in reinforcement learning is to develop "smart" agents – algorithms that possess the machinery to learn from their experiences. These agents must figure out the best course of action or policy through trial and error, gradually refining their strategies based on the cumulative feedback received from their environment. The challenge lies in the agent's ability to interpret reinforcement signals and adjust its actions to maximize the long-term reward, often without a clear or immediate indication of the best path forward. This process requires sophisticated learning mechanisms that enable the agent to make connections between actions and outcomes over time, leading to the development of intelligent behaviors that are adapted to the specific nuances of the environment in which the agent operates.

Figure 1.6 depicts a generalized representation of a system utilizing reinforcement learning. At the heart of this system is an agent, whose role is to experiment with various actions in a somewhat random manner, with the goal of understanding their impact on the system. The primary aim here is to discern whether a particular action leads to the desired effect within the context of the system's environment. The response of the environment to each action taken by the agent is communicated through a reward signal. This signal is crucial as it encodes the effectiveness of the

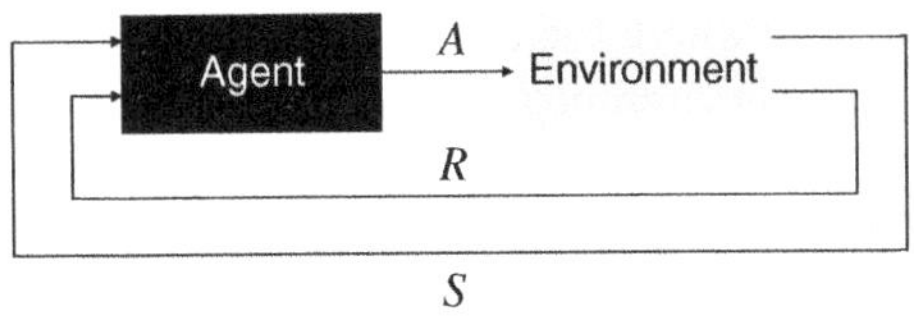

Figure 1.6 Generalized representation of a system utilizing reinforcement learning.

action – indicating whether the action had a positive (rewarding) or negative (penalizing) effect. Moreover, the evaluation and evolution of the system are understood in terms of states. The system exists in a particular state at any given time, and the objective of the agent's actions is to transition the system from its current state to a more desirable state in each iteration. This process involves a continuous cycle of action, feedback (via the reward signal), and adaptation, where the agent learns and refines its strategy based on the outcomes of its actions. The ultimate goal is for the agent to develop an understanding of which actions lead to the most favorable states, thereby maximizing the cumulative reward over time. This iterative learning and adaptation process, driven by the interaction between the agent and the environment and guided by the reward signal, is the essence of reinforcement learning as captured in Figure 1.6.

Reinforcement learning can be effectively applied to enhance metaheuristic methods, which are high-level strategies used for solving complex optimization problems. The integration of reinforcement learning into metaheuristics introduces a dynamic and adaptive learning component that can significantly improve the efficiency and effectiveness of these algorithms. Here's how this integration can work:

- **Dynamic Strategy Selection**: Metaheuristic algorithms often involve multiple strategies or operators (e.g., mutation, crossover in genetic algorithms, or local search strategies in simulated annealing). Reinforcement learning can be employed to dynamically select the most appropriate strategy based on the current state of the search. The reinforcement learning agent learns which strategies yield the best results in different scenarios, optimizing the search process over time.
- **Adaptive Parameter Tuning**: Many metaheuristic algorithms have parameters that need to be fine-tuned for optimal performance. Reinforcement learning can adaptively tune these parameters during the search process. By receiving feedback on the performance of the algorithm, the reinforcement learning agent can adjust parameters in real-time to improve efficiency and solution quality.
- **Learning from Past Searches**: Reinforcement learning can utilize the history of past search processes to inform current or future searches. This involves analyzing past solutions and search trajectories to identify patterns or strategies that led to successful outcomes, which can then be applied to new optimization problems.
- **Balancing Exploration and Exploitation**: One of the key challenges in metaheuristics is balancing exploration (searching new areas of the solution space) and exploitation (deepening the search around promising solutions). Reinforcement learning can help in making intelligent decisions about when to explore and when to exploit, based on the feedback received from the environment.
- **Automating Heuristic Selection**: In complex optimization problems, selecting the right heuristic can be crucial. Reinforcement learning can automate this

selection process by learning which heuristics work best for different types of problems or different stages of the problem-solving process.

- **Termination Criteria Optimization**: Deciding when to stop the search is another challenge in metaheuristics. Reinforcement learning can be used to develop intelligent termination criteria based on the likelihood of finding improved solutions, thus saving computational resources and time.

By applying reinforcement learning to metaheuristics, the algorithms can become more self-aware and adaptable, capable of learning from their environment and past experiences to make smarter decisions. This approach leads to a more efficient search process, potentially yielding better solutions to complex optimization problems.

1.6 Which Algorithm to Apply?

In the previous sections, we delved into the diverse landscape of machine learning algorithms, gaining an understanding of the foundational principles behind different techniques such as supervised, unsupervised, and reinforcement learning. Each of these methods offers unique approaches and tools for tackling various data-driven tasks. Having acquired this foundational knowledge, we now face a critical and often challenging question: "What is the right algorithm for my needs?" This query is pivotal in the journey of applying machine learning effectively. The answer depends on several factors, including the nature and structure of the data, the specific problem or task at hand, the desired outcome, and the computational resources available. For instance, if you have a well-defined task with labeled data, supervised learning might be the go-to choice. For exploratory data analysis or when dealing with unlabeled data, unsupervised learning, especially clustering, could be more appropriate. If the task involves making a series of decisions or learning from interactions within an environment, reinforcement learning might be the ideal fit. Ultimately, selecting the right algorithm is about aligning the strengths and capabilities of these techniques with the specific requirements and constraints of the problem you are aiming to solve.

Choosing the right machine learning algorithm for a specific task is a nuanced decision that often boils down to the broad but accurate answer: "It depends." The factors influencing this decision are varied and critical. Primarily, it depends on the characteristics of the data available: the size of the dataset (large or small), the quality (is it clean or noisy, well-structured or unstructured?), and the type of data (labeled or unlabeled, categorical or continuous). The choice also hinges on the specific goals of the analysis – whether the aim is to classify data, predict outcomes, discover patterns, or something else entirely. Additionally, the way the algorithm is formulated and translated into computer instructions plays a role, as some algorithms may be more complex and computationally demanding than others. Time constraints are another vital factor; some algorithms require lengthy periods for training and fine-tuning, which may not be feasible under tight deadlines. It's important to recognize that there is no universally best method that suits all situations. The diversity of machine learning algorithms means that each has its strengths and ideal use cases. Therefore, the most effective way to determine if a particular algorithm is suitable for your needs is through experimentation: applying it to your data, evaluating its performance, and iterating as needed. This hands-on approach is often the most reliable path to finding the algorithm that best aligns with your specific requirements and constraints.

To determine the most suitable machine learning algorithm for our specific needs, a preliminary analysis is a crucial first step. This process begins by thoroughly examining what we currently possess – the data. Understanding the size, quality, nature, and intricacies of our dataset is fundamental. Are we dealing with large or small datasets? Is the data clean or noisy, structured or unstructured, labeled or unlabeled? Next, we consider the tools at our disposal – the algorithms. Each algorithm has its strengths, weaknesses, and unique requirements, ranging from computational resources to the level of expertise needed for effective implementation. Lastly, we must clearly define our objectives – the results we aim to achieve with our machine learning project. Are we looking to predict outcomes, classify data, uncover hidden patterns, or something else? Defining clear objectives helps in aligning our choices with our end goals. By assessing these three critical aspects – data, algorithms, and objectives – we can gain valuable insights that guide us in choosing a path that best fits our specific circumstances and requirements. This informed approach allows us to narrow down our options and focus on strategies that offer the most promise for our unique situation.

When approaching a machine learning problem, starting with the data we have can lead to a clear classification of the type of problem and subsequently guide us to the appropriate algorithmic approach. This classification can be based on either the nature of the input or the expected output of the model (Gollapudi 2016).

Classifying Based on Input:

- **Supervised Learning**: If we can label the input data with corresponding outputs, then we're dealing with a supervised learning problem. This approach is suitable for tasks where the relationship between input data and output labels needs to be learned.
- **Unsupervised Learning**: In cases where we cannot label the input data, but our goal is to understand or uncover the underlying structure of the data, it falls under unsupervised learning. This method is ideal for discovering hidden patterns or groupings in the data.
- **Reinforcement Learning**: If the objective is to optimize an outcome or a function through interactions with an environment, then it's a reinforcement learning problem. This approach is about learning the best actions to take in different states to maximize a reward or achieve a specific goal.

Classifying Based on Output:

- **Regression**: If the output of the model is a numerical value (continuous and quantifiable), the problem is a regression one. Regression models predict quantities or magnitudes.
- **Classification**: When the model's output is a class or category, it's a classification problem. In this scenario, the model is used to categorize input data into predefined labels.
- **Clustering**: If the output is about grouping the input data into sets based on their features or characteristics, without pre-existing labels, then we are looking at a clustering problem. This is typically used to find natural groupings in the data.

By analyzing our data and clearly defining our problem in terms of input and output, we can more effectively choose the right machine learning approach, be it supervised, unsupervised, reinforcement learning, regression, classification, or clustering. This preliminary classification plays a critical role in guiding us towards the algorithm most likely to succeed in our specific context.

Once the problem is classified, the next step is to analyze the available tools suitable for addressing this specific issue. This involves identifying the applicable algorithms and focusing our efforts on the methods needed to implement these tools effectively. The selection of algorithms is determined by the nature of the problem, whether it's supervised, unsupervised, or reinforcement learning, and further, whether it involves regression, classification, or clustering.

After pinpointing the relevant algorithms, the crucial phase of performance evaluation begins. This is achieved by applying the selected algorithms to the datasets at our disposal. The application of these algorithms allows us to gather empirical data on their effectiveness and efficiency in handling the problem.

The evaluation process involves using a set of carefully chosen criteria to assess each algorithm's performance. These criteria could include accuracy, precision, recall, computational efficiency, scalability, and robustness against overfitting or noisy data, among others. The comparison of these metrics across different algorithms provides valuable insights into which algorithm performs best under specific conditions and constraints.

This systematic approach of applying, testing, and comparing helps in determining the most suitable algorithm for the problem at hand. It's a methodical process that involves both theoretical understanding and practical experimentation, ensuring a well-rounded evaluation of the tools' capabilities in real-world scenarios.

1.7 Recommendation to Build a Machine Learning Model

Once the decision is made on which algorithm to apply to our data, it's time to roll up our sleeves and get to work. However, before diving into the practical aspects, it's essential to thoughtfully plan and structure the workflow. Developing an application that incorporates machine learning involves a series of well-defined steps to ensure the process is efficient, effective, and yields the desired results.

The machine learning workflow is a structured process that typically involves seven key steps (Forsyth 2019), as likely depicted in Figure 1.7. It begins with (1) collecting the data, where relevant information is gathered for analysis. The next step is (2) preparing the data, which involves cleaning and formatting the data for use in machine learning models. This is followed by (3) performing data exploration, a crucial phase where patterns and insights are drawn from the data through various analytical techniques. The fourth step is (4) training the learning algorithm, where the model is built and taught to make predictions or classifications. Subsequently, (5) testing the model is conducted to evaluate its performance on unseen data. The sixth step, (6) evaluating the model, extends this assessment to real-world scenarios to ascertain the model's practical utility. The process culminates in (7) improving the model, where refinements and optimizations are made based on the evaluation outcomes. Each of these steps is integral to the development of a successful machine learning model, with Figure 1.7 likely providing a visual guide to this comprehensive process. All these operations will be described in detail below.

1. **The Collection of Data** is the foundational step in any machine learning project, as the entire analysis and subsequent insights are driven by this data. One might wonder about the origins of such data, which can be quite diverse. Often, data is acquired through extensive and meticulous procedures. This could involve measurement campaigns in various scientific or industrial settings, where data is gathered through sensors or instruments. Alternatively, data might be collected through more human-centric methods such as face-to-face interviews, surveys, or questionnaires, especially in fields like market research or social sciences.

   Regardless of the source, the collected data is systematically compiled into a database. This organized accumulation of data is crucial as it serves as the raw material from which knowledge and insights are extracted through analysis. The integrity, relevance, and quality of this data directly influence the effectiveness of the machine learning models developed from it.

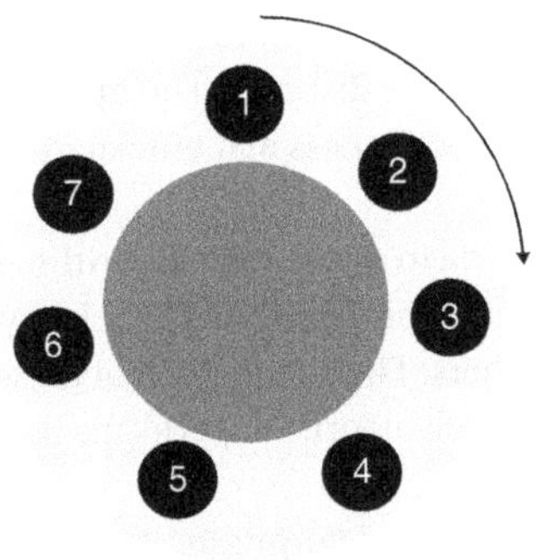

Figure 1.7 Visual guide to the comprehensive process of machine learning. The numbers represent operations that are described in the text.

For those who do not have specific data collection requirements, or to save on time and resources, utilizing publicly available datasets is a practical alternative. These datasets provide a rich and diverse range of data that can be used for various machine learning applications. A notable resource in this regard is the UCI Machine Learning Repository, which houses a comprehensive collection of datasets across different domains. This repository is a valuable asset for practitioners and researchers in machine learning, offering a wide array of data for experimentation and analysis. The accessibility of such resources greatly facilitates the data collection process, especially for those new to the field or working on projects where primary data collection is not feasible.

2. **Preparing the Data**: Having collected the data, the next crucial step in the machine learning workflow is data preparation, a phase that ensures the data is in a suitable format for the chosen algorithm. This stage is vital as the format and quality of data can significantly impact the performance and accuracy of the machine learning model. Data preparation typically involves a series of formatting and preprocessing tasks. These tasks can include converting data types, as different algorithms have varying requirements: some may require data in integer format, others might work best with string data, and yet others may need the data to be structured in a specific, unique format.

   In addition to type conversion, data preparation can also involve handling missing values, normalizing or scaling data, encoding categorical variables, and extracting or selecting relevant features. This process is about transforming raw data into a refined format that is optimized for analysis, ensuring that the machine learning algorithm can effectively learn from and make predictions based on this data.

   While data preparation can be intricate and requires careful consideration, it is generally less labor-intensive compared to the data collection process. However, its importance cannot be understated, as proper data preparation is a key determinant of the success of subsequent machine learning processes. The aim is to create a clean, accurate, and appropriately formatted dataset that aligns with the specific requirements of the algorithm and the objectives of the project.

3. **Exploration of Data**: Once the data is collected and prepared, the next crucial step in the machine learning workflow is data exploration. This stage is vital for understanding the characteristics and quality of the dataset before moving forward with more complex analyses. Data exploration involves a thorough examination of the dataset to ensure that it is complete, without significant gaps or a preponderance of empty values. This verification is essential to confirm that the data is indeed usable for the intended machine learning tasks.

   During data exploration, visualizations play a key role. Utilizing various types of plots allows us to visually inspect the data, uncovering potential patterns, trends, or anomalies. For instance, scatter plots, histograms, and box plots can reveal valuable insights about the distribution, variability, and overall structure of the data. Additionally, they can help in identifying outliers – data points that are significantly different from the rest of the dataset – which might influence the performance of machine learning models.

Plotting data in one, two, or three dimensions can provide different perspectives, each offering unique insights. One-dimensional plots can give a quick overview of individual features, two-dimensional plots can show relationships between pairs of features, and three-dimensional plots can offer a more holistic view of the data, albeit with increased complexity.

This exploratory phase is not just about ensuring data quality; it also sets the stage for making informed decisions about model selection, feature engineering, and the overall analytical approach. Understanding the data through exploration helps in tailoring the machine learning process more effectively to the specific nuances and characteristics of the dataset.

4. **Training Method**: The training phase is where the most important part of machine learning takes place, marking a transition from preparatory steps into the core activity of developing the model. In this phase, the chosen algorithm is applied to the data, and the process of learning from this data begins. For supervised learning models, this means the algorithm starts to discern patterns and relationships between the input data and the target outputs, effectively "learning" from the examples provided. The model undergoes a process of adjustment and refinement, tweaking its internal parameters to minimize the difference between its predictions and the actual target values. This training process is iterative, with the model progressively improving its accuracy and efficiency in predicting or classifying data.

   In contrast, unsupervised learning approaches, such as clustering or dimensionality reduction, do not involve a traditional training step with target values. Instead, these models focus on exploring the structure and distribution of the data itself, identifying patterns, groupings, or features inherent in the data without any predefined labels or outcomes. The "training" in unsupervised learning is more about the model uncovering and understanding the underlying characteristics of the dataset.

   This step is critical as it sets the foundation for the model's ability to make accurate predictions or classifications when faced with new, unseen data. The effectiveness of the training phase largely determines the overall success of the machine learning model in achieving its intended task, whether it's predicting future trends, classifying data into categories, or uncovering hidden structures within the dataset.

5. **Testing the Results**: The testing phase in machine learning is a critical step where the trained model is evaluated to determine its effectiveness and accuracy. This phase is about verifying whether the model, which has learned from the training data, can successfully apply this knowledge to new, unseen data. In supervised learning, this process involves using a separate dataset, often referred to as the testing set, which was not used during the training phase. The model's predictions or classifications are compared against known values or labels in this dataset, providing a measure of how well the model approximates the real system. Common metrics used for evaluation in supervised learning include accuracy, precision, recall, and the F1 score, among others.

   In unsupervised learning, where there are no predefined labels or target values, the evaluation process can be more nuanced. It may involve using metrics like the silhouette score, Davies–Bouldin index, or other cluster validation measures to assess the quality of the clusters or patterns identified by the model. These metrics can provide insights into how well-separated the clusters are or how cohesive the data points within each cluster are.

In both supervised and unsupervised learning scenarios, the testing phase is not just a final checkpoint; it's an iterative part of the process. If the model's performance is not satisfactory, it offers an opportunity to return to previous steps, such as revising the model, tweaking hyperparameters, or even re-examining and preprocessing the data. Adjustments can then be made based on the insights gained from testing, and the model can be retrained and tested again. This iterative approach is essential for refining the model and enhancing its ability to make accurate predictions or uncover meaningful patterns in the data.

6. **Evaluation**: Reaching the evaluation stage in the machine learning process signifies a pivotal moment where we can apply and assess the full extent of our model's capabilities. This stage is about gauging the model's ability to approximate and interpret real-world data, extending beyond the controlled environment of training and testing. After the model has been meticulously trained on a subset of data and rigorously tested on another, the evaluation phase involves applying the model to real, often more complex and varied, datasets. This is where the model's practical utility and robustness are truly put to the test.

   The evaluation might involve using the model to make predictions, classify new data, or uncover patterns in datasets that it hasn't encountered before. The key here is to observe how well the model performs in real-life scenarios, which often present challenges that are not encountered in the more sanitized training and testing environments. The success of the model in this phase is indicative of its generalizability and effectiveness in practical applications.

   Metrics and measures used in the testing phase are again employed here to quantify the model's performance. However, the emphasis is now on how these translate into actionable insights or accurate predictions in a real-world context. If the model performs well, it validates the effectiveness of the entire machine learning process, from data collection and preparation to training and testing. If not, it may necessitate a revisit to earlier stages for further refinement. This phase is crucial for confirming the model's value and readiness for deployment in actual applications.

7. **Improving the Performance of the Model**: After verifying the functionality of the model and evaluating its performance, the final phase in the machine learning process focuses on refinement and improvement. This stage is about taking a comprehensive look at the entire workflow to pinpoint areas where enhancements can be made. It involves a thorough analysis of each step of the process, from data collection and preparation to training, testing, and evaluation. The aim is to identify any inefficiencies, bottlenecks, or areas where the model's performance could be optimized.

   This might involve tweaking the model's architecture, adjusting hyperparameters, or experimenting with different algorithms to see if they yield better results. Data preprocessing methods can also be reexamined to ensure that the model is being fed the most relevant and clean data possible. Additionally, feature engineering – the process of selecting, modifying, or creating new features – is revisited to ascertain if the model can benefit from a different set of features.

Another critical aspect of this phase is considering new or updated data that might have become available, as machine learning models can significantly benefit from a richer or more diverse dataset. Furthermore, computational efficiency is evaluated, especially if the model is intended for deployment in a resource-constrained environment.

Improving algorithm performance is an iterative and continuous process, often involving several rounds of modifications and evaluations. This phase is crucial for ensuring that the model not only meets the current requirements but is also scalable and adaptable to future changes and challenges. The goal is to fine-tune the model to achieve the highest level of accuracy and efficiency possible, ensuring its long-term utility and effectiveness.

References

Alpaydin, E. (2021). *Machine Learning*. MIT Press.

Celebi, M.E. and Aydin, K. (ed.) (2016). *Unsupervised Learning Algorithms*, vol. 9, 103. Cham: Springer.

Forsyth, D. (2019). *Applied Machine Learning*. Cham: Springer International Publishing.

Gauci, J. and Stanley, K.O. (2008). A case study on the critical role of geometric regularity in machine learning. In: *AAAI*, 628–633.

Gollapudi, S. (2016). *Practical Machine Learning*. Packt Publishing Ltd.

Mahesh, B. (2020). Machine learning algorithms—a review. *International Journal of Science and Research* 9 (1): 381–386.

Menon, A., Tamuz, O., Gulwani, S. et al. (2013). A machine learning framework for programming by example. In: *International Conference on Machine Learning*, 187–195. PMLR.

Muhammad, I. and Yan, Z. (2015). Supervised machine learning approaches: a survey. *ICTACT Journal on Soft Computing* 5 (3): 946–952.

Sugiyama, M. (2015). *Statistical Reinforcement Learning: Modern Machine Learning Approaches*. CRC Press.

2

Introduction to Metaheuristics Methods

2.1 Introduction

This chapter delves into the fundamental concepts of optimization, with a special focus on the methodologies underlying metaheuristic optimization techniques. It offers a comparative analysis between traditional optimization methods and metaheuristic approaches, highlighting their differences and respective advantages. Additionally, the chapter provides an in-depth discussion on the taxonomy of metaheuristic methods, categorizing and defining various strategies under this broad umbrella. An important part of this chapter is the examination of several key mechanisms intrinsic to the methodology of metaheuristic techniques, enhancing the reader's understanding of how these methods function in practice. As illustrative examples, the chapter specifically analyzes two simple metaheuristic strategies: random search and simulated annealing, demonstrating their application and effectiveness. To aid in comprehension, the chapter is enriched with several MATLAB implementations. These practical code examples not only facilitate a deeper grasp of the discussed concepts but also serve as a valuable resource for readers to apply these techniques in their own optimization problems, bridging the gap between theoretical knowledge and practical application.

Optimization has increasingly become a pivotal aspect of various disciplines, driven by the universal aim to enhance quality while maintaining competitiveness in pricing. This surge in its relevance is anchored in the quest to create superior products or services without escalating costs. Fundamentally, optimization is about identifying the most effective solution from an extensive array of potential options (Baldick 2006). It involves a meticulous process of analyzing, comparing, and selecting the optimum choice that aligns with specific objectives, whether in engineering, business, healthcare, or other fields. This approach not only ensures efficiency and effectiveness but also fosters innovation and progress across sectors.

An optimization problem is typically structured as a process where the primary goal is to determine the optimal value, denoted as $\mathbf{x}^*$, which either minimizes or maximizes a given objective function, $f(\mathbf{x})$. This function represents a specific criterion that needs to be optimized, such as cost, efficiency, or performance. The process involves carefully adjusting the variables within the function, in this case $\mathbf{x}$, to find the value $\mathbf{x}^*$ that leads to the best possible outcome for $f(\mathbf{x})$. This optimal value is contingent upon satisfying a set of constraints or conditions that define the feasible region for the problem. These constraints might include resource limitations, physical laws, or specific requirements that the solution must adhere to. Thus, solving an optimization problem involves not

Machine Learning and Metaheuristic Computation, First Edition.
Erik Cuevas, Jorge Galvez, Omar Avalos, and Fernando Wario.

only maximizing or minimizing the objective function but also ensuring that the solution complies with all necessary constraints. This can be formulated as follows:

$$\begin{aligned} &\text{min/max} \quad f(\mathbf{x}), x = (x_1, \ldots, x_d) \in \mathbb{R}^d \\ &\text{Subject to:} \quad \mathbf{x} \in \mathbf{X} \end{aligned} \tag{2.1}$$

In the area of optimization, **x** is commonly used to denote the vector of decision variables, where each element in this vector represents a specific variable that can be adjusted or controlled within the problem. The number of these variables is represented by d, indicating the dimensionality of the problem. The set of all possible combinations of these decision variables is referred to as **X**, known as the candidate solutions set, search space, or solution space. This space encompasses all the potential solutions that can be considered for finding the optimal result. Often, the range of each decision variable in **x** is restricted by lower (l_i) and upper (u_i) bounds, which define the feasible region of the solution space. This can be mathematically expressed as $\mathbf{X} = \{\mathbf{x} \in \mathbb{R}^d | l_i \leq x_i \leq u_i, i = 1, \ldots, d\}$, where each x_i within the vector **x** must lie between its respective lower and upper bounds for all d dimensions. These boundaries ensure that the search for the optimal solution is conducted within a realistic and practical framework.

In optimization, the objective function $f(\mathbf{x})$ can either be subjected to minimization or maximization, depending on the specific goals of the problem. Whether the aim is to reduce costs, minimize error, maximize efficiency, or achieve the highest possible performance, the nature of the objective dictates the approach. Interestingly, these two types of optimization problems – minimization and maximization – are interconvertible through a simple mathematical relation. By negating the objective function, a minimization problem can be transformed into a maximization one, and vice versa. This is expressed as: if the goal is to maximize $f(\mathbf{x})$, it is equivalent to minimizing $-f(\mathbf{x})$, and if the task is to minimize $f(\mathbf{x})$, this can be approached as maximizing $-f(\mathbf{x})$. This relationship allows for flexibility in the formulation and solution of optimization problems, enabling problem-solvers to adapt the approach that best suits their computational tools or theoretical preferences. This convertibility is a fundamental aspect of optimization theory, broadening the applicability and versatility of optimization techniques across different scenarios. This concept can be formulated as follows (Pedregal 2004):

$$\begin{aligned} &\min_{\mathbf{x}^*} f(\mathbf{x}) \Leftrightarrow \max_{\mathbf{x}^*} [-1 \cdot f(\mathbf{x})] \\ &\max_{\mathbf{x}^*} f(\mathbf{x}) \Leftrightarrow \min_{\mathbf{x}^*} [-1 \cdot f(\mathbf{x})] \end{aligned} \tag{2.2}$$

To illustrate the above concepts, the following minimization problem is presented as an example:

$$\begin{aligned} &\text{min} \quad f(\mathbf{x}) = x^4 + 5x^3 + 4x^2 - 4x + 1 \\ &\text{Subject to:} \quad \mathbf{x} \in [-4, 1] \end{aligned} \tag{2.3}$$

In the presented formulation, we encounter an optimization problem centered around the minimization of a function that hinges on a single decision variable, denoted as $d = 1$. This simplifies the scenario to a one-dimensional optimization task. The search space **X**, in this case, is defined by a specific interval, extending from −4 to 1. This range delineates the boundaries within which the solution must be found. The core objective of the problem is to pinpoint the specific value of x within this interval for which the function $f(\mathbf{x})$ attains its minimum value. This value of x is the crux of the optimization process, and it is referred to as the optimal value, symbolized as x^*. To aid in understanding and visualizing this optimization task, a graphical representation of the function $f(\mathbf{x})$ is provided, typically in the form of a curve plotted within the defined interval of [−4, 1]. This visual depiction, often labeled as Figure 2.1 in texts, serves to illustrate how the

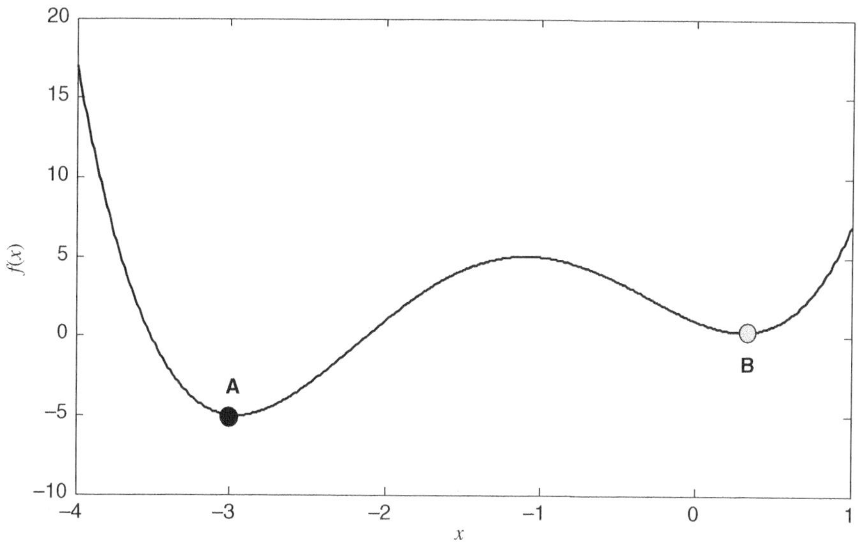

Figure 2.1 Graphical representation of the optimization problem formulated in Eq. 2.3.

function behaves across the search space and where its minimum value lies, thereby highlighting the optimal solution x^*.

From Figure 2.1, which graphically illustrates the function $f(\mathbf{x})$ in the optimization problem, we can observe two distinct points, labeled as solutions A and B. These points represent two different minima of the function $f(\mathbf{x})$. The presence of multiple prominent minima is a characteristic feature of what are known as multimodal functions. In multimodal functions, there are several points where the function reaches a minimum value, but these minima are of different natures. The minimum at point A is of particular significance as it represents the global optimal solution x^* for the problem, meaning it is the lowest point across the entire search space. On the other hand, point B signifies a local minimum. A local minimum, like B, is a point where the function reaches a minimum value in a nearby region but is not the absolute lowest when considering the entire search space. This distinction is crucial in optimization as the ultimate goal is often to find the global minimum (point A), which represents the best overall solution, rather than a local minimum (point B), which is only optimal in a limited context.

2.2 Classic Optimization Methods

Typically, the function $f(\mathbf{x})$ in optimization problems may exhibit a non-linear relationship with the decision variables $\mathbf{x}$, adding a layer of complexity to the problem-solving process. To navigate this intricacy, optimization methodologies often employ iterative processes that meticulously explore the search space to identify efficient solutions. There are two primary families of algorithms used for tackling such complex, non-linear optimization problems: classical techniques and metaheuristic schemes. Classical methods are grounded in mathematical rigor and often utilize the gradient of the function $f(\mathbf{x})$ to generate new candidate solutions. These techniques rely on differential calculus and are adept at navigating smoothly varying landscapes of the objective function. However, their effectiveness can be limited in scenarios where the function is not differentiable or is highly irregular. On the other hand, metaheuristic methods offer a more flexible approach. These methods do not require derivative information of the function for searching the optimal decision vector. Instead, they implement a set of heuristic rules to guide the search process. The beauty of metaheuristics lies in their inspiration from natural or societal phenomena. These algorithms mimic processes observed in nature, like evolution, or behaviors seen in social dynamics, enabling them to efficiently navigate complex, multimodal search spaces. This adaptability makes metaheuristics particularly useful in scenarios where classical methods falter, such as in problems with discontinuous or highly irregular objective functions.

Classical optimization algorithms, known for their specific performance characteristics, necessitate that the objective function $f(\mathbf{x})$ adheres to two fundamental requirements to be applicable. First, the function must be twice differentiable. This means that not only should the first derivative of $f(\mathbf{x})$ exist, but also its second derivative should be computable. The availability of these derivatives is crucial because classical algorithms often rely on gradient (first derivative) and curvature (second derivative) information to guide the search towards the optimal solution. The second requirement is that the function should be unimodal. In a unimodal function, there is only one local minimum or maximum, which is also the global minimum or maximum. This characteristic is important because classical algorithms are designed to converge to a single optimal point; in the presence of multiple local minima or maxima (as in multimodal functions), these algorithms may not reliably find the global optimum. Instead, they might converge to a local optimum that is not the best possible solution over the entire search space. Therefore, for classical optimization algorithms to perform effectively and as intended, both the twice differentiability and unimodality of the objective function $f(\mathbf{x})$ are imperative.

This section offers a foundational overview of gradient-based optimization techniques, a cornerstone of classical optimization methods. While the focus of the book is primarily on the in-depth exploration of metaheuristic methods, the inclusion of classical optimization is intended to provide a basic understanding of these traditional techniques. Gradient-based optimization is pivotal in understanding the broader landscape of optimization methods, as it relies on the use of derivatives to guide the search for optimal solutions. However, given that this book primarily delves into metaheuristics, the coverage of classical optimization is relatively brief and not exhaustive. For readers seeking a more comprehensive and detailed study of gradient-based and other classical optimization techniques, it is recommended to consult additional specialized texts. These texts can offer deeper insights into the mathematical foundations, algorithmic structures, and application contexts of classical optimization methods, thereby complementing the knowledge gained from this book's focus on metaheuristic approaches.

2.3 Descending Gradient Method

The gradient descent method (Dennis 1978), often referred to simply as the gradient method, stands as one of the earliest techniques employed for minimizing multidimensional objective functions. This method serves as the foundational pillar upon which several other more advanced optimization algorithms are built. The gradient descent method operates on a straightforward principle: it iteratively moves towards the minimum of the function by navigating in the direction of the steepest descent, as indicated by the negative of the function's gradient. Despite a notable drawback of slow convergence, especially in scenarios involving complex or high-dimensional functions, the gradient descent method remains the most frequently utilized approach for optimizing nonlinear functions. This enduring popularity is largely attributable to its simplicity and the relative ease with which it can be programmed. Its conceptual clarity and straightforward implementation make it an accessible and reliable choice for a wide range of optimization problems, particularly for those new to the field or in situations where more sophisticated methods are not necessary. The gradient descent method's enduring relevance in optimization underscores its importance in both theoretical and applied aspects of the field.

In the gradient descent method, the process begins with an initial point, denoted as $\mathbf{x}^0$, which serves as the starting position in the search for the optimal solution. From this point, the decision vector is iteratively updated through a series of steps, with the aim of progressively moving closer to the optimal solution, symbolized as $\mathbf{x}^*$. The number of iterations, referred to as *Niter*, is a crucial aspect of this process, as it determines how many times the decision vector is adjusted in pursuit of the optimal point. The iterative modification of the decision vector in the gradient descent method is governed by a specific mathematical expression. This expression encapsulates the essence of the method: at each step, the decision vector is updated by moving in the opposite direction of the gradient of the function at the current point. Mathematically, this update rule can be formulated as follows (Hocking 1991):

$$\mathbf{x}^{k+1} = \mathbf{x}^k - \alpha \mathbf{g}(f(\mathbf{x})) \tag{2.4}$$

where k represents the current iteration and represents the step size of the search.

In Eq. 2.4 the term $\mathbf{g}(f(\mathbf{x}))$ represents the gradient of the function $f(\mathbf{x})$. The gradient $\mathbf{g}$ of a function $f(\mathbf{x})$ at point $\mathbf{x}$ expresses the direction in which the function $f(\mathbf{x})$ shows its maximum growth. Thus, in the case of a minimization problem, the direction of descent can be obtained in the opposite direction of $\mathbf{g}$ (multiplying by -1). Under this rule, it is guaranteed that $f(\mathbf{x}^{k+1}) < f(\mathbf{x}^k)$, which implies that the new solution generated is better than the previous one.

In theoretical and didactic settings, the formulation of an optimization problem typically includes a well-defined objective function $f(\mathbf{x})$. This clear definition serves as a crucial component for demonstrating and teaching the principles of optimization. However, in practical applications, the exact formulation of $f(\mathbf{x})$ is often not deterministically known or explicitly defined. Instead, the values of the function are typically known only at specific points that are relevant or required by the optimization algorithm during its execution. This scenario is particularly common in real-world problems where the function might be based on empirical data, simulations, or complex systems where an analytical expression of $f(\mathbf{x})$ is not feasible.

Under these practical circumstances, where the function $f(\mathbf{x})$ and its gradient $\mathbf{g}$ are not analytically defined, numerical methods come into play for calculating the gradient. These methods estimate the gradient based on the function values at strategically chosen points. Techniques such as finite difference approximations are commonly used, where small perturbations are applied to the decision variables to estimate the rate of change of the function. This approach allows for the gradient estimation in situations where direct analytical computation is not possible. Although numerical methods for gradient calculation might introduce some approximation errors and require additional function evaluations, they are invaluable tools for tackling a wide range of optimization problems encountered in diverse practical scenarios. The ability to estimate gradients numerically broadens the applicability of optimization algorithms, making them versatile and effective even when dealing with complex, non-deterministic objective functions.

The gradient of a multidimensional function $f(\mathbf{x})$ $(\mathbf{x} = (x_1, \ldots, x_d) \in \mathbb{R}^d)$ represents the way in which the function varies with respect to one of its d dimensions. Thus, the gradient g_{x_1} expresses the way in which $f(\mathbf{x})$ varies with respect to x_1. Such a gradient is properly defined as:

$$g_{x_1} = \frac{\partial f(\mathbf{x})}{\partial x_1} \tag{2.5}$$

To calculate numerically the gradient g_{x_i} the following procedure is followed (Mathews and Fink 2000).

1. A new decision vector $\tilde{\mathbf{x}}_i$ is generated. This vector is the same in all decision variables as $\mathbf{x}$ except for x_i. This value will be replaced by $x_i + h$, where h is a very small value. Under these conditions, the new vector is defined as:

$$\tilde{\mathbf{x}}_i = (x_1, x_2, \ldots, x_i + h, \ldots, x_d) \tag{2.6}$$

2. The gradient g_{x_i} is calculated using the following model:

$$g_{x_i} = \frac{f(\tilde{\mathbf{x}}_i) - f(\mathbf{x})}{h} \tag{2.7}$$

Figure 2.2 shows a graphical representation of the process of numerical calculation of the gradient considering a simple example, where $f(\mathbf{x})$ has 2 dimensions (x_1, x_2).

To exemplify the operation of the gradient descent algorithm and its practical implementation in MATLAB, we intend to solve the following minimization problem:

$$\begin{array}{ll} \min & f(x_1, x_2) = 10 - e^{-(x_1^2 + 3x_2^2)} \\ \text{Subject to:} & -1 \leq x_1 \leq 1 \\ & -1 \leq x_2 \leq 1 \end{array} \tag{2.8}$$

In this formulation, a two-dimensional function $f(x_1, x_2)$ with a search space defined in the interval $[-1, 1]$ is considered for each of the decision variables x_1 and x_2. Figure 2.3 shows a representation of the objective function $f(x_1, x_2)$.

As can be seen, the function $f(x_1, x_2)$ can be derived twice and is unimodal (it has only one minimum). For these reasons, it meets the requirements to be minimized under the descending gradient method.

Principio del formulario.

The minimization process of a function $f(x_1, x_2)$ using the gradient descent method is succinctly encapsulated in pseudocode format, labeled as Algorithm 2.1. This algorithmic representation outlines the step-by-step procedure for applying gradient descent to a function with two decision variables. The procedure initiates by randomly selecting a decision vector $\mathbf{x}^k$ (where $k = 0$) within the defined search space. This search space for both variables x_1 and x_2 is delineated by the interval $[-1, 1]$. Once the initial decision vector $\mathbf{x}^k$ is established, the next step involves calculating the gradients g_{x_1} and g_{x_2} at the current point $\mathbf{x}^k$. These gradients represent the direction and rate of the steepest increase of the function at $\mathbf{x}^k$ for each variable separately. With the gradient information at hand, the algorithm proceeds to generate a new solution. This is achieved by applying the update equation, referred to as Eq. 2.4 in the pseudocode. Since the function $f(x_1, x_2)$ comprises two decision variables, the solution update process outlined in Eq. 2.4 considers each variable independently. This decoupled approach allows for the adjustment of each variable in the decision vector

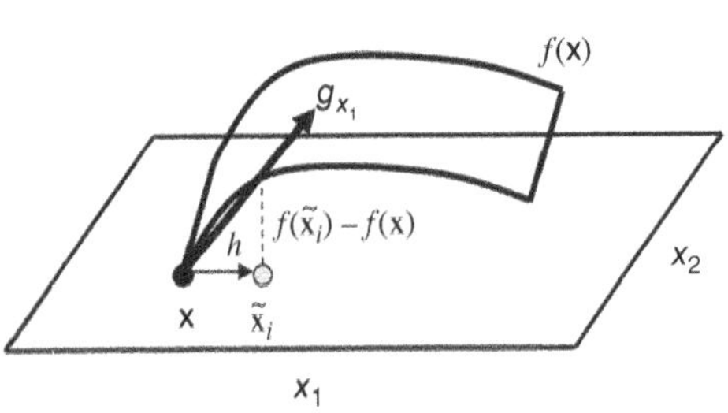

Figure 2.2 Graphical representation of the numerical calculation of the gradient.

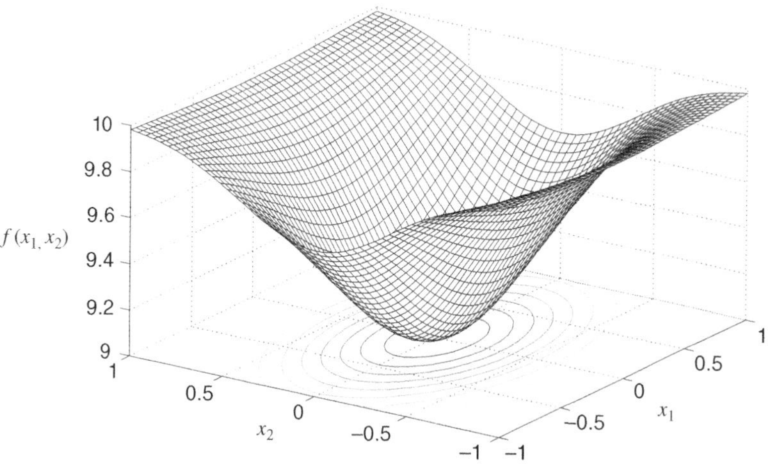

Figure 2.3 Graphical representation of the function $10 - e^{-(x_1^2+3x_2^2)}$.

Algorithm 2.1 ***Descending Gradient Method***

---

1. $k \leftarrow 0$
2. $x_1^k \leftarrow \text{rand}\,[-1, 1],\ x_2^k \leftarrow \text{rand}\,[-1, 1]$
3. **while** $(k < Niter)$ **{**
4. $g_{x_1} \leftarrow \frac{f(x_1^k+h,x_2^k)-f(x_1^k,x_2^k)}{h},\ g_{x_2} \leftarrow \frac{f(x_1^k,x_2^k+h)-f(x_1^k,x_2^k)}{h}$
5. $x_1^{k+1} \leftarrow x_1^k - \alpha g_{x_1},\ x_2^{k+1} \leftarrow x_2^k - \alpha g_{x_2}$
6. $k \leftarrow k+1$**}**

---

based on its respective gradient. The update, thus, is executed for each variable x_1 and x_2 separately, according to the calculated gradients and the specified update rule. This decoupled update mechanism ensures that both variables are optimally adjusted, leading to an effective search for the minimum of the function $f(x_1, x_2)$ in the multidimensional decision space. Under such conditions, the update rules are defined as follows:

$$\begin{aligned} x_1^{k+1} &= x_1^k - \alpha g_{x_1} \\ x_2^{k+1} &= x_2^k - \alpha g_{x_2} \end{aligned} \tag{2.9}$$

These equations are iteratively executed until a determined maximal number of iterations, *Niter*, has been reached.

To assist readers in practically implementing Algorithm 2.1, Code 2.1 provides a specific MATLAB script tailored for this purpose. This script is not just a direct translation of the pseudocode into MATLAB syntax; it also includes additional features that enhance understanding and visualization of the algorithm's operation. The first step in the MATLAB code involves plotting the function $f(x_1, x_2)$. This visualization is crucial as it allows readers to grasp the characteristics of the function they are attempting to minimize, such as its shape, gradients, and potential minima. Understanding these aspects is vital for comprehending how the gradient descent method navigates the search space. Following the visualization step, the code executes an iterative process. This process involves updating the candidate solutions starting from the initial value $\mathbf{x}^0$ and progressively moving towards the optimal value $\mathbf{x}^*$. During each iteration, the trajectory

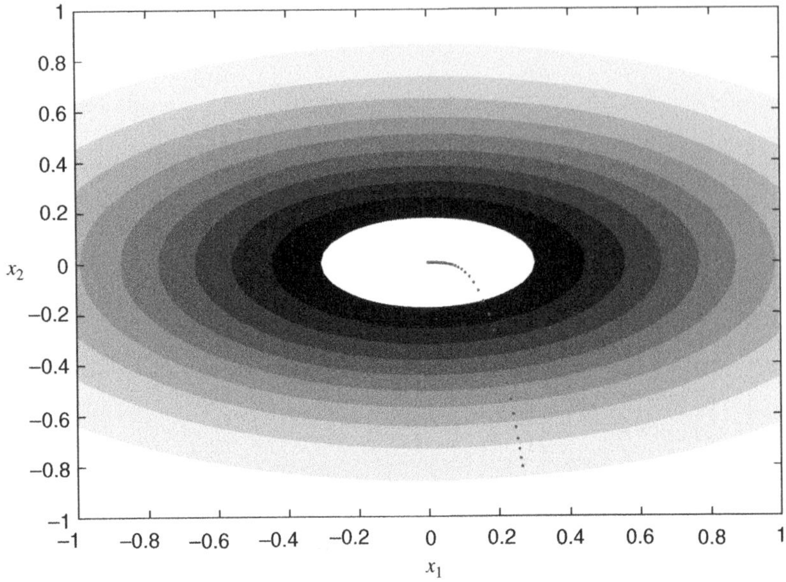

Figure 2.4 Path of the solutions obtained by the gradient descent algorithm when minimizing the function defined in 2.8.

of these candidate solutions is calculated and displayed. This dynamic representation shows how the algorithm explores the search space, adjusts its direction based on the gradients, and converges towards the minimum. To provide a concrete example of how the algorithm functions in practice, Figure 2.4, generated by Code 2.1, illustrates this trajectory on a MATLAB contour plot. This graphical representation demonstrates the path taken by the algorithm from its starting point to the point where it finds the optimal value $\mathbf{x}^*$. Such a visual aid is immensely helpful for readers, particularly those new to the concept of gradient descent, as it offers a clear, step-by-step illustration of the algorithm in action, showcasing the practical application of the theoretical concepts discussed earlier.

Code 2.1

```
% Descending gradient method
% Clear memory
clear all
% The function to be optimized 2.8 is defined as follows
funstr='10-(exp(-1*(x^2+3*y^2)))';
f=vectorize(inline(funstr));
range=[-1 1 -1 1];
% Function is plotted to reference
Ndiv=50;
dx=(range(2)-range(1))/Ndiv; dy=(range(4)-range(3))/Ndiv;
[x,y] =meshgrid(range(1):dx:range(2),range(3):dy:range(4));
z=(f(x,y));
```

```
figure(1);   surfc(x,y,z);
% The number of iterations is defined
k=0;
niter=200;
% The size of the disturbance for gradients is established.
hstep = 0.001;
% Optimization step is set
alfa=0.05;
% Generation of the starting point
xrange=range(2)-range(1);
yrange=range(4)-range(3);
x1=rand*xrange+range(1);
x2=rand*yrange+range(3);
figure
% The iterative optimization process is established
while (k<niter)
% The function is evaluated
zn=f(x1,x2);
% Gradients gx1 and gx2 are calculated.
vx1=x1+hstep;
vx2=x2+hstep;
gx1=(f(vx1,x2)-zn)/hstep;
gx2=(f(x1,vx2)-zn)/hstep;
% The solution produced is plotted
contour(x,y,z,15); hold on;
plot(x1,x2,'.','markersize',10,'markerfacecolor','g');
drawnow;
hold on;
% The new solution is calculated
x1=x1-alfa*gx1;
x2=x2-alfa*gx2;
k=k+1;
end
```

2.4 Metaheuristic Methods

Classical gradient-based methods are often considered among the fastest algorithms for nonlinear optimization problems (Reinhardt et al. 2013). A significant advantage of these techniques is their ability to guarantee the attainment of the optimal solution to the optimization problem under certain conditions. This assurance of reaching the optimal solution is a compelling feature, especially in scenarios where precision is paramount (Hussain et al. 2019). However, the applicability of these methods is notably constrained by specific prerequisites: the objective function must be twice differentiable and unimodal. In reality, many optimization problems present objective functions that do not meet one or both of these criteria. It's not uncommon for real-world objective functions to exhibit multimodal behavior, characterized by the presence of several local minima. In such cases, applying gradient-based methods can be problematic, as these methods might get

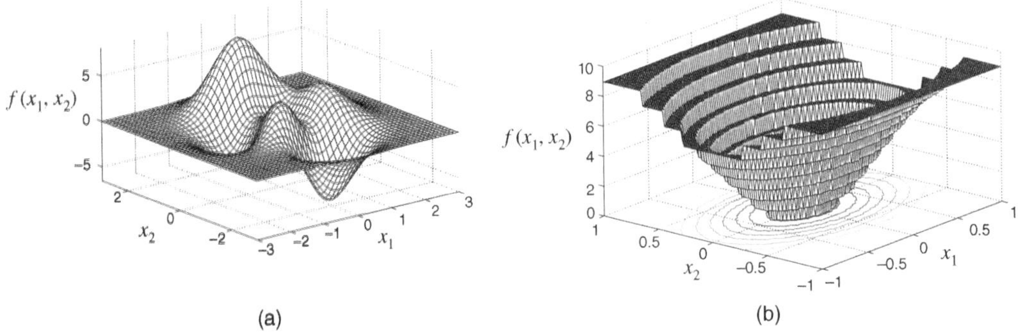

Figure 2.5 Examples of objective functions that (a) are multimodal or (b) are not differentiable.

trapped in one of the local minima, impeding any further exploration of the search space for a potentially better solution. An illustration of a multimodal function can be seen in Figure 2.5a, which exemplifies how multiple minima can exist within a single function. Additionally, there are numerous reasons why an objective function might not be differentiable, which further limits the suitability of gradient-based methods. Even a simple operation like rounding, for instance, can transform a differentiable function into a non-differentiable one. This is depicted in Figure 2.5b, where the rounded version of the function presented in Figure 2.3 is shown. Such transformations highlight the complexities and limitations encountered in real-world optimization scenarios, where objective functions may not always conform to the ideal conditions assumed by classical gradient-based optimization methods.

Metaheuristic methods (Simon 2013), a subset of metaheuristic methods, are distinguished by their non-reliance on the gradient information of the objective function. This characteristic significantly broadens their applicability, especially in complex optimization scenarios. By not being constrained to functions that are differentiable or have a clearly defined gradient, these methods can handle a wide array of objective functions, no matter how intricate or unconventional they may be. The flexibility of metaheuristic methods allows them to accommodate objective functions that are tailored to the specific requirements of the application at hand. This adaptability is particularly advantageous in cases where the objective function encompasses simulations or experimental models, scenarios often encountered in fields like engineering, biology, and economics. These functions might be too complex, noisy, or even discontinuous to fit the criteria necessary for gradient-based methods. In evolutionary computation, solutions evolve over time, following principles inspired by natural evolution, such as selection, mutation, and crossover. This process does not require any gradient information; instead, it evaluates the quality of solutions based on a fitness function, which is analogous to the objective function in optimization. The ability to work directly with the objective function, regardless of its mathematical properties, enables metaheuristic methods to tackle a diverse range of optimization problems, including those with complex, multimodal, and non-differentiable objective functions. This makes them highly versatile and powerful tools in the arsenal of optimization techniques, capable of addressing challenges that are beyond the reach of traditional gradient-based methods.

Metaheuristic methods, a key category of metaheuristic approaches, are uniquely characterized by their independence from derivative information of the objective function during the search for the optimal decision vector $\mathbf{x}$ that minimizes (or maximizes) a given objective function. Unlike gradient-based methods, which rely on the derivative information to guide their search, these methods utilize heuristic rules to create patterns for exploring the solution space. These heuristic rules often draw inspiration from simulations of various natural or social processes, such as biological evolution, social behavior patterns, or physical phenomena. The distinct advantage of metaheuristic methods lies in their ability to tackle a wide range of problems, including those where the objective function is complex, non-linear, non-differentiable, or even unknown. However, this advantage comes with a trade-off. Since metaheuristic methods do not leverage the derivative information of the objective function, they generally lack precise, immediate guidance on the direction and magnitude of search steps. This lack of direct, relevant information about the objective function's landscape means that these methods might require more iterations or evaluations to converge to an optimal or near-optimal solution, leading to slower convergence compared to gradient-based techniques. Despite this slower pace, the strength of metaheuristic methods lies in their robustness and versatility. They are particularly valuable in scenarios where traditional methods fail or are impractical, such as optimization problems with complex, irregular, or dynamic objective functions. By employing heuristic rules and mimicking natural or social processes, metaheuristic methods provide effective, though sometimes slower, strategies for finding solutions in diverse and challenging optimization landscapes.

Metaheuristic methods are inherently stochastic in nature (Bartholomew-Biggs 2008), meaning they employ random processes as a fundamental component in determining the directions and strategies of their search. This stochastic element introduces a level of unpredictability and diversity in the search process (Deb 2001), which is crucial for exploring complex and multimodal solution spaces effectively. However, the random nature of these methods also poses a significant challenge for their analytical study. Due to the inherent randomness, it becomes difficult to apply traditional analytical techniques to rigorously analyze and predict the behavior of such methods (Fletcher and Powell 1963). Consequently, many of the properties and understandings of metaheuristic methods have been gleaned through empirical means – experimentation and observation – rather than purely theoretical analysis (Yang 2010).

While some evolutionary computational algorithms are specifically designed to mimic biological phenomena – genetic algorithms, for example, are inspired by the process of natural selection – they are not confined to these biological paradigms in their operational principles. In their broader conception, these methods are fundamentally optimization techniques. They leverage concepts from biological evolution not as an end in themselves, but as a means to develop robust and versatile strategies for finding optimal or near-optimal solutions in complex optimization problems. This approach allows them to transcend the specifics of biological processes and function effectively as general-purpose optimization tools, adaptable to a wide array of problems across various domains. This versatility and the ability to handle diverse and challenging optimization scenarios underscore the significance of metaheuristic methods in the field of optimization.

The term "population optimization algorithms" is often used by some authors to describe metaheuristic techniques. This nomenclature highlights a key characteristic of many such methods: they typically operate with a population of candidate solutions to tackle the optimization problem. In this context, each candidate solution functions akin to an independent agent, each executing its own search strategy. The underlying concept is that over time, through processes reminiscent of natural selection and genetic variation, this population evolves, progressively improving the solutions until it converges to or nears the optimal solution. However, the term "population optimization algorithms" may not fully encapsulate the breadth of metaheuristic methods. This is because not all metaheuristic techniques rely on a population of solutions. For instance, methods like simulated annealing or certain evolutionary strategies work with a single candidate solution that is iteratively modified. In these methods, the focus is on the evolution of this single solution through successive iterations, rather than the evolution of a population of solutions. This distinction is crucial as it points to the more general nature of metaheuristic methods. While population-based approaches like genetic algorithms are a significant part of this category, the field also encompasses methods that operate on a single solution trajectory. Thus, metaheuristic methods, in their broader sense, extend beyond the concept of population-based optimization, encompassing a wider range of strategies and approaches. This more inclusive perspective acknowledges the diversity and flexibility of metaheuristic methods, recognizing their applicability across a spectrum of optimization scenarios, whether they involve single or multiple candidate solutions.

The term "computational intelligence" is sometimes employed to encompass metaheuristic techniques, distinguishing them from other areas within the broader domain of artificial intelligence, such as expert systems. This distinction is rooted in the differing fundamental approaches of these methodologies. Expert systems, a traditional discipline within artificial intelligence, primarily model deductive reasoning. They are designed to replicate the decision-making process of a human expert, relying on a predefined set of rules and logic to draw conclusions from specific inputs. In contrast, metaheuristic methods are more aligned with inductive reasoning. These methods, inspired by biological evolution, learn and evolve through a process of trial and error, exploration, and adaptation, rather than following rigid, pre-established rules. However, the scope of computational intelligence extends beyond just metaheuristic or metaheuristic methods. It is a broader concept that also includes approaches, such as neural networks and fuzzy systems. Neural networks, for instance, are designed to simulate the way the human brain processes information, and are widely used in areas like pattern recognition, classification, and prediction. Fuzzy systems, on the other hand, deal with reasoning that is approximate rather than precise, mimicking the way humans make decisions in a vague and uncertain environment. This wide spectrum of methodologies under the umbrella of computational intelligence is not limited to optimization problems. These approaches find applications across various domains, including data mining, machine learning, signal processing, and control systems, among others. The term "computational intelligence" thus represents a more comprehensive concept, acknowledging the diverse, adaptive, and often heuristic nature of these methods, and their applicability to a vast array of problems beyond just optimization.

The term "bio-inspired algorithms" is frequently used by researchers to refer to metaheuristic methods, but this characterization can be somewhat misleading. While it's true that many metaheuristic techniques draw inspiration from biological processes – such as genetic algorithms and particle swarm optimization – this is not universally the case. For instance, methods like differential evolution and the imperialistic competitive algorithm do not directly derive their mechanisms from natural phenomena. Differential evolution is based more on mathematical principles of optimization, and the imperialistic competitive algorithm models a socio-political process rather than a biological one. Furthermore, there are approaches within evolutionary computation, such as evolutionary strategies and oppositional learning, that maintain only a tenuous or abstract connection to biological processes. Evolutionary strategies, for example, focus on the optimization of strategy parameters and oppositional learning is based on mathematical concepts that do not necessarily mirror natural processes. Given these variations, it becomes evident that metaheuristic methods encompass a broader and more diverse set of algorithms than what the term "bio-inspired" might imply. While bio-inspired algorithms are a significant and well-recognized subset of evolutionary computation, the field as a whole extends beyond just mimicking biological processes. It includes a range of techniques and strategies, some of which are inspired by nature, others by different scientific or mathematical principles, making metaheuristic a more general and inclusive concept than the narrower category of bio-inspired algorithms. This diversity allows metaheuristic methods to be versatile and adaptable, capable of addressing a wide variety of problems across different disciplines.

The term "heuristic algorithms" is often used interchangeably with "evolutionary computation" by some authors, though the two encompass slightly different concepts. The word "heuristic" originates from the Greek term meaning "to find" or "to discover." Heuristic algorithms are methods that employ intuitive rules or strategies based on common sense or practical experience to solve problems. The primary goal of these algorithms is not necessarily to find the optimal solution but to discover a sufficiently acceptable or satisfactory solution within a reasonable timeframe and with feasible computational resources. Heuristic algorithms are characterized by their problem-solving approach, which is more about applying practical methods that work well in practice, rather than strictly following theoretical or mathematical guidelines. These methods are particularly useful in scenarios where an exhaustive search for the optimal solution is impractical due to complexity or computational constraints. The term "meta-heuristic" refers to a broader family of heuristic algorithms. Meta-heuristics are high-level frameworks or strategies that guide the search process, often incorporating mechanisms to escape local optima and explore the search space more diversely. These may include both population-based approaches and single-solution methods. Given these definitions, it can be argued that most, if not all, of the algorithms discussed in metaheuristic literature fall under the umbrella of meta-heuristics. This encompasses a wide range of algorithms, each with its unique strategies and mechanisms, but all sharing the common goal of efficiently and effectively finding good-enough solutions to complex problems. Therefore, while "evolutionary computation" and "heuristic algorithms" might sometimes be used synonymously, it's important to recognize that they represent a spectrum of approaches within the broader field of meta-heuristic methods.

Many researchers draw a distinction between evolutionary computational methods and swarm algorithms, although the two share some similarities. Swarm algorithms are based on the concept of collective intelligence, modeling the behavior of groups of animals or insects, such as ants, birds, or fish. This approach leverages the idea that simple rules followed by individuals can lead to complex, intelligent behavior emerging at the group level. Two notable examples in this category are Ant Colony Optimization (ACO), inspired by the foraging behavior of ants, and Particle Swarm Optimization (PSO), influenced by the social behavior of bird flocking or fish schooling. Despite their distinct inspiration, the operational mechanisms of swarm algorithms bear a resemblance to those of metaheuristic methods. Both involve a population of individuals (ants in ACO, particles in PSO, or candidate solutions in evolutionary algorithms) exploring the search space, albeit guided by different principles and processes. In swarm algorithms, the movement and decision-making of each individual are influenced by the collective experience of the group, whereas evolutionary methods typically rely more on mechanisms like mutation, crossover, and selection. Given their operational similarities and the shared goal of optimizing complex problems, this book considers swarm algorithms as a part of the broader category of metaheuristic methods. This classification is based on the perspective that the underlying principles of adaptation, learning, and evolution in a population, whether inspired by natural evolution or collective animal behavior, fall under the same overarching theme of evolutionary computation. This inclusive perspective allows for a more comprehensive understanding of these methods and their applications in solving a wide array of optimization problems.

The discussions above illuminate that the terminology used to define metaheuristic methods is notably imprecise and varies depending on the context. This lack of precise definition stems from the diverse origins and inspirations of these methods, as well as their evolving nature. In this book, with the intention of encompassing all perspectives and providing a unifying definition, metaheuristic methods are characterized in a broader sense. They are defined as algorithms that modify one or several candidate solutions over numerous iterations, without relying on the gradient information of the objective function. This approach to metaheuristic acknowledges the intrinsic variety within metaheuristic methods. The key element here is the combination of stochastic processes and deterministic models to guide the modification or search strategy. The stochastic component introduces randomness and diversity, allowing the algorithm to explore the solution space broadly and avoid getting trapped in local optima. On the other hand, deterministic models provide a structured approach to refining solutions and converging towards optimality. This blend of randomness and systematic strategy enables these methods to effectively tackle complex optimization problems that are intractable for traditional gradient-based approaches. By adopting this inclusive and integrative definition, the book aims to capture the essence of metaheuristic methods (Cuevas and Rodríguez 2020) as flexible, adaptive, and robust optimization tools. This perspective not only bridges various subfields within the domain of metaheuristics but also provides a coherent framework for understanding and applying these methods across a wide range of problem-solving scenarios.

A key focus here is to clearly define the nomenclature commonly employed by metaheuristic methods, which is essential for a comprehensive understanding. Metaheuristic algorithms, inspired by natural evolutionary processes (Venkataraman 2009), incorporate a variety of terms and concepts unique to their domain. These include notions, such as "population" (Matyas 1965), referring to a set of candidate solutions; "generation," indicating the iteration steps in the algorithm; "selection," describing the process of choosing more promising solutions; "mutation" and "crossover," mechanisms for introducing variability and new characteristics into the solutions; and "fitness," a measure of how well a solution satisfies the optimization criteria.

By dissecting these terms and concepts, the section aims to provide a clear and detailed overview of how metaheuristic algorithms function, how they approach the task of optimization, and the rationale behind their strategies. This elucidation not only aids in understanding the operational mechanics of these algorithms but also helps in appreciating their versatility and effectiveness in solving complex optimization problems. The goal is to present these concepts in a manner that is both accessible to newcomers and valuable to those with existing knowledge in the field, ensuring a comprehensive grasp of metaheuristics as a powerful tool in the optimization arsenal.

$$\begin{array}{ll} \text{min/max} & f(\mathbf{x}), x = (x_1, \ldots, x_d) \in \mathbb{R}^d \\ \text{Subject to:} & \mathbf{x} \in \mathbf{X} \end{array} \tag{2.10}$$

In optimization problems, **x** typically represents the vector of decision variables, and d specifies the number of these variables. This vector, **x**, is a crucial element as it encapsulates all the variables that can be adjusted or controlled in order to optimize a given objective function. The concept of d, the dimensionality of the problem, is equally important as it indicates how many such variables are involved in the problem, thereby defining the complexity and scope of the optimization task.

The set **X** is another fundamental concept, representing the set of all possible candidate solutions. This set is also referred to as the search space or solution space. It is essentially the domain within which the optimization algorithm operates, encompassing all the potential combinations of the decision variables that can be considered for arriving at the optimal solution.

In many instances, the search space is not unlimited but is instead bounded by lower and upper bounds for each of the decision variables. These bounds are denoted by l_i (the lower bound) and u_i (the upper bound) for each variable x_i in the decision vector **x**. The mathematical representation of this bounded search space can be expressed as $\mathbf{X} = \{\mathbf{x} \in \mathbb{R}^d | l_i \leq x_i \leq u_i, i = 1, \ldots, d\}$. This expression signifies that for every decision variable x_i in the vector **x**, there exists a permissible

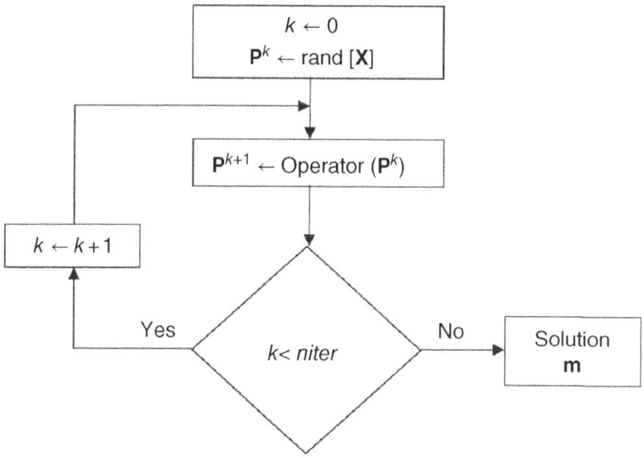

Figure 2.6 Optimization process from the point of view of metaheuristic algorithms.

range defined by its corresponding lower and upper bounds, l_i and u_i. These bounds ensure that the solutions explored by the optimization algorithm are feasible and within the practical constraints of the problem.

To tackle the optimization problem described in Eq. 2.10, a metaheuristic algorithm employs either a single candidate solution $\mathbf{x}^k$ or a population $\mathbf{P}^k$ consisting of N candidate solutions $\left(\mathbf{x}_1^k, \mathbf{x}_2^k, \ldots, \mathbf{x}_N^k\right)$. This population undergoes an evolutionary process, changing and adapting over a predetermined maximum number of iterations, *niter*, transitioning from an initial state to a final, optimally evolved state.

In the initial state of the algorithm, the set of candidate solutions is randomly initialized within the bounds of the search space $\mathbf{X}$. This initialization is crucial as it sets the starting point for the evolutionary process. At each subsequent generation or iteration (as it is often referred to in the nomenclature of metaheuristic algorithms), a set of evolutionary operators is applied to the current population $\mathbf{P}^k$ to create a new generation of candidate solutions $\mathbf{P}^{k+1}$.

The effectiveness of each candidate solution $\mathbf{x}_i^k$ (where i ranges from 1 to N) is assessed using the objective function $f\left(\mathbf{x}_i^k\right)$, which quantifies the quality of the solution with respect to the optimization problem. This value is known as the fitness value of $\mathbf{x}_i^k$ in the context of metaheuristic algorithms. During the evolution process, the algorithm typically tracks the best solution, denoted as $\mathbf{m}$, which emerges from the pool of all candidate solutions. This best solution holds a special designation and is continuously updated as the algorithm progresses.

The ultimate goal of this evolutionary process is that, by the final iteration, this position $\mathbf{m}$ will represent the optimal solution to the problem. Figure 2.6 in the reference material offers a graphical representation of this optimization process from the perspective of metaheuristic algorithms. This visual aid helps in understanding how the population of candidate solutions evolves and converges towards the best solution over time, providing a clear illustration of the dynamic and iterative nature of metaheuristic methods.

2.5 Exploitation and Exploration

Exploration and exploitation (Hussain et al. 2019) are two fundamental strategies in the realm of optimization, especially within metaheuristic and metaheuristic algorithms. Exploration is characterized by the search for new solutions in the solution space (Xu and Xu 2021). It involves venturing into uncharted or less-explored areas with the aim of discovering potentially better solutions. This approach is inherently risky, as the outcomes of exploring new possibilities are uncertain and can lead to solutions of varying quality, including those that may not improve upon existing ones. However, the potential reward of exploration is significant; it offers the chance to stumble upon the best possible solution, or at least, solutions that are substantially better than those previously known.

Exploitation, on the other hand, is a more conservative strategy (Morales-Castañeda et al. 2020). It focuses on utilizing existing solutions that have already proven to be effective in similar situations. This approach leverages the knowledge gained from past successes to refine and improve upon these solutions. Exploitation is less risky compared to exploration, as it relies on tried-and-tested solutions, making the outcomes more predictable. However, the downside is that the improvements made through exploitation are often incremental, leading to smaller gains in optimization.

For an optimization agent or search strategy, striking a balance between exploration and exploitation is crucial. On one hand, the ability to explore is necessary to discover novel and potentially superior solutions, despite the inherent risks. On the other hand, the ability to exploit is important for capitalizing on known successful solutions, albeit with marginal gains (Črepinšek et al. 2013). The optimal blend of exploration and exploitation depends on the specific characteristics of the problem and the stage of the search process. Initially, a greater emphasis on exploration may be beneficial to gain a broad understanding of the solution space, while later stages might benefit more from exploitation to fine-tune and enhance the already identified promising solutions. This dynamic interplay between exploration and exploitation is a key aspect of effective search strategies in optimization algorithms.

A metaheuristic approach, in its essence, is designed to orchestrate the dual processes of exploration and exploitation within the search space (Yang et al. 2022). In the context of metaheuristic methods, these two processes play distinct yet complementary roles. Exploration is the process of venturing into new areas of the search space to uncover novel solutions. It involves probing areas that are less known or entirely unknown, with the aim of discovering potentially better solutions that have not been considered before. This aspect of the search is crucial for broadening the scope of the solutions and avoiding premature convergence to suboptimal results.

Exploitation, in contrast, focuses on the local refinement of the best solutions already identified in the search process (Lin and Gen 2009). The goal here is to fine-tune these solutions, enhancing their quality and efficiency. This process leverages the information and insights gained from the successful solutions so far, to incrementally improve them. Exploitation is vital for intensifying the search around promising areas, thereby increasing the precision and effectiveness of the solutions.

However, focusing solely on either exploration or exploitation can be detrimental to the optimization process. Pure exploration, while opening up new possibilities, may degrade the accuracy of the solutions, as it tends to overlook the refinement of already good solutions. Conversely, pure exploitation, although effective in improving existing solutions, can severely limit the search strategy. It often leads to a scenario where the algorithm gets trapped in local optima, unable to escape and explore potentially better solutions elsewhere.

Therefore, the key challenge and strength of an evolutionary metaheuristic method lie in its ability to strike a delicate balance between exploration and exploitation (Binkley and Hagiwara 2008). This balance is critical for ensuring that the algorithm is able to thoroughly investigate the search space while also capitalizing on the promising solutions it finds. The exploration–exploitation balancing act has not been conclusively solved in the field, and as such, each metaheuristic method implements its own unique approach to address this challenge. Different algorithms employ various strategies and mechanisms to manage this balance, often tailored to the specific nature of the optimization problems they are designed to solve. This ongoing quest to effectively balance exploration and exploitation continues to be a central theme in the development and refinement of metaheuristic algorithms.

2.6 Acceptance and Probabilistic Selection

Acceptance and probabilistic selection are two fundamental operations commonly employed in virtually all metaheuristic methods, playing a crucial role in guiding the search process toward effective solutions.

The probabilistic acceptance operation is a strategy where the execution of a particular action is contingent upon a certain probability. This approach introduces a stochastic element into the decision-making process, allowing for a degree of randomness that can be vital for exploring the search space more broadly. For instance, in some algorithms, a worse solution might be accepted over a better one with a certain probability. This mechanism can help the algorithm escape from local optima by permitting moves that are not immediately beneficial but may lead to more promising areas of the search space in the long run.

Probabilistic selection, on the other hand, relates to the process of choosing an element from a set of possible solutions, where elements of higher quality have a greater likelihood of being selected compared to those of lower quality. This operation is central to the concept of "survival of the fittest" in evolutionary methods. It ensures that solutions which are closer to the optimal (or have better fitness) are more likely to be retained and propagated through generations. By preferentially selecting higher-quality solutions, the algorithm incrementally improves the overall quality of the population.

Both these operations – probabilistic acceptance and probabilistic selection – are instrumental in achieving a balance between exploration and exploitation. While probabilistic acceptance facilitates exploration by introducing randomness and flexibility, probabilistic selection steers the algorithm towards exploitation, concentrating the search around the most promising solutions found so far. The interplay of these operations allows metaheuristic methods to navigate complex search spaces effectively, adapting and evolving their strategies to find optimal or near-optimal solutions.

Probabilistic acceptance is a pivotal operation commonly employed in metaheuristic methods to guide the application of various operators in the solution search process. This operation hinges on the principle of executing a particular action, let's call it Action **A**, based on a predetermined probability, denoted as P_{A}.

The essence of probabilistic acceptance lies in the fact that P_{A} determines the frequency with which Action A is applied within the algorithm. To ensure this operation aligns with the principles of probability, P_{A} must fall within the range of valid probability values, which is the interval $[0, 1]$. In other words, P_{A} can take any value from 0 (indicating that Action A will never be executed) to 1 (implying that Action A will always be executed).

The process of deciding whether to accept or reject Action A under these conditions unfolds in the following manner: Firstly, a random number r_{A} is generated. This number is drawn from a uniform distribution spanning the interval $[0, 1]$, denoted as $\mathbf{U}[0, 1]$. The value of r_{A} is then compared to the probability P_{A}. If r_{A} is less than or equal to P_{A}, then Action A is executed. If, however, r_{A} is greater than P_{A}, Action A is not executed and therefore has no effect on the solution search process at that instance.

This probabilistic mechanism introduces an element of randomness and variability into the algorithm, which can be crucial for navigating complex solution spaces. It allows the algorithm to occasionally explore less optimal paths or accept less promising solutions, providing the flexibility needed to escape local optima and potentially discover more globally optimal solutions. This makes probabilistic acceptance an integral part of the dynamic and adaptive nature of metaheuristic algorithms.

Since metaheuristic algorithms operate iteratively, the probability P_{A} plays a pivotal role in dictating the frequency at which a certain action, referred to as Action A, is executed throughout the course of these iterations. This probability essentially determines how often the algorithm will opt to perform Action A.

When the value of P_{A} is set close to zero, it implies that Action A is designated to be a rare occurrence within the algorithm's execution. In this scenario, the algorithm will seldom resort to applying Action A, making it an infrequent aspect of the search process. Conversely, if P_{A} is set close to one, the situation is quite different. Here, Action A becomes a common event, being executed almost every time the opportunity arises. Such a high probability ensures that Action A is a regular and influential part of the algorithm's behavior.

From an implementation standpoint, the process of determining whether to execute Action A at each iteration is typically handled through the generation of a uniformly distributed random number (generated by the function *rand*). This is achieved using a function like rand which generates a random number in the range of [0, 1] (denoted as **U**[0, 1]). The generated random number is then compared to P_{A}. If the random number is less than or equal to P_{A}, Action A is executed in that iteration; otherwise, it is skipped. This use of a random number from a uniform distribution ensures that the decision to execute Action A maintains the stochastic nature inherent to metaheuristic algorithms, allowing these methods to balance exploration and exploitation effectively in their search for optimal solutions.

To demonstrate the concept of probabilistic acceptance in practice, a program, as illustrated in Code 2.2, was developed. This program is designed to run for a total of 10,000 iterations, with a set probability $P_A = 0.7$ dictating the execution frequency of a specific action, **ActionA**. According to this setup, **ActionA** is expected to be executed approximately 70% of the time throughout these iterations, while in the remaining 30% of the iterations, **ActionA** will not be executed.

In practical terms, when the program is run, a uniformly distributed random number between 0 and 1 is generated in each iteration. If this random number is less than or equal to 0.7 (reflecting the value of P_A), then **ActionA** is executed; if it is greater than 0.7, Action A is not executed. As a result, over the span of 10,000 iterations, one would expect the variable **ActionA** (which counts the number of times **ActionA** is executed) to reach a value close to 7000, given the 70% probability of execution. Correspondingly, the variable **NoActionA** (which counts the number of times **ActionA** is not executed) would approximate 3000, aligning with the 30% probability of non-execution.

This program exemplifies how probabilistic acceptance works in an iterative process. It highlights the impact of the chosen probability value on the frequency of an action's execution and provides a clear, quantifiable insight into how often an action occurs under specified probabilistic conditions. The outcome, with **ActionA** around 7000 and **NoActionA** around 3000, serves as a practical illustration of the probabilistic decision-making inherent in metaheuristic algorithms.

Code 2.2

```
% Probabilistic acceptance
% Clear memory
clear all
% Variables are initialized
ActionA=0;
NoActionA =0;
% Starts the iterative decision process
for i=1:10000
    % A random number is generated U[0, 1]
    rA=rand;
    % Probabilistic acceptance
    if (rA<=0.7)
        ActionA = ActionA +1;
    else
        NoActionA = NoActionA +1;
    end
end
```

Probabilistic selection (Lipowski and Lipowska 2012) is a key concept in metaheuristic and metaheuristic algorithms, focusing on the process of choosing elements from a set of available options based on their quality. In this approach, elements that exhibit higher quality – typically measured in terms of their fitness or suitability for the problem at hand – are given a greater probability of being selected compared to those of lower quality. This method introduces a bias towards better-performing elements, ensuring that the most promising solutions are more likely to be chosen and retained for future iterations of the algorithm.

The underlying principle of probabilistic selection is to strike a balance between maintaining diversity within the population and converging toward optimal or near-optimal solutions. By preferentially selecting higher-quality elements, the algorithm incrementally improves the overall quality of the population (Yu et al. 2016). However, by allowing elements with lower quality to be chosen with a smaller but non-zero probability, the algorithm retains a degree of diversity. This diversity is crucial for preventing premature convergence to local optima and ensuring that the search explores a broad range of the solution space.

Probabilistic selection can take various forms, such as roulette wheel selection, tournament selection, or rank-based selection, each with its own method of assigning selection probabilities based on quality (Chakraborty and Bhowmik 2015). Regardless of the specific technique, the core idea remains the same: elements that are better suited to solving the problem are more likely to be selected and propagated through the generations of the algorithm. This method of selection is fundamental to the success of many evolutionary algorithms, as it directly influences the trajectory and effectiveness of the search process.

In metaheuristic methods, particularly those involving a population of solutions, a common task is to select a particular solution $\mathbf{x}_e^k$ from the population $\mathbf{P}^k(\mathbf{x}_1^k, \mathbf{x}_2^k, \ldots, \mathbf{x}_N^k)$, where e is an index within the range $[1, 2, \ldots, N]$. This selection is not arbitrary; it is heavily influenced by the quality or fitness of the solutions in the population, denoted as $f(\mathbf{x}_1^k), f(\mathbf{x}_2^k), \ldots, f(\mathbf{x}_N^k)$. The principle guiding this selection process is that solutions with better quality (or higher fitness values) should have a higher probability of being chosen compared to those with lower quality.

Under such a selection process, the probability of choosing the solution $\mathbf{x}_e^k$ from the set of all N solutions is calculated based on its relative fitness compared to the fitness of the other solutions in the population. This probability is typically defined through a specific formula or mechanism which ensures that higher fitness solutions are more likely to be picked. One common approach is to assign selection probabilities proportional to the fitness of each solution. For instance, in a roulette wheel selection mechanism, each solution in the population is given a slice of the wheel, with the size of the slice proportional to its fitness. The higher the fitness, the larger the slice, and thus, the greater the chance of being selected.

This probabilistic selection method plays a crucial role in the dynamics of metaheuristic algorithms, as it directly influences the direction and efficiency of the search process. By preferentially choosing higher-quality solutions, the algorithm can quickly converge toward optimal or near-optimal solutions. However, by maintaining a non-zero probability of selecting lower-quality solutions, the algorithm also retains a degree of exploration and diversity, crucial for avoiding local optima and ensuring a comprehensive search of the solution space.

Under this selection process, the probability of choosing the solution $\mathbf{x}_e^k$ among the other $N-1$ solutions is defined as:

$$P_e = \frac{f\left(\mathbf{x}_e^k\right)}{\sum_{i=1}^{N} f\left(\mathbf{x}_i^k\right)} \tag{2.11}$$

Another important concept associated with the solution $\mathbf{x}_e^k$ is the cumulative probability P_e^A. This cumulative probability is defined as:

$$P_e^A = \sum_{i=1}^{e} P_i \tag{2.12}$$

Under these conditions, the cumulative probability P_N^A, of the last solution of the population $\mathbf{P}^k$, will be equal to one.

In metaheuristic algorithms, particularly those that involve a population-based approach, the selection of solutions is often guided by probabilistic methods. Once the selection probabilities $\{P_1, P_2, \ldots, P_N\}$ for each solution in the population $\mathbf{P}^k$ are calculated, along with their cumulative probabilities $\left\{P_1^A, P_2^A, \ldots, P_N^A\right\}$, the selection process unfolds in the following manner:

- **Generation of a Random Number**: The process begins with the generation of a random number r_S, uniformly distributed in the interval [0, 1]. This random number serves as a basis for selecting one of the solutions from the population.
- **Iterative Testing Process**: Starting with the first solution in the population, a test is conducted to check if the cumulative probability P_1^A is greater than r_S. If this condition is not met, the process continues to the next solution in the population.
- **Continuation of Testing**: This testing continues iteratively through the population. For each solution, the algorithm checks if its corresponding cumulative probability P_e^A meets the condition of being greater than r_S.
- **Selection of the Solution**: The iterative process concludes when it finds a cumulative probability P_e^A that satisfies the condition $P_e^A > r_S$. The solution $\mathbf{x}_e^k$ corresponding to this cumulative probability is then selected as the output of this process.

This approach to selection is widely used in various metaheuristic algorithms, especially in those employing mechanisms like roulette wheel selection. It ensures that solutions with higher

Table 2.1 Characteristics of the solutions used in the numerical example for probabilistic selection.

Solution	$f(\cdot)$	P_e	P_e^A
x_1^k	$f(x_1^k) = 25$	$P_1 = 0.25$	$P_1^A = 0.25$
x_2^k	$f(x_2^k) = 5$	$P_2 = 0.05$	$P_2^A = 0.30$
x_3^k	$f(x_3^k) = 40$	$P_3 = 0.40$	$P_3^A = 0.70$
x_4^k	$f(x_4^k) = 10$	$P_4 = 0.10$	$P_4^A = 0.80$
x_5^k	$f(x_5^k) = 20$	$P_5 = 0.20$	$P_5^A = 1.00$

probabilities (and typically higher fitness) have a greater chance of being chosen, while still allowing for the possibility of selecting less optimal solutions. This method of selection is key to maintaining a balance between exploration and exploitation, as it allows for both the intensification of the search around promising areas and the diversification of the search to explore new regions of the solution space.

In order to clarify this process, a numerical example is developed below. Suppose one has a population $\mathbf{P}^k$ with 5 elements $\left(\mathbf{x}_1^k, \mathbf{x}_2^k, \mathbf{x}_3^k, \mathbf{x}_4^k, \mathbf{x}_5^k\right)$, whose qualities (fitness values), probabilities and cumulative probabilities are represented in Table 2.1. Considering these values, the selection process would be as follows: A uniformly distributed random value $\mathbf{U}[0, 1]$ is generated. Assuming that the value produced was $r_S = 0.51$, it is tested using the first element if $P_1^A > r_S$, as this does not occur it is tested with the second solution, the same condition $P_2^A > r_S$, as the condition is still not satisfied, the third solution $P_3^A > r_S$ is tested. As the condition $P_3^A > r_S$ is satisfied, the element chosen is $\mathbf{x}_3^k$.

2.7 Random Search

The random search method (Zabinsky 2009), often recognized as one of the earliest optimization strategies grounded in a fully stochastic process, adopts a notably straightforward approach. In this method, the optimization process revolves around the evolution of a single candidate solution, denoted as $\mathbf{x}^k$. This method stands out for its simplicity and its reliance on randomness as the primary driver of the search process.

At each iteration of the random search method (Kaelo and Ali 2006), the current candidate solution $\mathbf{x}^k$ is modified through the addition of a random vector, denoted as $\Delta\mathbf{x}$. This random vector introduces variability into the solution, enabling the exploration of the search space in a stochastic manner. The process of updating the candidate solution can be expressed mathematically as follows:

$$\mathbf{x}^{k+1} = \mathbf{x}^k + \Delta\mathbf{x} \tag{2.13}$$

In this expression, $\mathbf{x}^{k+1}$ represents the new candidate solution for the next iteration. The vector $\Delta\mathbf{x}$ is generated randomly, and its addition to the current solution $\mathbf{x}^k$ results in a new solution that is a random variation of the existing one.

When employing the random search method in a multidimensional context, where the candidate solution $\mathbf{x}^k$ has d dimensions $\left(x_1^k, x_2^k, \ldots, x_d^k\right)$, each coordinate of the solution is subject to modification. This modification is implemented through a vector of random perturbations, denoted as

($\Delta\mathbf{x} = \{\Delta x_1, \Delta x_2, \ldots, \Delta x_d\}$). Each component of this perturbation vector, Δx_i (where i ranges from 1 to d), is individually generated and modeled using a Gaussian (or normal) probability distribution as follows:

$$p(\Delta x_i) = \frac{1}{\sigma_i \cdot \sqrt{2\pi}} exp\left(-0.5 \cdot \frac{(\Delta x_i - \mu_i)}{\sigma_i^2}\right) = N(\mu_i, \sigma_i) \tag{2.14}$$

The Gaussian distribution is characterized by its mean (often denoted as μ_i) and its standard deviation (σ_i), and it is a commonly used probability distribution in stochastic processes due to its natural occurrence in many real-world scenarios. In the context of the random search method, the Gaussian distribution is employed to generate each Δx_i, providing a controlled yet random influence on each dimension of the solution.

In this expression, $N(\mu_i, \sigma_i)$ denotes the Gaussian distribution with mean μ_i and variance σ_i. The choice of μ_i and σ_i can significantly impact the behavior of the random search method. Typically, μ_i is set to zero, centering the distribution around the current value of $\mathbf{x}^k$, while σ_i controls the spread or variability of the perturbation, influencing the extent of exploration in the search space.

By applying these Gaussian-distributed perturbations to each dimension of the candidate solution, the random search method facilitates a multidimensional exploration of the solution space. This approach allows for a comprehensive and unbiased search, although the randomness of the method may require a large number of iterations to locate optimal or near-optimal solutions, especially in complex, high-dimensional optimization problems.

In the random search method, once the new candidate solution $\mathbf{x}^{k+1}$ is computed, the subsequent step involves evaluating whether this new position represents an improvement over the previous candidate solution $\mathbf{x}^k$. This evaluation is crucial as it determines whether to accept $\mathbf{x}^{k+1}$ as the new candidate solution or to retain $\mathbf{x}^k$ for the next iteration.

The improvement test, particularly in the context of a minimization problem, can be defined by comparing the quality or fitness values of $\mathbf{x}^{k+1}$ and $\mathbf{x}^k$. The quality of a solution is typically assessed using an objective function, which quantifies how well the solution meets the criteria of the optimization problem. For a minimization case, the objective is to find the solution with the lowest possible value of this objective function.

The test for whether to accept $\mathbf{x}^{k+1}$ can be mathematically formulated as follows:

- If $f(\mathbf{x}^{k+1}) < f(\mathbf{x}^k)$, then accept $\mathbf{x}^{k+1}$ as the new candidate solution. This implies that $\mathbf{x}^{k+1}$ has a lower (and therefore better) value of the objective function compared to $\mathbf{x}^k$, signifying an improvement.
- If $f(\mathbf{x}^{k+1}) \geq f(\mathbf{x}^k)$, then retain $\mathbf{x}^k$ as the current candidate solution. In this scenario, $\mathbf{x}^{k+1}$ does not offer any improvement over $\mathbf{x}^k$ in terms of minimizing the objective function.

This process of testing and potentially updating the candidate solution ensures that the random search method progressively moves towards better solutions over successive iterations (Feng and Shen 2015). However, the stochastic nature of the modifications means that improvements are not guaranteed at every step. The algorithm relies on the random generation of new solutions and the systematic evaluation of their quality to gradually find a solution that minimizes the objective function, navigating the solution space in an unbiased and exploratory manner.

The random search method's reliance on stochasticity means that it does not follow any gradient or specific direction in the search space. Instead, it relies on random sampling to potentially stumble upon optimal or near-optimal solutions. While this method is conceptually simple and easy to implement, it may not be as efficient or effective as other more sophisticated metaheuristic algorithms, especially for complex or high-dimensional problems. However, its significance lies in its foundational role in the evolution of optimization techniques, demonstrating the potential of stochastic processes in searching for solutions.

The criterion used in the random search method for updating the candidate solution is commonly referred to as a "greedy" approach. This term implies that the algorithm only accepts changes to the solution that result in an immediate improvement in its quality. Specifically, in the context of the random search method, this means that a new candidate solution $\mathbf{x}^{k+1}$ is accepted only if it offers a better (lower for minimization, higher for maximization) objective function value compared to the current solution $\mathbf{x}^k$.

However, one challenge inherent to this method, especially due to its stochastic nature, is the possibility of the new solution $\mathbf{x}^{k+1}$ being generated outside the predefined search space $\mathbf{X}$. Since the objective function $f(\mathbf{x})$. is defined only within the bounds of this search space, a solution lying outside $\mathbf{X}$ has no valid objective function value. To manage this situation, the random search algorithm incorporates a safeguard mechanism. If a newly generated solution $\mathbf{x}^{k+1}$ falls outside the search space $\mathbf{X}$, the algorithm assigns it a very poor quality. This is represented by assigning an extremely large value to the objective function for minimization problems (i.e., $f(\mathbf{x}^{k+1}) = \infty$) or an extremely low value for maximization problems (i.e., $f(\mathbf{x}^{k+1}) = -\infty$).

By doing so, the algorithm ensures that any solution generated outside the viable search space is automatically deemed unfavorable and is not accepted as the new candidate solution. This approach effectively keeps the evolution of the solution within the bounds of the defined search space, maintaining the integrity and relevance of the search process. The greedy nature of the substitution criterion, combined with this safeguard against invalid solutions, helps guide the random search method in progressively and efficiently exploring the solution space toward finding an optimal or near-optimal solution.

In order to exemplify the operation of the randomized search algorithm and its practical implementation in MATLAB, we intend to solve the following maximization problem:

$$\begin{aligned} &\min && f(x_1, x_2) = 3(1-x_1)^2 + 10\left(\frac{x_1}{5} - x_1^3 - x_2^5\right)e^{(-x_1^2-x_2^2)} - \frac{1}{3}e^{(-(x_1+1)^2-x_2^2)} \\ &\text{Subject to:} && -3 \le x_1 \le 3 \\ &&& -3 \le x_2 \le 3 \end{aligned} \tag{2.15}$$

In this formulation, a two-dimensional function $f(x_1, x_2)$ with a search space defined in the interval $[-3, 3]$ is considered for each of the decision variables x_1 and x_2. Figure 2.7 shows a representation of the objective function $f(x_1, x_2)$.

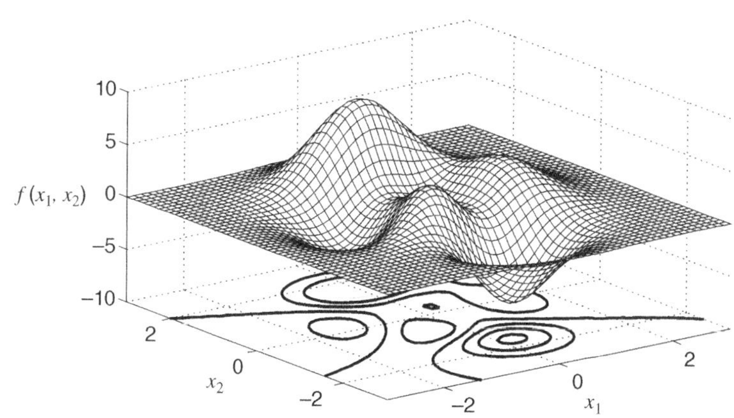

Figure 2.7 Representación gráfica de la función $f(x_1, x_2)$.

As can be seen, the function $f(x_1, x_2)$ can be derived twice, however, it is multimodal. For these reasons, it does not meet the requirements to be minimized under the gradient descent method. Under these circumstances, it is maximized by the random search method.

The process for the maximization of $f(x_1, x_2)$ by the random search method is presented in pseudocode form in Algorithm 2.2. The procedure starts by randomly selecting a decision vector $\mathbf{x}^k$ ($k = 0$), within the search space defined in the interval [−3, 3] for each of the variables x_1 and x_2. Then, the new candidate solution $\mathbf{x}^{k+1}$ is calculated, by including the random perturbation Δx. Once $\mathbf{x}^{k+1}$ is obtained, it is checked if it belongs to the search space. If it is not included in X, the solution is assigned a very poor quality ($f(\mathbf{x}^{k+1}) = \infty$). The idea is that points outside the search space cannot be chosen. Finally, it is decided whether the new point $\mathbf{x}^{k+1}$ formulates an improvement compared to its predecessor $\mathbf{x}^k$. So, if the quality of $\mathbf{x}^{k+1}$ is better than $\mathbf{x}^k$, the value of $\mathbf{x}^{k+1}$ is accepted as the new candidate solution, otherwise $\mathbf{x}^k$ remains unchanged. This process is repeated iteratively until a maximum number of Niter iterations have been reached.

Algorithm 2.2 ***Random Search Method for Solving 3.14***

$k \leftarrow 0$
$x_1^k \leftarrow \text{rand } [-3, 3],\ x_2^k \leftarrow \text{rand } [-3, 3]$
while $(k < Niter)$ {
$, \Delta x_2 = N(0, 1)$
$x_1^{k+1} = x_1^k + \Delta x_1, x_2^{k+1} = x_2^k + \Delta x_2$
$\mathbf{x}^k = (x_1^k, x_2^k), \mathbf{x}^{k+1} = (x_1^{k+1}, x_2^{k+1})$
If $(\mathbf{x}^{k+1} \notin \mathbf{X})\{f(x^{k+1}) = -\infty\}$
If $(f(\mathbf{x}^{k+1}) < (f(\mathbf{x}^k))\ \{\mathbf{x}^{k+1} = \mathbf{x}^k\}$
$k \leftarrow k + 1\}$

From the implementation point of view, the most critical part is represented by the calculation of $\Delta\mathbf{x} = (\Delta x_1, \Delta x_2)$. Such values are obtained by a Gaussian probability distribution. In MATLAB, a random sample r coming from a population with Gaussian distribution is calculated:

$$r = \mu + \sigma \text{ randn}$$

considering that μ and σ represent the mean and standard deviation of the population.

In order to provide the reader with an aid in the implementation of Algorithm 2.2, Code 2.3 shows the program in MATLAB. In the operation of code 1.4, first, the function $f(x_1, x_2)$ is plotted in order to appreciate its characteristics. Then, in an iterative way, the set of candidate solutions generated from its initial value $\mathbf{x}^0$ until the optimal value $\mathbf{x}^*$ is found is shown. Figure 2.8 shows an example of the set of solutions produced during the evolution of the algorithm, on two MATLAB contours, obtained by Code 3.4.

Code 2.3

```
% Random search method
% Clear memory
```

```
clear all
% The function to be optimized is defined
funstr='3*(1-x).^2.*exp(-(x.^2)-(y+1).^2)-10*(x/5-x.^3-y.^5).
*exp(-x.^2-y.^2)-...3*exp(-(x+1).^2 -y.^2)';
f=vectorize(inline(funstr));
range=[-3 3 -3 3];
% The function is drawn as a reference
Ndiv=50;
dx=(range(2)-range(1))/Ndiv; dy=(range(4)-range(3))/Ndiv;
[x,y] =meshgrid(range(1):dx:range(2),range(3):dy:range(4));
z=f(x,y);
figure(1);   surfc(x,y,z);
% The maximum number of iterations is defined
Niter=3000;
k=0;
% Starting point generation
xrange=range(2)-range(1);
yrange=range(4)-range(3);
xn=rand*xrange+range(1);
yn=rand*yrange+range(3);
figure
% The iterative optimization process is established
while(k<Niter)
% It is evaluated whether the solution belongs to the search space X
 if ((xn>=range(1))&(xn<=range(2))&(yn>=range(3))&(yn<=range(4)))
  % If it belongs, it is evaluated
  zn1=f(xn,yn);
 else
  % If it is not given a very low value
     zn1=-1000;
 end
  % The point is plotted
  contour(x,y,z,15); hold on;
  plot(xn,yn,'.','markersize',10,'markerfacecolor','g');
  drawnow;
  hold on;
  % The new solution is calculated
  xnc=xn+randn*1;
  ync=yn+randn*1;
  % It is evaluated whether the solution belongs to the search
  space X
  if ((xnc>=range(1))&(xnc<=range(2))&(ync>=range(3))&
  (ync<=range(4)))
  % If it belongs, it is evaluated
      zn2=f(xnc,ync);
  else
     % If it is not given a very low value
```

```
        zn2=-1000;
    end
    % Test whether the newly generated solution is accepted.
    if (zn2>zn1)
        xn=xnc;
        yn=ync;
    end
    k=k+1;
    end
```

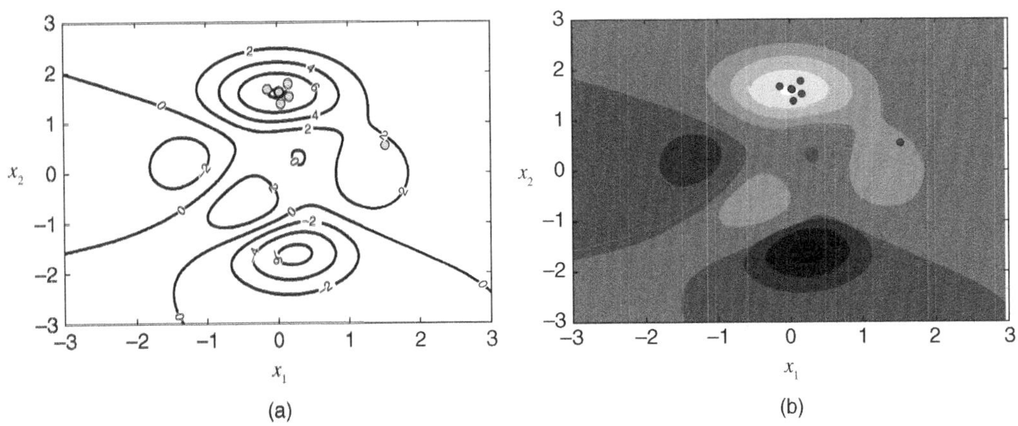

Figure 2.8 Solution map on (a) contour with level values and (b) with grayscale coding.

The random search method can be effectively used in machine learning, particularly in the context of hyperparameter optimization. Hyperparameter optimization is a critical step in building and fine-tuning machine learning models, as it involves selecting the optimal set of hyperparameters that govern the learning process and overall behavior of the model. Hyperparameters can include learning rates, the number of hidden layers and neurons in neural networks, regularization parameters, and many others, depending on the type of model being used.

The random search method can be applied in this context:

- **Defining the Hyperparameter Space**: The first step involves defining the range or space for each hyperparameter. For instance, if you're tuning a neural network, you might define ranges for the learning rate, number of layers, number of neurons per layer, etc.
- **Random Sampling of Hyperparameters**: Unlike grid search, which exhaustively tries all possible combinations of hyperparameters, random search randomly selects combinations of hyperparameters from the defined space. This is where the random search method shines, as it can explore a wide range of values without the computational expense of testing every possible combination.
- **Model Training and Evaluation**: For each randomly selected set of hyperparameters, the machine learning model is trained, and its performance is evaluated

using a predefined metric (such as accuracy, F1 score, mean squared error, etc.). This step is repeated for a specified number of iterations or until a satisfactory level of performance is achieved.

- **Selecting the Best Model**: After a series of iterations, the hyperparameter set that resulted in the best model performance is selected. This set of hyperparameters is considered optimal for the given task and dataset.
- **Final Model Training**: Finally, the model is retrained using the optimal set of hyperparameters on the entire training dataset to prepare it for deployment or further evaluation.

Advantages of Random Search in Machine Learning:

- **Efficiency**: Random search is more efficient than exhaustive search methods, especially when some hyperparameters are more important than others.
- **Scalability**: It scales well with the number of hyperparameters and the complexity of the model.
- **Flexibility**: It can navigate large and complex hyperparameter spaces, finding good combinations that might be missed by more deterministic methods.

Random search is particularly useful when the budget (time or computational resources) is limited, as it can often find a reasonably good set of hyperparameters in a fraction of the time it would take to perform an exhaustive search. However, it's worth noting that while random search can be more effective than grid search, it doesn't always guarantee finding the absolute best set of hyperparameters, especially in very large or complex hyperparameter spaces. In such cases, more advanced techniques like Bayesian optimization might be employed.

2.8 Simulated Annealing

Simulated annealing (Kirkpatrick et al. 1983) is a sophisticated optimization technique that takes inspiration from the physical process of annealing in metallurgy. This process involves heating and controlled cooling of a material, typically metal, to reduce defects in its crystalline structure and achieve a more ordered state. The concept of using this annealing process as a metaphor for an optimization algorithm was first proposed by Kirkpatrick et al. (1983), leading to a novel approach that diverges from traditional gradient-based methods.

The key principle behind simulated annealing is the analogy it draws between the objective function in optimization and the energy of a thermodynamic system. In this analogy, the goal of the optimization is akin to finding the lowest energy state of the system, which corresponds to the most stable and defect-free state in annealing.

One of the distinguishing features of simulated annealing is its ability to avoid getting trapped in local minima, a common drawback of gradient-based algorithms. This capability is achieved through the algorithm's unique temperature-controlled exploration of the search space. At high "temperatures," the algorithm is more willing to explore widely, accepting solutions that may not immediately seem to improve upon the current state. This broad exploration is akin to allowing the material to attain various states during the heating phase, encouraging a diverse range of configurations.

As the "temperature" lowers, akin to the cooling phase in annealing, the algorithm becomes more selective (Henderson et al. 2003). The generation of new solutions is restricted to points closer to the current solution, and the probability of accepting worse solutions decreases. This phase of the algorithm is more about refining and improving the current solution, analogous to the material forming a more ordered and defect-free structure as it cools.

This dynamic process of controlling "temperature" in simulated annealing allows for an effective balance between exploration (trying out new, possibly distant solutions) and exploitation (refining and improving near the current solution). It provides the algorithm with a robust mechanism to escape local minima and converge towards a global minimum, or at least a near-optimal solution, making it a powerful tool for a wide range of optimization problems. Since its inception, simulated annealing has been the subject of extensive research and application, demonstrating its versatility and effectiveness across various domains.

The simulated quenching algorithm, which is a variation of the simulated annealing method, operates by maintaining a single candidate solution, denoted as $\mathbf{x}^k$, throughout its process (Chopard et al. 2018). Similar to the random search method, the candidate solution in the simulated quenching algorithm is modified at each iteration. This modification involves the generation of a random vector, which is then used to perturb the current point, introducing variability and facilitating exploration of the solution space.

However, a distinctive aspect of the simulated quenching algorithm is its approach to accepting changes to the candidate solution. Unlike more traditional optimization methods that accept only improvements to the objective function, the simulated quenching algorithm employs a probabilistic mechanism that also allows for the acceptance of solutions that are worse than the current one. This feature is crucial for the algorithm's ability to effectively navigate complex solution spaces.

The rationale behind this probabilistic acceptance of inferior solutions lies in enhancing the algorithm's capability to escape from local minima. By occasionally accepting solutions that worsen the objective function, the algorithm avoids becoming trapped in local optima and continues its exploration for potentially better solutions. This approach mirrors the physical process of quenching, where rapid cooling can lead to states that are not necessarily the most stable or ordered but can be instrumental in achieving the desired properties in the final material.

The probability of accepting a worse solution typically depends on a parameter analogous to "temperature" in thermodynamics, which decreases over time. At higher temperatures, the algorithm is more likely to accept worse solutions, promoting exploration. As the temperature lowers, the likelihood of accepting worse solutions decreases, leading to a more focused exploitation of the solution space. This balance between exploration and exploitation, guided by the probabilistic acceptance of solutions, is what endows the simulated quenching algorithm with its robustness and effectiveness in solving optimization problems.

Under these circumstances, taking as an example a maximization problem, a new solution $\mathbf{x}^{k+1}$ will be accepted considering 2 different alternatives.

1. If its quality is superior to that of its predecessor $\mathbf{x}^k$. That is if $f(\mathbf{x}^{k+1}) > f(\mathbf{x}^k)$.
2. Under an acceptance probability p_a.

The second alternative determines that even if the quality of $\mathbf{x}^{k+1}$ is not superior to $\mathbf{x}^k$ ($f(\mathbf{x}^{k+1}) < f(\mathbf{x}^k)$), the solution $\mathbf{x}^{k+1}$ will be accepted according to an acceptance probability p_a defined as:

$$p_a = e^{-\frac{\Delta f}{T}} \tag{2.16}$$

where T represents the temperature controlling the tempering process, while Δf represents the energy difference between the points $\mathbf{x}^{k+1}$ and $\mathbf{x}^k$, which is defined as:

$$\Delta f = f(\mathbf{x}^{k+1}) - f(\mathbf{x}^k) \tag{2.17}$$

Thus, the acceptance or not of a new position $\mathbf{x}^{k+1}$ is performed under the following procedure. First, a random number r_1 uniformly distributed between [0, 1] is obtained, if $r_1 < p_a$, the point $\mathbf{x}^{k+1}$ is accepted as the new solution.

For a given energy difference Δf, if T is large, then $p_a \rightarrow 1$, which implies that all changes of $\mathbf{x}^{k+1}$ will be accepted regardless of whether their quality is greater than the previous candidate solution $\mathbf{x}^k$. If T is very small, then $p_a \rightarrow 0$, which means that only values of $\mathbf{x}^{k+1}$ that improve the quality of $\mathbf{x}^k$ will be accepted. When this happens the search strategy becomes the same as the one used by the random search method.

Thus, if T is large, the algorithm simulates a high thermal energy system, so the search space $\mathbf{X}$ is extensively explored. If T is very small, the system allows to locally refine the search to find the optimal point.

Under these conditions, the most important part of the simulated quenching algorithm is the so-called tempering control, which specifies the process in which the temperature is varied from a high to a low value (Shi et al. 2023). Such a process depends on the specific application and requires in most cases trial-and-error calibration. There are several ways to control the cooling process from an initial temperature T_{ini} to a final temperature T_{fin}. Two methods are known for this task, linear and geometric.

In the linear scheme, the temperature reduction is given under the following model:

$$T(k) = T_{ini} - \beta k \tag{2.18}$$

where β is the cooling ratio, which should be chosen such that $T \rightarrow 0$ when $k \rightarrow Niter$ (maximum number of iterations), this means that $\beta = (T_{ini} - T_{fin})/Niter$. On the other hand, in the geometric cooling scheme, the temperature is decremented by the use of a cooling factor β defined in the interval [0, 1]. The model specifying the geometric cooling strategy is specified by the following expression:

$$T(k) = T_{ini} \cdot \eta^k \tag{2.19}$$

The advantage of the geometric model is that $T \rightarrow 0$ when $k \rightarrow \infty$. In practice $\eta \in [0.7, 0.95]$. In order to show the complete computational procedure of the simulated annealing method, Algorithm 2.3 presents as pseudocode its generic structure.

The generic simulated annealing method starts with the configuration of its operating variables T_{ini}, T_{fin}, β, and $Niter$. Then, an initial point is randomly generated within the bounds of the search space $\mathbf{X}$. Next, the evolution process is generated, which is maintained until either the number of iterations has not been reached or the temperature has obtained its projected final value T_{ini}. During that process, the new candidate solution $\mathbf{x}^{k+1}$ is generated as a modification $\Delta\mathbf{x}$ of the original $\mathbf{x}^k$. Such modification $\Delta\mathbf{x}$ is computed similarly to the one performed by the randomized search algorithm explained in Section 4. Once $\mathbf{x}^{k+1}$ is generated, it is analyzed whether this new solution will be accepted or not. Two possibilities are considered for this purpose. (1) If the new solution improves the previous $\mathbf{x}^k$, it is accepted. Otherwise, if it does not improve it, (2) the acceptance of $\mathbf{x}^{k+1}$ is probabilistically tested with acceptance probability p_a. If the test is passed, $\mathbf{x}^{k+1}$ is accepted, otherwise, $\mathbf{x}^{k+1}$ is discarded and $\mathbf{x}^k$ is kept. At each iteration, in addition, the temperature is decreased by a factor β with the objective of reducing the degree of acceptance of new solutions $\mathbf{x}^{k+1}$ that do not exhibit better quality than their predecessor $\mathbf{x}^k$.

For the generation of new candidate solutions $\mathbf{x}^{k+1}$, the simulated annealing method uses the random modification $\Delta\mathbf{x}$. Because of this, many new solutions could fall outside the search space $\mathbf{X}$. The randomized search algorithm avoids this problem by assigning the new solution $\mathbf{x}^{k+1}$ a lousy quality, with the goal that $\mathbf{x}^{k+1}$ can never be selected. Since the simulated hardening method allows

Algorithm 2.3 ***Simulated Annealing Method***

1. Configure T_{ini}, T_{fin}, β, σ y *Niter*.
2. $k \leftarrow 0, T = T_{ini}$
3. $\mathbf{x}^k \leftarrow \text{rand}\ [\mathbf{X}]$
4. **while** $((T > T_{fin})$ **and** $(k < Niter))\{$
5. **while** $(\mathbf{x}^{k+1} \notin \mathbf{X})\{$
6. $\Delta\mathbf{x} \leftarrow \mathbf{N}(0, \sigma \cdot T)$
7. $\mathbf{x}^{k+1} \leftarrow \mathbf{x}^k + \Delta\mathbf{x}\}$
8. **If** $(\mathbf{x}^{k+1}$ is worse than $\mathbf{x}^k)$
9. $\{\Delta f \leftarrow f(\mathrm{x}^{k+1}) - f(\mathrm{x}^k)$
10. $p_a \leftarrow e^{-\frac{\Delta f}{T}}$
11. **If** $(p_a < rand)\{\mathbf{x}^{k+1} = \mathbf{x}^k\}\}$
12. $k \leftarrow \mathrm{k} + 1$
13. $T \leftarrow \beta \cdot T\}$

probabilistic acceptance of solutions that have poor quality, lousy quality solutions, such as these, could also be accepted. To avoid this problem, the simulated hardening algorithm implements a solution generation mechanism, which avoids constructing a new solution that falls outside of the search space $\mathbf{X}$. Normally such an implementation is realized by a **while** loop that runs perpetually until a point belonging to the search space $\mathbf{X}$ is found (see lines 5–7 of Algorithm 2.3).

A frequently implemented improvement in the simulated annealing method is the gradual reduction of the random perturbations $\Delta\mathbf{x}$, used for the production of the new solutions $\mathbf{x}^{k+1}$. The idea is that in the first iterations, large random jumps are allowed, with the objective of extensively exploring the search space. However, as the algorithm evolves, this capability decreases, until, in the last iterations, the exploration for a better solution is done only locally (with very small $\Delta\mathbf{x}$ values). As the perturbations $\Delta\mathbf{x}$ are computed by a Gaussian probability distribution of the form $\Delta\mathbf{x} \leftarrow N(0, \sigma \cdot T)$. Such behavior is easily implemented by multiplying the standard deviation with the current value of the temperature T. Thus, as the temperature decreases ($T \rightarrow 0$) during the evolution process, the magnitude of the perturbations will also decrease ($\Delta\mathbf{x} \rightarrow 0$).

To demonstrate the operation of the simulated annealing algorithm and its practical implementation in MATLAB, an example is provided where this algorithm is applied to solve a maximization problem, as formulated in Section 2.14. For this purpose, Program 2.4 in the material offers a detailed MATLAB code, which serves as a valuable resource for readers seeking to understand and implement the simulated annealing algorithm.

The implementation in Code 2.4 is carefully designed to follow the principles of the simulated annealing algorithm. It involves initializing a candidate solution and iteratively modifying it with random perturbations, while also employing a probabilistic mechanism to decide whether to accept each new solution. This mechanism is crucial for allowing the algorithm to occasionally accept solutions that do not immediately seem to improve the objective function, thereby facilitating the escape from local maxima in the context of a maximization problem.

Code 2.4

```
% Simulated annealing
% Clear memory
clear all
% The function to be optimized is defined
funstr='3*(1-x).^2.*exp(-(x.^2)-(y+1).^2)-10*(x/5-x.^3-y.^5).
*exp(-x.^2-y.^2)-1/3*exp(-(x+1).^2 -y.^2)';
f=vectorize(inline(funstr));
range=[-3 3 -3 3];
% The function is drawn as a reference
Ndiv=50;
dx=(range(2)-range(1))/Ndiv; dy=(range(4)-range(3))/Ndiv;
[x,y] =meshgrid(range(1):dx:range(2),range(3):dy:range(4));
z=f(x,y);
figure(1);   surfc(x,y,z);
% The maximum number of iterations is defined
k=1;
valido=0;
Niter=150;
% Define initial temperature
T_init =1.0;
% Define the final temperature
T_fin = 1e-10;
% Cooling ratio
beta=0.95;
% Generation of the starting point
xrange=range(2)-range(1);
yrange=range(4)-range(3);
xn=rand*xrange+range(1);
yn=rand*yrange+range(3);
% The temperature is initialized
T = T_init;
% The iterative optimization process is established
while (k<Niter)
% The point is plotted
  contour(x,y,z); hold on;
  plot(xn,yn,'.','markersize',10,'markerfacecolor','g');
  drawnow;
  hold off;
 % The quality of point x(k) is calculated.
  E_old = f(xn,yn);
  % The new solution x(k+1) is produced.
```

```
  % The while cycle applies until the new point is within X
 while(valido==0)
  % The standard deviation value is modified with T
  xnc=xn+randn*2.5*T;
  ync=yn+randn*2.5*T;
  if ((xnc>=range(1))&(xnc<=range(2))&(ync>=range(3))&
  (ync<=range(4)))
      valido=1;
  end
 end
  valido=0;
  % Information on temperature evolution is obtained
  data(k)=T;
  % The quality of the new solution is calculated
  E_new=f(xnc,ync);
 % The difference is calculated
 DeltaE=E_new-E_old;
 % If the new solution is better in quality than the previous one,
 %it is accepted.
if (DeltaE>0)
   xn=xnc;
    yn=ync;
end
% If their acceptance is not analyzed probabilistically
if (DeltaE<0 & exp(DeltaE/T)>rand );
    xn=xnc;
    yn=ync;
end
% Temperature is updated
T = beta*T;
if (T<T_fin)
    T=T_fin;
end
k=k+1;
end
```

To ensure the algorithm operates effectively, various parameters need to be configured, as outlined in Table 2.2. These parameters typically include the initial "temperature," the rate of "temperature" decrease (cooling schedule), the number of iterations, and other algorithm-specific settings that influence the behavior and performance of the simulated annealing process. The configuration of these parameters is critical, as they determine how aggressively the algorithm explores the solution space and how quickly it transitions from exploration to exploitation.

By following the MATLAB code in Program 2.4 and the parameter settings in Table 2.2, readers can gain a hands-on understanding of how the simulated annealing algorithm navigates the solution space. This practical example not only illustrates the implementation details of the algorithm but also showcases its unique capability to balance exploration and exploitation, making it an effective tool for solving complex optimization problems.

Table 2.2 Parameters of the simulated annealing method implemented in code 2.4.

Parameter	Value
T_{ini}	1
T_{fin}	1×10^{-10}
β	0.95
Niter	150
σ	2.5

The simulated annealing method, with its sophisticated approach to optimization, typically requires significantly fewer iterations to find the optimal solution, $\mathbf{x}^*$ compared to the random search algorithm. This efficiency stems from its strategic balance between exploration and exploitation, guided by a temperature-like parameter that methodically decreases over time. In metaheuristic methods, one of the persistent challenges is determining the appropriate number of iterations necessary to solve a given optimization problem effectively. This is a crucial aspect of algorithm design, as it directly impacts both the success of the optimization and the computational resources required. If the number of iterations is set too low, the algorithm may not have sufficient opportunity to thoroughly explore the solution space. As a result, there is an increased risk that the global optimum, or the best possible solution, will remain undiscovered. The algorithm might prematurely converge to a local optimum or not progress enough towards the most favorable solution. Conversely, setting the number of iterations too high leads to a different problem. While a higher number of iterations can increase the likelihood of finding the global optimum, it also incurs a greater computational cost. This can make the optimization process inefficient, especially in cases where computational resources are limited or when the algorithm is applied to large-scale or complex problems. Therefore, finding a balance in the number of iterations is essential. The goal is to allocate enough iterations to allow the algorithm to effectively explore and exploit the solution space, while also being mindful of the computational resources and time constraints. In the case of simulated annealing, this balance is further refined by the temperature schedule, which provides a structured approach to reducing the exploration over time, leading to a more focused and efficient search as the algorithm progresses. This dynamic adjustment is one of the key factors that contribute to the efficiency of simulated annealing compared to more straightforward methods like random search.

In the execution of Code 2.4, the process begins with the plotting of the function $f(x_1, x_2)$ to provide a visual understanding of its characteristics. This initial step is crucial as it helps to visualize the landscape of the optimization problem, including aspects like the location of peaks, valleys, and contours that represent potential optima. Understanding these characteristics is essential for interpreting the behavior and efficacy of the algorithm in navigating the solution space.

Following the visualization, the code then executes an iterative process where a set of candidate solutions is generated, starting from an initial value $\mathbf{x}^0$ and progressing towards the optimal value $\mathbf{x}^*$. This iterative process is central to the operation of the algorithm, involving the generation of new solutions and the application of the simulated annealing method to refine these solutions towards the global optimum.

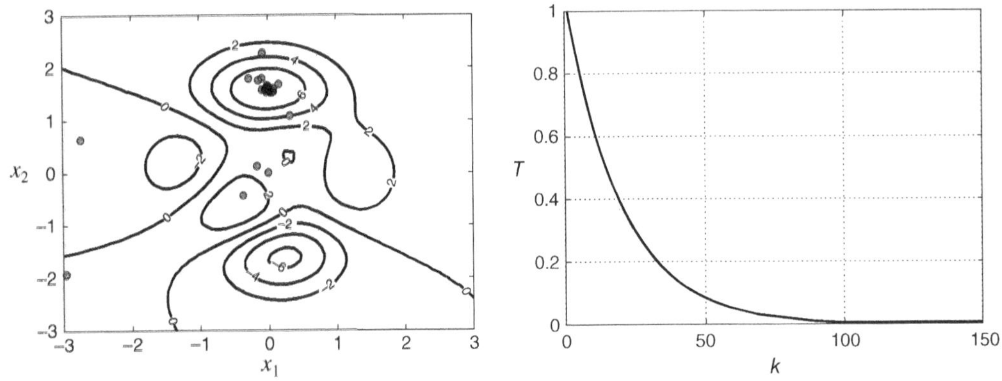

Figure 2.9 Solution map on (a) the contour with the values and (b) the cooling strategy (temperature decrease).

Figure 2.9a in the material illustrates an example of the set of solutions produced during the evolution of the algorithm. Displayed on two MATLAB contour plots, this figure provides a graphical representation of how the candidate solutions evolve over iterations. It shows the trajectory of the solutions in the search space, offering insight into how the algorithm explores and exploits different regions to find the optimal solution.

Additionally, Figure 2.9b presents the temperature decrease, or "tempering," process experienced during the evolution of the method. This graphical representation demonstrates the controlled reduction of the "temperature" parameter, a key aspect of the simulated annealing algorithm. The temperature schedule is pivotal in transitioning the algorithm from an exploratory phase (high temperature, where the algorithm is more likely to accept both better and worse solutions) to an exploitative phase (low temperature, where the algorithm becomes more selective, primarily accepting improvements). Observing this tempering process helps in understanding how the algorithm balances exploration and exploitation, gradually focusing its search on the most promising areas of the solution space. The visualizations provided in Figure 2.9a,b collectively offer a comprehensive view of the dynamic and adaptive nature of the simulated annealing algorithm in solving optimization problems.

The complementary use of the simulated annealing method and machine learning offers a powerful combination for solving complex optimization problems in model training and feature selection. In machine learning, model accuracy, and performance often hinge on fine-tuning hyperparameters and selecting the right features, tasks where simulated annealing can be particularly effective.

(A) **Simulated Annealing in Machine Learning**:

The simulated annealing method, inspired by the physical process of annealing in metallurgy, can be effectively utilized in machine learning, especially for hyperparameter optimization and feature selection. Here's how it can be applied:

1. **Hyperparameter Optimization**:
   - **Defining the Hyperparameter Space**: Just like in any optimization problem, you start by defining the range for each hyperparameter of the

machine learning model. For instance, this could include the learning rate, number of layers, and number of neurons for a neural network.

- **Initial Solution and Temperature**: Begin with an initially random set of hyperparameters and a high "temperature". The temperature in simulated annealing controls the probability of accepting worse solutions, facilitating broader exploration at the start.
- **Generating New Solutions**: At each iteration, slightly modify the current set of hyperparameters (akin to the generation of a new state in metallurgical annealing). This could involve small changes in the learning rate or altering the number of neurons.
- **Evaluating and Accepting Solutions**: Train the model with these hyperparameters and evaluate its performance. If the new solution (set of hyperparameters) performs better, accept it. If it performs worse, accept it with a probability that decreases with the temperature. This step is crucial as it allows the algorithm to escape local optima in the early stages.
- **Cooling Schedule**: Gradually decrease the temperature according to a predefined cooling schedule. As the temperature lowers, the algorithm becomes increasingly less likely to accept worse solutions, focusing more on exploiting the best solutions found so far.
- **Convergence**: The process is repeated until the system "cools down" to a low temperature or another stopping criterion is met, at which point the best set of hyperparameters found is selected.

2. **Feature Selection**:
   - **Initial Feature Set**: Start with a random selection of features.
   - **Iteration Process**: At each iteration, randomly add, remove, or modify features in the set.
   - **Model Evaluation**: Train the model on these features and evaluate its performance.
   - **Acceptance Criterion**: Similar to hyperparameter optimization, accept or reject the new set of features based on the model's performance and the current temperature, allowing for exploration and exploitation.
   - **Cooling and Convergence**: Lower the temperature over time, reducing the likelihood of accepting worse feature sets, until an optimal or satisfactory set of features is identified.

In both hyperparameter optimization and feature selection, simulated annealing offers a balance between exploration of the solution space (trying out a wide range of hyperparameters or feature sets) and exploitation (refining and focusing on the most promising solutions). This balance is particularly beneficial in complex machine learning models where the parameter space is vast, and the risk of getting trapped in local optima is high. Simulated annealing can navigate such spaces more effectively than simple random or exhaustive search methods, often leading to better overall model performance.

(B) **Machine Learning Techniques for Improving the Simulated Annealing Method**:

Machine learning techniques can be utilized to enhance the simulated annealing method, particularly in optimizing its operation and making it more efficient and effective for specific problems. Here are several ways in which machine learning can contribute:

1. **Adaptive Temperature Scheduling**: **Predictive Models**: Machine learning can be used to develop predictive models that determine the most effective temperature schedule based on the characteristics of the problem.

   Reinforcement Learning: This technique can help in dynamically adjusting the temperature based on the feedback received from the optimization process, leading to a more efficient cooling schedule.
2. **Feature-Based Problem Characterization**: Machine learning can analyze characteristics of the optimization problem (like landscape ruggedness or the number of local optima) to adapt the simulated annealing parameters accordingly.

   Clustering or classification algorithms can categorize problems into different types, each with tailored annealing parameters for improved performance.
3. **Optimizing Perturbation Strategies**: Machine learning can help in choosing or adapting the perturbation strategy (how new candidate solutions are generated) based on the problem's features or the current state of the optimization process.

   Neural networks or decision trees could predict the most effective perturbation methods (e.g., the magnitude of changes to apply) at different stages of the annealing process.
4. **Solution Space Analysis**: Machine learning algorithms can preprocess the solution space to identify regions of interest or potential optima, guiding the simulated annealing process to start from more promising areas.

   Techniques like dimensionality reduction can simplify complex solution spaces, making the annealing process more efficient.
5. **Performance Prediction**: Machine learning models can predict the performance of certain configurations of the annealing process, thus reducing the need for exhaustive trial-and-error experimentation.

   Regression models could estimate the quality of solutions based on different annealing parameters, helping to fine-tune the algorithm more quickly.
6. **Hybrid Approaches**: Combining simulated annealing with other optimization techniques (like genetic algorithms or gradient descent) guided by machine learning can lead to hybrid methods that leverage the strengths of each approach.

   Machine learning can determine when and how to switch between different methods or how to combine their outputs effectively.

Incorporating machine learning into simulated annealing opens up possibilities for self-tuning algorithms that adapt to specific problems and environments, making them more versatile and powerful. By leveraging predictive analytics, adaptive mechanisms, and intelligent decision-making, machine learning can significantly enhance the capabilities of traditional simulated annealing methods.

References

Baldick, R. (2006). *Applied Optimization*. Cambridge University Press.

Bartholomew-Biggs, M. (2008). *Nonlinear Optimization with Engineering Applications*. Springer.

Binkley, K.J. and Hagiwara, M. (2008). Balancing exploitation and exploration in particle swarm optimization: velocity-based reinitialization. *Information and Media Technologies* 3 (1): 103–111.

Broyden, C.G. (1970). The convergence of a class of double rank minimization algorithms: part 1 and 2. *Journal of Applied Mathematics* 6: 76–90 and 222–231.

Chakraborty, S. and Bhowmik, S. (2015). Blending roulette wheel selection with simulated annealing for job shop scheduling problem. Michael Faraday IET International Summit 2015.

Chopard, B., Tomassini, M., Chopard, B., and Tomassini, M. (2018). Simulated annealing. In: *An Introduction to Metaheuristics for Optimization*, 59–79. Springer.

Črepinšek, M., Liu, S.H., and Mernik, M. (2013). Exploration and exploitation in evolutionary algorithms: a survey. *ACM Computing Surveys (CSUR)* 45 (3): 1–33.

Cuevas, E. and Rodríguez, A. (2020). *Metaheuristic Computation with MATLAB®*. CRC Press.

Deb, K. (2001). *Multi-Objective Optimization Using Evolutionary Algorithms*. Wiley.

Dennis, J.E. (1978). A brief introduction to quasi-Newton methods. In: *Numerical Analysis: Proceedings of Symposia in Applied Mathematics* (ed. G.H. Golub and J. Öliger), 19–52. AMS.

Feng, J. and Shen, W.Z. (2015). Solving the wind farm layout optimization problem using random search algorithm. *Renewable Energy* 78: 182–192.

Fletcher, R. and Powell, M.J. (1963). A rapidly convergent descent method for minimization. *Computer Journal* 6: 163–168.

Henderson, D., Jacobson, S.H., and Johnson, A.W. (2003). The theory and practice of simulated annealing. In: *Handbook of Metaheuristics*, 287–319. Springer.

Hocking, L. (1991). *Optimal Control: An Introduction to the Theory with Applications*. Oxford University Press.

Hussain, K., Salleh, M.N.M., Cheng, S., and Shi, Y. (2019). On the exploration and exploitation in popular swarm-based metaheuristic algorithms. *Neural Computing and Applications* 31 (11): 7665–7683.

Kaelo, P. and Ali, M.M. (2006). Some variants of the controlled random search algorithm for global optimization. *Journal of Optimization Theory and Applications* 130: 253–264.

Kirkpatrick, S., Gelatt, C., and Vecchi, P. (1983). Optimization by simulated annealing. *Science* 220 (4598): 671–680.

Lin, L. and Gen, M. (2009). Auto-tuning strategy for evolutionary algorithms: balancing between exploration and exploitation. *Soft Computing* 13: 157–168.

Lipowski, A. and Lipowska, D. (2012). Roulette-wheel selection via stochastic acceptance. *Physica A: Statistical Mechanics and its Applications* 391 (6): 2193–2196.

Mathews, J. and Fink, K. (2000). *Metodos Numericos con Matlab*. Prentice Hall.

Matyas, J. (1965). Random optimization. *Automation and Remote Control* 26: 246–253.

Morales-Castañeda, B., Zaldivar, D., Cuevas, E. et al. (2020). A better balance in metaheuristic algorithms: does it exist? *Swarm and Evolutionary Computation* 54: 100671.

Pedregal, P. (2004). *Introduction to Optimization*, vol. 46. New York: Springer.

Reinhardt, R., Hoffmann, A., and Gerlach, T. (2013). *Nichtlineare Optimierung*. Springer.

Shi, K., Wu, Z., Jiang, B., and Karimi, H.R. (2023). Dynamic path planning of mobile robot based on improved simulated annealing algorithm. *Journal of the Franklin Institute* 360 (6): 4378–4398.

Simon, D. (2013). *Evolutionay Optimization Algorithms, Biologically Inspired and Population-Based Approaches to Computer Intelligence*. Wiley.

Venkataraman, P. (2009). *Applied Optimization with MATLAB Programming*, 2e. Wiley.

Xu, J. and Xu, L. (2021). Optimal stochastic process optimizer: a new metaheuristic algorithm with adaptive exploration-exploitation property. *IEEE Access* 9: 108640–108664.

Yang, X.-S. (2010). *Engineering Optimization*. Wiley.

Yang, H., Yu, Y., Cheng, J. et al. (2022). An intelligent metaphor-free spatial information sampling algorithm for balancing exploitation and exploration. *Knowledge-Based Systems* 250: 109081.

Yu, F., Fu, X., Li, H., and Dong, G. (2016). Improved roulette wheel selection-based genetic algorithm for TSP. In: *2016 International Conference on Network and Information Systems for Computers (ICNISC)*, 151–154. IEEE.

Zabinsky, Z.B. (2009). *Random Search Algorithms*. Department of Industrial and Systems Engineering, University of Washington, USA.

3

Fundamental Machine Learning Methods

3.1 Introduction

In this chapter, we delve into the core methodologies of machine learning, focusing particularly on algorithms that synergize well with metaheuristic methods or those frequently employed in systems where both paradigms are integrated. This exploration is critical because the fusion of machine learning techniques and metaheuristic approaches can lead to significant enhancements in problem-solving strategies. Specifically, we will scrutinize three fundamental machine learning techniques: regression, classification, and clustering.

Regression is: a fundamental technique in machine learning and statistics, used for modeling and analyzing relationships between variables. The primary goal of regression is: to understand how the typical value of the dependent variable changes when any one of the independent variables is varied, while keeping all other independent variables fixed. Essentially, it's about predicting a continuous outcome. For example, linear regression, one of the most basic and widely used forms of regression analysis, predicts a response using a linear combination of input features. Regression models are extensively used in fields like finance for predicting prices, in biology for growth rates, and in engineering for predicting the strength of materials, among others. These models can range from simple linear equations to complex neural networks and decision trees.

Classification, on the other hand, is a supervised learning approach where the aim is to categorize data into predefined classes or groups. Unlike regression, which predicts a continuous quantity, classification models predict discrete labels. For example, a classification algorithm might be used to identify whether an email is "spam" or "not spam," or to diagnose whether a tumor is "malignant" or "benign." These models work by learning from a dataset that has already been categorized (the training dataset) and then applying this learned decision-making process to new, unseen data. Common classification algorithms include logistic regression, support vector machines, k-nearest neighbors, and neural networks. Classification plays a critical role in a wide array of applications from medical diagnostics to image recognition.

Clustering is a type of unsupervised learning technique used to group a set of objects in such a way that objects in the same group (or cluster) are more similar to each other than to those in other groups. Unlike classification, clustering doesn't rely on predefined categories; instead, it identifies patterns and structures in the data to form groups. For instance, clustering can be used to segment customers into distinct groups based on buying patterns or to organize large databases of information into manageable clusters. Common clustering algorithms include K-means, hierarchical clustering, and DBSCAN. Clustering is particularly valuable in exploratory data analysis, as it can reveal hidden structures in data and is widely used in fields like market research, pattern recognition, data compression, and image analysis.

Machine Learning and Metaheuristic Computation, First Edition.
Erik Cuevas, Jorge Galvez, Omar Avalos, and Fernando Wario.

For each of these areas – regression, classification, and clustering – we aim to thoroughly examine the algorithms that have shown the most promise when combined with metaheuristic methods. This examination is not merely a review of these algorithms in isolation but an exploration of how their integration with metaheuristic approaches can boost their efficiency and effectiveness. Additionally, we will explore how the application of machine learning concepts has innovatively improved the search strategies of metaheuristic methods. This comprehensive analysis will provide insights into how the combination of these two fields – machine learning and metaheuristics – can lead to more robust and efficient problem-solving tools in various domains.

In this chapter, we not only explore the theoretical aspects of machine learning techniques but also provide practical insights through several MATLAB codes. These codes are meticulously designed to implement various machine learning algorithms, serving a dual purpose. Firstly, they offer the reader an immediate and tangible understanding of how these techniques function in a real-world programming environment. By interacting with the codes and observing their outputs, readers can grasp the nuances of these algorithms more effectively. Secondly, these codes are crafted to be easily adaptable for the reader's own projects and research.

3.2 Regression

Regression analysis (Draper and Smith 1998) is a fundamental statistical process used to examine and quantify the relationship between a set of independent variables, often referred to as explanatory variables or predictors, and a dependent variable, commonly known as the response variable or outcome. This powerful technique allows us to gain insights into how the value of the response variable changes when the explanatory variable is varied.

The primary objective of regression analysis is to model the relationship between the independent variables and the dependent variable. This modeling enables us to make predictions, understand the influence of each independent variable on the response variable, and identify patterns and trends in the data.

The process of conducting regression analysis involves several steps:

- **Data Collection**: The first step is to gather data on the variables of interest. The data should include observations of both the dependent and independent variables from various sources or experiments.
- **Data Preparation**: After collecting the data, it is essential to preprocess and clean it. This step includes handling missing values, removing outliers, and transforming variables if necessary.
- **Model Selection**: The next step is to choose the appropriate regression model that best suits the data and research question. There are different types of regression models, such as linear regression, multiple regression, polynomial regression, and more. The choice of the model depends on the nature of the variables and the research objectives.
- **Model Estimation**: Once the model is selected, the regression analysis estimates the coefficients (slopes) and intercepts that define the relationship between the independent and dependent variables. These coefficients represent the strength and direction of the relationship.
- **Interpretation of Results**: After obtaining the regression results, it is essential to interpret them in the context of the problem being studied. The coefficients reveal how much the dependent variable is expected to change concerning a one-unit change in each independent variable while keeping other variables constant.

- **Model Evaluation**: To assess the quality and validity of the regression model, various statistical measures, such as R-squared, p-values, and residual analysis, are employed. R-squared indicates how well the model fits the data, while p-values help determine the significance of each predictor's contribution.

Regression analysis finds applications in various fields, such as economics, social sciences, engineering, finance, and healthcare. Researchers and analysts utilize regression to make informed decisions, develop predictive models, and understand the underlying relationships within the data.

Let's consider a practical example of regression analysis in the context of predicting house prices. Imagine we have a dataset that contains information about various houses, including features such as the size of the house (in square feet), the number of bedrooms, the number of bathrooms, the location (represented by zip code or neighborhood), and the age of the house (in years). The dependent variable, in this case, would be the sale price of each house.

Our goal is to build a regression model that can predict the sale price of a house based on its features. We will use the dataset to perform regression analysis and develop a predictive model.

Here are the steps involved in the practical example of regression analysis:

- **Data Collection**: Obtain the dataset that includes information about houses, such as size, number of bedrooms, bathrooms, location, and age, along with their corresponding sale prices. The data may be collected from real estate agencies, online listings, or public records.
- **Data Preparation**: Preprocess and clean the data. Handle missing values, remove outliers (if any), and convert categorical variables like location into numerical representations (e.g., using one-hot encoding).
- **Data Exploration**: Explore the data to understand the relationships between the independent variables (house features) and the dependent variable (sale price). Visualize the data using scatter plots, histograms, and correlation matrices to identify any apparent trends or patterns.
- **Model Selection**: Choose an appropriate regression model that suits the data and problem. In this case, we might start with a multiple linear regression model since we have multiple independent variables that may collectively influence the sale price.
- **Model Training**: Split the dataset into two parts: a training set and a test set. The training set will be used to train the regression model, while the test set will be used to evaluate its performance. Fit the multiple linear regression model to the training data.
- **Model Evaluation**: Evaluate the performance of the regression model using metrics such as mean squared error (MSE), root mean squared error (RMSE), and R-squared (coefficient of determination) on the test set. These metrics will help us understand how well the model is predicting house prices compared to the actual sale prices.
- **Interpretation of Results**: Analyze the coefficients of the regression model to understand the impact of each independent variable on the sale price. Positive coefficients indicate that an increase in the respective feature leads to a higher sale price, while negative coefficients imply the opposite.
- **Prediction**: Once the regression model is trained and evaluated, it can be used to predict the sale price of new houses based on their features. By inputting the features of a house into the model, we can obtain a predicted sale price as the output.

For instance, the model might predict that a house with 2000 square feet, 3 bedrooms, 2 bathrooms, located in a certain zip code, and 10 years old would have a specific sale price based on the relationships learned from the training data. By applying regression analysis in this practical example, we can create a valuable tool for real estate agents, homeowners, or potential buyers to estimate house prices accurately and make informed decisions in the property market.

Regression analysis can serve a dual purpose, catering to both explanatory and predictive objectives. It is a versatile statistical technique that offers valuable insights into the relationships between variables and enables accurate predictions.

3.2.1 Explanatory Purpose

Regression analysis is often conducted with an explanatory intent, seeking to understand and assess the effects of independent variables on the dependent variable based on a specific theoretical model (Johannesson et al. 2023). By analyzing the data, researchers or analysts can determine the strength, direction, and significance of these effects.

The explanatory regression model helps answer questions such as:

- How does the dependent variable change concerning changes in each independent variable while keeping other variables constant?
- Which independent variables have a more substantial impact on the dependent variable, and which ones have a weaker influence?
- Are the relationships between the independent and dependent variables statistically significant?

For example, in the context of studying the impact of education level on income, a regression analysis may reveal how much income increases with each additional year of education, while other factors such as experience and location are controlled.

3.2.2 Predictive Purpose

Regression analysis is also widely used for predictive purposes. In this case, the primary goal is to build a regression model that can accurately predict the value of the dependent variable based on the values of the independent variables (McCarthy et al. 2019). The focus shifts from understanding relationships to finding an optimal linear combination of independent variables for making accurate predictions.

The predictive regression model helps address questions such as:

- Can we accurately forecast the value of the dependent variable for new data points using the model developed from existing data?
- How well does the regression model generalize to unseen data?

Continuing with the education and income example, a predictive regression model could be trained using historical data on individuals' education levels and corresponding incomes. This model can then be used to predict the income of new individuals based on their education level, allowing businesses or policymakers to make informed decisions.

It's important to note that while the explanatory and predictive purposes of regression analysis may overlap, they can also differ in their focus and application. Researchers often leverage regression analysis to gain a deeper understanding of the underlying relationships between variables, whereas predictive modeling aims to generate accurate forecasts for practical decision-making.

In this chapter, we delve into the introductory concepts of regression analysis. The main aspects of regression analysis will be thoroughly examined, providing a solid foundation for understanding its application in diverse fields. We will explore the fundamental concepts of independent and dependent variables, model selection, and the estimation of regression coefficients. Throughout the chapter, MATLAB and the Statistics and Machine Learning Toolbox will be utilized to implement and solve various regression problems. This hands-on approach will enable readers to gain practical experience and become proficient in using these tools for real-world regression analysis.

The coefficient of correlation r (Asuero et al. 2006) is a statistical measure that quantifies the strength and direction of the linear relationship between two quantitative variables, often denoted as X and Y. The model to compute the Pearson correlation coefficient for two variables X and Y is as follows:

$$r = \frac{\sum(X_i - \overline{X})(Y_i - \overline{Y})}{\sqrt{\sum(X_i - \overline{X})^2 \sum(Y_i - \overline{Y})^2}} \tag{3.1}$$

where X_i and Y_i are individual data points of variables X and Y, respectively. $\overline{X}$ and $\overline{Y}$ correspond to the means of the X and Y variables, respectively.

The coefficient of correlation provides valuable insights into the extent to which changes in one variable are associated with changes in the other variable. However, it is essential to recognize that correlation does not imply causation. In other words, the coefficient of correlation does not by itself determine whether X causes changes in Y, Y causes changes in X, or if there is a common underlying factor influencing both variables.

Consider the following scenarios to illustrate this point:

X Affects Y: If the coefficient of correlation indicates a positive correlation between X and Y, it means that as the values of X increase, the values of Y tend to increase as well. This might lead to the interpretation that X has an effect on Y. For instance, as the amount of study time (X) increases, test scores (Y) tend to improve.

Y Affects X: Conversely, a negative correlation between X and Y suggests that as X increases, Y tends to decrease. In this case, it might be inferred that Y has an effect on X. For example, as the number of hours spent watching television (Y) increases, physical activity levels (X) tend to decrease.

Common Underlying Factor: In some instances, both X and Y might be influenced by a third variable or a combination of factors that affect both variables. In such cases, the correlation between X and Y may be present, but neither variable directly causes the changes in the other (Chatterjee 2021).

Note

When analyzing the relationship between two variables X and Y, it is essential to recognize that a low value of the coefficient r does not automatically indicate independence between the variables. It is entirely possible for two variables to exhibit a meaningful connection without displaying a linear correlation. This is particularly true in cases where the relationship between the variables is nonlinear.

Correlation measures specifically evaluate the linear association between variables, meaning that they assess how well a straight line can approximate the relationship. If the variables have a nonlinear relationship, the correlation coefficient may not adequately capture the true connection, leading to a correlation close to zero. A nonlinear relationship implies that the change in one variable does not correspond proportionally to the change in the other variable. In such cases, the data points might follow a curved pattern, making the correlation coefficient less informative.

For example, consider a dataset where the *X* variable represents the number of hours a student studies for a test, and the *Y* variable represents the corresponding test scores. Initially, there might not seem to be a significant linear correlation between study hours and test scores, leading to a low or even zero correlation coefficient. However, there could still be a strong relationship between the two variables, with students scoring higher when studying a moderate amount and lower when studying too little or too much. To assess the potential presence of a nonlinear relationship, analysts may perform additional analyses, such as scatter plot visualizations or nonlinear regression techniques. These approaches can reveal underlying patterns and dependencies that may not be captured by simple correlation.

Calculating correlation and covariance is a valuable approach to explore the presence of a linear relationship between variables without assuming or fitting a specific model to the data. These statistical measures provide insights into the extent and direction of the association between two variables, enabling us to gain an initial understanding of their interdependence. In certain cases, two variables may exhibit a small or negligible linear correlation, indicating the possibility of a strong nonlinear relationship. This means that changes in one variable do not correspond to proportional changes in the other, and their connection might be better captured using nonlinear modeling techniques. On the other hand, a strong linear correlation between the two variables suggests a clear linear trend in their relationship. However, finding a model that approximates this trend is necessary to make accurate predictions or gain deeper insights into the data. Hence, calculating linear correlation before fitting a model serves as an excellent preliminary step to identify variables with simple relationships. It helps us discern whether a linear model is appropriate or if more sophisticated modeling techniques are needed to capture complex patterns.

Visualizing the observations in a Cartesian plane using scatter plots is a powerful way to examine correlations between pairs of variables. Scatter plots display data points as individual dots, with each dot representing a combination of values from the two variables. The stronger the correlation between the variables, the more pronounced the tendency of the points to cluster along a certain direction. For instance, if the scatter plot shows a relatively tight cluster of points forming a linear pattern, it suggests a strong positive or negative correlation, depending on whether the points slope upwards or downwards. Conversely, a scatter plot with points scattered randomly around the graph implies a weak or no linear correlation. By employing scatter plots and calculating correlation coefficients, we can initially assess the nature of the relationship between variables. If a linear relationship is evident, we can proceed with fitting a linear regression model or exploring other linear modeling techniques. If the relationship appears nonlinear, further analysis with nonlinear regression or more advanced methods becomes necessary.

Note

Covariance and correlation are fundamental statistical measures that play a crucial role in assessing the relationship between two variables. While both of them deal with the association between variables, they differ in their interpretations and the scale of their values.

Covariance quantifies the strength of a linear relationship between two variables. It indicates whether the two variables tend to vary together, meaning that when one variable increases, the other tends to increase as well, and vice versa. A positive covariance signifies a direct relationship, while a negative covariance indicates an inverse relationship. However, the magnitude of covariance is influenced by the units of the variables, making it challenging to interpret directly.

On the other hand, correlation provides a measure of the degree of a linear relationship between two variables but expresses it through a dimensionless quantity, making it easier to compare relationships across different datasets. The correlation coefficient r ranges between -1 and $+1$. A correlation coefficient of $+1$ indicates a perfect positive linear relationship, where both variables increase in direct proportion. A correlation coefficient of -1 represents a perfect negative linear relationship, where one variable increases as the other decreases. A correlation coefficient of 0 implies no linear relationship between the variables.

The key distinction between covariance and correlation lies in their scales: covariance values can vary widely based on the units of the variables being measured, while correlation coefficients remain standardized, allowing for straightforward comparison of relationships regardless of the measurement units.

Linear regression is: a powerful statistical method used to establish a linear relationship between two variables. Its primary objective is to find a straight line that best represents the distribution of data points. By doing so, linear regression enables us to understand and predict the connection between the variables.

Imagine a scatter plot of data points in a two-dimensional plane, where each point represents an observation of the two variables. The linear regression method aims to identify a line that fits the data points as closely as possible. When the points cluster near the line, it suggests that the chosen model can effectively describe the relationship between the variables.

The challenge in linear regression lies in selecting the best-fitting line from the infinite possibilities that could interpolate the data points. The goal is to find the line that minimizes the overall distance between the data points and the line. This distance is typically measured as the sum of squared vertical deviations (residuals) of the data points from the line.

In practice, several mathematical techniques are used to determine the unique line that optimizes the representation of the data. This line is commonly referred to as the "regression line" or "best-fit line." When a linear mathematical relationship exists between the two variables, it means that the observations of one variable (Y) can be obtained through a linear function of the observations of the other variable (X). The equation of the regression line is of the form:

$$Y = b_0 + b_1 X \tag{3.2}$$

where b_0 is the y-intercept (the value of Y when X is zero) and b_1 is the slope of the line (representing how much Y changes with a unit change in X). The slope (b_1) quantifies the direction and magnitude of the relationship between the variables. A positive slope indicates that as X increases, Y tends to increase, while a negative slope implies that as X increases, Y tends to decrease. Linear regression is: a versatile and widely used technique in various fields, such as economics, social sciences, engineering, and machine learning. It provides valuable insights into the relationship between variables and offers a powerful tool for predicting outcomes based on the observed data.

Note

The slope (b_1) in a linear regression model is of particular interest as it quantifies the variation of the mean response for every single increment of the explanatory variable. Understanding the slope's implications is crucial for comprehending the relationship between the variables being studied.

When examining the slope (b_1), its sign plays a pivotal role. If the slope is positive, it means that the regression line increases from left to right. In other words, as the value of the explanatory variable increases, the mean response (dependent variable) also tends to increase. For example, in the context of studying the relationship between study hours (explanatory variable) and exam scores (response variable Y), a positive slope would suggest that as students spend more time studying, their average exam scores also increase.

Conversely, when the slope is negative, the regression line decreases from left to right. Here, as the value of the explanatory variable increases, the mean response (dependent variable) tends to decrease. For instance, in the context of examining the relationship between pollution levels (explanatory variable) and lung health (response variable), a negative slope would indicate that as pollution levels rise, average lung health tends to deteriorate.

Moreover, if the slope is zero, it suggests that the explanatory variable has no effect on the value of the response. In other words, changes in the explanatory variable do not lead to any change in the mean response.

However, the significance of the slope goes beyond just its sign; its value is equally important. In the case of a positive slope, the magnitude of b_1 determines the rate at which the mean response increases concerning an increment in the explanatory variable. A larger positive b_1 indicates a steeper increase in the mean response for each unit change in the explanatory variable.

Similarly, with a negative slope, the magnitude of b_1 determines the rate at which the mean response decreases concerning an increment in the explanatory variable. A larger negative b_1 implies a steeper decline in the mean response for each unit change in the explanatory variable.

The Least Squares Regression method (Strejc 1981) is a popular approach for fitting a linear regression model to a given set of data points. Its main objective is to find the best-fitting line (regression line) that minimizes the sum of the squared vertical deviations (residuals) between the data points and the line.

When we have a set of observations in the form $((x_1, y_1), (x_2, y_2), \ldots, (x_n, y_n))$, each representing a pair of values for the independent variable (X) and the dependent variable (Y), we can use this data to formulate a linear equation. For each data pair, the equation will express the relationship between X and Y. This set of relationships can be represented in matrix form as:

$$\begin{bmatrix} y_1 \\ y_2 \\ \vdots \\ y_n \end{bmatrix} = \begin{bmatrix} x_1 & 1 \\ x_2 & 1 \\ \vdots & \vdots \\ x_n & 1 \end{bmatrix} [b_1 \ \ b_0] \tag{3.3}$$

Considering that

$$YO = \begin{bmatrix} y_1 \\ y_2 \\ \vdots \\ y_n \end{bmatrix}, \quad XE = \begin{bmatrix} x_1 & 1 \\ x_2 & 1 \\ \vdots & \vdots \\ x_n & 1 \end{bmatrix}, \quad P = \begin{bmatrix} b_1 & b_0 \end{bmatrix} \tag{3.4}$$

Under such conditions, the set of equations can be re-formulated as follows:

$$YO = XE \cdot P \tag{3.5}$$

Assuming the set of equations of Eq. 3.5, MATLAB, being a powerful computational tool, provides a specific operator (\) that efficiently locates the solution to this system of linear equations. Therefore, to determine the intercept (b_0) and the slope (b_1) of the regression line ($P = [b_0, b_1]$), we consider the following expression:

$$P = XE \backslash YO \tag{3.6}$$

In the context of regression analysis, the Least Square Method focuses on minimizing the sum of the squared residuals or errors between the actual data points and the values predicted by the regression equation. This approach is based on the assumption that the best-fitting line should be the one that comes closest to the observed data.

Consider a dataset with n points, where each data point consists of a pair of values (x_i, y_i). The Least Square Regression Line is mathematically represented as defined in Eq. 3.7. The coefficients (b_0 and b_1) in Eq. 3.7 are estimated by finding numerical values that minimize the sum of the squared deviations (residuals) between the observed responses (y_i) and the fitted responses (predicted values $\hat{y}_i$). The formula for the sum of squared deviations E is:

$$E = \sum_{i=1}^{n} (b_1 \cdot x_i + b_0 - y_i)^2 \tag{3.7}$$

By minimizing the sum of squared deviations E, the least square method ensures that the error between the determined regression model ($y = b_0 + b_1 x$) and the observed data (y_i) is minimal. In MATLAB, implementing the Least Squares Regression method involves a series of straightforward steps to find the best-fitting line that represents the relationship between two variables based on observed data points. Here are the steps to achieve Least Squares Regression using MATLAB:

Step 1: Set up the System of Linear Equations
For each data pair (x_i, y_i), we write a linear equation in the form of $Y = b_0 + b_1 X$. This gives us a set of equations based on the available data points.

Step 2: Formulate the Data as Matrices
Organize the X and Y values from the data pairs into matrices. The X matrix will contain the X values (x_i) as a column vector, and the Y matrix will contain the corresponding Y values (y_i) as a column vector.

Step 3: Solve the System of Linear Equations
To find the coefficients b_0 and b_1, we use the backslash operator (\) in MATLAB. By setting up the equation $Y = X *$ Coefficients, where Coefficients is a column vector containing [b_0, b_1], the backslash operator will efficiently compute the best-fitting values for b_0 and b_1 that minimize the sum of squared residuals.

The MATLAB code (in code 3.1) to find the coefficients b_0 and b_1 is as follows:

Code 3.1

```
% X and Y are column vectors containing the data points ((xi, yi))
X = [x1; x2; x3; ...; xn];
Y = [y1; y2; y3; ...; yn];

% Create the design matrix with a column of ones and the X vector
X_design = [ones(length(X), 1), X];
% Use the backslash operator to find the coefficients b0 and b1
Coefficients = X_design \ Y;

% Extract the intercept and slope from the Coefficients vector
b0 = Coefficients(1);
b1 = Coefficients(2);
```

To grasp the fundamental concepts of linear regression, let's begin with a straightforward example of a simple linear regression. In this example, we will use a set of data points artificially generated based on a known equation, $Y = 2X + 2$. This equation represents the underlying relationship we want to approximate with the help of linear regression. However, to emulate real-world conditions, we will add some noise to the data points. The artificially generated data points Y, combined with the added noise $N(0, \sigma)$, represent the observed data YO from which we will perform our estimation. In real-world scenarios, data is rarely perfectly clean and often contains random variations or errors. By adding noise to our data, we simulate the presence of such randomness, making our example more realistic and applicable to actual data analysis.

The primary objective is to find a line that best represents the relationship between the independent variable X and the observed data points YO. This line is known as the regression line or best-fit line. Through linear regression, we aim to approximate the actual relationship ($Y = 2X + 2$) using the observed data, despite the presence of noise.

Code 3.2 in MATLAB presents a set of instructions to solve the linear regression problem using the Least Squares method. This algorithm allows us to find the best-fitting line that approximates the relationship between two variables based on observed data points. The code implementation involves organizing the data, constructing the design matrix, calculating the regression coefficients, and visualizing the results.

Code 3.2

```
clear all
X=1:1:20;
%Ideal data
Y=2+2*X;
%Observed data (ideal data with noise)
YO=Y+randn(size(Y))*3;
```

```
plot(X,Y)
hold on
plot(X,YO,'o')
XE(:,2)=X;
XE(:,1)=ones(size(X));
%Estimation of intercept (b0) and the slope (b1)
Parameters= XE\YO'
```

Figure 3.1 displays both the ideal line and the observed data generated by adding noise to the original data. The purpose of this visualization is to showcase how well the regression line fits the noisy data, providing a visual representation of the relationship between the variables.

After executing Code 3.2, the results reveal the values of the slope and intercept as $b_0 = 1.99$ and $b_1 = 2.001$, respectively. Remarkably, these values are very close to their ideal counterparts. This outcome demonstrates the robustness of the Least Squares Regression method in determining the best possible line that approximates the relationship between the variables. The ideal values for the slope and intercept are the actual parameters of the linear equation representing the underlying relationship between the independent variable (X) and the dependent variable (Y). In our case, the ideal values are $b_0 = 2$ (intercept) and $b_1 = 2$ (slope), as per the original equation $Y = 2X + 2$.

The fact that the calculated values of b_0 and b_1 are nearly identical to their ideal values indicates the accuracy and effectiveness of the Least Squares Regression method. This method minimizes the sum of squared residuals between the observed data points and the regression line, resulting in coefficients that provide a close fit to the true relationship. The robustness of the Least Squares method is particularly valuable in real-world data analysis, where observed data often contains noise and random variations. Despite the presence of noise, the method manages to identify the best-fitting line that accurately represents the relationship between the variables. This makes the Least Squares Regression a widely adopted and reliable technique for various applications, including prediction, trend analysis, and model building. The proximity of the calculated coefficients to their ideal values also indicates the stability of the regression line

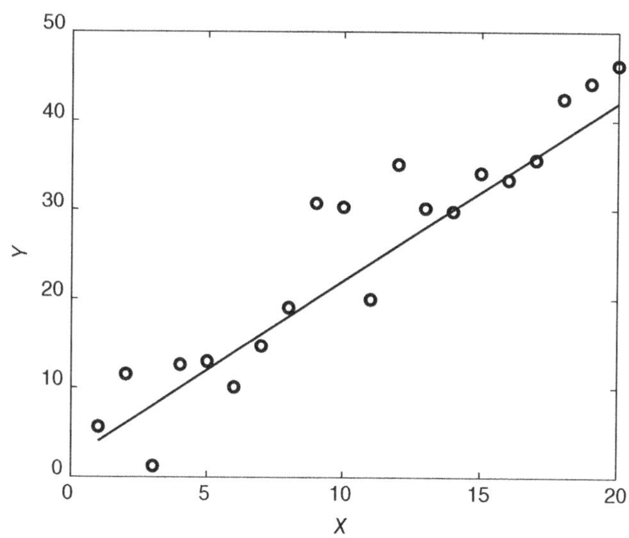

Figure 3.1 Ideal line and the observed data generated by adding noise to the original data.

when applied to different datasets with similar characteristics. As long as the data exhibits a linear relationship, the Least Squares method consistently produces reliable estimates for the slope and intercept, allowing researchers and analysts to make confident predictions and draw meaningful conclusions from their data.

Regression methods and metaheuristic algorithms are two powerful techniques used in different fields of study. However, they have also found complementary applications in each other's domains, leading to innovative approaches for problem-solving and optimization.

(A) Regression Methods in Metaheuristic Algorithms:

Regression methods have been integrated into metaheuristic algorithms to enhance their performance and adaptability. Metaheuristic algorithms are optimization techniques inspired by natural processes. These algorithms search for optimal solutions in complex and high-dimensional spaces, making them suitable for various real-world problems.

By incorporating regression methods within metaheuristic algorithms, researchers have achieved several benefits:

(I) **Enhanced Fitness Functions**: Regression methods (Bird and Li 2010) can be used to define more informative fitness functions, guiding the metaheuristic search towards solutions that closely approximate the desired outcomes. The fitness function, derived from the regression model, quantifies the quality of potential solutions based on the available data.

(II) **Handling Noisy Data (Fébba et al. 2020)**: In real-world applications, data may be noisy or contain uncertainties. Regression techniques can be employed to model the underlying trends in the data and filter out noise, thus improving the performance of metaheuristic algorithms in noisy environments.

(III) **Combining Data-Driven and Metaheuristic Approaches (Cisternas-Caneo et al. 2020)**: Regression methods allow metaheuristic algorithms to leverage existing data to inform the search process. This combination enables more efficient exploration of the solution space and faster convergence towards optimal solutions.

(B) Metaheuristic Algorithms for Improving Regression:

On the other hand, metaheuristic algorithms have been applied to improve regression models and enhance their predictive accuracy. Traditional regression methods, such as linear regression, may have limitations when dealing with complex or nonlinear relationships between variables. Metaheuristic algorithms can assist in finding better models and optimizing the model parameters.

Some key applications of metaheuristic algorithms in improving regression models include:

(I) **Feature Selection (Dokeroglu et al. 2022)**: Metaheuristic algorithms can be employed to select the most relevant features (independent variables) from a large pool, enhancing the model's interpretability and reducing overfitting.

(II) **Hyperparameter Optimization**: Tuning hyperparameters in regression models can be a challenging task (Nematzadeh et al. 2022). Metaheuristic algorithms can efficiently explore the hyperparameter space to find the best combinations, leading to more accurate models.

(III) **Nonlinear Regression**: Metaheuristic algorithms (Behnamian and Ghomi 2010) can be used to optimize the parameters of nonlinear regression models, such as support vector regression, artificial neural networks, and decision trees, improving their ability to capture complex relationships.

By integrating metaheuristic algorithms with regression methods, researchers have advanced the capabilities of both techniques, leading to more robust and accurate problem-solving approaches. These hybrid approaches have found applications in various domains, including engineering, finance, healthcare, and data science, addressing complex challenges and achieving superior results compared to traditional methods alone.

3.3 Classification

Classification algorithms (Umadevi and Marseline 2017) are a fundamental component of machine learning, as they enable automated learning to make accurate predictions based on observations or data inputs. The primary goal of classification is to assign each piece of data input to a specific class label based on patterns and relationships learned from a training dataset. This process allows the algorithm to make informed decisions and categorize new, unseen data.

The classification problem can be broadly categorized into two types: binary classification and multi-class classification. In binary classification, the algorithm distinguishes between just two distinct classes or categories, typically labeled as "positive" and "negative," "yes" and "no," or "1" and "0." On the other hand, multi-class classification deals with more than two classes, where each category represents a different label.

The process of classification is relatively straightforward. During the training phase, the algorithm is presented with a labeled dataset, where each data instance is associated with a specific class label. The algorithm learns from this labeled data, identifying patterns and relationships between the input features and their corresponding class labels. Once the learning process is complete, the algorithm builds a model that captures these patterns and can be used to classify new, unseen data. When presented with a new data instance, the classifier assigns a class label to that instance, indicating which category it belongs to.

In essence, the classification algorithm acts as a decision-maker, identifying the most appropriate class label for each data input based on the learned model. This process is akin to "teaching" the algorithm to recognize and classify different patterns, making it a valuable tool in various real-world applications.

This chapter provides a comprehensive exploration of various algorithms used for object classification. The main focus is on understanding how these algorithms work and how they can be applied to categorize objects into different classes. Several powerful classification methods will be discussed, each offering unique advantages in different scenarios. The algorithms covered in this chapter include:

Nearest Neighbors (Taunk et al. 2019): This method classifies objects based on their similarity to other objects in the training dataset. It assigns a class label to a new object by considering the class labels of its nearest neighbors in the feature space.

Discriminant Analysis (Ramayah et al. 2010): Discriminant analysis is a statistical technique used to find a linear combination of features that best separates different classes. It provides a probabilistic framework for classification based on the estimated class means and covariances.

Decision Trees (De Ville 2013): Decision trees are intuitive and versatile classification tools that create a tree-like model to make decisions based on feature values. The structure of the tree is built through a recursive partitioning process, resulting in an easily interpretable model.

Naive Bayes (Yang 2018): This probabilistic algorithm applies Bayes' theorem with a strong assumption of feature independence. Despite its simplicity, Naive Bayes often performs surprisingly well and is particularly useful when working with a large number of features.

Throughout the chapter, the principles of probability will be explored in the context of classification. Understanding the underlying probability distributions is essential for making informed decisions and achieving accurate predictions. One key aspect covered in this chapter is the usage of decision trees for classification. Decision trees are widely used due to their simplicity, interpretability, and ability to handle both categorical and continuous features. The process of building decision trees and handling data splits will be explained in detail.

Regression and classification are two essential branches of supervised machine learning, both aimed at making predictions and modeling relationships between variables. While they share similarities, they serve different purposes and have distinct characteristics.

3.3.1 Relationship Between Regression and Classification

Both regression and classification are types of supervised learning, where the algorithm learns from labeled training data to make predictions on new, unseen data. In both cases, the goal is to find a mapping between input features (independent variables) and their corresponding outputs (dependent variables or class labels). Both approaches involve learning from examples to generalize and make accurate predictions on new data points. The primary relationship between regression and classification lies in their common objective: predictive modeling. Both techniques aim to build models that can accurately predict outcomes based on input data. The primary difference lies in the nature of the output variable.

3.3.2 Differences Between Regression and Classification

According to the output, in regression, the output variable is continuous, representing a numeric value. The goal is to find a function that best fits the data points and can predict numerical values for new inputs. For example, predicting the price of a house based on its features or estimating a person's age based on certain attributes. In classification, the output variable is categorical, representing discrete classes or labels. The goal is to classify data instances into predefined classes based on the patterns learned during training. For example, classifying emails as "spam" or "not spam" or identifying different types of flowers based on their features.

According to the model type, Regression models use techniques such as linear regression, polynomial regression, support vector regression, and neural networks, among others. These models aim to fit a continuous function to the data. In classification, models include techniques like logistic regression, decision trees, random forests, support vector machines, k-nearest neighbors, and neural networks. These models are designed to classify data into discrete classes based on decision boundaries.

According to the Evaluation Metrics, in Regression, the Common evaluation metrics include mean squared error (MSE), mean absolute error (MAE), and *R*-squared (coefficient of determination), which measure the accuracy of the predictions. For classification, evaluation metrics include accuracy, precision, recall, F1-score, and area under the receiver operating characteristic curve (AUC-ROC), which assess the classifier's ability to correctly classify data into different classes.

3.4 Decision Trees

A decision tree (De Ville 2013) is a popular and widely used machine learning algorithm that serves as a graphical representation of decision-making processes. It mimics the structure of a tree, where each node represents a decision or a test on an attribute, each branch corresponds to the outcome of the test, and each leaf node represents a final decision or a class label. Decision trees are particularly valuable for classification and regression tasks, as they can be used to classify data into distinct categories or predict numerical values based on the input features.

The beauty of decision trees lies in their ability to capture complex decision-making processes and present them in an intuitive and interpretable format. Decision trees resemble flowcharts, where each node represents a decision or a condition, and the branches represent the potential outcomes or subsequent decisions based on those conditions. By following the path from the root of the tree to the leaf nodes, one can understand the sequence of choices and conditions leading to a final decision or classification.

In real-world scenarios, decision-making is often not a straightforward "yes" or "no" choice, but rather a series of conditional checks and evaluations. This waterfall-like process is ideally suited to be represented using decision trees. They provide a clear and concise visualization of how different factors influence the final outcome, allowing for easy interpretation and understanding of the decision-making rationale.

Using traditional tables and numbers to represent such complex decision processes can be cumbersome and confusing. Even if the data can be formally organized in tabular form, the explanation and justification of the choices made might not be immediately apparent to the reader. Decision trees, on the other hand, offer a visual representation that facilitates comprehension and reveals the logic behind the decision-making process.

Decision trees find applications in various fields, such as finance, medicine, marketing, and natural language processing. They are used for tasks like credit risk assessment, medical diagnosis, customer segmentation, sentiment analysis, and more. Their simplicity, interpretability, and ability to handle both categorical and numerical data make them a popular choice for decision-making and classification problems.

A decision tree is comprised of three essential components:

Nodes: The decision tree starts with a single node called the root node. Each node in the tree corresponds to an independent variable or a test on an attribute. The node contains the name of the independent variable that the algorithm evaluates to make a decision.

Branches: Connected to each node are branches that represent the possible values of the corresponding independent variable. When a decision is made based on the test at a node, the algorithm follows the branch that matches the observed value of the variable.

Leaf Nodes: At the end of each branch, there are leaf nodes. These leaf nodes represent the classes or categories into which the data is divided based on the tests performed at the nodes along the path. Each leaf node contains a collection of observations grouped together based on the values of the independent variables.

The decision tree algorithm uses a top-down, recursive approach called recursive partitioning to build the tree. It starts with the root node, selects the best attribute to split the data based on certain criteria (e.g., information gain, Gini impurity), and creates child nodes for each possible value of the selected attribute. This process is repeated for each child node until a stopping criterion is met, resulting in the creation of the leaf nodes that represent the final classes. The simplicity and interpretability of decision trees make them valuable for understanding complex decision processes and identifying the most influential features in the data. They are especially useful when transparency and explanation of the model's decision-making process are crucial.

3.4.1 Procedure of Classification

In a decision tree, the process of classifying an object involves traversing the tree from the root node to a specific leaf node. Each path followed represents a set of rules or conditions that determine the final classification or prediction for the object. As an object moves along the tree, it encounters nodes representing different attributes or features. At each node, the algorithm evaluates the value of the corresponding attribute for the given object. Based on the attribute's value, the algorithm decides which branch to follow, leading to the next node in the path. The branches in the decision tree represent the possible values that the attributes can assume. These branches guide the object's journey through the tree, navigating through different tests and decisions based on the attribute values. Eventually, the object reaches a leaf node, where the final classification is made. Each leaf node corresponds to a specific class or category, and the object is assigned to that class as the result of the decision-making process. The path followed from the root to the leaf node represents a set of classification rules, often referred to as "production rules" or "if-then" rules. These rules indicate the sequence of attribute tests that lead to the final classification. The rule is typically written along the tree path, specifying the attribute conditions and their corresponding branch values. In essence, each decision tree encompasses multiple production rules, with each path from the root to a leaf representing a distinct rule. The combination of all possible paths in the tree forms a comprehensive set of rules that cover various scenarios and outcomes. The ability to extract these rules from the decision tree is one of the key advantages of this model. Decision trees are highly interpretable, and by examining the paths and their corresponding rules, we can gain insights into the important features and decision patterns within the data.

In summary, classifying an instance with a decision tree involves a straightforward and step-by-step process that ensures the instance is correctly assigned to the appropriate class label. The following steps guide the classification procedure:

1. **Start from the Root.**
   The classification process begins at the root node of the decision tree. The root node represents the starting point of the decision-making process.
2. **Select the Instance Attribute.**
   At each node, an attribute is associated with a test or decision. For the instance being classified, the algorithm selects the attribute associated with the current node.
3. **Follow the Branch.**
   Having identified the attribute, the algorithm follows the branch that corresponds to the value assigned to that attribute in the instance. This decision determines the path the instance will take through the tree.

4. **Reach a Leaf Node.**
   The algorithm continues to traverse the tree by moving to the next node based on the values of the instance's attributes. The process is repeated until the algorithm reaches a leaf node.
5. **Return the Classification Label.**
   Once a leaf node is reached, the algorithm returns the class label associated with that leaf. The class label represents the final classification or prediction for the instance.
6. **Repeat if Necessary.**
   If the leaf node does not provide the final classification, the algorithm goes back to step 2, starting with the current node. It continues traversing the tree based on the instance's attribute values until it reaches a leaf node.

Through this step-by-step process, the decision tree determines the most appropriate class label for the instance being classified. The unique path taken from the root to the leaf node represents a set of decision rules specific to that instance.

To better understand the decision-making process in a classification tree, let's analyze a simple example. In this example, we will use two predictors, x_1 and x_2, to predict the class labels of the data instances. The goal is to generate artificial data and accurately characterize the class of each data point based on specific conditions. We'll classify an element as "true" when x_1 is less than 0.3 and x_2 is greater than 0.6, and "false" otherwise. To achieve this, we can utilize MATLAB to create the artificial dataset and perform the classification. The following MATLAB code presented in Code 3.3 demonstrates how to generate the data and implement the classification process:

Code 3.3

```
% Generating artificial data
rng('default'); % Set random seed for reproducibility
nSamples = 1000; % Number of data samples
x1 = rand(nSamples, 1); % Generate random values for x1
x2 = rand(nSamples, 1); % Generate random values for x2
X = [x1, x2]; % Combine x1 and x2 as the feature matrix

% Classifying data based on the given conditions
y_true = (x1 < 0.3) & (x2 > 0.6); % True when x1 < 0.3 and x2 > 0.6
y_false = ~y_true; % False otherwise

% Display the artificial data and their corresponding classes
disp('Artificial Data:')
disp([X, y_true])

% Train a decision tree classifier
tree = fitctree(X, y_true);

% Visualization of the decision tree
view(tree, 'Mode', 'graph');
```

```
% Example classification
example_instance = [0.2, 0.8]; % Example instance to classify
predicted_class = predict(tree, example_instance);
disp('Example Instance:')
disp(['x1: ', num2str(example_instance(1)), ', x2: ',
num2str(example_instance(2))])
disp(['Predicted Class: ', num2str(predicted_class)])
```

In this example, we generate 1000 samples for x_1 and x_2, each ranging between 0 and 1. We, then, combine x_1 and x_2 to create the feature matrix X. The class labels are determined based on the conditions $x_1 < 0.3$ and $x_2 > 0.6$. The "true" class is assigned to data points that satisfy these conditions, and the "false" class is assigned to the rest. Next, we use the `fitctree` function to train a decision tree classifier on the generated data. The decision tree will learn to identify the appropriate conditions to separate the data into the "true" and "false" classes. To visualize the decision tree, we use the view function, which generates a graphical representation of the tree. This visual representation helps us understand the sequence of decisions made at each node to arrive at the final classifications. By running this MATLAB code, we can observe Figure 3.2. It shows how the decision tree effectively separates the data into the specified classes, demonstrating the power of decision trees in performing classification tasks.

To make predictions using a decision tree, you can follow a step-by-step process starting from the top node of the tree, which is typically represented by a triangle symbol (Δ). This process is incredibly intuitive and demonstrates how the decision tree navigates through attribute tests to arrive at a final classification. Here is shown how the prediction process works using the example classification tree previously mentioned.

- **Start at the Top Node (Root)**:
  Begin at the top node of the decision tree, which is represented by a triangle (Δ). This node serves as the starting point for the prediction process.
- **First Check – Variable x_2**:
  The first decision point involves the variable x_2. Check whether the value of x_2 in the instance you're predicting is greater than 0.6. If it is, take the right branch from the top node.
- **Second Node – Right Branch**:
  Move to the next node, which corresponds to the right branch taken based on the x_2 condition. At this node, you have classified the data as a "true" type. This is the final prediction if the condition is: met.

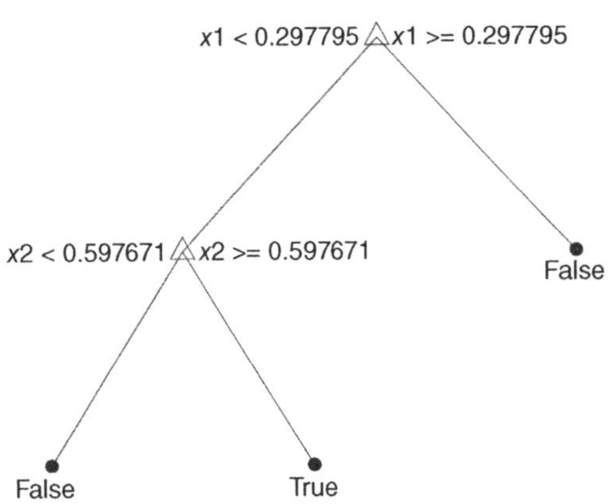

Figure 3.2 Decision tree that separates the data into the specified classes, demonstrating the power of decision trees in performing a classification task.

- **If $x_2 \leq 0.6$**:
  If the value of x_2 is not greater than 0.6 (i.e., $x_2 \leq 0.6$), then follow the left branch from the top node.
- **Third Node – Left Branch (Lower-Right Triangle)**:
  You arrive at the third node, represented by a lower-right triangle. At this point, the tree asks whether x_1 is smaller than 0.3. This represents the second condition that the tree evaluates.
- **If $x_1 < 0.3$**:
  If x_1 is indeed smaller than 0.3, take the left branch from the lower-right triangle node. Following this branch, the tree classifies the data as a "true" type.
- **If $x_1 \geq 0.3$**:
  If x_1 is not smaller than 0.3 (i.e., $x_1 \geq 0.3$), take the right branch from the lower-right triangle node. Following this branch, the tree classifies the data as a "false" type.

By tracing these steps, you can see how the decision tree uses attribute conditions to navigate from the root node to a specific leaf node, where the final classification is made. The tree's structure inherently captures the decision-making rules and conditions, making it a highly interpretable model. This process of predicting with decision trees is not only informative but also transparent, offering insights into how the algorithm arrives at its decisions. It's this transparency that makes decision trees popular for tasks that require explainable and interpretable models, such as auditing, medical diagnosis, and more.

During the classification process using a decision tree, a significant revelation occurs when we arrive at a leaf node. The conditions essential for determining the classification become apparent as we trace the path from the tree's root down to that specific leaf. This inherent property grants decision trees a remarkable level of transparency and interpretability. Each unique path from the root to a leaf, in essence, encapsulates a sequence of conditions that must be met to guide the algorithm to a precise classification outcome. This realization forms the foundation for transforming decision trees into a coherent set of rules. It's important to note that any decision tree, no matter its complexity, can be seamlessly converted into an organized collection of rules. Each individual rule corresponds directly to a specific path originating at the root and terminating at a leaf node. Consequently, the count of rules matches the count of leaf nodes present in the tree. This transformation renders a set of classification rules that mirrors the intricate structure of the original decision tree. The interpretability of these rules echoes the transparency of the tree itself, succinctly encapsulating the decision-making process and outlining the precise conditions governing each classification. The process of generating rules from the decision tree is a powerful approach, offering insights into decision logic in a readily understandable manner.

3.4.2 Determination of the Splitting Point

When constructing a decision tree for classification, the process of determining the optimal splitting point for each node is crucial. Two widely used methods for computing this optimal division point are the Gini index and entropy. These impurity measures play a pivotal role in guiding the decision tree algorithm's choice of attribute and threshold to split the data at each node.

3.4.2.1 Gini Index

The Gini index (Farris 2010) quantifies the impurity within a node by calculating the probability of a randomly selected data point being misclassified based on the distribution of classes in that node. The Gini index ranges from 0 (perfectly pure) to 0.5 (maximally impure). The algorithm evaluates different splitting points and selects the one that leads to the greatest reduction in Gini impurity across child nodes. The Gini impurity measurement for a partition P is determined by the following expression:

$$G(P) = 1 - \sum_{k=1}^{m} p_k^2 \tag{3.8}$$

where m represents the classes of the response variable so that $k = 1, \ldots, m$. p^k is the proportion of records in the partition P that belong to class k.

3.4.2.2 Entropy

Entropy is another measure of impurity that gauges the disorder or randomness in a node's class distribution. It calculates the uncertainty associated with classifying a randomly chosen instance in that node. The entropy ranges from 0 (pure) to 1 (maximally impure). Similar to the Gini index, the algorithm identifies the splitting point that maximizes the reduction in entropy across child nodes. The entropy for a particular partition P can be computed as follows:

$$E(P) = -\sum_{k=1}^{m} p_k \log_2 (p_k) \tag{3.9}$$

To illustrate the practical application of impurity measurements such as the Gini index and entropy, we will work through a numerical example. In this example, we'll consider a dataset of 24 data points that are visually distributed as depicted in Figure 3.2. In this figure, the black points signify elements belonging to class A, while the white points represent elements of class B. We will use the partition denoted as P to divide the space into two segments: left (L) and right (R). This partition forms the basis for evaluating the impurity using both the Gini index and entropy as measures of impurity within the resulting subsets. By examining this example, we can gain insight into how these impurity measurements inform the decision tree algorithm's choice of optimal splitting points.

Therefore, the Gini index and entropy for the left side (L), considering the partition P are computed as follows:

$$G_L(P) = 1 - \left(\frac{7}{8}\right)^2 - \left(\frac{1}{8}\right)^2 = 0.219 \tag{3.10}$$

$$E_L(P) = -\frac{7}{8}\log_2\left(\frac{7}{8}\right) - \frac{1}{8}\log_2\left(\frac{1}{8}\right) = 0.544 \tag{3.11}$$

For the right side (R):

$$G_R(P) = 1 - \left(\frac{11}{16}\right)^2 - \left(\frac{5}{16}\right)^2 = 0.430 \tag{3.12}$$

$$E_R(P) = -\frac{11}{16}\log_2\left(\frac{11}{16}\right) - \frac{5}{16}\log_2\left(\frac{5}{168}\right) = 0.896 \tag{3.13}$$

The combined impurity of the two regions formed by the partition is determined by calculating a weighted average of the impurity measures for each part (L and R). This weighting takes into account the number of records present in each region. For our specific example, we will compute this combined impurity using both the Gini index and entropy as follows (Figure 3.3):

$$G(P) = \frac{8}{24} \cdot G_L(P) + \frac{16}{24} \cdot G_R(P) = 0.359 \tag{3.14}$$

$$E(P) = \frac{8}{24} \cdot E_L(P) + \frac{16}{24} \cdot E_R(P) = 0.779 \tag{3.15}$$

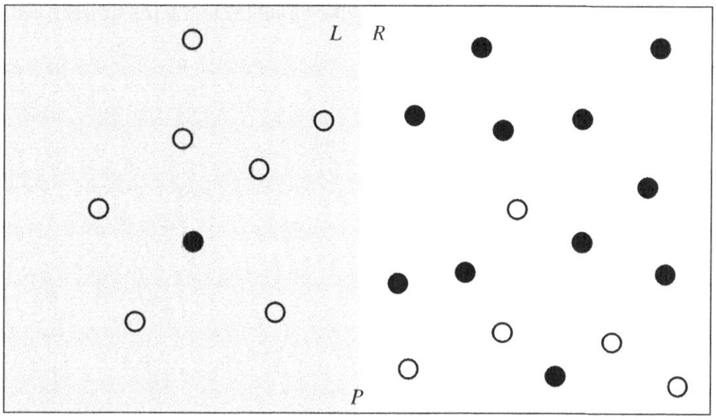

Figure 3.3 Distribution of an artificial dataset of 24 data points. The black points signify elements belonging to class A, while the white points represent elements of class B.

These impurity measures help the decision tree algorithm decide on the best splits to make, aiming to minimize impurity in the resulting child nodes. Both the Gini index and entropy serve as quantitative indicators of how well a particular splitting point separates classes within the node. The algorithm's objective is to select attributes and thresholds that yield subsets with the least possible impurity, thus enhancing the homogeneity of child nodes and improving the classification accuracy of the resulting decision tree. By considering these impurity measures, decision trees can effectively partition the data into subsets that exhibit greater purity and clearer class boundaries.

3.4.3 Example of Classification

In order to gain hands-on experience with decision trees, let's explore their implementation using MATLAB. The objective is to comprehend how decision trees work in a more intricate context, involving a real-world dataset. For this purpose, we'll turn to the well-known "Iris" flower dataset, a multivariate dataset introduced by the eminent British statistician and biologist Ronald Fisher in his groundbreaking 1936 paper. This dataset has become a staple in the machine learning community due to its diverse features and clearly defined classes.

Note

To access the dataset and obtain a brief overview of the variables it contains, you can visit the UCI Machine Learning Repository through this link: https://archive.ics.uci.edu/ml/datasets/iris. The dataset is readily available for download and provides valuable insights into the world of machine learning. Alternatively, it's worth noting that the MATLAB environment already includes the Iris dataset.

The Iris dataset is composed of 150 samples, with 50 samples belonging to each of the three distinct species of Iris: Iris setosa, Iris virginica, and Iris versicolor. From each sample, four features have been measured: the length and width of both the sepals and petals, all quantified in centimeters. The dataset encompasses the following variables: sepal length (cm), sepal width (cm),

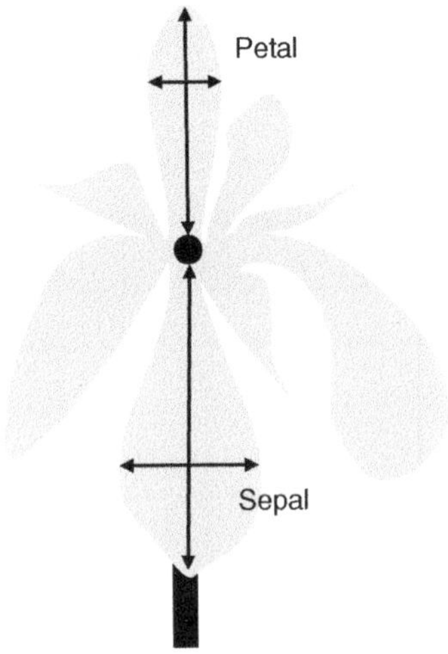

Figure 3.4 Relationship among the variables in the Iris flower dataset.

petal length (cm), and petal width (cm). In terms of classification, the three species serve as the classes: Setosa, Versicolour, and Virginica. The relationship among these variables is depicted in Figure 3.4, providing a visual representation of the interplay between the different measured attributes.

Our objective is to construct a classification tree capable of classifying flower species based on the dimensions of both the sepal and petal. The beauty lies in the fact that there's no need to establish a connection with the previously suggested archive to load the data into MATLAB's workspace. This is because MATLAB already includes the dataset within its software distribution. Importing the data into the MATLAB environment is as simple as executing the following command:

```
>> load fisheriris
```

After importing the dataset into MATLAB, two variables become readily accessible: `meas` and `species`. The former encapsulates the measurements of sepal and petal length and width, forming a 150 × 4 double array. The latter, `species`, embodies the classification information in a 150 × 1 cell array.

To comprehensively analyze the dataset, a series of graphs will be generated to illustrate the attributes of the species in pairs, effectively segregating observations into distinct groups. To achieve this, the `gplotmatrix()` function proves invaluable. This function is designed for creating a matrix of scatter plots, allowing you to visually explore relationships between multiple variables in a dataset. It's particularly useful when you want to understand how different variables interact and potentially influence each other. The normal syntax of the `gplotmatrix` function is as follows:

```
gplotmatrix(X,groups,species)
```

where `X` represents the data matrix where each column represents a different variable or feature. Groups is a vector specifying the group membership of each observation. This can be helpful for coloring or symbolizing points based on different groups. Finally, species corresponds to a categorical array or cell array containing labels for different classes or species. This parameter is useful for labeling different categories on the plots.

When the `gplotmatrix` function is used, the resulting figure comprises individual sets of axes, each presenting a scatter plot that contrasts a specific column of variable `X` with a corresponding column of variable `groups`. These plots are thoughtfully grouped according to the grouping variable `species`. In our present context, the variables we wish to juxtapose in pairs are housed within the meas variable (from the dataset), while the distinctive groups are defined by the `species` variable. This approach facilitates a clear and structured visualization of the interplay between different variables while discerning patterns within distinct species categories. To visualize this information, the following instruction is used:

```
gplotmatrix(meas, meas, species);
```

After executing this instruction, Figure 3.5 is shown. It displays the scatter plot of the dataset features of the three iris species.

After an analysis of Figure 3.5, it becomes evident that the values corresponding to the **setosa** species are distinctly segregated from those of the remaining two species. Conversely, the values associated with the other two species exhibit notable overlap across all the scatter plots. This initial visual assessment provides valuable insights into the differentiation and potential distinctiveness of the setosa species compared to the other iris species, highlighting a notable characteristic of the dataset's distribution.

To initiate our analysis, we first consider the variations in petal measurements across different species. For this exploration, we turn to the two columns housing the petal measurements, namely the third and fourth columns of the dataset. To depict the distribution of these measurements with respect to species, an effective choice is the utilization of the `gscatter` function. The MATLAB

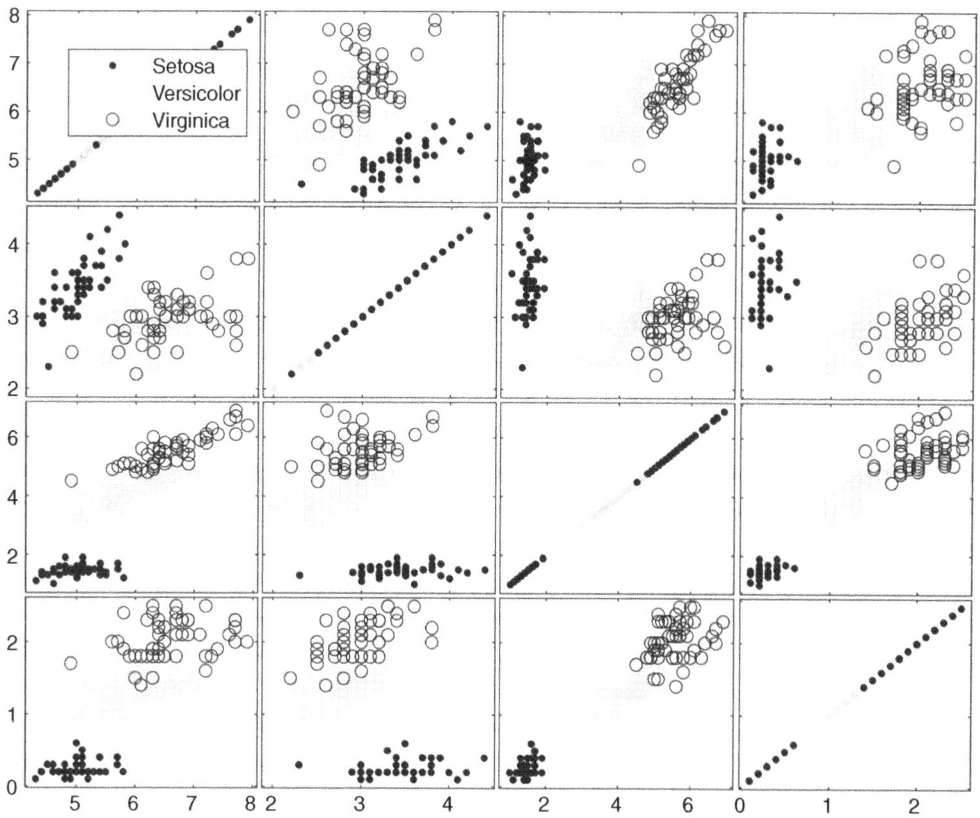

Figure 3.5 The scatter plot of the dataset features of the three iris species.

function `gscatter` is employed to generate scatter plots that are grouped by specific categories or classes. It is particularly useful when you want to visualize how data points of different groups are distributed across two or more dimensions. The syntax of the `gscatter` function is as follows:

```
gscatter(X, Y, group)
```

where X and Y correspond to the data arrays representing the coordinates of the data points. Group is a categorical array, vector, character array, or cell array of character vectors that indicates the group to which each data point belongs. Through the utilization of the `gscatter` function, we embark on an exploration of the distribution of petal measurements across various species. The objective is to harness visualization to uncover potential distinctions and patterns inherent within this specific dataset. By generating scatter plots that distinctly highlight the different species, we gain a clear insight into how petal measurements are distributed, facilitating the identification of any significant variations that might exist between the different iris species. To analyze the petal measurements, we need to use as instruction:

```
gscatter(meas(:,3), meas(:,4), species,'rgb','osd');
```

After executing this instruction, we obtain the feature distribution shown in Figure 3.6. Within this figure, an interesting distinction emerges as the three floral species are displayed. Their distribution across the plot is strikingly dissimilar, with each species occupying distinct areas. This visualization effectively highlights the separations between the species, providing a visual confirmation of their individual characteristics. The ability to visually discern these distinctions adds a layer of clarity and understanding to the dataset, aiding in the interpretation and analysis of the underlying botanical diversity.

The evident distribution of features strongly indicates the feasibility of a classification grounded in the attributes of the petals. With this insight in mind, the creation of a classification tree becomes a logical step forward. For this purpose, the MATLAB function `fitctree` proves to be invaluable. By employing `fitctree`, a binary decision tree is meticulously constructed, wherein the tree's structure is shaped by the input and output variables. This process culminates in a tree that is tailor-made to classify and predict, offering a structured approach to delineating the relationships

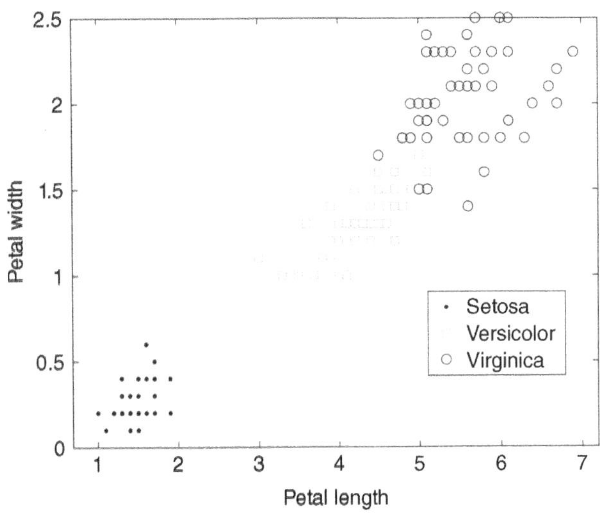

Figure 3.6 Feature distribution of the dataset according to petal length vs petal width.

between the input variables and the target classifications. Therefore, to classify each element, it is used:

```
ClassRes= fitctree(meas,species);
```

The binary tree generated by `fitctree` operates by partitioning branching nodes according to the values within a specific column of the `meas` matrix. At this point, we have the opportunity to inspect the tree that has been crafted. This can be accomplished using the `view` function, which offers two distinct modes for its utilization. To obtain a text-based description of the tree, the command `view(ClassRe)` can be employed. This provides a textual representation that offers insights into the tree's structure and branching decisions. Conversely, for a more visual and graphic understanding, the command `view(ClassTree, 'mode,' 'graph')` can be employed. This function call delivers a graphical depiction of the decision tree. This graphical representation offers a more intuitive and comprehensive view of the tree's architecture, enabling a deeper comprehension of its decision-making process. Therefore, the rules obtained by a decision tree can be seen as follows:

```
view(ClassRes)

Decision tree for classification
1  if x3<2.45 then node 2 elseif x3>=2.45 then node 3 else setosa
2  class = setosa
3  if x4<1.75 then node 4 elseif x4>=1.75 then node 5 else versicolor
4  if x3<4.95 then node 6 elseif x3>=4.95 then node 7 else versicolor
5  class = virginica
6  if x4<1.65 then node 8 elseif x4>=1.65 then node 9 else versicolor
7  class = virginica
8  class = versicolor
9  class = virginica
```

After an analysis of the generated decision tree, it becomes apparent that the resultant rules primarily involve the utilization of only two input variables for the classification process: specifically, x_3 and x_4. In the context of the Iris dataset, these variables correspond to the length and width of the petals, respectively. This strategic selection of input variables for classification aligns seamlessly with the findings derived from the visual analyses performed in the preceding paragraphs. The decision tree's inclination to rely on these specific attributes underscores the pivotal role that petal measurements play in distinguishing between the various species of iris flowers. This congruence between the decision tree's rules and the earlier exploratory analysis validates the tree's ability to discern and exploit the inherent patterns within the data. We can also visualize the structure of decision three by using the following instruction:

```
view(ClassRes,'mode','graph')
```

Figure 3.7 effectively shows the structure of the classification process as executed by the resultant decision tree. This visual representation serves as a tool for immediately comprehending the classification of the three distinct floral species. In a broader context, the construction of decision trees is often driven by the objective of predicting class labels or responses. The utility of these trees extends beyond mere classification; following their creation, we gain the capability to seamlessly predict responses for new, unseen data points. This predictive capacity enhances their applicability in various scenarios, ranging from species classification to a multitude of other fields where data-driven decision-making is imperative.

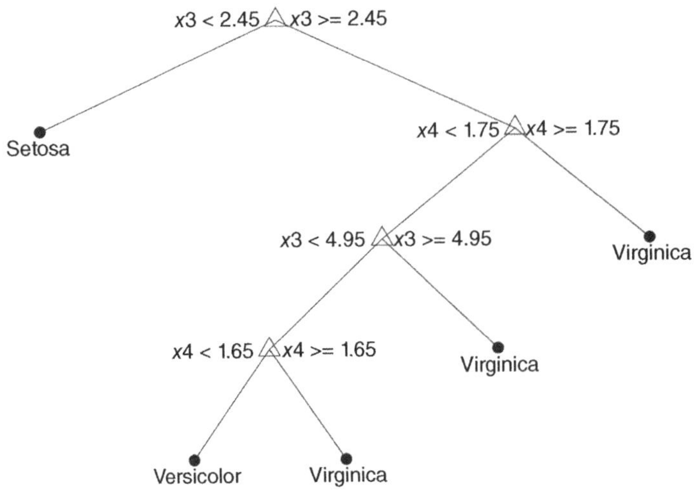

Figure 3.7 Structure of the classification process as executed by the resultant decision tree considering the three distinct floral species.

(A) Decision tree Methods in Metaheuristic Algorithms

- Decision tree methods can be applied within metaheuristic algorithms to enhance their performance, guide exploration, or aid in decision-making processes.
- **Feature Selection and Encoding (Rivera-Lopez et al. 2022)**: Decision trees can assist in selecting relevant features or encoding schemes for metaheuristic algorithms. By analyzing the importance of different features through tree-based techniques, metaheuristics can focus on the most influential variables, potentially improving convergence speed and solution quality.
- **Problem-Specific Strategies**: Decision trees can help metaheuristic algorithms adapt to problem-specific characteristics (Acampora et al. 2010). The decision rules learned from the training data can guide the algorithm's behavior, optimizing its search process based on the nature of the problem.
- **Combination with Local Search**: Many metaheuristic algorithms, such as Genetic Algorithms (GAs) or Particle Swarm Optimization (PSO), include local search to refine solutions. Decision trees can guide the local search process by identifying which regions of the solution space require more attention, potentially accelerating convergence and improving solution quality (Pavelski et al. 2018).
- **Early Termination**: Decision trees can serve as predictors of convergence. By monitoring the behavior of the algorithm and using learned rules, you can predict whether the algorithm is likely to find an optimal solution soon. If predicted to converge, the algorithm could be terminated early, saving computational resources (Kumar et al. 2021).
- **Diversity Maintenance**: Decision trees can guide metaheuristic algorithms to explore diverse regions of the solution space (Lee et al. 2024). By identifying unexplored regions based on historical data, the algorithm can prioritize

these areas, maintaining a better balance between exploration and exploitation.

- **Hyperparameter Tuning**: Metaheuristic algorithms often have various hyperparameters that impact their performance. Decision trees can be employed to optimize these hyperparameters based on their effect on the algorithm's behavior and solution quality (Shaheen et al. 2022).
- **Ensemble Techniques**: Decision trees can be combined with other metaheuristic algorithms to create ensemble approaches. These hybrid methods leverage the strengths of both techniques, potentially enhancing the robustness and efficiency of optimization.
- **Constraint Handling**: Decision trees can help manage constraints in optimization problems. By incorporating constraint-handling strategies into the decision tree learning process, metaheuristics can be guided to generate solutions that adhere to problem constraints.

(B) Metaheuristic Algorithms for Decision Trees:

Metaheuristic methods can be applied to decision tree approaches to enhance their performance, adaptability, and robustness. Integrating metaheuristics into decision tree algorithms can lead to improved feature selection, model tuning, and optimization of decision tree structures. Here's how metaheuristic methods can be used in decision tree approaches:

- **Hyperparameter Tuning**: Metaheuristic algorithms like Genetic Algorithms (GAs) or Particle Swarm Optimization (PSO) can be employed to optimize the hyperparameters of decision trees. This includes determining the optimal tree depth, the number of samples per leaf, and other parameters that impact the decision tree's performance.
- **Feature Selection**: Metaheuristics can assist in selecting the most relevant features for decision tree models. They can explore various subsets of features and assess their impact on the model's accuracy, leading to more efficient and interpretable trees.
- **Ensemble Methods**: Metaheuristics can be used to create ensemble methods with decision trees. For example, Genetic Programming (GP) can evolve decision trees and combine them into an ensemble, improving the overall performance and generalization ability.
- **Structure Optimization**: Metaheuristic techniques can optimize the structure of the decision tree. This includes determining the optimal split points and feature selections at each node, leading to more accurate and efficient trees.
- **Imbalanced Data Handling**: Decision trees can struggle with imbalanced datasets. Metaheuristic algorithms can be used to generate synthetic samples for the minority class, balancing the dataset and improving the tree's performance on the minority class.
- **Constrained Optimization**: If decision tree approaches need to satisfy certain constraints or requirements, metaheuristics can help find the optimal tree structure while adhering to these constraints.
- **Rule Extraction**: Decision trees can sometimes be overly complex (Shaheen et al. 2022). Metaheuristic techniques can simplify the tree by iteratively removing nodes or branches while maintaining model accuracy.

3.5 Bayesian Classification

In the following subsection, we consider the concept of the naive Bayes classifier (Yang 2018), a classification technique well-suited for datasets with categorical predictors. This approach capitalizes on conditional probabilities to make predictions. We first revisit the fundamentals of conditional probabilities and subsequently introduce the comprehensive Bayesian classifier, which is precise but can be challenging to apply practically due to its complexity. To address this, we explore the naive Bayes classifier as an alternative. The naive Bayes classifier is a more versatile solution that is widely applicable in various scenarios, offering a pragmatic approach to classification tasks involving categorical predictor variables.

The naive Bayes method, and a broader field of statistics, owe their names to the Reverend Thomas Bayes (1702–1761). To delve into the mechanics of the naive Bayes classifier, it's essential to begin by examining the comprehensive, or exact, Bayesian classifier. The underlying principle is straightforward and centers around these steps for each record intended for classification:

- Identify all other records sharing the same predictor profile, where predictor values are identical.
- Ascertain the classes to which these identified records belong and determine the class that appears most frequently.
- Allocate the most prevalent class to the new record.

While this process encapsulates the exact Bayesian classifier's approach, it's important to note that in many practical situations, implementing it becomes challenging due to its computational demands. As a solution to this, the naive Bayes classifier presents a more viable alternative, offering simplified calculations without sacrificing meaningful accuracy in a variety of applications.

Alternatively, or in tandem, there might be a need to modify the approach to address the question: "What is the likelihood of being a member of the class of interest?" as opposed to determining the most probable class. By obtaining class probabilities, the classifier can adopt a flexible cutoff strategy to assign a record to class C_i, even if C_i isn't the most probable class for that specific record. This adaptation proves valuable when pinpointing a particular class of interest is the priority, and there's a willingness to slightly "overidentify" records as belonging to this class. Such an approach is particularly relevant when certain classes carry higher significance or when precision in identifying specific classes takes precedence over overall probabilistic accuracy.

One prevalent classification method involves the establishment of a cutoff probability. This approach unfolds through the following series of steps:

- **Cutoff Probability Determination**: Set a predefined cutoff probability for the specific class of interest. This threshold signifies the minimum probability required for a record to be classified into that class.
- **Matching Predictor Profiles**: Identify all training records sharing the identical predictor profile as the new record, where predictor values align.
- **Class Probability Calculation**: Calculate the probability that these identified training records belong to the class of interest.
- **Classification Based on Cutoff**: If the computed probability surpasses the predetermined cutoff probability, allocate the new record to the class of interest.

Employing a cutoff probability strategy provides a mechanism to finely control the classification process. It allows for a flexible classification decision, especially when dealing with scenarios where certain classes have higher significance, and the emphasis is on identifying records that show a substantial propensity for belonging to a specific class.

3.5.1 Conditional Probability

Conditional probability is a fundamental concept in probability theory that measures the likelihood of an event occurring given that another related event has already occurred. In other words, it quantifies the probability of an event happening under a specific condition or constraint. Mathematically, the conditional probability of an event A occurring given that event B has occurred is denoted as $P(A|B)$.

When applied to classification, conditional probability helps answer questions like "What is the probability of a certain class given the observed features?" This probability informs the classifier's decision-making process by quantifying the likelihood of an instance belonging to a specific class C_i, given the observed values of its features $(x_1, \ldots, x_p)$. This can be expressed as follows:

$$P(C_i|x_1, \ldots, x_p) \tag{3.16}$$

In the process of classification, a fundamental step involves calculating the probability of a given record belonging to each of the available classes. This estimation is achieved by employing various techniques, often involving conditional probabilities and statistical models. Once these probabilities are computed for each class, the record is then assigned to the class that holds the highest probability value. Alternatively, the process can be tailored to make use of a predefined cutoff probability. This threshold guides the decision of whether the record should be assigned to a specific class of interest, irrespective of whether it holds the highest probability. This classification strategy ensures that each record is associated with the class that holds the greatest likelihood based on the calculated probabilities or adheres to predefined criteria if the cutoff probability is applied. This process underpins the foundation of classification algorithms, enabling accurate and informed categorization of records within various contexts.

3.5.2 Classification of Fraudulent Financial Reports

In the context of an accounting firm's operations, a crucial aspect revolves around the assessment and verification of annual financial reports submitted by its clientele, which predominantly consists of sizable companies. This process is fundamental, as it determines the accuracy and integrity of the financial information presented. For the sake of simplicity, the outcomes of these audits are categorized into two distinct classifications: "fraudulent" or "truthful," reflecting the accounting firm's determination of the authenticity of the financial reports.

Of paramount importance is the firm's commitment to precision in identifying fraudulent financial reports. This commitment is driven not only by professional ethics but also by legal ramifications. An erroneous classification, where a fraudulent report is inaccurately deemed truthful, could lead the accounting firm into legal jeopardy. Therefore, the firm operates under a stringent imperative to ensure that its classification decisions are meticulously accurate, safeguarding its reputation, legal standing, and the financial well-being of its clients and stakeholders. This exemplifies the profound significance of employing robust and dependable classification methods to address complex real-world scenarios.

The accounting firm realizes that their repository of information extends beyond financial records alone. They possess data pertaining to whether a customer has a history of legal issues, encompassing both criminal and civil charges. While this information has not been factored into their previous audits, the firm is contemplating its potential utility in enhancing their future audit processes. The central question that arises is whether a history of legal trouble, a priori unrelated to financial matters, could serve as a predictive indicator of potentially fraudulent financial reporting. This strategic consideration is rooted in the firm's desire to discern patterns that might warrant more thorough scrutiny during their auditing procedures, showcasing their commitment to adopting innovative and comprehensive approaches to ensure the integrity of financial reporting.

Approaching the analysis of this issue from a classification standpoint involves viewing each customer as a distinct record. The focal point is the outcome variable, denoted as Y, which comprises two distinct classes: "fraudulent" and "truthful." These classes, represented by C_1 and C_2 respectively, encapsulate the possible classifications of a given company. The predictor variable under consideration is the presence of "prior legal trouble," a binary attribute with values 0 (indicating no prior legal trouble) and 1 (indicating a history of legal issues). For the accounting firm's investigation, a dataset encompassing 1500 companies has been meticulously compiled. This dataset is rich with information derived from past audits, providing insights into the verdicts of whether a company's financial report was categorized as fraudulent or truthful, along with indications of whether the company had any previous legal encounters. This comprehensive dataset has been thoughtfully divided into two subsets: a training set containing records for 1000 firms and a validation set containing records for 500 firms. These subsets enable the accounting firm to train and validate classification models to predict whether a company's financial report should be flagged for potential fraud based on its history of legal issues. The frequency distribution of counts within the training set is illustrated in Table 3.1, offering an overview of the data's distribution across the defined classes and predictor values. This systematic approach underscores the firm's commitment to leveraging data-driven insights for more informed decision-making in their audit procedures.

Now, let's consider the scenario where a new company's financial report needs to be classified as either "fraudulent" or "truthful" based on the insights derived from the previously discussed dataset. To accomplish this classification task, a crucial step involves the computation of probabilities, akin to the method outlined earlier. Specifically, the aim is to estimate the probabilities associated with the new company's report belonging to each of the two classes: "fraudulent" and "truthful." By utilizing the information gathered from the historical dataset, which encompasses the outcome of previous audits and the presence or absence of prior legal trouble, the accounting firm can systematically calculate the probabilities that the new company's report falls within each classification category. This probability-based approach forms the foundation for making informed and data-driven decisions regarding the classification of the new company's financial report, thereby contributing to more accurate and principled auditing practices.

For instance, to ascertain the probability of the new company's report belonging to the "fraudulent" class given its prior legal history, the calculation involves considering the fraction of companies in the training set that had both prior legal trouble and were classified as fraudulent. Specifically, the probability $P(\text{fraudulent}|\text{prior legal})$ is derived as the ratio of 50 (the count of

Table 3.1 The frequency distribution of counts within the training set of fraudulent financial reports.

	No prior legal $X = 0$	Prior legal $X = 1$	Total
Fraudulent C_1	50	50	100
Truthful C_2	720	180	900
Total	770	230	1000

companies with prior legal trouble that were fraudulent) to 230 (the total count of companies with prior legal trouble in the training set). Conversely, the probability of the report belonging to the "truthful" class is complementary to the probability. In this case, it is calculated as the remaining fraction, which is 180 (the count of companies with prior legal trouble that were truthful) divided by 230.

This probability-driven approach reflects the accounting firm's endeavor to quantitatively assess the likelihood of the new company's financial report falling into specific classification categories based on historical patterns and data-driven insights.

In the classification process, when dealing with a company that has a history of prior legal trouble, a strategic decision must be made regarding its classification. In this scenario, a practical approach is to assign the company to a specific class based on its characteristics and probabilities. In our example, following the rule of "assign to the most probable class," when encountering a company with prior legal trouble, the classification decision leads to assigning it to the "truthful" class. This determination is influenced by the probability computations conducted earlier, where the calculated probability of belonging to the "truthful" class outweighs that of the "fraudulent" class. Interestingly, this outcome aligns with a more straightforward rule often referred to as the "majority class" rule. Under this naive rule, all records are assigned to the class that constitutes the majority within the dataset. Remarkably, in our present context, the application of the probability-based classification rule leads to the same conclusion as the majority class rule, further highlighting the significance of probability-based approaches in guiding classification decisions.

In the context of our example, the primary focus lies in identifying the potentially fraudulent reports, as the consequences of failing to do so could be severe, possibly leading to legal ramifications for the auditor. This recognition leads us to adopt a pragmatic approach that prioritizes the identification of fraudulent reports, even if it results in some truthful reports being mistakenly classified as fraudulent. It is understood that this approach might impact the overall classification accuracy, but the overarching objective of detecting fraudulent activities takes precedence. To execute this strategy, we employ a designated cutoff value for the probability of a record being classified as "fraudulent." All records surpassing this established cutoff are classified as fraudulent, allowing for a proactive stance toward identifying potential cases of concern. For the mathematical computation of this probability, we utilize the Bayesian formula, which involves the conditional probabilities and prior probabilities which is modeled as follows:

$$P(C_i|x_1,\dots,x_p) = \frac{P(x_1,\dots,x_p|C_i)\cdot P(C_i)}{P(x_1,\dots,x_p|C_i)\cdot P(C_i)+\dots+P(x_1,\dots,x_p|C_m)\cdot P(C_m)} \tag{3.17}$$

This formula serves as a robust framework to estimate the likelihood that a given record $(x_1, \dots, x_p)$ belongs to a specific class C_i, providing the analytical foundation for making informed decisions and driving the classification process.

In the specific scenario presented in our example, where instances of fraud are relatively uncommon, the determination of an appropriate cutoff value assumes critical significance. For instance, suppose we set the cutoff value at 0.20. If a record has a history of prior legal trouble, its calculated probability P(fraudulent|prior legal) would be 0.22, which exceeds the specified cutoff threshold. Consequently, the classification decision would label this record as "fraudulent." It's important to underscore that the selection of the cutoff value is not a fixed rule but rather a parameter that can be strategically adjusted by the user. Much like other parameters in any classification model, the cutoff value can be fine-tuned to optimize the performance and outcomes of the classification process. This dynamic flexibility empowers the user to strike an equilibrium between correctly identifying fraudulent cases and minimizing false positives, thus tailoring the classification approach to the specific goals and requirements at hand.

3.5.3 Practical Constraints by Using the Exact Bayes Method

The approach we have discussed entails identifying records within the dataset that closely match the new record intended for classification. This alignment is achieved when all predictor values of the records are entirely identical to those of the new record. While this method was straightforward to implement in the illustrative example provided earlier, it's worth noting that its feasibility can diminish as the complexity of the dataset increases. Particularly, this method becomes less practical in situations where there are multiple predictors contributing to the classification process. As such, more sophisticated techniques, such as the naive Bayes classifier, are commonly employed to navigate the complexities of high-dimensional datasets and deliver effective classification outcomes.

As the number of predictors increases, even moderately, the challenge of finding exact matches for records to be classified becomes more pronounced. This is particularly evident in scenarios involving a significant number of predictors, such as in predictive models that aim to forecast voting patterns based on demographic variables. In this context, even a substantial dataset might not yield a single record that precisely mirrors a new record possessing a unique combination of attributes. For instance, envision a case where a new record is characterized as a male Hispanic with a high income from the US Midwest. Furthermore, this individual voted in the last election, refrained from voting in the prior election, has three daughters and one son, and is divorced. Remarkably, these attributes constitute merely eight variables – a relatively modest number in the realm of data analysis. Even the introduction of a single additional variable, boasting five equally frequent categories, significantly reduces the likelihood of finding an exact match by a factor of five. This vividly illustrates the growing complexity and challenge of achieving accurate record classification in the face of a multitude of predictor variables.

3.5.4 Naive Bayes Method

In the naive Bayes approach, the conventional constraints on probability calculations have been relaxed. Instead of confining the probability assessment to records that precisely match the one being classified, the entire dataset is brought into play. Reflecting on the fundamental classification procedure introduced at the outset of this chapter, we recall the following steps for classifying a new record:

- Locate all other records sharing the same predictor profile, where predictor values align.
- Ascertain the classes to which these records belong and identify the class that is most prevalent.
- Allocate this prevalent class to the new record.

The classification procedure in the Naive Bayes method involves several steps:

- **Compute Class Probabilities**: Calculate the prior probabilities of each class based on the frequency of occurrence in the training dataset. These are the probabilities of encountering each class independently of any predictor variables.
- **Compute Conditional Probabilities**: For each predictor variable, calculate the conditional probabilities of each class given the value of that predictor. This involves determining how often each class occurs for a particular value of the predictor.
- **Calculate Likelihood**: For the new record to be classified, calculate the likelihood of it belonging to each class based on the conditional probabilities computed in the previous step. This involves multiplying the conditional probabilities for all predictor variables.

- **Apply Bayes' Theorem**: Apply Bayes' theorem to compute the posterior probabilities for each class. This is done by multiplying the likelihood of each class by the corresponding prior probability and then dividing by the sum of the products for all classes.
- **Normalize Probabilities**: Normalize the posterior probabilities so that they sum up to 1. This step ensures that the probabilities can be interpreted as probabilities of belonging to each class.
- **Assign Class**: Assign the new record to the class with the highest posterior probability. This is the class that is considered the most likely based on the available predictor information.
- **Optional Cutoff**: As an optional step, you can introduce a cutoff threshold for class assignment. If the probability of a class is above the cutoff, the record is assigned to that class. This can be useful when you prioritize certain classes over others or want to balance precision and recall.

Let's consider a simple example of using the Naive Bayes classification method to predict whether a person will play golf based on weather conditions. We have as a training dataset Table 3.2 which contains weather conditions and corresponding play golf outcomes.

Now let's say we want to predict whether we should play golf on a day with the following weather conditions: Outlook = Sunny, Temperature = Mild, Humidity = High, Windy = No. Here's how the Naive Bayes classification process works step by step:

Compute Class Probabilities:

$$P(\text{Play Golf} = \text{Yes}) = 9/14 = 0.6429$$
$$P(\text{Play Golf} = \text{No}) = 5/14 = 0.3571$$

Compute Conditional Probabilities:

$$P(\text{Outlook} = \text{Sunny} \mid \text{Play Golf} = \text{Yes}) = 2/9 = 0.2222$$
$$P(\text{Outlook} = \text{Sunny} \mid \text{Play Golf} = \text{No}) = 3/5 = 0.6000$$

The same computations should be done for the other predictor variables.

Table 3.2 Training dataset for a numerical example of the Naïve Bayes method.

Outlook	Temperature	Humidity	Windy	Play Golf
Sunny	Hot	High	No	No
Sunny	Hot	High	Yes	No
Overcast	Hot	High	No	Yes
Rain	Mild	High	No	Yes
Rain	Cool	Normal	No	Yes
Rain	Cool	Normal	Yes	No
Overcast	Cool	Normal	Yes	Yes
Sunny	Mild	High	No	No
Sunny	Cool	Normal	No	Yes
Rain	Mild	Normal	No	Yes
Sunny	Mild	Normal	Yes	Yes
Overcast	Mild	High	Yes	Yes
Overcast	Hot	Normal	No	Yes

Calculate Likelihood:

$$\begin{aligned}\text{Likelihood}(\text{Outlook} = \text{Sunny}) = P(&\text{Outlook} = \text{Sunny} \mid \text{Play Golf} = \text{Yes})\\ &\cdot P(\text{Outlook} = \text{Sunny} \mid \text{Play Golf} = \text{No})\\ &= 0.2222 \cdot 0.6000 = 0.1333.\end{aligned}$$

Calculate likelihoods for other predictor variables.

Apply Bayes' Theorem:

$$\begin{aligned}\text{Posterior}(\text{Play Golf} = \text{Yes}) &= \text{Likelihood}(\text{Outlook} = \text{Sunny}) \cdot P(\text{Play Golf} = \text{Yes})\\ &= 0.1333 \cdot 0.6429 = 0.0857.\\ \text{Posterior}(\text{Play Golf} = \text{No}) &= \text{Likelihood}(\text{Outlook} = \text{Sunny}) \cdot P(\text{Play Golf} = \text{No})\\ &= 0.1333 \cdot 0.3571 = 0.0476.\end{aligned}$$

Normalize Probabilities:

$$\text{Normalized Posterior}(\text{Play Golf} = \text{Yes}) = 0.0857/(0.0857 + 0.0476) = 0.6429.$$

$$\text{Normalized Posterior}(\text{Play Golf} = \text{No}) = 0.0476/(0.0857 + 0.0476) = 0.3571.$$

Assign Class:

The highest normalized posterior probability corresponds to Play Golf = Yes, so we predict that we should play golf.

3.5.5 Computational Experiment

In MATLAB, the Naive Bayes classifier operates in two distinct steps:

Training: In the training phase, the algorithm utilizes a labeled dataset, where the outcomes are known, to estimate the parameters of a probability distribution. This estimation is done under the assumption that the predictor variables are conditionally independent given the class label. The algorithm calculates the necessary probabilities based on the training data, and these probabilities form the basis for classification.

Prediction: Once the training is complete, the Naive Bayes classifier can predict the class label for new, unseen data. For a given set of predictor values, the classifier computes the posterior probability of the sample belonging to each class. The class with the highest posterior probability is then assigned as the predicted class for the new data point.

This two-step process allows the Naive Bayes classifier to make predictions on new data by utilizing the probability distributions learned during the training phase. MATLAB provides functions to create and train Naive Bayes models, as well as to perform predictions based on these models. The classifier is particularly useful for datasets with categorical or discrete predictors, where the assumption of conditional independence of the predictors given the class label simplifies the modeling process.

To illustrate the classification mechanisms of the Naïve Bayes method, we turn to Fisher's classic example involving three distinct types of iris flowers. For the sake of simplicity, we will continue using the same dataset, specifically aiming to classify iris types based on petal characteristics. In this instance, we'll employ a Bayesian classifier to demonstrate how this approach can effectively differentiate between different iris species using their petal attributes.

To establish a Naive Bayes classifier, the `fitcnb` function is utilized for training. This function returns a multiclass Naive Bayes model, which is trained based on the provided predictors.

To accommodate datasets with more than two classes, it's advisable to define the class order explicitly. In our case, the predictors encompass the petal length and petal width, while the classes pertain to setosa, versicolor, and virginica iris species. This training process readies the classifier to make informed classifications based on the attributes of the iris petals.

The syntax of the `fitcnb` function is as follows:

```
NaiveBayesModel = fitcnb(X, Y,);
```

Where `NaiveBayesModel` stores the classification model, `X` is a table of predictor variables (features) with dimensions $n \times p$, where n is the number of observations and p is the number of predictor variables. `Y` is a categorical array or cell array of strings containing the class labels for each observation.

The training procedure of the Naïve Bayes classifier using the Iris dataset is demonstrated in Code 3.4. The code begins by loading the relevant data from the iris dataset. Following this, the third and fourth columns of the `meas` variable, which signify petal length and petal width, are extracted. Subsequently, a table is constructed incorporating these variables, along with their respective predictor names, to form a foundational structure for the model. This setup prepares the data for training the Naïve Bayes classifier to make accurate predictions regarding the iris species based on petal characteristics.

Code 3.4

```
clear all
load fisheriris
PetalLength = meas(:,3);
PetalWidth = meas(:,4);
PetalTable = table(PetalLength,PetalWidth);
NaiveModelPetal
=fitcnb(PetalTable,species,'ClassNames',{'setosa','versicolor','virginica'})
```

Code 3.4 produces a `ClassificationNaiveBayes` object with several properties and methods. The elements of this object can be analyzed as follows:

```
NaiveModelPetal =

  ClassificationNaiveBayes
            PredictorNames: {'PetalLength'  'PetalWidth'}
              ResponseName: 'Y'
     CategoricalPredictors: []
                ClassNames: {'setosa'  'versicolor'  'virginica'}
            ScoreTransform: 'none'
           NumObservations: 150
         DistributionNames: {'normal'  'normal'}
    DistributionParameters: {3×2 cell}

  Properties, Methods
```

A ClassificationNaiveBayes object is created with several properties and methods. To access one of these elements, we can use dot notation. the `DistributionParameters` property in the object returned by `ClassificationNaiveBayes` stores the parameters of the probability distributions for each class in the Naive Bayes model. The DistributionParameters property is a cell array where each cell corresponds to the mean and variance values of each class. These elements can be visualized as follows:

```
NaiveModelPetal.DistributionParameters

ans =

  3×2 cell array

    {2×1 double}    {2×1 double}
    {2×1 double}    {2×1 double}
    {2×1 double}    {2×1 double}
```

In `DistributionParameters`, every row comprises data about different species (setosa, versicolor, and virginica), while each column includes information about specific features (such as petal length and petal width). Therefore, if you want to retrieve the mean and standard deviation associated with the versicolor species for petal length, you can use the following command:

```
NaiveModelPetal.DistributionParameters{2,1}

ans =

    4.2600
    0.4699
```

The initial value signifies the mean, while the subsequent value represents the standard deviation. To assess the model's efficacy, calculate the resubstitution error, which denotes the rate of misclassification or the portion of incorrectly classified instances within the training set. The resubstitution error rate primarily offers insights into the model's performance, indicating the quality of the algorithm employed and typically serving as a performance metric:

```
NaiveModelPetalResubErr = resubLoss(NaiveModelPetal)

NaiveModelPetalResubErr =

    0.0400
```

The outcome reveals that the Naive Bayes algorithm misclassifies approximately 4% of the observations. However, this straightforward calculation of the classification error does not provide insights into the specific nature of the errors made by the system. It falls short of addressing queries like whether the errors are evenly spread across all classes or if the system predominantly confuses certain classes while accurately classifying others.

To gain insight into the distribution of these errors, the computation of a confusion matrix can be employed. This matrix encapsulates details about the model's actual and predicted classifications. The evaluation of such systems frequently hinges on utilizing the information present in the matrix. Table 3.3 illustrates the structure of a confusion matrix for a two-class classifier.

The elements of the confusion matrix maintain a specific significance. *TP*, or True Positives, indicates the count of correct predictions where an instance is classified as positive. *FN*, or False Negatives, represents the count of incorrect predictions where an instance is misclassified as negative. *FP*, or False Positives, denotes the count of incorrect predictions where an instance is

Table 3.3 Confusion matrix for a two-class classifier.

	Predicted positive	**Predicted negative**
Real positive	*TP*	*FN*
Real negative	*FP*	*TN*

mistakenly classified as positive. Lastly, *TN*, or True Negatives, signifies the count of accurate predictions where an instance is rightly classified as negative.

The confusion matrix provides a clear representation of correct and incorrect predictions. The values along the main diagonal of the matrix signify accurate predictions, while the off-diagonal values represent errors. In MATLAB, the `confusionmat` function is employed to compute a confusion matrix. This function takes known and predicted group labels as inputs and produces the corresponding confusion matrix. Before using the function, it's essential to collect the model's predictions for the available data, allowing for the subsequent computation of the confusion matrix. The following code computes the confusion matrix for the case of the predictions of the iris dataset.

```
>> PredictedValue = predict(NaiveModelPetal,meas(:,3:4));
>> ConfMat = confusionmat(species,PredictedValue)

ConfMat =

    50     0     0
     0    47     3
     0     3    47
```

Based on the confusion matrix, there are a total of six errors, accounting for four percent of the available values. These errors are specifically related to the versicolor and virginica species. To gain insight into how the classifier makes its predictions with respect to the feature space, it's possible to visualize the decision regions within this space, which are defined by the petal length and petal width features. One effective approach to visualize these regions is by constructing a grid of (x, y) values and applying the classification function across this grid. To achieve this visualization, the process begins by computing the extremes of the grid. This involves determining the minimum and maximum values of the predictor variables, as outlined below:

```
>> min(meas(:,3:4))

ans =

    1.0000    0.1000

>> max(meas(:,3:4))

ans =

    6.9000    2.5000
```

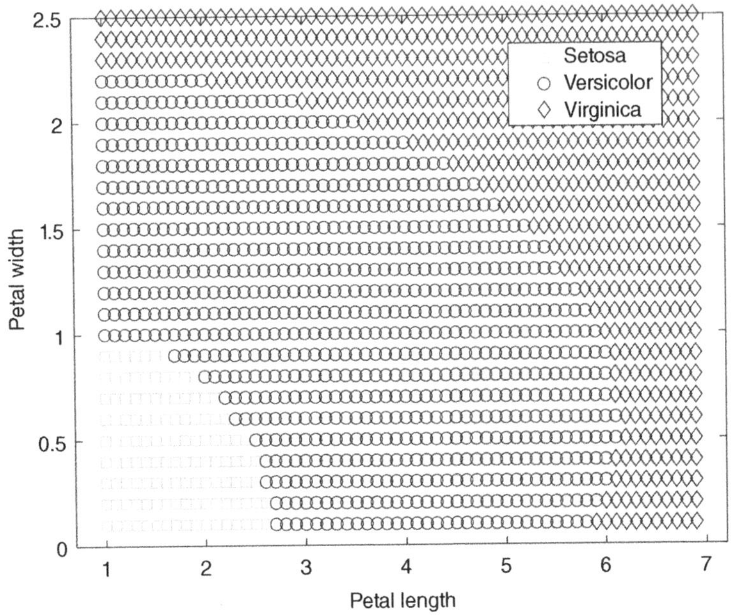

Figure 3.8 Classification regions produced by the Naïve Bayes method considering the iris data set.

to visualize the classification within the feature space, the implementation of Code 3.5 can be employed. This algorithm enables the visualization of regions in the feature space based on the classifications assigned by the Naïve Bayes method. The code is designed to effectively distribute these regions in accordance with the unique characteristics of each class, taking into account the features being analyzed. This visualization provides a clear representation of how the classification boundaries are defined within the feature space using the Naïve Bayes approach. Figure 3.8 shows the results after the execution of the Code 3.5.

Code 3.5

```
clear all
load fisheriris
PetalLength = meas(:,3);
PetalWidth = meas(:,4);
PetalTable = table(PetalLength,PetalWidth);
NaiveModelPetal
=fitcnb(PetalTable,species,'ClassNames',{'setosa','versicolor','virginica'});
[x y] = meshgrid(1:.1:6.9,0.1:.1:2.5);
PredictedGrid = predict(NaiveModelPetal, [x(:) y(:)]);
gscatter(x(:),y(:),PredictedGrid,'grb','sod')
```

(A) Naïve Bayes Method in Metaheuristic Algorithms

The application of the Naive Bayes algorithm to metaheuristic approaches involves combining the probabilistic reasoning of Naive Bayes with the optimization capabilities of metaheuristic algorithms. This integration aims to enhance the performance, adaptability, and efficiency of both paradigms across various problem domains. Here's an overview of how the Naive Bayes algorithm has been applied within metaheuristic frameworks:

- **Solution Encoding and Representation**: In metaheuristic optimization problems, solutions are often encoded as vectors or strings. The Naive Bayes algorithm can be utilized to model the probabilities of specific components or attributes within these solutions, allowing the metaheuristic to guide the search process toward more promising regions of the solution space.
- **Probabilistic Model-Based Metaheuristics (Shaheen et al. 2022)**: Some metaheuristic algorithms are model-based, meaning they build probabilistic models to capture the underlying problem landscape. The Naive Bayes algorithm can be integrated into these models to provide a probabilistic assessment of solution quality, guiding the exploration and exploitation phases of the metaheuristic.
- **Objective Function Modeling**: The Naive Bayes algorithm can be used to approximate the objective function of an optimization problem based on available data points (Chaudhuri and Sahu 2021). This can help the metaheuristic algorithm make informed decisions during the search process, reducing the number of expensive objective function evaluations.
- **Bayesian Optimization with Metaheuristics**: Bayesian optimization aims to find the global optimum of an expensive objective function (Nakib et al. 2015). Integrating Naive Bayes within a Bayesian optimization framework can provide probabilistic estimates of the objective function values, which can guide the metaheuristic to focus on promising regions of the search space.
- **Hybridization with Naive Bayes**: Hybrid algorithms that combine Naive Bayes with metaheuristic techniques create synergistic solutions. For instance, a metaheuristic can guide the exploration of the search space, while Naive Bayes provides probabilistic information to refine the decision-making process.
- **Data-Driven Problem Solving**: The Naive Bayes algorithm can assist metaheuristics in leveraging available data to make informed decisions. This is particularly useful in scenarios where the objective function is noisy or expensive to evaluate, enabling the metaheuristic to learn from data and adapt its search strategy.
- **Constraint Handling**: When optimization problems involve constraints, the Naive Bayes algorithm can model the feasibility of solutions. By combining Naive Bayes with a metaheuristic, feasible solutions can be more effectively explored, leading to improved convergence and better solutions.
- **Multi-Objective Optimization**: Naive Bayes can help in multi-objective optimization by providing insights into the relationships between different objectives. This information can guide the metaheuristic in generating a diverse set of Parcto-optimal solutions.
- **Adaptive Parameter Control**: Metaheuristic algorithms often involve tuning parameters to balance exploration and exploitation. The Naive Bayes algorithm can aid in dynamically adjusting these parameters based on probabilistic assessments of solution quality.

(B) Metaheuristic Algorithms for Naïve Bayes techniques

The application of metaheuristic methods to Naive Bayes approaches involves the integration of optimization capabilities of metaheuristics to enhance the accuracy, efficiency, and adaptability of Naive Bayes-based solutions. This integration aims to improve the performance of Naive Bayes algorithms across various problem domains by optimizing their parameters, feature selection, and classification rules. Here's an overview of how metaheuristic methods have been applied to Naive Bayes approaches:

- **Parameter Tuning**: Naive Bayes algorithms often have parameters that influence their performance. Metaheuristic optimization techniques can be employed to automatically tune these parameters, enhancing the algorithm's predictive accuracy. This is particularly useful when the optimal parameter values are complex to determine manually.
- **Feature Selection**: In datasets with a large number of features, not all attributes contribute equally to classification accuracy. Metaheuristics can aid in identifying the most relevant features for classification, reducing the dimensionality of the problem, and enhancing the efficiency and accuracy of Naive Bayes classifiers.
- **Hybrid Classification**: Hybrid methods that combine Naive Bayes algorithms with metaheuristics create synergistic solutions. For example, metaheuristics can guide the search for optimal feature subsets, while Naive Bayes provides probabilistic classification based on the selected features.
- **Optimization-Based Naive Bayes Learning**: Metaheuristics can be applied to learn the structure and parameters of Naive Bayes models from data. This optimization-driven learning process can lead to improved classification performance by tailoring the Naive Bayes model to the specific characteristics of the dataset.
- **Imbalanced Data Handling**: When dealing with imbalanced datasets, where one class is significantly underrepresented, Naive Bayes methods can struggle to predict the minority class accurately. Metaheuristics can assist in balancing the class distribution, thus improving the predictive performance of Naive Bayes algorithms.
- **Ensemble Techniques**: Metaheuristic algorithms can be used to create ensemble models that combine multiple Naive Bayes classifiers with varying parameter settings or feature subsets. This ensemble approach enhances the overall classification accuracy and robustness.
- **Hybrid Bayesian Optimization**: Bayesian optimization can be combined with metaheuristic algorithms to optimize the hyperparameters of Naive Bayes classifiers. This hybrid approach efficiently searches the hyperparameter space to achieve optimal classification performance.
- **Dynamic Adaptation**: Some metaheuristic algorithms, like genetic algorithms, can dynamically adapt their search strategies during runtime. This adaptability can be utilized to enhance the exploration-exploitation balance of Naive Bayes classifiers.
- **Customized Loss Functions**: Metaheuristics can assist in optimizing customized loss functions, allowing Naive Bayes classifiers to focus on specific aspects of classification errors that are critical in a given domain.

- **Uncertainty Estimation**: Metaheuristics can be employed to estimate uncertainties associated with Naive Bayes classifications. This is particularly useful when probabilistic confidence levels are required for decision-making.

3.6 k-Nearest Neighbors (k-NN)

In this section, we consider the k-nearest-neighbors (k-NN) algorithm (Taunk et al. 2019), a versatile tool applicable for both categorical classification and numerical prediction tasks. This method operates by locating comparable instances within the training dataset when faced with a new sample. These akin instances are referred to as "neighbors," and they play a crucial role in determining the classification or prediction of the new data point. For classification purposes, the method relies on a voting mechanism among neighbors, while prediction involves averaging their values. Our discussion includes elucidating the basis for gauging similarity, selecting an appropriate number of neighbors, and comprehending the mechanics of classification or prediction. The k-NN approach is notably automated and data-driven. We also deliberate on the strengths and limitations of the k-NN method, factoring in performance considerations and practical aspects like computational efficiency.

3.6.1 k-NN for Classification

The essence of k-nearest-neighbors (k-NN) methods revolves around the concept of identifying k records within the training dataset that bear resemblance to a fresh record awaiting classification. These analogous records, often referred to as neighbors, are then harnessed to determine the class assignment of the new record. This entails associating the new record with the prevailing class among these neighboring instances. If we denote the predictor values for the new record as $x_1, \ldots, x_p$, the objective is to seek out records in the training data that share proximity or "closeness" with the record to be classified within the predictor space (in essence, records exhibiting values proximate to $x_1, \ldots, x_p$). Subsequently, grounded in the classes affiliated with these neighboring records, we allocate a class label to the record under scrutiny. Figure 3.9 illustrates the visual representation of the k-Nearest Neighbors (k-NN) classification process. The diagram presents the distribution of elements belonging to two distinct classes: + and −. To comprehend the

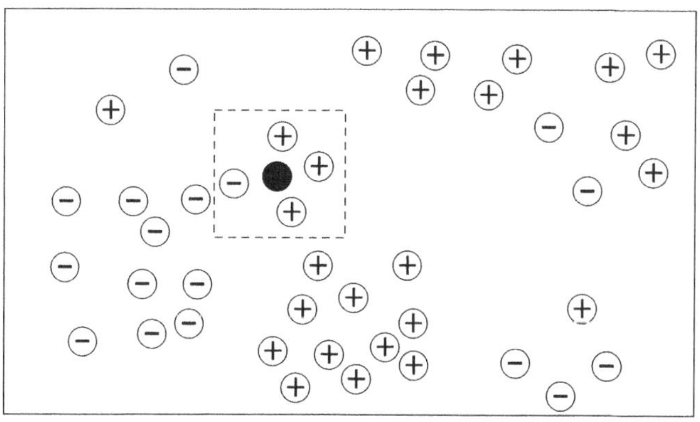

Figure 3.9 Visual representation of the k-Nearest Neighbors (k-NN) classification process.

classification of a new element, represented by the black point, let's assume we are utilizing a k value of 4. The k-NN approach involves identifying the four nearest data points to the new element, as indicated within the surrounding rectangle. Following this, we tally the classes of these nearest neighbors and assign the class + to the new point, since it is the most prevalent among the selected neighbors. This visual representation encapsulates the core concept of k-NN classification, where the class of an unknown data point is determined based on the majority class of its k nearest neighbors.

The k-nearest-neighbors (k-NN) algorithm is a classification approach that operates without presuming any particular structure for the connection between class membership (Y) and the predictors $x_1, \ldots, x_p$. It belongs to the category of nonparametric methods, signifying that it doesn't engage in parameter estimation within a predefined functional form, as observed in linear regression. Instead, k-NN harnesses the power of similarities present among the predictor values of the records contained within the dataset. This unique characteristic allows it to accommodate a wide range of data scenarios without imposing restrictive assumptions about the underlying relationship between the variables.

In the context of the k-nearest-neighbors algorithm, a crucial inquiry emerges: how should the distance between records be quantified based on their predictor values? The Euclidean distance is the most widely adopted measure for assessing such distances. Although there are other distance metrics for both numerical and categorical variables, the Euclidean distance, which is computationally cheap, is the most popular in k-NN.

In order to account for varying scales among different predictors, a common practice involves standardizing the predictors before computing the Euclidean distance. This step ensures that each predictor contributes uniformly to the distance calculation, preventing any undue influence from predictors with larger scales. Importantly, when standardizing new records, the means and standard deviations utilized are those derived from the training data. Notably, neither the new record nor the validation data is involved in these computations, reinforcing the independence and reliability of the standardization process.

After calculating the distances between the record to be classified and the existing records, we need a decision rule to assign a class to the record based on its neighboring records' classes. The simplest scenario is when $k = 1$; in this case, we identify the nearest neighbor and classify the new record into the same class as its closest neighbor. It's quite remarkable that this straightforward approach of using a single nearest neighbor for classification can be remarkably effective, particularly when dealing with a large training dataset. Astonishingly, this intuitive concept has been found to possess considerable power, even though it utilizes just a single nearest neighbor. Notably, the misclassification error associated with the 1-nearest neighbor strategy has a misclassification rate that is no more than twice the error rate achieved when the exact probability density functions for each class are known.

The concept of using k nearest neighbors can be expanded for cases where k is greater than 1. Here's how the extension works:

- Identify the k nearest neighbors to the record that needs classification.
- Utilize a majority decision rule to classify the record, where the record is assigned to the majority class among its k neighbors.

We consider a simple numerical example to demonstrate the k-Nearest Neighbors (k-NN) classification algorithm. Imagine we have a dataset of points in a two-dimensional space, and we want to classify a new point based on its proximity to the existing data points. Suppose we have the dataset shown in Table 3.4, where each point belongs to one of two classes: A or B.

Table 3.4 Data used in the numerical example for classification.

Point	x_1	x_2	Class
P_1	2	3	A
P_2	5	4	A
P_3	9	6	B
P_4	4	8	B

Assume that we have a new point, P_{new}, with coordinates (6, 5). Under such conditions, we want to classify it using the k-NN algorithm. Let's say we choose $k = 3$, which means we'll consider the three nearest neighbors to the new point.

Calculate the Euclidean distance between P_{new} and each existing point in the dataset:

$$\text{Distance}(P_{new}, P_1) = \sqrt{(6-2)^2 + (5-3)^2} = 4.47$$

$$\text{Distance}(P_{new}, P_2) = \sqrt{(6-5)^2 + (5-4)^2} = 1.41$$

$$\text{Distance}(P_{new}, P_3) = \sqrt{(6-9)^2 + (5-6)^2} = 3.16$$

$$\text{Distance}(P_{new}, P_4) = \sqrt{(6-4)^2 + (5-8)^2} = 3.61$$

Choose the $k = 3$ nearest neighbors based on the smallest distances. They correspond to P_2, P_3, and P_4 (since they have the smallest distances). Among the k nearest neighbors, count the occurrences of each class:

Class A: 1 occurrence (P_2)

Class B: 2 occurrences (P_3, P_4)

Since the majority class is B, we classify the new point P_{new} as Class B.

3.6.2 k-NN for Regression

The method of k-Nearest Neighbors (k-NN) can also be used for numerical prediction, not just classification. When used for numerical prediction, it's often referred to as "k-NN Regression." The basic idea is similar to the classification case, but instead of assigning a class label to the new data point, we predict a numerical value based on the values of its k-nearest neighbors.

To predict the value of a new element, the following steps are considered by the k-NN approach:

Distance Calculation: Calculate the distances between the new data point (the data point for which you want to make a prediction) and all other data points in the training dataset. The most common distance metric used is the Euclidean distance.

Select k Nearest Neighbors: Choose the k nearest neighbors with the smallest distances to the new data point.

Prediction: For k-NN regression, instead of majority voting, we take the average (or weighted average) of the target values of the k-nearest neighbors.

These weights reflect the proximity of each neighbor to the new data point. Neighbors that are closer to the new data point are given more weight in the average calculation, while neighbors that are farther away are given less weight.

Table 3.5 Data used in the numerical example for prediction.

Age	Income	Expense
25	50,000	1,200
30	60,000	1,500
35	55,000	1,400
40	75,000	1,800
45	80,000	2,000

Mathematically, the weighted average prediction for the new data point is calculated as follows:

$$Predicted\ Value = \frac{\sum_{i=1}^{k} w_i \cdot \text{Target Value}_i}{\sum_{i=1}^{k} w_i} \tag{3.18}$$

where w_i is an element that assigns a numerical weight to each neighbor i based on its distance from the new data point. Common weight functions include the inverse of the distance (closer neighbors have higher weights) or Gaussian weights (neighbors closer to the new data point have higher weights, and weights decrease as distance increases). Target Value_i is the numerical value of the i neighbor.

We consider a simple numerical example to demonstrate the k-Nearest Neighbors (k-NN) regression technique. Suppose we have a dataset with two variables, as it is shown in Table 3.5. The variables consider the elements "Age" and "Income," and we want to predict the component "Expense" based on these variables.

Assuming these data, we want to predict the expense for a new individual with age 33 and income 62,000 using k-NN regression with $k = 3$ (3 nearest neighbors).

Calculate Euclidean Distances:

Distance to (25, 50,000): $\sqrt{(33-25)^2 + (62{,}000 - 50{,}000)^2} = 12018.43$

Distance to (30, 60,000): $\sqrt{(33-30)^2 + (62{,}000 - 60{,}000)^2} = 2000.00$

Distance to (35, 55,000): $\sqrt{(33-35)^2 + (62{,}000 - 55{,}000)^2} = 7014.14$

Distance to (40, 75,000): $\sqrt{(33-40)^2 + (62{,}000 - 75{,}000)^2} = 13136.73$

Distance to (45, 80,000): $\sqrt{(33-45)^2 + (62, 000 - 80{,}000)^2} = 18344.69$

Select 3 Nearest Neighbors:

Neighbors: (30, 60,000), (35, 55,000), (25, 50,000)

Calculate Weights:

Inverse Distance Weighting:

Weight to (30, 60,000): 1/2000.00 = 0.0005

Weight to (35, 55,000): 1/7014.14 = 0.0001

Weight to (25, 50,000): 1/12018.43 = 0.0001

Weight to (25, 50,000): 1/12018.43 = 0.0001

Calculate Weighted Average Prediction:

$$\text{Prediction} = (0.0005 \times 1500) + (0.0001 \times 1400) + (0.0001 \times 1200)/(0.0005 + 0.0001 + 0.0001)$$

$$\text{Prediction} \approx 1462.96$$

So, based on the k-NN regression with $k = 3$, the predicted expense for an individual with age 33 and income 62,000 is approximately 1462.96. This prediction is a weighted average of expenses from the three nearest neighbors, where closer neighbors have a higher influence due to their higher weights.

(A) k-Nearest Neighbors Methods in Metaheuristic Algorithms

The k-Nearest Neighbors (k-NN) method is a versatile technique that finds applications not only in traditional machine learning but also within the realm of metaheuristic algorithms.

- **Initialization of Solutions**: In some metaheuristic algorithms, the initial solutions or population members play a crucial role in determining the quality of the final solution (Perim et al. 2008). The k-NN method can be used to generate diverse and promising initial solutions by considering the characteristics of existing solutions in the solution space.
- **Neighbor Selection**: Metaheuristic algorithms often involve exploring the solution space by generating neighboring solutions around a current solution. The k-NN method can be used to identify these neighbors, considering the similarity of their attributes or characteristics to the current solution. This approach can guide the algorithm to explore regions of the solution space with potentially better solutions.
- **Adaptive Parameter Tuning**: Many metaheuristic algorithms have parameters that influence their behavior, such as mutation rates or step sizes. The k-NN method can be utilized to adaptively adjust these parameters based on the characteristics of the solutions encountered during the optimization process. This dynamic parameter tuning can lead to improved convergence and solution quality.
- **Crossover or Combination**: Some metaheuristic algorithms involve combining or exchanging information between different solutions to create new ones. The k-NN method can help identify solutions that are similar or complementary, allowing for effective crossover or combination strategies that lead to diverse and high-quality solutions.
- **Constraint Handling**: Metaheuristic algorithms often encounter constrained optimization problems where solutions must satisfy certain constraints. The k-NN method can assist in identifying feasible solutions or guiding the search toward regions of the solution space that are likely to yield feasible solutions.
- **Local Search**: Metaheuristic algorithms can benefit from local search mechanisms that fine-tune solutions in the vicinity of the current solution. The k-NN method can guide local search by identifying nearby solutions that share similar characteristics, enabling more focused exploration.

(B) Metaheuristic Algorithms for k-NN:

Metaheuristic algorithms have been applied to k-NN approaches to enhance their performance, scalability, and adaptability in solving various types of problems. The combination of metaheuristics and k-NN techniques creates hybrid methodologies that increase the strengths of both paradigms. Here's an overview of how metaheuristic algorithms have been integrated with k-NN approaches:

- **Parameter Optimization**: Many machine learning algorithms, including k-NN, have hyperparameters that need to be set before training. Metaheuristic algorithms, such as genetic algorithms, particle swarm optimization, or simulated annealing, can be used to automatically tune these hyperparameters, leading to improved k-NN model performance and generalization.
- **Feature Selection**: In high-dimensional data, not all features are equally relevant. Metaheuristic algorithms can help identify the most informative subset of features for k-NN classification or regression, resulting in more efficient and accurate models by reducing noise and overfitting.
- **Distance Metric Learning**: The choice of distance metric in k-NN greatly influences its performance. Metaheuristic algorithms can be employed to learn an adaptive distance metric that best captures the underlying data distribution, improving the discrimination power of the k-NN classifier.
- **Imbalanced Data Handling**: In datasets with imbalanced class distributions, k-NN can suffer from bias towards the majority class. Metaheuristics can be used to re-sample the data, generating synthetic instances of the minority class or down-sampling the majority class to balance the distribution and enhance the classification accuracy.
- **Cluster-Based Optimization**: Metaheuristic algorithms often involve creating and refining solution clusters. These clusters can serve as local models for k-NN classification, where each cluster is associated with a different k-NN model, allowing for more accurate predictions within specific regions of the data space.
- **Hybrid Models**: Hybrid models combine the predictive power of different algorithms. Metaheuristics can be integrated with k-NN to build hybrid models that combine global optimization strategies from metaheuristics with the local refinement capabilities of k-NN. This leads to improved convergence and solution quality.
- **Ensemble Methods**: Metaheuristic algorithms can generate multiple diverse subsets of training data. By training multiple k-NN models on these subsets and combining their predictions, ensemble methods can enhance the robustness and generalization of k-NN-based classifiers.
- **Dynamic *k* Selection**: The value of k in k-NN affects the bias-variance trade-off. Metaheuristics can help in dynamically selecting an optimal k value for each data point based on its local characteristics, thus adapting k to the complexity of the data.
- **Parallelism and Scalability**: Metaheuristic algorithms are often parallelizable. When combined with k-NN, they can distribute the computation of distances or other tasks associated with k-NN across multiple processing units, improving scalability and reducing computational time

3.7 Clustering

This chapter considers the widely recognized task of unsupervised learning known as clustering. The main objective here is to organize a dataset into groups of similar records, forming what we call "clusters." This task serves a dual purpose: firstly, it helps us extract meaningful insights from the data, and secondly, it holds the potential to enhance the performance of supervised methods. By grouping similar records together, we can model each cluster separately, which often proves more effective than dealing with the entire mixed-up dataset. Clustering finds its footing in numerous business applications, spanning from crafting tailor-made marketing strategies to conducting thorough analyses of various industries. Within the realm of clustering, two popular approaches take the spotlight: hierarchical clustering and k-means clustering. Hierarchical clustering follows a step-by-step approach where records are gradually brought together into clusters. This process relies on measuring distances between individual records and the distances between clusters themselves. The algorithm's mechanics, centered around this clustering process, are explained in simple terms, with a nod to various common distance measurement methods. Hierarchical clustering brings forth an interesting visual aid called a "dendrogram." This graphical representation not only illustrates the clustering journey but also unveils valuable insights from the data organization. Shifting our focus to k-means clustering, a technique with widespread applications in handling large datasets, we encounter a more straightforward strategy. Here, a predefined set of clusters exists, and each record is assigned to a cluster based on how close it is to that cluster's center. The k-means algorithm is broken down into understandable steps, highlighting its efficiency in dealing with extensive datasets. However, the real effect of clustering lies in its outcomes. Once clusters are formed, the task of drawing insights begins. These insights extend beyond mere data segmentation, illuminating hidden patterns, refining business strategies, and guiding well-informed decisions.

Cluster analysis is a powerful tool designed to discover hidden patterns or groupings tucked away within a dataset. Unlike the supervised learning methods, these algorithms possess the remarkable ability to pinpoint groupings without relying on any predefined labels. Instead, they discern these clusters by assessing the similarities shared among individual elements. At its core, this constitutes an exemplary instance of unsupervised learning, a technique that sorts statistical units into groups with the objective of minimizing the distances within each group while simultaneously maximizing the distances between different groups. To quantify these inter-group distances, similarity or dissimilarity measures are employed, elucidating the relationships between these statistical units.

Notably, conducting cluster analysis doesn't demand a pre-existing interpretative model. Unlike certain other multivariate statistical methods, this approach refrains from making any a priori assumptions about the fundamental categories that may characterize the observed dataset. This distinguishing feature sets it apart from discriminant analysis, a technique that can predetermine groupings based on distinctive patterns assumed by specific characteristics. Instead, cluster analysis serves as an explorer. Its purpose is to discover latent structures that may be present yet unnoticed, enabling the deduction of the most probable groupings. As an analytical method, this approach is inherently empirical, leaning on induction to classify data. This chapter serves as your guide into the realm of data segmentation, demonstrating how to divide data into clusters—collections of similar items. In our journey, we'll delve into the intricacies of K-means and K-medoids methods, arming you with the knowledge to unearth data groups effectively. Furthermore, we'll consider the field of grouping techniques through hierarchical clustering, unveiling yet another potent tool for unraveling the complex relationships and patterns that lie within your data.

In this chapter, our focus will be on considering a range of crucial topics that will enhance your understanding of clustering techniques. We'll be covering the following key areas:

- **Hierarchical Clustering**: We'll explore the intricacies of hierarchical clustering, a method that sequentially groups data points to form clusters based on similarities.
- **K-means Method**: The K-means technique will be a highlight, demonstrating how it partitions data into clusters by iteratively assigning each point to the nearest cluster center.
- **K-medoids Method**: We'll dive into the K-medoids method, which refines the K-means approach by utilizing actual data points as cluster centers.
- **Gaussian Mixture Models**: Our exploration will extend to Gaussian mixture models, a probabilistic approach that models data as a combination of multiple Gaussian distributions.
- **Dendrograms**: The concept of dendrograms will come into play, providing graphical representations of hierarchical clustering processes and outcomes.

By the end of this chapter, you'll have a comprehensive grasp of diverse clustering techniques. You'll not only acquire the practical knowledge to apply these methods to your data but also develop a deep understanding of how these algorithms function. We will delve into the foundational concepts that underlie clustering methods, particularly their reliance on similarity measures to group data effectively. Furthermore, you'll gain insights into data preparation for clustering analysis, a crucial step that ensures accurate results. Our exploration will encompass essential topics, including detailed insights into the K-means and K-medoids techniques, the visual power of cluster trees and dendrograms, and, lastly, the sophistication of Gaussian mixture models.

Clustering, much like classification, revolves around the pursuit of uncovering the underlying pattern that guides the assignment of observations to appropriate groups. However, clustering presents an additional layer of complexity. Here, our task involves not only identifying this pattern but also discovering a logical partitioning of our groups. While classification benefits from the guidance of predefined classes provided by the target variable, clustering navigates without such assistance, relying solely on the spatial arrangement of data points for insights.

Within this landscape, the density of data plays a pivotal role. Areas where data aggregates represent clusters of similar observations. Identifying these clusters hinges on the recognition of observations that exhibit similarities within their own group while simultaneously differing from observations in other clusters. This recognition often signifies distinct underlying conditions for these clusters. Clustering involves two crucial elements:

- **Measuring Similarity**: This entails understanding how to quantify the likeness between observations. A robust measure of similarity is key to discerning meaningful patterns.
- **Defining Grouping**: Here, we consider the essence of grouping and how to establish meaningful clusters. This involves the knowledge for determining which observations belong together based on their similarity.

It's worth noting that these two elements – similarity measurement and group definition – constitute the foundation of a clustering algorithm. They are the driving forces behind the clustering process, allowing us to shape clusters that capture the intrinsic structures of the data. In essence, clustering navigates the intricate space of discovering both the hidden law that guides observations and the coherent subdivisions that give those observations context. As we journey through clustering, we explore the intricate dance of data, guided by the notions of similarity and grouping, ultimately leading to the revelation of inherent structures and insights within our dataset.

3.7.1 Similarity Indexes

Clustering is about figuring out how data should be grouped together. To do this, we use a measure of "closeness" between the data points. Closeness can mean how similar or different they are. This closeness helps us decide which data points should belong to the same group. Imagine you have a set of data, and you want to find clusters within it. To make this work, you need to decide what you mean by "similar" or "different." Once you've got that sorted out, you can group the data accordingly. In many cases, this "closeness" is thought of in terms of distance in a space with many dimensions. It's like figuring out how far apart the data points are in a space where each dimension represents a different aspect of the data. The trick here is that the quality of the clusters you find depends a lot on how you measure this distance. This choice of measurement is what we call a "metric." It's like using a specific ruler to measure distances. Different rulers can give you different results. Clustering algorithms work by grouping things based on how near or far they are from each other. So, whether something belongs to a group depends on how close it is to the other things in the same group. In simple terms, you can think of it like this: some observations (data points) form a cluster if they tend to be closer to each other than to observations in other groups. It's like grouping things that hang out together more than they do with things from different groups.

When we talk about similarity and dissimilarity, we're essentially discussing how much two things resemble or differ from each other. Similarity refers to a numeric measure of how much two objects are alike. It's like putting a number to how similar they are. The higher the similarity value, the more alike the objects are. These similarity values are usually non-negative and typically fall within the range of 0 (meaning no similarity) to 1 (indicating complete similarity).

Conversely, dissimilarity is a numeric measure of how different two objects are. It's like assigning a number to their differences. Lower dissimilarity values mean that the objects are more similar to each other. Quite often, the term "distance" is used interchangeably with dissimilarity. Just as with similarities, dissimilarity values can sometimes fit in the interval [0, 1]. However, it's also common for dissimilarities to range from 0 to infinity, capturing a broader spectrum of differences. In a nutshell, similarity quantifies how much two objects resemble each other, while dissimilarity gauges how much they differ. These measures play a crucial role in clustering, helping us determine which objects belong together and which stand apart.

Dissimilarities that exist between different data objects can often be quantified using the concept of distance. Distance serves as a way to capture how dissimilar or far apart two objects are from each other. It possesses specific properties that make it an effective measure of dissimilarity.

One common approach to measuring distance is through the use of the Euclidean distance. This method quantifies the distance, denoted as $d(\mathbf{x}, \mathbf{y})$ between two points, $\mathbf{x}$ and $\mathbf{y}$. The formula for calculating the Euclidean distance between these points involves squaring the differences between corresponding coordinates, summing up these squared differences, and then taking the square root of the total. This process is represented by the following formula:

$$d_E(\mathbf{x}, \mathbf{y}) = \sqrt{\sum_{i=1}^{n} (x_i - y_i)^2} \tag{3.19}$$

Here, n signifies the number of dimensions or attributes in the data. The Euclidean distance is just one of many distance metrics that can be employed to evaluate dissimilarity between data points. Ultimately, these distance metrics are invaluable tools in clustering, enabling us to accurately quantify the differences between objects and form cohesive clusters based on their relative distances.

Note

When working on a two-dimensional plane, the Euclidean distance plays a significant role as it signifies the shortest distance between two points or, in simpler terms, the straight-line distance connecting these points. This measurement is particularly useful for understanding the separation between points in a straightforward manner.

Beyond the Euclidean distance, there exist alternative methods for assessing distance, one of which is the Minkowski distance metric d_{MI}. This metric serves as a more flexible and generalized version of the Euclidean distance measure. In essence, the Minkowski distance metric offers a versatile way to gauge the separation between points or data objects. By adjusting a parameter r, you can tailor the metric to match the specific characteristics and nuances of your data and analysis needs. This adaptability is especially useful when dealing with complex datasets or scenarios where a one-size-fits-all distance measure might not be suitable. The Minkowski distance metric is computed as follows:

$$d_{MI}(\mathbf{x},\mathbf{y}) = \left(\sum_{i=1}^{n} |x_i - y_i|^r \right)^{\frac{1}{r}} \tag{3.20}$$

Another option is the Manhattan distance d_{MA}, also known as the "city block" distance or "taxicab" distance. It is a distance metric used to measure the distance between two points in a grid-like space, such as a two-dimensional plane. Unlike the straight-line "as-the-crow-flies" measurement of the Euclidean distance, the Manhattan distance considers movement only along the grid lines, akin to how a taxi would navigate through the streets of a city. The Manhattan distance metric is computed as follows:

$$d_{MA}(\mathbf{x},\mathbf{y}) = \sum_{i=1}^{n} |x_i - y_i| \tag{3.21}$$

The cosine distance d_C, often referred to as the cosine similarity distance, is a measure used to quantify the dissimilarity or similarity between two vectors, which represent data points or observations in a multi-dimensional space. Unlike other distance metrics, the cosine distance focuses on the angle between the vectors rather than their actual magnitudes. The cosine distance specifically examines the angle between two vectors, which can be thought of as arrows pointing from the origin of the coordinate system to the data points. The smaller the angle between the vectors, the closer they are in direction and, consequently, the more similar they are considered. The cosine distance metric is computed as follows:

$$d_C(\mathbf{x},\mathbf{y}) = \frac{\sum_{i=1}^{n} x_i \cdot y_i}{\left(\sum_{i=1}^{n} x_i^2\right)\left(\sum_{i=1}^{n} y_i^2\right)} \tag{3.22}$$

3.7.2 Methods for Clustering

After selecting a method to compute distances between data points, the next crucial step is determining how to create meaningful groups from the data. This involves employing specific algorithms to organize the data points into clusters. There are two primary families of clustering algorithms that take distinct approaches to achieve this:

- **Hierarchical Clustering**: It involves constructing a hierarchical structure or taxonomy of the data. This process is akin to creating a tree-like diagram, often referred to as a dendrogram. Similar to the taxonomic trees seen in biology, this dendrogram illustrates the relationships between data points. It starts with each data point as its own cluster and then iteratively combines clusters based on their proximity. The result is a branching structure that showcases how data points are grouped at different levels of similarity. This hierarchical organization provides insights into both finer and broader groupings within the data.
- **Partitioning Clustering**: It divides the data space into distinct partitions or sub-zones. Each partition constitutes a cluster, and collectively, these sub-zones cover the entire data space without overlap. This approach seeks to find the best way to divide the data into non-overlapping segments, ensuring that each data point is assigned to a single cluster. Common methods within partitioning clustering include K-means and K-medoids, where you determine the number of clusters you want beforehand, and the algorithm finds the most suitable divisions.

Both hierarchical and partitioning clustering have their strengths and applications. Hierarchical clustering is beneficial when understanding data relationships at different levels of granularity is important. Partitioning clustering, such as K-means, is useful when you want to explicitly define the number of clusters and create non-overlapping groups in the data space. Choosing the right clustering algorithm family depends on the nature of your data, the desired level of granularity, and the specific insights you aim to extract from the data's inherent structure.

Hierarchical clustering is a method that constructs clusters by iteratively breaking down instances in either a top-down or bottom-up manner. This approach can be categorized into two distinct algorithms:

- **Agglomerative Algorithm (Bottom-up)**: In the agglomerative algorithm, the process begins with each individual data point considered as its own cluster. At each subsequent iteration, the algorithm identifies the most closely related data points and merges them into a single cluster. This aggregation of similar points continues iteratively, resulting in larger and larger clusters. The process culminates when all data points are combined into a single overarching cluster. This method essentially builds up clusters from the individual data points.
- **Divisive Algorithm (Top-down)**: The divisive algorithm takes the opposite approach. It starts with all data points being part of a single cluster. In each subsequent iteration, the algorithm separates the data point that is most dissimilar from the rest and assigns it to a new, separate cluster. This process continues, gradually dividing the large initial cluster into smaller and more distinct subclusters. The divisive algorithm essentially deconstructs clusters from the whole dataset.

In essence, hierarchical clustering offers a flexible way to create clusters by progressively forming or breaking down groups of data points based on their similarities or dissimilarities. Whether starting from the individual points and building up (agglomerative) or starting from a single large cluster and dividing it (divisive), hierarchical clustering offers a nuanced perspective on data relationships that can reveal intricate structures within the data. The choice between these methods depends on the data characteristics and the insights sought from the analysis.

Both hierarchical clustering methods, agglomerative and divisive, result in the creation of a dendrogram. A dendrogram is a graphical representation that visually illustrates the arrangement of clusters in hierarchical clustering. It provides a hierarchical view of how data points are grouped together based on their similarities or dissimilarities. The term "dendrogram" originates from the Greek words "dendron," meaning tree, and "gramma," meaning drawing or representation. As such, a dendrogram is a tree-like diagram that showcases the branching structure of clusters.

In a dendrogram:

The vertical lines represent individual data points.
Horizontal lines or branches represent the process of merging clusters as we move up the diagram.
The height of each branch indicates the level of similarity or dissimilarity at which the clusters were merged. Lower branches suggest closer relationships, while higher branches indicate greater dissimilarity.

Dendrograms are particularly useful for interpreting hierarchical clustering results. They offer a visual summary of the data's hierarchical structure, helping analysts and researchers understand how the data points group together at different levels of similarity.

Imagine we have a dataset of animals, and we want to cluster them based on their characteristics. Let's say we use hierarchical clustering to analyze this data. After performing the hierarchical clustering algorithm, we obtain a dendrogram (see Figure 3.10) that illustrates how animals group together at different levels of similarity.

In this hypothetical dendrogram, **A** represents the entire dataset (all animals combined). **B, C,** and **D** represent clusters of animals that are more similar to each other compared to the rest of the dataset. **E, F, G,** and **H** represent subclusters within clusters B and D, each containing animals with even more specific similarities. Now, let's interpret this dendrogram step by step:

At the bottom: Each animal (data point) is represented as a separate entity, such as a species of animal. *As you move upward:* Similar animals begin to cluster together. For instance, B might group together carnivores like lions and tigers. *Higher up the dendrogram:* Clusters start to merge. C might combine herbivores like giraffes and elephants, which are somewhat less similar to carnivores. *Even higher:* The overarching **A** cluster includes all animals in the dataset. *Subclusters:* Within clusters **B** and **D**, smaller subclusters form. For example, **E** and **F** could group small carnivores, while **G** and **H** group larger ones. Cutting the dendrogram at a certain height would result in specific clusters. For instance, if we cut it between **C** and **D**, we'd have two main clusters: one containing herbivores and another containing carnivores. The dendrogram visually conveys how animals cluster based on their characteristics. As we move upward, the level of similarity decreases, reflecting broader groups. The branching points indicate where clusters merge or divide, and the distances between these points represent the degree of dissimilarity. This example demonstrates how dendrograms offer a clear way to comprehend hierarchical clustering outcomes and uncover meaningful insights from complex data relationships.

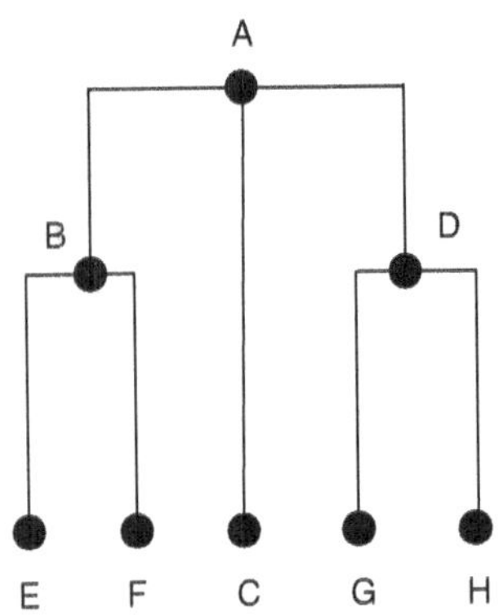

Figure 3.10 Hypothetical dendrogram considered as an example.

On the other hand, partitioning clustering is a technique that breaks down a dataset into distinct, non-overlapping clusters. In this method, the goal is to create partitions, with each partition forming a separate cluster. The process involves moving data instances from one cluster to another in an iterative manner, beginning with an initial partitioning. However, it's important to note that partitioning clustering requires the user to specify the desired number of clusters beforehand.

To achieve the best possible clustering arrangement using partitioning methods, an exhaustive exploration of all potential partitions is necessary. While this guarantees global optimality, it's a computationally intensive process involving the examination of all conceivable cluster combinations.

Figure 3.11 shows the partitioning clustering process considering three groups. As shown in the Figure, the objective was to rearrange these elements to form meaningful clusters. Therefore, starting from an initial cluster configuration (see Figure 3.11a), by iteratively transferring data points from one segment to another, the partitioning method creates distinct cluster configurations until it finds one that captures the inherent structure within the data (Figure 3.11b).

Keep in mind that determining the right number of clusters and achieving optimal results can be challenging in partitioning clustering. However, this approach remains valuable for tasks where explicit cluster counts are desired and can be set by the user.

Partitioning clustering involves a strategic pre-selection of parameters, followed by their fine-tuning to achieve an optimal balance between separation and compactness of clusters. This process revolves around adhering to a chosen criterion that effectively captures the distinctiveness of clusters. The goal is to bring to the forefront concealed underlying features of the data, effectively exposing the key patterns that drive the partitioning.

To achieve this, partitioning clustering seeks to minimize a measure of dissimilarity within the samples belonging to each cluster while maximizing the dissimilarity between different clusters. This balance is essential to ensure that clusters are internally cohesive while also being well-distinguished from one another.

For instance, a common approach involves designating cluster centers to represent the clusters. Initially, the data points are allocated to clusters based on their proximity to these centers. The process doesn't end here; instead, it progresses to iteratively refine the partitioning.

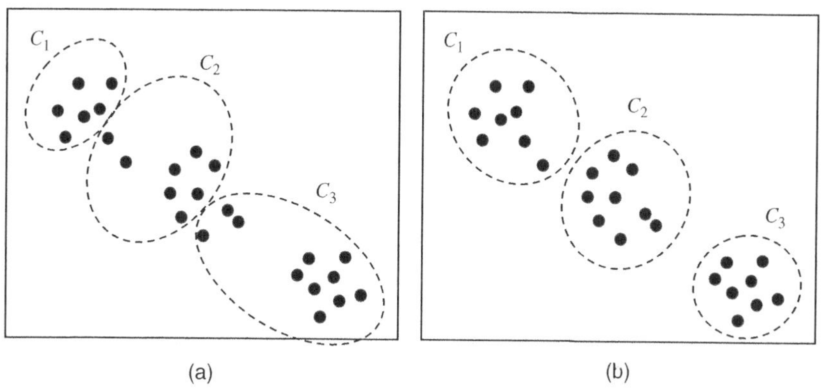

Figure 3.11 Partitioning clustering process considering three groups.

This refinement involves shifting objects between clusters, optimizing the arrangement to align with the chosen separation, and compactness criterion.

Consider an example where we're grouping customers based on their purchasing habits. The partitioning process might start by allocating customers to clusters based on their geographic location, represented by the cluster centers. However, as we iteratively adjust the allocation, we might observe that certain customers with similar purchasing behaviors in one location may fit better with a cluster in another region. This dynamic adjustment reveals hidden purchasing patterns that could be missed by simpler methods.

3.8 Hierarchical Clustering

Among all Hierarchical clustering approaches, Ward's method is one the most popular. Ward's method is a hierarchical clustering algorithm that focuses on minimizing the variance within clusters as it merges them. Named after its developer, Joe H. Ward Jr., this method is particularly effective when dealing with continuous variables and aims to create compact and internally coherent clusters.

The primary idea behind Ward's method is to quantify the increase in the total sum of squared distances (variance) within clusters when they are merged. It seeks to minimize the increase in variance, indicating that the newly formed cluster is as compact as possible, effectively minimizing the spread of data points within the cluster.

The Ward's method involves the following steps:

- **Initialization**: Start by treating each data point as its own cluster.
- **Merging Clusters**: Identify the two clusters that, when merged, result in the smallest increase in the sum of squared distances within clusters.
- **Update Cluster Distances**: Recalculate the distances between the merged cluster and the remaining clusters based on the increase in variance caused by the merger.
- **Repeat**: Continue merging clusters iteratively until all data points are part of a single cluster or until a predetermined number of clusters is reached.

Ward's method is particularly sensitive to the size of clusters and aims to minimize the "unwanted" variance introduced by merging clusters. As a result, it tends to create clusters that are relatively balanced in size and have lower internal variance.

This method is well-suited for cases where the underlying structure of the data includes spherical clusters of similar sizes. It's commonly used in various fields, including biology, psychology, and social sciences, as well as in machine learning and data analysis, where understanding the internal coherence of clusters is crucial.

In order to exemplify the operation of Ward's method, a numerical example is conducted. We'll use a small dataset with two-dimensional data points. Please note that this example is intentionally simplified for illustrative purposes. For the example consider the dataset of five data points shown in Table 3.6.

Step 1: Initialization:

Each data point is initially treated as its own cluster.

Clusters: [A], [B], [C], [D], [E].

Table 3.6 Data used in the numerical example for Ward's method.

Data	x_1	x_2
A	2	3
B	3	6
C	4	8
D	6	8
E	7	7

Step 2: Merging Clusters:

Calculate the pairwise distances between clusters using the Euclidean distance. Merge the clusters that result in the smallest increase in variance when merged. For example, let's calculate the distance between clusters [A] and [B]:

$$\text{Distance(A, B)} = \text{Euclidean Distance}([2,3],\ [3,6]) = \sqrt{1^2 + 3^2} = 3.16.$$

Similarly, calculate the distances between other clusters:

$$\text{Distance(A, C)} \approx 5$$

$$\text{Distance(A, D)} \approx 7.07$$

$$\text{Distance(A, E)} \approx 5.83$$

$$\text{Distance(B, C)} \approx 2.24$$

$$\text{Distance(B, D)} \approx 4.24$$

$$\text{Distance(B, E)} \approx 2.40$$

$$\text{Distance(C, D)} \approx 2.30$$

$$\text{Distance(C, E)} \approx 4.47$$

$$\text{Distance(D, E)} \approx 3.61$$

Merging [B] and [C] results in the smallest increase in variance (2.24).

Clusters: [A], [B, C], [D], [E]

Step 3: Update Cluster Distances

Recalculate the distances between the merged cluster [B, C] and the remaining clusters:

$$\text{Distance([B, C], A)} \approx 5.39$$

$$\text{Distance([B, C], D)} \approx 2.24$$

$$\text{Distance([B, C], E)} \approx 3.61$$

Merging [B, C] and [D] results in the smallest increase in variance.

Clusters: [A], [B, C, D], [E]

Step 4: Repeat

Continue merging clusters iteratively until all data points are part of a single cluster or until the desired number of clusters is reached. In this simplified example, we'll stop here.

Final Result:

The hierarchical clustering result using Ward's method is as follows:

Clusters: [A], [B, C, D], [E]

This result illustrates how Ward's method prioritizes minimizing the increase in variance within clusters as clusters are merged. In more complex scenarios, the process continues until a dendrogram is formed, and the choice of cluster cuts determines the final partitioning into clusters.

3.8.1 Implementation in MATLAB

In MATLAB, hierarchical clustering is a powerful technique for grouping data that results in a cluster tree, often visualized as a dendrogram. This multilevel hierarchy represents the process of combining clusters at one level into larger clusters at the next level. The approach begins with individual data points, and at each iteration, the algorithm merges the most closely related points or clusters to form new clusters.

To facilitate agglomerative hierarchical clustering in MATLAB, the Statistics and Machine Learning Toolbox provides a set of functions that streamline the process. The `pdist` function calculates pairwise distances between data points, and the linkage function computes linkage values that guide the merging process. The `clusterdata` function combines these components to perform agglomerative clustering efficiently. Finally, the resulting cluster tree can be visualized using the `dendrogram` function, which plots the dendrogram, highlighting the relationships between data points and clusters as they merge.

By employing these tools, MATLAB users can easily implement agglomerative hierarchical clustering to uncover hidden structures in their data, visualize the hierarchical relationships between clusters, and gain insights into the grouping patterns of their datasets.

In the context of hierarchical clustering in MATLAB, several key functions play integral roles in the process:

- **`Pdist`**: The initial step in clustering involves evaluating the potential similarities or dissimilarities between pairs of objects within the dataset. To accomplish this, the pdist function is utilized. This function computes the distances between objects, providing a fundamental measure of their relationship. With a range of distance calculation methods supported, `pdist` offers flexibility in assessing similarities based on diverse criteria. As we proceed, we will delve into practical applications of `pdist`.
- **`Linkage`**: Once the similarity measurements are established, the next phase revolves around arranging objects into a binary hierarchical cluster tree. This is where the linkage function becomes crucial. By connecting pairs of closely related objects, the linkage function employs the distance data derived from the prior step. This information determines the proximity of objects to each other, enabling the creation of binary clusters. These newly formed clusters are progressively aggregated into larger ones, eventually culminating in the hierarchical tree structure. This process is aptly termed cluster agglomeration.
- **`Cluster`**: After constructing the hierarchical cluster tree, the final step involves deciding where to make cuts to establish distinct clusters. The cluster function serves this purpose by segmenting the hierarchical tree from its lower branches. Objects situated beneath each cut are assigned to a singular cluster, thus partitioning the data. The cluster function presents two approaches for forming these clusters. One option involves identifying natural groupings within the hierarchical tree, while the other involves arbitrary cuts at different points in the hierarchy.

Table 3.7 Data used in the numerical example for the use of the MATLAB functions.

Data	x_1	x_2
A	10	10
B	9	9
C	1	1
D	1	2
E	9	7
F	5	5

With the objective to illustrate the use of the MATLAB functions, a simple clustering problem is solved. For the example, we will use the data shown in Table 3.7.

The first step is to introduce de data points through the following command.

```
>> DataPoints = [10 10;9 9;1 1;1 2;9 7;5 5]

DataPoints =

    10    10
     9     9
     1     1
     1     2
     9     7
     5     5
```

The next step involves the utilization of the `pdist` function. This function plays a pivotal role in calculating and furnishing distance-related insights. When invoked, the `pdist` function generates a vector that encapsulates distance data. Each element within this vector corresponds to the distance between a specific pair of points within the dataset. This collection of distances encapsulates the essential information needed to evaluate the relationships and dissimilarities between various data points, forming a fundamental basis for subsequent clustering analyses.

```
Distance = pdist(DataPoints)

Distance =

  Columns 1 through 11

    1.4142    12.7279    12.0416     3.1623     7.0711    11.3137
10.6301     2.0000     5.6569     1.0000    10.0000

  Columns 12 through 15

    5.6569     9.4340     5.0000     4.4721
```

The operation of the `pdist` function involves the computation of distances across pairs of points within the dataset. It meticulously calculates the distance between each data point, such as point A and point B, point A and point C, and so forth, exhaustively covering all conceivable pairs. While we previously discussed the concept of a matrix of distances, the output of the `pdist` function takes a different form. Specifically, it generates a vector wherein each element corresponds to a distinct distance calculation between two points. However, the resultant vector may not readily lend itself to straightforward analysis due to its arrangement. To effectively interpret and extract meaningful insights from this distance data, additional steps are often necessary. In subsequent stages of the clustering process, we employ various techniques and functions that utilize this vector to construct a comprehensive picture of the relationships between data points, facilitating the identification of patterns and groupings within the dataset.

To gain a more comprehensive understanding of the intricate interplay of distance information, a valuable strategy is to restructure the distance vector into a matrix form. This transformation is achieved using the `squareform` function, which assists in unveiling the relational intricacies between different data points. In the resulting matrix, each matrix element (i, j) signifies the distance between point i and point j. This matrix arrangement facilitates a clearer visualization of the distances between all pairs of points within the dataset. For instance, element 1,1 of the matrix indicates the distance between point 1 and itself, which invariably equates to zero. Similarly, element 1,2 of the matrix denotes the distance between point 1 and point 2, and so forth. By organizing distance information in this matrix format, analysts can more readily discern the varying degrees of similarity or dissimilarity between different data points, thereby forming a foundational basis for subsequent clustering analyses.

```
DistanceMatrix = squareform(Distance)

DistanceMatrix =

         0    1.4142   12.7279   12.0416    3.1623    7.0711
    1.4142         0   11.3137   10.6301    2.0000    5.6569
   12.7279   11.3137         0    1.0000   10.0000    5.6569
   12.0416   10.6301    1.0000         0    9.4340    5.0000
    3.1623    2.0000   10.0000    9.4340         0    4.4721
    7.0711    5.6569    5.6569    5.0000    4.4721         0
```

Upon closer examination of the distance matrix, a discernible pattern emerges: symmetry. The matrix exhibits a symmetrical structure, where the elements follow the relationship $a_{i,j} = a_{j,i}$. This symmetry highlights the dual nature of distances between pairs of points within the dataset.

In certain scenarios, it proves advantageous to normalize values within the dataset prior to calculating distance information. The rationale behind normalization stems from the inherent diversity in the scales of variables within raw data. Discrepancies in the magnitude of collected values can potentially distort proximity computations. To address this concern, normalization becomes a prudent step. By employing the `zscore` function, all values within the dataset undergo a transformation that aligns them onto a uniform proportional scale.

Why undertake such normalization? The answer lies in its ability to mitigate the effects of scale variations, ensuring that the ensuing distance calculations are robust and unbiased. This transformation unifies the scales of variables, rectifying potential distortions and fostering an accurate assessment of proximity between data points. In this way, the normalization process paves the way for more meaningful and reliable clustering analyses.

The essence of a clustering algorithm rests upon two fundamental elements: the concept of distance and the methodology for defining clusters. Following the calculation of proximity measures among objects within the dataset, the subsequent important step involves determining the arrangement of these objects into distinct clusters. To achieve this critical aspect, the `linkage` function assumes a pivotal role. Beginning with the distance measurements derived from the `pdist` function, the `linkage` function commences its task of forming pairs of closely related objects into binary clusters. This process unfolds iteratively: initial binary clusters are amalgamated, and progressively more objects are incorporated to construct larger clusters. This progression continues until all objects within the original dataset are seamlessly integrated into a comprehensive hierarchical tree structure. The linkage function acts as the bridge between the distance information and the hierarchical grouping of dataset objects. By assembling clusters based on proximity, it encapsulates the process of determining how objects should be organized to unveil inherent patterns within the data. As a result, the `linkage` function is a cornerstone of clustering algorithms, propelling the exploration of latent relationships and groupings concealed within complex datasets. Then, we apply the `linkage` function to the data already calculated in our example:

```
GroupsMatrix = linkage(Distance)

GroupsMatrix =

    3.0000    4.0000    1.0000
    1.0000    2.0000    1.4142
    5.0000    8.0000    2.0000
    6.0000    9.0000    4.4721
    7.0000   10.0000    5.0000
```

Executing this command accomplishes a substantial portion of the clustering process. The essence lies in the fact that the linkage function has adeptly identified potential groupings by leveraging the precomputed distance measurements. This critical step lays the groundwork for uncovering hidden patterns within the data. However, our exploration doesn't halt here. To delve deeper into the linkage function's mechanics, we turn our focus to the results encapsulated within the `GroupsMatrix`. This matrix offers insights into the intricate relationships between data points, the extent of their proximity, and the gradual formation of cluster hierarchies. By scrutinizing these results, we embark on a journey to comprehend the inner workings of hierarchical clustering, revealing the intricate interplay between calculated distances and the emergence of meaningful clusters.

In the matrix `GroupsMatrix`, each row encapsulates a distinctive cluster formation. By meticulously analyzing the matrix row by row, we can systematically trace the progression underpinning the construction of agglomerative clustering. The initial two columns of each row signify the paired points that are amalgamated, at least in the initial stages, followed by the newly formed clusters. It's important to reiterate that the hierarchical cluster in question adheres to the agglomerative approach, commencing with small clusters and progressively incorporating additional elements to engender larger clusters. The third column of the matrix contains the distance between the implicated points. In the context of the current example, the linkage function initiates the process by merging points 3 and 4 (corresponding to C and D, as outlined in the preceding numbered list of points). These two points exhibit the closest proximity, with a measured distance of 1. Subsequently, the linkage function proceeds to unite points 1 and 2 (representing A and B respectively), showcasing a measured distance of 1.41421. This step-by-step interpretation offers a granular understanding of how the agglomerative hierarchical clustering is systematically orchestrated, revealing the sequential assembly of clusters and the associated interplay of distances.

Upon initial examination, the `GroupsMatrix` matrix exhibits the identification of two distinct groups. However, additional rows within this matrix warrant closer analysis. What insights do these rows hold? The third row, for instance, signifies that the linkage function has combined points 5 and 8. Yet, a puzzle arises: the dataset originally consists of only six points. This anomaly can be resolved when we consider that Point 8 emerges as a newly constituted binary cluster, a direct consequence of amalgamating points 1 and 2. When the linkage function fuses two objects into a new cluster, a unique index value must be allocated to the cluster. This index value commences from the value $k+1$, where k symbolizes the points in the original dataset. Notably, indices 1 through 6 are already attributed to the initial dataset points. Analogously, Point 7 signifies the cluster obtained by merging points 3 and 4, corresponding to the very first cluster identified. Thus, the third row underscores the creation of a cluster involving Point E (the fifth point in the sequence), while Cluster 8 pertains to the amalgamation of points C and D (the first and second points in the sequence). This sequential unraveling offers a window into the intricate hierarchy of cluster formations and the underpinning indexing logic. Figure 3.12 presents the produced cluster from de data distribution. Figure 3.12a shows the initial data distribution while Figure 3.12b exhibits the cluster produced by the integration of different points.

The fourth row of the `GroupsMatrix` matrix offers a key insight into the clustering process. Here, the linkage function combines Point F (the sixth point in the order) with Cluster 9, representing the most recent cluster determination. This row signifies an important moment where various clusters come together. Notably, the linkage function unites Cluster 7 – the initial cluster found – with a fresh cluster created by amalgamating Cluster 9 and the original Point 6. This marks the final arrangement of clusters. It highlights how the clusters identified earlier and the newly formed ones interconnect, showing a comprehensive hierarchy that encapsulates the relationships between clusters and data points. Figure 3.13 illustrates the produced clusters.

The `linkage` function assumes an important role in the clustering process by harnessing the distances derived from the `pdist` function to orchestrate the sequencing of cluster identification. Following this initial phase, the linkage function assumes the task of computing distances between

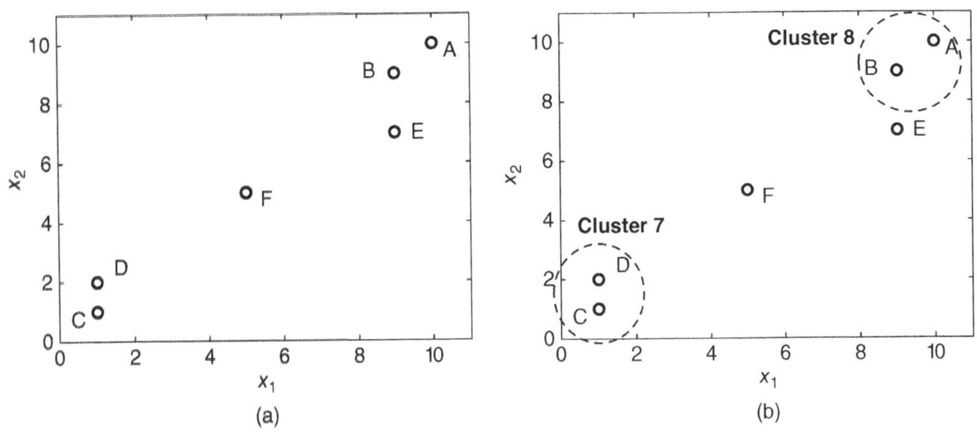

Figure 3.12 Produced cluster from de data distribution. (a) Initial data distribution while (b) the cluster produced by the integration of different points.

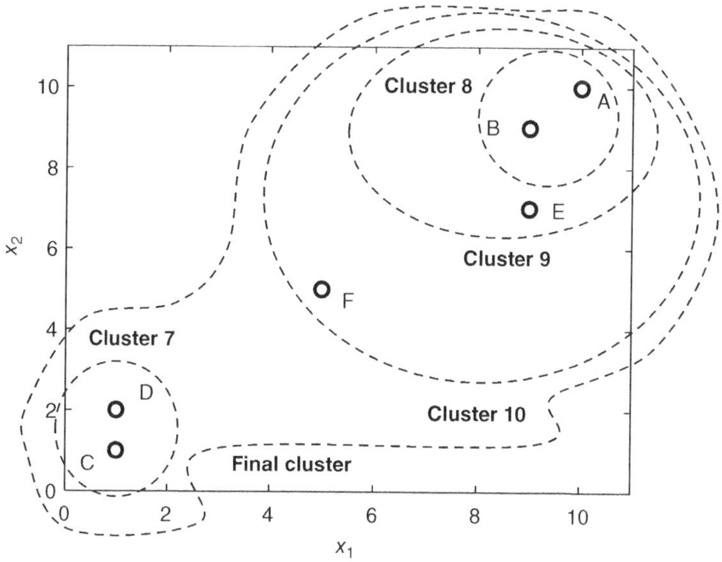

Figure 3.13 Produced clusters from the numerical example.

the newly established clusters. By default, the linkage function employs a method referred to as single linkage. However, it's worth noting that a diverse array of methods is at its disposal. These encompass techniques such as average, centroid, complete, median, single, ward, and weighted linkage. Each of these methods represents a distinct approach, offering a range of strategies to ascertain the distances and relationships between clusters. The choice of linkage method can profoundly impact the resultant clustering outcome, thereby shaping the interpretation of the data's inherent structure.

The culmination of the hierarchical clustering process is the creation of a dendrogram, a visualization that offers a comprehensive depiction of the binary cluster tree. The dendrogram() function assumes a pivotal role in this final phase. By invoking this function, we can generate a dendrogram plot that encapsulates the hierarchical relationships among the data points. The visual representation is composed of a series of U-shaped lines, each serving as a link between specific data points within the hierarchical tree. The height of each U shape within the dendrogram carries a profound significance – it symbolizes the distance that separates the pair of data points it connects. This visual portrayal serves as an invaluable tool for grasping the intricate hierarchy of clustering and the underlying relationships between the various data points.

```
>> dendrogram(GroupsMatrix)
```

Figure 3.14 presents an illustrative dendrogram that emerges as the outcome of hierarchical clustering. This dendrogram is constructed from a collection of points plotted on the Cartesian plane, as evidenced by the example under consideration. The figure vividly captures the arrangement of clusters that materialize through the hierarchical clustering algorithm. A cursory glance at the visual depiction allows us to discern the distinct clusters delineated by the algorithm's operations. However, to acquire a more comprehensive grasp of the underlying intricacies, it becomes imperative to delve further into the subject matter. Delving into the nuances of hierarchical clustering will enable a more profound understanding of the processes that have contributed to the formation of this visually compelling dendrogram.

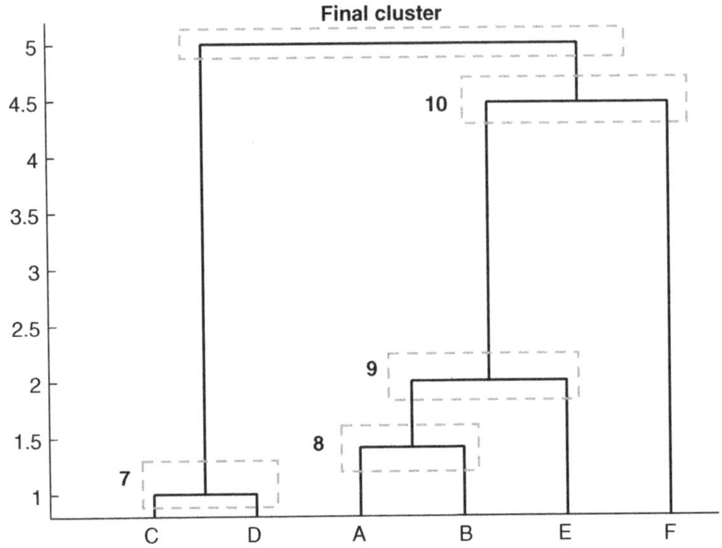

Figure 3.14 Illustrative dendrogram that emerges as the outcome of hierarchical clustering.

(A) Hierarchical clustering in Metaheuristic Algorithms

Hierarchical clustering is a valuable component in metaheuristic methods. Here's how hierarchical clustering is applied within the context of metaheuristic methods:

- **Solution Representation**: Metaheuristic methods work with a population of solutions or candidate solutions to a problem. Hierarchical clustering can be used to group these solutions based on their characteristics or attributes (Consoli et al. 2020). Each cluster represents a set of similar solutions in terms of their features.
- **Diversity Maintenance**: One of the key challenges in metaheuristic optimization is maintaining diversity within the population of solutions. Hierarchical clustering can help identify diverse clusters of solutions (Greistorfer and Voss 2005). When selecting solutions for the next iteration, metaheuristic algorithms can prioritize solutions from different clusters to ensure a diverse exploration of the solution space.
- **Initialization**: Many metaheuristic algorithms require an initial population of solutions to start their search. Hierarchical clustering can be used to generate an initial diverse population by selecting representatives from different clusters. This helps in providing a good starting point for the optimization process.
- **Neighborhood Search**: Metaheuristic methods often perform local search operations to explore the solution space. Hierarchical clustering can guide the selection of neighboring solutions. Solutions within the same cluster can be considered as potential neighbors, which can improve the efficiency of local search operations.
- **Adaptive Parameters**: Metaheuristic algorithms often have parameters that need to be adapted during the optimization process. Clustering can be used to adapt these parameters based on the characteristics of the solutions.

For example, the number of clusters or the size of clusters can be used to adjust exploration and exploitation strategies.

- **Termination Criteria**: Clustering can also be used to determine termination criteria for the metaheuristic algorithm. If the solutions are highly clustered and there is little diversity, it may indicate convergence, and the algorithm can be terminated.
- **Hybridization**: Metaheuristic methods are often combined with other optimization techniques to improve their performance. Hierarchical clustering can be used as a preprocessing step to group solutions before applying other optimization methods.

(B) Metaheuristic Methods in Hierarchical Clustering

Metaheuristic methods can be also used in hierarchical clustering to optimize the clustering process and improve the quality of the clustering results. Here's how metaheuristic methods can be applied to hierarchical clustering:

- **Optimal Number of Clusters**: Determining the optimal number of clusters (often denoted as K) is a critical step in hierarchical clustering. Metaheuristic methods, such as genetic algorithms or simulated annealing, can be employed to search for the optimal K value (José-García & Gómez-Flores 2016). They can explore different values of K and evaluate the quality of clusters using a fitness function. The goal is to find the K value that results in the best clustering solution according to the fitness function.
- **Initialization**: The initial placement of data points into clusters can significantly impact the final clustering outcome. Metaheuristic methods can be used to initialize the clustering process in a way that maximizes the overall quality of clusters. For example, they can find an initial assignment of data points to clusters that minimizes the within-cluster variance.
- **Distance Metric Optimization**: The choice of distance metric in hierarchical clustering (e.g., Euclidean distance, Manhattan distance) can influence the clustering results. Metaheuristic algorithms can optimize the selection of an appropriate distance metric by exploring various distance measures and their impact on clustering quality.
- **Outlier Handling**: Handling outliers or noise in the data is crucial for robust clustering. Metaheuristic methods can be employed to detect and manage outliers effectively (Larabi-Marie-Sainte 2021). By adapting the clustering process to identify and isolate outliers, metaheuristic algorithms can lead to more accurate cluster assignments.
- **Hierarchical Structure Optimization**: Hierarchical clustering produces a dendrogram representing a hierarchy of clusters. Metaheuristic methods can optimize the hierarchical structure by reorganizing the merging or splitting of clusters. This can be done to achieve a more interpretable or meaningful hierarchy that aligns with domain-specific objectives.
- **Cluster Validation**: Metaheuristic methods can be used to assess the quality of the clustering solution by optimizing cluster validation indices (e.g., silhouette score, Davies–Bouldin index). These methods can search for cluster configurations that maximize the chosen validation criterion.
- **Feature Selection and Dimension Reduction**: In some cases, it may be beneficial to perform hierarchical clustering on a reduced feature set

or lower-dimensional data. Metaheuristic techniques can be applied to optimize feature selection or dimensionality reduction methods, ensuring that the most relevant features are used for clustering.

- **Hybrid Approaches**: Metaheuristic methods can be integrated into the hierarchical clustering process as a part of hybrid approaches. These approaches combine the strengths of both hierarchical clustering and metaheuristic optimization to find high-quality clusterings in complex datasets.

3.9 K-Means Algorithm

The K-means algorithm, devised by MacQueen in 1967, stands as a foundational clustering method. Its primary objective is to partition groups of objects into K clusters based on their inherent attributes. This algorithm represents a variation of the expectation-maximization (EM) algorithm, renowned for its utility in ascertaining data clusters arising from Gaussian distributions. What sets the K-means algorithm apart is its distinctive approach to computing the Euclidean distance between pairs of data items, in stark contrast to EM's utilization of statistical methods. This fundamental distinction in distance calculation underpins the K-means algorithm's effectiveness in clustering data, making it a valuable tool in the realm of unsupervised machine learning and data analysis.

The K-means algorithm operates on the fundamental premise that object attributes can be effectively represented as vectors within a vector space. Within this framework, the primary objective is to minimize the cumulative intra-cluster variance or, equivalently, the standard deviation. To achieve this, the algorithm organizes data into clusters, with each cluster being characterized by a central point known as the centroid. By iteratively adjusting these centroids and assigning data points to the nearest centroid, K-means endeavors to create clusters that exhibit minimal variance within themselves while maximizing the separation between clusters. This process ultimately yields well-defined and distinct clusters within the dataset, making K-means a valuable tool for various data-driven applications.

The K-means algorithm unfolds through a systematic and iterative procedure that can be summarized as follows:

1. **Determine the Number of Clusters (K)**: The first step involves deciding how many clusters, denoted as K, the dataset should be divided into. This is a crucial decision and can significantly impact the quality of clustering.
2. **Initial Partitioning**: Initially, the algorithm creates K partitions and assigns each data point to one of these partitions. This assignment can be done either randomly or guided by heuristic information, depending on the implementation.
3. **Centroid Computation**: For each of the K partitions, the algorithm calculates the centroid. The centroid represents the geometric center of all the data points within a cluster.
4. **Distance Calculation**: The algorithm then proceeds to compute the distance between each data point and the centroids of all K clusters. This step quantifies how close each data point is to each cluster's centroid.
5. **Partition Refinement**: Based on the distance calculations, a new partition is constructed for the data. Each data point is associated with the cluster whose centroid is closest to it. This step essentially reassigns data points to the cluster that they are most similar to.

6. **Recalculation of Centroids**: After the new partition is formed, the centroids for the clusters are recalculated. These updated centroids represent the new geometric centers of their respective clusters.
7. **Iterative Process**: Steps 4 through 6 are repeated iteratively until the algorithm converges. Convergence occurs when the assignments of data points to clusters no longer change significantly, indicating that the clustering solution has stabilized.

This iterative procedure allows the K-means algorithm to iteratively refine the clustering solution, seeking to minimize the variance within clusters while maximizing the separation between them. The final result is a set of well-defined clusters that effectively group similar data points together.

The main objective of the K-means algorithm is to determine the optimal positions of K centroids, with each centroid representing a cluster. The positioning of these centroids is pivotal, and their placement can significantly influence the clustering outcome. Ideally, these centroids should be positioned as far apart from each other as possible to ensure distinct clusters. Once the initial centroid positions are established, each data point is assigned to the nearest centroid, forming an initial grouping. Following this initial grouping, the algorithm progresses to the next cycle by recalculating new centroids based on the barycenters (geometric centers) of the clusters resulting from the previous cycle. These newly located centroids serve as the basis for the subsequent clustering iteration. The algorithm then reassigns each data point to the closest centroid once again. This iterative process continues until there is minimal or no change in the positions of the centroids. At this point, the centroids have effectively settled into their final positions, and the algorithm has converged. The result is a set of K clusters, each defined by its centroid, representing well-separated and distinct groupings of data points.

The K-means algorithm is a data association algorithm that is perhaps the most widely used method in machine learning applications. The K-means approach divides a set of n vectors $(\mathbf{x}_1, \mathbf{x}_2, \ldots, \mathbf{x}_n)$ into m groups $(G_1, G_2, \ldots G_m)$. In K-means each group G_i is characterized by its centroid $\mathbf{c}_1$ which is computed such that a cost function is minimized. Assuming that the Euclidean distance is considered as a similarity criterion the cost function is defined as:

$$J = \sum_{i=1}^{m} J_i = \sum_{i=1}^{m} \sum_{(k,\mathbf{x}_k \in G_i)} \|\mathbf{x}_k - \mathbf{c}_i\|^2, \tag{3.23}$$

where J_i represents the cost attributed to group i. According to Eq. 3.24, the value of J_i depends on the spatial distribution of the vectors belonging to G_i and the position of its centroid $\mathbf{c}_i$.

The division of the elements in each group is defined by an element u_{ij}. This factor binary determines the correspondence of a vector to a group. Under these circumstances u_{ij} is 1 if the data $\mathbf{x}_j$ belongs to the group G_i and zero in case of non-membership. Thus considering u_{ij} Eq. 3.24 can be rewritten as follows:

$$J = \sum_{i=1}^{m} \sum_{j=1}^{n} u_{ij} \cdot \|\mathbf{x}_j - \mathbf{c}_i\|^2, \tag{3.24}$$

which represents the sum of the squared distances of each data $\mathbf{x}_j$ assigned to the group G_i.

In this way the data association problem is completely solved by finding the values of u_{ij} and $\mathbf{c}_i$ that minimize J. The K-means method minimizes J through an iterative process composed of two steps. In the first phase, the function J is optimized with respect to u_{ij} by keeping the positions of the centroids $\mathbf{c}_i$ fixed. In the second phase, the function J is minimized with respect to $\mathbf{c}_i$ considering the values of fixed u_{ij}. These phases are repeatedly applied until convergence is reached.

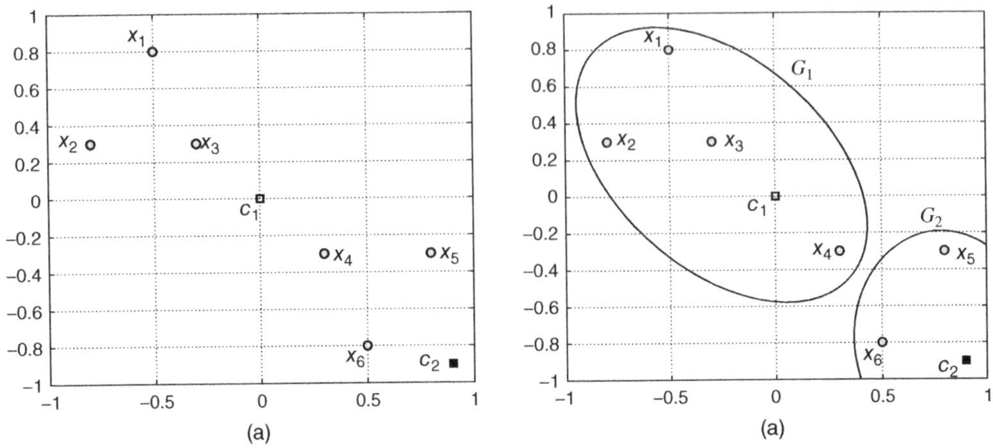

Figure 3.15 Data distribution (a) and region of influence under the first iteration (b).

In the first phase of this iterative process, the values of u_{ij} are first determined. Because the objective function J is linear with respect to u_{ij}, a closed form of computing the values of u_{ij} can then be obtained. Each term u_{ij} involves a different and independent group G_i, so it is possible to find each term u_{ij} separately. Under such circumstances, the value of one is chosen for u_{ij}whenever the centroid represents the minimum distance $\|\mathbf{x}_j - \mathbf{c}_i\|^2$. In other words, one simply maps the datum $\mathbf{x}_j$ to the centroid of the nearest group. This can be formally formulated as follows:

$$u_{ij} = \begin{cases} 1 & \text{if } i = \arg\min_i \|\mathbf{x}_j - \mathbf{c}_i\|^2 \\ 0 & \text{otherwise} \end{cases} \tag{3.25}$$

In the second phase, the values of $\mathbf{c}_i$ are determined by holding fixed the values of previously u_{ij} calculated in the first phase. Because the objective function J is quadratic in terms of $\mathbf{c}_i$, J can be minimized by equating the value of the derivative of J with respect to $\mathbf{c}_i$ to zero. From this process, one obtains:

$$2 \cdot \sum_{j=1}^{n} u_{ij} \cdot (\mathbf{x}_j - \mathbf{c}_i) = 0, \tag{3.26}$$

Considering this expression, the values of $\mathbf{c}_i$ can be calculated as follows:

$$\mathbf{c}_i = \frac{\sum_{j=1}^{n} u_{ij} \cdot \mathbf{x}_j}{\sum_{j=1}^{n} u_{ij}} \tag{3.27}$$

The denominator of this expression represents the total number of data assigned to group G_i. Considering this formulation, it is easy to interpret that the point $\mathbf{c}_i$ of represents the average position of all the data assigned to group G_i.

In order to exemplify the K-means method, we describe a numerical example that considers the grouping into two categories (G_1, G_2) of a set of six data $\mathbf{x}_1, \mathbf{x}_2, \mathbf{x}_3, \mathbf{x}_4, \mathbf{x}_5, \mathbf{x}_6$ two-dimensional data whose configuration is shown in Figure 3.15a. Their values are defined as:

$$\mathbf{x}_1 = (-0.5, 0.8) \qquad \mathbf{x}_2 = (-0.8, 0.3) \qquad \mathbf{x}_3 = (-0.3, 0.3)$$

$$\mathbf{x}_4 = (0.3, -0.3) \qquad \mathbf{x}_5 = (0.8, -0.3) \qquad \mathbf{x}_6 = (0.5, -0.8)$$

In the K-means clustering process, the first step is to select the initial value of the centroids $\mathbf{c}_1$ and $\mathbf{c}_2$ that characterize the two clusters. In this example, the initial values are $\mathbf{c}_1 = (0, 0)$ and $\mathbf{c}_2 = (0.9, -0.9)$.

The clustering process is iterative, alternating between two phases. In the first phase the membership of each data is determined, keeping fixed the values of the centroids $\mathbf{c}_1$ and $\mathbf{c}_2$. In this way and using the Euclidean distance, the distance from each point to the two different centroids is determined. These calculations are determined as marked below:

$\mathbf{x}_1$	$\mathbf{c}_1$	$\sqrt{(-0.5-0)^2+(0.8-0)^2}=0.94$
	$\mathbf{c}_2$	$\sqrt{(-0.5+0.9)^2+(0.8+0.9)^2}=2.2$
$\mathbf{x}_2$	$\mathbf{c}_1$	$\sqrt{(-0.8-0)^2+(0.3-0)^2}=0.85$
	$\mathbf{c}_2$	$\sqrt{(-0.8+0.9)^2+(0.3+0.9)^2}=2.08$
$\mathbf{x}_3$	$\mathbf{c}_1$	$\sqrt{(-0.3-0)^2+(0.3-0)^2}=0.42$
	$\mathbf{c}_2$	$\sqrt{(-0.3+0.9)^2+(0.3+0.9)^2}=1.69$
$\mathbf{x}_4$	$\mathbf{c}_1$	$\sqrt{(0.3-0)^2+(-0.3-0)^2}=0.42$
	$\mathbf{c}_2$	$\sqrt{(0.3+0.9)^2+(-0.3+0.9)^2}=0.84$
$\mathbf{x}_5$	$\mathbf{c}_1$	$\sqrt{(0.8-0)^2+(-0.3-0)^2}=0.85$
	$\mathbf{c}_2$	$\sqrt{(0.8+0.9)^2+(-0.3+0.9)^2}=0.68$
$\mathbf{x}_6$	$\mathbf{c}_1$	$\sqrt{(0.5-0)^2+(-0.8-0)^2}=0.94$
	$\mathbf{c}_2$	$\sqrt{(0.5+0.9)^2+(-0.8+0.9)^2}=0.41$

$\mathbf{x}_1$	$\mathbf{c}_1$	$\sqrt{(-0.5-0)^2+(0.8-0)^2}=0.94$	$\mathbf{x}_4$	$\mathbf{c}_1$	$\sqrt{(0.3-0)^2+(-0.3-0)^2}=0.42$
	$\mathbf{c}_2$	$\sqrt{(-0.5+0.9)^2+(0.8+0.9)^2}=2.2$		$\mathbf{c}_2$	$\sqrt{(0.3+0.9)^2+(-0.3+0.9)^2}=0.84$
$\mathbf{x}_2$	$\mathbf{c}_1$	$\sqrt{(-0.8-0)^2+(0.3-0)^2}=0.85$	$\mathbf{x}_5$	$\mathbf{c}_1$	$\sqrt{(0.8-0)^2+(-0.3-0)^2}=0.85$
	$\mathbf{c}_2$	$\sqrt{(-0.8+0.9)^2+(0.3+0.9)^2}=2.08$		$\mathbf{c}_2$	$\sqrt{(0.8+0.9)^2+(-0.3+0.9)^2}=0.68$
$\mathbf{x}_3$	$\mathbf{c}_1$	$\sqrt{(-0.3-0)^2+(0.3-0)^2}=0.42$	$\mathbf{x}_6$	$\mathbf{c}_1$	$\sqrt{(0.5-0)^2+(-0.8-0)^2}=0.94$
	$\mathbf{c}_2$	$\sqrt{(-0.3+0.9)^2+(0.3+0.9)^2}=1.69$		$\mathbf{c}_2$	$\sqrt{(0.5+0.9)^2+(-0.8+0.9)^2}=0.41$

In these calculations, the values corresponding to the smallest distances have been highlighted. Under these conditions, the membership values u_{ij} can acquire the following values:

$\mathbf{x}_1$	$\mathbf{c}_1$	$u_{1,1}=1$	$\mathbf{x}_4$	$\mathbf{c}_1$	$u_{1,4}=1$
	$\mathbf{c}_2$	$u_{2,1}=0$		$\mathbf{c}_2$	$u_{2,4}=0$
$\mathbf{x}_2$	$\mathbf{c}_1$	$u_{1,2}=1$	$\mathbf{x}_5$	$\mathbf{c}_1$	$u_{1,5}=0$
	$\mathbf{c}_2$	$u_{2,2}=0$		$\mathbf{c}_2$	$u_{2,5}=1$
$\mathbf{x}_3$	$\mathbf{c}_1$	$u_{1,3}=1$	$\mathbf{x}_6$	$\mathbf{c}_1$	$u_{1,6}=0$
	$\mathbf{c}_2$	$u_{2,3}=0$		$\mathbf{c}_2$	$u_{2,6}=1$

Under this configuration, group G_1 would be composed by the data $\mathbf{x}_1$, $\mathbf{x}_2$, $\mathbf{x}_3$, $\mathbf{x}_4$ while group G_1 by the points $\mathbf{x}_5$, $\mathbf{x}_6$. Figure 3.15b shows the region of influence of both groups on the data distribution.

Now in the second phase, keeping the membership values constant, the centroids $\mathbf{c}_1$ and $\mathbf{c}_2$ are calculated. Since this is a two-dimensional problem, the values will be decomposed into an x and a y component. In this way, one would have:

$$\mathbf{c}_1 = (c_1^x, c_1^y)$$

$$c_1^x = \frac{u_{1,1} \cdot 0.5 + u_{1,2} \cdot -0.8 + u_{1,3} \cdot -0.3 + u_{1,4} \cdot 0.3}{u_{1,1} + u_{1,2} + u_{1,3} + u_{1,4}} = \frac{-1.3}{4} = -0.3250$$

$$c_1^y = \frac{u_{1,1} \cdot 0.8 + u_{1,2} \cdot 0.3 + u_{1,3} \cdot 0.3 + u_{1,4} \cdot -0.3}{u_{1,1} + u_{1,2} + u_{1,3} + u_{1,4}} = \frac{1.1}{4} = 0.2750$$

$$\mathbf{c}_2 = (c_2^x, c_2^y)$$

$$c_2^x = \frac{u_{2,5} \cdot 0.8 + u_{2,6} \cdot -0.8}{u_{2,5} + u_{2,6}} = \frac{1.3}{2} = 0.6500$$

$$c_2^y = \frac{u_{2,5} \cdot -0.3 + u_{2,6} \cdot -0.8}{u_{2,5} + u_{2,6}} = \frac{-1.1}{2} = 0.5500$$

With the calculation of the centroids, the first iteration of the algorithm will end. In the second iteration, the method will again perform the first stage, keeping the centroids fixed and calculating the membership values according to the distances of the data to the new centroids. In this way we would have:

$\mathbf{x}_1$	$\mathbf{c}_1$	0.55	$u_{1,1} = 1$	$\mathbf{x}_4$	$\mathbf{c}_1$	0.84	$u_{1,4} = 0$
	$\mathbf{c}_2$	1.73	$u_{2,1} = 0$		$\mathbf{c}_2$	0.43	$u_{2,4} = 1$
$\mathbf{x}_2$	$\mathbf{c}_1$	0.47	$u_{1,2} = 1$	$\mathbf{x}_5$	$\mathbf{c}_1$	1.26	$u_{1,5} = 0$
	$\mathbf{c}_2$	1.68	$u_{2,2} = 0$		$\mathbf{c}_2$	0.29	$u_{2,5} = 1$
$\mathbf{x}_3$	$\mathbf{c}_1$	0.03	$u_{1,3} = 1$	$\mathbf{x}_6$	$\mathbf{c}_1$	1.35	$u_{1,6} = 0$
	$\mathbf{c}_2$	1.27	$u_{2,3} = 0$		$\mathbf{c}_2$	0.29	$u_{2,6} = 1$

With these values, it can be seen that with the calculation of the new centroids, the algorithm is able to cluster the data as can be seen in Figure 3.16. If the method were to continue calculating, no significant difference in the clustering would be found.

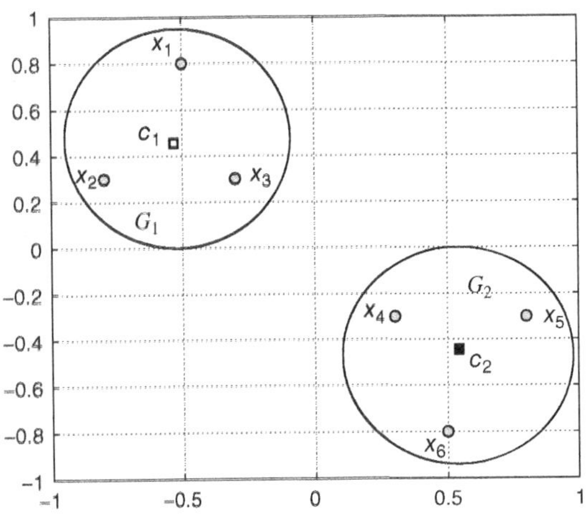

Figure 3.16 Clustering of data after one iteration of the K-means algorithm.

3.9.1 Implementation of K-Means Method in MATLAB

The K-means algorithm is implemented as part of the MatLAB functions within the Statistics and Machine Learning Toolbox. Its generic syntax is specified as:

```
idx = kmeans(X,k)
```

The function performs the division of the data specified in the matrix `X` into k groups. The data are stored in `X` in such a way that each row specifies the element number, while the columns represent the values of the decision variables. Under these conditions, the matrix `X` is of dimension n-dimensional. The result of the grouping is delivered in the vector `idx` of dimension k. This vector groups the data $\mathbf{x}_j$ ($j = 1, \ldots, n$) in one of the k groups.

In the grouping example that will be discussed in this section, an auxiliary function called `arffparser` will be used. This function can be obtained from the site with extra material provided by the publisher for this book. The function has the following syntax:

```
C=arffparser('read', 'datos.arff');
```

The function allows to associate databases already created in the `C` data structure. The data are specified by the `.arff` file type. As a result of the execution of this function, the data are stored in the `C` data structure. Considering two-dimensional data the data are obtained by using the following lines of code:

```
x=C.x.values;
y=C.y.values;
```

Another important auxiliary function for the data exercise to be verified in this section is the MatLAB function find. This function has the following syntax:

```
num = find(V);
```

The function reports in the vector `num` the row and column indices corresponding to the non-zero elements contained in the matrix `V`. Normally the matrix `V` comes from a logical operation that allows it to have only two categories of elements 0 or 1. A simple reference to this function would be the detection of the elements that are in the matrix `B` that are equal to 10:

```
num = find(B==10);
```

Once these auxiliary functions have been explained, we proceed to explain the example in data of the K-means method. In the example, the data stored in the shapes.arff file (which is available in the supplementary material of this book provided by the publisher) will be grouped into four different groups. This example is presented in Code 3.6.

Code 3.6

```
%% Clear variables
clear all
% The data are read
C=arffparser('read', 'shapes.arff');
```

```
% The data are assigned
x=C.x.values;
y=C.y.values;
% The original data are plotted
plot(x,y,'o')
% Another window is opened to present the results
figure
D(:,1)=x;
D(:,2)=y;
% The K-means method is run for 4 groups
idx = kmeans(D,4);
% The indexes are obtained for each group
D1 = find(idx==1);
D2 = find(idx==2);
D3 = find(idx==3);
D4 = find(idx==4);
% The results are plotted
plot(D(D1,1),D(D1,2),'o');
hold on
plot(D(D2,1),D(D2,2),'or');
plot(D(D3,1),D(D3,2),'ok');
plot(D(D4,1),D(D4,2),'oy');
```

The results of Code 3.6 are shown in Figure 3.17, which shows the data to be grouped (a) and the result obtained by K-means (b).

(A) K-means clustering in Metaheuristic Algorithms
Using K-means within metaheuristic methods involves integrating the K-means clustering algorithm as part of the optimization process driven by a metaheuristic technique. Here's a step-by-step explanation of how K-means can be used within metaheuristic methods:

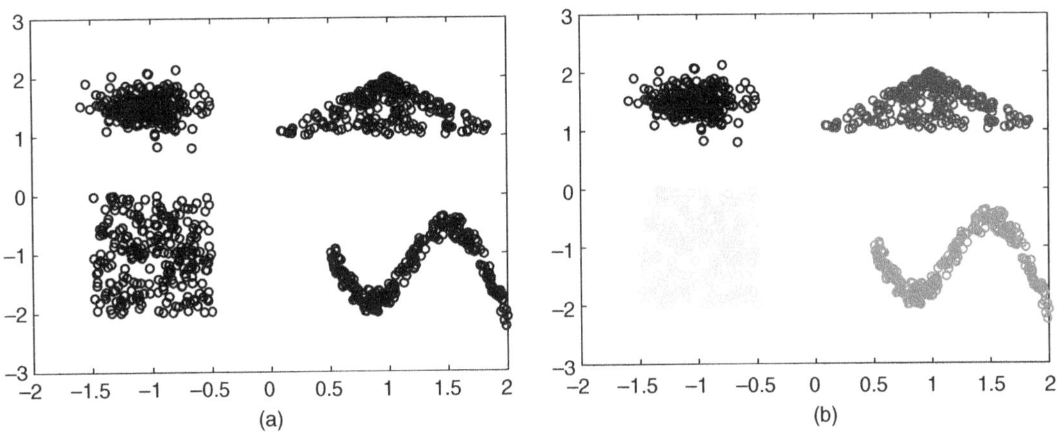

Figure 3.17 Result of running Code 3.6 showing the example data of the K-means method.

- **Metaheuristic Selection**: Choose an appropriate metaheuristic optimization algorithm based on the problem at hand. Common metaheuristic methods include Genetic Algorithms (GA), Particle Swarm Optimization (PSO), Simulated Annealing, Ant Colony Optimization (ACO), and Differential Evolution, among others. The choice of metaheuristic depends on the problem's characteristics, such as its dimensionality, constraints, and optimization goals.
- **Encoding Data**: To apply K-means within a metaheuristic framework, you need to encode the problem-specific information. In the context of clustering, this typically involves encoding the initial centroids for K-means and, if necessary, the value of K (the number of clusters).
- **Objective Function**: Define an objective function that represents the optimization goal. For clustering problems, the objective function often quantifies the quality of the clustering solution. It can be based on criteria like minimizing the within-cluster variance or maximizing a cluster validity index (e.g., silhouette score).
- **Initialization**: Within the metaheuristic optimization algorithm, include a mechanism to initialize the K-means clustering algorithm. The initial centroids can be generated randomly, or more sophisticated techniques can be employed to improve the quality of initialization.
- **K-means Optimization**: Embed the K-means clustering algorithm as part of the metaheuristic's search process. The metaheuristic generates candidate solutions and applies K-means to cluster data points based on the centroids provided by the metaheuristic. The clustering quality, as determined by the objective function, is used to evaluate the fitness of each candidate solution.
- **Solution Representation**: Define how the solutions will be represented within the metaheuristic. For K-means, a solution consists of the centroid positions and, optionally, the cluster assignments for each data point.
- **Crossover and Mutation**: If the chosen metaheuristic involves genetic or evolutionary components, implement crossover and mutation operations tailored to the K-means representation. These operations can manipulate the centroids to explore different cluster configurations.
- **Evaluation and Fitness**: Evaluate the fitness of each candidate solution by applying the K-means clustering algorithm to the data based on the provided centroids. The objective function quantifies the quality of the clustering solution.
- **Search Strategy**: The metaheuristic's search strategy guides the exploration of the solution space. It may involve mechanisms like population-based exploration (in GAs or PSO), neighborhood search (in local search-based methods), or temperature control (in simulated annealing).
- **Termination Criteria**: Specify termination criteria for the metaheuristic algorithm. This could be a maximum number of iterations, a convergence threshold, or a fixed runtime.

(B) Metaheuristic Algorithms in K-means Clustering

Using metaheuristic methods within the K-means clustering algorithm involves enhancing the standard K-means process by incorporating elements of optimization, exploration, and heuristic search. Here's a step-by-step explanation of how metaheuristic methods can be applied within K-means:

- **Initialization**: K-means is sensitive to initial centroid placement, which can lead to suboptimal solutions. A metaheuristic algorithm, such as Genetic Algorithms (GAs) or Particle Swarm Optimization (PSO), can be used to optimize the initial centroid selection. Metaheuristics can intelligently choose initial centroids that lead to better convergence.
- **Enhanced Centroid Update**: Traditional K-means uses a simple centroid update rule based on point assignments, which can get stuck in local optima. Embed a metaheuristic optimization process within each centroid update step. Therefore, the metaheuristic can explore different centroid configurations to minimize the clustering objective function, which is typically the within-cluster variance.
- **Calibration of the K Parameter**: K-means requires specifying the number of clusters (K) in advance, which can be challenging to determine accurately. Metaheuristic techniques can be applied to search for the optimal number of clusters (K). This can involve trying different values of K and evaluating their impact on clustering quality using a fitness function.
- **Outlier Handling**: K-means is sensitive to outliers, which can distort cluster centroids. Metaheuristic methods can be used to identify and handle outliers. Outliers can be detected based on their impact on the clustering objective function, and metaheuristics can assist in determining how to address them, such as by reassigning them to the nearest cluster.
- **Parameter Optimization**: K-means has hyperparameters like the maximum number of iterations and convergence tolerance. Metaheuristic algorithms can be applied to search for optimal hyperparameter settings. This can involve optimizing parameters like the maximum number of iterations, convergence criteria, or tolerance levels.
- **Convergence Improvement**: K-means may converge to local optima, leading to suboptimal cluster assignments. Metaheuristic techniques can be incorporated to escape local optima by allowing the algorithm to explore alternative solutions. For example, Simulated Annealing can introduce randomness into the search process to avoid premature convergence.
- **Cluster Validity Assessment**: K-means does not inherently provide information about the quality of the clustering solution. Metaheuristics can be used to optimize cluster validity indices (e.g., silhouette score or Davies–Bouldin index). These indices can guide the search for the best clustering configuration.

3.10 Expectation-Maximization Method

The K-means algorithm (Jiménez 2021) is an example of fixed grouping where each object can belong to one and only one group. In this section, we will discuss an approach that is more flexible in assigning an object to a certain group. Under this scheme, an object can belong to several groups at different levels.

Consider a set **D** of n points $\mathbf{x}_j$ defined in a d-dimensional $\mathbb{R}^d$ space. If a random variable x_a is defined which corresponds to the decision variable a of each point, the random vector $\mathbf{X} = (x_1, \ldots, x_d)$ corresponds to the generator of the d attributes of each point $\mathbf{x}_j$ of the set **D**.

3.10.1 Gaussian Mixture Models

In this section, it is considered that each group or cluster G_i is characterized by a multi-variate normal distribution defined as:

$$f_i(\mathbf{x}) = f(\mathbf{x}|\boldsymbol{\mu}_i, \Sigma_i) = \frac{1}{(2\pi)^{d/2}|\Sigma_i|^{1/2}} \exp\left\{ -\frac{(\mathbf{x} - \boldsymbol{\mu}_i)^T \Sigma_i^{-1} (\mathbf{x} - \boldsymbol{\mu}_i)}{2} \right\} \tag{3.28}$$

Where the center point $\boldsymbol{\mu}_i \in \mathbb{R}^d$ of the cluster and its covariance matrix $\Sigma_i \in \mathbb{R}^{dxd}$ represent unknown parameters in this model. $f_i(\mathbf{x})$ represents the probability density of the sample $\mathbf{x}$ attributable to the cluster G_i. If the probability density of $\mathbf{X}$ is assumed to be given by a Gaussian mixture model for all m clusters, it is defined by the following composition of functions:

$$f(\mathbf{x}) = \sum_{i=1}^{m} f_i(\mathbf{x}) P(G_i) = \sum_{i=1}^{m} f(\mathbf{x}|\boldsymbol{\mu}_i, \Sigma_i) P(G_i) \tag{3.29}$$

Where the a priori probabilities $P(G_i)$ are referred to in this context as the mixture weights satisfying the following condition:

$$\sum_{i=1}^{m} P(G_i) = 1 \tag{3.30}$$

3.10.2 Maximum Likelihood Estimation

Considering the data set **D**, we define the probability of θ as the conditional probability $P(\mathbf{D}|\theta)$ of obtaining the data **D** given the configuration of the model defined by the parameters \theta. Because the n points of **D** are considered the random samples of the distribution **X**, the probability $P(\mathbf{D}|\theta)$ is defined as:

$$P(\mathbf{D}|\theta) = \prod_{j=1}^{n} f(\mathbf{x}_j) \tag{3.31}$$

The idea with maximum likelihood estimation is to choose parameters that maximize the likelihood such that:

$$\theta^* = \arg\max_{\theta} (P(\mathbf{D}|\theta)) \tag{3.32}$$

To facilitate the solution of Eq. 3.32 it is typical to better consider the maximization of its logarithm. With this modification, it is possible to transform the multiplications into a series of additions. From this modification, the following expressions are produced:

$$\theta^* = \arg\max_{\theta} (\ln(P(\mathbf{D}|\theta)))$$

$$\ln(P(\mathbf{D}|\theta)) = \sum_{j=1}^{n} \ln(f_i(\mathbf{x})) = \sum_{j=1}^{n} \ln\left(\sum_{i=1}^{m} f(\mathbf{x}|\boldsymbol{\mu}_i, \Sigma_i) P(G_i) \right) \tag{3.33}$$

Maximizing these equations directly to obtain the parameters θ is complicated from a classical optimization point of view. A better option is to use the Expectation–Maximization (EM) method.

The EM scheme is an iterative process that divides the problem into two distinct steps: expectation and maximization. The method starts with an initial estimate of the parameters θ. With these values, in the expectation phase, the algorithm calculates the posterior probabilities $P(G_i|\mathbf{x}_j)$ by using Bayes' theorem:

$$P(G_i|\mathbf{x}_j) = \frac{P(G_i \cap \mathbf{x}_j)}{P(\mathbf{x}_j)} = \frac{P(\mathbf{x}_j|G_i)P(G_i)}{\sum_{c=1}^{m} P(\mathbf{x}_j|G_c)P(G_c)} \tag{3.34}$$

In this clustering technique, each cluster is characterized as a multi-variate Gaussian distribution, the probability of obtaining the samples $\mathbf{x}_j$ considering that they come from group G_i can be obtained from the calculation of that distribution:

$$P(\mathbf{x}_j|G_i) = f(\mathbf{x}_j|\boldsymbol{\mu}_i, \Sigma_i) \tag{3.35}$$

Thus the a posteriori probability $P(G_i|\mathbf{x}_j)$ of Eq. 3.35 can be redefined as:

$$P(G_i|\mathbf{x}_j) = \frac{f_i(\mathbf{x}_j|G_i)P(G_i)}{\sum_{c=1}^{m} f_c(\mathbf{x}_j|G_c)P(G_c)} \tag{3.36}$$

The value of $P(G_i|\mathbf{x}_j)$ can be considered as the contribution or importance of the point $\mathbf{x}_j$ with respect to the grouping characterized by G_i.

Then, in the maximization step, the EM algorithm re-estimates the values of the parameters θ using the previously calculated contributions $P(G_i|\mathbf{x}_j)$. That is, with the new information, the values of $\boldsymbol{\mu}_i$, Σ_i and $P(G_i)$ of each of the m groups ($i \in 1, \dots, m$) are recalculated. The estimate of the new mean $\boldsymbol{\mu}_i$ is computed as the weighted mean of all n points. On the other hand, the covariance matrix Σ_i is estimated with the values of the covariances modified by the relative importance of the contributions $P(G_i|\mathbf{x}_j)$. Finally, the new values of $P(G_i)$ are calculated as the average of the contributions $P(G_i|\mathbf{x}_j)$ associated with each cluster.

3.10.3 EM in One Dimension

In order to illustrate the main features of the EM method, this subsection presents its use in a one-dimensional case. Under these conditions, the dataset $\mathbf{D}$ consists of n data with a single attribute x, such that each point $x_j \in \mathbb{R}$ is a random sample of x. Each cluster G_i of the m characterizing the distribution of the data is modeled by a Gaussian function of the form:

$$f_i(x) = f\left(x|\mu_i, \sigma_i^2\right) = \frac{1}{\sqrt{2\pi}} \exp\left(-\frac{(x-\mu_i)^2}{2\sigma_i^2}\right) P(G_i) \tag{3.37}$$

The method is divided into three steps: initialization, expectation, and maximization.

3.10.3.1 Initialization

For each cluster G_i, such that $i = 1, \dots, m$ its parameters μ_i, σ_i^2 and $P(G_i)$ are set randomly. The value of μ_i is selected as a random value uniformly distributed among the range of possible x values. The initial value of σ_i^2 is typically set to 1. Finally, the mixture parameters are initialized such that each cluster maintains the same importance within the combination $P(G_i) = 1/m$.

3.10.3.2 Expectation

Assuming the initial values for each cluster of the parameters μ_i, σ_i^2 and $P(G_i)$, the a posteriori probability $P(G_i|\mathbf{x}_j)$ of each cluster are calculated according to the following expression:

$$P(G_i|\mathbf{x}_j) = \frac{f_i\left(x_j|\mu_i, \sigma_i^2\right) P(G_i)}{\sum_{c=1}^{m} f_c\left(x_j|\mu_c, \sigma_c^2\right) P(G_c)} \tag{3.38}$$

In order to facilitate the notation, it will be selected from now on that $w_{i,j} = P(G_i|\mathbf{x}_j)$. Such a notation is convenient from the point of view that $w_{i,j}$ represents the weight or influence of the point $\mathbf{x}_j$ in the cluster G_i.

3.10.3.3 Maximization

Once the values of the a posteriori probability or weights $w_{i,j} = P(G_i|\mathbf{x}_j)$ have been calculated, the values of the parameters μ_i, σ_i^2 and $P(G_i)$ of each Gaussian distribution modeling each cluster are updated. These values are chosen in such a way as to perform a posteriori likelihood maximization.

The value of the mean is recalculated μ_i as the weighted mean of all points with respect to the cluster in question G_i according to the following expression:

$$\mu_i = \frac{\sum_{j=1}^{n} w_{i,j} x_j}{\sum_{j=1}^{n} w_{i,j}} \tag{3.39}$$

The variance value is re-estimated by calculating the weighted variance of all the points with respect to the cluster in question. This calculation is performed under the following formulation:

$$\sigma_i^2 = \frac{\sum_{j=1}^{n} w_{i,j} (x_j - \mu_i)^2}{\sum_{j=1}^{n} w_{i,j}} \tag{3.40}$$

Finally, the value of the a priori probabilities or mixing coefficients $P(G_i)$ are calculated for each cluster G_i as follows:

$$P(G_i) = \frac{\sum_{j=1}^{n} w_{i,j}}{n} \tag{3.41}$$

Thus the clustering process can be summarized as follows. First, the parameters of m Gaussian distributions are initialized randomly. Considering k as the iteration number, this initial state is defined as $k = 0$. Under these conditions, the data set $\mathbf{D}$ will be tried to be modeled with m Gaussian functions according to their initial parameters. Then, the expectation and maximization steps are applied alternatively. This process is repeated, until there are no changes in the estimation of the parameters (convergence).

3.10.4 Numerical Example

Figure 3.18 presents the operation process of the expectation-maximization algorithm for the one-dimensional clustering case. The data set $\mathbf{D}$ is defined by the following list of elements:

$$\begin{array}{lllll} x_1 = 10 & x_2 = 1.3 & x_3 = 2.2 & x_4 = 2.6 & x_5 = 2.8 \\ x_6 = 5.0 & x_7 = 7.3 & x_8 = 7.4 & x_9 = 7.5 & x_{10} = 7.7 \\ x_{11} = 7.9 & & & & \end{array}$$

According to the distribution of the data $\mathbf{D}$ it is assumed that these can be grouped through two clusters ($m = 2$). Thus the initial parameters of the two Gaussian functions that characterize both clusters are defined as:

$$\begin{array}{lll} \mu_1 = 6.63 & \sigma_1^2 = 1 & P(G_1) = 0.5 \\ \mu_2 = 7.57 & \sigma_2^2 = 1 & P(G_2) = 0.5 \end{array}$$

After the first application of the process ($k = 1$), the parameter values of the distributions have been updated with the following values:

$$\begin{array}{lll} \mu_1 = 3.72 & \sigma_1^2 = 6.13 & P(G_1) = 0.71 \\ \mu_2 = 7.40 & \sigma_2^2 = 0.69 & P(G_2) = 0.29 \end{array}$$

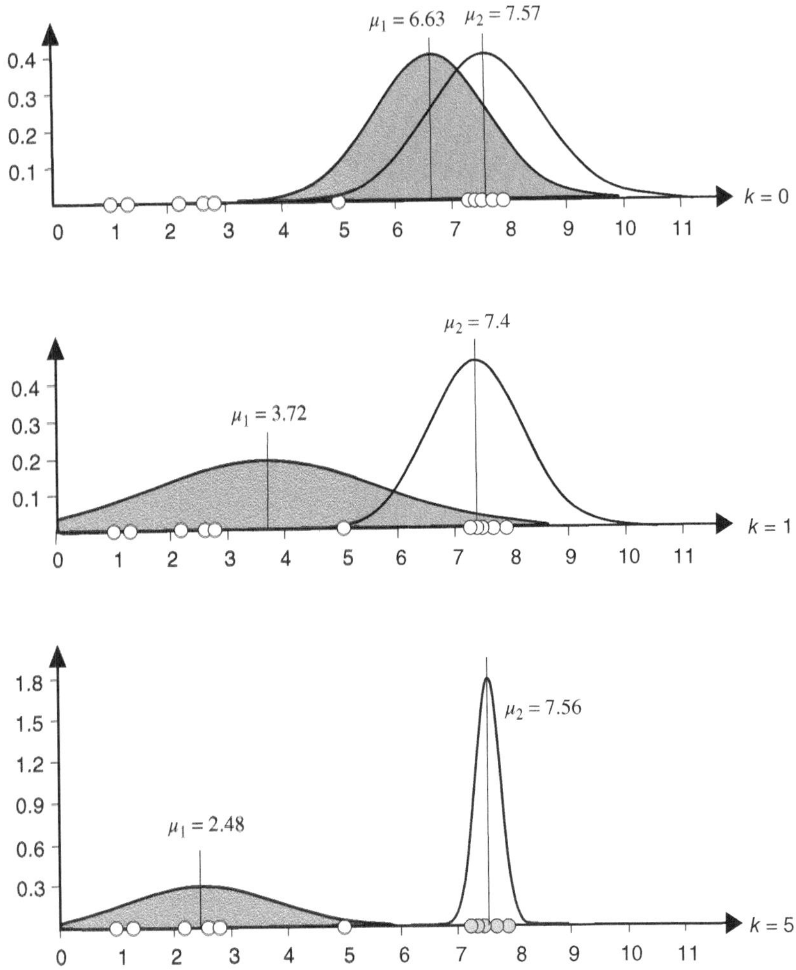

Figure 3.18 Clustering process using the expectation-maximization (EM) method.

After five iterations ($k = 1$) the parameter values have converged. This means that their values undergo practically imperceptible changes. Thus, the final values are obtained:

$$\mu_1 = 2.48 \qquad \sigma_1^2 = 1.69 \qquad P(G_1) = 0.55$$
$$\mu_2 = 7.56 \qquad \sigma_2^2 = 0.05 \qquad P(G_2) = 0.45$$

An interesting advantage of the EM method is that it yields the a posteriori values $w_{i,j} = P(G_i|x_j)$ which represent the degree of membership of data x_j to group G_i. Under these conditions, selecting the value of $w_{i,j} = P(G_i|x_j)$ for which data x_j yielded the highest value, the following grouping would be obtained:

$$G_1 = \{x_1, x_2, x_3, x_4, x_5, x_6\}$$
$$G_2 = \{x_7, x_8, x_9, x_{10}, x_{11}\}$$

This final grouping can be seen in Figure 3.18 in the image corresponding to iteration $k = 5$. The white dots correspond to group G_1, while the gray dots correspond to group G_2.

3.10.5 EM in Several Dimensions

The vast majority of applications require a grouping of data with multiple attributes or decision variables. In this section, the EM operation and calculation process will be generalized for d dimensions. Under these conditions, the parameters of the Gaussian distributions modeling each cluster will be extended to match the attributes of the data. Thus, one has:

$$\boldsymbol{\mu}_i = (\mu_1, \dots, \mu_d), \Sigma_i = \begin{bmatrix} \sigma_1^2 & \cdots & \sigma_{1,d} \\ \vdots & \ddots & \vdots \\ \sigma_{d,1} & \cdots & \sigma_d^2 \end{bmatrix}, P(G_i) \tag{3.42}$$

The steps for the operation of the EM method in several dimensions are the same: Initialization, expectation, and maximization.

Initialization in *d* Dimensions

For each cluster G_i, the values of the dimensions of the mean vector $\boldsymbol{\mu}_i$ are randomly set within the feasible range of the variables. The covariance matrix Σ_i is initialized as an identity matrix $\mathbf{I}$ of dimension dxd. Finally, the values of the a priori probabilities are set as como $P(G_i) = 1/m$, where m is the number of clusters into which the data set $\mathbf{D}$ will be divided.

Expectation in *d* Dimensions

This step is similar to the one-dimensional case. Thus, a posteriori probabilities $w_{i,j} = P(G_i|x_j)$ corresponding to the relative importance of point $\mathbf{x}_j = \left(x_j^1, \dots, x_j^d\right)$ to a respective cluster G_i are computed. These values are calculated by using Eq. 3.38.

Maximization in *d* Dimensions

Once the weights have been computed, the values of the parameters $\boldsymbol{\mu}_i$, Σ_i and $P(G_i)$ are recalculated. However, since these values represent a vector $\boldsymbol{\mu}_i$, a matrix Σ_i, and a scalar $P(G_i)$, the calculation equations are slightly different from the one-dimensional case. These equations are as follows:

$$\boldsymbol{\mu}_i = \frac{\sum_{j=1}^{n} w_{i,j}\mathbf{x}_j}{\sum_{j=1}^{n} w_{i,j}} \tag{3.43}$$

$$\Sigma_i = \frac{\sum_{j=1}^{n} w_{i,j}(\mathbf{x}_j - \boldsymbol{\mu}_i)^T(\mathbf{x}_j - \boldsymbol{\mu}_i)}{\sum_{j=1}^{n} w_{i,j}} \tag{3.44}$$

$$P(G_i) = \frac{\sum_{j=1}^{n} w_{i,j}}{n} \tag{3.45}$$

All steps of the EM method for d dimensions are summarized in Program 3.1 as pseudocode.

Program 3.1 ***Clustering Process Using the Expectation-Maximization Method.***

---

1. Input data $\mathbf{D} = \{\mathbf{x}_1, \dots, \mathbf{x}_n\}$, $\mathbf{x}_j = \left(x_j^1, \dots, x_d^1\right)$, m, tolerance.
2. Initialization, $k = 0$

   $\boldsymbol{\mu}_i = (\mu_1, \dots, \mu_d)$, $\Sigma_i = \mathbf{I}$, $P(G_i) = 1/m$

3. **repeat**

$k = k + 1$

4. Expectation

for $i = 1$ to m

for $j = 1$ to n

$$w_{i,j} \leftarrow \frac{f_i(\mathbf{x}_j|G_i)P(G_i)}{\sum_{c=1}^{m} f_c(\mathbf{x}_j|G_c)P(G_c)}$$

end j

end i

5. Maximization.

for $i = 1$ to m

$$\boldsymbol{\mu}_i = \frac{\sum_{j=1}^{n} w_{i,j}\mathbf{x}_j}{\sum_{j=1}^{n} w_{i,j}},\ \Sigma_i = \frac{\sum_{j=1}^{n} w_{i,j}(\mathbf{x}_j-\boldsymbol{\mu}_i)^T(\mathbf{x}_j-\boldsymbol{\mu}_i)}{\sum_{j=1}^{n} w_{i,j}},\ P(G_i) = \frac{\sum_{j=1}^{n} w_{i,j}}{n}$$

end i

6. **until** $\sum_{i=1}^{m} \left\| \mu_i^k - \mu_i^{k+1} \right\| \leq$ tolerance

---

Then, we analyze the operation and implementation of the EM algorithm in MatLAB. The idea is to consider the structure of a program that allows the clustering of multidimensional data using the EM technique.

The first step for an implementation of a clustering method is to produce the data to be clustered. This action is important because, since the data production process is known, it is easy to qualify the clustering results.

Under these conditions, to test the performance of the EM algorithm, a two-dimensional data set ($d = 2$) corresponding to the random samples drawn from the mixture of three Gaussians with the following parameters will be produced:

$$\boldsymbol{\mu}_1 = (-2.1, 1.28) \quad \boldsymbol{\mu}_2 = (-1.2, -1.40) \quad \boldsymbol{\mu}_3 = (2.64, 0.19)$$

$$\Sigma_1 = \begin{bmatrix} 0.59 & 0 \\ 0 & 0.11 \end{bmatrix} \quad \Sigma_2 = \begin{bmatrix} 0.49 & 0 \\ 0 & 0.11 \end{bmatrix} \quad \Sigma_3 = \begin{bmatrix} 0.05 & 0 \\ 0 & 0.21 \end{bmatrix}$$

$$P(G_1) = 1/3 \quad P(G_2) = 1/3 \quad P(G_3) = 1/3$$

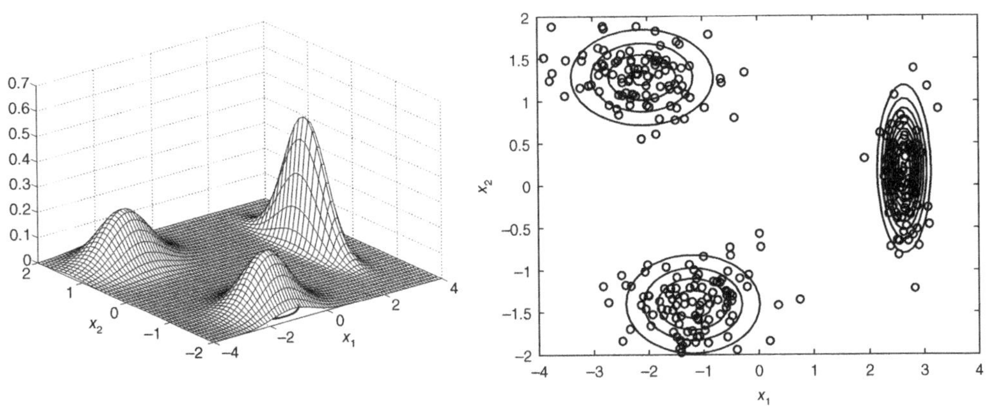

Figure 3.19 Generation of the data set, (a) mixture probability distribution, and (b) the set of 300 data drawn as samples from the distribution.

The generation of this data is performed by Program 3.2. This program is organized in two parts. In the first part, information is obtained to display the mixture of Gaussians as the probability distribution. The MatLAB function `mvnpdf` is used to obtain the value of a multidimensional Gaussian function. In the second part, the function `gmdistribution` is used to define the mixture of Gaussians as a probability distribution. Once this function is defined, the `random` function is used to obtain 300 samples from the mixture of three Gaussians as a probability distribution. Figure 3.19 illustrates (a) the probability distribution obtained and (b) the set of 300 data **D** drawn from it.

Code 3.7

```
%First part
mu1 = [-2.1 1.28];
Sigma1 = [0.59 0; 0 0.11];
mu2 = [-1.2 -1.40];
Sigma2 = [0.49 0; 0 0.11];
mu3 = [2.64 0.19];
Sigma3 = [0.05 0; 0 0.21];
x1 = -4:.1:4; x2 = -2:.1:2;
[X1,X2] = meshgrid(x1,x2);
F1 = mvnpdf([X1(:) X2(:)],mu1,Sigma1);
F2 = mvnpdf([X1(:) X2(:)],mu2,Sigma2);
F3 = mvnpdf([X1(:) X2(:)],mu3,Sigma3);
F=F1*(1/3)+F2*(1/3)+F3*(1/3);
F = reshape(F,length(x2),length(x1));
meshc(X1,X2,F);
%Second part
muD = [-2.1 1.28;-1.2 -1.40; 2.64 0.19];
sigmaD = cat(3,[0.59 0; 0 0.11],[0.49 0; 0 0.11],[0.05 0; 0 0.21]);
p = ones(1,3)/3;
gm = gmdistribution(muD,sigmaD,p);
rng('default');
X = random(gm,300);
figure
plot(X(:,1),X(:,2),'o')
```

Once the data set **D** has been obtained, the EM method is executed to find the parameters of the distribution that gave rise to them. Program 3.3 is used for this purpose. This program implements the EM algorithm for two dimensions considering the parameters of the mixture of 3 Gaussian functions. Finally, the clustering is achieved by exploring the maximum values of the weights $w_{i,j} = P(G_i|\mathbf{x}_j)$. This is because the weights represent the degree of membership of a point $\mathbf{x}_j$ to a given cluster G_i. Figure 3.20 illustrates (a) the distribution obtained with the estimated parameters and (b) the clustering of the data in each group or cluster.

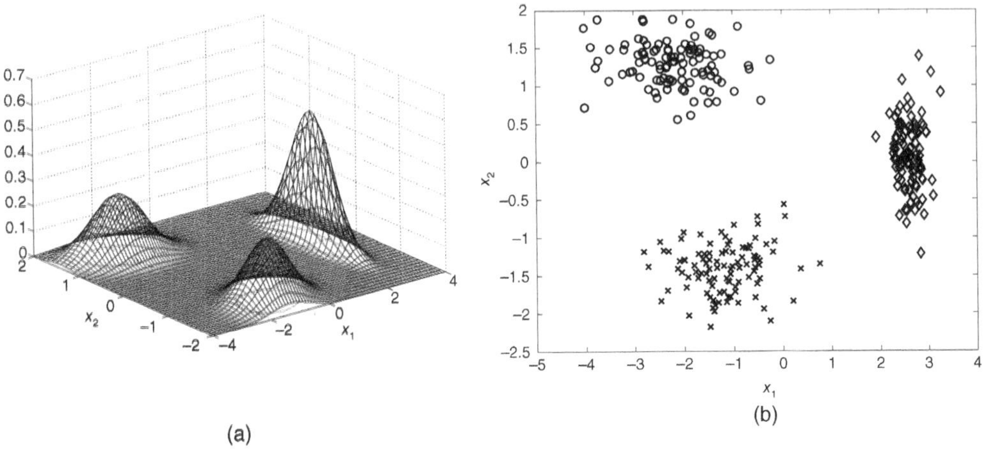

Figure 3.20 Results of clustering with the EM method, (a) mixture probability distribution and (b) clustering by each cluster.

Code 3.8

```
[n d]=size(X);
c=3;
%Initialization
pi=ones(1,3)/3;
M = [-3.59 0.25;-1.09 -0.46; 0.75 1.07];
W=zeros(c,n);
P=zeros(size(W));
V=zeros(d,d,c);
V(:,:,1)=[1 0;0 1];
V(:,:,2)=[1 0;0 1];
V(:,:,3)=[1 0;0 1];

for k=1:1:100
 %Expectation
    for da=1:n
   for cu=1:3
%Equation 3.39
P(cu,da)= mvnpdf([X(da,1) X(da,2)],M(cu,:),V(:,:,cu))*pi(cu);
   end
   Tot=sum(P(:,da));
   W(:,da)=P(:,da)/Tot;
    end
  %Maximization
 T=zeros(c,d);
 for cu=1:3
   for da=1:n
```

```
   %Ecuación 5.21
   T(cu,:)=T(cu,:)+W(cu,da)*X(da,:);
    end
    M(cu,:)=T(cu,:)/(sum(W(cu,:)));
    end
   B=zeros(size(V));
   for cu=1:3
    for da=1:n
    dxm=X(da,:)-M(cu,:);
    %Equation 3.44
    B(:,:,cu)=B(:,:,cu)+W(cu,da)*dxm'*dxm;
    end
     V(:,:,cu)=B(:,:,cu)/(sum(W(cu,:)));
    end
   for cu=1:3
    %Equation 3.46
    pi(cu)=sum(W(cu,:))/n;
    end
    end
figure
G1 = mvnpdf([X1(:) X2(:)],M(1,:),V(:,:,1));
G2 = mvnpdf([X1(:) X2(:)],M(2,:),V(:,:,2));
G3 = mvnpdf([X1(:) X2(:)],M(3,:),V(:,:,3));
G=G1*pi(1)+G2*pi(2)+G3*pi(3);
GT = reshape(G,length(x2),length(x1));
 meshc(X1,X2,GT)
%Clasification
[d1,Id]=max(W);
Indice1=find(Id==1);
Indice2=find(Id==2);
Indice3=find(Id==3);
figure
plot(X(Indice1,1),X(Indice1,2),'o')
hold on
plot(X(Indice2,1),X(Indice2,2),'x')
plot(X(Indice3,1),X(Indice3,2),'D')
```

(A) Expectation-Maximization (EM) in Metaheuristic Algorithms

The EM method is a statistical technique used for estimating parameters in models when there is missing or incomplete data. It is commonly applied in the context of unsupervised machine learning and statistics. While EM itself is not typically used as a standalone metaheuristic optimization method, it can be incorporated into metaheuristic algorithms to enhance their performance in certain scenarios. Here's how EM can be used in conjunction with metaheuristic methods:

- **Initialization**: Many metaheuristic algorithms require an initial solution to start the optimization process. EM can be used to provide an initial estimate of the solution, especially when dealing with data-driven optimization problems. For example, if you have incomplete or noisy data, EM can be used to estimate the missing values or clean the data, which can then be used as an initial solution for your metaheuristic algorithm.
- **Fitness Evaluation**: Metaheuristic algorithms evaluate the quality of solutions using a fitness function. EM can be employed to improve the accuracy of the fitness function by providing a more accurate estimate of the parameters of the underlying data distribution (Santos et al. 2016). This can lead to better-informed decisions during the search process.
- **Constraint Handling**: Some optimization problems involve constraints that are difficult to incorporate directly into the objective function. EM can help model and handle these constraints separately. The metaheuristic algorithm can then explore the solution space while respecting these constraints more effectively.
- **Parameter Estimation**: Metaheuristic algorithms often have several parameters that need to be tuned for optimal performance. EM can be used to estimate these parameters from historical data or during the optimization process itself. This dynamic parameter adaptation can help the metaheuristic algorithm converge faster and find better solutions.
- **Combining with Population-Based Methods**: In population-based metaheuristics like genetic algorithms or particle swarm optimization, EM can be used to improve the diversity and quality of the initial population. By generating diverse individuals with EM, the algorithm can start with a more promising set of solutions, potentially accelerating convergence.
- **Hybridization**: Metaheuristic algorithms can be hybridized with other optimization techniques. EM can serve as one of the components in a hybrid optimization approach, where it handles specific aspects of the optimization problem while the metaheuristic focuses on exploring the solution space efficiently.
- **Dynamic Modeling**: In some optimization problems, the underlying data distribution or problem characteristics may change over time. EM can be used to adapt the model to these changes, allowing the metaheuristic algorithm to continually adjust its search strategy.
- **Local Search Enhancement**: EM can be applied to perform a local search within the neighborhoods of candidate solutions generated by the metaheuristic. This can help refine solutions and overcome local optima more effectively.

(B) Metaheuristic Algorithms in Expectation-Maximization (EM)

Metaheuristic methods can be used to enhance the performance of the EM algorithm, especially when EM is applied to complex or high-dimensional optimization problems. The integration of metaheuristic techniques can help EM find better solutions faster. Three important elements in this integration are:

- **Random Initialization**: EM is sensitive to initial parameter values. By using a metaheuristic algorithm like a genetic algorithm, simulated annealing, or particle swarm optimization, you can perform a search in the parameter space to find promising initial values. This can help EM converge to better solutions as it starts from a more favorable starting point.

- **Convergence Enhancement**:
- **Local Search**: After running EM for several iterations, the algorithm may converge to a local optimum. To improve the final solution, you can use a metaheuristic's local search capabilities to explore the neighborhood of the current solution. For example, hill climbing or a local search guided by a mutation operator in a genetic algorithm can help EM escape local optima and find a globally better solution.
- **Constraint Handling**: EM may not inherently handle constraints well, especially in optimization problems with constraints. Metaheuristic methods can be used to enforce constraints during the optimization process, ensuring that the solutions generated by EM are feasible. This can be done by incorporating constraint-handling techniques like penalty functions or repair operators into the metaheuristic.
- **Robustness Improvement**: EM can be sensitive to noisy or incomplete data. Metaheuristic methods can be used to enhance the robustness of the optimization process. For instance, you can incorporate robust optimization techniques into the metaheuristic to make the EM algorithm less susceptible to data outliers or modeling errors.

References

Acampora, G., Cadenas, J.M., Loia, V., and Muñoz, E. (2010). Achieving memetic adaptability by means of fuzzy decision trees. In: *International Conference on Fuzzy Systems*, 1–8. IEEE.

Asuero, A.G., Sayago, A., and González, A.G. (2006). The correlation coefficient: an overview. *Critical Reviews in Analytical Chemistry* 36 (1): 41–59.

Behnamian, J. and Ghomi, S.F. (2010). Development of a PSO–SA hybrid metaheuristic for a new comprehensive regression model to time-series forecasting. *Expert Systems with Applications* 37 (2): 974–984.

Bird, S. and Li, X. (2010). Improving local convergence in particle swarms by fitness approximation using regression. In: *Computational Intelligence in Expensive Optimization Problems* (ed. Y. Tenne and C.-K. Goh), 265–293. Springer.

Chatterjee, S. (2021). A new coefficient of correlation. *Journal of the American Statistical Association* 116 (536): 2009–2022.

Chaudhuri, A. and Sahu, T.P. (2021). Feature weighting for naïve Bayes using multi objective artificial bee colony algorithm. *International Journal of Computational Science and Engineering* 24 (1): 74–88.

Cisternas-Caneo, F., Crawford, B., Soto, R. et al. (2020). A data-driven dynamic discretization framework to solve combinatorial problems using continuous metaheuristics. In: *International Conference on Innovations in Bio-Inspired Computing and Applications*, 76–85. Cham: Springer International Publishing.

Consoli, S., Korst, J., Pauws, S., and Geleijnse, G. (2020). Improved metaheuristics for the quartet method of hierarchical clustering. *Journal of Global Optimization* 78: 241–270.

De Ville, B. (2013). Decision trees. *Wiley Interdisciplinary Reviews: Computational Statistics* 5 (6): 448–455.

Dokeroglu, T., Deniz, A., and Kiziloz, H.E. (2022). A comprehensive survey on recent metaheuristics for feature selection. *Neurocomputing* 494: 269–296.

Draper, N.R. and Smith, H. (1998). *Applied Regression Analysis*, vol. 326. John Wiley & Sons.

Farris, F.A. (2010). The Gini index and measures of inequality. *The American Mathematical Monthly* 117 (10): 851–864.

Fébba, D.M., Bortoni, E.C., Oliveira, A.F., and Rubinger, R.M. (2020). The effects of noises on metaheuristic algorithms applied to the PV parameter extraction problem. *Solar Energy* 201: 420–436.

Greistorfer, P. and Voss, S. (2005). Controlled pool maintenance for metaheuristics. In: *Metaheuristic Optimization via Memory and Evolution: Tabu Search and Scatter Search*, 387–424.

Jiménez, E.C. (2021). *Introducción al Machine Learning con MATLAB.* Marcombo.

Johannesson, E., Ohlson, J.A., and Zhai, S.W. (2023). The explanatory power of explanatory variables. In: *Review of Accounting Studies* (ed. R. Sharda, S. Voß, C. Rego, and B. Alidaee), 1–31. Springer.

José-García, A. and Gómez-Flores, W. (2016). Automatic clustering using nature-inspired metaheuristics: a survey. *Applied Soft Computing* 41: 192–213.

Kumar, S., Ratnoo, S., and Vashishtha, J. (2021). Hyper heuristic evolutionary approach for constructing decision tree classifiers. *Journal of Information and Communication Technology* 20 (2): 249–276.

Larabi-Marie-Sainte, S. (2021). Outlier detection based feature selection exploiting bio-inspired optimization algorithms. *Applied Sciences* 11 (15): 6769.

Lee, J., Yoon, Y., Kim, J., and Kim, Y.H. (2024). Metaheuristic-based feature selection methods for diagnosing sarcopenia with machine learning algorithms. *Biomimetics* 9 (3): 179.

McCarthy, R.V., McCarthy, M.M., Ceccucci, W. et al. (2019). Predictive models using regression. In: *Applying Predictive Analytics: Finding Value in Data* (ed. R.V. McCarthy, M.M. McCarthy, W. Ceccucci, and L. Halawi), 89–121.

Nakib, A., Thibault, B., and Siarry, P. (2015). Bayesian based metaheuristic for large scale continuous optimization. In: *2015 IEEE International Parallel and Distributed Processing Symposium Workshop*, 314–322. IEEE.

Nematzadeh, S., Kiani, F., Torkamanian-Afshar, M., and Aydin, N. (2022). Tuning hyperparameters of machine learning algorithms and deep neural networks using metaheuristics: a bioinformatics study on biomedical and biological cases. *Computational Biology and Chemistry* 97: 107619.

Pavelski, L., Delgado, M., and Kessaci, M.E. (2018). Meta-learning for optimization: a case study on the flowshop problem using decision trees. In: *2018 IEEE Congress on Evolutionary Computation (CEC)*, 1–8. IEEE.

Perim, G.T., Wandekokem, E.D., and Varejão, F.M. (2008). K-means initialization methods for improving clustering by simulated annealing. In: *Advances in Artificial Intelligence–IBERAMIA 2008: 11th Ibero-American Conference on AI*, Lisbon, Portugal, October 14–17, 2008. Proceedings 11, 133–142. Berlin, Heidelberg: Springer-Verlag.

Ramayah, T., Ahmad, N.H., Halim, H.A., and May-Chiun, S.R.M.Z. (2010). Discriminant analysis: an illustrated example. *African Journal of Business Management* 4 (9): 1654.

Rivera-Lopez, R., Canul-Reich, J., Mezura-Montes, E., and Cruz-Chávez, M.A. (2022). Induction of decision trees as classification models through metaheuristics. *Swarm and Evolutionary Computation* 69: 101006.

Santos, A., Silva, M., Santos, R. et al. (2016). A global expectation-maximization based on memetic swarm optimization for structural damage detection. *Structural Health Monitoring* 15 (5): 610–625.

Shaheen, M.A., Hasanien, H.M., Mekhamer, S.F. et al. (2022). Probabilistic optimal power flow solution using a novel hybrid metaheuristic and machine learning algorithm. *Mathematics* 10 (17): 3036.

Strejc, V. (1981). Least squares and regression methods. In: *Trends and Progress in System Identification*, 103–143. Pergamon.

Taunk, K., De, S., Verma, S., and Swetapadma, A. (2019). A brief review of nearest neighbor algorithm for learning and classification. In: *2019 International Conference on Intelligent Computing and Control Systems (ICCS)*, 1255–1260. IEEE.

Umadevi, S. and Marseline, K.J. (2017). A survey on data mining classification algorithms. In: *2017 International Conference on Signal Processing and Communication (ICSPC)*, 264–268. IEEE.

Yang, F.J. (2018). An implementation of naive Bayes classifier. In: *2018 International Conference on Computational Science and Computational Intelligence (CSCI)*, 301–306. IEEE.

4

Main Metaheuristic Techniques

4.1 Introduction

A metaheuristic algorithm is an advanced computational strategy designed to solve complex optimization problems that are difficult to tackle using traditional methods. These algorithms are characterized by their ability to escape local optima, a common pitfall in optimization problems, thereby increasing the chances of finding a near-optimal or globally optimal solution. Unlike exact algorithms that guarantee an optimal solution but often at the cost of high computational time, metaheuristics provide a good balance between solution quality and computational efficiency.

The strength of metaheuristic algorithms lies in their flexibility and adaptability, making them applicable to a wide range of problems, from logistics and scheduling to machine learning and engineering design. They are particularly useful when dealing with large, complex, and multi-modal landscapes where traditional methods are inefficient or infeasible. Despite their heuristic nature, which does not guarantee a perfect solution, their ability to consistently find high-quality solutions in a reasonable time frame makes them invaluable tools in the field of computational optimization.

In this chapter, we delve into the most prominent metaheuristic algorithms as identified in the literature: genetic algorithms (GAs), particle swarm optimization (PSO), and differential evolution (DE). These methods stand out for their widespread use and effectiveness in solving complex optimization problems. Given their extensive application, it's not surprising that these techniques are frequently used in tandem with machine learning methods, creating powerful hybrid approaches. The chapter offers a detailed exploration of these algorithms, with a particular focus on the underlying mechanisms that enable the integration of machine learning elements to enhance their performance. Additionally, the chapter is enriched with numerous MATLAB code segments. These codes are not just implementations of the GA, PSO, and DE algorithms; they also encompass various other significant mechanisms that represent advancements in these techniques. This comprehensive approach provides readers with both the theoretical understanding and practical tools needed to apply and improve these metaheuristic algorithms in a wide range of problem-solving scenarios.

4.1.1 Use of Metaphors

Metaphors play a crucial role in the development and understanding of metaheuristic algorithms. These algorithms often draw inspiration from natural or social phenomena, and metaphors serve as a bridge between these real-world processes and computational methods. For instance,

Machine Learning and Metaheuristic Computation, First Edition.
Erik Cuevas, Jorge Galvez, Omar Avalos, and Fernando Wario.

the metaphor of natural evolution underpins GAs, where concepts of selection, crossover, and mutation are used to evolve solutions to optimization problems. Similarly, PSO is based on the metaphor of social behavior in flocks of birds or schools of fish, where the collective intelligence of the group leads to effective problem-solving strategies.

The use of metaphors in metaheuristics is not just a creative exercise; it provides several significant benefits. Firstly, it facilitates the conceptualization and design of algorithms by providing a familiar framework to model complex computational processes. This approach can lead to innovative solutions that might not be discovered through conventional mathematical or algorithmic thinking. Secondly, metaphors make these algorithms more accessible and easier to understand for a broader audience, including those without deep technical backgrounds. By relating to natural or familiar processes, the underlying principles of these complex algorithms become more relatable and easier to grasp.

Moreover, metaphors encourage interdisciplinary collaboration by bridging gaps between fields. For example, insights from biology have directly influenced the development of evolutionary algorithms. Lastly, metaphors stimulate continuous innovation in the field of optimization. As researchers draw inspiration from different sources, new metaheuristic algorithms are developed, broadening the scope and efficiency of computational methods available for solving diverse and challenging optimization problems. Thus, metaphors are not just a superficial layer over these algorithms but are fundamental to their conceptualization, development, and application.

4.1.2 Problems of the Use of Metaphors

While metaphors in metaheuristic algorithms offer conceptual and educational benefits, their use also presents notable challenges and criticisms. One primary issue is the potential for oversimplification. Metaphors, by their nature, simplify complex natural or social phenomena to make them more relatable. This simplification can lead to misunderstandings about how these algorithms function, potentially causing users to overlook important computational details or to misapply the algorithms in inappropriate contexts. Additionally, the reliance on metaphors can sometimes lead to a form of "narrative fallacy," where the attractiveness of the metaphor overshadows the algorithm's actual performance and robustness. This can result in the development of algorithms that are more appealing conceptually than they are effective in practice.

Another criticism is that metaphor-based design can limit creativity and innovation in algorithm development. Researchers might become constrained by the specifics of the metaphor, inhibiting the exploration of novel algorithmic structures that do not fit within the metaphorical framework. This can lead to a proliferation of "novel" algorithms that are essentially minor variations of existing ones, offering little in the way of genuine innovation or improved performance.

Furthermore, the validation and comparison of these algorithms become challenging. The metaphor can sometimes be used to justify algorithmic choices without rigorous theoretical or empirical backing, making it difficult to objectively assess and compare the efficacy of different metaheuristic algorithms.

In summary, while metaphors in metaheuristic algorithms aid in conceptual understanding and interdisciplinary inspiration, they can also lead to oversimplification, narrative fallacies, reduced innovation, and challenges in validation and comparison. These issues highlight the need for a balanced approach that appreciates the value of metaphors while maintaining rigorous standards of algorithm development and evaluation.

4.1.3 Metaheuristic Algorithms

Metaheuristic algorithms have gained significant attention in the field of computational optimization due to their ability to efficiently solve complex and diverse problems. This survey aims to analyze some of the most important metaheuristic algorithms, highlighting their unique features, applications, and comparative effectiveness.

Genetic Algorithms (GAs): Inspired by the principles of natural selection and genetics, GAs are widely used for their robustness and ability to find global optima in complex landscapes. They are particularly effective in problems where the solution space is vast and not well understood. GAs have been successfully applied in fields like bioinformatics, engineering design, and artificial intelligence (Goldberg 1989).

Differential Evolution (DE): This algorithm is a robust and efficient metaheuristic used for solving complex optimization problems, particularly those involving continuous variables. Developed by Storn and Price in 1997, DE stands out for its simplicity, ease of use, and effectiveness in handling non-linear, non-differentiable, and multi-modal objective functions. The algorithm operates through a population-based approach, similar to GAs, but with a unique mechanism of generating trial solutions.

Particle Swarm Optimization (PSO): Mimicking the social behavior of birds and fish, PSO has been noted for its efficiency in continuous optimization problems. Its ability to adaptively tune its parameters makes it suitable for dynamic environments (Kennedy and Eberhart 1995).

Ant Colony Optimization (ACO): Drawing inspiration from the foraging behavior of ants, ACO excels in combinatorial optimization problems like the traveling salesman problem and network routing (Dorigo and Di Caro 1999).

Tabu Search (TS): TS stands out for its use of memory structures to escape local optima. It is effective in large-scale combinatorial problems and has been widely used in logistics and scheduling (Glover 1986).

Each of these algorithms has its strengths and ideal application areas. For instance, Gas, DE, and PSO are often preferred for their versatility and ease of implementation, while ACO and SA are chosen for specific problem types where their respective mechanisms offer distinct advantages.

Considering the vast array of metaheuristic algorithms available, it becomes impractical, if not impossible, to delve into each one in great detail within a single chapter. The field of computational optimization has seen the development of numerous algorithms, each with its unique approach and application domain. However, to provide a focused and in-depth understanding, this chapter will concentrate on three specific algorithms: GAs, PSO, and DE. The rationale behind selecting these three is twofold.

Firstly, GA, PSO, and DE are among the most popular and widely used metaheuristic algorithms. Their prominence in both academic research and practical applications has made them foundational to the study and application of optimization techniques. Their popularity also means that they have been extensively tested and applied across a myriad of problem domains, thus providing a wealth of knowledge and insights into their capabilities and limitations.

Secondly, the search structures and strategies employed by these three algorithms have been influential in the development of many other metaheuristic algorithms. GA, with its evolutionary approach; PSO, with its social behavior-inspired mechanism; and DE, with its differential mutation strategy, each represent a distinct and powerful approach to optimization. By understanding these algorithms, one gains insight not only into their specific mechanics but also into the broader principles and strategies that underpin the field of metaheuristics. This understanding is invaluable for both the development of new algorithms and the application of existing ones to complex optimization problems.

4.2 Genetic Algorithms

The initial concept of the GA was first introduced by John Holland at the University of Michigan, marking a significant milestone in the field of evolutionary computation (Baldick 2006). Since its inception, GA has evolved and diversified, leading to the emergence of numerous variants that either modify the original structure or amalgamate it with other computational strategies. This evolution of GA reflects its adaptability and effectiveness in addressing a wide range of complex problems. Today, these innovative GA approaches are extensively documented in recent publications across various specialized journals. Key journals contributing to this evolving discourse include "Evolutionary Computation," "Transactions on Evolutionary Computation," "Swarm and Evolutionary Computation," "Applied Soft Computing," "Soft Computing," "Evolutionary Intelligence," "Memetic Computing," and "Neural Computing and Applications," among others. These publications not only demonstrate the ongoing relevance and advancement of GAs but also highlight the vibrant and dynamic nature of research in this area. They serve as a testament to the continuous refinement and application of GAs in diverse fields, ranging from engineering and economics to artificial intelligence and beyond, showcasing the enduring impact of Holland's foundational work.

GAs derive their computational principle from natural genetics (Yang 2010). In this subsection, we explore the operational characteristics of GAs, which are essentially search strategies inspired by the principles of natural selection. At the heart of GAs is the adaptation of central concepts from genetics, such as chromosomes, genes, mutation, crossover (recombination), and selection, into an artificial context to create robust search mechanisms. These mechanisms emulate the evolutionary process seen in nature, where the fittest individuals are more likely to pass their genetic material to the next generation. In GAs, potential solutions to an optimization problem are encoded as "chromosomes" and a population of these solutions undergoes evolution over successive generations. The process involves selecting the fittest solutions, recombining them to produce offspring, and introducing mutations to maintain diversity within the population. This evolutionary cycle continues until a termination condition is met, often yielding highly optimized solutions. The strength of GAs lies in their ability to efficiently search large, complex solution spaces and their robustness in handling a variety of problem types. Unlike traditional optimization methods that may require detailed information about the problem's landscape, GAs can perform well with minimal information, relying on the power of evolution-inspired processes to guide the search toward optimal or near-optimal solutions.

GAs are structured around three fundamental operators (Venkataraman 2009): Selection, Crossover, and Mutation. These operators are crucial in guiding the evolutionary process that characterizes GAs.

Selection is responsible for choosing the fittest individuals from the current population to pass their genetic information to the next generation. The selection process typically favors individuals with higher fitness values, ensuring that the best solutions have a higher chance of contributing to the next generation. Crossover is the process of combining the genetic information of two parent solutions to produce new offspring. This operator is vital for introducing variability in the population, allowing for the exploration of new areas in the solution space. Mutation introduces random changes to the genetic information of the offspring. This operator is essential for maintaining diversity within the population, preventing premature convergence to local optima, and ensuring a thorough exploration of the solution space.

The operational process of a GA begins with the generation of an initial population of random solutions, rather than starting with a single candidate solution. This population-based approach is one of the distinguishing features of GAs. Once the initial population is generated, each solution is evaluated based on the optimization problem, typically represented by a cost function. The value derived from this cost function is referred to as the fitness value, which is assigned to each candidate solution. The fitness evaluation of a solution involves assessing both its cost function value and its respective constraint violation. The combination of these two factors yields a relative score that reflects the efficacy of the solution in addressing the optimization problem. This score is then used in the selection process to determine which solutions are most suited to propagate their genetic material to the subsequent generation, thereby driving the evolutionary process inherent in GAs.

In GA, the population of solutions undergoes transformation through the three main operations: selection, crossover, and mutation. These operations are pivotal in evolving the population toward optimal or near-optimal solutions. The crossover and mutation operations are stochastic processes executed based on certain probabilities. The crossover operator is applied with a probability denoted as p_c, which is typically set high. This operator facilitates the exchange of spatial information between candidate solutions, allowing the combination of different solutions' features. Crossover plays a crucial role in exploring the solution space and generating potentially better offspring. In contrast, the mutation process is executed with a probability p_m, which is generally low compared to crossover probability. Mutation introduces random alterations to the genetic makeup of the candidate solutions. This operator is essential for maintaining genetic diversity within the population, helping to avoid premature convergence to local optima and potentially improving the accuracy of solutions. The combined effect of crossover and mutation is to develop a robust search strategy capable of localizing promising regions within the solution space. Following the application of these operators, an iteration counter is incremented, marking the completion of a GA cycle. The algorithm then evaluates a termination criterion. If this criterion is not met, the algorithm proceeds to a new cycle, continuing the evolutionary process. However, if the termination condition is fulfilled, the algorithm concludes its execution. This entire GA process, from initialization to termination, can be comprehensively understood through a flowchart representation, as illustrated in Figure 4.1. The flowchart delineates each step of the GA, from generating the initial population to the final output, providing a clear and structured overview of the algorithm's operational flow.

4.2.1 Canonical Genetic Algorithm

To demonstrate the working mechanism of GAs, we engage in a practical, hand-simulation of one generation of the algorithm, focusing on a problem involving two variables. This problem, sourced from reference (Dennis 1978), serves as a concrete example to illustrate the GA's processing method. Alongside this hands-on example, we delve into a theoretical discussion on various GA parameters and their interplay within the algorithm.

For a more tangible understanding, we consider a basic design problem of a cylindrical can, involving two parameters: the height (h) and the diameter (d) of the can. The optimization scenario posited here involves designing a can that must hold a minimum volume of 500 ml. The primary objective of this design challenge is to minimize the cost of the metal used in manufacturing the can. This requirement establishes the basis of our optimization problem, where the goal is to find

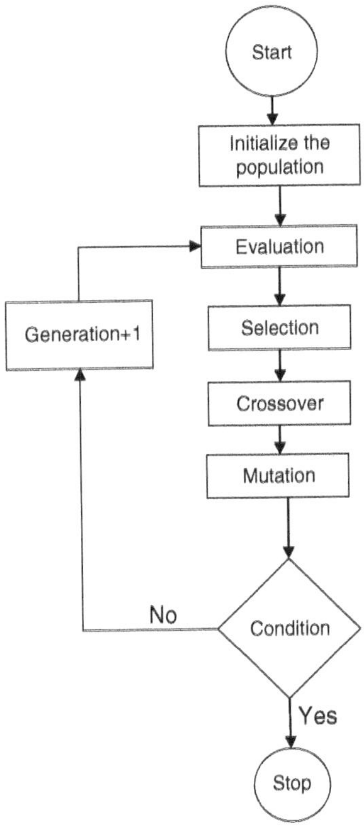

Figure 4.1 Operational process diagram of genetic algorithms.

the optimal values of height and diameter that satisfy the volume constraint while minimizing material cost.

Through this example, we aim to explore and explain the fundamental operating principles of a GA. By applying the algorithm to a simple yet practical problem, the concepts of selection, crossover, mutation, and the overall evolutionary process of GAs become clearer. This hands-on approach not only aids in comprehending the mechanics of GAs but also illustrates how they can be effectively applied to real-world optimization problems. Therefore, the optimization problem can be formulated as follows:

$$\begin{aligned}
&\text{Minimize} \quad f(d,h) = c\left(\frac{\pi d^2}{2} + \pi dh\right) \\
&\text{Subject to} \quad g(d,h) = \frac{\pi d^2 h}{4} \geq 500 \\
&\qquad d_{\min} \leq d \leq d_{\max} \\
&\qquad h_{\min} \leq h \leq h_{\max}
\end{aligned} \tag{4.1}$$

In the optimization problem concerning the design of a cylindrical can, where the objective is to minimize the cost of the metal used, the cost per square centimeter of the can's metal is denoted as c. The design variables in this problem, the height (h) and diameter (d) of the can, are constrained to specific ranges. Specifically, the diameter d varies within the range $[d_{\min}, d_{\max}]$ and the height h within $[h_{\min}, h_{\max}]$, measured in centimeters.

The initial step in employing GAs to determine the optimal values of d and h is to represent these decision variables as binary strings. For instance, if we decide to use five bits to represent each

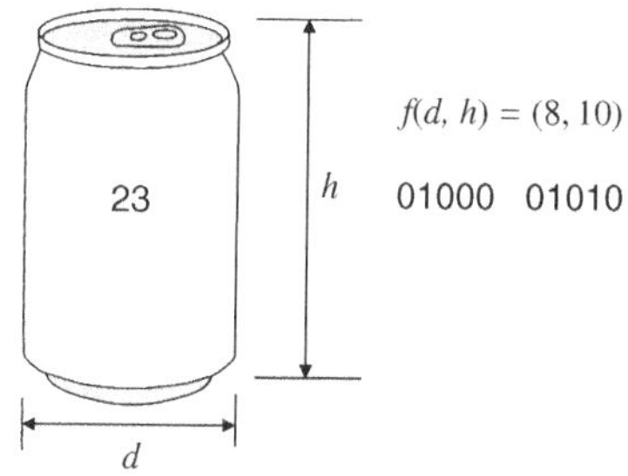

Figure 4.2 Representation of a Potential Solution for the can design optimization task, with the calculated cost of the can as 23 units.

of the decision variables, a total of ten bits would be needed to encode a complete chromosome representing a solution. This binary representation is crucial for the GA's process of selection, crossover, and mutation.

To illustrate, consider a scenario where the solution corresponds to a can with a diameter of 8 cm and a height of 10 cm. This specific solution would be represented as a combination of binary strings in the chromosome, with each string encoding the respective value of d and h. Such a representation is depicted in Figure 4.2, showcasing how the GA translates the physical dimensions of the can into a format suitable for the evolutionary optimization process. This binary encoding is the key to how GAs manipulate and evolve potential solutions in the quest for optimal can design, balancing the constraints of volume and cost efficiency.

In the binary representation used for the can optimization problem, both design variables – the diameter (d) and height (h) of the can – are coded within a range of [0, 31], using five bits for each decision variable. This range is chosen to accommodate the binary format, where five bits can represent any integer from 0 to 31. This encoding allows for a broad spectrum of candidate solutions to be considered and tested in the search for the optimal design. When a candidate solution is generated in the form of a binary string, it represents a specific combination of diameter and height within the predefined range. The next critical step in the GA process is to evaluate this solution based on the cost function and any potential constraint violations. In scenarios where constraints are not explicitly defined, the fitness value of the candidate solution depends solely on the cost function. For our can design example, both the cost function and any applicable constraints are evaluated to determine the fitness of each candidate solution. This evaluation process involves converting the binary-encoded values of diameter and height back into their numerical form and then assessing these values against the cost function and the constraints of the problem. In cases where constraints are involved, solutions that violate these constraints may be penalized or deemed unfit, depending on the specific implementation of the GA. This evaluation step is crucial as it directly influences the selection process in the GA, guiding the algorithm toward solutions that not only minimize cost but also adhere to the necessary design constraints. In our specific case, the evaluation of the cost function and any constraints is conducted in the following manner:

$$f(d,h) = 0.065\left(\frac{\pi \cdot 8^2}{2} + \pi \cdot 8 \cdot 10\right) = 23 \tag{4.2}$$

$$g(d,h) = \frac{\pi \cdot 8^2 \cdot 10}{4} = 502.656 \tag{4.3}$$

where $c = 0.065$ represents the unit cost of the can's metal per square centimeter.

The primary goal of our optimization problem is to minimize the total material cost while ensuring that the can's capacity is no less than 300 ml. Consequently, in this context, a solution with a

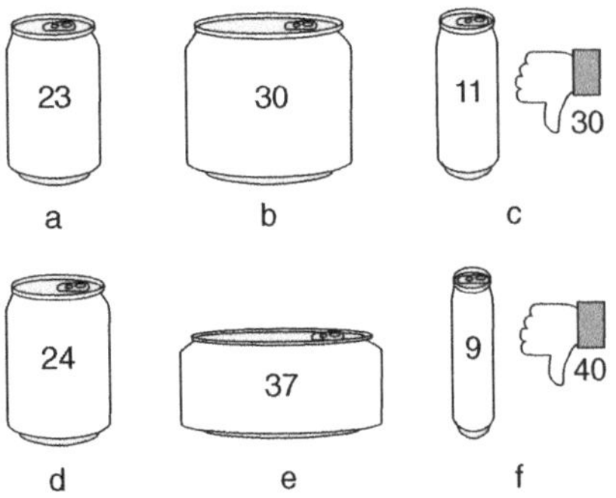

Figure 4.3 A randomly generated group of six cans and the calculation of their individual quality.

lower fitness value is considered superior. Figure 4.3 presents a set of six random solutions to the can design problem, showcasing both feasible and unfeasible solutions. Feasible solutions meet the constraint requirement of containing at least 300 ml, whereas unfeasible solutions fail to meet this criterion to varying degrees, as dictated by the constraint function $g(d, h)$.

Feasible solutions are evaluated solely based on the cost function $f(d, h)$. In contrast, the fitness of unfeasible solutions incorporates a penalty in addition to the cost function, reflecting the degree of constraint violation. In our example, two solutions fail to achieve the 300 ml volume requirement and are thus penalized with an additional constraint cost. This penalty must be calculated based on the extent of the constraint violation and should be significant enough to ensure that all infeasible solutions are less desirable than any feasible solution.

In Figure 4.3, cans labeled a, b, d, and e represent feasible solutions, as they meet the minimum volume requirement. Their evaluation is based purely on the cost function $f(d, h)$. However, the solutions corresponding to cans c and f are deemed infeasible, as they do not fulfill the 300 ml criterion. These solutions are penalized accordingly. The overall quality of these solutions is determined by adding their cost function values (11 and 9 for c and f, respectively) to their constraint violation penalties (30 and 40 for c and f, respectively), ensuring that the penalization reflects their inability to meet the volume requirement effectively.

4.2.2 Selection Process

The primary goal of the selection process in GAs is to enhance the proliferation of high-quality solutions and suppress the presence of poor solutions within a population while keeping the total number of candidate solutions unchanged (Hocking 1991). The selection operator is integral to the evolutionary process of GAs and it executes several key tasks:

- **Identify High-Quality Solutions**: The first task is to assess and identify the solutions in the population that exhibit superior quality based on their fitness values.
- **Reproduction of Superior Solutions**: Once the high-quality solutions are identified, the next step is to reproduce these solutions. This reproduction is crucial for passing on the desirable traits of these solutions to subsequent generations.
- **Exclusion of Inferior Solutions**: Concurrently, the selection process aims to avoid choosing poor solutions from the population. The idea is that new copies of the superior solutions will gradually replace the less desirable ones, thus improving the overall quality of the population over successive generations.

There are several selection schemes utilized in GAs, each with its unique approach to achieving these tasks. The most common methods include:

- **Tournament Selection** (Mathews and Fink 2000): This method involves randomly selecting a small subset of the population and then choosing the best individual from this group to be a parent. The process is repeated until the desired number of parents is selected.
- **Proportional Selection** (Baldick 2006): Also known as Roulette wheel selection, this method selects individuals based on their fitness proportionate to the total fitness of the population, giving higher fitness individuals a greater chance of being selected.
- **Ranking Selection** (Reinhardt et al. 2013): In this approach, individuals are ranked based on their fitness, and the selection probability is then determined based on this ranking, rather than directly on fitness values.
- **Pure Random Selection**: As the name suggests, this method involves selecting individuals entirely at random, regardless of their fitness.

Each of these selection methods has its advantages and is chosen based on the specific requirements and dynamics of the problem being solved. They play a pivotal role in guiding the evolutionary process toward convergence on optimal or near-optimal solutions.

In the tournament selection method, two candidate solutions are randomly chosen from the population, and a "contest" is conducted between them. The process involves comparing the fitness values of these two solutions, and the one with the better fitness is selected for further processing. When this method is repeated multiple times across the population, it naturally leads to the selection of the best solutions multiple times, while the less fit solutions are gradually phased out due to their inability to win these "tournaments." An advantageous feature of tournament selection is its straightforward applicability to both minimization and maximization problems, achieved by simply altering the comparison operator used in the contest.

Another prominent method is proportional selection, where the probability of choosing a solution x_i is directly proportional to its fitness value $f(x_i)$. For example, if the average fitness of all population members is f_{avg}, then a solution x_i with a fitness $f(x_i)$. is likely to be chosen approximately $(f(x_i)/f_{\text{avg}})$ times over multiple selection iterations. This mechanism is often implemented using a Roulette-wheel simulation (RWS), where the wheel is divided into sections corresponding to each solution in the population. The size of each section is proportional to the fitness value $f(x_i)$ of the respective solution.

The selection process in RWS involves spinning the wheel and randomly selecting a solution based on where the pointer lands, reflecting the stochastic nature of the outcome. For instance, Figure 4.4 might depict a Roulette wheel for five candidate solutions with varying fitness values. In this scenario, if the third solution has the highest fitness compared to the other four, the RWS is more likely to select this solution more frequently. This is due to its larger section on the wheel, representing a higher probability of being chosen. The RWS method can be effectively simulated in a computer program, making it a practical and commonly used approach in GAs for selecting solutions based on their relative fitness.

To simulate the RWS method, the likelihood of choosing the solution x_i from N elements is calculated in the following way:

$$P_i(x_i) = \frac{f(x_i)}{\sum_{j=1}^{N} f(x_j)} \tag{4.4}$$

i	$f(x_i)$	$P_i(x_i)$
1	25.0	0.25
2	5.0	0.05
3	40.0	0.40
4	10.0	0.10
5	20.0	0.20

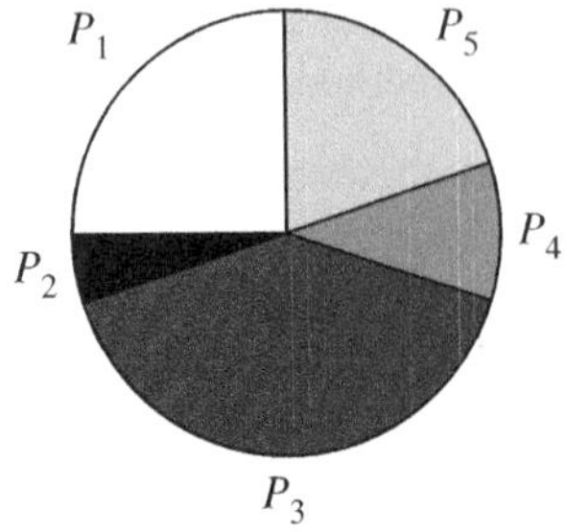

Figure 4.4 A roulette wheel representation for five solutions, segmented based on their respective fitness values.

After determining the probabilities for all solutions, the cumulative probability P_i^A for each element x_i is derived by summing up the individual probabilities starting from the first solution x_1 up to the specific element x_i, as follows:

$$P_i^A(x_i) = \sum_{j=1}^{i} P_j(x_j) \tag{4.5}$$

Consequently, the cumulative probability P_N^A for the final element x_N in the sequence is equal to one. In this scenario, the cumulative probability P_i^A for a given solution x_i represents the range of occurrence probabilities between P_{i-1} and P_i. A notable instance is the cumulative probability P_1^A for the first solution, which is equivalent to the probability range from 0 to P_1.

To select a solution using the RWS method, a random number u, which is uniformly distributed, is first generated. The chosen solution is then the one whose cumulative probability range most closely matches the generated number u.

For instance, Figure 4.5 depicts the cumulative probability distribution of five solutions, with values ranging from zero to one, as exemplified in Figure 4.4. In this setup, once a uniformly distributed random number u is generated, the selection of a solution is based on where u falls within these cumulative probability ranges. Given that the probability P_3 for solution x_3 is the highest among all five elements, it is more probable that the random number u will fall within the range between P_2 and P_3, hence selecting solution x_3.

One of the limitations of the proportional selection method, however, is its dependency on calculating the average fitness of all members in the population. This requirement can make the process slower in comparison to the tournament selection method, where such comprehensive calculations are not necessary. The tournament method's relative simplicity and efficiency in selection make it a preferred choice in scenarios where computational speed is a significant consideration.

In certain metaheuristic approaches, there's a need to choose a subset of N elements from an initial group of M individuals, where M is equal to or greater than N. Opting for multiple individuals in a single selection step is often more efficient and robust than selecting just one individual at a time. This approach is particularly evident in Evolutionary Strategies, where a group of μ elements is chosen in one go from the original population. During this procedure, the number of copies N_i

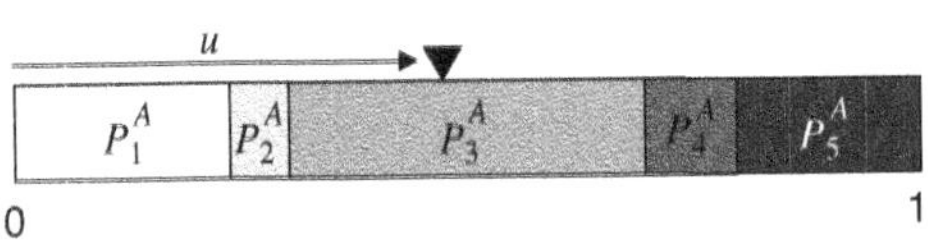

Figure 4.5 Execution of the Roulette-Wheel Selection mechanism.

that each solution x_i will have in the final selected set is calculated in the following manner:

$$N_i = int(N \cdot P_i) \tag{4.6}$$

where $int(\cdot)$ refers to the function that returns the integer part of its input. In cases where the total number of copies for all solutions, given by $\sum_{j=1}^{N} N_j < N$), does not reach the full quota of N elements, the remaining slots (calculated as $N - \sum_{j=1}^{N} N_j$) are filled using the RWS method.

Despite its effectiveness, the proportional selection scheme has a significant drawback. It operates under the assumption that all fitness values are positive, ensuring that Eq. 4.3 yields valid probability values. However, if fitness values are negative, the assigned probabilities become invalid. This issue can be addressed by adding a sufficiently large positive value, denoted as θ, to each fitness value, ensuring all are positive. Determining the appropriate θ value can be challenging, as the specific nature of the optimization problem is often unknown.

In the ranking selection method, solutions are sorted based on their fitness values, with the lowest-ranked solution receiving a rank of 1 and the highest-ranked solution a rank of N. This method then applies the proportional selection operator using these ranks rather than fitness values. The advantage of this approach is that it bypasses the issue of negative values, as it only considers ranks. However, a notable downside is reduced selection pressure due to the potential discrepancy between rank and actual fitness values. For instance, two solutions may have a substantial difference in fitness but only a one-rank difference, leading them to be considered almost equally likely for selection despite their varying fitness.

Pure random selection, on the other hand, is the simplest method, where a solution is chosen randomly without any consideration of fitness or rank. While easy to implement, this method often yields suboptimal results as it does not facilitate the propagation of superior solutions or the elimination of inferior ones, essentially treating all solutions with equal likelihood regardless of their quality.

4.2.3 Binary Crossover Process

The crossover operation in GAs plays a crucial role in exchanging information between solutions (Bartholomew-Biggs 2008). Its primary purpose is to facilitate the transfer of spatial information among members of the population, thereby serving as a strategic tool in the search for optimal solutions. It's important to note that the selection operator, by itself, does not generate new solutions within the population. Instead, its function is to reproduce copies of well-performing solutions while simultaneously filtering out the less effective ones.

Crossover and mutation are the two key binary operators responsible for producing new candidate solutions. In the crossover process, two solutions from the original population, referred to as parents, are randomly selected. A segment of their binary strings is then exchanged between them, resulting in the creation of two new offspring solutions.

The crossover operation for binary representations typically involves the combination of two selected parents, denoted as $\mathbf{p}_1$ and $\mathbf{p}_2$. To simplify the explanation of this process, a mask $\mathbf{m}$ is often used. This mask determines which bits from the parent solutions should be swapped or combined. In the mask, bits marked as "one" are swapped, while those marked as 'zero' remain unchanged. The result of this crossover process is the production of two new solutions, $\mathbf{c}_1$ and $\mathbf{c}_2$. This book will discuss three crossover schemes for binary representations: one-point crossover, two-point crossover, and uniform crossover.

The crossover operation is stochastic and is executed based on a certain probability, denoted as p_c. This probability, which is typically set high, determines the likelihood of the crossover

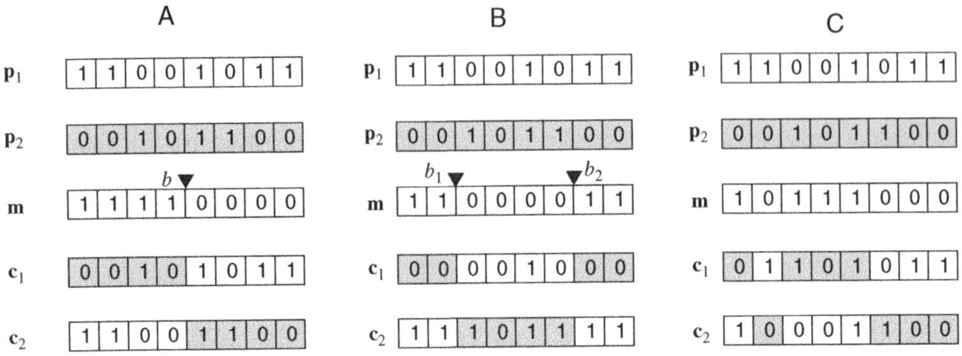

Figure 4.6 Variety of crossover mechanisms.

operator being applied in any given generation. This stochastic nature of crossover allows for the introduction of new genetic combinations into the population, thereby contributing to the exploration of the solution space and the overall effectiveness of the genetic algorithm.

In GAs, the crossover operation can be performed in three primary ways, each with its unique method of combining genetic information from parent solutions to create offspring.

One-Point Crossover: In this method, a single-bit position, denoted as b, is randomly chosen as the crossover point. The segments of the binary strings after this point are swapped between the two parent solutions, $\mathbf{p}_1$ and $\mathbf{p}_2$, to produce offspring $\mathbf{c}_1$ and $\mathbf{c}_2$. This process effectively splits the parent chromosomes at point b and exchanges their tails. An example of one-point crossover is shown in Figure 4.6a. This operation can also be defined using a mask $\mathbf{m}$, which is configured with zeros and ones, with the distribution centered around the crossover point b.

Two-Point Crossover: This operation involves selecting two-bit positions, b_1 and b_2, randomly. The segments of the binary strings between these two points are then swapped between the parents. Similar to one-point crossover but with an additional bit position, the mask $\mathbf{m}$ in this case contains two segments of ones within the complete bit string. The process of two-point crossover is illustrated in Figure 4.6b, highlighting how it allows for more complex recombination of parental genes compared to one-point crossover.

Uniform Crossover: The uniform crossover method randomizes the combination of bits from the parents more extensively. Here, each bit position has an equal probability (typically 0.5) of being chosen for crossover. For each bit of the mask $\mathbf{m}$, a random number r, uniformly distributed, is generated. If $r > 0.5$, the corresponding bit position i in the mask is set to one; otherwise, it is set to zero. This method results in a more randomized and diverse mixture of parental genes in the offspring. Figure 4.6c demonstrates the process of uniform crossover, underscoring its stochastic nature in generating offspring solutions.

Each of these crossover methods has its strengths and applications, and the choice among them depends on the specific requirements of the problem and the desired balance between exploration and exploitation in the genetic algorithm.

4.2.4 Binary Mutation Process

The mutation operation in GAs involves randomly altering one or more bits in a binary string to their opposite values. This process plays a crucial role in introducing diversity to the population and ensuring the algorithm does not become trapped in local minima. Like crossover, mutation

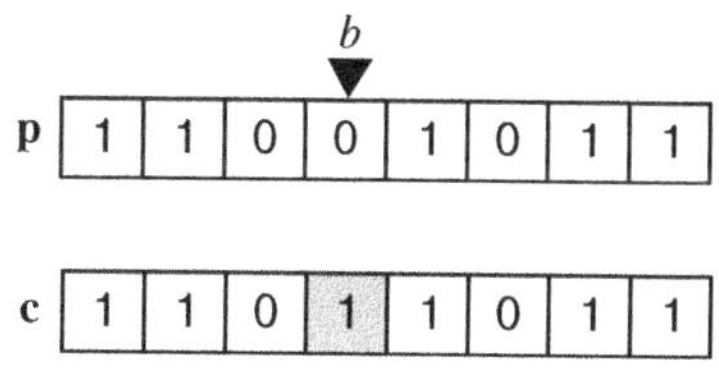

Figure 4.7 Process of mutation.

is a stochastic process and is governed by a mutation probability, denoted as p_m. The probability p_m is typically kept low to ensure that high-quality candidate solutions are not drastically altered, maintaining a balance between introducing variability and preserving acquired good traits.

One of the most common forms of mutation is uniform mutation. In this approach, one or several bit positions, such as b or $b_1 \ldots b_m$, are randomly selected from the binary string $\mathbf{p}$. A new solution $\mathbf{c}$ is then created by flipping these selected bits. Essentially, if a selected bit is "one", it is changed to "zero", and vice versa. This method allows for random, yet controlled, alterations in the genetic makeup of the solutions, thereby contributing to the exploration of new areas in the solution space.

Figure 4.7 demonstrates the process of uniform mutation. In this illustration, the random selection and inversion of bits are shown, highlighting how this mutation process can subtly yet effectively modify a candidate solution. The implementation of mutation, particularly the uniform mutation, ensures that the genetic algorithm avoids premature convergence and maintains a healthy diversity of solutions, crucial for finding optimal or near-optimal solutions in complex optimization problems.

4.2.5 Implementation of the Binary GA

In this section, we integrate and implement the entire binary genetic algorithm process. To demonstrate its assembly, we consider minimizing the following problem:

$$\begin{aligned} &\text{Minimize} \quad f(x) = (x-2)^4 + 5(x-2)^3 + 4(x-2)^2 - 4(x-2) + 1 \\ &\text{Subject to} \quad -2 \le x \le 3 \end{aligned} \tag{4.7}$$

The cost function under consideration is visually represented in Figure 4.8. As observed in the figure, the cost function features two minima: a global minimum at approximately $x_g \approx -1$ and a local minimum near $x_l \approx 2.25$. Given that GAs are designed for global optimization, they are expected to locate the global minimum solution x_g. However, it's notable that this cost function

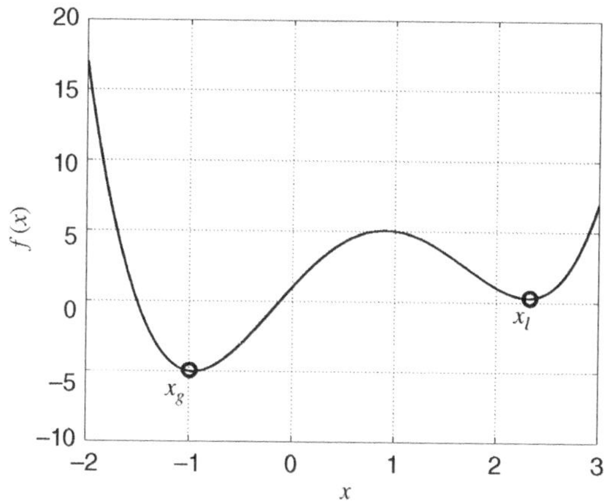

Figure 4.8 Cost function example for the implementation of the binary GA.

includes negative fitness values, which suggests that the use of the proportional selection method might not be ideal in this scenario.

Program 4.1 presents the full implementation of the binary GA. This implementation incorporates various functions to facilitate easier analysis and understanding. The optimization process encapsulated in the program can be broken down into five distinct sections, each corresponding to a specific function within the algorithm: initialization, conversion from binary to decimal values, ranking selection, crossover, and mutation.

Each of these sections plays a critical role in the functioning of the GA. The initialization step sets up the initial population of solutions. The conversion function translates binary representations to decimal values, crucial for evaluating the fitness of solutions. The ranking selection method is used to select superior solutions, particularly important given the negative values in the cost function. Crossover and mutation are then applied to generate new solutions and maintain diversity within the population, guiding the algorithm toward the global optimum solution. This structured approach allows the GA to systematically explore and exploit the solution space, demonstrating its capability as a powerful tool for global optimization.

Program 4.1 ***Development of the Binary Genetic Algorithm Using MATLAB***

```
%Algorithm 4.1
% Binary GA implementation
clear all
global solnew sol pop popnew fitness fitold f range;
% Objective function
funstr='(x-2)^4+5*(x-2)^3+4*(x-2)^2-4*(x-2)+1';
%Search space range
range=[-2 3];
f=vectorize(inline(funstr));
% Parameter Initialization
popsize=10;     % Population size N
MaxGen=120;       % maximal number of generations
nsite=2;         % bits to be mutated
pc=0.95;         % Crossover probability
pm=0.05;         % Mutation probability
nsbit=16;        % Binary string size (bits)
%The initial population is generated
popnew=init_genA(popsize,nsbit); % Section A
fitness=zeros(1,popsize);    % Memory is kept
% Binary string are converted into a decimal value
 for i=1:popsize,
solnew(i)=bintodecA(popnew(i,:)); % Section B
fitness(i)=f(solnew(i));
 end
% The optimization process begins
 for i=1:MaxGen,
fitold=fitness; pop=popnew; sol=solnew;
```

```
% A new population is generated applying the ranking selection
      for z=1:popsize
      e=seleccionR(fitold); % Section C
      MP(z,:)=pop(e,:);
      end

for z1=1:2:popsize
% The parents p1 and p2 are selected
     p1=floor(popsize*rand)+1;
     p2=floor(popsize*rand)+1;
% Crossover is applied
     if pc>rand,
   % Products c1 and c2 are generated
     [NP(z1,:),NP(z1+1,:)]=crossoverA(MP(p1,:),MP(p2,:))  ; % Section 4
     else
     % Otherwise the parents remain
         NP(z1,:)=MP(p1,:);
         NP(z1+1,:)=MP(p2,:);
     end
% Mutation is executed
if pm>rand,
% Products n1 y n2 are generated
mu1=NP(z1,:);
mu2=NP(z1+1,:);
NP(z1,:)=mutate(mu1,nsite); % Section D
NP(z1+1,:)=mutate(mu2,nsite);
end
end
% The binary strings are converted into decimal
for i=1:popsize,
solnew(i)=bintodecA(NP(i,:)); % Section B
fitness(i)=f(solnew(i));
 end
popnew=NP;
 end
% The final results are shown
 x=range(1):0.001:range(2);
 plot(x,f(x));
hold on
 plot(solnew,fitness,'or');
```

In Section A of the optimization process, everything starts with the creation of an initial population. When specific information about the candidate solutions is lacking, the most effective approach to establish this initial population is through the generation of random binary strings. In this specific case, a binary string of 17 bits is utilized. Of these, 16 bits are allocated for representing the numeric value, and one bit is designated for indicating the sign. To randomly determine the composition of these 17 bits in each string, a set of 17 random numbers, uniformly distributed, is generated. Since these numbers fall within the range of [0, 1], those that are greater than 0.5 are assigned the binary value of one, while the rest are set to zero. This method ensures a diverse and unbiased initial population, critical for the effectiveness of the genetic algorithm. This process of initializing the genetic population is encapsulated in the function init_genA, as detailed in Program 4.2. The function's role is to randomly create these initial binary strings, laying the foundational groundwork for the subsequent steps of the genetic algorithm. This initial population is then subject to further processes like selection, crossover, and mutation, driving the algorithm toward finding an optimal solution for the given optimization problem.

Program 4.2 ***Development of the `init_genA` Function***

```
function pop=init_genA(np,nsbit)
% np solutions with nsbits to describe the numerical value
% an extra bit is also define to indicate the sign
pop=rand(np,nsbit+1)>0.5;
```

The binary GA operates by utilizing binary strings to represent candidate solutions. Given this framework, it becomes essential to have a routine that can convert these binary strings into decimal data. Section B of the implementation addresses this requirement. The primary purpose of this conversion is to evaluate each candidate solution in terms of the cost function, translating the binary-encoded solution into a format that can be quantitatively assessed. This conversion routine is an integral part of the binary GA process and is invoked at various stages of the implementation whenever such a transformation is needed. By converting the binary strings to decimal values, the algorithm can apply the cost function to these values, thereby determining the fitness of each solution in the population. This evaluation is crucial for the subsequent steps of selection, crossover, and mutation, as it guides the algorithm in identifying and propagating superior solutions while discarding inferior ones. The specifics of this binary-to-decimal conversion process are encapsulated in the function bintodecA, as detailed in Program 4.3. This function systematically takes each binary string from the population and converts it into its corresponding decimal value, thereby preparing the solution for fitness evaluation. The accuracy and efficiency of bintodecA are vital for the overall effectiveness of the binary GA, as it ensures that the evolutionary process is based on a reliable and meaningful assessment of each candidate solution.

Program 4.3 ***Implementation of the Function `bintodecA`***

```
function [dec]=bintodecA(bin)
 global range;
% It is evaluated the size of the string
% this part corresponds to the numeric part
 nn=length(bin)-1;
 num=bin(2:end);
% This is the part that determines the sign
sign=1-2*bin(1);
% Accumulator is initialized
dec=0;
% It is determined the maximal number to represent
 dp=floor(log2(max(abs(range))));
% Here the number is converted
 for i=1:nn,
```

```
dec=dec+num(i)*2^(dp-i);
 end
 dec=dec*sign;
```

In the implementation of the binary GA, the first genetic operator applied is the selection operation, which is carried out in Section C. The primary aim of this selection process is to encourage the propagation of good solutions within the population and to eliminate poorer solutions, all while keeping the total number of candidate solutions constant. This step is crucial in guiding the evolutionary progress of the algorithm. In the specific problem being addressed, the cost function includes negative fitness values. This characteristic makes the proportional selection method less suitable, as it typically assumes positive fitness values for effective operation. Consequently, the ranking selection method is chosen for this implementation. This method involves organizing all solutions based on their fitness values, where the solution with the lowest fitness is given the rank of 1, and the solution with the highest fitness is assigned the rank of N. This ranking system allows for a more equitable and effective selection process, especially in cases involving negative fitness values. To implement this ranking selection method, the following segment of MATLAB code is utilized:

```
1. [D I] = sort(fP,'descend');
2. r = 1:length(D);
3. r(I) = r;
```

This code segment is designed to assess the fitness of each solution in the population, rank them accordingly, and then use these ranks to guide the selection of solutions for the next generation. By doing so, the algorithm systematically favors solutions that are more likely to lead toward an optimal or near-optimal solution, while also maintaining a diverse and robust population of candidate solutions.

In the MATLAB code for the ranking selection process, the initial step involves organizing the fitness values of the population, denoted as fP, in descending order. This arrangement is accomplished in the first line of the code. Subsequently, lines 2 and 3 are dedicated to assigning an appropriate rank to each element in the sorted list. This ranking is inverse to the fitness order, meaning the solution with the highest fitness receives the highest rank.

Once the solutions are ranked, the proportional selection operator is applied, but with a twist: instead of using the fitness values directly, the ranks of the solutions are used. This approach is particularly useful when dealing with negative fitness values, as it circumvents the issues associated with the proportional selection method under such conditions.

To execute this modified proportional selection process, the selection probabilities P_i for each solution i are first determined. Following this, the cumulative probability P_i^A for each element x_i is calculated. This step is crucial as it sets the stage for the selection of solutions based on their cumulative probabilities.

The selection of a solution emulating the proportional selection process involves generating a uniformly distributed random number u. The solution whose cumulative probability range is most closely aligned with the random number u is then chosen. This methodology ensures that solutions with higher ranks (and therefore better fitness) have a higher probability of being selected, while still maintaining an element of randomness.

This entire process is encapsulated in the function seleccionR, as outlined in Program 4.4. The function seleccionR effectively demonstrates the integration of ranking with proportional selection, showcasing an innovative approach to selection in GAs, especially in scenarios where fitness values might be negative or where a more equitable selection process is desired.

Program 4.4 ***Implementation of the function*** `seleccionR`

```
function [iE] = seleccionR(fP)
% It is assigned a rank to each solution
% The worst has the rank 1
% the best the rank N
Ps=length(fP);
[D I] = sort(fP,'descend');
r = 1:length(D);
   r(I) = r;
fP=r;
suma=0;
% The roulette-wheel process
for k=1:Ps
 P(k)=fP(k)/(sum(fP));
 suma=suma+P(k);
 A(k)=suma; % cumulative probability
end
R=rand;
for u=1:Ps
    if (A(u)>=R)
      break
    end
end
% iE is the selected element
iE=u;
end
```

Section D of the binary GA implementation focuses on the crossover operation. This key process involves the selection of two candidate solutions, labeled as a and b, which are randomly chosen from the population to act as parent solutions. The crossover operation is fundamental in combining the genetic material of these parent solutions to produce new offspring, thereby contributing to the genetic diversity and evolution of the population.

The next step in the crossover operation is the random selection of a crossover point, denoted as cpointcpoint. This point can be any number from 1 to 17, corresponding to the positions in the binary string. The crossover point determines where the segments of the binary strings from the two parent solutions will be exchanged or swapped. This exchange of genetic material is crucial as it creates new combinations of traits, which could potentially lead to better solutions.

Program 4.5 ***Implementation of the Function*** `crossoverA`

```
function [c,d]=crossoverA(a,b)
nn=length(a);
```

```
% two new individuals are generated by crossover
% cpoint represents the point where both
% solutions are swapped
cpoint=floor(nn*rand)+1;
c=[a(1:cpoint) b(cpoint+1:end)];
d=[b(1:cpoint) a(cpoint+1:end)];
```

The detailed procedure of the crossover operation is encapsulated in the function crossoverA, as presented in Program 4.5. The function crossoverA systematically executes the crossover process by first selecting the parent solutions, then determining the crossover point, and finally performing the swapping of the binary string segments at and beyond this point. The design of this function ensures that the crossover process is conducted efficiently and effectively, allowing for the exploration of new areas in the solution space and enhancing the overall capability of the GA to find optimal or near-optimal solutions.

In Section E of the binary GA implementation, the focus is on the mutation operation, which plays a critical role in maintaining genetic diversity within the population. The mutation process begins by determining a fixed number of mutation sites, denoted as nsitensite. This number represents how many bits in the original binary string will undergo mutation, essentially serving as a control for the extent of genetic alteration in each iteration.

Once nsitensite is established, the algorithm initiates a loop that runs for nsitensite iterations. During each iteration of this loop, two key operations are performed to mutate the binary string. The first step involves randomly selecting a bit position in the string, which can be any position from 1 to 17. The second step is to flip this selected bit to its opposite logic state; if the bit is currently a '1', it is changed to a '0', and vice versa. This bit-flipping introduces small, random changes to the genetic makeup of the solutions, aiding in the exploration of the solution space and preventing the algorithm from converging prematurely to local optima.

This mutation process is encapsulated in the function mutate, detailed in Program 4.5. The mutate function systematically executes these operations, ensuring that each solution in the population has a chance to undergo slight genetic modifications. This controlled alteration of the genetic structure is crucial for the effectiveness of the GA, as it allows for the continuous introduction of new traits and characteristics into the population, fostering robustness and adaptability in the search for optimal solutions.

Program 4.6 ***Implementation of the Function*** `mutate`

```
function anew=mutate(a,nsite)
nn=length(a); anew=a;
% A new solution is generated with nsite modifications
% from the original binary string
for i=1:nsite,
j=floor(rand*nn)+1;
anew(j)=mod(a(j)+1,2);
 end
```

After executing Program 4.1, the system outputs the final solution as depicted in Figure 4.9.

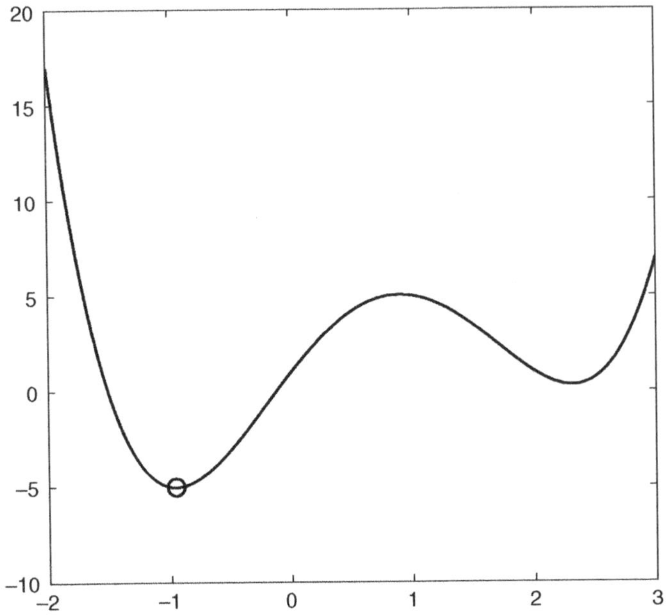

Figure 4.9 The outcome produced upon executing Program 4.1.

4.2.6 Genetic Algorithm Utilizing Real-Valued Parameters

The binary GA encounters specific challenges when optimizing continuous cost functions. In binary GAs, a fixed coding scheme is used to represent all decision variables, requiring the binary strings to be designed in such a way that they can encompass the minimum value of the cost function. However, as this minimum value is often unknown beforehand, this can lead to accuracy issues in the application of binary GAs.

To address these challenges, several implementations of GA with real parameters have been developed. In these versions, mutation and crossover operations are directly performed on real parameter values, eliminating the need for string coding. This approach is particularly advantageous when solving continuous optimization problems, as it does away with the conversion step from binary to real values, thus speeding up the execution compared to binary-coded GAs. Unlike their binary counterparts, GAs with real parameters can directly evaluate candidate solutions in terms of the cost function without an intermediate conversion step.

Despite these benefits, a significant challenge lies in adapting the original binary operators for use with real values. In the binary context, crossover and mutation operations are search mechanisms that are straightforward to conceptualize and implement. The objective is to develop equivalent operations for real-parameter candidate solutions, which can effectively serve as a search strategy. For instance, in this context, the crossover operation is no longer about swapping information but can be reinterpreted as a blending operator for real parameters.

In this section, we will discuss the most popular operators for crossover and mutation in the context of real-parameter GAs. These discussions aim to illuminate how these operators can be effectively adapted and applied in continuous optimization scenarios, leveraging the advantages of real-parameter representation while maintaining the robust search capabilities of GAs.

4.2.7 Crossover Operator for Real-Valued Parameters

One of the earliest and simplest crossover operators for floating-point representation is the linear crossover (Simon 2013). In this approach, two n-dimensional parent solutions, $\mathbf{p}_1 = \{p_1^1, \dots, p_1^n\}$ and $\mathbf{p}_2 = \{p_1^1, \dots, p_1^n\}$, are linearly combined to generate three distinct offspring solutions, $\mathbf{c}_1$, $\mathbf{c}_2$ and $\mathbf{c}_3$. The computation of these offspring solutions is as follows:

$$
\begin{aligned}
\mathbf{c}_1 &= \mathbf{p}_1 + \mathbf{p}_2 \\
\mathbf{c}_2 &= 1.5\mathbf{p}_1 - 0.5\mathbf{p}_2 \\
\mathbf{c}_3 &= -0.5\mathbf{p}_1 + 1.5\mathbf{p}_2
\end{aligned}
\tag{4.8}
$$

Out of these three solutions, the two with the best performance according to the objective function are chosen as the offspring resulting from the crossover process (forming new candidate solutions).

In the arithmetic crossover method (Simon 2013), two-parent candidate solutions, $\mathbf{p}_1$ and $\mathbf{p}_2$, are merged to create a new solution based on the following formula:

$$\mathbf{c}_1 = (1 - \gamma)\mathbf{p}_1 + \gamma\mathbf{p}_2 \tag{4.9}$$

where γ is a value within the range $[0, 1]$. The new solution $\mathbf{c}_1$ is essentially a weighted sum of its parent solutions $\mathbf{p}_1$ and $\mathbf{p}_2$.

Through the blend crossover method (BLX-α) (Deb 2001), a new solution $\mathbf{c}_1$ emerges from the merging of two parent solutions, $\mathbf{p}_1$ and $\mathbf{p}_2$, exhibiting the following characteristics:

$$\mathbf{c}_1 = (1 - \rho)\mathbf{p}_1 + \rho\mathbf{p}_2 \tag{4.10}$$

Contrary to the arithmetic crossover, the value of ρ is established in the following manner:

$$\rho = (1 - 2\alpha)U(0, 1) - \alpha \tag{4.11}$$

where $U(0, 1)$ denotes a random number uniformly distributed between 0 and 1, and α is a constant that falls within the range $[0, 1]$.

The blend crossover (BLX-α) generates a new solution in its first dimension, c_1^1, which is randomly positioned within the interval $\left[p_1^1 - \alpha\left(p_2^1 - p_1^1\right), p_2^1 - \alpha\left(p_2^1 - p_1^1\right)\right]$. In the context of the BLX-α, it is generally assumed that $p_1^1 < p_2^1$.

A notable feature of the BLX-α blending operator is that the location of the new solution $\mathbf{c}_1$ depends on the distance $d(\mathbf{p}_1, \mathbf{p}_2)$ between the parent solutions $\mathbf{p}_1$ and $\mathbf{p}_2$. Essentially, if the distance between $\mathbf{p}_1$ and $\mathbf{p}_2$ is substantial, the distances $d(\mathbf{c}_1, \mathbf{p}_1)$ and $d(\mathbf{c}_1, \mathbf{p}_2)$ between the new solution $\mathbf{c}_1$ and its parents will also be significant. This characteristic of the BLX-α facilitates a more extensive exploration of the search space compared to the weighted approach used in arithmetic crossover. The reason for this enhanced exploration capability lies in the stochastic component incorporated in the blend crossover, as outlined in Eq. 4.11. By allowing for a broader range of potential solution positions within the interval, the BLX-α crossover can traverse more diverse areas of the search space, potentially leading to more effective solutions in optimization problems.

The Simulated Binary Crossover (SBX) method (Matyas 1965) mimics the mechanics of the one-point crossover used in binary representations but is adapted for real-valued parameters. In the SBX approach, two parent solutions, $\mathbf{p}_1$ and $\mathbf{p}_2$, are selected to generate two new offspring solutions, $\mathbf{c}_1$ and $\mathbf{c}_2$. A key aspect of the SBX process is the inclusion of a dispersion factor, denoted as n_c, which significantly influences the outcome of the crossover operation.

The value of n_c plays a crucial role in determining the proximity of the new solutions to their parents. When n_c is set to a large value, there's a higher likelihood that the offspring solutions $\mathbf{c}_1$ and $\mathbf{c}_2$ will be located close to their parent solutions $\mathbf{p}_1$ and $\mathbf{p}_2$. Conversely, smaller values of n_c

tend to result in the new solutions being positioned farther away from the parents. This parameter thus controls the extent to which the offspring solutions explore the search space relative to their parents.

The generation of the new solutions $\mathbf{c}_1$ and $\mathbf{c}_2$ in SBX is executed through a specific process. This process involves calculations that take into account the values of the parent solutions, the dispersion factor n_c, and potentially other factors that govern the dynamics of the crossover. The SBX method is particularly effective in ensuring a balanced exploration of the search space, as it can be tuned to produce offspring that are either close to the parent solutions, facilitating local search, or further away, promoting the exploration of new areas in the search space. This adaptability makes SBX a versatile and powerful crossover technique in the realm of GAs with real-valued parameters. Firstly, a quasi-random factor β is generated by the following formulation:

$$\beta = \begin{cases} (2r)^{\frac{1}{n_c+1}} & \text{if } r \leq 0.5 \\ \left(\dfrac{1}{2(1-r)}\right)^{\frac{1}{n_c+1}} & \text{otherwise} \end{cases} \tag{4.12}$$

where r is random number uniformly distributed $U(0, 1)$. Once computed β, the new solutions $\mathbf{c}_1$ and $\mathbf{c}_2$ are generated as follows:

$$\begin{aligned} \mathbf{c}_1 &= 0.5[(1+\beta)\mathbf{p}_1 + (1-\beta)\mathbf{p}_2] \\ \mathbf{c}_2 &= 0.5[(1-\beta)\mathbf{p}_1 + (1+\beta)\mathbf{p}_2] \end{aligned} \tag{4.13}$$

To demonstrate the impact of the SBX method in generating new individuals, a carefully structured experiment has been conducted. In this experiment, a series of 1000 crossover operations were performed, each considering varying values of the dispersion factor n_c. The objective was to analyze how different settings of n_c influence the distribution of offspring solutions.

To quantitatively assess the distribution of the new solutions generated by the SBX, a probability density analysis was conducted. This analysis involved creating a histogram with 100 bins, which provides a visual representation of the frequency distribution of the new solutions. By examining this histogram, insights into the spread and concentration of the offspring solutions relative to their parents can be gained.

For the purpose of this experiment, the parent solutions denoted as $\mathbf{p}_1$ and $\mathbf{p}_2$, were held constant at positions 2 and 5, respectively. This fixed positioning allows for a controlled examination of the effects of the SBX operator, as it eliminates variability arising from different parent locations.

The implementation of the SBX crossover, along with the experimental setup, is detailed in Program 4.7, written in MATLAB. This program not only executes the SBX crossover multiple times under various n_c values but also compiles and presents the resulting data in a histogram format. Through this experimental approach, a deeper understanding of the dynamics and effectiveness of the SBX method in real-parameter GAs can be attained, particularly in terms of how it navigates the search space to create diverse yet potentially viable new solutions.

Program 4.7 ***Execution of the Simulated Binary Crossover (SBX) Operation***

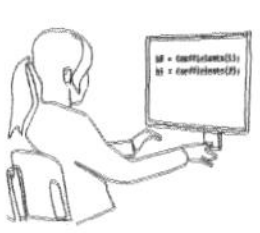

```
%Algorithm 4.7
% SBX crossover effect experiments
% Initialization
```

```
nc=2; % Dispersion factor
p1=2; % Parent 1
p2=5; % Parent 2
% Cycle of 1000 executions
for k=1:1000
% Random number U[0,1]
r=rand;
% SBX crossover
if r<=0.5
    mu=(2*r)^(1/(nc+1));
else
    mu=(1/(2*(1-r)))^(1/(nc+1));
end
c1(k)=((1+mu)*p1+(1-mu)*p2)*0.5;
c2(k)=((1-mu)*p1+(1+mu)*p2)*0.5;
end
CT=[c1 c2];
% Histogram of 100 bins
hist(CT,100)
```

Figure 4.10a and b present the outcomes of running Program 4.7, specifically illustrating the effects of varying the dispersion factor n_c in theSBX operation. These figures demonstrate the results for two different settings: $n_c = 2$ and $n_c = 5$, respectively.

From the data shown in Figure 4.10a, it is evident that when n_c is set to 2, the resultant solutions are widely distributed, showing a tendency to be located far from the values of their parent solutions. This indicates a greater explorative capability of the SBX operation under this setting, as it generates offspring that span a broader range of the search space.

Conversely, Figure 4.10b reveals a different scenario when n_c is increased to 5. In this case, the solutions are more densely clustered around the values of their parent solutions. This closer distribution suggests a more exploitative approach by the SBX operation, with offspring being generated

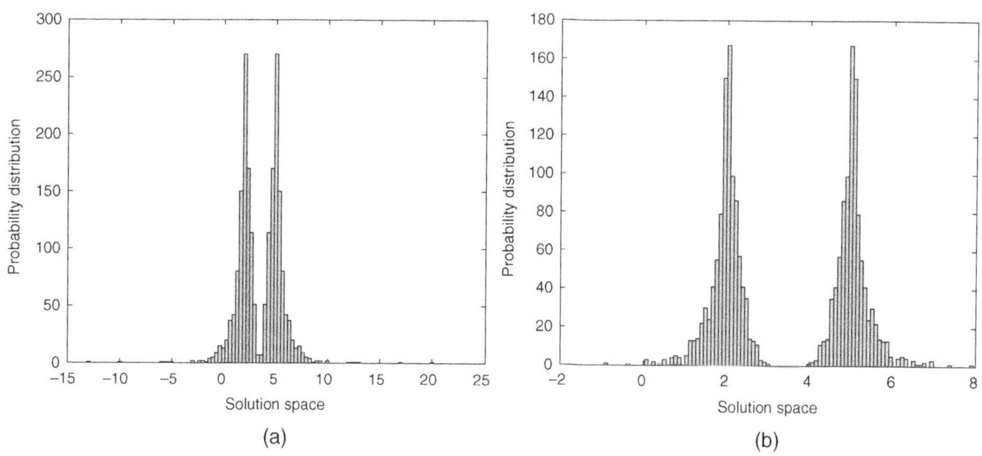

Figure 4.10 Impact of the Simulated Binary Crossover (SBX) Operation with (a) $n_c = 2$ and (b) $n_c = 5$.

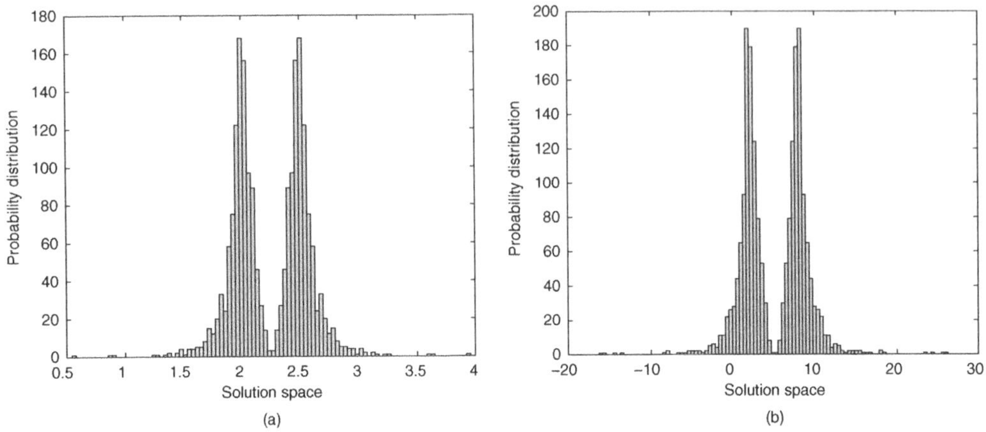

Figure 4.11 Impact of the Simulated Binary Crossover (SBX) Operation with (a) $\mathbf{p}_1 = 2, \mathbf{p}_2 = 2.5$ and (b) $\mathbf{p}_1 = 2, \mathbf{p}_2 = 8$.

in closer proximity to their parents, thus concentrating the search in the region around the parent solutions. These results highlight the influence of the dispersion factor n_c in the SBX process. By adjusting n_c, the balance between exploration and exploitation in the generation of new solutions can be controlled, making SBX a versatile and effective crossover technique in GAs for a wide range of optimization problems.

The SBX operation also exhibits a notable effect based on the proximity of the parent solutions to each other. Specifically, when the parent solutions are located close to one another, the newly generated candidate solutions tend to be produced near these parental positions. In contrast, if the parents are situated at a considerable distance from each other, the resultant offspring solutions are typically generated farther away from the parent locations. This behavior occurs even when the dispersion factor n_c is held constant.

To demonstrate this aspect of the SBX crossover, an additional experiment was designed. In this experiment, a total of 1000 crossover operations were conducted, all with the dispersion factor set to $n_c = 2$. The probability density of the newly created solutions was then analyzed using a histogram comprising 100 bins. For this experiment, the parent solutions, $\mathbf{p}_1$ and $\mathbf{p}_2$, were fixed at two different sets of positions: (a) $\mathbf{p}_1 = 2, \mathbf{p}_2 = 2.5$ and (b) $\mathbf{p}_1 = 2, \mathbf{p}_2 = 8$. This setup was chosen to observe the effects of varying distances between parent solutions on the offspring distribution.

Modifications were made to Program 4.7 to facilitate this experiment. Figure 4.11 presents the resulting distribution of solutions for both scenarios. The figure is expected to reveal distinct patterns of offspring distribution in relation to the proximity of their parents. Such findings underscore the sensitivity of the SBX crossover to parent solution positioning, highlighting its capability to adapt the search strategy based on the spatial arrangement of solutions within the optimization landscape. This adaptability is a crucial feature, particularly in optimization problems where the landscape's topography varies significantly.

Observations from Figure 4.11 reveal significant insights into the behavior of the new solutions generated by the SBX operation. In case (b), where the parent solutions are closer together ($\mathbf{p}_1 = 2$, $\mathbf{p}_2 = 2.5$), the offspring solutions are found to be distributed near the parents. Conversely, in case (b), with a larger distance between the parents ($\mathbf{p}_1 = 2$, $\mathbf{p}_2 = 8$.), the new solutions are distributed farther away from the original parent solutions.

This pattern strongly suggests that the distribution of new solutions in SBX is heavily influenced by the proximity of the parent solutions. The effect can be interpreted as a dynamic shift between exploration and exploitation mechanisms, depending on the distance between the parent solutions. When the parents are positioned far apart, the SBX crossover acts as an exploration mechanism, spreading the search across a wider area of the solution space. This approach is beneficial for discovering diverse and potentially better areas of the search landscape that have not been previously examined.

On the other hand, when the parent solutions are situated close to each other, the SBX crossover functions more as an exploitation operator. In this scenario, the search is concentrated around the vicinity of the parent solutions, intensively examining the local area for optimal or near-optimal solutions. This focused approach is advantageous for fine-tuning and refining solutions in a specific region of the search space.

Thus, the SBX crossover's ability to modulate between exploration and exploitation based on parent proximity makes it a versatile and effective tool in the optimization process, adept at navigating diverse and complex solution landscapes.

The crossover operations discussed previously predominantly involve the blending of two parent solutions to create new offspring. However, in the realm of GAs, there's an evolving exploration of multi-parent crossover operators. These operators, by incorporating more than two parents in the blending process, can significantly enhance the explorative capabilities of the algorithm, compared to traditional two-parent operators.

Multi-parent crossover allows for a more comprehensive interchange of spatial information, facilitating the generation of new solutions in potentially promising regions of the search space. This approach leverages the diverse genetic information from multiple parents, thereby creating a richer pool of candidate solutions.

One such multi-parent crossover operator is the Unimodal Normal Distribution Crossover (UNDX) (Kirkpatrick et al. 1983), which specifically requires three parents to produce new individuals. The UNDX generates new candidate solutions based on an ellipsoidal probability distribution, characterized by two principal axes. The first axis (A) aligns with the line connecting two of the parents. The second axis (B) is orthogonal to the first, determined by the perpendicular distance from the third parent to axis A.

Although the UNDX operator can technically operate with more than three parents, its most common application in practical scenarios involves just three. In the UNDX process, n_μ parents (typically $n_\mu = 3$) are randomly chosen from the population. The resulting offspring are then produced based on this ellipsoidal distribution, which considers the spatial relationship between these selected parents. By doing so, the UNDX method effectively navigates the search space, utilizing the collective attributes of multiple parents to explore new solution territories that might not be reachable with traditional two-parent crossover methods. Subsequently, the mean calculation is performed using only $n_\mu - 1$ parents, as described below:

$$\overline{\mathbf{p}} = \frac{1}{n_\mu - 1} \sum_{i=1}^{n_\mu - 1} \mathbf{p}_i \tag{4.14}$$

Following this, the direction vectors $\mathbf{d}_i$ for all $n_\mu - 1$ parents are determined using the formula $\mathbf{d}_i = \mathbf{p}_i - \overline{\mathbf{p}}$. Subsequently, the direction cosines are calculated through the equation below:

$$\mathbf{e}_i = \frac{\mathbf{e}_i}{|\mathbf{e}_i|} \tag{4.15}$$

where $|\mathbf{e}_i|$ represents the magnitude of the vector $\mathbf{e}_i$. Utilizing these vectors, one of the axes of the ellipsoidal probability distribution is constructed. Subsequently, the final (third) parent, n_μ, is taken

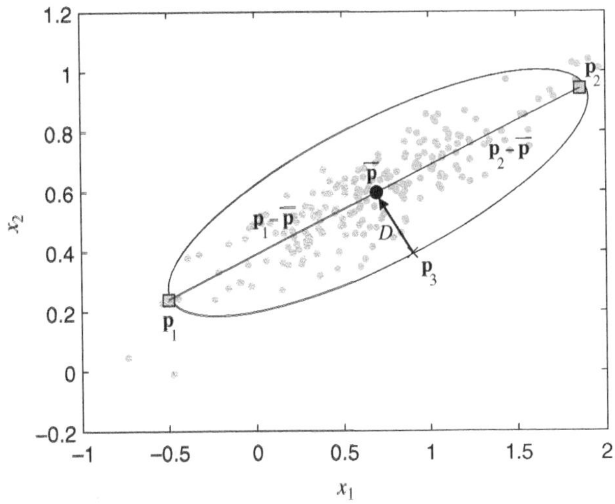

Figure 4.12 The Ellipsoidal Probability Distribution in the UNDX Method.

into account to determine the other orthogonal axis D. The value of D is calculated based on the positions of the three parents, $\mathbf{p}_1$, $\mathbf{p}_2$ and $\mathbf{p}_3$, in the following manner:

$$D = |\mathbf{p}_3 - \mathbf{p}_1| \cdot \left(1 - \left(\frac{(\mathbf{p}_3 - \mathbf{p}_1)^T(\mathbf{p}_2 - \mathbf{p}_1)}{|\mathbf{p}_3 - \mathbf{p}_1||\mathbf{p}_2 - \mathbf{p}_1|}\right)\right)^{\frac{1}{2}} \tag{4.16}$$

Figure 4.12 provides a visual representation of the ellipsoidal probability distribution. In this figure, the square points indicate the positions of parents $\mathbf{p}_1$ and $\mathbf{p}_2$, while the cross point represents parent $\mathbf{p}_3$. As depicted in Figure 4.12, the probability distribution encompasses two axes. The first axis, which is the major axis, is formed by the vectors $\mathbf{p}_1 - \overline{\mathbf{p}}$ and $\mathbf{p}_2 - \overline{\mathbf{p}}$. The second axis, considered the minor axis, is defined by the orthogonal vector D.

After establishing the ellipsoidal probability distribution, the generation of new solutions follows this model:

$$\mathbf{c}_i = \overline{\mathbf{p}} + \sum_{j=1}^{n_\mu - 1} N\left(0, \sigma_1^2\right) |\mathbf{d}_j| \mathbf{e}_j + N\left(0, \sigma_2^2\right) D\mathbf{e}_{n_\mu}, \tag{4.17}$$

where

$$\sigma_1 = \frac{0.30}{\sqrt{n_\mu - 2}}, \qquad \sigma_2 = \frac{0.35}{\sqrt{n_\mu - 2}}, \tag{4.18}$$

To demonstrate the impact of the UNDX on the creation of new individuals, a specific experiment has been designed. This experiment involves generating a set of 500 new individuals, with the parent solutions randomly selected from the search space. For the purposes of this study, a two-dimensional scenario is considered to simplify the visualization and analysis of the results.

Program 4.8, written in MATLAB, details the implementation of the UNDX method as well as the setup for the experiment. This program not only executes the UNDX operation but also sets the parameters and conditions under which the parent solutions are chosen, and new individuals are generated. By randomizing the selection of parents within the search space, the experiment aims to provide a comprehensive view of how UNDX navigates and explores the solution landscape.

Through this experimental approach, insights can be gained into the efficacy of UNDX in diversifying the population and enhancing the search process. By examining the distribution and characteristics of the newly generated individuals, the strengths and potential limitations of the UNDX method in real-world optimization scenarios can be better understood. This experiment, therefore, serves as a valuable tool for evaluating the performance of UNDX in GAs, particularly in terms of its ability to effectively combine and utilize genetic information from multiple parents.

Program 4.8 ***Execution of the Unimodal Normal Distribution Crossover (UNDX) Operation***

```
%Algorithm 4.8
% UNDX crossover effect experiments
% Initialization
clear all
% Number of new solutions generated
Npts=500;
% Selection of parents
p1=randn(1,2);
p2=randn(1,2);
p3=randn(1,2);
% The parents are highlighted
plot(p1(1),p1(2),'or');
hold on
plot(p2(1),p2(2),'or');
% The mean of the first two parents
m=(p1+p2)/2;
% Directions vectors
    d1=p1-m;
    d2=p2-m;
    d3=p3-m;
% Direction cosines
    e1=d1/(norm(d1));
    e2=d2/(norm(d2));
    e3=d3/(norm(d3));
% The orthogonal axis
  D= norm(p3-p1)*((1-((((p3-p1)*(p2-p1)')/(norm(p3-p1)*
       norm(p2-p1)))^2))^0.5);
for it=1:Npts
    t1=0.30*randn*norm(d1)*e1+0.30*randn*norm(d2)*e2;
    t2=0.35*randn*D*e3;
    c(it,:)=m+t1+t2;
end
% The solutions are shown
plot(p1(1),p1(2),'o','MarkerSize',10,'MarkerFaceColor','r');
```

```
hold on
plot(p2(1),p2(2),'o','MarkerSize',10,'MarkerFaceColor','k');
plot(p3(1),p3(2),'o','MarkerSize',10,'MarkerFaceColor','g');
plot(c(:,1),c(:,2),'ob');
```

Figure 4.13 showcases the results of several runs of Program 2.8, highlighting some intriguing configurations produced by the UNDX operation. In this figure, the square points denote the parent solutions $\mathbf{p}_1$ and $\mathbf{p}_2$, while the cross point represents the third parent, $\mathbf{p}_3$.

In Figure 4.13a, the distribution of the new solutions predominantly aligns along the major axis, which is defined by the vector connecting the parents $\mathbf{p}_1$ and $\mathbf{p}_2$. This alignment indicates that the offspring solutions are being generated in a manner that closely follows the line of descent from these two parent solutions, emphasizing the genetic influence of $\mathbf{p}_1$ and $\mathbf{p}_2$ on the new solutions.

Conversely, Figure 4.13b illustrates a different scenario where the new solutions are more broadly dispersed in the direction of the orthogonal axis D. This distribution suggests a more explorative approach of the UNDX, as it produces offspring solutions that deviate from the direct lineage of $\mathbf{p}_1$ and $\mathbf{p}_2$, and instead, incorporate more influence from the position of the third parent, $\mathbf{p}_3$.

These different configurations of solution distributions in Figure 4.13 provide valuable insights into the dynamics of the UNDX crossover. They illustrate how the positioning and relationship of the parent solutions can significantly influence the areas of the search space being explored by the generated offspring, demonstrating the versatility and adaptability of the UNDX method in exploring and exploiting the solution landscape in GAs.

The Parent Centric Crossover (PCX) (Fletcher and Powell 1963) is a multi-parent crossover operation designed to generate new solutions in close proximity to a selected parent. Although PCX can involve several parents in its process, it is typically implemented with three parents. In this operation, n_μ parents are randomly chosen from the current population, where n_μ is usually set to 3.

Once the parents are selected, one parent, denoted as $\mathbf{p}_i$, is randomly picked from these n_μ parents. The new individual $\mathbf{c}_i$ is then created in the vicinity of this chosen parent $\mathbf{p}_i$. The generation process of $\mathbf{c}_i$ in PCX is structured into five distinct stages:

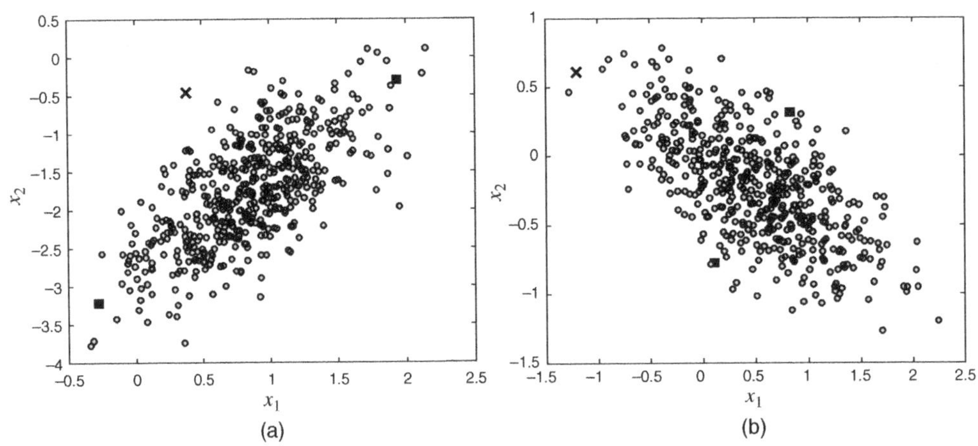

Figure 4.13 Different Sets of solutions generated across two generations using the UNDX crossover method.

The first stage (Central Point Calculation) involves calculating the central point $\overline{\mathbf{p}}$ of all the selected parents. This central point represents the average position of all the parent solutions in the solution space.

The next step (Direction Vector Computation) is to compute a direction vector between the selected parent $\mathbf{p}_i$ and the central point $\overline{\mathbf{p}}$. This is achieved with the formula $\mathbf{d}_i = \mathbf{p}_i - \overline{\mathbf{p}}$, which essentially measures the relative position of $\mathbf{p}_i$ with respect to the central point.

Subsequently, the direction cosines for all parents are calculated (Calculation of Direction Cosines). The direction cosine for each parent, $\mathbf{e}_i$, is normalized by dividing by its magnitude $|\mathbf{e}_i|$, resulting in $\mathbf{e}_i = \mathbf{e}_i/|\mathbf{e}_i|$.

In the fourth stage, the orthogonal distances δ_j (for j ranging from 1 to n_μ, excluding i) of the remaining $n_\mu - 1$ parents to the vector $\mathbf{d}_i$ are determined. Subsequently, the mean orthogonal distance is computed in the following manner:

$$\overline{\delta} = \frac{\sum_{j=1, j\neq i}^{n_\mu} \delta_j}{n_\mu - 1} \tag{4.19}$$

Ultimately, in the fifth and final step, a new solution is generated using this model:

$$\mathbf{c}_k = \mathbf{p}_i + N\left(0, \sigma_1^2\right) |\mathbf{d}_i| + \sum_{j=1, j\neq i}^{n_\mu} N\left(0, \sigma_2^2\right) \overline{\delta}\, \mathbf{e}_j \tag{4.20}$$

These steps collectively set the foundation for the PCX operation. The central point and direction vectors play a crucial role in determining the region of the search space where the new solution $\mathbf{c}_i$ will be located. This parent-centric approach of PCX ensures that the offspring solutions are not just random variants but are strategically positioned near one of the parent solutions, thereby maintaining a balance between exploring new areas and exploiting the known good regions of the search space.

In the PCX operation, the parameters σ_1 and σ_2 are crucial as they determine the extent or size of dispersion in the generation of new solutions. Figure 4.14 provides a visual depiction of this process, illustrating the generation of 500 new individuals. Within this figure, the square points represent the parent solutions $\mathbf{p}_1$, $\mathbf{p}_2$ and $\mathbf{p}_3$.

In this particular example, parent $\mathbf{p}_1$ is consistently selected as the basis for generating new candidate solutions. Consequently, when calculating a new individual $\mathbf{c}_k$, the focus is on determining the orthogonal distances δ_2 and δ_3. These distances are measured in relation to the vector $\mathbf{d}_i$, which represents the directional vector from the central point of the parents to the selected parent $\mathbf{p}_1$. This method of generating new solutions ensures that they are influenced significantly by the position and characteristics of the chosen parent, $\mathbf{p}_1$, while also taking into account the spatial information provided by the other parents. This approach facilitates the creation of offspring that are not only diverse but also closely aligned with the promising regions of the search space identified by the parent solutions. Subsequently, after determining the average orthogonal distance $\overline{\delta}$, the position of $\mathbf{c}_i$ is calculated using the model:

$$\mathbf{c}_k = \mathbf{p}_1 + N\left(0, \sigma_1^2\right) |\mathbf{d}_1| + N\left(0, \sigma_2^2\right) \overline{\delta}\mathbf{e}_2 + N\left(0, \sigma_2^2\right) \overline{\delta}\mathbf{e}_3 \tag{4.21}$$

To demonstrate the effectiveness of the PCX in generating new individuals, a specific experiment has been set up. This experiment involves performing 300 crossover operations, each with a random selection of parent solutions. The primary focus is to observe and plot the positions of the solutions generated through these operations.

In this experimental setup, three parent solutions are assumed, and the dispersion factors are set as $\sigma_1 = 0.15$ and $\sigma_2 = 0.15$. These parameters are chosen to provide insight into how the PCX

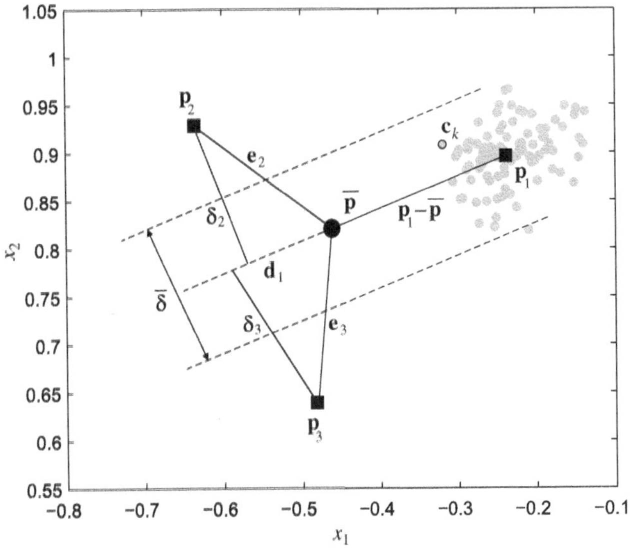

Figure 4.14 Creation of Solutions Using the PCX Crossover Method.

method navigates the solution space and how it influences the dispersion of offspring solutions around the parent solutions.

Program 4.9, implemented in MATLAB, demonstrates the execution of the PCX crossover in a two-dimensional context. This program not only carries out the crossover operations but also includes the functionality to visualize the resulting solution positions. By analyzing these plots, one can gain a deeper understanding of the spatial dynamics of the PCX method, particularly in terms of how it balances the exploration and exploitation aspects in the generation of new solutions. The experiment, therefore, serves as a practical example to evaluate the PCX crossover's ability to effectively utilize parent information in producing diverse yet promising candidate solutions in GAs.

Program 4.9 ***Execution of the Parent Centric Crossover (PCX) Operation***

```
%Algorithm 4.9
% PCX crossover effect experiments
% Initialization
clear all
% Number of generated points
Npts=300;
% Dispersion factors sigma 1 and sigma 2
sigma1=0.15;
sigma2=0.15;
% Parents are randomly produced
p1=randn(1,2);
p2=randn(1,2);
p3=randn(1,2);
% Calculate the parent central point
```

```
m=(p1+p2+p3)/3;
% Direction vector
    d1=p1-m;
    d2=p2-m;
    d3=p3-m;
% Direction cosines
    e1=d1/(norm(d1));
    e2=d2/(norm(d2));
    e3=d3/(norm(d3));
% Cycle of 300 executions
for it=1:Npts
   % One parent is randomly selected
    N = randi(3);
   % If the selected parent is one
   if N==1
    % Orthogonal distance are computed
    D2=norm(p3-p1)*((1-((((p3-p1)*(m-p1)')/(norm(p3-p1)*norm(m-p1)))^2))^0.5);
    D3=norm(p2-p1)*((1-((((p2-p1)*(m-p1)')/(norm(p2-p1)*norm(m-p1)))^2))^0.5);
    % The average orthogonal value
    D=(D2+D3)/2;
    c(it,:)=p1+sigma1*randn*d1+sigma2*randn*D*e2+sigma2*randn*D*e3;
   end
    % If the selected parent is two
    if N==2
     D1=norm(p3-p2)*((1-((((p3-p2)*(m-p2)')/(norm(p3-p2)*norm(m-p2)))^2))^0.5);
     D3= norm(p1-p2)*((1-((((p1-p2)*(m-p2)')/(norm(p1-p2)*norm(m-p2)))^2))^0.5);
     D=(D1+D3)/2;
     c(it,:)=p2+sigma1*randn*d2+sigma2*randn*D*e1+sigma2*randn*D*e3;
    end
     % If the selected parent is three
     if N==3
     D1= norm(p2-p3)*((1-((((p2-p3)*(m-p3)')/(norm(p2-p3)*norm(m-p3)))^2))^0.5);
     D2= norm(p1-p3)*((1-((((p1-p3)*(m-p3)')/(norm(p1-p3)*norm(m-p3)))^2))^0.5);
     D=(D1+D2)/2;
     c(it,:)=p3+sigma1*randn*d3+sigma2*randn*D*e1+sigma2*randn*D*e2;
     end
end
% Results are shown
plot(c(:,1),c(:,2),'ob');
hold on
plot(p1(1),p1(2),'o','MarkerSize',10,'MarkerFaceColor','r');
plot(p2(1),p2(2),'o','MarkerSize',10,'MarkerFaceColor','k');
plot(p3(1),p3(2),'o','MarkerSize',10,'MarkerFaceColor','g');
```

Figure 4.15 displays the outcomes from several runs of Program 4.9, showcasing a range of interesting configurations. In the figure, square points denote the parent solutions $\mathbf{p}_1$, $\mathbf{p}_2$ and $\mathbf{p}_3$, while the other points represent the newly generated individuals.

In Figure 4.15a, the new solutions are created using dispersion factors $\sigma_1 = 0.15$ and $\sigma_2 = 0.15$. Conversely, Figure 4.15b illustrates the scenario where the new solutions are generated with higher dispersion factors, $\sigma_1 = 0.35$ and $\sigma_2 = 0.35$.

The results in Figure 4.15 demonstrate how the values of σ_1 and σ_2 influence the distribution of new solutions in relation to the parent positions. Specifically, when σ_1 and σ_2 are set low, the resultant solutions tend to be located closer to the parent solutions, indicating a more concentrated or exploitative search around the parent's region. In contrast, with higher values of σ_1 and σ_2, the solutions are generated further away from the parents, suggesting a broader, more exploratory

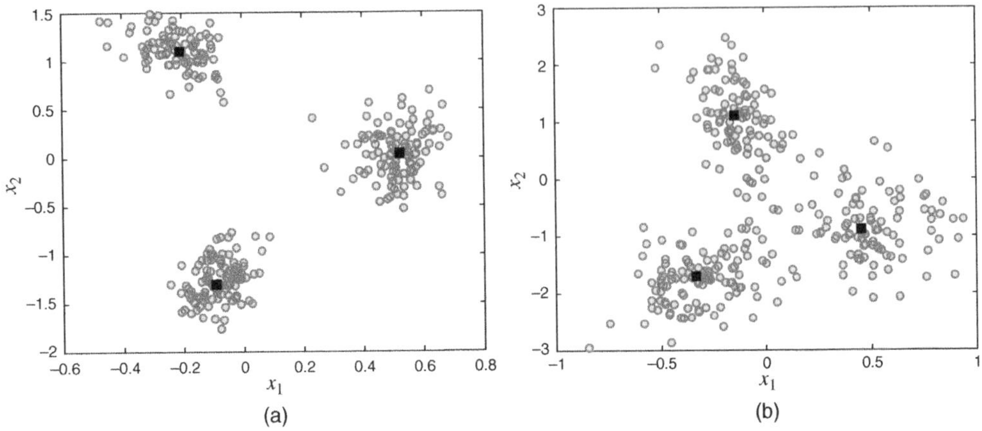

Figure 4.15 Distinct Sets of Solutions Generated by the PCX Crossover: (a) utilizing $\sigma_1 = 0.15, \sigma_2 = 0.15$, (b) using $\sigma_1 = 0.35, \sigma_2 = 0.35$.

search across the solution space. This variation in solution proximity based on the dispersion factors illustrates the adaptability of the PCX method in GAs, allowing it to effectively balance between local search and exploration of new areas in the search space.

4.2.8 Mutation Operator for Real-Valued Parameters

Mutation is a crucial operation in GAs, serving to alter candidate solutions with the primary aim of enhancing the diversity within the population. This search mechanism plays a key role in preventing the algorithm from becoming trapped in local minima. In this sub-section, we delve into the principal mutation operators specifically tailored for real-parameter optimization problems.

One of the most straightforward approaches to mutation in the realm of real-parameter GAs is the uniform mutation. In uniform mutation, a new solution, denoted as $\mathbf{c}_1^U$, is generated in the vicinity of an existing parent solution $\mathbf{p}_1$. This new solution is created based on a uniform probability distribution (Simon 2013). The uniform mutation strategy operates under the principle of equal probability, meaning that any value within the defined neighborhood of the parent solution has an equal chance of being selected. This approach is particularly effective in introducing random, yet controlled, variations to the solutions, thereby contributing to a broader exploration of the search space and reducing the likelihood of convergence to suboptimal solutions.

The simplicity of the uniform mutation method makes it a popular choice, especially due to its ease of implementation and its effectiveness in maintaining genetic diversity. By subtly altering the solutions, it ensures that the GA continually probes different areas of the solution space, which is crucial for finding optimal or near-optimal solutions in complex optimization problems. The uniform mutation method can be modeled as follows:

$$\mathbf{c}_1^U = \mathbf{p}_1 + (r - 0.5)\delta \tag{4.22}$$

where δ acts as a calibration factor that determines the extent of permissible perturbation. During the mutation process, there's a possibility that the value of $\mathbf{c}_1^U$ might exceed the predefined lower and upper bounds. In such scenarios, it is crucial to incorporate safeguards in the code implementation to prevent such occurrences.

One of the most widely used mutation methods is Normal mutation, which employs a zero-mean Gaussian probability distribution (Simon 2013). In this approach, a new solution $\mathbf{c}_1^N$ is derived from the parent solution $\mathbf{p}_1$ by adding a random number that is drawn from a normal Gaussian distribution. The normal mutation is generated by the following equation:

$$\mathbf{c}_1^N = \mathbf{p}_1 + N(0, \sigma) \tag{4.23}$$

where σ is a user-defined parameter, and $N(0, \sigma)$ represents a normal Gaussian distribution. The parameter σ dictates the magnitude of the alteration experienced by $\mathbf{p}_1$. Additionally, σ can be adaptively adjusted in each iteration following a specific predefined rule. This aspect of adaptability bears a strong resemblance to the mutation operation commonly used in Evolution Strategies (ES).

To examine the impact of both uniform and normal mutation operators, a MATLAB program has been developed. This program, outlined in Program 4.10, aims to visually present the results of mutation operations. In the program, the parent solution $\mathbf{p}_1$ is positioned at 1. For the uniform mutation, the parameter δ is set to 0.7, while for normal mutation, σ is configured at 0.1. Under these settings, a series of mutation operations are executed, with the results being compiled into a vector. A substantial number of mutations are necessary to ensure an accurate convergence toward a specific distribution pattern. The final output of the program is a set of histograms that display these distributions, providing a clear visual representation of the effects and tendencies of both mutation methods. This visual analysis serves as a useful tool for understanding the different dynamics and characteristics of uniform and normal mutation within the context of GAs.

Program 4.10 ***Uniform and Normal Mutation Methods***

```
%Algorithm 4.10
% Uniform and normal mutation
clear all
% Parent location
p1=1;
% Parameter configuration
delta=0.7; % For uniform
sigma=0.1; % For normal
% Cycle of mutations
for i=1:1000000
    c1(i)=p1+(rand-0.5)*delta; % For uniform
    c2(i)=p1+randn*sigma; % For normal
 end
% Histograms for both cases
hist(c1,50)
figure
hist(c2,50)
```

Program 4.10 demonstrates the application of MATLAB's rand and randn functions for generating random numbers corresponding to uniform and Gaussian distributions, respectively. These functions are integral to the implementation of uniform and normal mutation methods within the program. rand is utilized for uniform mutation, producing random numbers with a uniform distribution, while randn is employed for normal mutation, generating numbers based on a Gaussian distribution.

Figure 4.16 presents the histograms resulting from the execution of Program 2.10. These histograms visually represent the distributions of the mutated solutions generated by the program. They provide a clear and informative view of how each mutation method – uniform and normal – influences the distribution of solutions in the search space. By comparing these histograms, one can gain valuable insights into the characteristics and effects of each mutation strategy, observing the spread and concentration of solutions and how they vary between the two methods. This visual analysis is a crucial part of understanding the practical implications of using uniform and normal mutations in GAs and their impact on the exploration and exploitation balance in the search for optimal solutions.

The Simulated Binary Mutation (SBM) shares a similar conceptual foundation with the SBX, in that it seeks to mimic the characteristics of binary mutation within the context of real-parameter optimization (Broyden 1970). In the SBM approach, a new solution, denoted as $\mathbf{c}_1^B$, is derived by making probabilistic adjustments to a parent solution $\mathbf{p}_1$, keeping in mind the real-value nature of the solution space.

In this method, it is essential to recognize the bounds of the solution space, characterized by a defined minimum ($v_{\min}$) and maximum ($v_{\max}$) value. These boundaries ensure that the mutations remain within feasible limits of the problem being solved.

The key aspect of the SBM is its ability to emulate the effects of binary mutation in a probabilistic manner while operating in a real-parameter space. This emulation is achieved through the parameter p_B, which acts as a proxy for a binary mutation factor. Essentially, p_B determines the likelihood and extent of the mutation applied to the parent solution. By manipulating this parameter, the SBM can control the degree of variation introduced in the offspring solution, thus emulating the randomness and variability characteristic of traditional binary mutation, but in a real-valued optimization setting. This approach allows the SBM to effectively explore the solution space, introducing new

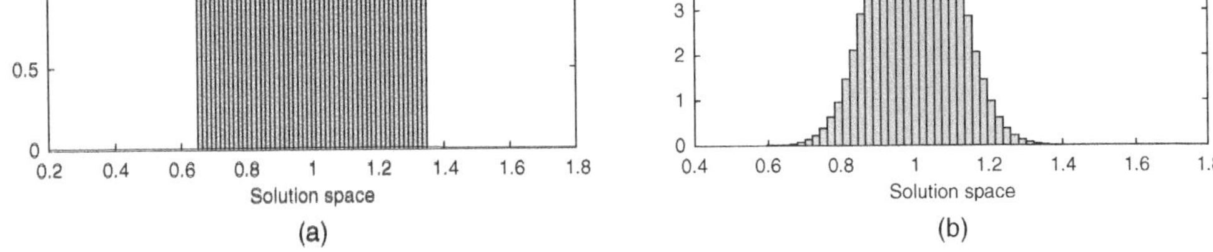

Figure 4.16 Impact of mutation operations in the scenarios of (a) uniform and (b) normal distributions.

variations that can lead to the discovery of better solutions, while still maintaining a tangible link to the principles of binary mutation. Consequently, the SBM process is executed through the following operation:

$$\mathbf{c}_1^B = \begin{cases} \mathbf{p}_1 + (1 - 2 \cdot \text{rand}(\cdot)) \cdot (v_{\max} - \mathbf{p}_1) & \text{rand}(\cdot) \leq p_B \\ \mathbf{p}_1 + (1 - 2 \cdot \text{rand}(\cdot)) \cdot (\mathbf{p}_1 - v_{\min}) & \text{otherwise} \end{cases} \tag{4.24}$$

where rand(·) generates a random number with a uniform distribution. To examine the impact of the SBM, a MATLAB program has been developed, enabling visualization of its mutation results. This program is outlined in Program 2.11. Within this program, the parent solution $\mathbf{p}_1$ is initially positioned at 1. The solution space for $\mathbf{p}_1$ is defined within the interval $[-3, 3]$. Moreover, the binary probability p_B is established at 0.5. To ensure accurate convergence to a specific distribution, a large number of mutations are required. The results are then presented in the form of histograms, offering a clear visual representation of the distribution patterns.

Figure 4.17 displays the histograms obtained after running Program 2.11. This figure showcases the results across four different scenarios: (a) $p_B = 0.1$, (b) $p_B = 0.25$, (c) $p_B = 0.5$ and (d) $p_B = 0.9$. Each of these cases represents a different setting for the binary probability p_B, allowing for an analysis of how varying levels of mutation probability affect the distribution of solutions. By comparing these histograms, one can discern the subtleties and nuances of the SBM process, particularly in relation to how the parameter p_B influences the exploration of the solution space and the diversity of the generated solutions.

Program 4.11 ***Simulated Binary Mutation Method***

```
%Algorithm 4.11
% Simulated binary mutation and normal mutation
clear all
% Parent location
p1=1;
% Parameter configuration
rangeMax=3; % Max value
rangeMin=-3; % Min Value
pB=0.5; % Binary probability
% Cycle of mutations
for i=1:1000000
    if rand<=pB
    c1(i)=p1+(1-2*rand)*(rangeMax-p1);
    else
    c1(i)=p1+(1-2*rand)*(p1-rangeMin);
    end
 end
% Histograms for both cases
hist(c1,50)
```

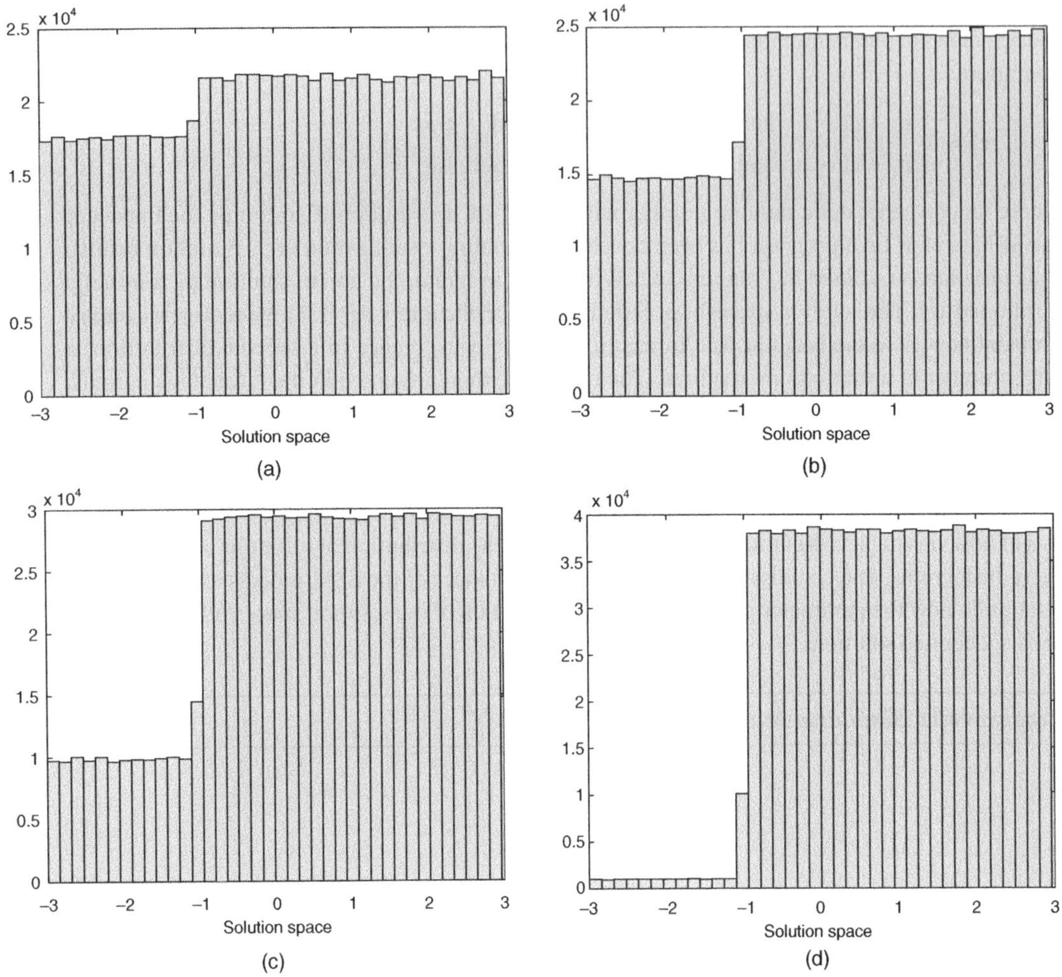

Figure 4.17 Impact of Simulated Binary Mutation operations in scenarios of (a) $p_B = 0.1$, (b) $p_B = 0.25$, (c) $p_B = 0.5$ and (d) $p_B = 0.9$.

Observations from Figure 4.17 distinctly show that the value of p_B (binary probability) significantly influences the generation of new solutions in the SBM process. Notably, as p_B increases, there is a corresponding increase in the likelihood of the new solution $\mathbf{c}_1^B$ falling within the interval $[-3, -1]$. This trend highlights the direct impact of the mutation probability on the dispersion and location of the mutated solutions.

The figure demonstrates that with lower values of p_B, the mutations tend to be more conservative, resulting in new solutions that are relatively close to the original parent position. However, as p_B is raised, the mutations become more aggressive, pushing the solutions further away from the parent and into wider regions of the solution space. This behavior underscores the role of p_B as a key parameter in controlling the exploration extent of the mutation process. By adjusting p_B, the algorithm can effectively navigate between localized search (exploitation) and wide-ranging search (exploration), making the SBM a versatile tool in the optimization process.

4.2.9 Computational Implementation of the GA with Real Parameters

This section integrates and implements the entire process of the real-parameter GA. To demonstrate how it is constructed, we consider the maximization of the following two-dimensional problem:

$$\begin{aligned} &\text{Maximize} \quad f(x_1, x_2) = 3(1 - x_1)^2 e^{-(x_1^2 - x_2^2)} - 10\left(\frac{x_1}{5} - x_1^3 - x_2^5\right) e^{(-x_1^2 - x_2^2)} - 1/3e^{(-(x_1+1)^2 - x_2^2)} \\ &\text{Subject to} \quad -3 \leq x_1, x_2 \leq 3 \end{aligned} \tag{4.25}$$

The graphical depiction of the specified cost function is provided in Figure 4.18. From the analysis of Figure 4.18, it's evident that the cost function encompasses three maxima: a global maximum situated at approximately $x_g \approx (0.0, 1.5)$ and two additional local maxima. Being a global optimization technique, GAs are designed to seek out solutions like x_g, the global maximum in this case.

An important characteristic of this cost function is the presence of negative fitness values. This aspect has significant implications for the choice of selection method within the GA framework. Specifically, the existence of negative fitness values suggests that the proportional selection method may not be the most suitable approach. Proportional selection typically operates on the principle of fitness proportionality, which can become problematic or less effective when dealing with negative fitness values. Therefore, alternative selection strategies that can handle such scenarios effectively are preferable to ensure the robust performance of the GA in identifying and converging on the global maximum solution x_g.

Program 4.11 provides a comprehensive implementation of the real-parameter GA. This implementation is structured to include several distinct functions, each designed to facilitate ease of analysis and understanding. The entire optimization process within this program is organized into four key sections, each corresponding to a specific function within the algorithm:

Initialization: This section is responsible for setting up the initial population of solutions. It involves generating the initial set of real-valued candidate solutions that will undergo the evolutionary process.

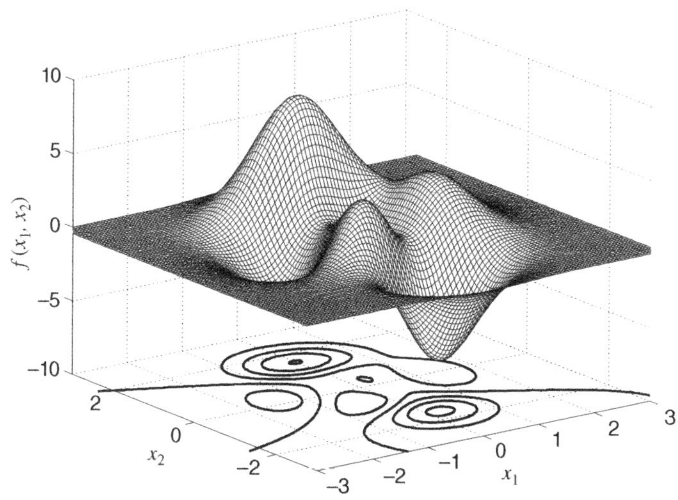

Figure 4.18 Example of a cost function for implementing the real-parameter genetic algorithm.

Ranking Selection: This part of the process involves the ranking of solutions based on their fitness values. The ranking selection method is particularly useful when dealing with negative fitness values, as it ranks solutions based on their relative performance rather than absolute fitness scores.

Crossover: The crossover function facilitates the combination of genetic material from parent solutions to create new offspring. This step is critical in introducing diversity and new traits into the population.

Mutation. Finally, the mutation function introduces random changes to the solutions, further contributing to the diversity of the population. This step is essential in preventing premature convergence and ensuring a thorough exploration of the solution space.

Together, these sections form a cohesive and efficient real-parameter GA, allowing for a systematic and effective approach to solving optimization problems. The modular nature of the implementation, with distinct functions for each key process, enhances the clarity and flexibility of the algorithm, making it adaptable to a wide range of optimization scenarios.

Program 4.12 ***Real-Parameter Genetic Algorithm Using MATLAB***

```
%Algorithm 4.12
% Real-parameter GA implementation
clear all
% Two-dimensional Objective function
funstr='3*(1-x).^2.*exp(-(x.^2)-(y+1).^2)-10*(x/5-x.^3-y.^5).*
      exp(-x.^2-y.^2)- 1/3*exp(-(x+1).^2 - y.^2)';
% Search space range
range=[-3 3 -3 3];
f=vectorize(inline(funstr));
% Parameter initialization
n=20;    %Population size N
MaxGen=300;       % Maximal number of generations
pc=0.95;          % Crossover probability
pm=0.05;          % Mutation probability
% The objective function is shown
Ndiv=100;
dx=(range(2)-range(1))/Ndiv; dy=(range(4)-range(3))/Ndiv;
[x,y]=meshgrid(range(1):dx:range(2),range(3):dy:range(4));
zin=f(x,y);
figure(1);    surfc(x,y,zin); figure(2);
% Generation of the first population (Section 1)
xrange=range(2)-range(1);
yrange=range(4)-range(3);
xn=rand(1,n)*xrange+range(1);
yn=rand(1,n)*yrange+range(3);
```

```
% The optimization process begins
 for i=1:MaxGen,
contour(x,y,zin,15); hold on;
% Fitness evaluation
zn=f(xn,yn);
% A new population is generated applying the ranking selection
     for z=1:n
     e=seleccionRM(zn);    % Section 2
     MP(z,1)=xn(e);
     MP(z,2)=yn(e);
     end

for z1=1:2:n
%The parents p1 and p2 are selected
    p1=floor(n*rand)+1;
    p2=floor(n*rand)+1;
%Crossover is applied (simulated binary crossover SBX)
    if pc>rand,
   % Section 3
    [NP(z1,:),NP(z1+1,:)]=crossoverRE(MP(p1,:),MP(p2,:)) ;
    else
    %Otherwise the parents remain
        NP(z1,:)=MP(p1,:);
        NP(z1+1,:)=MP(p2,:);
    end
% Mutation is executed (Normal mutation)
if pm>rand,
mu1=NP(z1,:);
mu2=NP(z1+1,:);
% Section 4
NP(z1,:)=mutateRE(mu1);
NP(z1+1,:)=mutateRE(mu2);
end
end
% The new population is integrated
xn=NP(:,1);
yn=NP(:,2);
% The final results are shown
plot(xn,yn,'.','markersize',22,'markerfacecolor','g');
drawnow;
hold off;
 end
```

In Section 1 of the optimization process using the real-parameter GA, everything commences with the generation of an initial population. When specific information about the candidate solutions is not available, the most effective method to establish this initial population is by generating random numbers within the defined interval range for each variable. In this specific scenario, each variable is confined to a range extending from −3 to 3.

Given these parameters, the population consisting of n individuals is created by utilizing a specific code segment, as detailed in Program 4.12. This code is responsible for randomly generating values for each individual within the specified range for every variable. This approach ensures that the initial population is diverse and covers a broad spectrum of the solution space, setting a solid foundation for the subsequent evolutionary processes of the GA. By initiating the population in this manner, the GA is better equipped to explore the solution space more thoroughly from the onset, increasing the likelihood of finding optimal or near-optimal solutions.

Program 4.13 ***Initialization of the Population***

```
% Generation of the first population
xrange=range(2)-range(1);
yrange=range(4)-range(3);
xn=rand(1,n)*xrange+range(1);
yn=rand(1,n)*yrange+range(3);
```

In Section 2 of the real-parameter GA implementation, the selection process mirrors the approach used in the binary implementation, albeit with adaptations for real-parameter scenarios. The primary goal of this selection phase remains the same: to encourage the propagation of good solutions within the population and to eliminate inferior solutions, all while maintaining a constant number of candidate solutions.

A significant aspect to consider in this problem is the presence of negative fitness values within the cost function. This characteristic renders the proportional selection method less effective, as it typically assumes positive fitness values for optimal operation. Consequently, the ranking selection method is employed instead. In this approach, all solutions are organized based on their fitness values, with the lowest-ranked solution receiving rank 1 and the highest-ranked solution receiving rank N.

However, there is a notable difference from the binary implementation. While the binary case often involves minimization, the real-parameter GA in this context is focused on the maximization of the objective function. This shift necessitates a modification in the selection operator, altering the ranking order to ascend. As a result, solutions with higher fitness values (larger numbers in the case of maximization) are given a greater likelihood of being selected. This adjustment ensures that the selection process aligns with the maximization objective, effectively prioritizing solutions that are closer to the desired optimal outcome and thereby steering the evolutionary process in the right direction. The specific code segments responsible for achieving this effect are outlined below:

```
1. [D I] = sort(fP,'ascend');
2. r = 1:length(D);
3. r(I) = r;
```

The entire process for Section 2 is encapsulated in the seleccionRM function, as detailed in Program 4.14.

Program 4.14 ***Function*** `seleccionRM` ***that Implements the Selection Process of Section 2***

```
function [iE] = seleccionRM(fP)
% It is assigned a rank to each solution
% The worst has the rank 1
% the best the rank N
Ps=length(fP);
[D I] = sort(fP,'ascend'); % Configured for maximization
r = 1:length(D);
   r(I) = r;
fP=r;
suma=0;
% The roulette-wheel process
for k=1:Ps
 P(k)=fP(k)/(sum(fP));
 suma=suma+P(k);
 A(k)=suma; % cumulative probability
end
R=rand;
for u=1:Ps
    if (A(u)>=R)
      break
    end
end
% iE is the selected element
iE=u;
end
```

In Section 3 of the implementation, the crossover operation is conducted with a specific crossover probability, denoted as p_c. For this operation, the SBX method is utilized. In the SBX approach, two-parent solutions, $\mathbf{p}_1$ and $\mathbf{p}_2$, are selected to produce two new solutions, $\mathbf{c}_1$ and $\mathbf{c}_2$, which are regarded as the offspring. A key aspect of the SBX process is the inclusion of a dispersion factor, n_c, which plays a significant role in influencing the outcome of the crossover operation.

In the program under discussion, the crossover probability p_c is set at 0.95, and the dispersion factor n_c is chosen as 1. These parameters have been selected to optimize the effectiveness of the SBX method in this specific context. The value of p_c ensures a high likelihood of crossover occurring, while the choice of n_c determines the spread of the offspring solutions around the parents.

The details of the crossover process are meticulously coded in the function crossoverRE, as provided in Program 4.15. This function is responsible for executing the SBX operation, applying the specified parameters to generate offspring solutions that are not only diverse but also closely aligned with the promising regions of the search space identified by the parent solutions. Through this approach, the crossover process in the real-parameter GA is optimized to balance exploration and exploitation effectively.

Program 4.15 ***Implementation of the Function*** `crossoverRE` ***that Implements Section 3***

```
function [c,d]=crossoverRE(a,b)
% Dispersion factor
nc=1;
% Random number U[0,1]
r=rand;
% SBX crossover
if r<=0.5
    mu=(2*r)^(1/(nc+1));
else
    mu=(1/(2*(1-r)))^(1/(nc+1));
end
% Generation of individuals for each dimension
c1x=((1+mu)*a(1)+(1-mu)*b(1))*0.5;
c1y=((1+mu)*a(2)+(1-mu)*b(2))*0.5;
c2x=((1-mu)*a(1)+(1+mu)*b(1))*0.5;
c2y=((1-mu)*a(2)+(1+mu)*b(2))*0.5;

c(1)=c1x;
c(2)=c1y;
d(1)=c2x;
d(2)=c2y;
```

In Section 4 of the implementation, the mutation operation is carried out stochastically, based on a predetermined mutation probability, p_m. While there are various schemes available for mutation, this particular implementation utilizes the normal mutation for its simplicity and effectiveness. In the normal mutation approach, a new solution $\mathbf{c}_1^N$ is created from an existing parent solution $\mathbf{p}_1$ by adding a random number that is drawn from a normal Gaussian distribution.

A crucial aspect of this mutation process is the definition of the parameter σ, which determines the magnitude of the modification applied to $\mathbf{p}_1$. This parameter essentially controls the extent of the perturbation introduced in the parent solution during the mutation process. For this implementation, the mutation probability p_m and the parameter σ are set to 0.05 and 0.1, respectively. These values have been chosen to provide a balanced approach to mutation, introducing enough variability to explore the solution space effectively without causing drastic changes that might lead to instability in the optimization process.

The coding of this mutation process is detailed in the function mutateRE, as presented in Program 4.16. The mutateRE function systematically executes the normal mutation operation, applying the set parameters to subtly alter the parent solution and generate a new solution. This incorporation of mutation is vital in maintaining the diversity of the population and in preventing the GA from converging prematurely to local optima, thereby enhancing the overall effectiveness of the optimization process.

Program 4.16 ***Implementation of the Function*** `mutateRE` ***that Implements Section 4***

```
function anew=mutateRE(a)
% Perturbation size
  sigma=0.1;
  % Two-dimesnional mutation
  mx=a(1)+randn*sigma;
  my=a(2)+randn*sigma;
anew(1)=mx;
anew(2)=my;
 end
```

Figure 4.19 illustrates the progression of the optimization process undertaken by the GA as it attempts to solve the problem defined in Eq. 4.7. This figure captures the evolving distribution of solutions across different generations within the GA's run. Specifically, it showcases the distribution of solutions at various stages of the algorithm's execution, including the (1) initial population, (2) after 40 iterations, (3) following 100 iterations, (4) post 180 iterations, (5) subsequent to 230 iterations, and (6) upon completion of 300 iterations.

From the visual data presented in Figure 4.19, it is evident that as the number of iterations increases, the GA steadily progresses toward finding the best solutions, eventually converging on or near the global maximum value. This progression demonstrates the algorithm's ability to effectively navigate the solution space and refine its search over time.

The figure also highlights the dynamic nature of the GA, where its performance is influenced by various configuration parameters. Adjustments to these parameters, such as population size, crossover and mutation rates, and selection methods, can significantly impact the algorithm's efficiency and its ability to locate the optimal solution. The adaptability of the GA to different parameter settings is a key strength, allowing it to be tailored to a wide range of optimization problems and solution landscapes. This flexibility is crucial for optimizing the GA's performance to meet specific requirements or constraints of the problem at hand.

Genetic algorithms (GAs) and machine Learning (ML) have a synergistic relationship where each can significantly enhance the capabilities of the other. GAs can be instrumental in machine learning by optimizing ML models, particularly in selecting features, tuning hyperparameters, and evolving neural network architectures. By navigating complex solution spaces to find optimal configurations, GAs help in constructing more efficient and accurate ML models. Conversely, machine learning techniques can be employed to improve the performance of GAs. ML algorithms can analyze patterns in the evolution of GA populations, predicting and guiding the evolutionary process toward more promising solution spaces. This integration of ML in GAs can lead to faster convergence and better adaptation, especially in dynamically changing environments or in solving complex, multi-dimensional problems. The interplay between these two fields opens up innovative avenues for advanced problem-solving and optimization in various domains.

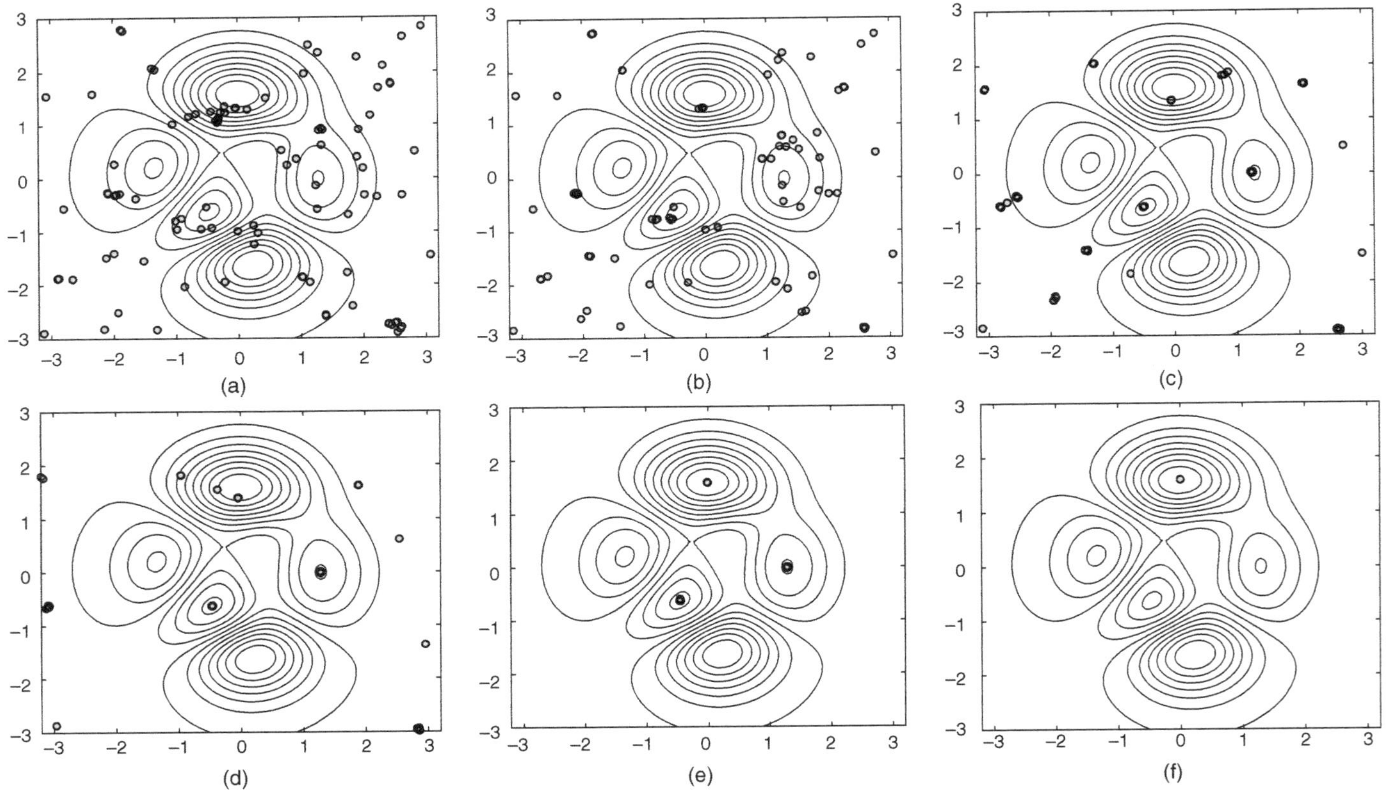

Figure 4.19 Progression of the optimization process conducted by the GA, displaying the distribution of solutions at various stages: (a) initial population, (b) after 40 iterations, (c) following 100 iterations, (d) post 180 iterations, (e) subsequent to 230 iterations, and (f) upon completion of 300 iterations.

4.3 Particle Swarm Optimization (PSO)

PSO, introduced in 1995 by J. Kennedy and R. Eberhart, has emerged as a prominent metaheuristic algorithm. Drawing inspiration from the collective behaviors observed in animal groups like schools of fish or flocks of birds, PSO mimics these natural phenomena to enhance problem-solving efficiency. By harnessing the concept of collective intelligence, where individuals collaborate for greater survival, PSO optimizes solutions through group interactions. This algorithm's main features, search strategies, and application in solving optimization problems are thoroughly discussed in this chapter. It delves into the specific operators used in PSO, analyzing their theoretical underpinnings that facilitate computational implementation, particularly in the MATLAB® environment. Furthermore, the chapter showcases PSO's practical applications through examples, demonstrating its effectiveness in addressing problems both with and without constraints.

In the natural world, collective intelligence is a widespread phenomenon, especially evident in animals that live in groups. These animals leverage their group dynamics for various essential activities, such as defense against predators, efficient foraging, constructing shelters, and safely traversing long distances. In such systems, intelligence is not an attribute of individual members but emerges from their interactions aimed at a shared objective: survival.

One striking advantage of group living is evident in the increased likelihood of evading predator attacks. The 'confused predator effect,' as highlighted by Milinski and Heller in 1978, suggests that predators find it more challenging to target and capture prey within a group than an isolated individual. This collective defense mechanism significantly enhances the survival chances of group members.

Furthermore, group living proves advantageous in food acquisition. At first glance, this might seem counterintuitive; a group cannot hunt stealthily or go unnoticed, potentially alerting prey to imminent danger. However, despite these apparent drawbacks, the success rate of group foraging or hunting is notably higher. This can be attributed to the 'many eyes hypothesis,' proposed by Lima in 1995, which posits that a group, with its cumulative vigilance, has a higher probability of locating food due to the increased number of individuals engaged in the search. Additionally, collaborative efforts in a group enable strategies like surrounding and cornering prey, tactics that would be impossible for a solitary hunter.

The PSO algorithm draws inspiration from these aspects of animal behavior, focusing on collaboration for enhanced collective and individual performance. PSO principles are observable in both animal and human behaviors. Humans, like animals, often form groups to tackle tasks more effectively, achieving both collective goals and individual objectives. In pursuing a common goal, the exchange of information among group members is pivotal. This collaborative approach allows for the refinement of strategies based on individual experiences and observations. If one member's strategy is unsuccessful, sharing this information with the group can lead to a collective adjustment of tactics, increasing the likelihood of achieving the desired outcome. This process is reflective of decision-making improvements in humans, where strategies are adapted based on personal success, the success of peers (local influence), and the success of the wider group or society (global influence). These dynamics of local and global influence form the core principles of PSO, highlighting the algorithm's roots in the natural world's collective intelligence.

4.3.1 Strategy for Searching in Particle Swarm Optimization

In the PSO framework, a collection of elements, referred to as a swarm, is used, with each element signifying a potential solution. This concept aligns with metaheuristic computation, where a swarm is analogous to a population, and individual particles represent separate entities. These particles traverse a multidimensional search space, with their locations changing based on personal experiences and influences from nearby particles.

PSO comprises a group of **X** particles, each modeling the cooperative behavior of N agents working together on a collective task. Every agent is depicted as a particle, $\mathbf{x}_i$, with the whole group represented as $\mathbf{X} = \{\mathbf{x}_1, \mathbf{x}_2, \ldots, \mathbf{x}_N\}$. The collective aim of these particles is to find a viable solution to a specified optimization problem within a clearly defined and bounded search space. Here, each particle is not only a search agent but also a potential evolving solution within the iterative process. The position of each particle, denoted as $\mathbf{x}_i$, marks its place in the search space, and these positions are periodically updated at discrete time intervals.

During their evolutionary journey, the particles communicate spatial information gleaned from their exploration. Additionally, they possess a memory feature, allowing them to record and recall the most effective solutions they have discovered so far. The movement of each particle through the search space is influenced by its velocity, which in turn is determined by information shared among the swarm's agents. Thus, a particle's trajectory is guided by both its previous positions (local influence) and the positions of other particles within the swarm (global influence).

This setup enables PSO to model the dynamics of particle movement driven by the collective behavior of the swarm. The model takes into account both local and global influences on the particles, influencing the degree and direction of each agent's movement. Such a strategy enhances the quality of solutions; as particles interact and evolve with each iteration, they experience changes influenced by the dynamics of both local and global mechanisms. This iterative process of adaptation and interaction sharpens the search strategy, leading to progressively refined and optimal solutions.

At the outset of the PSO algorithm, an initial population, denoted as $\mathbf{X}^0$, is created, consisting of N particles. This initial population is represented as $\mathbf{X}^0 = \{\mathbf{x}_1^0, \mathbf{x}_2^0, \ldots, \mathbf{x}_N^0\}$, where each particle $\mathbf{x}_i^0$ is a vector in a d-dimensional search space. The initialization process involves generating each particle's initial position randomly within predefined bounds. Specifically, each particle $\mathbf{x}_i^0$ is represented by $\left[x_{i,1}^0, x_{i,2}^0, \ldots, x_{i,d}^0\right]$, with each component $x_{i,j}^0$ being randomly chosen within a range set by the lower bound (lb) and upper bound (ub) for that dimension.

These bounds, lb and ub, vary for each dimension j and are tailored to the specific problem being optimized. They define the feasible region of the search space, essentially setting the limits within which potential solutions can exist. This setup ensures that the initial positions of the particles are spread out across the range of possible solutions, giving the algorithm a broad and diverse starting point for the optimization process. The equation below outlines the method used for initializing particles.

$$
\begin{aligned}
&x_{ij}^0 = lb_j + r_{ij}(ub_j - lb_j) \\
&i = 1, 2, \ldots, N; \quad j = 1, 2, \ldots, d
\end{aligned}
\tag{4.26}
$$

In this context, x_{ij}^0 represents the starting value of particle i in dimension j. The terms lb_j and ub_j are the minimum and maximum boundaries for dimension j, respectively. Furthermore, r_{ij} denotes a random value, uniformly distributed between [0, 1], specific to particle i in its dimension j.

In the preliminary phase of the PSO algorithm, alongside the initialization of the population, the parameters for the optimization problem are also established. These parameters are essential for tailoring the algorithm to the specific problem at hand. They include the number of particles (N), the number of dimensions (d) in the search space, the maximum number of iterations (k_{max}), and any equality or inequality constraints that form part of the problem's generic parameters.

The exact definition of these parameters varies depending on the nature and requirements of the optimization problem being addressed. In the context of the chapter under discussion, the focus is on solving optimization problems that do not involve constraints. As such, the essential parameters for initializing the PSO in this scenario are limited to the number of particles in the swarm, the dimensionality of the search space, the defined limits of this space, and the maximum number of iterations allowed for the algorithm. This setup ensures that the PSO is adequately configured to effectively tackle the specific optimization challenges presented.

In the approach to searching, every particle traverses the solution space at a particular velocity, denoted as $\mathbf{v}_i$. This velocity also needs to be assigned an initial value. In the most basic form of the PSO algorithm, the initial velocity for each particle is set to zero, leading to the following setup:

$$\mathbf{v}_i^0 = 0 \tag{4.27}$$

Throughout the evolutionary phase, the velocity is determined by taking into account the data from the best global particle, $\mathbf{g}$, and the best local particle, $\mathbf{p}_i$. The best global particle signifies the top-performing particle across the entire population and is indicative of the optimal global solution, as follows:

$$\mathbf{g} = \mathbf{x}_i \in \{\mathbf{X}\} \mid f(\mathbf{x}_i) = \min\{f(\mathbf{x}_1), f(\mathbf{x}_2), \dots, f(\mathbf{x}_N)\} \tag{4.28}$$

Concerning the best local particle, this term relates to the record of its highest achievement to date. It represents the optimal solution that has not been surpassed yet. In academic discussions, this local particle is often termed as the best neighboring particle. Hence, the identification of the best-performing particle so far is established in the following manner:

$$\mathbf{p}_i^{k+1} = \mathbf{x}_i^k \in \{\mathbf{X}^k\} \mid \mathbf{x}_i^k = \min\left\{\mathbf{p}_i^k, \mathbf{x}_i^k\right\} \tag{4.29}$$

In this scenario, the leading particles, symbolizing the optimal solutions, significantly impact the search process by steering the entire population toward the best outcomes within the solution space.

The calculation of velocity is influenced by both the global and local impacts of these top-performing particles. These influences are modulated by distinct factors, commonly referred to as cognitive and social constants. The cognitive constant impacts the local influence, whereas the social constant influences the global aspect. Equation 4.27 illustrates the method for computing velocity:

$$\mathbf{v}_i^{k+1} = \mathbf{v}_i^k + c_1 \cdot \left(\mathbf{r}_1^k \cdot \left(\mathbf{p}_i^k - \mathbf{x}_i^k\right)\right) + c_2 \cdot \left(\mathbf{r}_2^k \cdot \left(\mathbf{g}^k - \mathbf{x}_i^k\right)\right) \tag{4.30}$$

In this context, k denotes the ongoing iteration, $\mathbf{v}_i^{k+1}$ is the updated velocity for particle $\mathbf{x}_i^k$ in the forthcoming generation $k+1$, and $\mathbf{v}_i^k$ is the current velocity of the same particle. The symbol $\mathbf{g}^k$ represents the best global particle identified to this point, while $\mathbf{p}_i^k$ denotes the top local value discovered so far for particle $\mathbf{x}_i^k$ (up to iteration k). Additionally, $\mathbf{r}_1^k$ and $\mathbf{r}_2^k$ are two d-dimensional random vectors, each element of which is derived from uniformly distributed random numbers within the range [0, 1]. The terms c_1 and c_2 correspond to the cognitive and social constants, respectively.

The PSO algorithm has gained significant success and popularity, leading to numerous modifications from its original form. Many of these alterations focus on enhancing the calculation of particle speed. Another key aspect often revised in newer versions is the initialization of velocity, with the aim of refining the particles' movement speed for improved performance in the search process.

Various methods exist for initializing velocity, as noted by Helwig and Wanka in 2008. The most prevalent approaches include random initialization and setting the initial velocity to zero.

In the PSO's original formulation, the initial velocity is set to zero. Concurrently, the values of the cognitive and social constants are typically fixed at $c_1 = 1$ and $c_2 = 1$. The chosen values for these parameters significantly influence the algorithm's effectiveness. Therefore, it's crucial to fine-tune these parameters specifically for each problem. The optimal values for c_1 and c_2 are those that yield the best results in the given context. This customization ensures that the PSO algorithm is adequately adapted to the unique challenges and requirements of each optimization problem.

Particles navigate through the search space to uncover potential solutions. The trajectory of each particle is dictated by the velocity computed as per Eq. 4.31. Thus, in each iteration k, the position of every particle within the population is revised in line with the subsequent expression:

$$\mathbf{x}_i^{k+1} = \mathbf{x}_i^k + \mathbf{v}_i^{k+1} \tag{4.31}$$

In this context, $\mathbf{v}_i^{k+1}$ signifies the updated velocity for particle $\mathbf{x}_i^k$, as derived from Eq. 4.31. The movement mechanism of particles is a key aspect that various PSO adaptations have modified, acknowledging the significant impact particle displacement has on the algorithm's efficiency. Although there are numerous versions of the PSO, this chapter introduces a simplified version of the algorithm. This approach is taken to facilitate an easier understanding of PSO's fundamental attributes for the reader.

4.3.2 Analysis of the PSO Algorithm

In PSO, the modification of the position of each particle $\mathbf{x}_i^{k+1}$ is governed by its corresponding velocity vector $\mathbf{v}_i^{k+1}$. The calculation of this velocity, $\mathbf{v}_i^{k+1}$, incorporates three distinct elements: the particle's prior velocity $\mathbf{v}_i^k$, a cognitive component $\mathbf{r}_1^k \cdot (\mathbf{p}_i^k - \mathbf{x}_i^k)$, and a social factor $\mathbf{r}_2^k \cdot (\mathbf{g}^k - \mathbf{x}_i^k)$.

The concept of previous velocity in PSO acts as a repository of past directional movement. It can also be seen as a form of momentum, helping to prevent abrupt directional shifts. This aspect ensures that particles maintain a trajectory consistent with their current direction.

The cognitive factor is a crucial component that reflects the individual performance of particle i throughout the optimization process. It essentially mimics the particle's memory of the location where it previously achieved its best performance. Thanks to this cognitive element, particles are able to be influenced by their own optimal positions, providing them the opportunity to revisit these spots as they evolve.

On the other hand, the social term represents the collective influence exerted by the entire population on each individual particle. Generally, this factor steers the search toward the most successful element found within the entire group. As a result, each particle is not only influenced by its own history but is also drawn toward the best-identified position in the swarm.

Both the cognitive and social components are modulated by random numbers, ensuring that their impact varies throughout the search process. This variability adds a dynamic aspect to the strategy, allowing the influences to adapt and change as the search progresses.

4.3.3 Inertia Weighting

One of the simplest yet efficient adaptations of PSO is the integration of the inertia weight ω. With this addition, the modification of each particle's position is governed by the subsequent model:

$$\mathbf{v}_i^{k+1} = \omega \cdot \mathbf{v}_i^k + c_1 \cdot \left(\mathbf{r}_1^k \cdot \left(\mathbf{p}_i^k - \mathbf{x}_i^k\right)\right) + c_2 \cdot \left(\mathbf{r}_2^k \cdot \left(\mathbf{g}^k - \mathbf{x}_i^k\right)\right) \tag{4.32}$$

By incorporating it, the possibility of the velocity escalating boundlessly in each iteration is mitigated. Despite the stabilizing effects of ω, it does influence the search strategy by decelerating its convergence rate. The value of ω is dynamically adjusted, starting from 0.9 in the initial generation and gradually decreasing to 0.4 in the final iteration.

4.3.4 Particle Swarm Optimization Algorithm Using MATLAB

The PSO algorithm has been executed within the MATLAB environment to demonstrate its search methodology. This specific implementation is showcased in Algorithm 6.1. The primary goal in this process is to minimize an objective function in order to locate the global minimum. The optimization problem selected for this example isn't representative of an engineering challenge or a real-world application. Rather, it is a mathematical construct known as the peaks function. This function is defined as follows:

$$f(x_1, x_2) = 3(1 - x_1)^2 e^{-(x_1^2 - x_2^2)} - 10\left(\frac{x_1}{5} - x_1^3 - x_2^5\right) e^{(-x_1^2 - x_2^2)} - 1/3e^{(-(x_1+1)^2 - x_2^2)} \tag{4.33}$$

The peaks function, defined in a two-dimensional space, is extensively utilized due to its interesting properties. This function is characterized by the presence of both minima and maxima, which include local and global points. These features make it an ideal candidate for swiftly assessing the efficacy of various metaheuristic algorithms. Notably, the peaks function possesses a global minimum, which is approximately −6.54. This distinct landscape of peaks and valleys provides a comprehensive testbed for evaluating the performance and robustness of optimization algorithms like PSO in navigating complex solution spaces.

To visually demonstrate the PSO search process, its implementation has been tailored for the two-dimensional peaks function problem. For those looking to apply this method in higher-dimensional spaces, necessary modifications need to be made. These adjustments include altering key algorithm parameters, such as the number of dimensions (d), the lower (lb), and upper (ub) limits for each dimension, as well as revising the number of particles (N) and the maximum number of iterations (k_{max}).

It's important to note that increasing the dimensionality of the problem adds to the complexity of the search. Having more search agents and extended time for conducting the search can significantly enhance the optimization process in such cases. Therefore, modifying the number of particles and iterations is advisable to fine-tune the performance of the optimization.

Algorithm 6.1 details the PSO implementation. Within the algorithm's code, there are several explanatory comments that assist in understanding how PSO functions. These annotations are particularly helpful in clarifying the adjustments needed for different dimensions and how they influence the overall effectiveness of the PSO in navigating more complex optimization challenges.

Program 4.17 ***Implementation of the PSO Method by Using MATLAB***

```
%Algorithm 4.17
% Implementation of the PSO algorithm
%% Clear memory and close Matlab Windows
clear all % Clear memory
close all % close Matlab Windows
%% Problem to optimize (minimize), the definition of the objective function
    funObj = @(xi) 3*(1-xi(1))^2*exp(-(xi(1)^2)-(xi(2)+1)^2) ...
                   -10*(xi(1)/5-xi(1)^3 - xi(2)^5)*exp(-xi(1)^2-xi(2)^2)...
                   -1/3*exp(-(xi(1)+1)^2 - xi(2)^2);
```

```
%% Parameter configuration
    N = 10;             % Particle number
    d = 2;              % Dimensions
    lb = [-3 -3];       % Lower limit of search the space
    ub = [3 3];         % Upper limit of search the space
    k = 0;              % Current iteration
    kmax = 100;         % Maximum number of iterations
    c1 = 2;             % Cognitive constant
    c2 = 2;             % Social constant
%% Initialization of particles and velocity
    for i = 1:N
        x(i,:) = rand(1,d).*(ub-lb)+lb; % Initialization of particles
        v(i,:) = zeros(1,d);            % Initialization of velocities
    end
%% Evaluation of the initial particles in the objective function
    for i = 1:N
        xi=x(i,:);              % Extraction of the particle xi
        fx(i,:) = funObj(xi); % Evaluation of the particle xi
    end
%% Record of the best global particle and the best local particles
    [gfit, ind] = min(fx); % Fitness of the best global particle
    g = x(ind,:);          % Position of the best global particle
    fp = fx;               % Fitness of the best local particles
    p = x;                 % Position of the best local particles
%% Calculation of the search space for graphical proposes
    ejex=linspace(min(lb),max(ub),50); % Solutions for vector d = 1
    ejey=ejex;                         % Solutions for vector d = 2
    ejez=[];                           % Fitness matrix
    for i = 1:length(ejex)
        for j = 1:length(ejey)
            ejez(i,j) = funObj([ejex(i) ejey(j)]);
        end
    end
    [ejey ejex] = meshgrid(ejex,ejey); % Computation of the meshgrid
%% Iterative process
    while k < kmax % Stop criterion
        k = k + 1; % new iteration
        %% Draw the search space Surface
            figure(1);             % Show Figure 1
            surf(ejex,ejey,ejez) % Draw the function surface
            hold on                % Hold the figures
        %% Draw the particles
            % Draw the particles in red color
            plot3(x(:,1),x(:,2),fx,'o','MarkerFaceColor','m','MarkerSize',10)
            % Dibuja las mejores partículas locales en color verde
            plot3(p(:,1),p(:,2),fp,'o','MarkerFaceColor','g','MarkerSize',10)
            % Pause to allow viewing the graph
            pause(0.3)
            % Release figure 1
            hold off
        %% Draw the function contour
            figure(2)                    % Show figure 2
            contour(ejex,ejey,ejez,20) % The cfunction contour is redraw
            hold on                      % Hold figure 2 for graphical proposes
        %% Draw the particles in the contour
            % Draw the particles in red color
            plot(x(:,1),x(:,2),'o','MarkerFaceColor','m');
            % Dibuja las mejores partículas locales en color verde
```

```
            plot(p(:,1),p(:,2),'o','MarkerFaceColor','g');
            % Pause to allow viewing the graph
            pause(0.3)
            % Release figure 2
            hold off
        %% Computation of the new velocity for each particle
            for i= 1:N
                % Extraction of the particle xi
                xi = x(i,:);
                % Extraction of the local particle pi
                pi = p(i,:);
                % Determination of the new velocity for each particle vi
                v(i,:) = v(i,:)+c1*rand(1,d).*(pi-xi)+c2*rand(1,d).*(g-xi);
            end
        %% Determination of the new position of each particle
            x = x + v;
        %% Verify that the particles do not leave the limits lb and ub
            for i = 1:N                        % For each particle
                for j=1:d                      % For each dimension
                    if x(i,j) < lb(j)          % Check the lower limit
                        x(i,j) = lb(j);
                    elseif x(i,j) > ub(j) % Check the upper limit
                        x(i,j) = ub(j);
                    end
                end
            end
        %% Evaluation of the new particles with the objective function
            for i = 1:N
                xi = x(i,:);            % Extraction of the particle xi
                fx(i,:) = funObj(xi); % Evaluation of the particle xi
            end
        %% Record of the best global particle and the best local particles
            [gfitkmas1, ind] = min(fx);
            % If a better solution was found, update the global particle
            if gfitkmas1 < gfit
                % Update the fitness of the best global particle
                gfit = gfitkmas1;
                % Update the position of the best global particle
                g = x(ind,:);
            end
            for i = 1:N
                % If any particle is a better solution than the previous,
                % update your best local particle
                if fx(i,:) < fp(i,:)
                    % Update the fitness of the best local particles
                    fp(i,:) = fx(i,:);
                    % Update the position of the best local particles
                    p(i,:) = x(i,:);
                end
            end
%% Historical record of the best solutions found in each generation
            Evolucion(k) = gfit;
    end
%% End of the iterative process, display of results
    Figure
    % Graph of the evolutionary process of the PSO
    plot(Evolucion)
```

```
%% Results of PSO
    disp([The best solution : ', num2str(g)])
    disp(['The best fitness  : ', num2str(gfit)])
```

The particle swarm optimization (PSO) algorithm finds significant utility in machine learning, particularly in optimizing machine learning models and algorithms. PSO can effectively fine-tune hyperparameters, select features, and enhance the performance of various machine learning techniques. Conversely, machine learning methods can also augment PSO. By employing machine learning techniques, such as reinforcement learning or neural networks, the efficiency and accuracy of the PSO algorithm can be significantly improved. These enhancements might include better decision-making in particle movement or more effective adaptation to complex optimization landscapes, leading to a synergistic relationship where both domains benefit from each other's strengths.

4.4 Differential Evolution (DE) Algorithm

In 1997, Kenneth Price and Rainer Storn introduced the metaheuristic algorithm known as DE, marking a significant advancement in optimization techniques. DE operates as a population-based algorithm, employing a straightforward and direct search strategy. This innovative method generates new parameter vectors by adding the weighted difference between two randomly selected population members, fostering efficient exploration and exploitation of the solution space. This Section considers the operational mechanics of the DE algorithm. It not only elaborates on the mathematical underpinnings of DE's operators but also discusses its practical implementation in MATLAB, a popular programming environment for algorithmic development. The primary aim of this section is to equip the reader with a thorough understanding of DE's mathematical framework and its application potential in solving various optimization challenges.

In 1995, Rainer Price tackled the Chebyshev polynomial adjustment problem, as documented by Rozenberg et al. in 2005. Price approached this challenge using the Genetic Annealing algorithm, a method he co-developed with K.V in 1994. Although he successfully resolved the problem, Price recognized that the algorithm fell short of the performance benchmarks essential for a competitive optimization technique. These benchmarks included robust global search capabilities, rapid convergence, and ease of implementation.

In response to these shortcomings, Price, collaborating with Storn in 1997, innovated a new strategy rooted in vector calculus and evolutionary computation principles. This novel approach involved the creation of parameter vectors by adding the weighted difference between two population members to a third member. This operation, known as differential mutation, marked a significant advancement in the field of metaheuristic algorithms.

DE, as this new method was called, demonstrated superior performance compared to other metaheuristic schemes in solving optimization problems. Its key strengths include straightforward implementation, effective convergence properties verified through independent tests, and the ability to parallelize for tackling high-computational-cost problems. The DE algorithm's most notable feature is its adeptness at finding optimal global solutions for multimodal, non-differentiable, and non-linear functions.

The DE algorithm has showcased its capabilities in prestigious forums such as the IEEE Congress on Evolutionary Computation (CEC) and has been applied successfully in various real-world optimization scenarios. Like other metaheuristic methods, DE operates iteratively, utilizing exploration-exploitation operators such as mutation and crossover throughout the optimization process to identify the best solution.

In the realm of metaheuristic algorithms, maintaining a balance between exploration and exploitation is crucial. Without this equilibrium, the effectiveness of evolutionary optimization techniques diminishes, especially in practical applications. To circumvent this issue, DE incorporates specific mechanisms to prevent getting trapped in local optima. The mutation operator in DE employs a direct strategy to probe unexplored areas of the search space, while the crossover operator enhances population diversity, increasing the likelihood of locating the global optimum.

Through these thoughtful design choices, DE stands out as a robust and efficient tool in the field of evolutionary optimization, capable of addressing a wide range of complex optimization challenges.

4.4.1 The Search Strategy of DE

DE shares similarities with the PSO method in being a population-based algorithm where each member is represented as a parameter vector. The evolutionary process of DE unfolds through four distinct phases, each critical to the optimization process.

The initial phase involves the creation of a population. Here, parameter vectors are stochastically generated, ensuring a random yet controlled distribution over the search space of the problem at hand. This random generation lays the groundwork for a diverse and robust starting population.

In the second phase, DE employs differential mutation. This process involves recombining elements of the population to foster genetic diversity and enable the exploration of new solution spaces. This mutation is not random but is guided by the differences between the population members, allowing for a more directed and effective search.

The third stage introduces the crossover operator. By combining information from different population elements, this operator significantly enhances the diversity within the population. This increase in diversity is crucial for avoiding local optima and ensuring that the population explores a wide range of potential solutions.

The final, fourth step involves an elitist selection mechanism. This process is designed to ensure that the most promising solutions, or the 'best' individuals, are carried over to the next generation. By doing so, DE ensures that each generation improves upon the last, steadily moving toward an optimal solution.

To visualize this process, consider Figure 4.20, which illustrates the distribution of nine solutions on a two-dimensional surface. This figure highlights the operational mechanics of DE by showing how the difference between two randomly selected points (for instance, points 7 and 9,

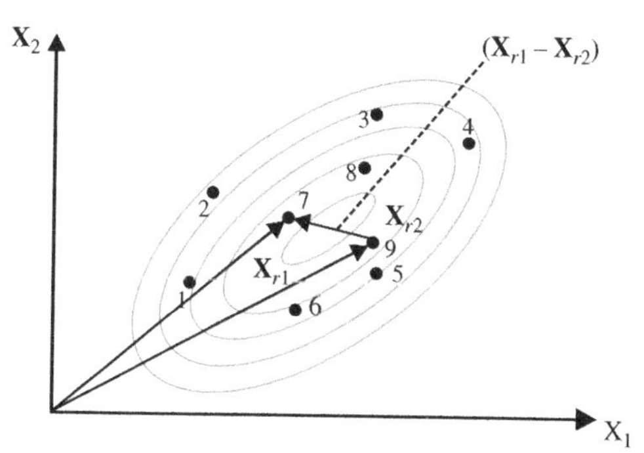

Figure 4.20 Visual representation of the disparity between two randomly selected vectors employed in the search mechanism of the DE algorithm.

corresponding to vectors $\mathbf{x}_{r_1}$ and $\mathbf{x}_{r_2}$, respectively) is used to guide the evolutionary process. This visual representation helps in understanding how DE navigates the search space, constantly adapting and evolving its population toward the optimal solution.

Following the process described earlier, the DE algorithm takes the next step by scaling the calculated difference between the two randomly chosen vectors and adding it to a third vector, $\mathbf{x}_{r_3}$, which is also selected randomly (in this instance, corresponding to point five on the graphical representation). The magnitude of the addition is determined by a scaling factor, denoted as F, which specifies the extent to which the difference between points $\mathbf{x}_{r_1}$ and $\mathbf{x}_{r_2}$ is incorporated into the third vector, $\mathbf{x}_{r_3}$. The result of this operation is the creation of a new vector, referred to as the mutant vector $\mathbf{v}_1$. This entire process, encompassing the scaling and addition to generate the mutant vector, is visually detailed in Figure 4.21. The figure serves to illustrate the systematic approach of the DE algorithm in evolving the vectors within its population, highlighting the methodical progression toward finding an optimal solution.

Figure 4.22 effectively demonstrates a key aspect of the DE algorithm's process. It shows how the newly created mutant vector $\mathbf{v}_1$, derived from the earlier steps, exhibits a better fitness value compared to the original point, labeled as point 1 in the illustration. This superior fitness value is significant because, in the DE algorithm, vectors with better quality – indicated by their fitness – are selected to replace their predecessors in the population. This ensures that the population evolves toward increasingly optimal solutions.

The DE algorithm continues to execute this process of evolution and replacement until it meets a predetermined stopping criterion. This criterion is often based on the maximum number of generations deemed necessary for the optimization process. Essentially, the algorithm iterates through generations, continuously refining its population, until it reaches this set limit.

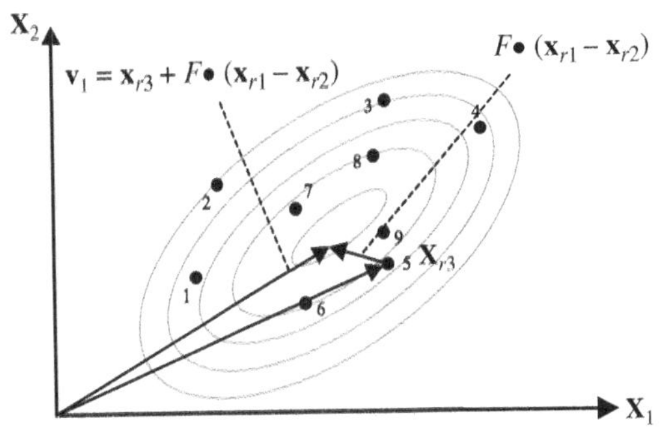

Figure 4.21 Visual depiction of combining the scaled difference of two vectors with a third randomly chosen vector, as utilized in the search methodology of the DE algorithm.

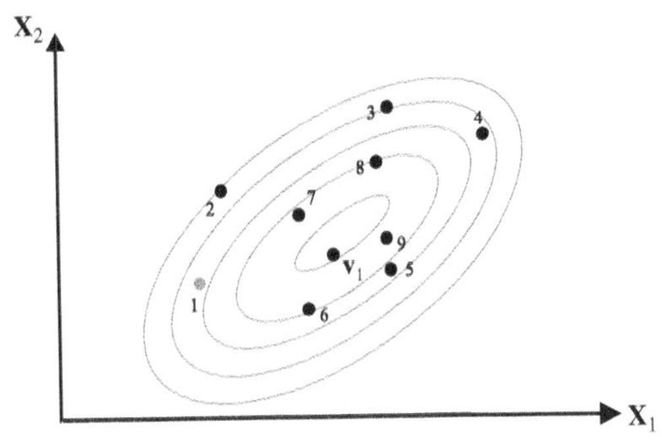

Figure 4.22 Visual depiction of the replacement of the original vector by the mutant vector.

Upon completing the stipulated number of iterations, the DE algorithm arrives at its final phase. The best solution from the last generation is identified as the optimal solution for the problem at hand, be it a maximization or minimization issue. This solution represents the culmination of the algorithm's systematic search and optimization process, effectively addressing the formulated optimization problem with the best possible outcome derived from the evolving population.

In the DE algorithm, the population consists of N parameter vectors, each situated within a d-dimensional space of real values. Represented as $\mathbf{X}$, this population comprises vectors $\{\mathbf{x}_1^k, \mathbf{x}_2^k, \dots \mathbf{x}_N^k\}$, where each $\mathbf{x}_i^k$ denotes a specific position in the d-dimensional space, represented as $\{x_1, x_2, \dots x_d\}$. Throughout each generation (iteration) k, these vectors undergo manipulation through a trio of operators: mutation, crossover, and selection. The aim of these operations is to steer the search strategy toward the global optimum.

Each operator in the DE algorithm plays a crucial role in generating new candidate solutions, striking a balance between exploration and exploitation. This balance is key to enhancing the population's diversity. After initializing the population positions randomly and uniformly, the DE algorithm iteratively applies the mutation, crossover, and selection operators.

The mutation operation is pivotal for exploring the search space, creating a direct pathway toward the global optimum. Conversely, the crossover operation is tasked with augmenting the diversity of the positions within the parameter vectors. The selection operation then focuses on retaining the best individuals in the population. In each iteration, the fitness value of the vector produced by the mutation and crossover operations is assessed. If this new vector demonstrates better performance than its predecessor, it replaces the latter; if not, the original vector remains.

This selection mechanism ensures that only the most promising solutions are preserved for future generations, facilitating the exchange of information among the best candidates. As a result, the DE algorithm achieves effective convergence toward the global optimum of the optimization problem, continually refining the population toward the most efficient solutions.

Initialization is the initial phase of the DE algorithm. During this phase, it's crucial to define the boundaries of the search space for the optimization problem. These boundaries are essentially vectors that set the minimum and maximum limits for each dimension of the problem, commonly referred to as box constraints. The lower boundary is denoted by the vector $\mathbf{lb} = [lb_1, lb_2, \dots, lb_d]$, and the upper boundary is represented by $\mathbf{ub} = [ub_1, ub_2, \dots, ub_d]$.

After establishing these boundaries for the search space, the next step is to create a random number generation method. This method relies on a uniform distribution to generate sample values. Utilizing this distribution, the method assigns values to each position in every member of the population. The values are determined within the confines of the lower and upper limits as established, thereby ensuring that each population member is initialized within the specified search space. For this, the following model is employed:

$$\mathbf{X} = \mathbf{lb} + \mathbf{r}(\mathbf{0}, \mathbf{1}) \cdot (\mathbf{ub} - \mathbf{lb}) \tag{4.34}$$

In the context of initializing the DE algorithm's population, the terms **lb** and **ub** refer to the vectors that define the lower and upper limits of the search space, respectively. Each element in these vectors sets the boundaries for the corresponding dimension of the problem. Alongside these, $\mathbf{r}(\mathbf{0}, \mathbf{1})$ represents a vector composed of random numbers. These numbers are generated within the range of 0 to 1 and follow a uniform distribution. This mechanism ensures that each member of the population is assigned initial values that are both random and constrained within the defined limits of the search space, providing a diverse and well-distributed starting point for the optimization process.

4.4.2 The Mutation Operation in DE

After completing the initialization phase, the DE algorithm proceeds to employ the mutation operator. This operator plays a crucial role in recombining population elements, thereby creating modified versions of each individual. One of the reasons for the popularity of the DE algorithm is the mathematical simplicity underlying this mutation process. It effectively allows for straightforward yet powerful manipulation of candidate solutions.

In the DE algorithm, the mutation process is specifically termed 'differential mutation'. This designation reflects the operator's reliance on the differences between various candidate solutions within the population. By leveraging these differences, the algorithm promotes an exchange of information among all elements, facilitating a more dynamic and effective search process.

The DE algorithm, as covered in existing literature, has seen various adaptations and improvements, particularly in the operation of the mutation operator. These enhancements often involve altering the mutation process to optimize performance in real-world applications. Section 4.6 of the referenced material will delve into the most commonly employed modifications of the mutation operator used in practical scenarios. However, the fundamental mathematical model that underpins the differential mutation in its standard form is outlined in the subsequent discussion. This model lays the foundation for understanding how differential mutation operates within the DE algorithm, setting the stage for exploring its more advanced modifications.

The basic model of differential mutation in the DE algorithm involves merging the randomly scaled difference of two population vectors with a third vector from the same population. This process results in the creation of a new entity, termed the mutant vector. Hence, the mathematical formulation of the differential mutation can be described as follows:

$$\mathbf{v}^k = \left\{\mathbf{x}_{r3}^k + F * \left(\mathbf{x}_{r1}^k - \mathbf{x}_{r2}^k\right) \tag{4.35}$$

In this context, $\mathbf{x}_{r_1}^k$, $\mathbf{x}_{r_2}^k$ and $\mathbf{x}_{r_3}^k$ $(r_1, r_2, r_3 \in \{1, 2, \ldots, N\}$ and $r_1 \neq r_2 \neq r_3 \neq i)$ denote randomly chosen candidate solutions from the population. The scaling factor, F, which lies within the range [0, 2], is referred to as the differential weight. This factor plays a critical role in controlling the extent of variation based on the difference $(\mathbf{x}_{r1}^k - \mathbf{x}_{r2}^k)$. Essentially, the scaling factor is a numerical value that influences the rate at which the population evolves, thereby aiding in the maintenance of a balanced optimization process. A scaling value close to zero results in faster convergence of the process, whereas a higher value leads to slower convergence. The setting of this parameter is typically predetermined and varies depending on the specific requirements of the application being addressed.

Figure 4.23 serves as a visual aid to elucidate the mutation process in the DE algorithm, specifically illustrating the differential mutation operator. The figure displays three parameter vectors, labeled as $\mathbf{x}_{r_1}^k$, $\mathbf{x}_{r_2}^k$ and $\mathbf{x}_{r_3}^k$. These vectors undergo a transformation through the mutation procedure, leading to the generation of a fourth vector, known as the mutant vector $\mathbf{v}^k$. This mutant vector is the resultant candidate solution formed by adding the scaled difference between $\mathbf{x}_{r_1}^k$ and $\mathbf{x}_{r_2}^k$ to the vector $\mathbf{x}_{r_3}^k$.

A key aspect evident from the figure is that the mutant vector $\mathbf{v}^k$ is positioned differently within the search space compared to the existing vectors of the population. This shift in position underscores the efficiency of the mutation operator in exploring new areas of the search space. By enabling the generation of a vector in a distinct area, the differential mutation operator significantly contributes to the thorough and effective exploration of the solution space, which is crucial for the overall success of the optimization process in the DE algorithm.

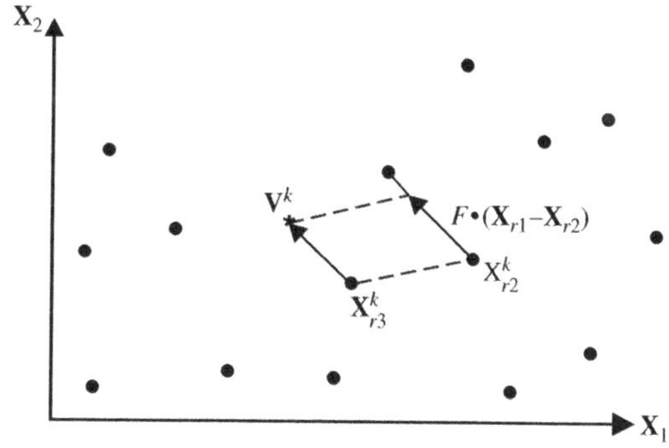

Figure 4.23 Visual depiction of the mutation operator employed in the differential evolution algorithm's search mechanism.

Equation 4.35 presents the most straightforward and commonly used method to amalgamate three randomly chosen candidate solutions from population X, resulting in the formation of a new, fourth parameter vector. The selection of vectors with subscripts r_1, r_2 and r_3 can vary considerably, and the manner of this selection significantly influences the behavior of the DE algorithm.

The DE algorithm's various iterations primarily stem from alterations to the mutation operator. These variations have been developed by researchers and practitioners who have meticulously examined how the mutation operator performs in different scenarios, particularly in cases involving the optimization of complex surfaces (as noted by Qing in 2009). The mutation strategies discussed in the subsequent sections are based on the assumption of a population X comprising solutions that are uniformly distributed across the search space. Additionally, the notation used here refers specifically to the mutation process occurring in a given generation, denoted as k. This focus on mutation underscores its critical role in the evolution and effectiveness of the DE algorithm, highlighting how even minor adjustments to this operator can yield diverse behaviors and outcomes in optimization tasks.

4.4.2.1 Mutation Rand/1

This mutation strategy within the DE algorithm involves selecting the parameter vectors $\mathbf{x}^k_{r_1}$, $\mathbf{x}^k_{r_2}$, and $\mathbf{x}^k_{r_3}$ from the population in a random manner. A crucial aspect of this selection is ensuring that each of these vectors is distinct from the others, adhering to the condition $r_1, r_2, r_3 \in \{1, 2, \ldots, N\}$ and $r_1 \neq r_2 \neq r_3 \neq i$. This approach to mutation is notably popular in real-world applications because it effectively maintains a high level of diversity within the population. Besides enhancing diversity, this method is also favored for its low computational cost, making it an efficient choice for a wide range of optimization tasks. The combination of diversity maintenance and computational efficiency is key to the success and widespread adoption of this mutation strategy in practical applications. This mutation strategy can be modeled as follows:

$$\mathbf{v}^k = \{\mathbf{x}^k_{r3} + F * (\mathbf{x}^k_{r1} - \mathbf{x}^k_{r2}) \tag{4.36}$$

4.4.2.2 Mutación Best/1

In this particular mutation strategy employed by the DE algorithm, the individuals $\mathbf{x}^k_{r_1}$ and $\mathbf{x}^k_{r_2}$ are chosen randomly from the population. It is essential that these individuals are distinct from each other, fulfilling the condition r_1 and $r_2 \in \{1, 2, \ldots, N\}$ and $r_1 \neq r_2 \neq i$. Alongside these, the vector $\mathbf{x}^k_{best}$ is identified as the best element within the population for that specific iteration, denoted as k.

This strategy is widely utilized due to its tendency to facilitate rapid convergence toward the global optimum in many scenarios. By incorporating the current best solution in the population ($\mathbf{x}^k_{best}$) into the mutation process, the algorithm often accelerates its progress toward the most optimal solution. However, this approach does come with a drawback. The reliance on $\mathbf{x}_{best}^k$ can lead to a decrease in the diversity of the population over time. As a result, the candidate solutions might be increasingly drawn toward a local optimum instead of exploring the broader search space. This attraction to a local optimum can be a significant challenge, especially in complex optimization problems where global optimum search is essential. Therefore, while this strategy enhances convergence speed, it requires careful consideration and balancing to ensure that it doesn't compromise the overall effectiveness of the search process in finding the most optimal solution. This mutation is implemented as follows:

$$\mathbf{v}^k = \{\mathbf{x}_{best}^k + F * (\mathbf{x}_{r1}^k - \mathbf{x}_{r2}^k) \tag{4.37}$$

4.4.2.3 Mutation Rand/2

In this variant of the mutation strategy used in the DE algorithm, five parameter vectors are utilized: $\mathbf{x}_{r_1}^k, \mathbf{x}_{r_2}^k, \mathbf{x}_{r_3}^k, \mathbf{x}_{r_4}^k$ and $\mathbf{x}_{r_5}^k$. These vectors are chosen randomly from the population, adhering to the condition that r_1, r_2, r_3, r_4, and $r_5 \in \{1, 2, \ldots, N\}$ and are all distinct from each other $(r_1 \neq r_2 \neq r_3 \neq r_4 \neq r_5 \neq i)$. This strategy is particularly advantageous for problems characterized by high dimensionality, where maintaining a greater degree of diversity within the population is crucial.

By incorporating information from five different individuals, the mutant vector $\mathbf{v}^k$ becomes a more comprehensive representation of the population's diversity. This approach effectively broadens the communication channel among the individuals in the population. As a result, the algorithm is better equipped to explore a more diverse set of solutions, enhancing its ability to navigate complex, high-dimensional search spaces. This increase in diversity and the consequent enhancement in exploratory capacity make this five-vector mutation strategy a valuable tool for tackling intricate optimization problems that demand a more extensive search approach. This mutation strategy can be modeled as follows:

$$\mathbf{v}^k = \{\mathbf{x}_{r5}^k + F * (\mathbf{x}_{r1}^k - \mathbf{x}_{r2}^k) + F * (\mathbf{x}_{r3}^k - \mathbf{x}_{r4}^k) \tag{4.38}$$

4.4.2.4 Mutation Best/2

In this specific mutation strategy of the DE algorithm, four distinct solutions are employed, selected randomly from the population with the condition that they must be different from each other, fulfilling r_1, r_2, r_3, and $r_4 \in \{1, 2, \ldots, N\}$ and $r_1 \neq r_2 \neq r_3 \neq r_4 \neq i$. This approach is particularly effective when dealing with multimodal functions, where rapid convergence toward the global optimum is essential.

The inclusion of four unique individuals in this variant offers a compelling blend of characteristics. It not only increases the diversity within the population but also enhances the exploitation phase of the algorithm. By integrating diverse perspectives from multiple solutions, the algorithm can more effectively navigate complex landscapes and identify optimal solutions. This increased diversity aids in avoiding premature convergence to local optima, ensuring a more thorough exploration of the search space. Simultaneously, the improved exploitation capability allows the algorithm to effectively refine and focus on promising areas, thereby accelerating the convergence process. This balance between exploration and exploitation makes this four-solution strategy particularly advantageous for tackling complex optimization problems that demand both depth and speed in the search process. This mutation is implemented as follows:

$$\mathbf{v}^k = \{\mathbf{x}_{best}^k + F * (\mathbf{x}_{r1}^k - \mathbf{x}_{r2}^k) + F * (\mathbf{x}_{r3}^k - \mathbf{x}_{r4}^k) \tag{4.39}$$

4.4.2.5 Mutation Current-to-Best/1

In this particular mutation operator within the DE algorithm, the process involves two distinct solutions, chosen randomly from the population. The selection criteria ensure that these solutions are different from each other, adhering to the condition r_1 and $r_2 \in \{1, 2, \ldots, N\}$ and $r_1 \neq r_2 \neq i$. Additionally, this strategy incorporates the vector $\mathbf{x}_i^k$, representing the current individual in the population undergoing the mutation operation, and the vector $\mathbf{x}_{best}^k$, which signifies the best-performing member of the population in iteration k.

This mutation strategy, by taking into account two random elements from the population, manages to maintain a certain level of diversity within the population. The differential aspect of the operation, which is the difference between the best individual ($\mathbf{x}_{best}^k$) and the current individual ($\mathbf{x}_i^k$), drives the convergence toward the best individual. This approach ensures that the algorithm steadily moves toward an optimal solution.

However, a challenge arises with this strategy when a significant number of individuals cluster around the best individual, potentially leading to a reduction in population diversity. This concentration in the vicinity of the best solution can limit the algorithm's ability to explore new and diverse areas of the search space. As a result, while this strategy is effective in converging toward the best solution, it needs to be balanced with mechanisms that ensure continued exploration and avoid the risk of stagnation in local optima, thus maintaining the overall health and diversity of the population. This mutation is implemented as follows:

$$\mathbf{v}^k = \{\mathbf{x}_i^k + F * (\mathbf{x}_{\text{best}}^k - \mathbf{x}_i^k) + F * (\mathbf{x}_{r1}^k - \mathbf{x}_{r2}^k) \tag{4.40}$$

4.4.3 The Crossover Operation in DE

The crossover operation in the DE algorithm serves a pivotal role, primarily aimed at enhancing the diversity of each solution vector. This operation acts as a complement to the mutation strategy, effectively contributing to an increase in the overall diversity of the population. In the crossover process, the mutant vector $\mathbf{v}^k$ and the individual $\mathbf{x}_i^k$ from the population are subjected to a recombination procedure. This procedure involves an element-to-element exchange between the two vectors. During this exchange, elements from the mutant vector $\mathbf{v}^k$ and the individual $\mathbf{x}_i^k$ are combined to form a new vector, referred to as the trial vector $\mathbf{u}^k$. The creation of this trial vector through crossover ensures that new genetic material is introduced into the population, which helps in exploring new regions of the search space and prevents the population from converging prematurely on local optima. By continuously introducing such variations, the crossover operation plays a crucial role in maintaining a healthy level of genetic diversity within the population, which is essential for the effective search and optimization capabilities of the DE algorithm. This procedure is computed based on the following framework:

$$\mathbf{u}^k = u_j^k \begin{cases} v_{i,j}^k & \text{if } j = j_{\mathbf{rand(0,1)}} \text{ ó } \mathbf{rand}\ (\mathbf{0}, \mathbf{1}) \leq CR \\ x_{i,j}^k & \text{otherwise} \end{cases} \tag{4.41}$$

In this context, $j_{\mathbf{rand(0,1)}} \in \{1, 2, \ldots, d\}$ signifies a specific position within the i-th solution vector. The term rand(0,1) is used to denote a randomly selected number that falls within the uniform distribution range of (0,1). The crossover rate, denoted as CR, is a crucial parameter in this process, governing the extent to which the mutant vector $\mathbf{v}^k$ influences the formation of the trial vector $\mathbf{u}^k$. As a key configuration parameter of the DE algorithm, the crossover rate CR is assigned a value that lies within the range [0, 1]. This parameter plays a significant role in balancing the contribution of the mutant vector to the trial vector, thereby impacting the diversity and exploration capabilities of the DE algorithm.

In the crossover phase of the DE algorithm, there is a random exchange of positions between the individual vector $\mathbf{x}_i^k$ from the population and the mutant vector $\mathbf{v}^k$, as formulated in Eq. 4.35. The crossover rate, denoted as CR, acts as a probabilistic factor in this process. It determines which positions from the mutant vector $\mathbf{v}^k$ are to be incorporated into the creation of the trial vector $\mathbf{u}^k$, and which positions will be retained from the individual vector $\mathbf{x}_i^k$.

The decision of whether to use a parameter from the mutant vector $\mathbf{v}^k$ or the individual's vector $\mathbf{x}_i^k$ in forming the trial vector $\mathbf{u}^k$ is based on the outcome of a random number generator, rand(0,1). If this randomly generated number is less than or equal to the CR value, then the corresponding parameter for the trial vector $\mathbf{u}^k$ is taken from the mutant vector $\mathbf{v}^k$. Conversely, if the random number exceeds the CR value, the parameter for $\mathbf{u}^k$ is derived from the individual's vector $\mathbf{x}_i^k$. This method of selectively combining elements from both the mutant and individual vectors introduces a strategic level of variability and diversity in the population, which is essential for the efficient exploration and optimization capabilities of the DE algorithm.

Figure 4.24 serves as a visual aid to demonstrate the crossover operation involved in the mutation process of the DE algorithm, particularly as outlined in Eq. 4.39. The figure illustrates the interaction between the parameter vector $\mathbf{x}_i^k$ and the mutant vector $\mathbf{v}^k$. Notably, both vectors are situated within a 5-dimensional space (d = 5). Each position within these vectors is symbolized by boxes aligned next to the labels corresponding to each vector.

In this depicted example, the creation of the trial vector $\mathbf{u}^k$ is influenced by both $\mathbf{x}_i^k$ and $\mathbf{v}^k$. Specifically, the first ($j = 1$) and fourth ($j = 4$) positions of the trial vector $\mathbf{u}^k$ are derived from the parameter vector $\mathbf{x}_i^k$, whereas the second ($j = 2$), third ($j = 3$), and fifth ($j = 5$) positions are sourced from the mutant vector $\mathbf{v}^k$. The arrows in the figure represent the evaluation process described in Eq. 4.41. During this process, if a randomly generated value falls below the crossover probability CR, the corresponding parameter value for the trial vector $\mathbf{u}^k$ is taken from the mutant vector $\mathbf{v}^k$. If the random value exceeds the *CR* threshold, the parameter is instead sourced from the individual's vector $\mathbf{x}_i^k$.

This graphical representation effectively depicts how the crossover operation blends elements from both the individual and mutant vectors to form the trial vector $\mathbf{u}^k$. This process of selective combination and exchange is critical for introducing new genetic material and variations into the population, a key factor in the DE algorithm's ability to explore and optimize within multidimensional solution spaces.

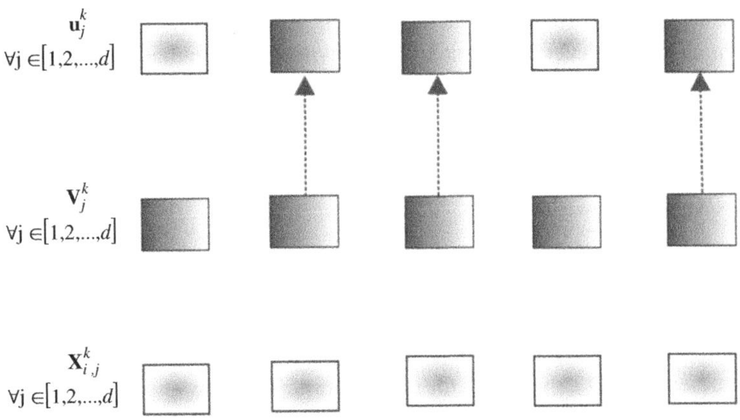

Figure 4.24 Visual depiction of the crossover mechanism employed in the search strategy of the DE algorithm.

4.4.4 The Selection Operation in DE

The selection operation in the DE algorithm is crucial for ensuring that the best solutions are retained within the population throughout the optimization process. After the mutation and crossover operations have been performed, the newly formed test vector $\mathbf{u}^k$ emerges as a potential candidate for inclusion in the population. However, its incorporation is contingent upon meeting a specific quality selection criterion.

This selection process evaluates whether the test vector $\mathbf{u}^k$ offers an improvement over its predecessor. The criterion for this evaluation involves comparing the fitness values of the test vector $\mathbf{u}^k$ and the existing individual $\mathbf{x}_i^k$ it is poised to replace. The fitness of each vector is a measure of its solution quality. The decision rule is straightforward: if the fitness value of the test vector $f(\mathbf{u}^k)$ is superior (which typically means lower in optimization problems) to the fitness of the current individual $f\left(\mathbf{x}_i^k\right)$, then $\mathbf{u}^k$ will supplant $\mathbf{x}_i^k$ in the population for the subsequent generation. On the other hand, if the test vector does not demonstrate a better fitness value, the existing individual $\mathbf{x}_i^k$ will retain its position in the population for at least another generation.

This selection mechanism plays a pivotal role in the DE algorithm, as it ensures that only improvements or equally competent solutions are carried forward. This approach is essential for the continuous improvement and evolution of the population toward the optimal solution, maintaining the overall quality and efficacy of the population across generations. This selection process is encapsulated in the equation presented below:

$$\mathbf{x}_i^k = \begin{cases} \mathbf{u}^k, & si\ f(\mathbf{u}^k) \leq f\left(\mathbf{x}_i^k\right) \\ \mathbf{x}_i^k, & \text{de otra forma} \end{cases} \tag{4.42}$$

In this context, $f()$ denotes the objective function that the algorithm aims to optimize. This selection procedure is methodically repeated in every generation of the algorithm and continues until a predefined stopping criterion is met. Typically, the stopping criterion most frequently employed is the maximum number of generations, $K_{\max}$, which is determined by the user at the outset of the optimization process.

4.4.5 Implementation of DE in MATLAB

Code 4.1 showcases the implementation of the DE algorithm in MATLAB®, following the procedural guidelines detailed in Section 4.2. To demonstrate the DE algorithm's operation, Code 4.1 incorporates a test function commonly utilized in assessing optimization methods, known as the sphere function. This function is characterized by its unimodal, convex, and multidimensional surface. It possesses a singular global minimum at the zero position of each dimension that constitutes the function's surface. The function's multidimensional nature serves as a testbed to examine the scaling effects of a metaheuristic algorithm's operators in high-dimensional environments. Furthermore, the sphere function's continuous and convex features suggest that nearly all optimization techniques, both classical and evolutionary, can reach the global optimum relatively easily.

The DE algorithm operates with a population size of 50 individuals ($N = 50$) and the iterative process is designed to cease when it reaches a maximum of 1000 iterations ($k_{\max} = 1000$). In order to visually demonstrate the behavior of individuals on the sphere function's surface, the movement of these individuals is plotted in each iteration. This aspect of the implementation is crucial for allowing users to observe the algorithm's performance in real time. Consequently, the DE algorithm is tested within a two-dimensional search space ($d = 2$), making it easier to visualize and comprehend the dynamics of the algorithm and the effectiveness of its various operators in navigating and optimizing within the specified search space.

Program 4.18 ***Implementation of the DE method by Using MATLAB.***

```
%Algorithm 4.18
% Implementation of the DE algorithm
    %% Clearing memory and closing Matlab windows
    clear all
    close all
% The function to be optimized, in this case, the sphere
function is considered.
fitness = @(xi) (xi(1)^2) + (xi(2)^2);
Kmax = 1000;
N = 50;
F = 0.2;
CR = 0.5;
dim = 2;
lb = -100;
ub = 100;
% Initialization of the population
if size(ub,2)==1
    X=rand(N,dim).*(ub-lb)+lb;
end
if size(ub,2)>1
    for j = 1:N
        for i=1:dim
            high=ub(i);down=lb(i);
            X(j,i)=rand(1,1).*(high-down)+down;
        end
    end
end
% The fitness values of the initial population are obtained.
for i = 1:N
    fitnessX(i,1) = fitness(X(i,:));
end
% The best overall individual is obtained
[fitnessXbest,Index] = min(fitnessX);
xBest = X(Index,:);
% The values are obtained to plot the function
 if dim<=2
        rango=ub-lb;
        figure(1)
```

```
        x1=[lb:rango/100:ub];
        y1=x1;
        [X1,Y1]=meshgrid(x1,y1);
        [row1,col1]=size(X1);
        for q=1:col1
            for hh=1:row1
                zz(hh,q)=fitness([X1(hh,q),Y1(hh,q)]);
            end
        end
 end
 evaluations = 1;
% Iterative process of the algorithm
    while (evaluations <= Kmax)
        for i = 1:N

            Indexes = randperm(N);
        a = Indexes(1);
        b = Indexes(2);
        c = Indexes(3);
        %Mutation
        v = X(c,:) + F * (X(a,:) - X(b,:));

        if size(ub,2)==1
            for it = 1:dim
                if (v(it) < lb)
                    v(it) = lb;
                end
                if (v(it) > ub)
                    v(it) = ub;
                end
            end
        end
        if size(ub,2) > 1
            for it = 1:dim
                high=ub(it);down=lb(it);
                if (v(it) < down)
                    v(it) = down;
                end
                if (v(it) > high)
                    v(it) = high;
                end
            end
        end
            %Crossover
          u=zeros(1,dim);
        j0 = randi([1 dim]);
        for j=1:dim
```

```
                if j==j0 || rand<= CR
                    u(j)=v(j);
                else
                    u(j)=X(i,j);
                end
            end
            % The fitness of the i-th vector is obtained
            fitnessI = fitness(X(i,:));
            % The fitness of the test vector u
            fitnessU = fitness(u);
            % The selection operation is performed
            if fitnessU < fitnessI
                X(i,:) = u;
                if fitnessU < fitnessXbest
                    fitnessXbest = fitnessU;
                    xBest = u;
                end
            end
        end
        % Current population graph
        if dim <= 2
            surf(X1,Y1,zz);
            hold on
            for iStruct = 1 : N
                plot(X(iStruct,1),X(iStruct,2),...
                    'o','markersize',6,'markerfacecolor','r');
            end
            plot(xBest(1),xBest(2),...
            'o','markersize',10,'markerfacecolor','g');
            drawnow;
            hold off
        end
        evaluations = evaluations + 1;
        fprintf('Iteration: %d\n',evaluations);
        end
    fprintf('Best agent: (%d,%d)\n',xBest(1),xBest(2));
    fprintf('Best fitness: %d\n',fitnessXbest);
```

The differential evolution (DE) algorithm holds significant potential in the realm of machine learning, primarily as an efficient tool for optimizing complex models, such as neural networks, and fine-tuning hyperparameters. Its ability to navigate multi-dimensional search spaces makes it well-suited for tasks like feature selection and model optimization, which are integral to machine learning workflows. Conversely, machine learning techniques can greatly enhance the DE method itself. For instance, machine learning models can be employed to predict the performance of different parameter combinations in DE, thereby reducing the computational load. They can also be used to adaptively adjust DE's control parameters in real-time, based on the learning from previous iterations. This symbiotic relationship between DE and machine learning techniques not only amplifies the effectiveness of DE in solving complex optimization problems but also opens up innovative ways to leverage machine learning for algorithmic improvements, leading to more robust and efficient optimization processes.

References

Baldick, R. (2006). *Applied Optimization*. Cambridge University Press.

Bartholomew-Biggs, M. (2008). *Nonlinear Optimization with Engineering Applications*. Springer.

Broyden, C.G. (1970). The convergence of a class of double rank minimization algorithms: part 1 and 2. *Journal of Applied Mathematics* 6: 76–90 and 222–231.

Deb, K. (2001). *Multi-Objective Optimization Using Evolutionary Algorithms*. Wiley.

Dennis, J.E. (1978). A brief introduction to quasi-Newton methods. In: *Numerical Analysis: Proceedings of Symposia in Applied Mathematics* (ed. G.H. Golub and J. Öliger), 19–52. American Mathematical Society.

Dorigo, M. and Di Caro, G. (1999). *Ant Colony Optimization: A New Metaheuristic*.

Fletcher, R. and Powell, M.J. (1963). A rapidly convergent descent method for minimization. *Computer Journal* 6: 163–168.

Glover, F. (1986). *Future Paths for Integer Programming and Links to Artificial Intelligence*.

Goldberg, D.E. (1989). *Genetic Algorithms in Search, Optimization, and Machine Learning*. Oxford Press.

Hocking, L. (1991). *Optimal Control: An Introduction to the Theory with Applications*. Oxford University Press.

Kennedy, J. and Eberhart, R. (1995). *Particle Swarm Optimization*. IEEE.

Kirkpatrick, S., Gelatt, C., and Vecchi, P. (1983). Optimization by simulated annealing. *Science* 220 (4598): 671–680.

Mathews, J. and Fink, K. (2000). *Metodos Numericos con Matlab*. Prentice Hall.

Matyas, J. (1965). Random optimization. *Automation and Remote Control* 26: 246–253.

Reinhardt, R., Hoffmann, A., and Gerlach, T. (2013). *Nichtlineare Optimierung*. Springer.

Simon, D. (2013). *Evolutionary Optimization Algorithms, Biologically Inspired and Population-Based Approaches to Computer Intelligence*. Wiley.

Venkataraman, P. (2009). *Applied Optimization with MATLAB Programming*, 2e. Wiley.

Yang, X.-S. (2010). *Engineering Optimization*. Wiley.

5

Metaheuristic Techniques for Fine-Tuning Parameter of Complex Systems

5.1 Introduction

The nature of all real problems in engineering and the real world tends to the nonlinearity. Moreover, to analyze and control them is necessary to define the model that represents such a problem or plant. On the other hand, determining the model that represents a specific problem to be treated becomes a titanic task that usually is not feasible. Under such considerations, alternative models can represent the response of several problems and plants which can be highly difficult to approximate (Piroddi et al. 2012). The adaptive neuro-fuzzy inference system (ANFIS) (Jang 1993) is a suitable type of flexible network for nonlinear systems that has acquired notoriety as a soft computing approach that combines the strengths of two areas of artificial intelligence, the learning capability of adaptive networks through the partial truth reasoning of the Fuzzy system Takagi-Sugeno (Takagi and Sugeno 1985), and the inference employing Fuzzy procedure to obtain an accurate and generalization relationship of input and output pairs.

ANFIS and similar approaches contain in their structure optimizers which are responsible for determining the internal parameters that better fit the system or plant to be approximated. Nevertheless, in many cases, these optimizers cannot perform proper parameter tuning due to their own structure limitations which commonly present different flaws in their search strategy. As an efficient alternative, different authors report in the literature different modifications to the main structures of these approaches in which metaheuristic techniques are considered to improve the fine-tuning of the internal parameters considering their good performance in several complex applications.

5.2 Differential Evolution (DE)

Differential Evolution (DE) is one of the most famous optimization approaches due to its capabilities for determining competitive solutions to complex problems and its relatively simple implementation. DE was proposed by Storn and Price (1997) which is based on the difference between two elements represented as vectors $\mathbf{x}_{r_1}$ and $\mathbf{x}_{r_2}$ corresponding to points 7 and 9 as is shown in Figure 5.1a.

Once the distance is determined, it is scaled and added to a third vector randomly selected $\mathbf{x}_{r_3}$ (in the graphical representation is considered as the element 5) where the scaling factor is represented as F and indicates the magnitude of the difference between elements that is considered to add to the third vector in order to generate a fourth vector $\mathbf{v}_1$ known as a mutant vector as can be

Machine Learning and Metaheuristic Computation, First Edition.
Erik Cuevas, Jorge Galvez, Omar Avalos, and Fernando Wario.

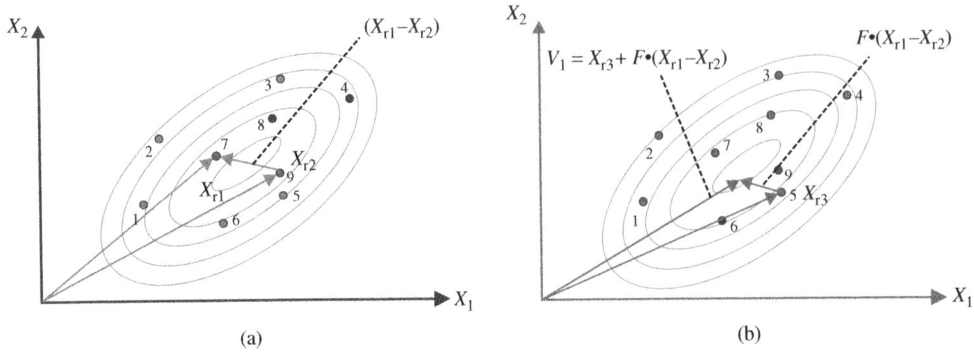

Figure 5.1 Graphical description of two vectors randomly selected by the DE in its search strategy (a) Random vectors selection and (b) Generation of new vector V_1.

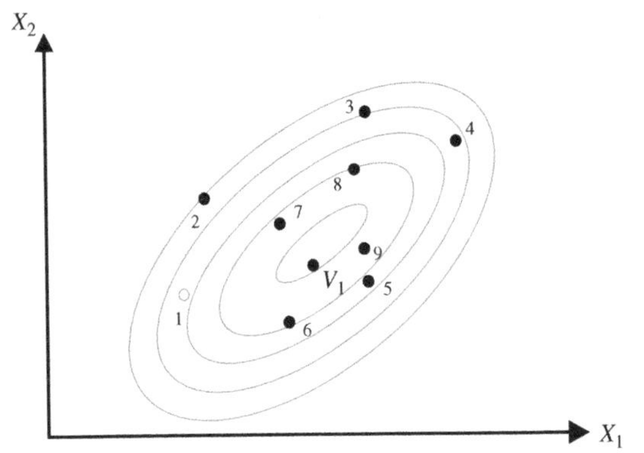

Figure 5.2 Graphical representation of the substitution of element 1 by the new mutant vector.

seen in Figure 5.1b. Finally, in Figure 5.2 the new mutant vector is evaluated using a cost function showing a better quality than element 1 which means that the new element replaces element 1 in the optimization process.

As typical optimization approaches, the population of the DE is represented as a set of N vectors (elements) in which the parameters are defined on the d-dimensional real values search space. Computationally, the population is symbolized by $\mathbf{X}$ and is formed by a set of vectors $\{\mathbf{x}_1^k, \mathbf{x}_2^k, \ldots, \mathbf{x}_N^k\}$ where each vector $\mathbf{x}_i^k$ represents a position in the d-dimensional vectoral space $\{x_1, x_2, \ldots, x_d\}$. These parameter vectors are manipulated by the DE operators: mutation, crossover, and selection through the optimization process at each iteration k for determining the global solution. The operators employed in the search strategy by the DE are described below.

5.2.1 Mutation

Once the initialization is performed (randomly) the mutation is employed to change the elements into the population to generate a modified population version. This modification is better known as differential mutation because it is based on the difference between vectors promoting the information exchange. The differential mutation is computed as follows:

$$\mathbf{v}^k = \{\mathbf{x}_{r3}^k + F * (\mathbf{x}_{r1}^k - \mathbf{x}_{r2}^k)\} \tag{5.1}$$

where $\mathbf{x}_{r1}^k, \mathbf{x}_{r2}^k$, and $\mathbf{x}_{r3}^k$ (being $r_1, r_2, r_3 \in \{1, 2, \ldots, N\}$ and $r_1 \neq r_2 \neq r_3 \neq i$) are the vectors randomly selected while $F \in [0, 2]$ is known as the differential weight which adjusts the magnitude regarding the difference between $(\mathbf{x}_{r1}^k - \mathbf{x}_{r2}^k)$. Equation 5.1 shows the most common combination of three vectors randomly selected from the population to generate a fourth element (vector). Nevertheless, different variations mainly are focused on the operator of the DE that can generate distinct behavior in the mutation stage modifying the search strategy. It is worth mentioning that the mutation Eq. 5.1 is also known as *Mutation rand/1*. To exemplify the different options of mutation operators, the most used mutation operators are briefly described below.

5.2.1.1 Mutation Best/1

$$\mathbf{v}^k = \left\{\mathbf{x}_{best}^k + F * \left(\mathbf{x}_{r1}^k - \mathbf{x}_{r2}^k\right)\right\} \tag{5.2}$$

In this strategy, the elements $\mathbf{x}_{r1}^k$ and $\mathbf{x}_{r2}^k$ (r_1, $r_2 \in \{1, 2, \ldots, N\}$ and $r_1 \neq r_2 \neq i$) are randomly selected from the population, and $\mathbf{x}_{best}^k$ is the best element of the iteration k. This mutation increases the convergence rate to the optimal solution but decreases the population diversity which generates that the candidate solutions could be attracted to local solutions.

5.2.1.2 Mutation Rand/2

$$\mathbf{v}^k = \left\{\mathbf{x}_{r5}^k + F * \left(\mathbf{x}_{r1}^k - \mathbf{x}_{r2}^k\right) + F * \left(\mathbf{x}_{r3}^k - \mathbf{x}_{r4}^k\right)\right\} \tag{5.3}$$

In this variation on the mutation operator, five vectors are considered to generate a sixth element where $\mathbf{x}_{r1}^k, \mathbf{x}_{r2}^k, \mathbf{x}_{r3}^k, \mathbf{x}_{r4}^k$, and $\mathbf{x}_5^k$ ($r_1, r_2, r_3, r_4, r_5 \in \{1, 2, \ldots, N\}$, and $r_1 \neq r_2 \neq r_3 \neq r_4 \neq r_5 \neq i$) are randomly selected from the population. This mutation is appropriate when the dimensionality of the problem to be treated is high due to increases in the diversity by considering more elements for generating the mutant vector.

5.2.1.3 Mutation Best/2

$$\mathbf{v}^k = \left\{\mathbf{x}_{best}^k + F * \left(\mathbf{x}_{r1}^k - \mathbf{x}_{r2}^k\right) + F * \left(\mathbf{x}_{r3}^k - \mathbf{x}_{r4}^k\right)\right\} \tag{5.4}$$

In this strategy, four elements randomly selected are considered under the same restrictions as the last variations. This modification is useful in problems with a nature multimodal in which a fast convergence into the global solution is required maintaining the information between elements increasing the diversity of the population.

5.2.1.4 Mutation Current-to-Best/1

$$\mathbf{v}^k = \left\{\mathbf{x}_i^k + F * \left(\mathbf{x}_{best}^k - \mathbf{x}_i^k\right) + F * \left(\mathbf{x}_{r1}^k - \mathbf{x}_{r2}^k\right)\right\} \tag{5.5}$$

This mutation considers $\mathbf{x}_{r1}^k$ and $\mathbf{x}_{r2}^k$ ($r_1, r_2 \in \{1, 2, \ldots, N\}$ and $r_1 \neq r_2 \neq i$) randomly selected from the population, $\mathbf{x}_i^k$ is the current element that is being modified by the operator, and $\mathbf{x}_{best}^k$ is the best element at iteration k. Considering that just two elements are randomly selected, the diversity remains in a certain grade but as the difference is regarding the best element the convergence is guaranteed in the best current element.

5.2.2 Crossover

The crossover operator has the main objective of increasing the diversity of the population. This operation complements the mutation to balance the exploration and exploitation in the search strategy. In this stage, the elements $\mathbf{v}^k$ and $\mathbf{x}_i^k$ combine their information to generate a new element $\mathbf{u}^k$ and is described as follows.

$$\mathbf{u}^k = u^k \begin{cases} v_{i,j}^k & \text{if } j = j_{\text{rand}(0,1)} \text{ or } \text{rand}(0,1) \leq CR \\ x_{i,j}^k & \text{otherwise} \end{cases} \tag{5.6}$$

where $j_{\text{rand}(0,1)}$ represents one of the positions of the *i-th* vector and rand(0, 1) is a normally distributed random number between the interval (0,1). The parameter CR controls the balance between the exploration and exploitation which determines if the operator of mutation or the crossover is performed.

5.2.3 Selection

This stage determines whether a solution $\mathbf{u}^k$ can be considered as part of the population, for this purpose an elitist selection is carried out, in this process, it is considered if the last element is replaced by the new mutant vector or remains. To determine which element is replaced, a cost function is employed where the new mutant vector is evaluated $f(\mathbf{u}^k)$ as well as the current element $f(\mathbf{x}_i^k)$, if the fitness value of the new element is better than the current vector is replaced,

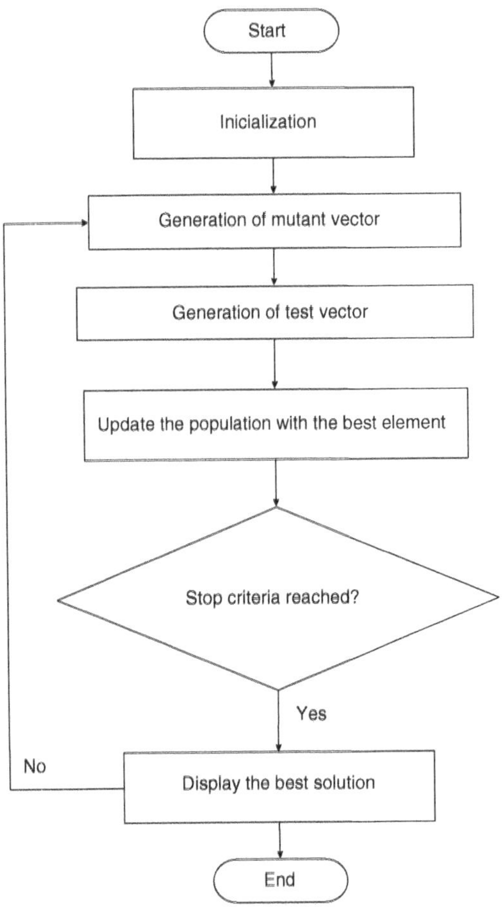

Figure 5.3 Differential Evolution (DE) main functioning flowchart.

otherwise remains. To determine the candidate solution to be selected the following expression is employed. For a better understanding of the complete functioning of the DE, the flowchart in the Figure 5.3

$$\mathbf{x}_i^k = \begin{cases} \mathbf{u}^k & \text{if } f(\mathbf{u}^k) \leq f\left(\mathbf{x}_i^k\right) \\ \mathbf{x}_i^k & \text{otherwise} \end{cases} \tag{5.7}$$

For a better understanding of the main functioning of the DE, Algorithm 5.1 presents step-by-step the optimization process over a well-known test function called the sphere function which exhibits unimodal surface, convex, and multidimensional characteristics. Under such conditions, the cost function has just one minimum in zero. In step 1 the function to be optimized is declared, considering that the optimization process is going to be plotted the example must contemplate two dimensions. Step two sets the maximum number of iterations, population size, dimensions number, and DE parameters. In the DE just two parameters are needed, the CR which represents the threshold value between the mutation and crossover, and the F which represents the scaling factor in the mutation stage. In steps 3 and 4 the population is initialized employing a uniform distribution and the fitness value is computed respectively.

After evaluating the population, a memory is generated to store the fitness values and their positions. The best element of each iteration is stored for visualizing the evolution of the optimization process. In step 5 the iterative process of the search strategy where three vectors are randomly selected and the mutation and crossover are performed, at the same time the limits of each particle are verified considering the lower and upper bounds. Step 6 determines by an elitist selection the elements that are able to shape the next population.

```
%Algorithm 5.1
%Clean data
clear all
close all

%Step 1, The problem to be optimized is defined (Sphere function)
fitness = @(xi) (xi(1)^2) + (xi(2)^2);

% Step 2, DE parameters declaration
Kmax = 100;
N = 50;
F = 0.2;
CR = 0.5;
dim = 2;

% Stet 3, randomly initialization of the vectors (elements) between
%lower and upper bounds
lb = -100;
ub = 100;
```

```
if size(ub,2)==1
   X=rand(N,dim).*(ub-lb)+lb;
end
if size(ub,2)>1
   for j = 1:N
       for i=1:dim
           high=ub(i);down=lb(i);
           X(j,i)=rand(1,1).*(high-down)+down;
      end
   end
end

% Step 4, evaluation of the population using the cost function
for i = 1:N
    fitnessX(i,1) = fitness(X(i,:));
end

% Save the best element and they fitness in memory
[BestfitnessX,index] = min(fitnessX);
xBest = X(index,:);

%Plotting the particles in the iteration process
if dim<=2
          rango=ub-lb;
         figure(1) % Plotting current population
         x1=[lb:rango/100:ub];
         y1=x1;
         [X1,Y1]=meshgrid(x1,y1);
         [row1,col1]=size(X1);
         for q=1:col1
             for hh=1:row1
                 zz(hh,q)=fitness([X1(hh,q),Y1(hh,q)]);
             end
         end
end
eval = 1;

%Step 5, iterative process of the optimization
while (eval <= Kmax)
      for i = 1:N
% Three vectors randomly selected, mutant vector generation
          index = randperm(N);
          a = index(1);
          b = index(2);
          c = index(3);
          v = X(c,:) + F * (X(a,:) - X(b,:));
```

```
        if size(ub,2)==1
           for it = 1:dim
               if (v(it) < lb)
                   v(it) = lb;
               end
               if (v(it) > ub)
               v(it) = ub;
               end
           end
        end
        if size(ub,2) > 1
           for it = 1:dim
               high=ub(it);down=lb(it);
               if (v(it) < down)
                  v(it) = down;
               end
                  if (v(it) > high)
                  v(it) = high;
               end
            end
         end
%Crossover
         u=zeros(1,dim);
        j0 = randi([1 dim]);
        for j=1:dim
            if j==j0 || rand<= CR
               u(j)=v(j);
            else
               u(j)=X(i,j);
            end
        end

%Cost function evaluation to the population and the test vector
         fitnessI = fitness(X(i,:));
         fitnessU = fitness(u);

%Step 6, Elitist selection is performed
    if fitnessU < fitnessI
            X(i,:) = u;
      if fitnessU < BestfitnessX
          BestfitnessX = fitnessU;
          xBest = u;
      end
    end
end
```

```
%Plotting the current iteration
if dim <= 2
   surf(X1,Y1,zz);
   hold on
   for iStruct = 1 : N
   plot(X(iStruct,1),X(iStruct,2),...
        'o','markersize',6,'markerfacecolor','r');
   end
   plot(xBest(1),xBest(2),...
        'o','markersize',10,'markerfacecolor','g');
   drawnow;
   hold off
end
eval = eval + 1;
fprintf('Iteration: %d\n',eval);
end

%Step 7, Display the best vector and its fitness value
fprintf('Best individual: (%d,%d)\n',xBest(1),xBest(2));
fprintf('Best fitness: %d\n',BestfitnessX);
```

Finally, in step 7 the best vector and its fitness value are displayed as the optimal solution while the cost function and the particles are plotted at each iteration in order to visualize the search strategy and the convergence at the global solution of the vectors in the function surface. Figure 5.4 shows graphically the vector result of the optimization process.

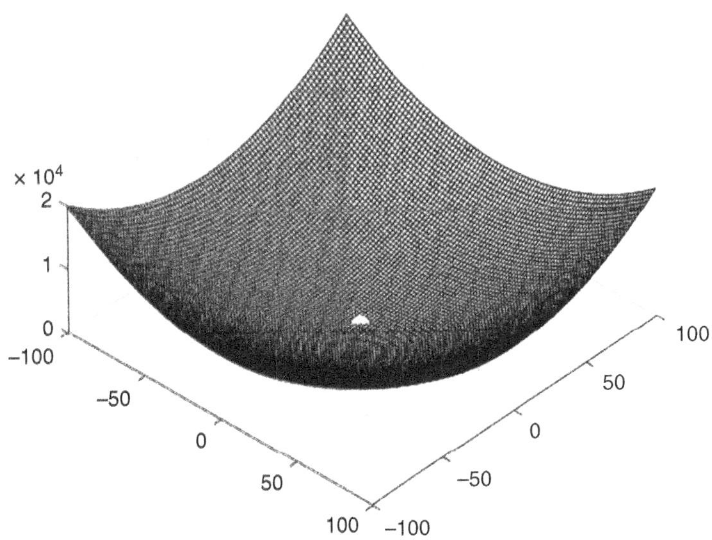

Figure 5.4 Differential Evolution (DE) optimal value to sphere function.

5.3 Adaptive Network-Based Fuzzy Inference System (ANFIS)

The Adaptive Network-based Fuzzy Inference System, better known as ANFIS model, is a suitable variety of adaptable networks for nonlinear systems that has reached notoriety as a soft computing method. ANFIS approach takes advantage of the strengths of two fields of artificial intelligence, the first adaptable learning process of neural networks through the partial knowledge of the Fuzzy logic system Takagi-Sugeno, and the inference based on the Fuzzy approach by the accurate generation of the relation between the input and output pairs.

According to the main structure of the ANFIS model, this structure can be considered as two different models, a non-linear system followed by a linear block as can be seen in Figure 5.5. Under such considerations, in the ANFIS model, the nonlinear system represents the antecedent of the complete structure while the linear block involves the linear functions of the consequent.

Structurally, the ANFIS structure can be represented into five different layers, each one of which develops a particular purpose in the system. Each layer is described below.

Layer 1: In this layer each node i defines the degree of the input u satisfying the linguistic concept characterized by A_i.

$$O_i^1 = \mu_{A_i}(u) \tag{5.8}$$

The linguistic correspondence is determined by a member function described below:

$$\mu_{A_i}(u) = e^{-\frac{(u-\sigma_i)}{(2s_i)^2}} \tag{5.9}$$

where $\{\sigma_i, s_i\}$ are the adaptable parameters of the member function which are better known as the premise parameters.

Layer 2: In this layer, each node i is labeled with $\prod$ which represents the firing strength of its corresponding fuzzy rule $\left(O_i^2 = w_i\right)$.

Layer 3: In this point each node i is represented as N which implies the normalization of the firing strength and is computed as below:

$$O_i^3 = \overline{w}_i = \frac{w_i}{\sum_{j=1}^{h} w_j}, \tag{5.10}$$

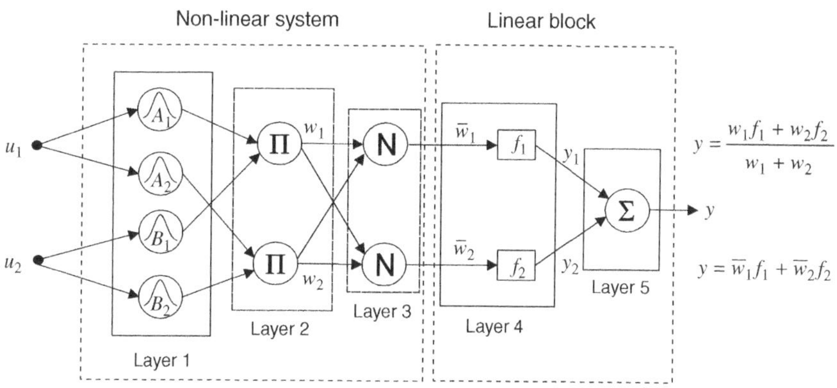

Figure 5.5 Adaptive Network-based Fuzzy Inference System (ANFIS) structure.

Layer 4: In this stage, each node i is operated by a linear function that acts as a processing unit and can be performed employing the following expression:

$$O_i^4 = \overline{w}_i f_i = \overline{w}_i(p_i u_1 + q_i u_2 + r_i) \tag{5.11}$$

Layer 5: In this final stage the node i is labeled as $\sum$ which represents the sum of all signals and is computed as below:

$$y = O_i^5 = \sum_i \overline{w}_i \cdot f_i = \frac{\sum_i w_i \cdot f_i}{\sum_i w_i} \tag{5.12}$$

The internal parameters of the ANFIS model can be divided into two groups, non-linear parameters that consider the elements $P_{Nl} = \{\sigma_i, s_i\}$ and the linear parameters that correspond to $P_l = \{p_i, q_i, r_i\}$. Considering that Nu is the total number of inputs of the ANFIS model and FM_q is the number of member functions related to the inputs q ($q = 1, \ldots, Nu$), and the number of non-linear and linear parameter are computed as follow:

$$P_{NL} = 2 \cdot \sum_{q=1}^{Nu} FM_q, \quad P_L = \left[\prod_{q=1}^{Nu} FM_q\right] \cdot (Nu + 1), \tag{5.13}$$

$$P_T = P_p + P_c \tag{5.14}$$

5.4 Differential Evolution for Fine-Tuning ANFIS Parameters Setting

In this subsection the implementation of the hybridization between the DE and the ANFIS model, under such circumstances, the internal optimizer of the ANFIS is replaced by the DE to improve the model's response regarding complex applications. In order to perform this example, the mathematical optimization model can be represented as the minimization approach as described below:

$$\begin{aligned} &\text{minimize} && f(\mathbf{x}), \ \mathbf{x} = (x^1, \ldots, x^d) \in \mathbb{R}^d, \\ &\text{subject to} && g_i(\mathbf{x}) \le 0, \ i = \{1, \ldots, m\}, \\ &&& h_j(\mathbf{x}) = 0, \ j = \{1, \ldots, p\}, \end{aligned} \tag{5.15}$$

where the DE employs its search strategy for determining the scalar $f(\mathbf{x})$ where $\mathbf{X} = \{\mathbf{x} \in \mathbb{R}^d \mid l_h \le x_h \le u_h, h = 1, \ldots, d\}$ is the feasible bounded space considered within the upper and lower limits. The main goal of the optimization process is to determine the best solution (global solution) for a specific problem in which the following definition is fulfilled: $f : \mathbf{X} \in \mathbb{R}^d \to \mathbb{R}, \mathbf{X} \neq 0$, for $\mathbf{x} \in \mathbf{X}$ the value $f^* \triangleq f(\mathbf{x}^*) > -\infty$ is the best solution if and only if $\forall \mathbf{x} \in \mathbf{X} : f(\mathbf{x}^*) \le f(\mathbf{x})$ where $\mathbf{x}^*$ is the global solution.

For simplicity, the example is explained in the flowchart of Figure 5.6, and it can be divided into two main parts: forward and backward pass of the model. In the figure, the first element of the process is represented in section A1, and this stage considers the initial parameters of the complete process and the generation of the connection nodes array as is presented in Figure 5.5. For this specific example, the dataset considers 5 inputs which represent that is, necessary to achieve 112 nodes in total, this process is performed in section A2 of Figure 5.6 in which an iterative process is necessary where a set of values of the inputs is employed in the first three layers of the ANFIS structure. Once the training data are located in their respective nodes, the premise values

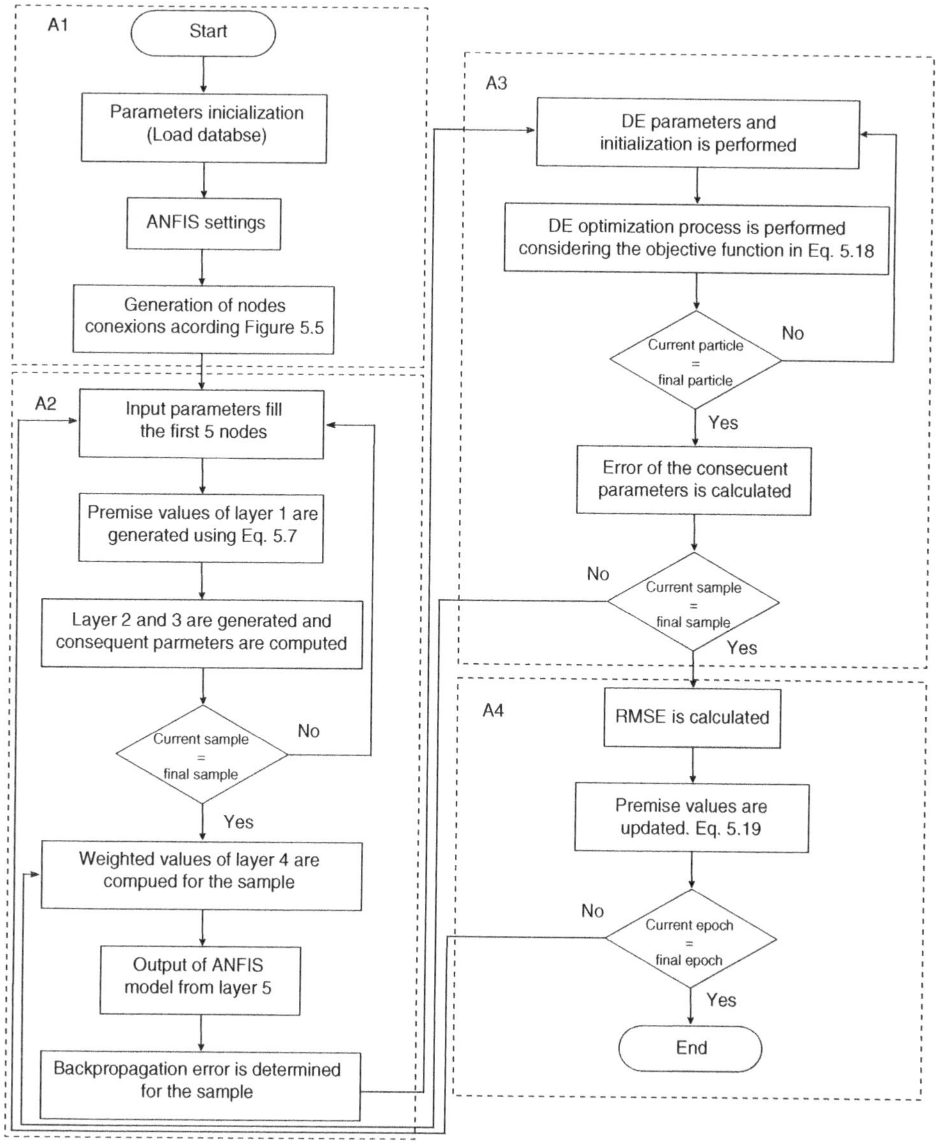

Figure 5.6 Flowchart of the ANFIS hybridization structure.

of layer 1 are computed using a deterministic method while the connection between nodes 1 and 2 is determined using the expression 5.16.

$$\text{if} \rightarrow \frac{x-c}{a}\begin{cases} = 0 & \mu_{A_i}(x) = 1 \\ \neq 0 & \mu_{A_i}(x) = \dfrac{1}{1+\left(\left(\frac{x-c}{a}\right)^2\right)^b} \end{cases} \tag{5.16}$$

where x, a, b, and c are the premise values that define the generalized bell of the member functions, while $\mu_{A_i}(x)$ represents the node to be filled. Subsequently, the firing strengths and the normalized values of their ratios in layers 2 and 3 are determined as Section 5.3 explains. Then, the consequent values are computed which correspond to six parameters estimated by a first-order polynomial expression represented in Eq. 5.17. When the consequent parameters are determined for each input of the dataset, the iterative process for achieving the weights of layer 4 is performed, and the output of the ANFIS model is computed in layer 5. After this procedure, the first output of the ANFIS model is used for determining the backpropagation error and modifying the premise values of layer 1 in order to improve the approximation task.

$$\text{if} \rightarrow \frac{x-c}{a} \begin{cases} = 0 & den = 1 \\ \neq 0 & den = \left(\left(\frac{x-c}{a}\right)^2\right)^b \end{cases} \tag{5.17}$$

$$\text{if} \rightarrow mf_i \begin{cases} x \ \ mf_i = \dfrac{2b \times den}{a \times (1 + 2den + den^2)} \\ c \begin{cases} \text{if} \rightarrow den = 1 & mf_i = 0 \\ \text{if} \rightarrow den \neq 1 \ \ mf_i = \dfrac{-\log\left(\frac{x-c}{a}\right)^2 \times den}{1 + 2den + den^2} \end{cases} \\ a \begin{cases} \text{if} \rightarrow x = c & mf_i = 0 \\ \text{if} \rightarrow x \neq c \ \ mf_i = \dfrac{2b \times den}{(x-c) \times (1 + 2den + den^2)} \end{cases} \end{cases} \tag{5.18}$$

In the same scheme, the expression 5.18 is employed for determining the actual premise values and the backpropagation errors, where mf_i is the current member function in layer 1 while x, a, b, and c are the new premise values for each member function. Under these considerations, the DE is employed in this stage to improve the strategy of determining these values. As mentioned before, to perform the optimization method is necessary to determine a quality metric of solutions achieved by the DE, in this case, the cost function used to measure the feasible solutions is described below (section A3 Figure 5.6).

$$\mu_{A_{i,j}} = \sum_{i=n_i+1}^{n_i x n_{MF}} \sum_{j=1}^{3} Be_i \times mf_i \tag{5.19}$$

where n_i and n_{MF} are the previous number of inputs and the number of member functions respectively. The subindexes i and j represent the current node and the parameters of the respective member function and Be_i is the backpropagation error while $\mu_{A_{i,j}}$ is the value of the cost function. Once the premise parameters of layer 1 are determined, the consequent values of layer 4 are modified considering the backpropagation error and the proposed consequence values from nodes of layers 1 and 4.

Section A4 shows that the backward pass process finishes; and the Root Mean Square Error (RMSE) is determined by the current epoch considering the difference between the output of the hybridization of the ANFIS model and the actual sample of the database. Subsequently, the premise values are updated in order to know the evolution of the optimization process at each epoch employing the following expression.

$$\mu_B(x) = \frac{\mu_B(x) - S_s \times \mu_A(x)}{\ell} \tag{5.20}$$

where $\mu_B(x)$ and $\mu_A(x)$ represent the current updated and estimated premise parameters, S_s is the step size which is determined by the user in the initialization of the problem, and ℓ is the square

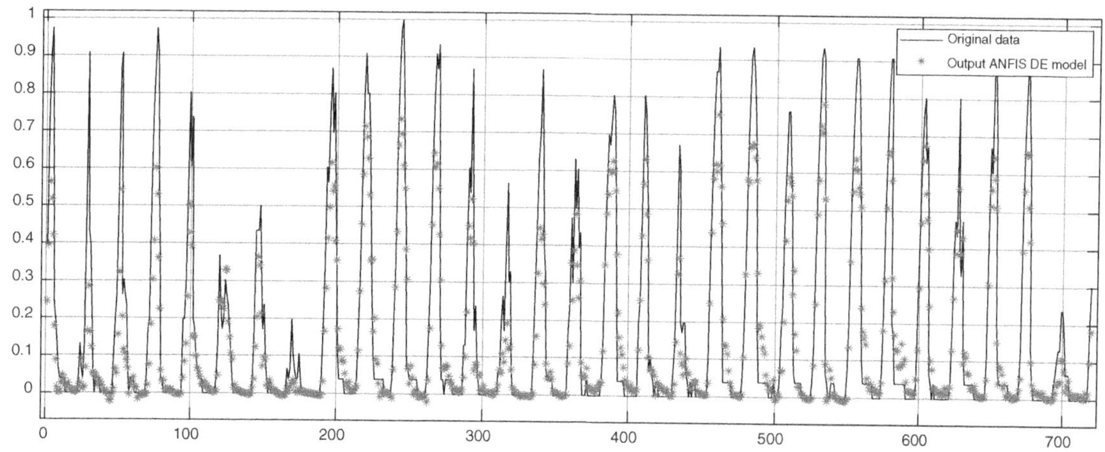

Figure 5.7 ANFIS_DE response after training method regarding original data.

root sum of difference from the premise values. In Algorithm 5.2 the hybridization of the ANFIS model and DE approach are performed. In step 1, the initial parameter setting of the ANFIS model, and the dataset used for this experiment are declared. Once the initial parameters are configured by the user, the main structure of the ANFIS model and the network generation is performed in step 2, in this specific example the number of iterations and epochs are considered as 35 and 100 respectively. After step 2 in the function declaration, the complete structure configuration of the ANFIS model is constructed. In step 3, the complete training process where basically two main inter steps are performed; the DE optimization method, and the Kalman filter technique in which the premise and consequent parameters are achieved in the complete process. Finally, in step 4 the test of the trained model is performed, and the process is ended. The approximation test of the trained model is shown in Figure 5.7.

```
%Algorithm 5.2
%Clean data
clear all
close all

%% Step 1, ANFIS data initialization and dataset uploading
mf=2;
step_size=0.1;
decrease_rate=0.9;
increase_rate=1.1;

Dataset='datos_prom.xlsx';
data=xlsread(Dataset);
Sdata=data;
aux=[data(:,1:4) data(:,end)];
```

```
data=aux;

Irun=1;
Frun=35;

%% Step2, Main ANFIS structure
while Irun<=Frun
    if Irun>1
        fprintf('\n\n')
    end
    disp(['Run
',num2str(Irun),'___________________________________________________'])

    epoch_n=100;

%Step 3, Complete ANFIS training and optimization process
[bestnet,RMSE]=myanfis(data,epoch_n,mf,step_size,...
decrease_rate,increase_rate);

%Step 4, Evaluation of the training model.
 y_myanfis=evalmyanfis(bestnet,data(:,1:end-1));

    if Irun==1
        Net.M1_RMSE=zeros(epoch_n,Frun);
        Net.M1_ANFIS=zeros(size(data,1),Frun);
    end

    Net.M1_RMSE(:,Irun)=RMSE;
    Net.M1_ANFIS(:,Irun)=y_myanfis;

    if Irun==Frun
        Net.M1_config=bestnet.config;
        Net.M1_mparam=bestnet.mparams;
        Net.M1_kparams=bestnet.kparams;
        Net.M1_Premisa=bestnet.Premisa;
        Net.M1_Consecuente=bestnet.Consecuente;
    end

    Irun=Irun+1;
end

% Functions declaration
%% MyANFIS configuration construction.
function [bestnet,RMSE] =
myanfis(data,epoch_n,mf,step_size,decrease_rate,increase_rate)
inputs=data(:,1:end-1);
```

```
output=data(:,end);
ndata=size(data,1);

mn=min(inputs);
mx=max(inputs);
mm=mx-mn;
ni=size(inputs,2);
nc=mf^ni;
Node_n = ni + ni*mf + 3*nc + 1;

min_RMSE=999999999999;
mparams=[];
kparams=zeros(nc,(ni+1));

for i=1:ni
    tmp=linspace(mn(1),mx(1),mf)';
    mparams=[mparams;repmat([mm(i)/6 2],mf,1) tmp];
end

mynet.Premisa=mparams;
config=zeros(Node_n);
nodes=zeros(Node_n,1);

st=ni;
for i=1:ni
    config(i,st+[1:mf])=1;
    st=st+mf;
end

st=ni+ni*mf+1;
if size(inputs,2)==2
    for i=1:mf
        for j=1:mf
            config(ni+i,st)=1;
            config(ni+mf+j,st)=1;
            st=st+1;
        end
    end
elseif size(inputs,2)==3
    for i=1:mf
        for j=1:mf
            for k=1:mf
                config(ni+i,st)=1;
                config(ni+mf+j,st)=1;
                config(ni+2*mf+k,st)=1;
                st=st+1;
            end
```

```
            end
        end
    elseif size(inputs,2)==4
        for i=1:mf
            for j=1:mf
                for k=1:mf
                    for l=1:mf
                        config(ni+i,st)=1;
                        config(ni+mf+j,st)=1;
                        config(ni+2*mf+k,st)=1;
                        config(ni+3*mf+l,st)=1;
                        st=st+1;
                    end
                end
            end
        end
    elseif size(inputs,2)==5
        for i=1:mf
            for j=1:mf
                for k=1:mf
                    for l=1:mf
                        for m=1:mf
                            config(ni+i,st)=1;
                            config(ni+mf+j,st)=1;
                            config(ni+2*mf+k,st)=1;
                            config(ni+3*mf+l,st)=1;
                            config(ni+4*mf+m,st)=1;
                            st=st+1;
                        end
                    end
                end
            end
        end
    else
        return;
    end

    for i=1:nc
        for j=1:nc
            config(ni+ni*mf+i,ni+ni*mf+nc+j)=1;
        end
    end

    for i=1:nc
        config(ni+ni*mf+nc+i,ni+ni*mf+2*nc+i)=1;
    end
```

```
for i=1:nc
    config(ni+ni*mf+2*nc+i,end)=1;
end

for i=1:ni
    for j=1:nc
        config(i,ni+ni*mf+2*nc+j)=1;
    end
end

mynet.config=config;
mynet.mparams=mparams;
mynet.kparams=kparams;
mynet.nodes=nodes;
mynet.ni=ni;
mynet.mf=mf;
mynet.nc=nc;
mynet.last_decrease_ss=1;
mynet.last_increase_ss=1;

%% Layer from 1 to 3 construction and the epochs staring
layer_1_to_3_output=zeros(Node_n,ni+1);
for iter=1:epoch_n
    for j=1:ndata
        mynet.nodes(1:mynet.ni)=inputs(j,:)';

        mynet=calculate_output1(mynet);
        mynet=calculate_output2(mynet);
        mynet=calculate_output3(mynet);

        layer_1_to_3_output(:,j)=mynet.nodes;

        kalman_data=get_kalman_data(mynet,output(j));
        mynet=mykalman(mynet,kalman_data,j);

        if j==1 && iter==1
            mynet.Consecuente=kparams;
        end
    end

    mynet.mparam_de_do=zeros(mynet.ni*mynet.mf,3);
    mynet.kparam_de_do=zeros(mynet.nc,mynet.ni+1);

    for j=1:ndata
        mynet.nodes=layer_1_to_3_output(:,j);

        mynet=calculate_output4(mynet);
```

```
        mynet.nodes(end)=sum( mynet.nodes(end-mynet.nc:end-1));

        anfis_output(j,1)=mynet.nodes(end);
        target=output(j);
        de_dout = -2*(target - anfis_output(j,1));

        mynet=calculate_de_do(mynet,de_dout);
        mynet=update_de_do(mynet);
    end

    diff=anfis_output-output;
    [tse]=es_lev(anfis_output,output);
    total_squared_error=tse;
    RMSE(iter,1) = sqrt(total_squared_error/ndata);

    if rem(iter,10)==0 && rem(iter,50)~=0
        fprintf('* ')
    elseif rem(iter,10)==0 && rem(iter,50)==0
        fprintf('*\n')
    else
        fprintf('*')
    end

    if RMSE(iter,1)<min_RMSE
        bestnet=mynet;
        min_RMSE=RMSE(iter,1);
    end

    tmp=mynet.mparam_de_do;
    tmp=tmp.*tmp;
    len=sqrt(sum(tmp(:)));
    mynet.mparams=mynet.mparams - step_size * ...
        mynet.mparam_de_do/len;

    [mynet step_size]=update_step_size(mynet,RMSE,iter,...
         step_size,decrease_rate,increase_rate);
end
end

%% Calculation of the output 1
function mynet=calculate_output1(mynet)

mparams=mynet.mparams;
for i=1:mynet.ni
    for j=1:mynet.mf

        ind=mynet.ni+(i-1)*mynet.mf+j;
```

```
        x = mynet.nodes(i);                         % Input node i
        a = mparams((i-1)*mynet.mf+j,1);
        b = mparams((i-1)*mynet.mf+j,2);
        c = mparams((i-1)*mynet.mf+j,3);

        tmp1 = (x - c)/a;
        if tmp1 == 0
            tmp2=0;
        else
            tmp2 = (tmp1*tmp1)^b;
        end
        mynet.nodes(ind)=1/(1+ tmp2);
    end
end
end

%% Calculation of the output 2
function mynet=calculate_output2(mynet)

st=mynet.ni+mynet.ni*mynet.mf;

for i=st+1:st+mynet.nc
    I=find(mynet.config(:,i)==1);           % Find nodes of layer 2
    tmp=cumprod(mynet.nodes(I));
    mynet.nodes(i)=tmp(end);
end
end

%% Calculation of the output 3
function mynet=calculate_output3(mynet)

st=mynet.ni+mynet.ni*mynet.mf +mynet.nc ;

for i=st+1:st+mynet.nc
    I=find(mynet.config(:,i)==1);
    denom=sum(mynet.nodes(I));
    mynet.nodes(i)=mynet.nodes(i-mynet.nc)/denom;
end
end

%% Calculation of the output 4
function mynet=calculate_output4(mynet)

st=mynet.ni+mynet.ni*mynet.mf +2*mynet.nc ;
inp=mynet.nodes(1:mynet.ni)';
kparam=mynet.kparams;
```

```
for i=1:mynet.nc
    mynet.nodes(i+st)=wn*...
          (sum(kparam(i,1:end-1).*inp)+ ...
          Kparam(i,end));
end
end

%% Obtaining the Kalman data (Deterministic approach)
function kalman_data=get_kalman_data(mynet,target)

kalman_data=zeros((mynet.ni+1)*mynet.nc+1,1);
st=mynet.ni+mynet.ni*mynet.mf +mynet.nc ;

j=1;
for i=st+1:st+mynet.nc
    for k=1:mynet.ni
        kalman_data(j)=mynet.nodes(i)*mynet.nodes(k);
        j=j+1;
    end
    kalman_data(j)=mynet.nodes(i);
    j=j+1;
end

kalman_data(j)=target;
end

%% Performing Kalman method
function mynet=mykalman(mynet,kalman_data,j)

k_p_n= (mynet.ni+1)*mynet.nc;
alpha = 1000000;

if j==1
    mynet.P=zeros(k_p_n,1);
    mynet.S=alpha*eye(k_p_n);
end

x=kalman_data(1:end-1);
y=kalman_data(end);

tmp1=(x'*mynet.S)';
denom=1+sum(tmp1.*x);
tmp2=(mynet.S*x);

tmp_m=tmp2*tmp1';
tmp_r=-1/denom*tmp_m;
mynet.S=mynet.S+tmp_r;
```

```
diff=y-sum(x.*mynet.P);
tmp3=diff*(mynet.S*x);
mynet.P=mynet.P+tmp3;
mynet.kparams=reshape(mynet.P,[mynet.ni+1 mynet.nc])';
end

%% DE optimization approach
function mynet=calculate_de_do(mynet,de_dout)

mynet.de_do=zeros(size(mynet.nodes));
mynet.de_do(end)=de_dout;

for i=length(mynet.nodes)-1:-1:mynet.ni+1
    de_do=0;
    II=find(mynet.config(i,:)==1);
    I=find(II>i);
    for j=1:length(I)
        jj=II(I(j));
        tmp1=mynet.de_do(jj);
        tmp2=derivative_o_o(mynet,i, jj);
        de_do = de_do+tmp1*tmp2;
    end
    mynet.de_do(i)=de_do;
end
end

%% Derivative function of DE
function tmp=derivative_o_o(mynet,i,j)

if i>mynet.ni+mynet.ni*mynet.mf +2*mynet.nc
    tmp=1;
elseif i>mynet.ni+mynet.ni*mynet.mf +mynet.nc
    tmp=do4_do3(mynet, j);
elseif i>mynet.ni+mynet.ni*mynet.mf
    tmp=do3_do2(mynet,i, j);
elseif i>mynet.ni
    tmp=mynet.nodes(j)/mynet.nodes(i);
end
end

%% DE operator 1
function tmp=do4_do3(mynet, j)
kparam=mynet.kparams;
inp=mynet.nodes(1:mynet.ni)';
jj=j-mynet.ni-mynet.ni*mynet.mf -2*mynet.nc;
tmp=sum(kparam(jj,1:end-1).*inp)+kparam(jj,end);
end
```

```
%% DE operator 2
function tmp=do3_do2(mynet,i, j)
II=find(mynet.config(:,j)==1);
I=find(II<j);
total=sum(mynet.nodes(II(I)));
if j-i==mynet.nc
    tmp=(total-mynet.nodes(i))/(total*total);
else
    tmp=-mynet.nodes(j-mynet.nc)/(total*total);
end
end

%% Update DE information
function [mynet] = update_de_do(mynet)

s=1;
for i=mynet.ni+1:mynet.ni+mynet.ni*mynet.mf
    for j=1:3
        I=find(mynet.config(:,i)==1);
        x=mynet.nodes(I);
        a=mynet.mparams(i-mynet.ni,1);
        b=mynet.mparams(i-mynet.ni,2);
        c=mynet.mparams(i-mynet.ni,3);
        tmp1 = (x - c)/a;
        if tmp1==0
            tmp2=0;
        else
            tmp2 = (tmp1*tmp1)^b;
        end
        denom = (1 + tmp2)*(1 + tmp2);
        if j==1
            do_dp=(2*b*tmp2/(a*denom));
        elseif j==2 && tmp1==0
            do_dp=0;
        elseif j==2 && tmp1~=0
            do_dp=(-log(tmp1*tmp1)*tmp2/denom);
        elseif j==3 && x==c
            do_dp=0;
        elseif j==3 && x~=c
            do_dp=(2*b*tmp2/((x - c)*(denom)));
        end

        mynet.mparam_de_do(s,j)=...
            mynet.mparam_de_do(s,j)+...
            mynet.de_do(i)*do_dp;
    end
    s=s+1;
end
```

```
s=1;

for i=1+mynet.ni+mynet.ni*mynet.mf+2*mynet.nc:size(mynet.config)-1
    for j=1:mynet.ni+1
        wn=mynet.nodes(i-mynet.nc);
        inp=mynet.nodes(1:mynet.ni)';
        inp=[inp 1];
        do_dp=wn*inp(j);
        mynet.kparam_de_do(s,j)=...
             mynet.kparam_de_do(s,j)+...
             mynet.de_do(i)*do_dp;
    end
    s=s+1;
end
end


%% Difference between ANFIS output and current sample
function[tse]=es_lev(anfis_output,output)
step=0.1;
instep=0;
F=0.8;
ngen=100;
cr=1-F;
pop=100;
dim=size(anfis_output,1);

x=instep+(step-instep).*rand(pop,dim);
x=x';

for i=1:dim
    for j=1:pop
        if x(i,j)<instep
            x(i,j)=instep;
        elseif x(i,j)>step
            x(i,j)=step;
        end
    end
end

Diff=zeros(dim,1);
lev=zeros(1,pop);
nlev=lev;

for i=1:pop
    for j=1:dim
        Diff(j,1)=x(j,i)+anfis_output(j,1);
```

```
        end
        diff=Diff-output;
        error=sum(diff.*diff);
        lev(1,i)=error;
    end

    x=x';
    lev=lev';
    gen=1;

    while ngen<=gen
        for i=1:pop
            A=randperm(pop);
            r1=x(A(1),:);
            r2=x(A(2),:);
            r3=x(A(3),:);

            Pmut=r3+F*(r1-r2);
            for j=1:dim
                if Pmut(1,j)<instep
                    Pmut(1,j)=instep;
                elseif Pmut(1,j)>step
                    Pmut(1,j)=step;
                end
            end
            Pcros=zeros(1,dim);

            for j=1:dim
                aux=rand();
                if aux<cr
                    Pcros(1,j)=Pmut(1,j);
                else
                    Pcros(1,j)=x(i,j);
                end
            end

            Pcros=Pcros';
            for j=1:dim
                Diff(j,1)=Pcros(j,1)+anfis_output(j,1);
            end

            diff=Diff-output;
            error=sum(diff.*diff);
            nlev(1,i)=error;
            lev=lev';
            x=x';
            if nlev(i,1)<lev(i,1)
```

```
            x(:,i)=Pcros(:,1);
            lev(1,i)=nlev(1,i);
        end

        x=x';
        lev=lev';
    end
    gen=gen+1;
end
tse=min(lev);
end

%% Evaluation of the proposed ANFIS_DE
function yhat=evalmyanfis(mynet,inputs)

ndata=size(inputs,1);

for j=1:ndata
    mynet.nodes(1:mynet.ni)=inputs(j,:)';
    mynet=calculate_output1(mynet);
    mynet=calculate_output2(mynet);
    mynet=calculate_output3(mynet);
    mynet=calculate_output4(mynet);
    mynet.nodes(end)=sum( mynet.nodes(end-mynet.nc:end-1));
    yhat(j,1)=mynet.nodes(end);
end
end

%% Update the stepsize of DE
function [mynet step_size]=...
    update_step_size(mynet,error_array,iter,...
    step_size,decrease_rate,increase_rate)

if check_decrease_ss(error_array, mynet.last_decrease_ss, iter)
    step_size = step_size*decrease_rate;
      mynet.last_decrease_ss = iter;
elseif check_increase_ss(error_array, mynet.last_increase_ss, iter)
    step_size = step_size*increase_rate;
      mynet.last_increase_ss = iter;
end
end

function sts=check_decrease_ss(error_array, last_change, current)
if (current - last_change < 4)
      sts=false;
elseif ((error_array(current)     < error_array(current - 1)) && ...
         (error_array(current - 1) > error_array(current - 2)) && ...
```

```
          (error_array(current - 2) < error_array(current - 3)) && ...
         (error_array(current - 3) > error_array(current - 4)))
    sts=true;
else
    sts=false;
end
end

function sts=check_increase_ss(error_array, last_change, current)
if (current - last_change < 4)
   sts=false;
elseif ((error_array(current)     < error_array(current - 1)) && ...
         (error_array(current - 1) < error_array(current - 2)) && ...
         (error_array(current - 2) < error_array(current - 3)) && ...
         (error_array(current - 3) < error_array(current - 4)))
    sts=true;
else
    sts=false;
end
end
```

References

Jang, J.S.R. (1993). ANFIS: adaptive-network-based fuzzy inference system. *IEEE Transactions on Systems, Man, and Cybernetics* 23 (3): 665–685. https://doi.org/10.1109/21.256541.

Piroddi, L., Farina, M., and Lovera, M. (2012). Black box model identification of nonlinear input–output models: a Wiener–Hammerstein benchmark. *Control Engineering Practice* 20 (11): 1109–1118. https://doi.org/10.1016/J.CONENGPRAC.2012.03.002.

Storn, R. and Price, K. (1997). Differential evolution—a simple and efficient heuristic for global optimization over continuous spaces. *Journal of Global Optimization* 341–359. https://doi.org/10.1023/A:1008202821328.

Takagi, T. and Sugeno, M. (1985). Fuzzy identification of systems and its applications to modeling and control. *IEEE Transactions on Systems, Man, and Cybernetics* SMC-15 (1): 116–132. https://doi.org/10.1109/TSMC.1985.6313399.

6

Techniques of Machine Learning for Producing Metaheuristic Operators

6.1 Introduction

Metaheuristic algorithms have been developed to solve minimization/maximization problems. Based on our scientific understanding of biological, ecological, or even social systems, a variety of metaheuristics have been proposed by scientific communities. The performance of metaheuristic method in finding an optimal solution typically depends on its capacity to achieve a suitable balance between its evolutionary stages. The exploration stage and the exploitation stage are two frequent phases of the evolutionary strategy.

Exploration stage entails inspecting new areas in the search space, whereas exploitation entails doing local searches in areas that have already been explored with the goal of enhancing the quality of the solutions. The optimization process loses accuracy when mostly exploratory work is done, but it gains the ability to identify new possible solutions over the search space. On the other hand, if exploitation is privileged, existing solutions are mostly improved. However, adversely, this fact produces that the algorithm can be trapped in local minima due to scarce exploration. Under such circumstances, a balance among these two stages is decisive for the proper functioning of the method.

Since the performance of an evolutionary computation (EC) algorithm highly depends on the balance of exploration and exploitation procedures, different combination of operators may lead to unbalance the optimization process.

To alleviate such issues researchers have suggested the combination of different metaheuristic operators for obtaining new performance levels. Recently, a large variety of approaches that do not entirely adhere to the idea of a single EC approach have been developed. These techniques associate different algorithmic structures, commonly extracted from other computation techniques. These methods have been referred as hybrid EC algorithms (Blum et al. 2008). The main goal of hybridization is to increase the performance of single EC methods by combining complementing computational techniques. The goal of hybridization is to overcome the shortcomings of each individual approach and, via their fusion, produce a synergetic result (Blum et al. 2011). The incorporation of many techniques into hybrid EC approaches enables the blending of the advantages of each method. It has been demonstrated that the appropriate selection of algorithmic elements and fusion strategies, hybrid EC methods can overtake their algorithmic elements because of their synergetic effect (Ma et al. 2014; Niknam and Azad Farsani 2010).

In the last decade, several EC algorithms have been suggested by different scientific communities for enhancing the search capabilities of original EC based on machine learning techniques, fuzzy logic, neural networks and support vector machine (Dash and Dash 2016; Illias et al. 2016).

Machine Learning and Metaheuristic Computation, First Edition.
Erik Cuevas, Jorge Galvez, Omar Avalos, and Fernando Wario.

Although most of these approaches are convincing, the study and construction of new hybrid EC methods need further and extensive research.

In this chapter, two different methods are combined to produce a hybrid metaheuristic approach. The produced metaheuristic combines clustering and chaotic sequences. Clustering (Ezugwu et al. 2022) Clustering is the process of grouping together datapoints into clusters that are distinct from one another. Scarcely, the division of the population into different groups has been documented in the literature in order to alter the search mechanism for a metaheuristic algorithm. The proposed metaheuristic method uses a clustering method to divide the population into individual groups at the initial stage of the optimization process. Therefore, the proposed algorithm creates groups based on the spatial associations of datapoints without considering a fixed distance among them or a necessary number of them.

On the other hand, chaotic sequences are increasingly being used to improve existing EC approaches in order to promote population diversity by avoiding premature convergence. Chaos is recognized by its interesting stochastic characteristics (Yang et al. 2007). In order to enhance the performance of an EC approach, chaotic sequences have frequently been utilized rather than random numbers.

In this chapter, a hybrid optimization algorithm for solving optimization problems is presented. The approach, called Cluster-Chaotic-Optimization (CCO), combines the stochastic properties of chaotic sequences with the grouping capabilities of a clustering algorithm to create metaheuristic operators. In the optimization procedure, CCO divides the population into clusters according to spatial associations. Then, two different operations are computed to update the position of each datapoint. The first operation, called intra-cluster, locally explores the search space inside each cluster. This operation modifies the position of all datapoints belonging a cluster. Under such conditions, datapoints belonging to the same cluster are locally modified considering the position of best datapoint inside the cluster. The second operation, called extra-cluster, explores the entire search space among the clusters. This procedure modifies only the best datapoint inside a given cluster whereas the remaining datapoints. Hence, in the extra-cluster procedure, the best datapoint for a given cluster is attracted by the best datapoint of the entire population. In both operations, the position adjustment on each datapoint is generated by using cluster-based operations and chaotic sequences. With such hybridization, the CCO locally and globally examines the entire search space through the optimization process.

In this chapter, we delve into the concept of hierarchical clustering and chaotic sequences. The main aspects of clustering and chaotic sequences will be thoroughly examined, providing a solid foundation for understanding its application in the generation of evolutionary operators. Throughout the chapter, MATLAB will be used to implement these methodologies. This hands-on approach will enable readers to gain practical experience and become proficient in using these techniques to produce metaheuristic operators in their own projects.

6.2 Hierarchical Clustering

Clustering is one of the most used techniques to create homogeneous groups of objects or entities. For a given set of datapoints $D = \{x_1, \ldots, x_n\}$, where $x_j \in R^d$ grouping the datapoints into X number of clusters so that similar datapoints in the clusters are close to each other. In most of the analytical projects, after the data cleaning process and preparation, clustering methods are often carried out before any analytical modeling.

Clustering falls under the category of unsupervised learning. That means there is no labeled class for a given dataset. We are only interested in grouping similar entities or objects in a cluster. In this chapter, we focus on hierarchical clustering. Hierarchical clustering constructs an association tree over the data, where tree leaves are considered as individual clusters, while the root is a single cluster which contains all the remaining datapoints. Between the tree root and the tree leaves, there are subset of clusters. The goal of hierarchical clustering is to create a series of nested partitions that can be viewed as a tree structure commonly called a dendrogram. The groups within this structure maintain a configuration such that, at the lowest level of the tree, each element represents a group while at the highest level, all points form a single group. Under these conditions, at intermediate levels of the tree, different groupings can be found, depending on the relative distances between elements. There are two schemes under the hierarchical clustering: divisive hierarchical clustering also known as a top-down clustering approach, and agglomerative hierarchical clustering also known as a bottom-up clustering approach.

In divisive clustering, the entire set of datapoints is assigned to a single cluster. Once there is one cluster, the cluster is further divided until there is one cluster for each single datapoint. On the other hand, the agglomerative process operates in the opposite way. At starting point, each single datapoint is treated as a cluster then a pair of clusters are combined until all clusters are merged into a single cluster. In this chapter, it will be focused on the agglomerative clustering for producing metaheuristic operators for exploration and exploitation stages.

6.2.1 Agglomerative Hierarchical Clustering Algorithm

In this section, a detailed description of the algorithmic design of the agglomerative hierarchical clustering technique is presented. The design of the agglomerative algorithm considers each single datapoint as a cluster at the starting point then, it will combine a pair of clusters until all clusters are merged into a single big cluster. Since the agglomerative method involves a series of straightforward steps. Here are the steps for designing an agglomerative approach:

Step 1: Set up Initial Clusters:
Assign each observation as a single point cluster to begin with, so that if there are N observations, there will be N clusters, each containing a single observation.

Step 2: Find Similar Pair of Clusters:
Find the most similar pair of clusters and merge them into one cluster. (Many similarity and dissimilarity metrics can be used in this step. The metric used in this step can produced different clusters.) In this chapter, Euclidean distance is used for producing metaheuristic operators.

Step 3: Merge Closest Clusters:
Find the two closest clusters for producing one cluster. (Many linkage techniques can be used in this step. The linkage technique used in this step can produced different clusters). In this chapter, the Ward method is used for merge clusters for producing metaheuristic operators.

Step 4: Repeat Steps 2 and 3 Until all Datapoints are Clustered into a Single Cluster:

Note

The algorithmic design of an agglomerative clustering is a simple and generic scheme. For that, given a particular clustering application, the algorithm can be adjusted by modifying the Steps 2 and 3. Steps 2 and 3 are computed based on similarity indexes and linkage techniques, respectively. Similarity and dissimilarity indexes commonly refer to the relationship among datapoints by a distance measurement. These indexes indicate a way of measuring how datapoints are related or closed to each other. On the other hand, linkage techniques refers how datapoints are merge between two clusters to produce a new cluster.

In agglomerative clustering, the most used similarity and dissimilarity metrics are:

- Euclidean distance
- Manhattan distance
- Minkowski distance
- Jaccard similarity coefficient
- Cosine similarity
- Gowe's similarity coefficient
- Pearson correlation

In agglomerative clustering, the most used linkage techniques are:

- Single linkage
- Complete linkage
- Average linkage
- Centroid method
- Ward method

In this chapter the Ward method is used for producing metaheuristic operators. Ward method is computed based on the minimization of the cluster variance. Related literature suggests the use of Ward method as the most suitable method for quantitative variables.

The previously described algorithm generates a dendrogram. A dendrogram is a tree diagram that shows the clusters and levels of similarity that result from the hierarchical clustering process at each step. The individual observations are presented along the horizontal axis, and the similarity level is measured along the vertical axis. Figure 6.1 shows an example of the structure of a dendrogram.

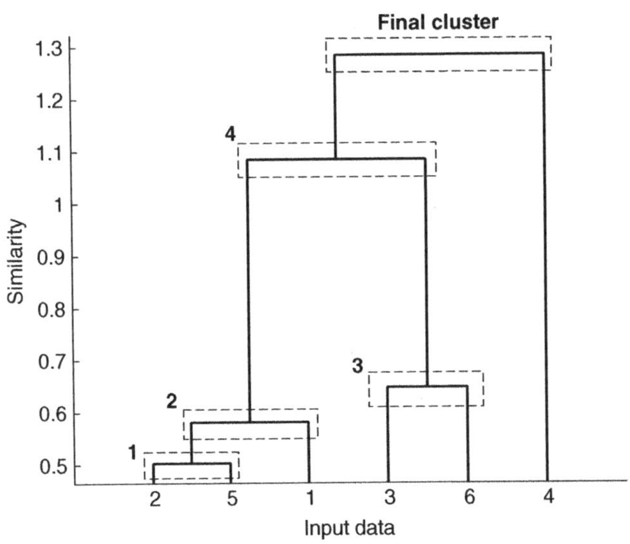

Figure 6.1 Dendrogram structure.

Selecting the final grouping for your data is called cutting the dendrogram. Cutting the dendrogram refers to draw a horizontal line (link) to specify the final grouping, different cuts determine which final grouping makes sense for the data to be clustered. In cluster analysis, to determine the natural cluster divisions the comparison among heights of each link with the heights of neighboring links is used. Commonly, to define a cutting threshold for a dendrogram the height of inconsistent links (links whose height differs noticeably from the height of the links below it is used as cutting criterion.

In Figure 6.1, it is represented an example dendrogram, where each rectangular dashed shape represents different types of cuts to form a cluster. In the figure, the first cluster is obtained by the datapoints 2 and 5. Then, the datapoint 1 is merge into the first cluster to form the second cluster. This process continues until the final cluster which corresponds to the highest hierarchical level.

The MATLAB code (in Algorithm 6.1) is presented by using the built-in functions of MATLAB as follows:

```
%Algorithm 6.1
% Step 1: Set a default random sequence generator to produce
standard random values
rng('default');

% Step 2: Set 50 datapoints, this will be the dataset
X = [(randn(50,2)*0.75)+1;
    (randn(50,2)*0.25)-1];

% Step 3: Compute distances among datapoints
Y = pdist(X,"euclidean");

% Step 4: Merge clusters using Ward method
Z = linkage(X,"ward");

% Step 5: Plot the dendrogram from the agglomerative process
figure(1)
dendrogram(Z);

% Step 6: Cut the dendrogram into 2 clusters
T = cluster(Z,'maxclust',2);

% Step 7: Plot the datapoints clustered by Step 6
figure(2)
gscatter(X(:,1),X(:,2),T)
```

In Algorithm 6.1, Step 1 indicates which random number generators will be used. The `'default'` instruction from rng function uses a random generator whose output will be the same at each execution of the code. This scheme is used for reproducibility purpose, so

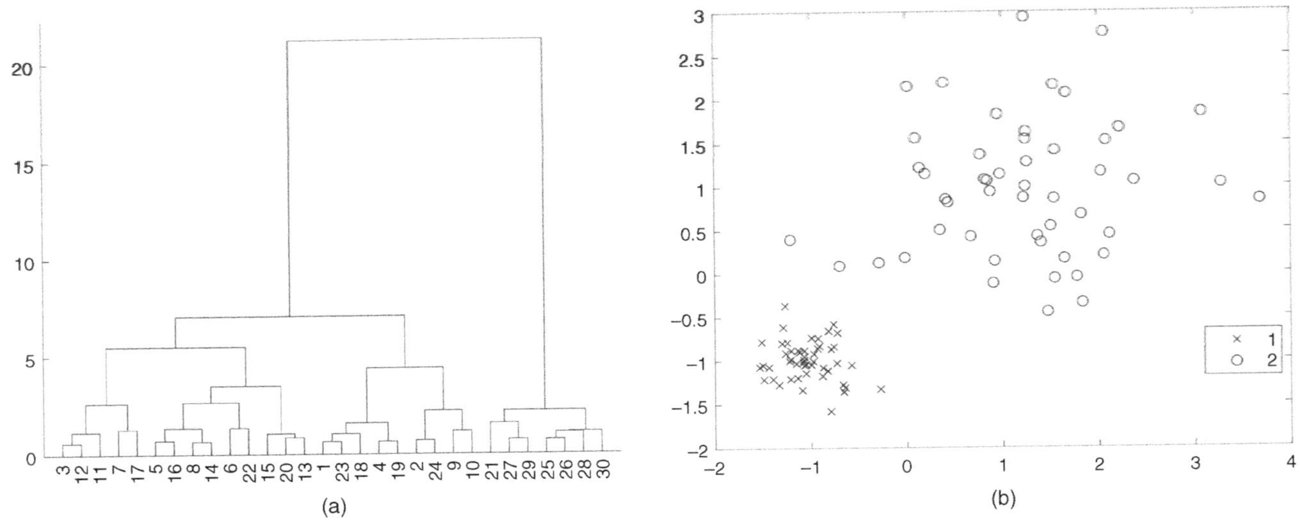

Figure 6.2 Output from Algorithm 6.1. (a) Shows the produced dendrogram from the datapoints. (b) Shows the clustered datapoints by cutting the dendrogram to produced two clusters.

the reader can follow a generic output from the clustering process. Step 2, generates 50 datapoints in a random fashion. This datapoints will be the dataset used for clustering process. In the Step 3, all the Euclidean distances among each datapoint is computed. The output from this step, will be the input to the linkage scheme from Step 4 where the ward's method is used to merge clusters. The plot from de dendrogram is then produced by using the built-in function `dendrogram()`. In Step 6, the dendrogram is cut considering a maximum number of clusters set to 2. Finally, Step 7 plots a scatterplot based on the cutting scheme from Step 6. The output of the Algorithm 6.1 can be seen in Figure 6.2.

In Figure 6.2a, the produced dendrogram from the dataset of Step 2 in the Algorithm 6.1 is shown. As it can be shown, the dendrogram associate natural associations among each datapoint, then it will merge pair of clusters until one single cluster is produced at the root of the tree. Since the Step 6 cuts the dendrogram to produced two clusters from the datapoints, Figure 6.2b shows the result scatter plot.

The agglomerative clustering process is simple to implement but powerful technique since user can define the natural division of groups. According to the characteristics of a given dataset, the user can use a cutting scheme to better model the datapoint divisions.

6.3 Chaotic Sequences

Chaos is a type of characteristic nonlinear dynamic system, which presents interesting properties such as ergodicity, pseudo-randomness, and sensibility of initial values in its control parameters. In the last decade, chaotic sequences are increasingly considered rather than random numbers in several engineering applications. Recently, many researchers have adopted the use of chaotic sequences for producing metaheuristic operators. In engineering optimization methods, the use of randomness can be replaced by a chaotic sequence to improve their performance. Related literature reveals that the experimental analysis of several metaheuristic methods performs better chaotic sequences rather than random numbers (Huang et al. 2016; Snaselova and Zboril 2015).

The simplest systems that can generate chaotic values are one-dimensional, non-invertible sequences. In related literature, several chaotic sequences have been proposed. However, most of them hold a randomness behavior considering specific configurations. An exception to those is the Iterative Chaotic Map with Infinite Collapses (ICMIC) due to ICMIC behaves chaotically throughout a wider configuration range. Under such configurations, The ICMIC sequence regulates the bias and dispersion of the generated random numbers. Due of these properties, the ICMIC sequence was used in this chapter to create random perturbations in the optimization process. The following mathematical model is used to compute the ICMIC sequence:

$$z(t+1) = \sin\left(\frac{\varphi\pi}{z(t)}\right), \varphi\varepsilon(0, \infty) \tag{6.1}$$

Figure 6.3 illustrates the pseudo-random behavior produced by the chaotic map of Eq. 6.1. The figure shows a portion of the time period from within the interval [3.5–4.4]. In this chapter, the chaotic parameter φ has been set to $\varphi = 4$. The dynamic reaction produced by ICMIC is represented by this value. With this value, ICMIC produces pseudo-random values around zero with a deviation in the interval [−1 −1]. These characteristics describe the primary behavior of a random number generator.

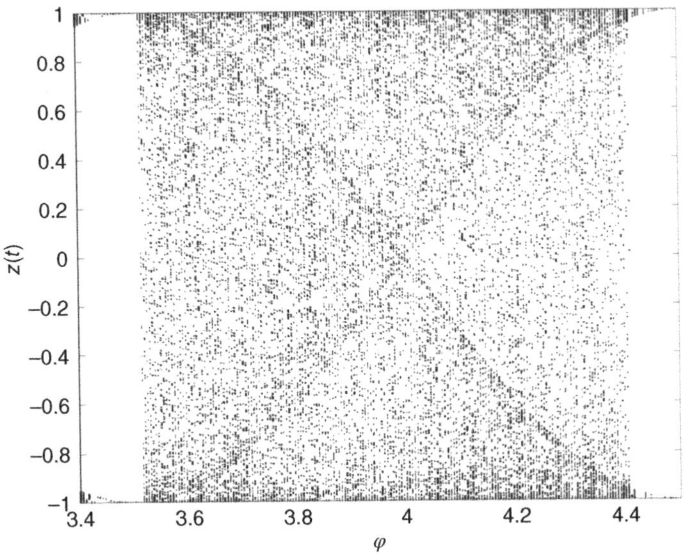

Figure 6.3 Chaotic map of the ICMIC.

The MATLAB code (in Algorithm 6.2) presents the simulation of one-dimensional chaotic sequence. The chaotic sequence is given by the following mathematical description:

$$x_1 = \lambda x_0(1 - x_0) \tag{6.2}$$

```
%Algorithm 6.2
%% INITIAL CONFIGURATION
%Clear memory and Close Matlab windows
clear all
close all

%% Step 1 Definition of initial conditions
x = 0.400000;
y = 0.399999;
x1 = x;
x2 = x;
x3 = x;
y1 = y;
y2 = y;
y3 = y;
lambda1 = 2.0;
lambda2 = 1 + sqrt(5);
lambda3 = 4.0;
```

```
%% Step 2 Chaotic sequence emulation
for i = 1:20
    fprintf('%f %f %f %f %f %f\n',x1,x2,x3,y1,y2,y3);
    x1 = lambda1 * x1 * (1-x1);
    y1 = lambda1 * y1 * (1-y1);
    x2 = lambda2 * x2 * (1-x2);
    y2 = lambda2 * y2 * (1-y2);
    x3 = lambda3 * x3 * (1-x3);
    y3 = lambda3 * y3 * (1-y3);
end
```

The Algorithm 6.2, represents the simulation of one-dimensional chaotic sequence considering three different lambda values to show the chaotic behavior given from initial conditions. The output of the code clearly indicates that the values from the first and fourth columns represents an attraction point, while the second and fifth columns represents a limit cycle.

6.4 Cluster-Chaotic-Optimization (CCO)

Clustering using population is assumed as the main goal of the CCO. With the clustering procedure, the goal is to determine which search regions should receive more attention during the evolution process. This idea establishes an alternative methodology to produced metaheuristic operators to conduct a search mechanism where spatial associations guide the optimization process. The majority of EC algorithms employ techniques that take into account each individual without taking into account their spatial relationship among the rest of elements in the population. Under such conditions, Traditional metaheuristic operators struggle to locate promising search areas, and even when they do, they hardly exploit such areas. On the other hand, On the other hand, employing chaotic sequences to carry out random perturbations is another essential feature of the presented hybrid strategy. It has been shown that using chaotic sequences instead of random numbers can significantly improve the effectiveness of optimization techniques. With its inclusion, EC algorithms improve its convergence by avoiding local minima stagnation.

CCO has been designed to locate the global solution of a nonlinear optimization problem in the following form:

$$\begin{array}{lll} \text{Minimize/Maximize} & J(x), & x = (x_1, \dots, x_n) \in R^n \\ \text{subject to} & & x \, \varepsilon \, S \end{array} \tag{6.3}$$

where $J : R^n \rightarrow R$ is a nonlinear optimization problem whereas $S = \{x \, \varepsilon \, R^n \mid l_j \leq x_j \leq u_j, j = 1, \dots, n\}$ is a bounded search space, restricted by the lower (l_j) and upper (u_j) bounds. Additionally, x is a solution within the set of possible solutions.

In order to solve an optimization problem using the CCO, it considers a population of datapoints $D^k = \left\{ d_1^k, d_2^k, \dots, d_{N_D}^k \right\}$ containing N_D number of possible solutions. These solutions will evolve from initial iteration ($k = 0$) until a total number of iterations is reached ($k = Max\_Iter$). Each datapoint $d_i^k = \left\{ d_{i,1}^k, d_{i,1}^k, \dots, d_{i,n}^k \right\}$ represents an n-dimensional decision variable vector. After a random initialization for the population, each datapoint is modified by two metaheuristic operators based on a hierarchical clustering scheme: intra-cluster and extra-cluster.

Since CCO method involves a series of straightforward steps. Here are the steps:

Step 1: Initialization:
Initialize a population D containing N_D datapoints. Each datapoint corresponds to a candidate solution for a given optimization problem.

Step 2: Clustering:
Compute an agglomerative clustering approach using the population D of datapoints as the input data to generate a dendrogram. Then, use a cutting method to generate clusters that will be evolved.

Step 3: Intra-Cluster Procedure:
Explores the search space within each formed cluster from Step 2. This procedure adjusts the position of all datapoints inside each cluster. This metaheuristic operators can be considered as the exploitation stage in the optimization process.

Step 4: Extra-Cluster Procedure:
Explores the search space outside among clusters from Step 3. This procedure adjusts the best datapoint in term of fitness value to be attracted to the best datapoint in the entire population. This metaheuristic operator can be considered as the exploitation stage in the optimization process.

Step 5: Repeat Steps 2–4 until the Maximum Number of Iterations is Reached.
In the following subsections, a detailed description of each main procedure for the CCO method is described.

6.4.1 Initialization

At this stage the population D of N_D datapoints is randomly and uniformly initialized. The values of each decision variable are randomly and uniformly distributed among a predefined the lower (l_j) and upper (u_j) bounds. The initialization procedure is defined as:

$$d_{i,j}^k = l_j + \text{rand}(0,1) \cdot (u_j - l_j), \ \ j = 1, \dots, n; \ \ i = 1, \dots, N_D \tag{6.4}$$

where $d_{i,j}^k$ represents to the j-th decision variable of the i-th datapoint at the k-th iteration.

6.4.2 Clustering

The primary method of data analysis employed by CCO is clustering. The goal of the clustering is to determine which search areas should receive more attention throughout the evolution process. With this idea, a new approach for conducting search strategies is established, one in which each unique association conducts the optimization process.

The Ward linkage method has been employed as a clustering approach for producing metaheuristic operators: intra-cluster and extra-cluster evolutionary operators. The generation of the dendrogram from the population D is computed at each iteration before the inter-cluster and extra-cluster procedures. After the execution of the Ward method at k-th iteration, the complete population D^k is divided into g clusters, where each cluster c_q^k, $(q \in 1, \dots, g)$ contains $|c_q^k|$ number of datapoints.

For producing g clusters, a cutting scheme based on the inconsistency links is considered. Commonly, in cluster analysis, the final grouping is achieved by considering the maximum number of inconstant links. That means, in the proposed methodology, there are considered the maximum number of links whose height differs noticeably from the height of the links below it.

6.4.3 Intra-Cluster Procedure

Under this procedure, each cluster produced by the Ward linkage technique is independently treated. The Intra-Cluster operator involves two different phases: the local attraction movement and a local perturbation process. Both phases are executed over each datapoint, except for the best element inside the cluster. This process increases the search capabilities by exploiting the search space within the cluster.

6.4.3.1 Local Attraction Movement

Assuming that the cluster c_q^k is integrated by a set of $|c_q^k|$ datapoints, each datapoint d_i^k is attracted to the best datapoint (solution) $d_b^k = \left\{ d_{b,1}^k, d_{b,1}^k, \ldots, d_{b,n}^k \right\}$ inside the cluster. The best datapoint inside the cluster is computed based on fitness value. In this chapter, it is considered a minimization problem, which can be expressed as follows:

$$d_b^k = \arg \arg J\left(d_i^k\right), \quad i \in c_q^k \tag{6.5}$$

The local attraction metaheuristic operator updates the position of the datapoint d_i^k in terms of the j-th decision variable as follows:

$$d_{i,j}^{k+1} = d_{i,j}^k + \rho_{C_q}^k \cdot z \cdot \left(d_{b,j}^k - d_{i,j}^k\right) \tag{6.6}$$

where z, corresponds to the output from the ICMIC chaotic map. Additionally, the term $\rho_{C_q}^k$ represents the cluster density. Cluster density is computed as follows:

$$\rho_{C_q}^k = \frac{|c_q^k|}{N_D} \tag{6.7}$$

The density cluster term $\rho_{C_q}^k$ can be considered as a velocity factor. This term emulates small movements to clusters containing few datapoints. On the other hand, clusters containing larger number of datapoints produce high movements of its datapoints. Figure 6.4 illustrates the effect of the local attraction movement considering two study cases. Figure 6.4a shows the velocity vectors as small arrows to represent small movements inside the cluster since it contains high number of datapoints. This process contributes to the exploitation inside the cluster induced by small movement. On the other hand, Figure 6.4b illustrates the velocity vectors as large arrows to represent larger movements inside the cluster. This process contributes to the exploration inside the cluster induced by larger movements.

6.4.3.2 Local Perturbation Strategy

The local perturbation strategy is executed after the movements produced by the local attraction procedure. This mechanism is applied to each datapoint for each cluster. The goal of this procedure

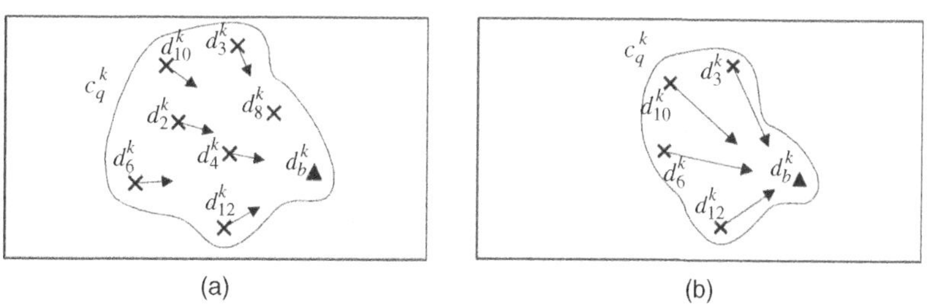

Figure 6.4 Local attraction movement. (a) Cluster with a high density and (b) cluster with small density.

is to increase the search capabilities inside each cluster promoting population diversity. Under this operation, new datapoints d_i^{k+1} are locally modified following a circular path to produce two new different solutions (datapoints) $h_i^A = \left\{ h_{i,1}^A, \ldots, h_{i,n}^A \right\}$ and $h_i^B = \left\{ h_{i,1}^B, \ldots, h_{i,n}^B \right\}$. Both solutions are generated following the model:

$$h_{i,j}^A = d_{i,j}^{k+1} + \left(d_{i,j}^{k+1} \cdot z_A \cdot v_A \right);$$
$$h_{i,j}^B = d_{i,j}^{k+1} - \left(d_{i,j}^{k+1} \cdot z_B \cdot v_B \right) \tag{6.8}$$

where z_A and z_B are values obtained by the ICMIC chaotic map. Additionally, the circular neighborhood represented by the v_A and v_B values are computed according to:

$$v_A = \cos(\alpha \cdot r);$$
$$v_B = \cos(\alpha \cdot r); \tag{6.9}$$

where r is a random number within the interval $(0, 2\pi)$, and α corresponds to a perturbation parameter which is modified during the evolution process.

Note

Some configuration parameters of metaheuristic algorithms, evolve considering the actual stage of the optimization process.

The final step is to use an elitist criterion to determine which element will prevail in the population. The elitist criterion is described as follows:

$$d_i^{k+1} = \{h_i^A \text{ if} J\left(h_i^A\right) < J\left(d_i^{k+1}\right) \; h_i^B \text{ if } J\left(h_i^B\right) < J\left(d_i^{k+1}\right) \; d_i^{k+1} \text{ otherwise} \tag{6.10}$$

Figure 6.5 illustrates the process of the local perturbation strategy. The figure shows the case of study when a datapoint is modified by generating two new datapoints h_i^A and h_i^B. In the figure, the fitness value of the datapoint h_i^B presents a better fitness value than d_i^{k+1}, h_i^B will replace it for the next iteration $k+1$.

6.4.3.3 Extra-Cluster Procedure

Under this metaheuristic operation, the best datapoints d_b^k of the set clusters ($b \in 1, \ldots, g$) are evolved based on the best global solution d_B^k (datapoint) being so far in the entire current population. The best global solution is defined as:

$$d_B^k = \arg\arg J\left(d_i^k\right), \; i \in (1, \ldots, N_D) \tag{6.11}$$

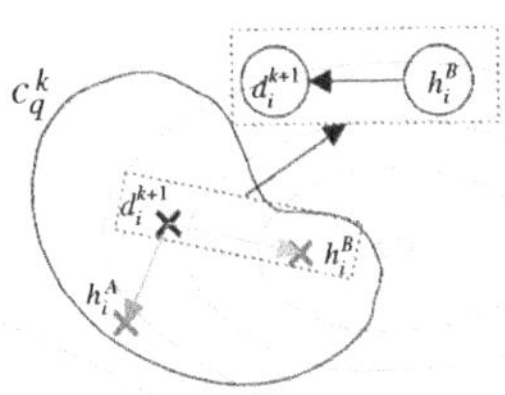

Figure 6.5 Process of local perturbation for a generic individual configuration.

The best global solution d_B^k is then used to compute two different subprocesses: Global attraction and global perturbation.

6.4.3.4 Global Attraction Movement

The global attraction operator adjusts the position of each best datapoint d_b^k among all clusters. This procedure reorganized the best elements for each cluster, to explore into a wider zone within the search space. The attraction model can be described as follows:

$$d_{b,j}^{k+1} = d_{b,j}^k + \left(d_{B,j}^k - d_{b,j}^k\right) \cdot \text{rand}(\cdot) \cdot v_G \tag{6.12}$$

where rand$(\cdot)$ is a random number within the interval [0, 1], while the term v_G represents a circular neighborhood computed by Eq. 6.9. Figure 6.6a shows the global attraction movement. In the figure, it is quite evident how the best cluster datapoints are attracted to the best global solution d_B^k for the current k-th iteration.

6.4.3.5 Global Perturbation Strategy

In this operation, a circular perturbation is applied once the new locations generated by the global attraction procedure. The goal of the global perturbation operation is to improve the exploitation of the search space around d_b^{k+1}. Under this operation two different solutions (datapoints) $h_b^R = \left\{h_{b,1}^R, \dots, h_{b,n}^R\right\}$ and $h_b^S = \left\{h_{b,1}^S, \dots, h_{b,n}^S\right\}$ are generated based on the following model:

$$\begin{aligned} h_{b,j}^R &= d_{b,j}^{k+1} + \left(d_{b,j}^{k+1} \cdot r_R \cdot v_R\right); \\ h_{b,j}^S &= d_{b,j}^{k+1} - \left(d_{b,j}^{k+1} \cdot r_S \cdot v_S\right); \end{aligned} \tag{6.13}$$

where r_R and r_S represent two random numbers within the interval [0, 1]. Additionally, the terms v_R and v_S represent circular neighborhoods as the Equation 6.9 describes. The final step is to use an elitist criterion to determine which element will prevail in the population. The elitist criterion is described as follows:

$$d_b^{k+1} = \{h_b^R \; if J\left(h_b^R\right) < J\left(d_b^{k+1}\right) \; h_b^S \; if J\left(h_b^S\right) < J\left(d_b^{k+1}\right) \; d_b^{k+1} \text{ otherwise} \tag{6.14}$$

Figure 6.6b illustrates the process of global perturbation strategy. The figure shows the study case when the best element for each cluster d_b^k is modified to generate two new candidate datapoints h_b^R and h_b^S within a circular neighborhood. In the figure, since the fitness value of the datapoint h_b^R presents a better fitness value than d_b^{k+1}, h_b^R replaces d_b^{k+1} for the next iteration $k+1$.

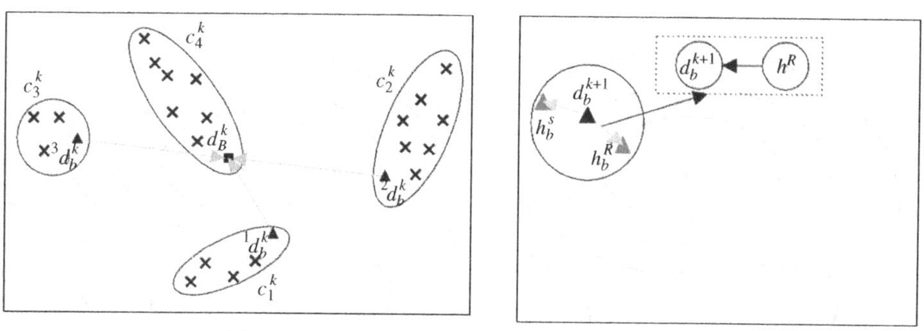

(a) (b)

Figure 6.6 Extra-cluster procedure. (a) Global attraction movement and (b) global perturbation strategy.

6.5 Computational Procedure

The algorithmic structure of the CCO follows an iterative process, in which intra-cluster and extra-cluster metaheuristic operators are executed. Such procedures can be summarized in the Pseudo-code 6.1.

Pseudo-code 6.1 ***Computational Procedure of the Cluster Chaotic Optimization (CCO) Method***

Input: N_D, gen, $k = 0$	
$\mathbf{D}^k \leftarrow$ **Initialize**(N_D);	**Step 1**
while $k<=gen$ **do**	
$\mathbf{d}_B^k \leftarrow$ **SelectBestParticle**($\mathbf{D}^k$);	
$[c_q^k, g] \leftarrow$ **Clustering**($\mathbf{D}^k$);	**Step 2**
$\alpha \leftarrow$ **CalculatePerturbation**(gen);	
for ($q = 1;q>g;q$++)	**Step 3**
$\mathbf{d}_b^k \leftarrow$ **BestElementCluster**(c_q^k);	
$\mathbf{d}_l^{k+1} \leftarrow$ **LocalAttractionMovement**(c_q^k); $l \in c_q^k$	
$\mathbf{d}_l^{k+1} \leftarrow$ **LocalPerturbationStrategy**($\mathbf{d}_l^{k+1}$);	
end **for**	
for (all best cluster elements of c_q^k)	**Step 4**
$\mathbf{d}_b^{k+1} \leftarrow$ **GlobalAttractionMovement**($\mathbf{d}_b^k$);	
$\mathbf{d}_b^{k+1} \leftarrow$ **GlobalPerturbationStrategy**($\mathbf{d}_b^{k+1}$);	
end **for**	
$k = k + 1$;	
end while	**Step 5**
Output: $\mathbf{d}_B^k$	

In the Pseudo-code 6.1, the Step 1 initialize the population of datapoints. Then, the Ward's method is computed to produce clusters using the current population. Step 3 and 4 executes the intra-cluster and extra-cluster procedures respectively. Finally, the Step 5 repeats Steps 2–4 until a maximum number of iterations is reached.

6.6 Implementation of the CCO Algorithm in MATLAB

In Algorithm 6.3, it is described the MATLAB code for the CCO algorithm. To observe the functionality of the algorithm, the code encodes a benchmark function commonly used in performance testing related to the optimization of continuous functions. In this example, the Ackley function is implemented, so that the reader can observe the functionality of the CCO algorithm considering a minimization process.

The Ackley function exhibits a non-convex unimodal surface in a 2-dimensional space, and has a single global minimum located at position 0 of each of the decision variables used in the search space. The non-convex feature is used to test the scaling of the metaheuristic operators of the CCO algorithm when operates over surfaces that contain multiple local optima. On the other hand, the Ackley function is continuous and non-convex, which indicates that not any optimization technique either classical or metaheuristic can reach the global optimum. The mathematical model of the Ackley function is as follows:

$$f(x) = -20\ \exp\left(-0.2\sqrt{\frac{1}{d}\sum_{i=1}^{d} x_i^2}\right) - \exp\left(\sqrt{\frac{1}{d}\sum_{i=1}^{d} \cos\left(2\pi\ x_i\right)}\right) + 20 + \exp(1) \tag{6.15}$$

Finally, so that the reader can see the behavior of the datapoints on the Ackley surface, at each iteration the movement of the solutions (datapoints) on the Ackley surface is plotted.

```
%Algorithm 6.3
%% INITIAL CONFIGURATION FOR THE OPTIMIZATION PROCESS
%Clear memory and Close Matlab windows
clear all;
close all;
%The maximum number of iterations is established
Max_Iter = 1000;
%The size of the population is established
Np = 50;
%The number of decision variables is established
dim = 2;
%The limits of the search space are defined.
lb = -32;
ub = 32;
%Adaptive parameters are calculated to control
%the optimization process in terms of iterations
sum = 0;
if size(ub,2)==1
    for i = 1:dim
        sum = sum + (ub - lb);
    end
end
if size(ub,2) > 1
    for i = 1:dim
        high=ub(i); down=lb(i);
        sum = sum + (high-down);
    end
end
%Initial alpha term is computed
alphaTotal = (sum/dim);
if alphaTotal > min(ub)
    alphaTotal = alphaTotal-ub;
    alphaTotal = alphaTotal / norm(alphaTotal);
end
```

```
%The maximum number of iterations is divided into three phases
%Phase 1 considers the 70%, Phase 2 considers the 20% and
%Phase 3 considers the last 10%.
EP = [70, 20, 10];
IT = zeros(1,3);
i = EP(1);
IT(1) = round((Max_Iter * i) / 100);
i = EP(1) + EP(2);
IT(2) = round(((Max_Iter * i) / 100));
IT(3) = round(Max_Iter);

%% Step 1 INITIALIZATION
%Initialization of the initial population,
%X is the variable representing the population of N elements
if size(ub,2)==1
    X=rand(Np,dim).*(ub-lb)+lb;
end
if size(ub,2)>1
    for i=1:dim
        high=ub(i);down=lb(i);
        X(:,i)=rand(Np,1).*(high-down)+down;
    end
end
%The fitness values of the initial population are obtained
fitness=ObjectiveFunction(X,dim);

%The population is sorted in ascending order
[Lightn,Index]=sort(fitness,'ascend');
sortedPop = X(Index, :);
%The best solution is obtained from the population
xbest = sortedPop(1,:);
fobj=Lightn(1);
fitness=ObjectiveFunction(sortedPop,dim);
[LightnBest,IndexBest]=sort(fitness,'ascend');
sortedPop = sortedPop(IndexBest, :);
%The plot the function to be optimized is computed
if dim<=2
    rangeUpLb=ub-lb;
    figure(1)
    x=[lb:rangeUpLb/100:ub];
    y=x;
    [xg,yg]=meshgrid(x,y);
    [row,col]=size(xg);
    for l=1:col
        for h=1:row
            z(h,l)=ObjectiveFunction([xg(h,l),yg(h,l)],dim);
        end
```

```
    end
end
cutmean = 1;
count = 0;
phase = 1;
div = 100;
%Iterative process of the algorithm
while count <= Max_Iter
    %The adaptive alpha term is computed according to the actual
    %in the optimization process based on the number of
    %phase iterations
    alfAdaptive =  alphaTotal * (EP(phase) / div);

    %% Step 2 CLUSTERING
    Z = linkage(sortedPop,'ward',{'euclidean'});
    %Dendrogram cutting process
    I = inconsistent(Z);
    cutAux = cutmean;
    cutmean = max(I(:,4));
    cutmean = cutmean - (cutmean* 0.001);
    if cutmean <= 0
        cutmean = cutAux;
    end
    clust = cluster(Z,'cutoff',cutmean);
    aux_clust = max(clust);
    %The computation of each cluster centroid is performed
    [n,m] = size(sortedPop);
    aux_clust = max(clust);
    for k = 1: m
        for j = 1: aux_clust
            centroid(j,k) = mean(sortedPop(j==clust,k));
        end
    end
    %The density term for each cluster is computed
    for i = 1: aux_clust
        sum = 0;
        index = find(clust==i);
        xAux = sortedPop(index,:);
        for j = 1: size(xAux,1)
            d(j) = (norm(xAux(j,:) - centroid(i)));
            sum = d(j) + sum;
        end
        maxDist = max(max(d));
        minDist = min(min(d));
        dis(i) = (sum/aux_clust) ;
        if maxDist == 0
            density(i) = size(xAux,1) / 50;
```

```
        else
            density(i) = (size(xAux,1)/50) *  aux_clust;
        end
    end
    density = sort(density,'ascend');

    %% Step 3 INTRA-CLUSTER PROCEDURE
    for k = 1:aux_clust
        f = find(clust==k,1);
        bestCluster(k,:) = sortedPop(f,:);
        index = find(clust==k);
        index = index(2:end);
        if ~isempty(index)
            for i = 1 : size(index,1)
                xAux = sortedPop(index(i),:);
                %Local Attraction movement
                sortedPop(index(i),:) = xAux + ...
((bestCluster(k,:) - xAux).* ...
chaosVector(lb,ub,dim).*...
(density(k)));
                sortedPop(index(i),:) =
findrange(sortedPop(index(i),:),lb,ub,dim,1);
                fitnessO = ...
ObjectiveFunction(sortedPop(in ex(i),:), dim);
                LightnBest(1,index(i)) = fitnessO;
                %Local Perturbation Strategy
                vT = vTransform(dim,alfAdaptive,lb,ub);
                left =  sortedPop(index(i),:) -
(sortedPop(index(i),:).*(chaosVector(lb,ub,dim))).*vT;
                left = findrange(left,lb,ub,dim,1);
                vT = vTransform(dim,alfAdaptive,lb,ub);
                right = sortedPop(index(i),:) +
(sortedPop(index(i),:).*(chaosVector(lb,ub,dim))).*vT;
                right = findrange(right,lb,ub,dim,1);
                fitnessLR=ObjectiveFunction([left;right],dim);
                if fitnessLR(1) < fitnessO
                    sortedPop(index(i),:) = left;
                    LightnBest(1,index(i))  = fitnessLR(1,1);
                end
                if fitnessLR(2) < fitnessO
                    sortedPop(index(i),:) = right;
                    LightnBest(1,index(i))   = fitnessLR(1,2);
                end
            end
        end
        %% Step 4 EXTRA-CLUSTER PROCEDURE
        vT = vTransform(dim,alfAdaptive,lb,ub);
        %Global Attraction movement
```

```
        bestCluster(k,:) =  bestCluster(k,:)  + (xbest -
bestCluster(k,:)).* vT.*(chaosVector(lb,ub,dim));
        bestCluster(k,:) = findrange(bestCluster(k,:),lb,ub,dim,1);
        fitnessOBC =     ObjectiveFunction(bestCluster(k,:),dim);
        sortedPop(f,:) = bestCluster(k,:);
        LightnBest(1,f) = fitnessOBC;
        %Global Perturbation Strategy
        vT = vTransform(dim,alfAdaptive,lb,ub);
        left =   bestCluster(k,:) -
(bestCluster(k,:).*(chaosVector(lb,ub,dim))).*vT;
        left = findrange(left,lb,ub,dim,1);
        vT = vTransform(dim,alfAdaptive,lb,ub);
        right =  bestCluster(k,:) +
(bestCluster(k,:).*(chaosVector(lb,ub,dim))).*vT;
        right = findrange(right,lb,ub,dim,1);
        fitnessLR= ObjectiveFunction([left;right],dim);
        if fitnessLR(1) < fitnessOBC
            sortedPop(f,:)  = left;
            LightnBest(1,f) = fitnessLR(1,1);
        end
        if fitnessLR(2) < fitnessOBC
            sortedPop(f,:) = right;
            LightnBest(1,f) = fitnessLR(1,2);
        end
    end
    [LightnBest,IndexBest]=sort(LightnBest,'ascend');
    sortedPop = sortedPop(IndexBest, :);
    %Selection of the best solution so far
    if LightnBest(1)  < fobj
        xbest = sortedPop(1,:);
        fobj = LightnBest(1);
    end
    %Iteration and phase counters
    count = count + 1;
    if count > IT(phase)
        phase = phase + 1;
        div = div * Max_Iter;
    end
    %The plot the population is generated
    if dim<=2
        surf(xg,yg,z);
        title('Ackley function')
        hold on
        plot3(sortedPop(:,1),sortedPop(:,2),LightnBest(1,:),'o',
'markersize',6,'markerfacecolor','r');
        plot3(xbest(1,1),xbest(1,2),fobj,'o','markersize',10,
'markerfacecolor','g');
        drawnow;
```

```
        hold off
    end
    fprintf('Iteration: %d\n',count);
    fprintf('Best solution: (%d,%d)\n',xbest(1,1),xbest(1,2));
    fprintf('Best fitness: %d\n',fobj);
end

%%OBJECTIVE FUNCTION
%Ackley function implementation
function fit = ObjectiveFunction(L,dim)
    [N,~]=size(L);
    for i=1:N
        fit(i)= -20*exp(-.2*sqrt(sum( L(i,:).^2)/dim))-
exp(sum(cos(2*pi.* L(i,:)))/dim)+20+exp(1);
    end
end

%Circular perturbation strategy
function vT = vTransform(dim,r,lb,ub)
    vT = ones(1,dim);
    [~,col]=size(lb);
    for i = 1: dim
        if col > 1
            vT(1,i) = 1*cos(r(i)*rand);
        else
            vT(1,i) = 1*cos(r*rand);
        end
    end
end

%Iterative Chaotic Map with Infinite Collapses function
function y = chaosVector(low,up,dim)

    if size(up,2)==1
        for i = 1:dim
            aux = rand;
            for j =1:50
                aux = sin((pi*4)/aux);
            end
            y(1,i) = aux;
        end
    end
    if size(up,2) > 1
        for i = 1:dim
            high=up(i);down=low(i);
            aux = rand;
            for j =1:50
```

```
                    aux =  sin((pi*4)/aux);
                end
                y(1,i) = aux;
            end
        end
    end

%Find range function
function X = findrange(X,low,up,dim,N)
    if size(up,2)==1
        for j = 1 : N
            for i = 1:dim
                if (X(j,i) < low)
                    X(j,i) = rand(1,1).*(up-low)+low;
                end
                if (X(j,i) > up)
                    X(j,i) = rand(1,1).*(up-low)+low;
                end
            end
        end
    end
    if size(up,2) > 1
        for j = 1 : N
            for i = 1:dim
                high=up(i);down=low(i);
                if (X(j,i) < down)
                    X(j,i) = rand(1,1).*(high-down)+down;
                end
                if (X(j,i) > high)
                    X(j,i) = rand(1,1).*(high-down)+down;
                end
            end
        end
    end
end
```

The Algorithm 6.3 graphically shows the evolution of the population using the iterative structure of the CCO method. The plotted graph is shown in Figure 6.7.

In Algorithm 6.3, the first stage indicates the initial parameters configuration required by the optimization process. Such configuration relies on setting the maximum number of iterations, the population size, the number of decision variables involved in the optimization process and the definition of the limits of the search space. During the optimization process of the CCO it is also introduced an adaptive mechanism to regulate the balance between exploration and exploitation operators. Under this scheme, the maximum number of iterations is divided into three phases: Phase 1 considers the 70%, Phase 2 considers the 20% and Phase 3 considers the last 10% of iterations. This mechanism cannot be considered as a metaheuristic operator since it only regulates the optimization procedure.

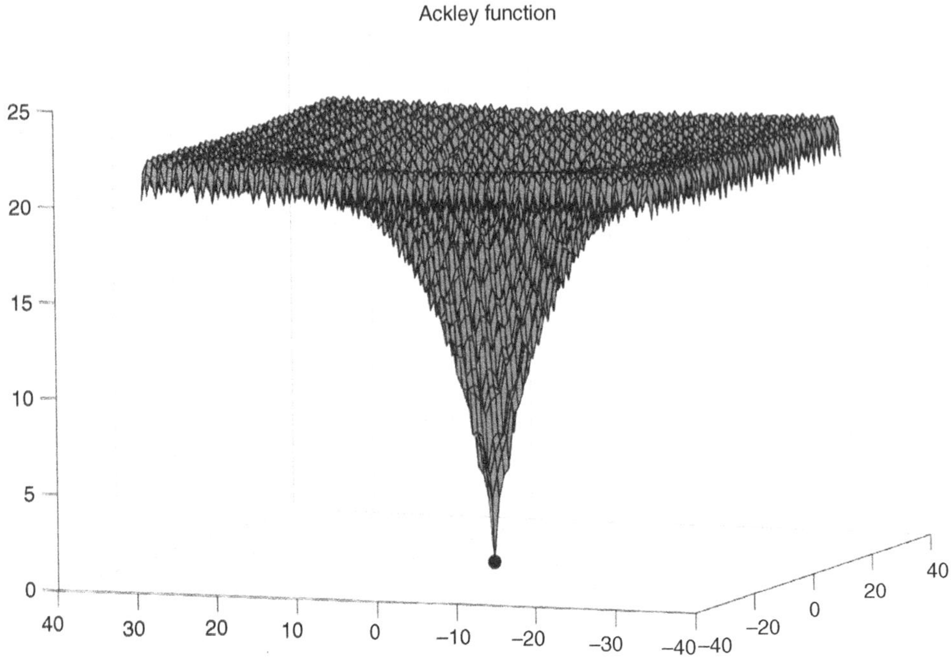

Figure 6.7 The graph of the Ackley function produced by CCO.

The algorithm describes the Step 1, in this step the initialization of the population is achieved. Each datapoint is randomly generated within the limits of the search space. Additionally, the fitness value for each datapoint is then obtained. The main loop of the algorithm begins to the Step 2 that means to compute the dendrogram of the population followed by the Ward's method. Once the dendrogram is generated, a cutting scheme is applied based on the maximum number of inconsistencies of the dendrogram. Step 3 implements the Intra-cluster procedure, where the local attraction movement and local perturbation strategy explores the space inside each cluster. Step 4 implements the Extra-cluster procedure, where the global attraction movement and global perturbation strategy is explores the space outside each cluster to promote exploration into wider search zones. In the algorithm, the objective function to be optimized is implemented above the main loop. The objective function considered in this chapter is the well-known Ackley function. Also it is implemented the circular perturbation mechanism and the iterative chaotic map with infinite collapses to produce chaotic sequence values.

6.7 Spring Design Optimization Problem Using the CCO Algorithm in MATLAB

Optimization problems involve finding an optimal solution within a possible set of solutions that pose maximization or minimization problems. Most areas in engineering can present optimization problems to find the optimal solution to planning problems, operations research, or even engineering design problems, among others. From this perspective, the need to develop optimization techniques that solve these problems is of great interest within the scientific and engineering community. In Section 6.5, the code related to the implementation of the CCO algorithm using a synthetic benchmark function that exhibits a unimodal and convexities was presented. However, in such example the CCO is tested using a mathematical function that is part of a set of test functions that do not represent a real application. Under this circumstance, this section analyzes an engineering design problem and describes how the CCO method can be used to solve real world applications.

The simple spring design problem is a complex engineering problem where the objective is to design a spring for tension or compression. For this problem, a set of specific design requirements (also called constraints) must be addressed to include the minimum deflection and frequency, as well as the maximum diameter and shear stress of the spring.

The main objective of simple spring design is to minimize the weight of the tension or compression spring. To do this, the mathematical description of the model is formulated as an optimization problem taking the following form:

$$\min_{x_1, x_2, x_3} \quad f(x) = (x_3 + 2)x_2 x_1^2$$

Subject to:

$$\begin{aligned} g_1(x) &= 1 - \frac{x_2^3 x_3}{71{,}785 x_1^4} \leq 0 \\ g_2(x) &= \frac{4x_2^2 - x_1 x_2}{12{,}566\left(x_2 x_1^3 - x_1^4\right)} + \frac{1}{5108 x_1^2} - 1 \leq 0 \\ g_3(x) &= 1 - \frac{140.45 x_1}{x_2^2 x_3} \leq 0 \\ g_4(x) &= \frac{x_1 + x_2}{1.5} - 1 \leq 0 \end{aligned} \tag{6.16}$$

where x_1, x_2 and x_3 represent the thickness of the rod (W), the average diameter of the coil (D), and the number of active coils (L), respectively. These values are distributed in a three-dimensional space $(d = 3)$ and define the decision variables of the problem. In turn, $g_1(x), \ldots, g_4(x)$, correspond to the four non-linear restrictions that must be met for the spring design to be optimal. The limits of the search space corresponding to each dimension of the problem are defined as: $0.05 \leq x_1 \leq 2$, $0.25 \leq x_2 \leq 1.3$ and $2 \leq x_3 \leq 15$. The design parameters for the spring problem are graphically illustrated in Figure 6.8, where D corresponds to the average diameter of the coil, L represents the number of active coils, and W the thickness of the rod. The optimization process of this engineering problem using the CCO algorithm is shown in Algorithm 6.4.

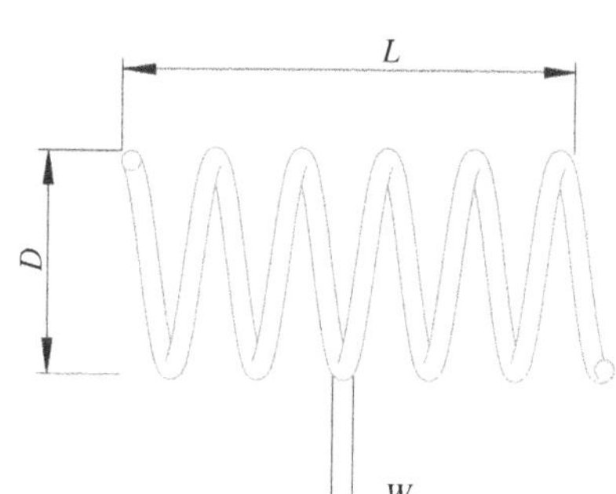

Figure 6.8 Design parameters of the simple spring design problem.

```
%Algorithm 6.4
%% INITIAL CONFIGURATION FOR THE OPTIMIZATION PROCESS
%Clear memory and Close Matlab windows
clear all;
close all;
%The maximum number of iterations is established
Max_Iter = 1000;
%The size of the population is established
Np = 50;
%The number of decision variables is established
dim = 3;
%The limits of the search space are defined.
lb = [0.05 0.25 2];
ub = [2 1.3 15];
%The penalization parameters are defined.
rg = 100;
cg = 2;
%Adaptive parameters are calculated to control
%the optimization process in terms of iterations
sum = 0;
if size(ub,2)==1
    for i = 1:dim
        sum = sum + (ub - lb);
    end
end
if size(ub,2) > 1
    for i = 1:dim
        high=ub(i); down=lb(i);
        sum = sum + (high-down);
    end
end
%Initial alpha term is computed
alphaTotal = (sum/dim);
if alphaTotal > min(ub)
    alphaTotal = alphaTotal-ub;
    alphaTotal = alphaTotal / norm(alphaTotal);
end
%The maximum number of iterations is divided into three phases
%Phase 1 considers the 70%, Phase 2 considers the 20% and
%Phase 3 considers the last 10%.
EP = [70, 20, 10];
IT = zeros(1,3);
i = EP(1);
```

```
IT(1) = round((Max_Iter * i) / 100);
i = EP(1) + EP(2);
IT(2) = round(((Max_Iter * i) / 100));
IT(3) = round(Max_Iter);

%% Step 1 INITIALIZATION
%Initialization of the initial population,
%X is the variable representing the population of N elements
if size(ub,2)==1
    X=rand(Np,dim).*(ub-lb)+lb;
end
if size(ub,2)>1
    for i=1:dim
        high=ub(i);down=lb(i);
        X(:,i)=rand(Np,1).*(high-down)+down;
    end
end
%The fitness values of the initial population are obtained
fitness=ObjectiveFunction(X,dim,rg,cg);

%The population is sorted in ascending order
[Lightn,Index]=sort(fitness,'ascend');
sortedPop = X(Index, :);
%The best solution is obtained from the population
xbest = sortedPop(1,:);
fobj=Lightn(1);
fitness=ObjectiveFunction(sortedPop,dim,rg,cg);
[LightnBest,IndexBest]=sort(fitness,'ascend');
sortedPop = sortedPop(IndexBest, :);
%The plot the function to be optimized is computed
if dim<=2
    rangeUpLb=ub-lb;
    figure(1)
    x=[lb:rangeUpLb/100:ub];
    y=x;
    [xg,yg]=meshgrid(x,y);
    [row,col]=size(xg);
    for l=1:col
        for h=1:row
            z(h,l)=ObjectiveFunction([xg(h,l),yg(h,l)],dim,rg,cg);
        end
    end
end
cutmean = 1;
count = 0;
phase = 1;
div = 100;
```

```
%Iterative process of the algorithm
while count <= Max_Iter
    %The adaptive alpha term is computed according to the actual
    %phase in the optimization process based on the number of
    %iterations
    alfAdaptive =  alphaTotal * (EP(phase) / div);

    %% Step 2 CLUSTERING
    Z = linkage(sortedPop,'ward',{'euclidean'});
    %Dendrogram cutting process
    I = inconsistent(Z);
    cutAux = cutmean;
    cutmean = max(I(:,4));
    cutmean = cutmean - (cutmean* 0.001);
    if cutmean <= 0
        cutmean = cutAux;
    end
    clust = cluster(Z,'cutoff',cutmean);
    aux_clust = max(clust);
    %The computation of each cluster centroid is performed
    [n,m] = size(sortedPop);
    aux_clust = max(clust);
    for k = 1: m
        for j = 1: aux_clust
            centroid(j,k) = mean(sortedPop(j==clust,k));
        end
    end
    %The density term for each cluster is computed
    for i = 1: aux_clust
        sum = 0;
        index = find(clust==i);
        xAux = sortedPop(index,:);
        for j = 1: size(xAux,1)
            d(j) = (norm(xAux(j,:) - centroid(i)));
            sum = d(j) + sum;
        end
        maxDist = max(max(d));
        minDist = min(min(d));
        dis(i) = (sum/aux_clust) ;
        if maxDist == 0
            density(i) = size(xAux,1) / 50;
        else
            density(i) = (size(xAux,1)/50) *  aux_clust;
        end
    end
    density = sort(density,'ascend');
```

```
    %% Step 3 INTRA-CLUSTER PROCEDURE
    for k = 1:aux_clust
        f = find(clust==k,1);
        bestCluster(k,:) = sortedPop(f,:);
        index = find(clust==k);
        index = index(2:end);
        if ~isempty(index)
            for i = 1 : size(index,1)
                xAux = sortedPop(index(i),:);
                %Local Attraction movement
                sortedPop(index(i),:) = xAux +  ((bestCluster(k,:) -
xAux) .* chaosVector(lb,ub,dim) .*(density(k)));
                sortedPop(index(i),:) =
findrange(sortedPop(index(i),:),lb,ub,dim,1);
                fitnessO =
ObjectiveFunction(sortedPop(index(i),:),dim,rg,cg);
                LightnBest(1,index(i)) = fitnessO;
                %Local Perturbation Strategy
                vT = vTransform(dim,alfAdaptive,lb,ub);
                left =  sortedPop(index(i),:) -
(sortedPop(index(i),:).*(chaosVector(lb,ub,dim))).*vT;
                left = findrange(left,lb,ub,dim,1);
                vT = vTransform(dim,alfAdaptive,lb,ub);
                right = sortedPop(index(i),:) +
(sortedPop(index(i),:).*(chaosVector(lb,ub,dim))).*vT;
                right = findrange(right,lb,ub,dim,1);
                fitnessLR=ObjectiveFunction([left;right],dim,rg,cg);
                if fitnessLR(1) < fitnessO
                    sortedPop(index(i),:) = left;
                    LightnBest(1,index(i))  = fitnessLR(1,1);
                end
                if fitnessLR(2) < fitnessO
                    sortedPop(index(i),:) = right;
                    LightnBest(1,index(i))   = fitnessLR(1,2);
                end
            end
        end
        %% Step 4 EXTRA-CLUSTER PROCEDURE
        vT = vTransform(dim,alfAdaptive,lb,ub);
        %Global Attraction movement
        bestCluster(k,:) =  bestCluster(k,:)  + (xbest -
bestCluster(k,:)).* vT.*(chaosVector(lb,ub,dim));
        bestCluster(k,:) = findrange(bestCluster(k,:),lb,ub,dim,1);
        fitnessOBC = ...
ObjectiveFunction(bestCluster(k,:), dim,rg,cg);
        sortedPop(f,:) = bestCluster(k,:);
        LightnBest(1,f) = fitnessOBC;
```

```
        %Global Perturbation Strategy
        vT = vTransform(dim,alfAdaptive,lb,ub);
        left =   bestCluster(k,:) -
(bestCluster(k,:).*(chaosVector(lb,ub,dim))).*vT;
        left = findrange(left,lb,ub,dim,1);
        vT = vTransform(dim,alfAdaptive,lb,ub);
        right =  bestCluster(k,:) +
(bestCluster(k,:).*(chaosVector(lb,ub,dim))).*vT;
        right = findrange(right,lb,ub,dim,1);
        fitnessLR= ObjectiveFunction([left;right],dim,rg,cg);
        if fitnessLR(1) < fitnessOBC
            sortedPop(f,:)  = left;
            LightnBest(1,f) = fitnessLR(1,1);
        end
        if fitnessLR(2) < fitnessOBC
            sortedPop(f,:) = right;
            LightnBest(1,f) = fitnessLR(1,2);
        end
    end
    [LightnBest,IndexBest]=sort(LightnBest,'ascend');
    sortedPop = sortedPop(IndexBest, :);
    %Selection of the best solution so far
    if LightnBest(1)  < fobj
        xbest = sortedPop(1,:);
        fobj = LightnBest(1);
    end
    %Iteration and phase counters
    count = count + 1;
    if count > IT(phase)
        phase = phase + 1;
        div = div * Max_Iter;
    end
    %The plot the population is generated
    if dim<=2
        surf(xg,yg,z);
        title('Ackley function')
        hold on

        plot3(sortedPop(:,1),sortedPop(:,2),...
LightnBest(1,:),'o','markersize',6,...
'markerfacecolor','r');
        plot3(xbest(1,1),xbest(1,2),fobj,...
'o','markersize',10,...
'markerfacecolor','g');
        drawnow;
        hold off
    end
```

```
        fprintf('Iteration: %d\n',count);
        fprintf('Best solution: (%d,%d)\n',xbest(1,1),xbest(1,2));
        fprintf('Best fitness: %d\n',fobj);
    end

%%OBJECTIVE FUNCTION
%Implementation of the Spring design optimization problem
function fit = ObjectiveFunction(L,dim,rg,cg)
    [N,~]=size(L);
    for i=1:N
        fitnessX = (L(3) + 2) * L(2)* (L(1)^2);
        g1= 1-((L(i,2)^3*L(i,3))/(71785*L(i,1)^4) );
        p1=4*L(i,2)^2-L(i,1)*L(i,2)/12566*(L(i,2)*L(i,1)^3-L(i,1)^4);
          p2=1/(5108*L(i,1)^2);
        g2=(p1+p2-1) ;
          g3=(1-( (140.45*L(i,1))/(L(i,2)^2*L(i,3)) ) );
          g4=(((L(i,2)+L(i,1))/1.5)-1);
        P = (rg * min(0,g1)^2) +...
(rg * min(0,g2)^2) +...
(rg * min(0,g3)^2) +...
(rg * min(0,g4)^2);
        fitnessX = fitnessX + P;
        rg = rg * cg;
        fit(i)= fitnessX;
    end
end

%Circular perturbation strategy
function vT = vTransform(dim,r,lb,ub)
    vT = ones(1,dim);
    [~,col]=size(lb);
    for i = 1: dim
        if col > 1
            vT(1,i) = 1*cos(r(i)*rand);
        else
            vT(1,i) = 1*cos(r*rand);
        end
    end
end

%Iterative Chaotic Map with Infinite Collapses function
function y = chaosVector(low,up,dim)

    if size(up,2)==1
        for i = 1:dim
            aux = rand;
            for j =1:50
```

```
                aux = sin((pi*4)/aux);
            end
            y(1,i) = aux;
        end
    end
    if size(up,2) > 1
        for i = 1:dim
            high=up(i);down=low(i);
            aux = rand;
            for j =1:50
                aux =  sin((pi*4)/aux);
            end
            y(1,i) = aux;
        end
    end
end

%Find range function
function X = findrange(X,low,up,dim,N)
    if size(up,2)==1
        for j = 1 : N
            for i = 1:dim
                if (X(j,i) < low)
                    X(j,i) = rand(1,1).*(up-low)+low;
                end
                if (X(j,i) > up)
                    X(j,i) = rand(1,1).*(up-low)+low;
                end
            end
        end
    end
    if size(up,2) > 1
        for j = 1 : N
            for i = 1:dim
                high=up(i);down=low(i);
                if (X(j,i) < down)
                    X(j,i) = rand(1,1).*(high-down)+down;
                end
                if (X(j,i) > high)
                    X(j,i) = rand(1,1).*(high-down)+down;
                end
            end
        end
    end
end
```

In Algorithm 6.4, the initial configuration declares the dimensionality and the limits of the search space according to the spring design problem. The spring design optimization problem contains 4 constraints. These constraints refer to physical requirements for designing a spring. Commonly in metaheuristics a penalization term is added to the fitness value. For that the variables *rg* and *cg* are defined to control the penalization for the objective function. The objective function implements each of the constraints in Eq. 6.16. The penalization term is added to the actual fitness value. The penalized fitness value incorporates information in future iterations of the optimization process.

References

Blum, C., Blesa, J., Roli, A., and Sampels, M. (2008). *Hybrid Metaheuristics: An Emerging Approach to Optimization*. https://doi.org/10.1007/978-3-540-78295-7.

Blum, C., Puchinger, J., Raidl, G.R., and Roli, A. (2011). Hybrid metaheuristics in combinatorial optimization: a survey. *Applied Soft Computing* 11 (6): 4135–4151. https://doi.org/10.1016/J.ASOC.2011.02.032.

Dash, R. and Dash, P.K. (2016). An evolutionary hybrid fuzzy computationally efficient EGARCH model for volatility prediction. *Applied Soft Computing* 45: 40–60. https://doi.org/10.1016/J.ASOC.2016.04.014.

Ezugwu, A.E., Ikotun, A.M., Oyelade, O.O. et al. (2022). A comprehensive survey of clustering algorithms: state-of-the-art machine learning applications, taxonomy, challenges, and future research prospects. *Engineering Applications of Artificial Intelligence* 110: 104743. https://doi.org/10.1016/J.ENGAPPAI.2022.104743.

Huang, L., Ding, S., Yu, S. et al. (2016). Chaos-enhanced Cuckoo search optimization algorithms for global optimization. *Applied Mathematical Modelling* 40 (5–6): 3860–3875. https://doi.org/10.1016/J.APM.2015.10.052.

Illias, H.A., Chai, X.R., and Abu Bakar, A.H. (2016). Hybrid modified evolutionary particle swarm optimisation-time varying acceleration coefficient-artificial neural network for power transformer fault diagnosis. *Measurement* 90: 94–102. https://doi.org/10.1016/J.MEASUREMENT.2016.04.052.

Ma, H., Simon, D., Fei, M. et al. (2014). Hybrid biogeography-based evolutionary algorithms. *Engineering Applications of Artificial Intelligence* 30: 213–224. https://doi.org/10.1016/J.ENGAPPAI.2014.01.011.

Niknam, T. and Azad Farsani, E. (2010). A hybrid self-adaptive particle swarm optimization and modified shuffled frog leaping algorithm for distribution feeder reconfiguration. *Engineering Applications of Artificial Intelligence* 23 (8): 1340–1349. https://doi.org/10.1016/J.ENGAPPAI.2010.02.005.

Snaselova, P. and Zboril, F. (2015). Genetic algorithm using theory of Chaos. *Procedia Computer Science* 51 (1): 316–325. https://doi.org/10.1016/J.PROCS.2015.05.248.

Yang, D., Li, G., and Cheng, G. (2007). On the efficiency of chaos optimization algorithms for global optimization. *Chaos, Solitons & Fractals* 34 (4): 1366–1375. https://doi.org/10.1016/J.CHAOS.2006.04.057.

7

Techniques of Machine Learning for Modifying the Search Strategy

7.1 Introduction

Extracting knowledge is the process of finding new information in data. For extracting significant information, a set of multiple techniques can be applied. Some techniques include neural networks, decision trees, and clustering. Knowledge extraction is the main part of building artificial intelligence applications since it allows machines to learn the intrinsic characteristics of the data and make predictions or recommendations. One of the most interesting techniques is based on the Self-Organization Maps (SOMs) introduced by Teuvo Kohonen (1982).

A SOM is an unsupervised neural network which has been extensively employed in fields including information extraction and machine learning. In SOM, vector quantization is used to condense a large number of data vectors into a manageable subset of representative vectors grouped in a fixed lattice. SOM has several advantages over other methods for extracting knowledge. SOMs enable for the discovery of unexpected patterns in input data by mapping complicated, high-dimensional data onto a predefined lattice (topology). In order to keep the lattice map's spatial relationships between neighboring items in the original data and the neural units, SOM preserves the data organization. The visualization of complicated data structures is thus made intuitive by the association of numerous input data with a single neural unit (Akinduko et al. 2016). These properties make it possible to identify unexpected data structures, determine if groups of vectors are similar or dissimilar, and examine their intrinsic patterns.

The learning process of the SOM involves the concept of competitive learning. In competitive learning, a set of neural units compete with each other to produce a winning neuron, which is often the neuron that best matches the input data. Then, the weights of each neuron are updated according to their activation response. The importance of this kind of learning relies on its capacity to automatically group similar data inputs into clusters in input data when no prior information or labels are provided. The main goal of the competitive learning strategy of SOMs is to classify input data without the use of input-labeled data.

The inherent characteristics of the competitive learning mechanism of the SOMs can be employed to produce interesting search strategies for developing metaheuristic algorithms.

Most of the metaheuristic algorithms are proposed as metaphors of natural, biological, or even social phenomena as a source of inspiration to construct search strategies into computational algorithms for finding optimal solutions in complex optimization problems. Recently, the scientific community has focused their attention on how to improve the existing search strategies by introducing some kind of knowledge in their metaheuristic operators. Under such circumstances, the metaheuristic approaches can be categorized into two groups. The first class incorporates knowledge before the beginning of the optimization process. These methods are known as Evolutionary

Machine Learning and Metaheuristic Computation, First Edition.
Erik Cuevas, Jorge Galvez, Omar Avalos, and Fernando Wario.

Methods with a Prior Information (EMAI). Under these techniques, the incorporated information remains fixed during the entire optimization process (Deveci and Demirel 2018; Kobeaga et al. 2018). On the other hand, the second class incorporates knowledge of each iteration of the optimization process. These methods are known as Evolutionary Techniques with Dynamic Information (ETDI) (Mobin et al. 2018; Nobile et al. 2018; Yeguas et al. 2014).

ETDI methods extract information from the optimization process using some techniques such as: statistical analysis methods, regression trees, and genetic programming (Hong et al. 2018; Hu et al. 2017). The extracted information of these methods modifies the search strategy of the metaheuristic algorithm. Most of these approaches use straightforward machine learning techniques that only take into account a few population members as well as the best current element as complete representations of the optimization process. Under such circumstances, the development of novel metaheuristic algorithms where the knowledge extraction is not based only on the population but on the entire search strategy is an emerging research topic.

This chapter describes the EA-SOM metaheuristic optimization algorithm, which uses information gained from the optimization process at each generation to control its search strategy. The proposed method employs a SOM as an extracting knowledge method to identify potential locations. The proposed strategy trains the SOM using a subset of the entire group of produced solutions seen thus far for each generation. The neural unit from lattice that corresponds to the best solution is found after the training stage. Then, a full population of potential solutions is generated using a local knowledge mechanism.

In this chapter, we delve into the concept of competitive learning. Competitive learning model is the mechanism employed by the structure of SOMs for training a lattice of neural units. The main aspect of involving the concept of competitive learning during the optimization process relies on extracting information of the optimization process at each generation. This methodology produces evolutionary strategies for improving the search mechanism of metaheuristic algorithms by guiding the search process through the gained information by the optimization process iteratively. Throughout the chapter, MATLAB will be used to implement this methodology. This hands-on approach will enable readers to gain practical experience and become proficient in using SOM structure to produce metaheuristic operators in their own projects.

7.2 Self-Organization Map (SOM)

The SOMs, also called Kohonen's maps, were introduced by Teuvo Kohonen. A SOM is a technique that analyzes data in many dimensions with complex relationships between them and reduces them to represent them in, usually, one, two, or three dimensions. SOMs are mathematical models based on the abstraction process of the topographic mapping between the human visual system to the cerebral cortex. Analyzing and modeling the topographic mapping are important to understand how the human brain recognizes and processes the pattern it receives from the human visual system to make decisions. A SOM is an unsupervised neural network which is an extensively used technique for extracting knowledge in machine learning tasks. This kind of neural networks are effective methods for analyzing complex multidimensional data.

SOMs have several significant advantages over other methods for extracting knowledge, one of which is that the processed data keeps the original elements' topology (data organization) intact. SOMs are frequently used as data reduction or clustering methods due to this property.

Vector quantization is used by SOM to condense a large number of data vectors into a manageable subset of representative vectors arranged in a predetermined lattice. SOMs allow for the discovery of unexpected patterns in input data by mapping complex, high-dimensional data into a fixed lattice. SOM maintains the data organization so that similar elements in the original data remain close to neural units in the output layer. In order to facilitate the visualization of complex data structures, SOMs link multiple input data to a single prototype neural unit. These characteristics make it possible to identify unexpected data structures, determine whether groups of vectors are similar or dissimilar, and examine their natural patterns.

A SOM can be illustrated as a two-layer neural network that only contains input layer and output layer. The input layer contains the input (training data), while the output layer represents a rectangular grid of neural units called lattice (Figure 7.1).

The objective of SOMs is to find a mapping between input data and the lattice through a competitive learning model. SOMs perform unsupervised learning model, where labels and prior classifications are not necessary for the input data. Due to this approach, SOMs can operate under unlabeled or sparsely labeled data to form clusters from input data. The learning process of SOMs is based on the concept of competitive learning model, where a set of neural units competes with each other to produce a winning neuron that best matches the input data. The importance of this kind of learning model relies on its capacity to automatically group similar input data without the necessity of prior labels for each input data.

The competitive learning strategy used in SOMs can be defined into three main procedures: Competition, cooperation, and synaptic adaptation. In the competition phase, the SOM structure finds the correspondence among input data and each neural unit in the output layer, producing a winning neuron in the lattice. The winning neuron is the neural unit in the lattice that best matches the input data. The cooperation phase determines the spatial relationship also called neighborhood relation, so adjacent neural units to the winning neuron share knowledge locally. Finally, the

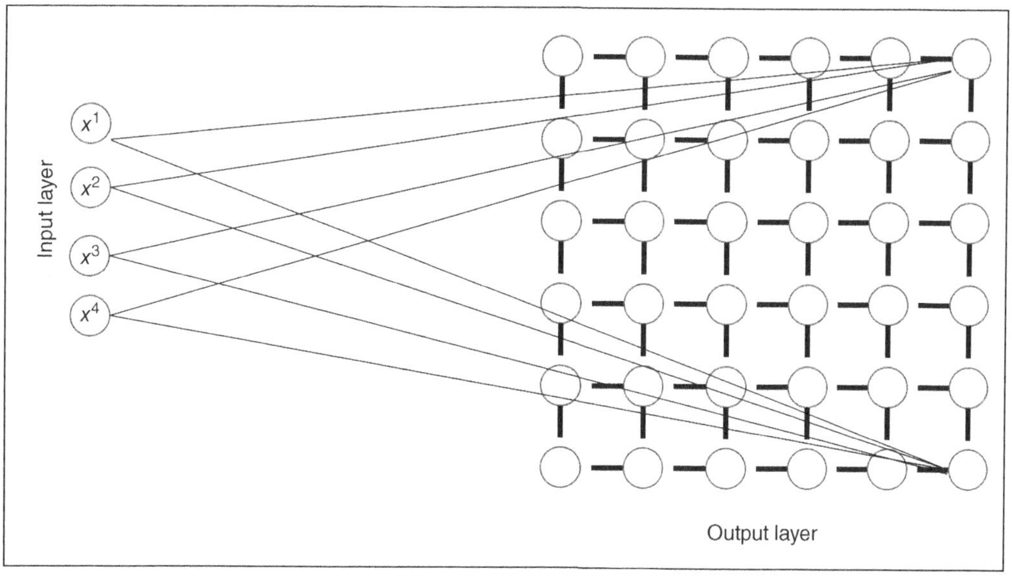

Figure 7.1 Representation of a Self-Organization Map (SOM).

synaptic adaptation phase updated the weights of the neural units according to their importance in the neighborhood. Closer neurons to the winning neuron will share more information than distant neurons. This fact follows the neurobiological studies which indicate that biological neurons are excited following a local and decreasing interaction over time.

In the following sections, the network architecture, and the competitive learning model of a SOM are detailed.

7.2.1 Network Architecture

The SOM is composed by a set of neurons, commonly arranged in a 2-D rectangular or hexagonal grid, to form a discrete topological map (lattice) where the input data will be mapped. A SOM integrates two different layers: an input layer and a competitive layer (output layer). The network architecture of a SOM networks can be shown in Figure 7.2.

The network is made by the input layer which represents the training data set, and the output layer which corresponds to the mapping learned through the competitive learning strategy. In this structure, SOM considers as input data an n-dimensional vector $\mathbf{x}$. Each node (neural unit) in the lattice is fully connected to each node in the input layer. The output lattice involves $Z = z * z$ competitive neural units. Associated with each neural unit in the lattice, there is a weight vector which is equal in size to an input vector $\mathbf{x}$. The weight vector of each neural unit represents the input data to which it is associated.

The learning model of SOMs consists of finding the best neural unit in the lattice (topology) that best matches an input data vector. Once the winning neuron is obtained, a definition of a neighborhood relation can be computed for the cooperative phase in the learning model. The importance of obtaining the winning neuron is the representation of the best knowledge from the input data, and the importance of the neighborhood is that closer neural units to the winning neuron will represent important knowledge, rather than distant neurons.

The topology of a SOM is dictated by the adjacent neurons by a neighborhood relation. This relationship affects the way data is associated. Complex neighborhood relationships result in

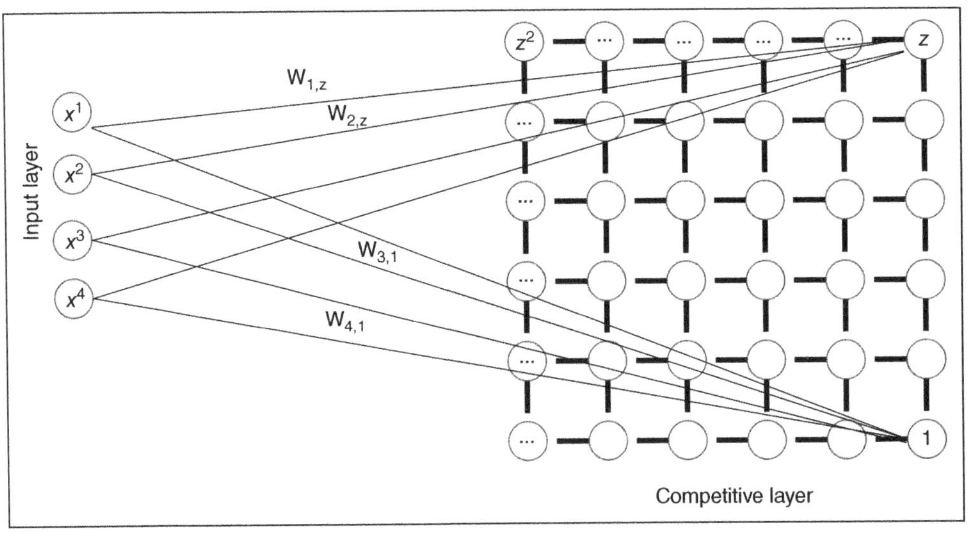

Figure 7.2 Representation of a SOM considering initial weights for each input variable.

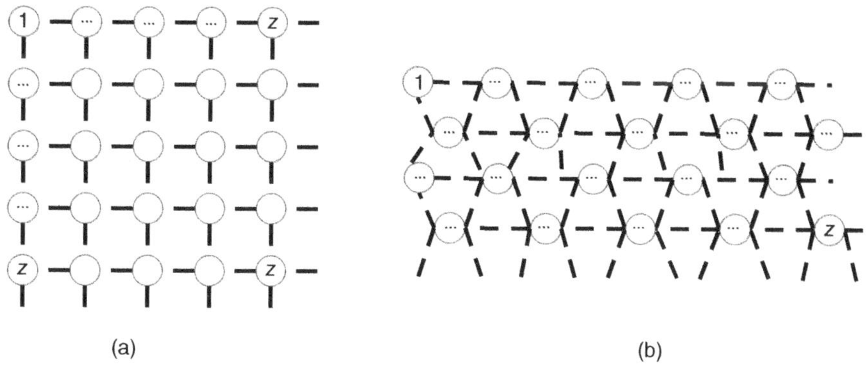

Figure 7.3 Topological structure of a Self-Organization Map (SOM). (a) Rectangular topology, (b) hexagonal topology.

more complex extensions of the neighborhood. Commonly, the topology employed in SOMs is a rectangular or hexagonal grid to maintain simple neighborhood relations over the entire lattice. Since SOMs are based on the abstraction process of how the human visual system maps into the cerebral cortex, the neurobiological field suggests that the neighborhood relationship among biological neurons can be modeled as a decreasing function of time. Under such circumstances, the neighborhood relation in SOMs should be a symmetric and monotonically decreasing function of time considering the spatial relation of the winning neuron. In Figure 7.3a, a rectangular topology of a SOM is presented. In Figure 7.3b, a hexagonal topology of an SOM is described.

7.2.2 Competitive Learning Model

Unsupervised learning model learns the intrinsic nature of the input data without prior knowledge from the input dataset. These techniques learn by their own without external assumptions. In SOMs, the unsupervised learning process produces clusters formed for the input data, which allows data compression from the input space. This process is achieved by introducing the concept of competitive learning in which the neurons from the output layer compete with each other to be activated, as a result, only one neuron (winning neuron) is activated through each generation. The aim of SOMs is to transform input data in n-dimensional space into a discrete lattice. This mechanism compresses input data into low-dimensional feature space. For that, SOMs are considered neural networks that selectively transform data into a low-dimensional representation of the entire input data.

The competitive learning model from SOMs is considered as the training stage of the algorithm. The objective of the training stage is to find the final topology of the lattice, which will represent the main features of the input data into a low-dimensional representation. In order to train a SOM, three important processes must be executed. Competition procedure, cooperation procedure, and synaptic adaptation.

7.2.2.1 Competition Procedure

In this procedure, each input data vector computes its correspondence to each neural unit in the output layer. The correspondence value is computed by a discriminant function. Commonly, SOMs employ the Euclidean distance between input vectors with the weights of each neural unit in the lattice. The neural unit with the smallest discriminant value is declared as the winning neuron.

Note

In competitive learning, the most commonly used discriminant functions are:

- Euclidean distance.
- Manhattan distance.
- Minkowski distance.
- Cosine similarity

In this chapter, the Euclidean distance is employed as a discriminant function. Euclidean distance is the most common measurement to implement the competition mechanism of SOMs. However, readers can implement any discriminant function for their own applications. One important aspect to consider is the fact that different discriminant functions can obtain different clusters in the output layer in SOMs. We encourage readers to experiment with different discriminant functions considering the input dataset.

7.2.2.2 Cooperation Procedure

Under this procedure, the winning neuron determines its spatial associations in terms of neighborhood relation. That is, neighbor neurons around the winner are also excited. This mechanism mimics the basis of knowledge cooperation since closer neurons respect the winner and will share important information rather than distant neurons from the winner. This mechanism is also called as lateral interaction. According to neurobiological studies, biological neurons are excited following a local and decreasing interaction over time among neighbor neurons. Under such circumstances, in the cooperation procedure neurons will share information following a symmetric and monotonically decreasing function of time around the winner.

Note

In competitive learning, the most common topological neighborhood relations for producing cooperative behavior among the lattice are:

- Exponential decay.
- Average rate.
- Gaussian curve.
- Mexican-hat curve.

In this chapter, the combination of Gaussian curve and exponential decay is employed to obtain the cooperative behavior of the competitive learning model. Gaussian curve defines the neighborhood in terms of a Gaussian function, where the winning neuron is the highest value of the Gaussian shape function. Additionally, an exponential decay is also employed to mimic a monotonically decreasing function to indicate that neighbor neurons closer to the winner will share more important information than distant neurons.

7.2.2.3 Synaptic Adaptation Procedure

Under this procedure, the weight vectors of the winning neuron and its neighbors are updated following the Hebbian learning rule. The effect of employing this weight adaptation strategy is to move the weight vectors of both the winning neuron and its neighbors toward the input vector to construct a final lattice representation of the entire dataset.

Note

In neural networks, the most common rule used for updating weights is the Hebbian rule based on the studies of the neuroscientific Donald Heeb in his publication in 1949, *"The Organization of Behaviour."* The idea behind the theory is that when human brains learn something new, neurons become activated and linked together to form neural networks. These connections are initially weak, but as the stimulus is repeated, they become increasingly strong, making the action more intuitive.

7.2.3 Self-Organization Map (SOM) Algorithm

The algorithmic design to implement a SOM involves a series of straightforward steps. Here are the steps:

Step 1: Initialization:
In this step, the weight vectors for each neural unit of the output layer are randomly initialized with small values. For this stage, it is required the definition of a lattice. The lattice used in this chapter is a rectangular grid representation.

Step 2: Competition Procedure:
In this step, the Euclidean distance between the input data vector with the weight vector associated with each neural unit is computed. Afterward, the neural unit representing the smallest distance in the lattice is selected and considered as the winning neuron.

Step 3: Cooperation Procedure:
In this step, the neighborhood of the winning neuron is computed. The neighborhood is defined based on a gaussian function. Also, an exponential decay function is computed.

Step 4: Synaptic Adaptation Procedure:
In this step, the weight vectors of the winning neuron, and its neighbors are updated. The adaptation process follows the Hebbian learning rule.

Step 5: Repeat Steps 2–4 until the Stop Criterion is Reached:
The complete algorithm for SOMs can be summarized as follows:

1. Define the initial topological structure.
2. Initialize all weight vectors from the lattice.
3. Set the number of generations *Max_Gen*.
4. Set the initial generation counter $k = 0$.
5. From the dataset, select an input data vector $\mathbf{x}$.
6. Perform the competition procedure.
   Compute the Euclidean distances among $\mathbf{x}$ and each weight vector of a neural unit $\mathbf{w}_j$.
   Obtain the winning neuron according to the following scheme:

$$i(\mathbf{x}) = \arg\min_{j} \|\mathbf{x} - \mathbf{w}_j\| \tag{7.1}$$

Where $i(\mathbf{x})$ represents the index of the neural unit from the lattice which is the closest element to the input vector.

7. Perform cooperative procedure.
   Compute the neighborhood function $h_{j,i(x)}$ following equations:

$$h_{j,i(\mathbf{x})}(k) = \exp\left(-\frac{d_{j,i}^2}{2\sigma^2(k)}\right) \tag{7.2}$$

   where $d_{j,i}^2$ is the distance between the winning neuron and each neighbor neuron. And σ is the neighborhood radius at k-th iteration.
8. Perform synaptic adaptation procedure
   Adjust the weights of both the winner unit and its neighbor elements considering this model:

$$\mathbf{w}_j(k+1) = \mathbf{w}_j(k) + \eta(k)\, h_{j,i(\mathbf{x})}(k)\, (\mathbf{x}(k) - \mathbf{w}_j(k)) \tag{7.3}$$

   where $\eta(k)$ is the learning rate at k-th iteration and it is computed as exponential decay as:

$$\eta(k) = \eta_0 \exp\left(-\frac{k}{\tau_2}\right) \tag{7.4}$$

   Where η_0 is the initial learning rate and τ_2 is a decay constant.
9. Update $k = k + 1$. If $k <$ Max_Gen repeat Step 5 to Step 9, otherwise STOP

7.2.4 Application of Self-Organization Map (SOM)

The MATLAB code (in Algorithm 7.1) is presented by using the built-in functions of MATLAB as follows:

```
%Algorithm 7.1
%% INITIAL CONFIGURATION
%Clear memory and Close Matlab windows
clear all
close all

%% Step 1 Load Sample Dataset from Matlab
load simplecluster_dataset;
%Obtain the input data from the previous
x = simpleclusterInputs;

%% Step 2 Create the Self-Organization Map
%Create a 10x10 lattice
dim1 = 10;
dim2 = 10;
net = selforgmap([dim1 dim2]);
```

```
%% Step 3 Train the Network
[net,tr] = train(net,x);

%% Step 4 Plot the network lattice and hits
figure(1)
plotsompos(net,x)
figure(2)
plotsomhits(net,x)
```

In Algorithm 7.1, Step 1 loads a synthetic dataset from Matlab. The `simplecluster_dataset` contains 1000 sample datapoints. In Step 2, the architecture of the SOM is defined. In this example, it is considered a lattice containing 10 × 10 neurons. The built-in function `selforgmap` creates the lattice. Then, in Step 3 the training stage from the SOM is defined in Step 2. Finally, after the training stage, Step 4 plots the network final lattice and the network hints. The output of Algorithm 7.1 can be seen in Figure 7.4.

From Figure 7.4a, it can be shown that synthetic data is grouped by the SOM lattice. The built-in function `plotsompos` represents the weight positions from the trained SOM. The built-in function `plotsomhits` represents a layer in which each neuron counts the number of input vectors it classifies. This can be shown in Figure 7.4b.

7.3 Evolutionary-SOM (EA-SOM)

The competitive learning model in SOMs allows data input to be clustered into low-dimensional space. This characteristic categorizes SOMs as data reduction techniques. SOMs are considered as exploratory data analysis method, where no prior information of the input data is required. Under such circumstances, the structure of SOMs can be reformulated to create metaheuristic operators to propose interesting search strategies to contribute to the optimization process.

Most of the metaheuristic algorithms published in the literature contemplate the iterative nature of evolutionary principles. One of the pillars of metaheuristic algorithms is based on sampling the search space by using exploration and exploitation operations through generations. The sampling scheme in metaheuristic algorithms is one of the most critical aspects to solve any optimization problem since there is no guarantee that the evolutionary operators are reevaluating solutions from past generations. In this section, it is presented a strategy search scheme which combines the most important features of the competitive learning model in SOMs to learn information related to previous solutions from past generations to improve the search capabilities in future generations. Utilizing previous data from a process reduces the need to acquire new data in order to infer its internal properties and relationships. In metaheuristic methods, using knowledge to conduct the search strategy is an intriguing idea that has the potential to improve the effectiveness of optimization techniques.

In this section, a proposed metaheuristic called Evolutionary-SOM (EA-SOM) is presented. This metaheuristic algorithm has been developed to locate the global solution (global minimum/maximum) of a nonlinear optimization problem. A nonlinear optimization problem can be mathematically described as follows:

$$\begin{array}{lll} \text{Minimize/Maximize} & J(\mathbf{x}), & \mathbf{x} = (x_1, \dots, x_n) \in \mathbb{R}^n \\ \text{subject to} & \mathbf{x} \, \varepsilon \, \boldsymbol{S} & \end{array} \tag{7.5}$$

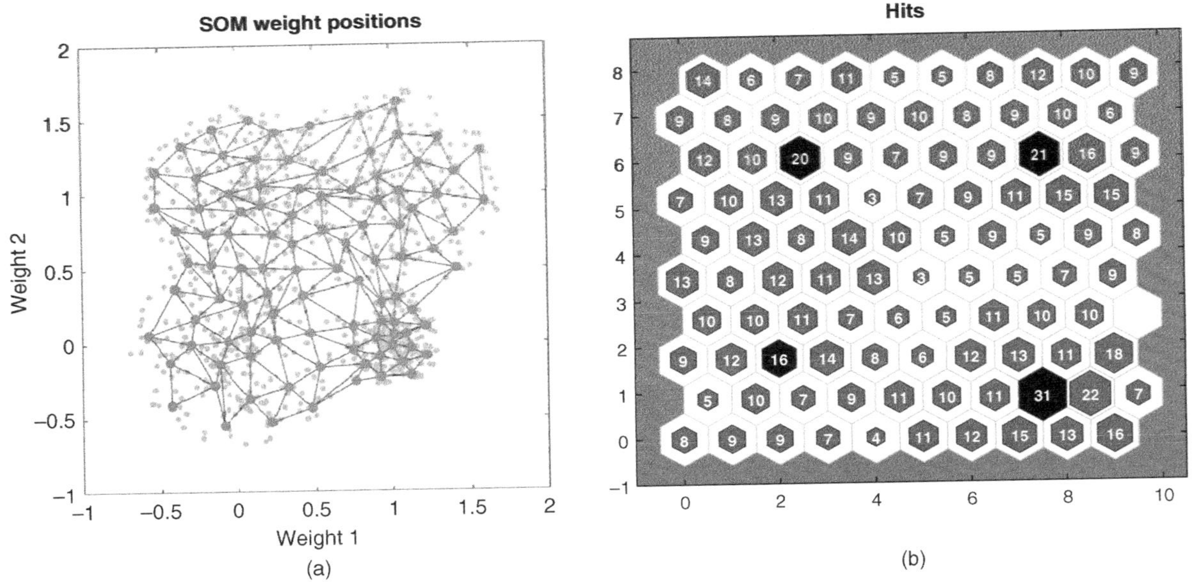

Figure 7.4 Output from Algorithm 7.1. (a) Shows the datapoints and the network lattice from the training stage from the SOM. (b) shows the hints from the neurons.

where $J : \mathbb{R}^n \rightarrow \mathbb{R}$ is a nonlinear objective function whereas $\mathbf{S} = \{\mathbf{x} \in \mathbb{R}^n \mid l_j \leq x_j \leq u_j, j = 1, \ldots, n\}$ represents the entire set of solution vectors $\mathbf{x}$ within a search space bounded by the lower (l_j) and upper (u_j) limits. The objective of the optimization process is achieved once the optimization method finds the $\mathbf{g}$-th solution which represents the best global solution within the set of possible solutions.

In order to solve an optimization problem using the EA-SOM, it considers a population of datapoints $\mathbf{D}^k = \left\{\mathbf{d}_1^k, \mathbf{d}_2^k, \ldots, \mathbf{d}_{N_D}^k\right\}$ containing N_D number of possible solutions. These solutions will evolve from initial iteration $(k = 0)$ until a total number of iterations is reached $(k = Max\_Iter)$. Each datapoint $\mathbf{d}_i^k = \{\mathrm{d}_{i,1}^k, \mathrm{d}_{i,1}^k, \ldots, \mathrm{d}_{i,n}^k\}$ represents an n-dimensional decision variable vector. After a random initialization for the population, promising areas are found by the extracted information by the SOM. As a result, to train the SOM, the proposed method uses a portion of the past solutions observed thus far in each iteration. After training, the winning neuron of the output layer that best matches the best solution is identified. Then, by using neighborhood information, the SOM produces new population members for the next generation.

To get an intuition of the EA-SOM, Figure 7.5a shows a benchmark optimization function, containing several datapoints. These datapoints are considered as the input data for the input layer of a SOM. Once the SOM is trained, promising areas within the search space can be located in Figure 7.5b. The internal mechanism of the competitive learning of the SOM generates the lattice from Figure 7.5c. In this figure, it is shown the mapping from the input data to the data reduction of the search space. This mechanism provides information to the metaheuristic operators to guide the search strategy into the promising areas of the search space.

Since EA-SOM method involves a series of straightforward steps. Here are the steps:

Step 1: Initialization:
Initialize a population $\mathbf{D}$ containing N_D datapoints. Each datapoint corresponds to a candidate solution $\mathbf{x}$ for a given optimization problem. Also, all the initial datapoints of $\mathbf{D}$ are stored in two different memory structures: Historical memory $\mathbf{H}$, and initial training set memory $\mathbf{T}(0)$. An important aspect in the $\mathbf{T}(0)$ is that each initial input data vector is built combining the candidate solution and its respective initial fitness value $\mathbf{t}_i = \{\mathbf{d}_i^0, J(\mathbf{d}_i^0)\}$. During the optimization process, the memory structures $\mathbf{H}$ and $\mathbf{T}$ will be updated according to the following steps.

Step 2: Training:
In this stage, the SOM is trained to identify promising areas by compressing the search space of the objective function. Therefore, a lattice of $[z, z]$ neural units is defined. By using the competitive learning model, the SOM is trained considering a set $\mathbf{T}$ datapoints. During the training process, each input data vector is built combining the candidate solution and its respective fitness value $\mathbf{t}_i = \left\{\mathbf{d}_i^k, J\left(\mathbf{d}_i^k\right)\right\}$.

Step 3: Knowledge Extraction:
In this step, the knowledge extraction mechanism is based on the data organization features of SOMs. That is, elements in the original data remain close to neural units in the output layer. For that, once trained the promising regions are mapped in the competitive layer of $(z \cdot z)$ lattice. This process represents the data reduction scheme for the search space.

Step 4: Solution Production:
Once the promising regions of the output layer are obtained, new solutions are generated considering the winning neuron and its neighborhood. These generated solutions will be part of the next population for the optimization process.

Step 5: New Training set Construction:
Once the generated solutions from Step 4 were generated, the new training set $\mathbf{T}(k+1)$ is created incorporating the produced solutions. Also, the generated solutions will be stored in the historical memory structure $\mathbf{H}(k+1)$.

Step 6: Repeat Steps 2–5 until the Maximum Number of Iterations is Reached:
In the following subsections, a detailed description of each main procedure for the EA-SOM method is described.

7.3.1 Initialization

At this stage, the population $\mathbf{D}$ of N_D datapoints is randomly and uniformly initialized. The values of each decision variable are randomly and uniformly distributed among a predefined lower (l_j) and upper (u_j) bounds. The initialization procedure is defined as:

$$\mathrm{d}_{i,j}^{k} = l_j + \mathrm{rand}(0,1) \cdot (u_j - l_j), \quad j = 1, \dots, n; \quad i = 1, \dots, N_D \tag{7.6}$$

where $\mathrm{d}_{i,j}^{k}$ represents the j-th decision variable of the i-th datapoint at the k-th iteration.

All the initial datapoints (where $k = 0$) in the population $\mathbf{D}(k)$ are also stored in the historical memory $\mathbf{H}(k)$, and the training set memory structure $\mathbf{T}(k)$. The historical memory structure $\mathbf{H}(k)$ will store solutions since the initial population through the last iteration. The training set memory structure $\mathbf{T}(k)$ will store training data to feed the SOM model. The elements in $\mathbf{T}(k)$ will change considering the information of actual k-th iteration.

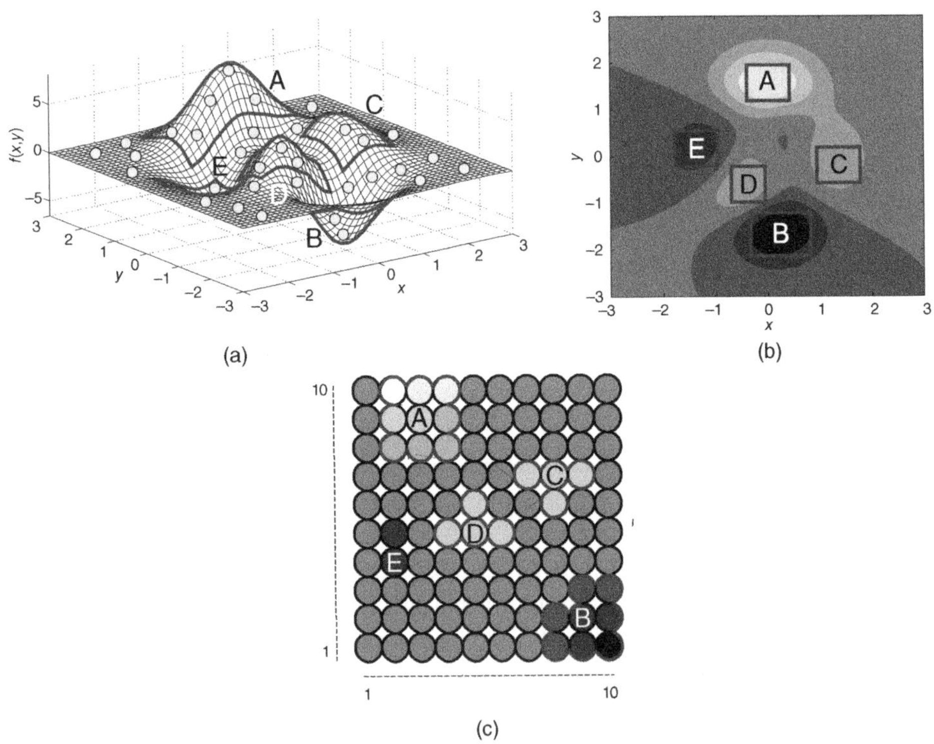

Figure 7.5 Effect of the data-reduction and clustering in EA-SOM. (a) Benchmark function used for the training process, (b) contour representation, and (c) data-reduction and clustering result considering a rectangular lattice of 10×10 neural units.

At the beginning, the $\mathbf{T}(0)$ contemplates that each initial input data vector is built combining the candidate solution and its respective initial fitness value $\mathbf{t}_i = \{\mathbf{d}_i^0, J(\mathbf{d}_i^0)\}$.

7.3.2 Training

In this step, a lattice composed by $[z, z]$ neural units is defined (z, corresponds to the number of neurons, since rectangular lattice is considered in this chapter, the total number of neural units is $z * z$).

Following the competitive learning model in SOMs, in this procedure, the SOM is trained considering the competition, cooperative, and synaptic adaptation procedures (Section 7.2.3). For the training scheme, each input data vector is built combining the candidate solution and its respective fitness value $\mathbf{t}_i = \left\{\mathbf{d}_i^k, J\left(\mathbf{d}_i^k\right)\right\}$.

Note

An important aspect in the training stage is that the number of training samples that are used in the learning process affects the quality of the reduced search space. The use of all available historical data would produce the best approximation. However, the use of this big amount of data increases the computational effort. For that, depending on the application, the reader must consider using a reasonable number of samples, and neurons to avoid computational overload.

7.3.3 Knowledge Extraction

Once trained, several information can be extracted from the previous step such as: The promising areas by the output layer of the SOM, the winning neuron, and the information about its neighborhood.

To summarize, at the end of the training step, it is assumed the following model:

$$w = \underset{w \in [z, z]}{\arg\min} \|\mathbf{g} - \mathbf{w}_w\| \tag{7.7}$$

where w represents the w-th winning neuron from the $[z, z]$ lattice. And $\mathbf{g}$ represents the best datapoint solution in the optimization problem for the k-th iteration (Eq. 7.5). That means, that the index of the winning neuron is obtained and therefore its neighborhood information.

In this step, to extract more information codified in the output layer of the trained SOM, neighborhood information around the winning neuron $\mathbf{w}_w$ is also obtained. In EA-SOM, the two closest neurons from the winning neuron are also identified $\mathbf{w}_A$ and $\mathbf{w}_B$. These close neurons also represent competitive neurons that contain minimal distances around the best solution $\mathbf{g}$ without considering the existence of unit $\mathbf{w}_w$. Along with the neurons $\mathbf{w}_w$, $\mathbf{w}_A$, and $\mathbf{w}_B$, their respective distances to $\mathbf{g}$ are also preserved due to the data organization feature of the SOM.

The distances of the neurons $\mathbf{w}_w$, $\mathbf{w}_A$, and $\mathbf{w}_B$ can be computed as:

$$D_w = \|\mathbf{g} - \mathbf{w}_w\|, \quad D_A = \|\mathbf{g} - \mathbf{w}_A\|, \quad D_B = \|\mathbf{g} - \mathbf{w}_B\| \tag{7.8}$$

With the information obtained by Eqs. 7.7 and 7.8, the idea is to relate the position of the original input data with the information mapped in the output layer. The relation to this case, is defined as a rank function which is calculated as:

$$R = 1 - \frac{|m - w|}{z} \tag{7.9}$$

where m corresponds to the central unit of the lattice ($m = (z * z)/2$). The objective of the rank function is to keep a value near to one in the middle of the lattice, whereas in the border of the lattice a value near to zero.

The extracted information from Eqs. 7.7 to 7.9 will be used in the production of new solutions by the next step.

7.3.4 Solution Production

The main idea in the EA-SOM is that extracted information during the optimization process can be employed to guide the search strategy based on past information not only keeping the population elements through iterations but also maintaining local information of the output layer to improve the entire optimization process. For that, extracted information in the previous step is used to generate new solutions based on the detection of the promising regions in the output layer.

In this step, a set N of new solutions is generated. Since SOM maintains relationships between input data with the mapping of the lattice, new solutions can be produced considering that the original positions of the input data contain a high probability to be inside of the influence neighborhood by the winning neuron $\mathbf{w}_w$. This influence neighborhood acts as a radius among the neurons $\mathbf{w}_w$, $\mathbf{w}_A$, and $\mathbf{w}_B$ which corresponds to promising search zones in the search space. The influence radius δ, is computed as:

$$\delta = \frac{\mathbf{D}_w + \mathbf{D}_A + \mathbf{D}_B}{3} \tag{7.10}$$

Figure 7.6 graphically presents the intuition of the influence radius δ.

Finally, to produce N new solutions, the following model computed each:

$$\mathbf{N} = \mathbf{w}_w + \delta \cdot R \cdot (r \cdot 2 - 1) \tag{7.11}$$

where r represents a uniformly distributed random number in [0, 1].

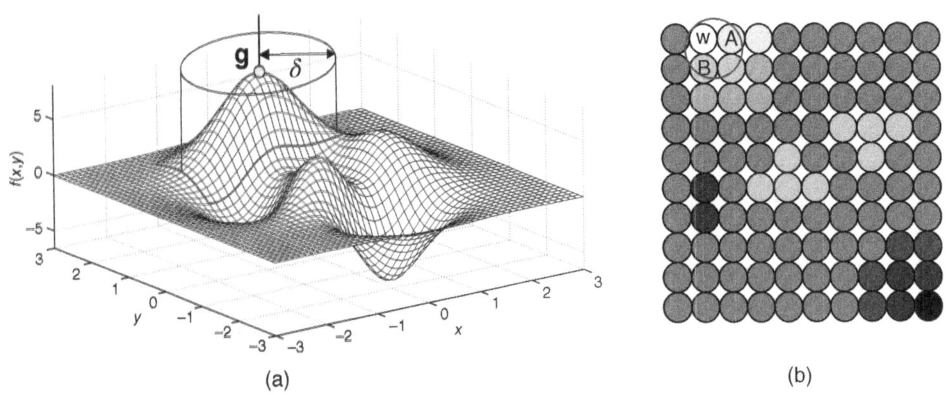

Figure 7.6 Visual representation of δ considering a benchmark function, (a) objective function, and (b) lattice composed by 10×10 neurons.

Note

An important aspect of the solution production scheme is that all the functionality of the proposed methodology relies on the relationship between the best solution in the optimization problem and the winning neuron as well as its neighborhood. The reader can design another search strategy contemplating different aspects of the extracted information. In this chapter, authors keep the simplest strategy in order to show the potential of extracting information during the optimization process.

7.3.5 New Training Set Construction

The produced $\mathbf{N}$ solutions from Eq. 7.11 contain solutions generated by the extracted information of the competitive learning model in SOM. The final step is to construct the new training set $\mathbf{T}(k+1)$ for the next iteration of the EA-SOM. At each iteration, a new set containing N solutions will be produced. After a certain number of iterations, a large number of solutions will be generated. Under such circumstances, it is impractical to add the $\mathbf{N}$ generated solutions to the new training set. Therefore, considering that the size of the $\mathbf{T}(k+1)$ will be the same as the population size, that is N_D elements. It is assumed that $\mathbf{N}$ must be much less than N_D. Under this scheme, only the first N elements will be part of $\mathbf{T}(k+1)$. The rest of the elements will be randomly selected from the historical data $\mathbf{H}$.

After the construction of $\mathbf{T}(k+1)$, the historic memory will be updated as follows:

$$\mathbf{H}(k+1) = \mathbf{H}(k) \cup \mathbf{N} \tag{7.12}$$

7.4 Computational Procedure

The algorithmic structure of the EA-SOM follows an iterative process, in which the steps from the previous are executed. Such procedures can be summarized in the Pseudo-code 7.1.

Pseudo-code 7.1 ***Computational Procedure of the Evolutionary-SOM (EA-SOM) Method***

Input: N_D, N, *Maxgen*, $k = 0$.	
$\mathbf{D}^k \leftarrow$ **Initialize**(N_D);	**Step 1**
$\mathbf{H}(k) \leftarrow \mathbf{D}^k$, $\mathbf{T}(k) \leftarrow \mathbf{D}^k$	
while k<=*Maxgen* **do**	
SOM $\leftarrow$ **TrainSOM**($\mathbf{T}(k)$)	**Step 2**
$\mathbf{g} \leftarrow$ **SelectBestParticle**($\mathbf{T}(k)$);	
$\{\mathbf{w}_w, \mathbf{w}_A, \mathbf{w}_B\} \leftarrow$ **DetectNeuralUnits(SOM)**	**Step 3**
$\{R, \delta\} \leftarrow$ **CalculateInf**($\mathbf{w}_w, \mathbf{w}_A, \mathbf{w}_B$)	
$\mathbf{N} \leftarrow$ **GenerateNewSolutions**($\mathbf{N}, R, \delta$);	**Step 4**
$\mathbf{T}(k+1) \leftarrow$ **ConstructT**($\mathbf{N}$,$\mathbf{H}(k)$)	**Step 5**
$\mathbf{H}(k+1) \leftarrow \mathbf{H}(k) \cup \mathbf{N}$	
$K \leftarrow k+1$	
end **while**	
Output: $\mathbf{g}$	

In Pseudo-code 7.1, Step 1 initializes the population of datapoints, as well as the historic memory, and the training set memory structure. Then, the competitive learning is executed in Step 2. Step 3 extracts information from the training stage. Step 4 generates new solutions. Finally, Step 5 constructs the new training set and updates the historical memory. This process repeats until a maximum number of iterations is reached.

7.5 Implementation of the EA-SOM Algorithm in MATLAB

In Algorithm 7.2, it is described the MATLAB code for the EA-SOM algorithm. To observe the functionality of the algorithm, the code encodes a benchmark function commonly used in performance testing related to the optimization of continuous functions. In this example, the Bird function is implemented, so that the reader can observe the functionality of the EA-SOM algorithm considering a minimization process.

The Bird function exhibits a non-convex unimodal surface in a 2-dimensional space and contains six global minima. The non-convex feature is used to test the scaling of the search strategy of the EA-SOM method when operates over surfaces that contain multiple global optima. On the other hand, the Bird function is continuous and non-convex, which indicates that no optimization technique either classical or metaheuristic can reach the global optimum. The mathematical model of the Bird function is as follows:

$$f(x_1, x_2) = \sin(x_1) \cdot e^{[1-\cos(x_2)]^2} + \cos(x_2) \cdot e^{[1-\sin(x_1)]^2} + (x_1 - x_2)^2$$
$$-2\pi \leq x_i \leq 2\pi, i = 1, 2 \tag{7.13}$$

Finally, so that the reader can see the behavior of the datapoints on the Bird function surface, at each iteration the movement of the solutions (datapoints) on the Bird surface is plotted.

```
%Algorithm 7.2
%% INITIAL CONFIGURATION FOR THE OPTIMIZATION PROCESS
%Clear memory and Close Matlab windows
clear all;
close all;

%% Step 1 INITIALIZATION
%The maximum number of iterations is established
Max_Iter = 1000;
%The size of the population is established
Np = 50;
%The number of decision variables is established
dim = 2;
%The limits of the search space are defined
lb = -2*pi;
ub = 2*pi;
%Initialization of the initial population,
%X is the variable representing the population of Np elements
if size(ub,2)==1
    X=rand(Np,dim).*(ub-lb)+lb;
```

```
end
if size(ub,2)>1
    for i=1:dim
        high=ub(i);down=lb(i);
        X(:,i)=rand(Np,1).*(high-down)+down;
    end
end
%The fitness values of the initial population are obtained
fitness = ObjectiveFunction(X,dim);
%The population is sorted in ascending order
[fitnessA, indexSorted] = sort(fitness,'ascend');
%The best solution is obtained from the initial population
bestX = X(indexSorted(1),:);
bestFitness = fitnessA(1);
count = 0;
%Initialization of the SOM, in this example a lattice is composed by
% 20 * 20 neurons
dimM = 20;
rSampling = 20;
%The topology of the SOM is created
net = selforgmap([dimM dimM]);
%The plot the function to be optimized is computed
if dim<=2
    rangeUpLb=ub-lb;
    figure(1)
    x=[lb:rangeUpLb/100:ub];
    y=x;
    [xg,yg]=meshgrid(x,y);
    [row,col]=size(xg);
    for l=1:col
        for h=1:row
            z(h,l)=ObjectiveFunction([xg(h,l),yg(h,l)],dim);
        end
    end
end
%Iterative process of the algorithm
while count < Max_Iter

    %% Step 2 TRAINING
    P = [X';fitness];
    net = configure(net,P);
    %The number of epochs is established
    net.trainParam.epochs = 25;
    %This instruction disables the convergence
    %graph of the learning process
    net.trainParam.showWindow = 0;
    %The train is achieved by the MATLAB function train
    net = train(net,P);
    %The fitness values are sorted
    [fitness, indexSorted] = sort(fitness,'ascend');
    XTemp = X(indexSorted(1),:);
    FTemp = fitness(1);
    %Selection of the best solution so far
```

```
    if FTemp < bestFitness
        bestX = XTemp;
        bestFitness = FTemp;
    end
    data = [XTemp';FTemp];
    %SOM output
    out= net(data);
    %The index of the winning neuron is obtained
    neuron_aux=find(out==1);
    %The weight vector of the winning neuron is obtained
    Mat=net.IW{1,1};
    %The Euclidean distance among the winning neuron respect the
    %remaining neural units from the lattice is obtained. This
    %mechanism will be used in order to find the two closest neurons
    %around the winning neuron
    for Idx = 1 : dimM*dimM
        dis(Idx)= pdist2(Mat(Idx,1:end), Mat(neuron_aux,1:end));
    end
    [disS, ID]=sort(dis,'ascend');
    aux = find(disS,1);
    sd1 = (ID(aux))/(dimM*dimM);
    sd = mean(disS(aux:aux+2))/(max(disS(aux:end))-min(disS(aux:end)));
    sd = ((disS(aux)^2)/(sd1))*sd;
    sd = sd^(exp(-count/(1000-count)));
    %The weight vector of the winning neuron is perturb (this mechanism,
    %will promote solution diversity)
    Mat(neuron_aux,1:dim) = ...
(XTemp - Mat(neuron_aux,1:dim)) + ...
sd.*rand(1,dim);
    Mat(neuron_aux,1:dim) = ...
findrange( Mat(neuron_aux,1:dim),...
lb,ub,dim,1);
    Mat(neuron_aux,end) = ObjectiveFunction(Mat(neuron_aux,1:dim),dim);

    %% Step 3 KNOWLEDGE EXTRACTION
    %Based on the extracted information, a subset of neurons around the
    %winning neuron is created
    XNew = Mat(neuron_aux,1:dim);
    fitnessNew = Mat(neuron_aux,end);
    xSub = repmat(Mat(neuron_aux,1:dim),...
rSampling,1) + sd .* ...
rand(rSampling,dim);
    xSub = findrange(xSub,lb,ub,dim,size(xSub,1));
    fitnessSub = ObjectiveFunction(xSub,dim);
    XNew = [XNew;xSub];
    fitnessNew = [fitnessNew, fitnessSub];

    %% Step 4 SOLUTION PRODUCTION
    %The two closest neurons around the winning neuron are obtained
    T = ID(aux:aux+3);
    xSubNeurons = Mat(T,1:dim);
    xSubNeurons = findrange(xSubNeurons(:,1:dim), ...
lb,ub,dim,size(xSubNeurons,1));
    fitnessSubNeuronas = ObjectiveFunction(xSubNeurons,dim);
```

```
    %% Step 5 NEW TRAINING SET CONSTRUCTION
    XNew = [XNew;xSubNeurons];
    fitnessNew = [fitnessNew, fitnessSubNeuronas];
    %Since EA-SOM tend to produce several solutions at each generation,
    %a cleaning process is applied to avoid overfitting
    remaining = Np - size(XNew,1);
    if size(ub,2)==1
        XAux=rand(remaining,dim).*(ub-lb)+lb;
    end
    if size(ub,2)>1
        for i=1:dim
            high=ub(i);down=lb(i);
            XAux(:,i)=rand(remaining,1).*(high-down)+down;
        end
    end
    FAux = ObjectiveFunction(XAux,dim);
    X = [XNew;XAux];
    fitness = [fitnessNew,FAux];
    %The plot the population is generated
    if dim<=2
        surf(xg,yg,z);
        title('Bird function')
        hold on
        plot3(X(:,1),X(:,2),fitness(1,:),'o',...
             'markersize',6,'markerfacecolor','r');
        plot3(bestX(1,1),bestX(1,2),bestFitness,'o',...
             'markersize',10,'markerfacecolor','g');
        drawnow;
        hold off
    end
    %Iteration counters
    count = count + 1;
    fprintf('Iteration: %d\n',count);
    fprintf('Best solution: (%d,%d)\n',bestX(1,1),bestX(1,2));
    fprintf('Best fitness: %d\n',bestFitness);
end

%%OBJECTIVE FUNCTION
%Bird function implementation
function fit = ObjectiveFunction(L,dim)
    [N,~]=size(L);
    for i=1:N
        fit(i) = sin(L(i,1))*exp((1-cos(L(i,2)))^2) + ...
             cos(L(i,2))*exp((1-sin(L(i,1)))^2) + ...
             (L(i,1)-L(i,2))^2;
    end
end

%Find range function
function X = findrange(X,low,ub,dim,N)
    if size(ub,2)==1
        for j = 1 : N
```

```
                for i = 1:dim
                    if (X(j,i) < low)
                        X(j,i) = rand(1,1).*(ub-low)+low;
                    end
                    if (X(j,i) > ub)
                        X(j,i) = rand(1,1).*(ub-low)+low;
                    end
                end
            end
        end
        if size(ub,2) > 1
            for j = 1 : N
                for i = 1:dim
                    high=ub(i);lb=low(i);
                    if (X(j,i) < lb)
                        X(j,i) = rand(1,1).*(high-lb)+lb;
                    end
                    if (X(j,i) > high)
                        X(j,i) = rand(1,1).*(high-lb)+lb;
                    end
                end
            end
        end
    end
```

The Algorithm 7.2 graphically shows the evolution of the population using the iterative structure of the EA-SOM method. The plotted graph is shown in Figure 7.7.

In Algorithm 7.2, the Step 1 configures the initial parameters required by the optimization process. Such configuration relies on setting the maximum number of iterations, the population

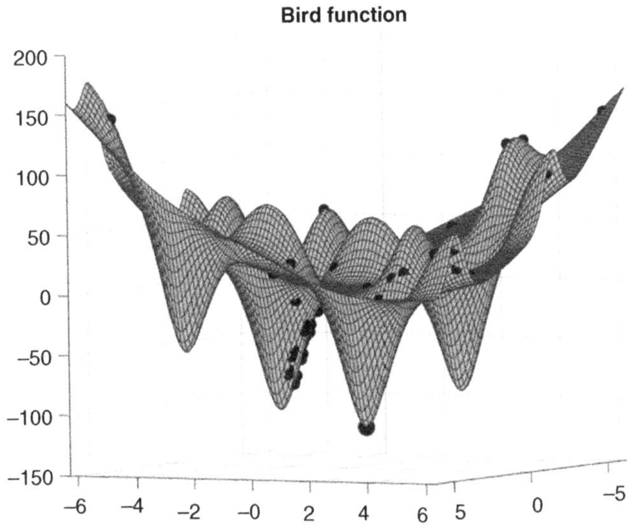

Figure 7.7 The graph of the Bird function produced by EA-SOM.

size, the number of decision variables involved in the optimization process, and the definition of the limits of the search space. Additionally, in this step, the structure of a SOM is defined. In the code, the built-in function `selforgmap` creates a lattice containing 20 * 20 neurons. The Step 2 defines the training phase of the EA-SOM. In this step, the competitive learning method is implemented to obtain the winning neuron. Then, in Step 3 the knowledge extraction mechanism is employed considering the algorithmic structure in Section 7.3.3. Step 4 defines the procedure for solution production which by the definition of the three closest neighbor neurons to the winning neuron. Finally, in Step 5 the new training set is built considering past solutions and produced solutions of Step 4. In the algorithm, the objective function to be optimized is implemented after the definition of the main loop. The objective function considered in this chapter is the well-known Bird function. Also, it is implemented a `findrage` function as an auxiliary function to limit the produced solutions maintained inside the limits of the search space.

7.6 Gear Design Optimization Problem Using the EA-SOM Algorithm in MATLAB

Most areas in engineering can present optimization problems to find the optimal solution to complex problems. From this perspective, the extensive necessity to apply an optimization algorithm to find the optimal solution is a required step for defining a solution. In Section 7.5, the code related to the implementation of the EA-SOM algorithm using a benchmark function that exhibits a multimodal complexity was presented. However, in such example, the EA-SOM performs over synthetic functions that do not represent a real application. Under this circumstance, this section analyzes an engineering design problem and describes how the EA-SOM method can be used to solve real-world applications. In this section, a gear design optimization problem is defined in order to be solved by the EA-SOM algorithm.

The design problem of a gear train is considered as a complex engineering problem where the objective is to design a gear train that can transmit maximum power. The mathematical description of the model is formulated as an optimization problem taking the following form:

$$\begin{aligned} &\text{Min} \quad f(\mathbf{x}) = \left(\left(\frac{1}{6.931}\right) - \left(\frac{x_3 x_2}{x_1 x_4}\right)\right)^2 \\ &x_1, x_2, x_3, x_4 \\ &\text{Subject to:} \end{aligned} \tag{7.14}$$

where x_1, x_2, x_3 and x_4 represent the number of teeth for each of the gears. These values are distributed in a four-dimensional space ($d = 4$) and define the decision variables of the problem. Also, the limits of the search space corresponding to each dimension of the problem are defined as: $12 \leq x_i \leq 60$, $i = 1, \ldots 4$. Figure 7.8 illustrates the design parameters for the assembly train. In the figure, the A corresponds to x_1, B represents x_2, D is represented by x_3, and finally, F corresponds to x_4.

The optimization process of this engineering problem using the EA-SOM algorithm is shown in Algorithm 7.3.

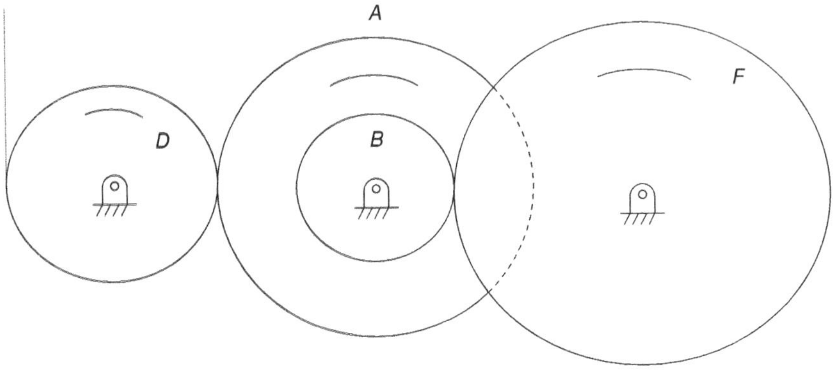

Figure 7.8 Design parameters of the gear train design problem.

```
%Algorithm 7.3
%% INITIAL CONFIGURATION FOR THE OPTIMIZATION PROCESS
%Clear memory and Close Matlab windows
clear all;
close all;

%% Step 1 INITIALIZATION
%The maximum number of iterations is established
Max_Iter = 1000;
%The size of the population is established
Np = 50;
%The number of decision variables is established
dim = 4;
%The limits of the search space are defined
lb = 12;
ub = 60;
%Initialization of the initial population,
%X is the variable representing the population of Np elements
if size(ub,2)==1
    X=rand(Np,dim).*(ub-lb)+lb;
end
if size(ub,2)>1
    for i=1:dim
        high=ub(i);down=lb(i);
        X(:,i)=rand(Np,1).*(high-down)+down;
    end
end
%The fitness values of the initial population are obtained
fitness = ObjectiveFunction(X,dim);
```

```
%The population is sorted in ascending order
[fitnessA, indexSorted] = sort(fitness,'ascend');
%The best solution is obtained from the initial population
bestX = X(indexSorted(1),:);
bestFitness = fitnessA(1);
count = 0;
%Initialization of the SOM, in this example a lattice is composed by
% 20 * 20 neurons
dimM = 20;
rSampling = 20;
%The topology of the SOM is created
net = selforgmap([dimM dimM]);
%The plot the function to be optimized is computed
if dim<=2
    rangeUpLb=ub-lb;
    figure(1)
    x=[lb:rangeUpLb/100:ub];
    y=x;
    [xg,yg]=meshgrid(x,y);
    [row,col]=size(xg);
    for l=1:col
        for h=1:row
            z(h,l)=ObjectiveFunction([xg(h,l),yg(h,l)],dim);
        end
    end
end
%Iterative process of the algorithm
while count < Max_Iter

    %% Step 2 TRAINING
    P = [X';fitness];
    net = configure(net,P);
    %The number of epochs is established
    net.trainParam.epochs = 25;
    %This instruction disable the convergence graph of the learning
    %process
    net.trainParam.showWindow = 0;
    %The train is achieved by the MATLAB function train
    net = train(net,P);
    %The fitness values are sorted
    [fitness, indexSorted] = sort(fitness,'ascend');
    XTemp = X(indexSorted(1),:);
    FTemp = fitness(1);
    %Selection of the best solution so far
    if FTemp < bestFitness
        bestX = XTemp;
        bestFitness = FTemp;
```

```
    end
    data = [XTemp';FTemp];
    %SOM output
    out= net(data);
    %The index of the winning neuron is obtained
    neuron_aux=find(out==1);
    %The weight vector of the winning neuron is obtained
    Mat=net.IW{1,1};
    %The Euclidean distance among the winning neuron respect the
    %remaining neural units from the lattice is obtained. This
    %mechanism will be used in order to find the two closest
    %neurons around the winning neuron
    for Idx = 1 : dimM*dimM
        dis(Idx)= pdist2(Mat(Idx,1:end), Mat(neuron_aux,1:end));
    end
    [disS, ID]=sort(dis,'ascend');
    aux = find(disS,1);
    sd1 = (ID(aux))/(dimM*dimM);
    sd = mean(disS(aux:aux+2))/...
(max(disS(aux:end))-min(disS(aux:end)));
    sd = ((disS(aux)^2)/(sd1))*sd;
    sd = sd^(exp(-count/(1000-count)));
    %The weight vector of the winning neuron is perturb (this
    %mechanism, will promote solution diversity)
    Mat(neuron_aux,1:dim) = (XTemp - Mat(neuron_aux,1:dim)) + sd.*
rand(1,dim);
    Mat(neuron_aux,1:dim) = ...
findrange( Mat(neuron_aux,1:dim),lb,ub,dim,1);
    Mat(neuron_aux,end) = ...
ObjectiveFunction(Mat(neuron_aux,1:dim),dim);

    %% Step 3 KNOWLEDGE EXTRACTION
    %Based on the extracted information, a subset of neurons around
    %the winning neuron is created
    XNew = Mat(neuron_aux,1:dim);
    fitnessNew = Mat(neuron_aux,end);
    xSub = repmat(Mat(neuron_aux,1:dim),rSampling,1) + sd .*
rand(rSampling,dim);
    xSub = findrange(xSub,lb,ub,dim,size(xSub,1));
    fitnessSub = ObjectiveFunction(xSub,dim);
    XNew = [XNew;xSub];
    fitnessNew = [fitnessNew, fitnessSub];

    %% Step 4 SOLUTION PRODUCTION
    %The two closest neurons around the winning neuron are obtained
    T = ID(aux:aux+3);
    xSubNeurons = Mat(T,1:dim);
```

```
    xSubNeurons =
findrange(xSubNeurons(:,1:dim),lb,ub,dim,size(xSubNeurons,1));
    fitnessSubNeuronas = ObjectiveFunction(xSubNeurons,dim);

    %% Step 5 NEW TRAINING SET CONSTRUCTION
    XNew = [XNew;xSubNeurons];
    fitnessNew = [fitnessNew, fitnessSubNeuronas];
    %Since EA-SOM tend to produce several solutions at each
    %generation, a cleanning process is applied to avoid overfitting
    remaining = Np - size(XNew,1);
    if size(ub,2)==1
        XAux=rand(remaining,dim).*(ub-lb)+lb;
    end
    if size(ub,2)>1
        for i=1:dim
            high=ub(i);down=lb(i);
            XAux(:,i)=rand(remaining,1).*(high-down)+down;
        end
    end
    FAux = ObjectiveFunction(XAux,dim);
    X = [XNew;XAux];
    fitness = [fitnessNew,FAux];
    %The plot the population is generated
    if dim<=2
        surf(xg,yg,z);
        title('Bird function')
        hold on
        plot3(X(:,1),X(:,2),fitness(1,:),'o',...
            'markersize',6,'markerfacecolor','r');
        plot3(bestX(1,1),bestX(1,2),bestFitness,'o',...
            'markersize',10,'markerfacecolor','g');
        drawnow;
        hold off
    end
    %Iteration counters
    count = count + 1;
    fprintf('Iteration: %d\n',count);
    fprintf('Best solution: (%d,%d)\n',bestX(1,1),bestX(1,2));
    fprintf('Best fitness: %d\n',bestFitness);
end

%%OBJECTIVE FUNCTION
%Bird function implementation
function fit = ObjectiveFunction(L,dim)
    [N,~]=size(L);
    for i=1:N
        fit(i) = ((1/6.931) - (L(3)*L(2)/L(1)*L(4))^2);
```

```
    end
end
%Find range function
function X = findrange(X,low,ub,dim,N)
    if size(ub,2)==1
        for j = 1 : N
            for i = 1:dim
                if (X(j,i) < low)
                    X(j,i) = rand(1,1).*(ub-low)+low;
                end
                if (X(j,i) > ub)
                    X(j,i) = rand(1,1).*(ub-low)+low;
                end
            end
        end
    end
    if size(ub,2) > 1
        for j = 1 : N
            for i = 1:dim
                high=ub(i);lb=low(i);
                if (X(j,i) < lb)
                    X(j,i) = rand(1,1).*(high-lb)+lb;
                end
                if (X(j,i) > high)
                    X(j,i) = rand(1,1).*(high-lb)+lb;
                end
            end
        end
    end
end
```

In Algorithm 7.3, the initial configuration declares the dimensionality and the limits of the search space according to the gear train design problem. The objective function implements the constraints mathematical formulation of Eq. 7.14.

References

Akinduko, A.A., Mirkes, E.M., and Gorban, A.N. (2016). SOM: stochastic initialization versus principal components. *Information Sciences* 364–365: 213–221. https://doi.org/10.1016/J.INS.2015.10.013.

Deveci, M. and Demirel, N.Ç. (2018). Evolutionary algorithms for solving the airline crew pairing problem. *Computers & Industrial Engineering* 115: 389–406. https://doi.org/10.1016/J.CIE.2017.11.022.

Hong, L., Drake, J.H., Woodward, J.R., and Özcan, E. (2018). A hyper-heuristic approach to automated generation of mutation operators for evolutionary programming. *Applied Soft Computing* 62: 162–175. https://doi.org/10.1016/J.ASOC.2017.10.002.

Hu, Z., Yang, J., Sun, H. et al. (2017). An improved multi-objective evolutionary algorithm based on environmental and history information. *Neurocomputing* 222: 170–182. https://doi.org/10.1016/J.NEUCOM.2016.10.014.

Kobeaga, G., Merino, M., and Lozano, J.A. (2018). An efficient evolutionary algorithm for the orienteering problem. *Computers & Operations Research* 90: 42–59. https://doi.org/10.1016/J.COR.2017.09.003.

Kohonen, T. (1982). Self-organized formation of topologically correct feature maps. *Biological Cybernetics* 43 (1): 59–69. https://doi.org/10.1007/BF00337288/METRICS.

Mobin, M., Mousavi, S.M., Komaki, M., and Tavana, M. (2018). A hybrid desirability function approach for tuning parameters in evolutionary optimization algorithms. *Measurement* 114: 417–427. https://doi.org/10.1016/J.MEASUREMENT.2017.10.009.

Nobile, M.S., Cazzaniga, P., Besozzi, D. et al. (2018). Fuzzy self-tuning PSO: a settings-free algorithm for global optimization. *Swarm and Evolutionary Computation* 39: 70–85. https://doi.org/10.1016/J.SWEVO.2017.09.001.

Yeguas, E., Luzón, M.V., Pavón, R. et al. (2014). Automatic parameter tuning for evolutionary algorithms using a Bayesian case-based reasoning system. *Applied Soft Computing* 18: 185–195. https://doi.org/10.1016/J.ASOC.2014.01.032.

8

Techniques of Machine Learning Mixed with Metaheuristic Methods

8.1 Introduction

Artificial Neural Networks (ANNs) are, arguably, the most popular machine learning (ML) technique among nonspecialists. This popularity is significantly due to recent developments in Deep Neural Networks (DNN), in particular Generative Adversarial Networks (GANs) and Large Language Models (LLMs). The success of text and image generators based on DNNs has been such that artificial intelligence (AI) and ANNs have practically become interchangeable terms in the popular vocabulary. Although ANNs are perceived as a relatively new technique for this population sector, this is not the case. ANNs, as a branch of ML, can be dated back to the 1950s, particularly to the work of Frank Rosenblatt (1958), who invented the perceptron, the first implemented ANN.

The perceptron consists of only one layer of input nodes that send weighted inputs to a receiving node, generating an output value based on the activation function of choice. Although the ANNs currently in use are significantly more complex than the perceptron, the general functioning remains the same, where the efficacy of the network relies on choosing an appropriate architecture and finding the combination of weights that allows the network to generate the expected output for each presented input. Although significant efforts have been made to solve these two tasks, these are still open problems. Choosing the correct network architecture has proven difficult to automate, remaining primarily a craft where the designer's expertise plays a central role in the network's success. On the other hand, training the network, which is adjusting its weights, has well-established methods, such as backpropagation. During the training phase, the network is presented with labeled training data, and the weights are iteratively updated to minimize a defined loss function, ultimately allowing the network to generalize to unseen data.

Metaheuristic methods have been used to solve the network's architecture automatic selection and the training process. To illustrate the hybridization of machine learning techniques and metaheuristic methods, this chapter presents the training of an ANN using a metaheuristic method. Namely, a Feedforward Neural Network (FNN), also known as a multilayer perceptron, is trained using the Flower Pollination Algorithm (FPA). We begin by presenting the FPA algorithm and its computational procedure. Then, we explain the generalities of ANNs and their training process. Finally, we explain how an ANN can be trained using a metaheuristic method, namely the FPA.

Machine Learning and Metaheuristic Computation, First Edition.
Erik Cuevas, Jorge Galvez, Omar Avalos, and Fernando Wario.

8.2 Flower Pollination Algorithm (FPA)

FPA, initially proposed by Yang (2012), takes inspiration from the pollination process of flowering plants as it occurs in natural environments. In general, flower pollination refers to the transferring of pollen between flowers of the same or different plants, a process so effective that it has allowed flowering plants to dominate the landscape. Pollination can be carried out in two ways: abiotic and biotic. Abiotic pollination refers to those cases where environmental agents such as wind or water carry the pollen from one flower to another. About 10% of the pollination processes fall into the abiotic case. The remaining 90% of pollination processes are of the biotic type; this is, the pollen is transported between flowers by living organisms like insects, bats, and birds. At the same time, pollination is divided into two groups according to their source: self-pollination and cross-pollination. These classifications are summarized in Table 8.1. In the context of FPA, while abiotic and self-pollination are associated with local search, biotic processes and cross-pollination are related to global search. One interesting phenomenon observed in biotic pollinators, and essential to the FPA, is the called flower constancy, a tendency of some pollinators to visit flowers of the same species.

Idealizing the above characteristics of the different types of pollination and pollinators and incorporating the flower consistency phenomenon, the FPA proposes the following rules:

1. **Global Rule:** Biotics and cross-pollination are considered global pollination processes. Pollen-carrying pollinators performing Lévy flights.
2. **Local Rule:** Abiotics and self-pollination are considered local pollination processes.
3. **Reproduction Rule:** Flower constancy is considered as the reproduction probability proportional to the similarity of the two flowers involved.
4. **Switch Rule:** The transition between local pollination and global pollination is controlled by a switch probability $p \in [0, 1]$.

8.2.1 Global Rule and Lévy Flight

When the global rule is selected, the pollen is considered to be carried out by biotic pollinators such as insects and birds. Under this rule, the pollinators' capacity to travel long distances and cover

Table 8.1 Types of pollination.

Types of Pollinators	Description
Biotic pollinators	The pollen is transferred by an animal or insect from one flower to another, usually in a different plant
Abiotic pollinators	The pollen is transferred from one flower to another by the wind, diffusion in water, or gravity

Types of Pollination	Description
Cross-pollination	The pollen is transferred from one flower to another in a different plant
Self-pollination	The pollen is transferred from one flower to another in the same plant

longer ranges ensures the reproduction of the fittest. To portray the behavior of biotic pollinators, taking pollen from one flower to the next and eventually flying over long distances, it is a common practice to resort to the Levy flight, mathematically defined in Eq. 8.1.

$$L \sim \frac{\lambda \Gamma(\lambda) \sin(\pi\lambda/2)}{\pi} \frac{1}{s^{1+\lambda}}, \quad (s \gg s_0 > 0) \tag{8.1}$$

where $\Gamma(\lambda)$ is the standard gamma distribution, and it is valid for large steps. It is possible to numerically simulate a Lévy stable process following the algorithm proposed by Mantegna (1994). To implement Mantegna's algorithm are necessary the following computations:

$$s_i = \frac{U}{|V|^{1/\beta}} \tag{8.2}$$

where $U = \{u_1, \cdots, u_d\}$ and $V = \{v_1, \cdots, v_d\}$ are d-dimensional vectors and $\beta = 3/2$. Each element of both vectors are drawn from normal distributions, as indicated in Eq. 8.3.

$$\begin{aligned} u &\sim N\left(0, \sigma_u^2\right), & v &\sim N\left(0, \sigma_v^2\right) \\ \sigma_u &= \left(\frac{\Gamma(1+\beta)\sin(\pi\cdot\beta/2)}{\Gamma((1+\beta)/2)\cdot\beta\cdot 2^{(\beta-1)/2}}\right)^{1/\beta}, & \sigma_v &= 1 \end{aligned} \tag{8.3}$$

Finally, the Lévy flight value is obtained by:

$$L_i = 0.01 \cdot s_i \left(x_i^k - x_{best}\right) \tag{8.4}$$

where x_i^k is the solution vector x_i at iteration k, and x_{best} is the best solution found among all explored solutions up to the current generation/iteration. This way, under the global rule, the solutions updated following Eq. 8.5.

$$x_i^{k+1} = x_i^k + L_i \tag{8.5}$$

8.2.2 Local Rule

The local rule aims to mimic self-pollination and the process carried out by abiotic pollinators. This rule, including flower constancy, is given by Eq. 8.6.

$$x_i^{k+1} = x_i^k + \in \left(x_j^k - x_z^k\right) \tag{8.6}$$

where x_j^k and x_z^k represent different flowers from the same species and $\in$ is a local random walk in the range [0, 1].

The switching rule is controlled by the parameter p. Usually, a parametric study must be conducted to find the most appropriate p-value to the problem at hand. The search begins with $p = 0.5$ for a balanced search. As p approaches 1, the probability of selecting the global rule increases. Otherwise, p values below 0.5 result on more frequent selection of the local rule.

8.2.3 Elitist Selection Procedure

The elitist selection procedure updates the solution population, one at a time, based on their fitness. This rule guarantees that the evolution of all solutions is always toward better performance. Under such circumstances, this operation indicates that only reasonable solutions will be stored through future generations. To accomplish elitist selection, a simple rule is applied. If the fitness value of the produced solution by the Eq. 8.5 or Eq. 8.6 is better than the current solution; the former replaces the latter. This mechanism is resumed in the following rules:

$$x_i^{k+1} = \begin{Bmatrix} x_i^{k+1} & if\ J\left(x_i^{k+1}\right) < J\left(x_i^{k}\right) \\ x_i^{k} & \text{Otherwise} \end{Bmatrix} \quad (8.7)$$

The overall functioning of the FPA algorithm is shown in the flowchart in Figure 8.1.

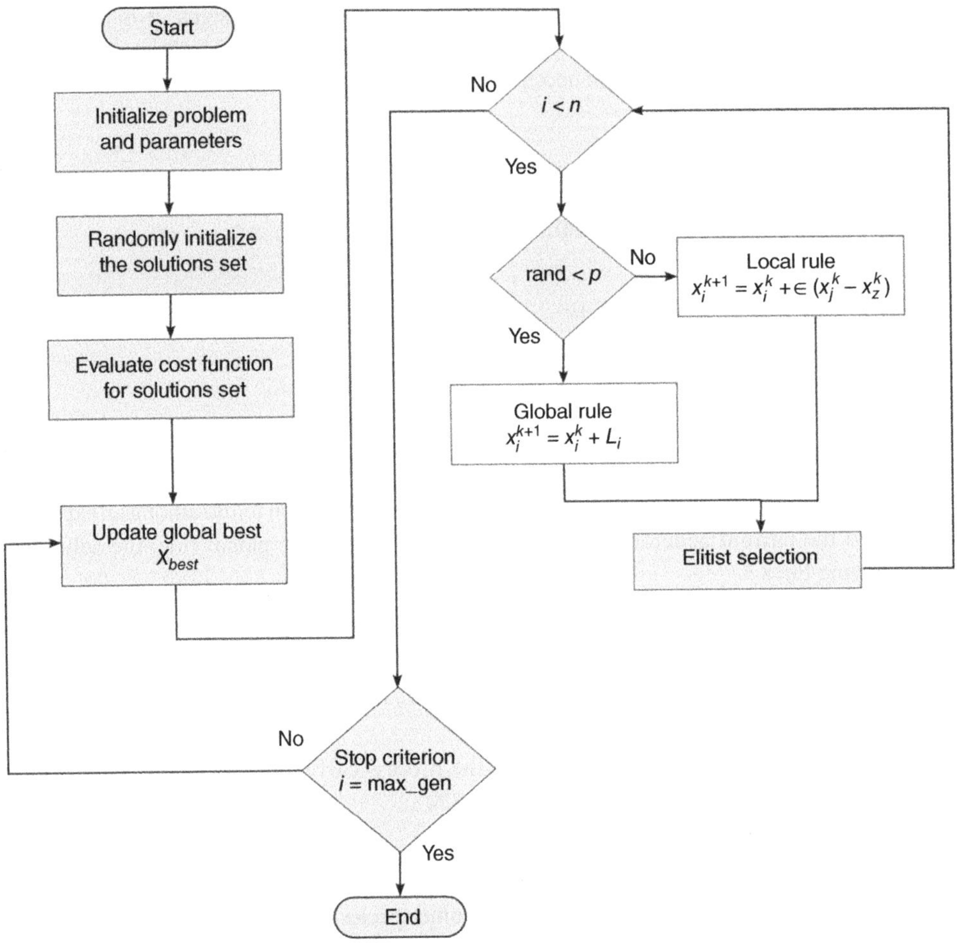

Figure 8.1 Flower pollination algorithm (FPA) flowchart.

The implementation in MATLAB of the FPA algorithm to find the minimum of the Rosenbrock's test function is presented in Algorithm 8.1. The code is divided into six steps that can also be found in the FPA flowchart (see Figure 8.1).

```
%Algorithm 8.1
%Clean data
close all
clear all
```

```
% Step 1, problem, and FPA parameters declaration
% problem parameters
dim = 2;                          % dimensionality
l_bound = -2*ones(1,dim);         % lower boundary
u_bound =  2*ones(1,dim);         % upper boundary

% FPA parameters
max_it = 3000;              % Maximum number of iterations
n = 20;                     % Population size
p = 0.8;                    % Switching probability

% Create aux structure
aux_ant.Position = [];
aux_ant.Cost = [];

% Step 2, 3 randomly initialization of the solutions set
% within the search space bounds and cost function evaluation
for i=1:n
    % Random solution
    POL(i).Position = unifrnd(l_bound, u_bound, [1,dim]);
    % Evaluation
    POL(i).Cost = fitness_function(POL(i).Position);
end

%
S = POL;

% Init fitness history
fitness_history = zeros(max_it,1);

% FPA main loop
for k=1: max_it
    % Step 4, get best solution so far
    [fmin, I]= min([POL.Cost]);
    best = POL(I);
    fitness_history(k) = best.Cost;

    % Step 5, update solutions set
    for i=1:n
    % select between global and local rule
    if rand > p
        % Global rule case
        % Get Levy step for number of dimensions
        L = Levy(dim);
        dS = L.*(POL(i).Position - best.Position);
        S(i).Position = POL(i).Position + dS;
    else
```

```
            % Local rule case
            epsilon = rand;
            % Find two random flowers
            JK = randperm(n);
            ds = epsilon*(POL(JK(1)).Position - POL(JK(2)).Position);
            S(i).Position = POL(i).Position + ds;
        end
        % Check if within bounds
        S(i).Position = simplebounds(S(i).Position, l_bound, u_bound);
        % Step 6, Elitist selection
        % Cost function evaluation
        S(i).Cost = fitness_function(S(i).Position);
        if S(i).Cost <= POL(i).Cost,
            POL(i) = S(i);
        end
    end

    % Update fitness history
    [fmin, I]= min([POL.Cost]);
    best = POL(I);
    fitness_history(k) = best.Cost;

    %*****************************************************************
    % PLOT COST FUNCTION AND BEST SOLUTION
    %*****************************************************************
    % Graphic representation Rosenbrock
    range=u_bound - l_bound;
    figure(1)
    x1=[l_bound:range/100:u_bound];
    y1=x1;
    [X1,Y1]=meshgrid(x1,y1);
    [row1,col1]=size(X1);
    for q=1:col1
        for hh=1:row1
            vector = [X1(hh,q),Y1(hh,q)];
            zz(hh,q)=(1-vector(1))^2+100*(vector(2)-vector(1)^2)^2;
        end
    end
    mesh(X1,Y1,zz, 'edgecolor', [0.5,0.5,0.5]);
    hold on

    % Add best solution
    plot(best.Position(1),best.Position(2),'o', . . .
        'markersize',6,'markerfacecolor','r');
```

```
%************************************************************************
% FUNCTIONS
%************************************************************************

%************************************************************************
% Lévy function
%************************************************************************
function L=Levy(d)
   beta=3/2;
   sig_num = gamma(1+beta)*sin(pi*beta/2);
   sig_den = gamma((1+beta)/2)*beta*2^((beta-1)/2)
   sigma=(sig_num/ sig_den)^(1/beta);
    u=randn(1,d)*sigma;
    v=randn(1,d);
    step=u./abs(v).^(1/beta);
    L=0.01*step;
end

%************************************************************************
% Rosenbrock's cost function
%************************************************************************
function ft = fitness_function(xn)
   ft = (1-xn(1))^2+100*(xn(2)-xn(1)^2)^2;
end
```

In Step 1 of the algorithm, the parameters of the problem and the FPA algorithm are defined, including the problem's dimensionality, lower and upper boundaries, maximum number of iterations, population size, and switching probability (p). In Step 2, the solutions are randomly initiated, considering a uniform probability distribution across the entire search space. In Step 3, the fitness values are computed. The main loop takes place from Steps 4 to 6. First, the best solution so far is updated in Step 4. In Steps 5 and 6, the solutions are updated either by global or local rules and following an elitist selection principle. The algorithm iterates over Steps 4 to 6 till the stop criteria are met. Figure 8.2 shows the function and the best solution found by the FPA optimization.

8.3 Feedforward Neural Networks (FNNs)

Although certainly not a new type of machine learning algorithm, ANNs have gained popularity in recent years, mainly since the introduction of DNNs. ANNs are loosely based on the operation of biological neural systems. An ANN consists of an interconnected group of units called artificial neurons. In an ANN, neurons are aggregated into layers, and signals travel from the input layer to the output layer, passing through as many intermediate layers (hidden layers) as the model considers. The connections between artificial neurons aim to mimic synapses and have associated weights

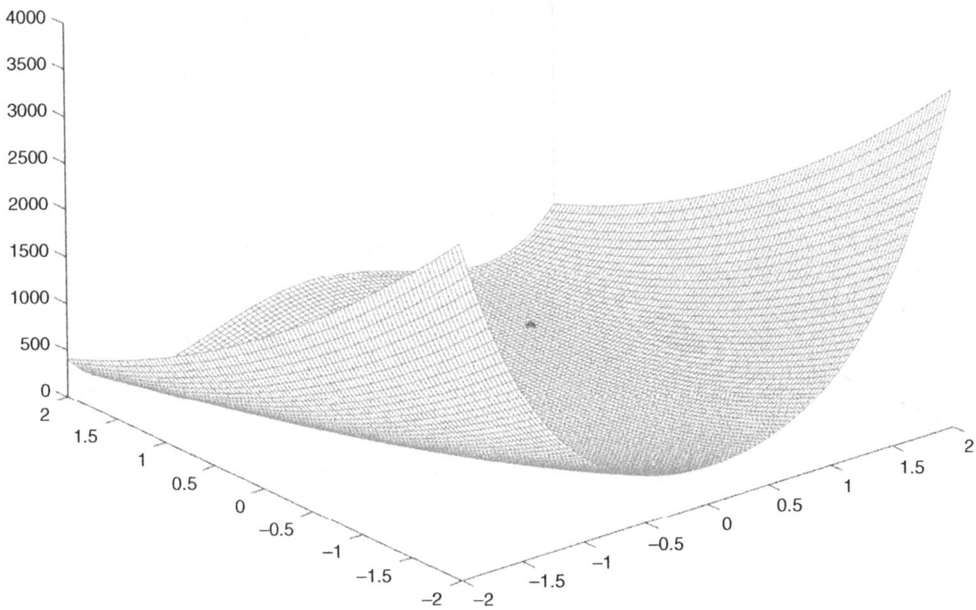

Figure 8.2 The Rosenbrock fitness function employed for the optimization process and the best solution found by FPA.

that increase or decrease the strength of the signal flowing through. Each artificial neuron receives input signals from one or multiple connected neurons; these signals are summed and internally processed by some nonlinear function (activation function) to generate an output signal, which is sent to other connected neurons.

ANNs are, in most cases, feedforward networks; this is, connections only allow signals to flow in one direction without any type of loops. However, it is also possible to find Recurrent Neural Networks (RNNs), a type of ANN with connections that allow signals to flow in both directions. These types of connections render RNNs with memory and make them ideal for applications such as speech and handwriting recognition.

For an ANN to produce the expected output, both architecture and weights must be optimized according to the problem at hand. Neither selecting the optimal architecture nor finding its weights are trivial tasks. Selecting the optimal architecture for an ANN; this is the number of layers, number of neurons per layer, type of connections, and activation function of each network is generally a trial-and-error process in which the designer's expertise plays a central role. On the other hand, finding the weights to optimize the network's performance is done through training, a process during which weights are adjusted iteratively. Undoubtedly, backpropagation is among the most popular training algorithms. The effectiveness of backpropagation depends on a series of decisions such as weights' initialization, number of iterations, and learning rate.

Significant efforts have been made to optimize the ANN's parameters, both related to its architecture and its weights. As a representative case, this chapter presents the optimization of an FNN's weights using an FPA. A series of concepts must first be further covered to understand this process operation better.

8.3.1 Perceptron

In the early 1940s, Warren McCullochs and Walter Pitts, neurophysiologist and mathematician, respectively, proposed for the first time a model that aimed to describe how neurons interact with each other to classify an input into two different classes (McCulloch and Pitts 1943). Later, this model was improved by Rosenblatt (1958), who was also responsible for its first hardware implementation.

In the context of machine learning, the perceptron is a linear classifier that maps its input X (a vector of real values) to an output value $f(X)$ (a single binary value) (Figure 8.3). Hence, the perceptron's output can be represented using Eq. 8.8.

$$f(X) = H(W \cdot X) \tag{8.8}$$

where H is the Heaviside step function and W is the vector of weights. The dot product $W \cdot X = \sum_{i=1}^{n} w_i x_i$, where n is the number of inputs to the perceptron, including the bias, which is used to shift the decision boundary and it is independent of any other input.

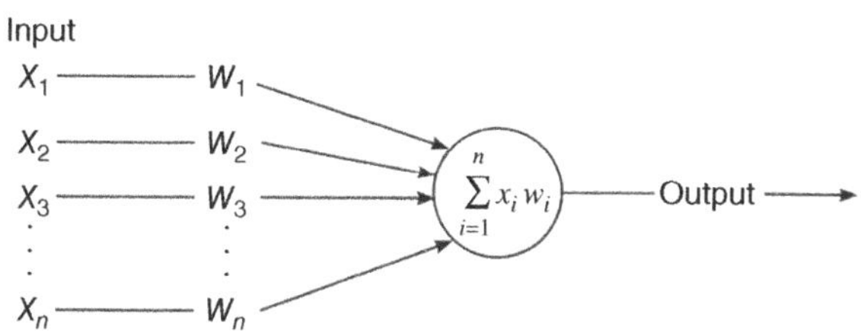

Figure 8.3 Schematic of the perceptron.

8.3.2 Feedforward Neural Networks (FNNs)

The perceptron's limitation to exclusively solve linear classification problems (Minsky and Papert 1969) led to an eventual loss of interest in the topic of artificial neural networks among researchers. It was not until several years later, when it was proved that networks with two or more layers of neurons (FNNs) were significantly more potent than single (layer) perceptrons, that the field of NN experienced a resurgence. The extra layers of perceptrons, conferred FNNs the ability to classify nonlinearly separable data groups, being the first to report on it Shun'ichi Amari (1967). The general structure of an FNN (Figure 8.4) consists of:

- An input layer.
- At least one hidden layer.
- An output layer.
- Connections between consecutive layers.

Instead of the Heaviside function found on the perceptron, FNNs mainly rely on two sigmoidal activation functions:

$$f(v_i) = \tanh(v_i) \tag{8.9}$$

$$f(v_i) = \left(1 + e^{-v_i}\right)^{-1} \tag{8.10}$$

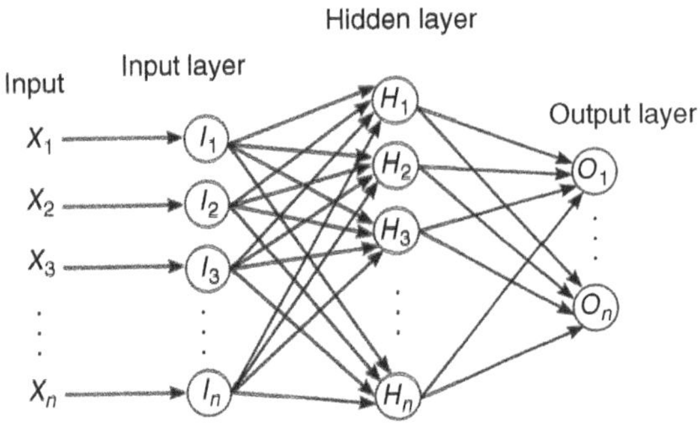

Figure 8.4 Feedforward neural network.

where $v_i = \sum_{i=1}^{n} w_i x_i$ is the weighted input to the neuron. The hyperbolic tangent (Eq. 8.9) ranges from −1 to 1, while the logistic function (Eq. 8.10) ranges from 0 to 1. To reduce the computational cost of the training procedure and overcome numerical problems related to the saturation in sigmoids, these have been frequently substituted with the rectified linear unit (ReLU), particularly in the context of deep learning, where the number of layers and neurons has increased significantly with every new development.

Note

It is worth noting the difference between the terms **feedforward neural network (FNN)** and **multilayer perceptron (MLP)**, which, although sometimes used interchangeably, are not equivalent. The FFN is one of two broad groups in which ANNs are classified and refers to any artificial neural network consisting of three or more successive layers, where the signals flow unidirectionally, from input to output, and through the hidden layers. An MLP, on the other hand, is a type of FNN consisting of fully connected neurons with the Heaviside step function as an activation function. More modern FNN architectures include not-fully connected layers and use nonlinear activation functions. The other broad group in which ANNs are classified is recursive neural networks (RNNs), whose connections allow signals to flow in both directions.

8.4 Training an FNN Using FPA

Although ANNs can be trained following any of the three main learning paradigms in machine learning (supervised, unsupervised, and reinforcement learning), the supervised learning approach allows for a straightforward understanding of how learning occurs in ANNs.

Under supervised learning, ANNs aim to minimize empirical risk, reducing the difference between the desired outputs and the actual outputs delivered by the model. During the training phase, ANNs are presented with a large number of labeled data, known as training set. The value of a defined loss function is obtained for each input–output pair. The ANN's weights are updated at each turn to minimize the loss function. Usually, gradient-based methods are used to estimate the network's weights update, with backpropagation being the most popular (Rumelhart et al. 1986).

As an alternative to backpropagation, the use of metaheuristic algorithms to train ANN has gained traction in the last decades. In specialized literature, it is possible to find examples of particle

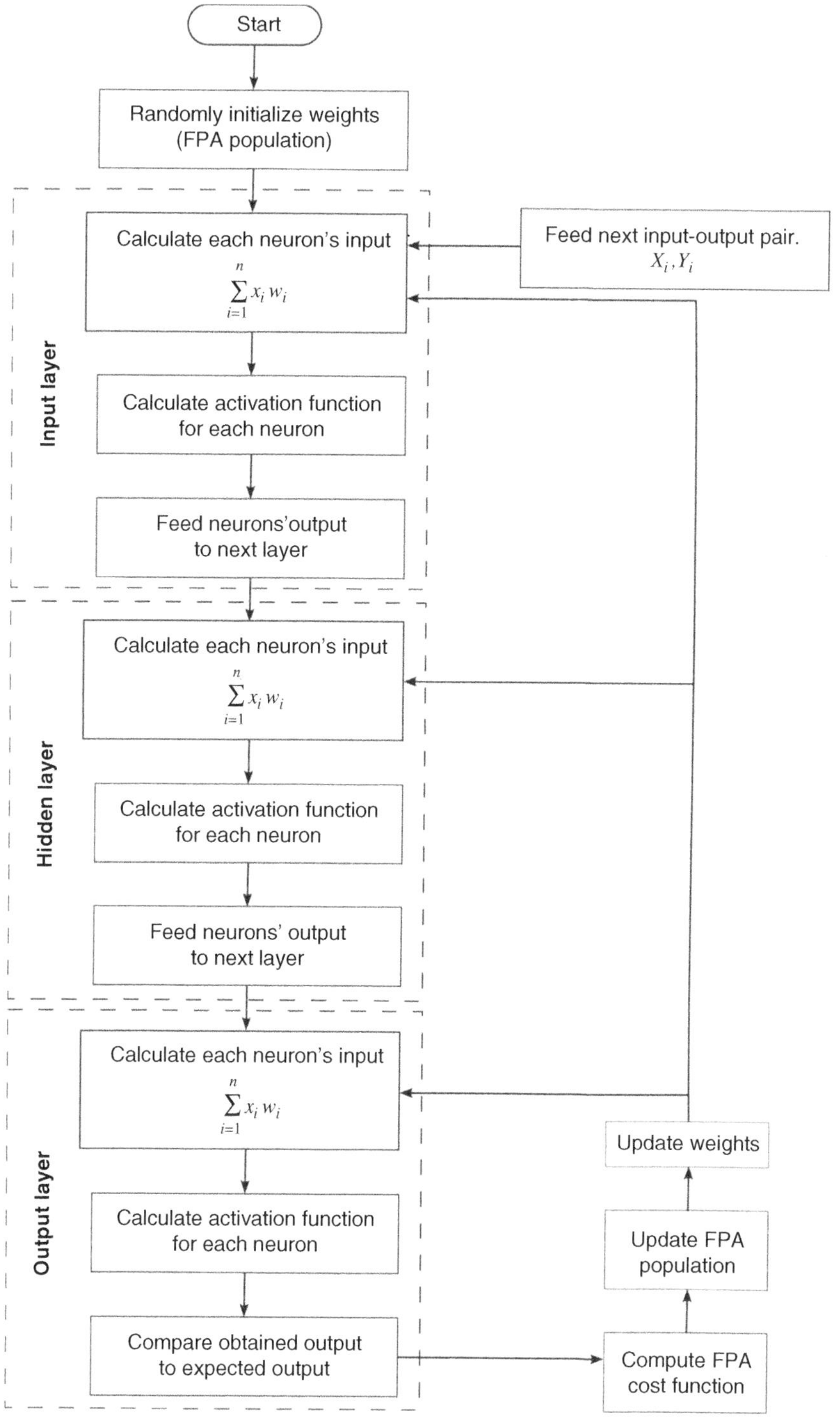

Figure 8.5 Flowchart of the training process using the flower pollination algorithm (FPA).

swarm optimization (PSO) (Yu et al. 2008), differential evolution (DE) (Ilonen et al. 2003), artificial bee colony (ABC) (Taheri et al. 2017), genetic algorithms (GA) (Harpham et al. 2004), and FPA (Kaya and Kaya 2021; Wang et al. 2019).

The learning process when using a metaheuristic algorithm instead of backpropagation remains the same overall. The major change resides in how the network's weights are iteratively updated. In the particular case of the FPA, illustrated in Figure 8.5, each of the solutions in the FPA population represents a candidate set of weights for the NN. At each iteration, all candidate solutions are put to the test with a training set and its corresponding fitness value is obtained. Based on the solutions' performance, the population is updated, keeping record of the best global solution. As with any implementation of the FPA, the optimization procedure ends when a fitness threshold is surpassed or the maximum number of iterations is met.

Note

It is common to assume that ANNs can only be trained under a supervised learning approach. This might be because many texts only cover this case when explaining how ANNs learn, which is an understandable decision since supervised learning might be the most straightforward paradigm associated with ANNs' training procedure. However, ANNs can also be trained following an unsupervised or reinforcement learning approach. As always, the type of learning paradigm of choice will depend on the task at hand. Maybe the most common case for unsupervised learning on ANN is clustering, standing out the Self-organized maps (SOM), an ANN type of architecture designed explicitly for clustering (Kohonen 1982).

With mixing machine learning and metaheuristic methods, it is crucial to keep in mind the advantages and limitations of both in order to make the most out of their hybridization. Training an ANN using a metaheuristic algorithm can be particularly beneficial when approaches based on gradient descent get stuck in local minima or plateaus of the loss function. However, metaheuristic algorithms are, in the rule, more computationally expensive than their gradient-based counterparts; hence, it is also important to consider the number of parameters (weights to adjust) when deciding for one of the approaches.

It is important to remember that, as mentioned in the introduction to this chapter, the hybridization of machine learning and metaheuristic methods is not limited to the training of ANNs using metaheuristic algorithms. Thanks to the large availability of training data, modern ANNs have become larger, and although in these scenarios of high-dimensional parameter space, the gradient descent might struggle to find the loss function's global minimum, this might be preferred over the high cost of implementing an alternative methodology. However, adjusting hyperparameters to avoid overfitting can still be solved using metaheuristic algorithms or, even more critical, finding the right topology for the network (Stanley and Miikkulainen 2002).

References

Amari, S. (1967). A theory of adaptive pattern classifiers. *IEEE Transactions on Electronic Computers* EC-16 (3): 299–307. https://doi.org/10.1109/PGEC.1967.264666.

Baştemur Kaya, C. and Kaya, E. (2021). A novel approach based to neural network and flower pollination algorithm to predict number of COVID-19 cases. *Balkan Journal of Electrical and Computer Engineering*. https://doi.org/10.17694/bajece.932391.

Harpham, C., Dawson, C.W., and Brown, M.R. (2004). A review of genetic algorithms applied to training radial basis function networks. *Neural Computing and Applications* 13 (3): 193–201. https://doi.org/10.1007/S00521-004-0404-5/METRICS.

Ilonen, J., Kamarainen, J.K., and Lampinen, J. (2003). Differential evolution training algorithm for feed-forward neural networks. *Neural Processing Letters* 17 (1): 93–105. https://doi.org/10.1023/A:1022995128597/METRICS.

Kohonen, T. (1982). Self-organized formation of topologically correct feature maps. *Biological Cybernetics* 43 (1): 59–69. https://doi.org/10.1007/BF00337288/METRICS.

Mantegna, R.N. (1994). Fast, accurate algorithm for numerical simulation of Lévy stable stochastic processes. *Physical Review E* 49 (5): 4677. https://doi.org/10.1103/PhysRevE.49.4677.

McCulloch, W.S. and Pitts, W. (1943). A logical calculus of the ideas immanent in nervous activity. *The Bulletin of Mathematical Biophysics* 5 (4): 115–133. https://doi.org/10.1007/BF02478259/METRICS.

Minsky, M. and Papert, S. (1969). *Perceptrons*. MIT Press.

Rosenblatt, F. (1958). The perceptron: a probabilistic model for information storage and organization in the brain. *Psychological Review* 65 (6): 386–408. https://doi.org/10.1037/H0042519.

Rumelhart, D.E., Hinton, G.E., and Williams, R.J. (1986). Learning representations by back-propagating errors. *Nature* 323 (6088): 533–536. https://doi.org/10.1038/323533a0.

Stanley, K.O. and Miikkulainen, R. (2002). Evolving neural networks through augmenting topologies. *Evolutionary Computation* 10 (2): 99–127. https://doi.org/10.1162/106365602320169811.

Taheri, K., Hasanipanah, M., Golzar, S.B. et al. (2017). A hybrid artificial bee colony algorithm-artificial neural network for forecasting the blast-produced ground vibration. *Engineering with Computers* 33 (3): 689–700. https://doi.org/10.1007/S00366-016-0497-3/METRICS.

Wang, M., Lin, J., Yue, L. et al. (2019). Flower pollination neural network for heart disease classification. *IOP Conference Series: Materials Science and Engineering* 551 (1): 012072. https://doi.org/10.1088/1757-899X/551/1/012072.

Yang, X.-S. (2012). Flower pollination algorithm for global optimization. In: *Unconventional Computation and Natural Computation. UCNC 2012*, Lecture Notes in Computer Science, vol. 7445 (ed. J. Durand-Lose and N. Jonoska), 240–249. Berlin, Heidelberg: Springer-Verlag.

Yu, J., Wang, S., and Xi, L. (2008). Evolving artificial neural networks using an improved PSO and DPSO. *Neurocomputing* 71 (4–6): 1054–1060. https://doi.org/10.1016/J.NEUCOM.2007.10.013.

9

Metaheuristic Methods for Classification

9.1 Introduction

Classification is one of the most important topics in machine learning. In the classification task, the main goal is to label the inputs to a respective output such as $y \in (1, 2, \ldots C)$, where C determines the number of classes. If the problem involves two classes the classification becomes a binary classification, otherwise, if the task considers more than two classes the problem becomes a multiclass classification. The classification can be determined into two different types: parametric models, which can be described employing statistical models with a fixed number of parameters, while the nonparametric models can change the number of parameters regarding the amount of training parameters.

On the other hand, metaheuristic approaches have been widely used in several areas because they employ different search strategies to determine optimal solutions to complex problems. Most metaheuristic techniques are based on the behavior of some species considering that they must overcome several difficulties over millions of years to survive developing the strategies for success. Under such considerations, computationally we emulate these behaviors to determine the best solution to different problems. In this chapter, we focus on the most employed techniques for classification and the Crow Search Algorithm (CSA) to improve the accuracy of classification techniques.

9.2 Crow Search Algorithm (CSA)

The CSA is a metaheuristic approach based on the intelligent conduct of crows and was presented by Askarzadeh (2016). Despite being a recent technique, the CSA has drawn the research community's attention and has been employed and adjusted for solving comprehensive engineering problems (dos Santos Coelho et al. 2018; Meraihi et al. 2021). In the CSA, the goal is to emulate specific intelligent conducts of crows that have been considered one of the most brilliant birds in nature (Buniyaadi et al. 2020). Four principal conducts stand out in CSA: the ability to live in a flock, the capacity to hide food and remember the place of the hiding position, the capability to steal other crows' food, and the self-awareness of being robbed.

Computationally, the CSA is conformed for a flock with N search particles (crows) where each of them is an n-dimensional vector, which n is related to the problem dimension. Each agent (crow) has a related memory for remembering the best position (hidden place) known until the current

Machine Learning and Metaheuristic Computation, First Edition.
Erik Cuevas, Jorge Galvez, Omar Avalos, and Fernando Wario.

iteration. The position $P_{i,k}$ and the memory $M_{i,k}$ of the crow i at iteration k are described in Eqs. 9.1 and 9.2.

$$P_{i,k} = \left[p_{i,k}^1, p_{i,k}^2, \dots, p_{i,k}^n\right] \tag{9.1}$$

$$M_{i,k} = \left[m_{i,k}^1, m_{i,k}^2, \dots, m_{i,k}^n\right] \tag{9.2}$$

$$i = 1, 2, \cdots, N; \quad k = 1, 2, \dots, \text{maxIter}$$

where maxIter is the stop criteria in the evolutionary process.

The new position for crow i on iteration $k+1$ is carried out by either tracking or evasion. In both conducts, a crow i follows a crow j to discover its hidden place. In tracking, the crow i reaches its target and approaches the hiding location. In evasion, crow j detects the tracking crow i and assumes a random position. Equation 9.3 computationally describes these conducts.

$$P_{i,k+1} = \begin{cases} P_{i,k} + r_i{}^* fl^* (M_{j,k} - P_{i,k}) & r_j \geq AP \\ \text{random} & \text{otherwise} \end{cases} \tag{9.3}$$

where AP is the awareness probability parameter that manipulates the crow conducts if a random number r_i (uniformly distributed between 0 and 1) is higher or equal than AP, then the pursuit is performed; otherwise, evasion is executed. In the pursuit stage, fl is the flight distance parameter which indicates the closeness degree toward the best position of crow j, $M_{j,k}$ is the best location of crow j, and r_j is uniformly distributed in the range [0, 1]. The new crow location is computed in the objective function $F(\bullet)$ and its memory is calculated by Eq. 9.4.

$$M_{i,k+1} = \begin{cases} F(P_{i,k+1}) & F(P_{i,k+1}) < F(M_{i,k}) \\ M_{i,k} & \text{otherwise} \end{cases} \tag{9.4}$$

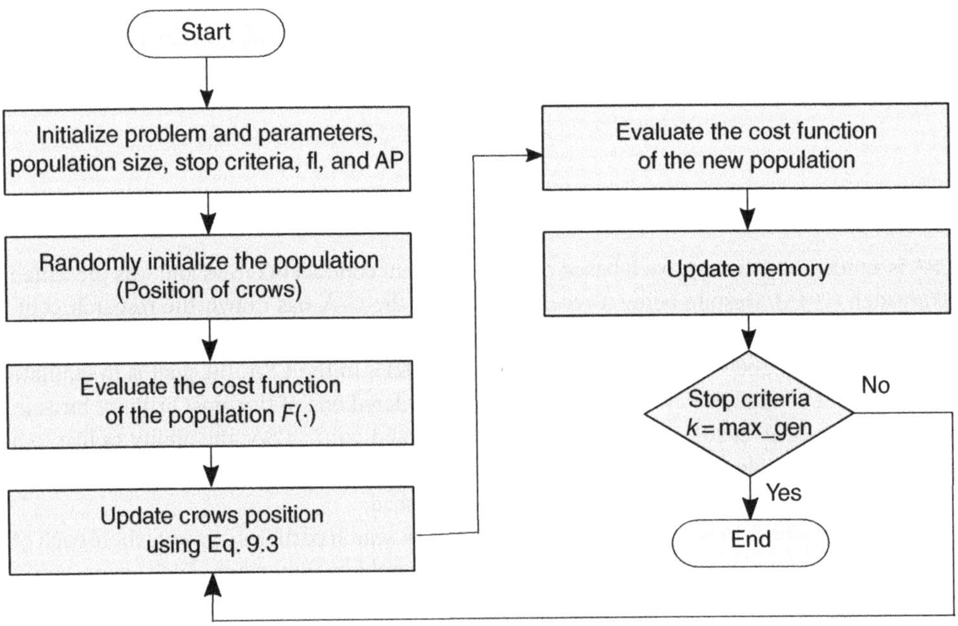

Figure 9.1 Crow search algorithm (CSA) flowchart.

The required stages of CSA are shown in the flowchart of Figure 9.1. In the first stage the problem is initialized (dimensions and limits) and the parameters of the CSA (fl, AP, stop criterion) are defined. In the next stage, the position of the population (crows) is initialized randomly through the search space and then each solution is evaluated employing the cost function of the problem. Then, new positions are calculated using Eq. 9.3 and their feasibility is proved. Once the new positions are generated, they are evaluated by the cost function, and the memory is updated. Finally, the stop criterion is verified to determine if the algorithm terminates or continues with the iterative process. The stop criterion is related directly to the application of the CSA, but two typical rules are employed: (1) the use of a maximum number of iterations, and (2) when the objective function value of the best particle converges and there are no changes along the iterations.

```
%Algorithm 9.1
%Clean data
close all
clear all

% Step 1, problem, and CSA parameters declaration
pd=2;
N=20;
AP=0.1;
fl=2;
l=-5.12;
u=5.12;

% Step 2, randomly initialization of the particles (crows)
% between lower and upper bounds
for i=1:N
    for j=1:pd
        x(i,j)=l-(l-u)*rand;
    end
end

% Step 3, evaluation of the population using the cost function
xn=x;
ft=fitness(xn,N);

% Save the population and they fitness in memory
mem=x;
fit_mem=ft;

% Step 4, the CSA generates new solutions where crows chase other
% crows and flying randomly through the search space
tmax=500;
```

```
for k=1:tmax
    num=ceil(N*rand(1,N));
    for i=1:N
        if rand>AP
            xnew(i,:)= x(i,:)+fl*rand*(mem(num(i),:)-x(i,:));
        else
            for j=1:pd
                xnew(i,j)=l-(l-u)*rand;
            end
        end
    end

% Step 5, evaluation of the new population using the cost function
xn=xnew;
ft=fitness(xn,N);

% Update position and memory
    for i=1:N
        if xnew(i,:)>=l & xnew(i,:)<=u
            x(i,:)=xnew(i,:);
            if ft(i)<fit_mem(i)
                mem(i,:)=xnew(i,:);
                fit_mem(i)=ft(i);
            end
        end
    end
end

% Step 6, display the best particle and its fitness value
[a, b] = min(fit_mem); respf = ['Best fitness:'];
respp = ['Best particle (crow):'];
disp (respf); min(fit_mem)
disp (respp); mem(b,:)

% Cost function
function ft=fitness(xn,N)
    for i=1:N
        ft(i)=sum(xn(i,:).^2); % Sphere function
    end
end
```

In order to represent the main functioning of the CSA, Algorithm 9.1 shows the implementation in MATLAB and the Statistics and Machine Learning Toolbox. As we mentioned in the flow chart, the first step is determining the problem parameters (number of variables), lower and upper bounds (physics or design limitations in the parameters of certain applications), and the algorithm parameters setting (each metaheuristic approach has its own parameter setting). In Step 2, the population (crows) is generated using random numbers drawn from a uniform distribution. In Step 3 each element (crow) of the population must be evaluated, this evaluation indicates the quality of the solution, to determine this evaluation is necessary a metric better known as cost function or objective function. Once the particles have been evaluated, they are saved into a memory where the best solutions are collected.

In Step 4, the operators of the CSA are employed to generate the chasing behavior of crows or flying randomly through the search space to determine feasible solutions. To carry out this step, an awareness probability (AP) and flight length (fl) are set previously, if a number randomly generated is higher than the AP the chasing behavior is performed, otherwise, the random flight is conducted. In Step 5, the new population is evaluated employing the cost function and is compared with the population previously stored in the memory, if the new position of the particle $j+1$ has a better quality than the same particle at iteration j then is replaced, otherwise, remains.

In this case, the test function known as the sphere function is employed. To perform this experiment, the number of dimensions (variables of the problem) and the upper and lower bounds must be set by the user considering the characteristics of the problem to be treated. For this experimental example, the upper and lower bounds are 5.12 and −5.12 respectively, and the dimensions are set in 2 for a good appreciation of the reader. Under such circumstances, the CSA employs its search strategy to determine the values between these ranges that better results provide considering that the goal is the minimization of the cost function (in this case the optimal solution is zero). Figure 9.2 shows the graphical representation of the sphere function, Figure 9.2a is the 3D representation while Figure 9.2b is the same representation but in a view of 2D from the bottom.

9.3 CSA for Nearest-Neighbor Method (k-NN)

The Nearest-Neighbor Method is one of the most straightforward techniques for classification in machine learning, and due to its easy implementation, it is widely employed in several applications. In this approach, the data from different groups are labeled during the training stage while once a new observation x_0 is acquired, the distance between the closest N samples $x_i, \dots, x_N$ regarding the new data x_0 is determined. Under such an approach, this new observation is labeled to a group K_i by considering the consensus of the closest neighbors (Biau and Devroye 2015).

In this example, the CSA is employed to improve the classification task of the k-NN approach using the operators to perform a search in the space of feasible solutions. As we mentioned before, k-NN is the simplest classification technique where some parameters can be determined by the user in order to obtain a better outcome. Under such considerations, the main element is the number of the k-elements that better train the model for a specific dataset. In this case, the employed data is the Iris dataset which is widely used for academic tasks. This is a small dataset that MATLAB already includes within its software distribution in which the elements are easily distinguished between them.

This database considers 150 samples that include four characteristics of different flowers, to get this database, we use the follow command:

```
>> load fisheriris
```

After the database is loaded, the information is separated into a matrix that contains the four characteristics of the flowers, and a vector that labels the types of flowers with such traits.

```
>> X = meas;
>> Y = species;
```

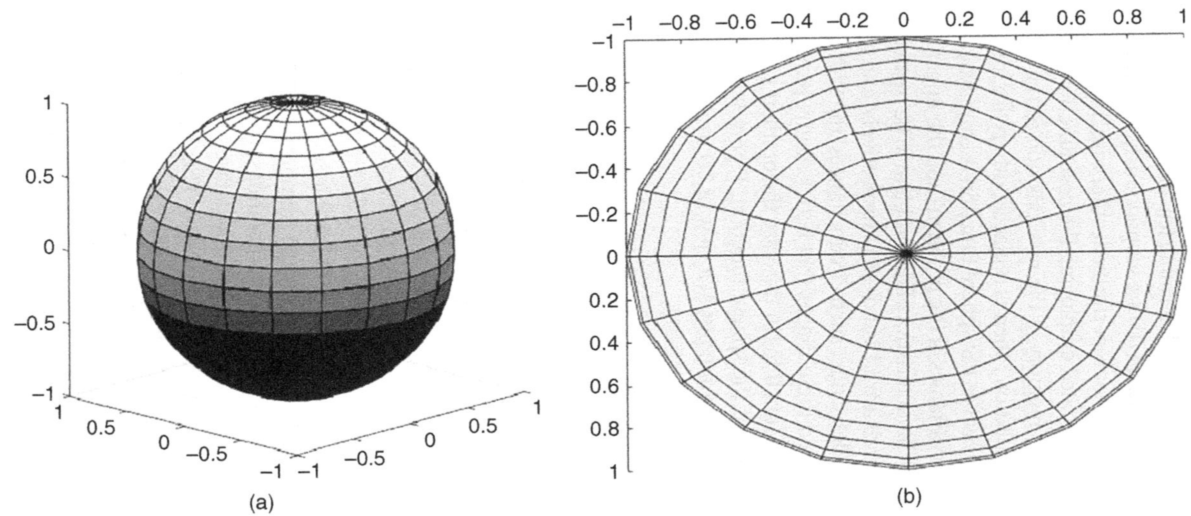

Figure 9.2 Sphere test function graphical representation.

When the matrix X and vector Y are defined, 70% of the data contained are used in the training stage of the k-NN method, and the left 30% in the test stage (Xtrain, SpeciesTrain, Xtest, Speciestest) as is shown in Step 1. Under such circumstances, the CSA must be modified in terms of this new application where the number of dimensions is set in 1 considering that the number of neighbors must be determined by the optimization approach, lower and upper bounds are set in 1 and 20 respectively as is indicated in Step 2, here the initialization remains as in Algorithm 9.1.

To perform the k-NN classification with the CSA, the main structure of Algorithm 9.1 remains but the cost function (objective function) must be replaced by one that considers the specifications of the problem, in this case, the cost function is replaced by Algorithm 9.2.

```
%Algorithm 9.2
%Clean data
close all
clear all

% Step 1, problem, and CSA parameters declaration
pd=1;
N=1;
AP=0.1;
fl=1.5;
load fisheriris
X = meas;
a1 = X(1:35,:);  a11 = X(36:50,:);
a2 = X(51:85,:);   a22 = X(86:100,:);
a3 = X(101:135,:);   a33 = X(136:150,:);
Xtrain = [a1; a2; a3];  Xtest= [a11; a22; a33];
b1 = species (1:35,:);  b11 = species (36:50,:);
b2 = species (51:85,:);   b22 = species (86:100,:);
b3 = species (101:135,:);   b33 = species (136:150,:);
SpeciesTrain = [b1; b2; b3];   Speciestest= [b11; b22; b33];

% Step 2, randomly initialization of the particles (crows)
% between lower and upper bounds

% Step 3, evaluation of the population using the cost function

% Save the population and they fitness in memory

% Step 4, the CSA generates new solutions where crows chase other
% crows and flying randomly through the search space

% Step 5, evaluation of the new population using the cost function
```

```
% Update position and memory

% Step 6, display the best particle and its fitness value
gscatter(Xtrain(:,1), Xtrain(:,2), SpeciesTrain,'rgb','osd');
xlabel('Sepal length');
ylabel('Sepal width');
hold on
plot(Xtest(1:15,1), Xtest(1:15,2), '*', 'markersize',...
10, 'markerfacecolor','r');
hold on
plot(Xtest(16:30,1), Xtest(16:30,2), '+', 'markersize',...
10, 'markerfacecolor', 'g');
hold on
plot(Xtest(31:45,1), Xtest(31:45,2), '.', 'markersize',...
10, 'markerfacecolor','g');
legend ('Setosa', 'Vericolor', 'Virginica', 'SetosaTest',...
'VericolorTest', 'VirginicaTest')


% Cost function
function ft=fitness(xn, N, Xtrain, YTrain, Xtest, Ytest)
   for i=1:N
      Mdl = fitcknn(Xtrain, YTrain,'NumNeighbors', xn(i));
      ypredict = predict(Mdl, Xtest);
      T = strcmp (ypredict, Ytest); incorrect = find (T == 0);
      ft (i) = (length(Ytest) - length (incorrect))/length(Ytest);
   end
end
```

For this example, we use the MATLAB software distribution k-NN technique which can be employed by the following command.

```
>> Mdl = fitcknn (Features, Labels, 'NumNeighbors', k)
```

This command needs at least two input arguments that represent the characteristics of the elements to be classified, the labels of the objects, and optionally the k elements to train the technique, otherwise, the technique determines a fixed number of elements. In Algorithm 9.2, the k-NN train is determined by *Mdl* where the features (4 features available in the database) and labels are introduced from the database previously loaded, and the number of k elements is determined by the CSA for each particle (crow). Once the data is complete and the model trained, we employ the left 30% of the data to test the k-NN model using the predict command. When the trained model is tested, the metric employed as the new cost function is the accuracy of the model determined in Eq. 9.5.

$$ft = \frac{trp}{tp} \tag{9.5}$$

where *trp* expresses the true prediction determined by the model, and *tp* is the total of predictions. Under this consideration, the CSA has a metric that helps to determine the next step in the search

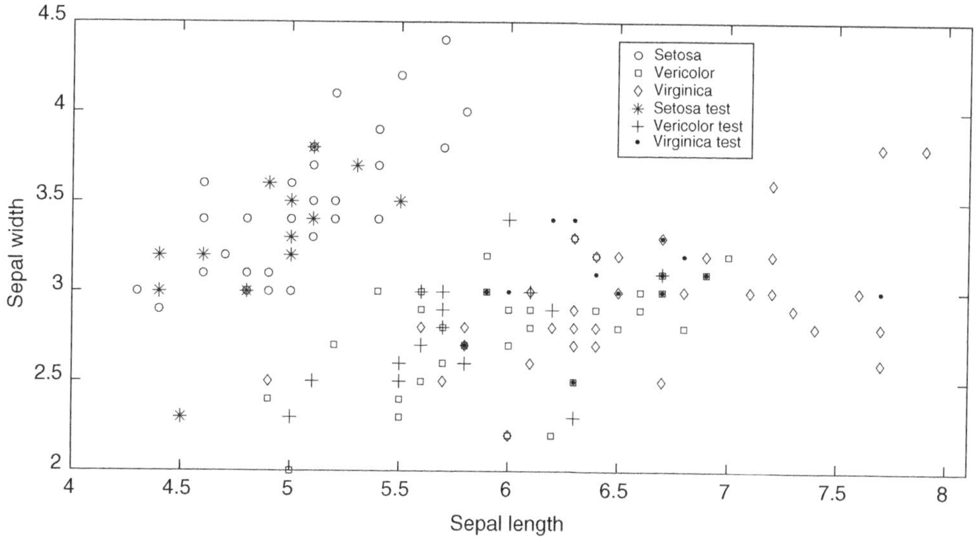

Figure 9.3 Graphical result of classification of CSA-k-NN.

strategy. For this example, the CSA is able to determine the necessary number of k elements that better perform the classification set in 5 to get the 100% of true classification. Figure 9.3 shows the result of the training and test classification in the case of the Iris database, where the circle, square, and rhomb represent the training data while star, plus sign, and dot represent the test data.

Note

When a specific application is performed employing a metaheuristic approach, the user must be careful of the specification, constrains, and specifications of the problem. In this example, the particles (crows) must be integers positives due to the number of k neighbors cannot be decimal.

9.4 CSA for Logistic Regression

Logistic regression is an example of a parametric approach, this technique is similar to linear regression, but the main difference is laid out in the binary outcome [0, 1] as well as in the parametric model and the hypothesis (Hosmer et al. 1989). This regression employs the expression $\mu(x) = \text{logit}(\mathbf{wx})$ also known as the logistic function or sigmoidal due to its peculiar "S" shape shown in Figure 9.4. As we mentioned before, this function can map all real numbers scale into the interval [0, 1] and can be described as in the following expression.

$$\mu(x) = \frac{1}{1 + \exp(-\mathbf{wx})} = \frac{\exp(\mathbf{wx})}{1 + \exp(\mathbf{wx})} \tag{9.6}$$

In this example as well as in the k-NN, the CSA approach is employed to determine the best classification process in a binary dataset that describes the score of two tests on the scale of [0, 100]

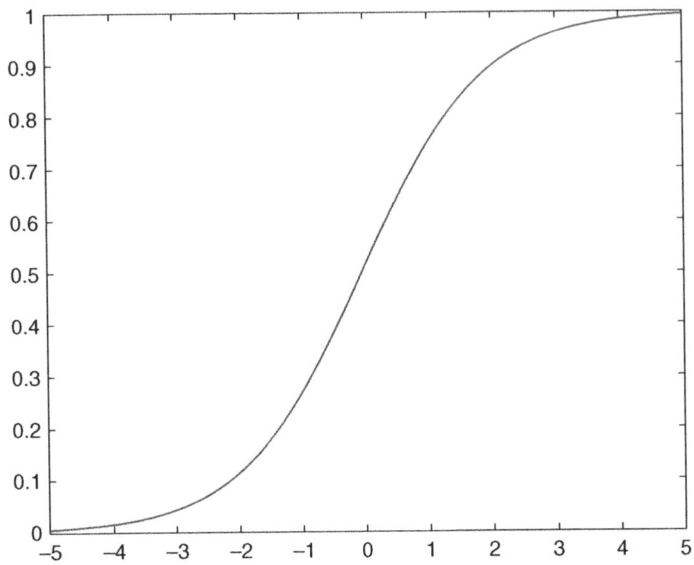

Figure 9.4 Logistic function or sigmoidal.

Table 9.1 Test scores and results of the applicants.

Test 1	Test 2	Result
65	50	0
70	85	1
80	79	1
70	60	0
55	40	0
36	70	0
68	72	1
79	94	1
10	15	0
84	80	1
69	72	1
18	46	0
68	93	1
44	36	0
59	68	0
99	71	1
15	65	0
79	89	1
17	63	0
65	65	1

and in a binary result [0, 1] which represents if the participants were or not accepted for a certain job. The dataset employed in this example is presented in Table 9.1 and the implementation is presented in Algorithm 9.3.

```
%Algorithm 9.3
%Clean data
close all
clear all

% Step 1, problem, and CSA parameters declaration
pd=3;
N=10;
AP=0.1;
fl=1.5;
x1 = readmatrix('logitdata.xlsx');
X = x1(:, [1,2]); X = zscore(X);
Y = x1(:, 3);
in = find (Y ==1); out = find(Y==0);
[m,n] = size(X);
X =  [ones(m,1) X];

% Step 2, evaluation of the population using the cost function
x=zeros(N,pd);
xn=x;
[ft, S]=fitness(xn, X, Y, N);

% Save the population and they fitness in memory
mem=x;
fit_mem=ft;

% Step 4, the CSA generates new solutions where crows chase other
% crows and flying randomly through the search space

% Step 5, evaluation of the new population using the cost function

% Step 6, display the best particle and its fitness value
[a, b] = min(fit_mem); respf = ['Best fitness:'];
respp = ['Best particle (crow):'];
disp (respf); min(fit_mem)
disp (respp); mem(b,:)
```

```
syms x1 x2
fnn=mem(b,1)+mem(b,2)*x1+mem(b,3)*x2-0.5;
plot (X(in, 2), X(in, 3),'*k'); hold on
plot (X(out, 2), X(out, 3),'+b');
fimplicit (fnn);
legend('Accepted','Rejected','Decision boundary')

% Cost function
function [ft, S]=fitness(xn, X, Y, N)
     for i=1:N
       m = length (Y);
       S = sigm(X*xn');
       ft  = (-1/m) * sum (Y.* log(S) + (1-Y).*log(1-S));
     end
end

% Logistic function
function S = sigm(z)
     S = zeros (size(z) );
     [m , n] = size(z) ;
     for i = 1:m
         for j = 1:n
             S (i,j) = 1 / (1 + exp(-z(i,j)) );
         end
     end
end
```

In Step 1 all parameters of the CSA are initialized, and the database is loaded from an xlsx file which is located in the same directory of the script. Once the data is loaded, two different sets are generated in order to train our model the information data and the labels, as the classification task involves two possible results, true or false, the labels are in a binary format [0, 1]. For simplicity, after the data separation, the training data are standardized and identify the true and false cases. In Step 2, for simplicity, the initial parameters are set to zero and evaluated using the cost function described in Eq. 9.7. After that, the fitness value is stored in the memory.

$$J(\theta) = \frac{1}{m}\sum_{i=1}^{m} \text{Cos}\, t(h_\theta(x_i), y_i) = -\frac{1}{m}\left[\sum_{i=1}^{m} y_i \log h_\theta(x_i) + (1 - y_i)\log(1 - h_\theta(x_i))\right] \tag{9.7}$$

Steps 4 and 5 remain with no modifications, the algorithm iterates until the stop criteria is reached. Step 6 plots the elements that are rejected and the accepted considering the qualification obtained in the two tests while the line represents the decision boundary due to the logistic classification. The graphical representation is presented in Figure 9.5.

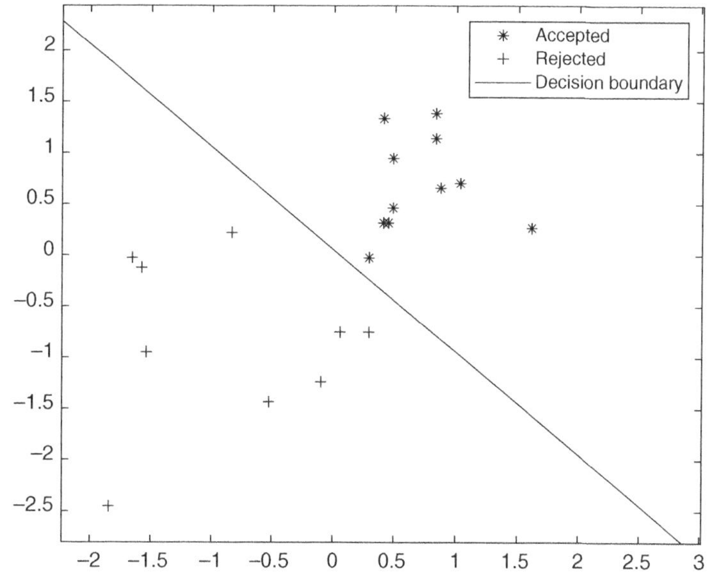

Figure 9.5 Logistic regression of accepted, rejected positions, and the decision boundary.

9.5 CSA for Fisher Linear Discriminant

The Fisher linear discriminant is a classification approach that has been widely employed in two-dimensional problems for simple applications, on the other hand, as the difficulty of the problem increases the computational complexity considerably increases. Fisher linear discriminant (FLDA) is a supervised parametric classification that employs dimensionality reduction approaches to perform the classification task. For this example, the simplest case where two classes are considered, after the analysis, the study can be generalized into N different classes (Shalev-Shwartz and Ben-David 2013).

Suppose that we have a set of data $\mathbf{x} = [x_1, \dots, x_N]$ which are conformed for two classes, the main objective is determine the vector defined by $\mathbf{w}$ such that the N-dimensional space better separate the defined classes projected in $\mathbf{w}$ (Figure 9.6).

Note

As we mentioned before, the FLDA is an approach that can be used for dimensionality reduction and classification approaches. The FLDA shares some features regarding the Principal Component Analysis (PCA) in which the dimensions are reduced by considering the elements (dimensions) that more variations contribute to the study. On the other hand, the most variation of data is not crucial in the FLDA approach, instead, the variation of data in this technique focuses on maximizing the separability between two groups in order to make the best decision when new data is considered in such an analysis.

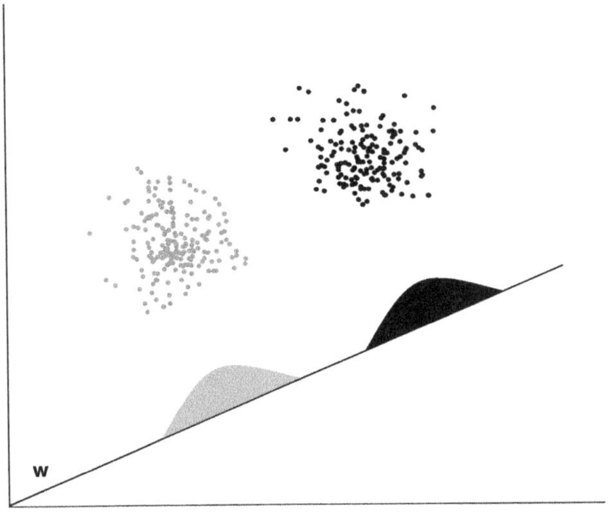

Figure 9.6 Two-class data projected in **w**.

To clarify the functioning of the FLDA employing the CSA, we are required to generate a dataset, for simplicity, the number of characteristics is 2 and we consider 25 samples. In Step 1 of Algorithm 9.4, the CSA initial parameters and the dataset are generated and separated into two groups that are labeled with [1, 0].

Step 2 generates the initial population; in this specific application, a single particle is used for simplicity. However, the population can be increased as the user considers appropriate where the upper and lower bounds are set in 1 and −1, respectively. After the initialization, the population is evaluated using the cost function which must be generated by considering the application's specific requirements. In the case of the FLDA, the main goal is to determine the line that better separates the classes. Under such circumstances, the cost function maximizes the distance between classes. The cost function is represented in Eq. 9.8, where $m1$ and $m2$ are the means of groups 1 and 2, respectively.

$$\max\ J(\mathbf{x}) = \sqrt{m1^2 - m2^2} \tag{9.8}$$

```
%Algorithm 9.4
%Clean data
clear all
close all
% Step 1, problem, and CSA parameters declaration
pd=2;
N=2;
```

```
AP=0.1;
fl=1.5;

% Generate the database

X = [randn(10,2); randn(15,2) + 1.5];  Y = [zeros(10,1); ones(15,1)];
Xaux1 = find (Y==1); X1 = (X(Xaux1,:));
Xaux2 = find (Y==0); X2 = (X(Xaux2,:));

% Step 2, randomly initialization of the particles (crows) between
% lower and upper bounds
[-1,1]
l= -1;
u= 1;
for i=1:N
    for j=1:pd
        x(i,j)=l-(l-u)*rand;
    end
end

% Step 3, evaluation of the population using the cost function

% Save the population and they fitness in memory

% Step 4, the CSA generates new solutions where crows chase other
% crows and flying randomly through the search space

% Step 5, evaluation of the new population using the cost function

% Update position and memory

% Step 6, display the best particle and its fitness value

[a, b] = min(fit_mem); respf = ['Best fitness:'];
respp = ['Best particle (crow):'];
disp (respf); min(fit_mem)
disp (respp); mem(b,:)

xaux = [xn(1,1:2); xn(1,3:4)];
a1=X1 * xaux; a2=X2 * xaux;
plot (X2(:, 1), X2(:, 2),'*r');
hold on
plot (X1(:, 1), X1(:, 2),'+b');
legend ('Group 1', 'Group 2');
```

```
figure
plot (a2(:, 1), a2(:, 2),'*r');
hold on
plot (a1(:, 1), a1(:, 2),'+b');
legend ('Group 1', 'Group 2');

% Cost function
function [ft]=fitness(xn, X1, X2)

    x = [xn(1,1:2); xn(1,3:4)];
    G1 = X1 * x; G2 = X2 * x;
    m1 = mean (G1); m2 = mean (G2);
    ft = (norm (m1-m2));

end
```

Once the CSA determines the best elements of the matrix w, the data is plotted in two graphics, Figure 9.7a shows the original database where the groups are represented with '*' and '+' while Figure 9.7b shows the data representation after the FLDA analysis. Under such circumstances, the experimental results generate new positions of the data where the distance between means is bigger.

9.6 CSA for Naïve Bayes Classification

Naïve Bayes (NB) classification approach is a classification technique based on the likelihood of belonging to a certain group due to the features of an element. The NB technique classifies the k values of a N number of features $x \in \{1, \dots, k\}^N$. This approach does not consider the possible correlation between elements, or in other words, NB considers that the data are conditionally independent (Wickramasinghe and Kalutarage 2021). In order to perform an example of NB employing the CSA to improve the performance of the classification approach, the command of the MATLAB software distribution employed is described below.

```
Mdl = fitcnb(Tbl,ResponseVarName)
```

As the NB approach is based on probabilities, the optimization technique must be employed for a different consideration. In Algorithm 9.5 the complete optimization process is presented, nevertheless as in the last examples, the steps that change regarding the original CSA are shown while the steps that are the same as the original CSA are omitted but are mentioned in the code.

In this example, a dataset of 1200 samples randomly generated is employed. Step 1 shows the data generation where 80% are used for training while the last 20% are employed to test the trained model. Under the characteristics of the NB technique, the CSA is employed to determine the number of elements that better classify the train data considering the lower quantity of elements. In the data generation, the 480 elements are considered for training and 120 for testing, the data are separated into two groups labeled with [0, 1] as seen in Figure 9.7.

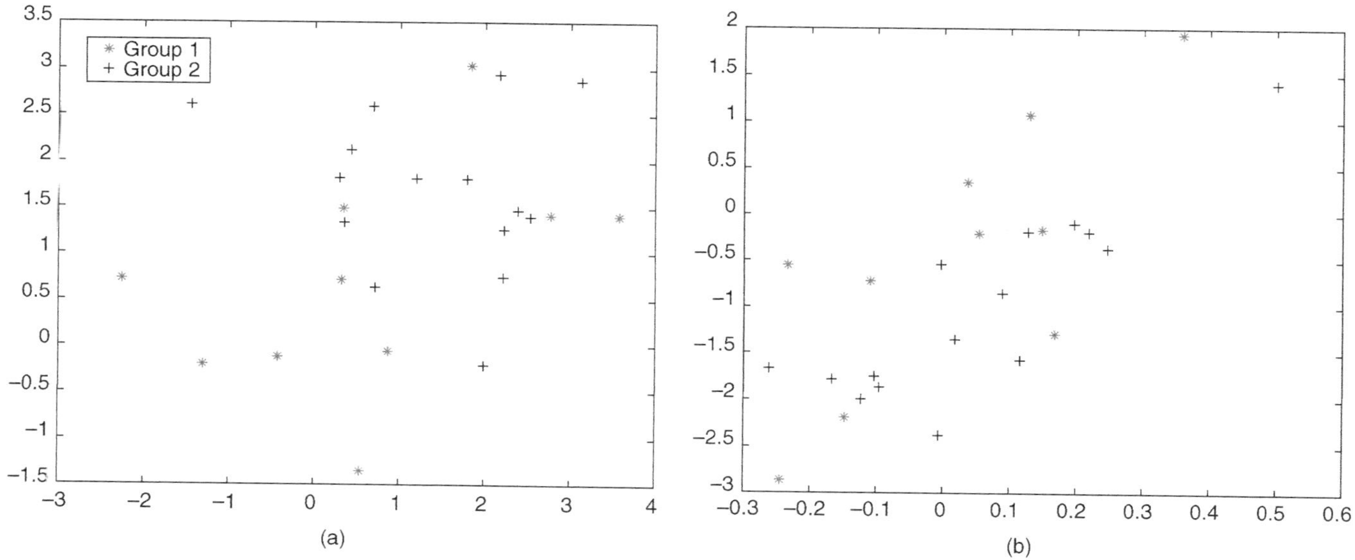

Figure 9.7 (a) Original data distribution, (b) data representation after the FLDA and optimization process.

```
%Algorithm 9.5
%Clean data
clear all
close all

% Step 1, problem, and CSA parameters declaration
pd=480;
N=10;
AP=0.1;
fl=1.5;

% Generate database

X = [randn(600,2); randn(600,2) + 1.5];
Y1test = [zeros(120,1)]; Y2test = [ones(120,1)];
X1train = X((1:480),:); X1test = X((481:600),:);
X2train = X((601:1080),:); X2test = X((1081:1200),:);
Xtest = [X1test; X2test];
Y1train = [zeros(480,1)]; Y2train = [ones(480,1)];
Ytest = [zeros(120,1); ones(120,1)];

% Step 2, Randomly initialization of the particles (crows) between
% lower and upper bounds
l= 1;
u= 480;
for i=1:N
    for j=1:pd
        x(i,j)=l-(l-u)*rand;
    end
end

% Step 3, Evaluation of the population using the cost function

xn=x;
[X, Mdl, ft, Tind] = fitness(xn, X1train, X2train, N,...
Xtest, Y1train, Y2train, Ytest);

% Save the population and they fitness in memory

% Step 4, the CSA generates new solutions where crows chase other
% crows and flying randomly through the search space

% Step 5, evaluation of the new population using the cost function
```

```
% Update position and memory

% Step 6, Display the best particle and its fitness value
[a, b] = min(fit_mem); respf = ['Best fitness:'];
respp = ['Best particle (crow):'];
disp (respf); min(fit_mem)
disp (respp); resp = mem(b,:);
best = resp(ind_mem(:,b))

% Cost function
function [X, Mdl, ft, Tind]=fitness(xn, X1train, X2train, ...
N, Xtest, Y1train, Y2train, Ytest)

    xn1 = round(xn);
    for i=1:N
        for j=1: length(xn1)
    if (0<=xn1(i,j)) & (xn1(i,j) >= 480)
       xn1 (i,j)=479;
   else
       xn1 (i,j) =  xn1 (i,j);
    end
        end
    end
    mi = min(min(xn1(:,1)));
    ma = max(max(xn1(:,1)));

    for i=1:N
        indx = randi ([mi ma],1, xn1(N,1) ); %indx = round(indx)';
        tr1 = X1train(indx,:); tr2 = X2train(indx,:);
        y1 = Y1train(indx); y2 = Y2train(indx);
        Y = [y1 ; y2];
        X = [tr1; tr2];
        Mdl = fitcnb(X,Y);
        pred = predict(Mdl, Xtest);
        good = 0; bad = 0;
        for j = 1 : length (pred)
            if pred (j) == Ytest(j)
                good = good + 1;
            else
                bad = bad + 1;
            end
        end
        ft(i) = (1 / (good / length (pred)));
        Tind (:,i) = indx;
    end
end
```

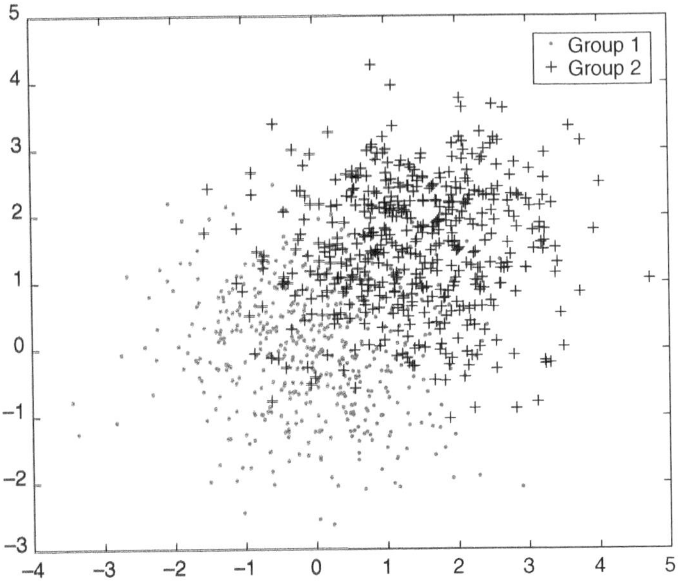

Figure 9.8 Training data distribution used in Algorithm 9.5.

In Step 2 the CSA and problem parameters are configured, where the population size is 10 and the number of dimensions is considered the same number of elements that are included in the study (480) that represent the number of elements of each group as is shown in Figure 9.8. Step 3 evaluates the objective function in which the model is trained considering the number of elements that the CSA determines optimal for the classification task. In Steps 4 and 5, the optimization process is performed employing the search strategy of the CSA until the stop criterion is reached. In the cost function, a validation step is included to guarantee that all particles are within the bounds of the problem. Once the best solution is determined by the CSA, the result is displayed where the final elements employed to determine the best classification as well as the fitness value are shown.

9.7 CSA for Support Vector Machine

The support vector machine (SVM) is an unsupervised classification technique which generates a hyperplane that maximizes the distance between groups for a better generalization. Originally the SVM was generated to solve binary problems, nevertheless, can be extended for multiclass classification (Farhat 1992; Shalev-Shwartz and Srebro 2008). Considering a pair of training data $(x_1, y_1), (x_2, y_2), \dots, (x_N, y_N)$ which are considered as linearly separable labeled into two different groups $[1, -1]$ in the case of binary classification where the separation class maximizes the distance between them as can be shown in Figure 9.9.

In order to perform the example considering that the CSA improves the model's internal parameters, the data and main structure of the CSA_NN employed is reported in the literature by Mousavi (2017). Under such circumstances, the functioning algorithm is shown in Algorithm 9.6. Due to this example's characteristics, the algorithm's corresponding steps are considered in the generation of the network and for the result display instead of the main CSA functioning.

In Step 1, training data is loaded from a previously generated data file containing 40 elements with 300 features each. The elements are labeled with their respective groups (6 groups for this

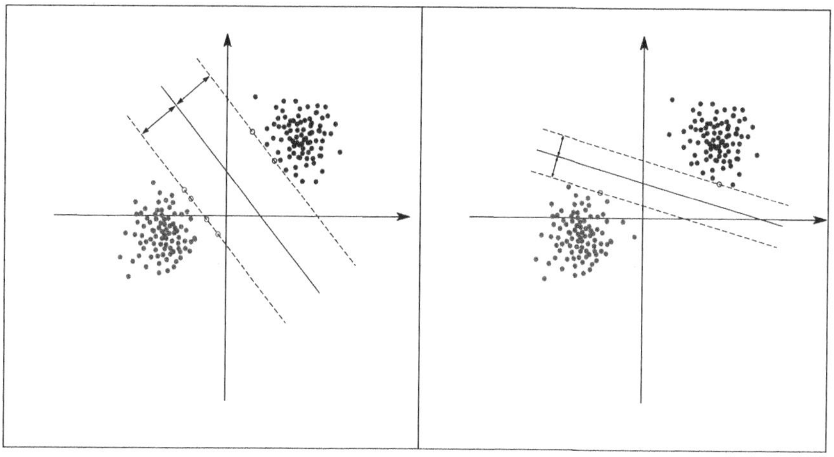

Figure 9.9 Hyperplane adjustment considering the support vectors represented as the empty dots.

example) and the dimensions of the problem to generate the network are defined. Once the number of hidden layers is set, the construction of the network is performed in Step 2 employing the MATLAB command described below.

```
net = newff(P,T,S)
```

where P represents the features of the elements, T is the target or the labels of each element, and S is the data of the network such as the parameters number and hidden layers.

```
%Algorithm 9.6
%Clean data
clear all
close all

% Step 1, Generate the data for the training and test.
netdata=load('Test.mat');
netdata=netdata.FinalReady;
% Data, groups, and variable change
network=netdata(:,1:end-1); netlbl=netdata(:,end);
inputs = network; targets = netlbl;
% Dimension of the problem
InputNum = size(inputs,2);
OutputNum = size(targets,2);
pr = [-1 1];
PR = repmat(pr,InputNum,1);

% Number of Hidden Layers
NH=5;
```

```
% Step 2, Generation of the first Network
Network1 = newff(PR,[NH OutputNum],{'tansig' 'tansig'});

% Step 3, CSA for improving the network training
Network1 = CSA_NN(Network1,inputs,targets);

% Step 4, Obtain the Outputs of the CSA_NN model
outputs = Network1(inputs');
outputs=outputs';
sizenet=size(network);
sizenet=sizenet(1,1);

% Computing the error in of the CSA_NN
MSE=mse(outputs);
% Bias Output for Confusion Matrix
outputs=outputs-(MSE*0.1)/2;

% Detecting Mislabeled Data
for i=1 : 50
            if outputs(i) <= 0.9
               out(i)=0;
        elseif outputs(i) >= 0.9
               out(i)=1;              end;end;
for i=51 : 100
            if outputs(i) <= 0.9
               out(i)=0;
        elseif outputs(i) >= 0.9
               out(i)=2;              end;end;
for i=101 : 150
            if outputs(i) <= 0.9
               out(i)=0;
        elseif outputs(i) >= 0.9
               out(i)=3;              end;end;
for i=151 : 200
            if outputs(i) <= 0.9
               out(i)=0;
        elseif outputs(i) >= 0.9
               out(i)=4;              end;end;
for i=201 : 250
            if outputs(i) <= 0.9
               out(i)=0;
        elseif outputs(i) >= 0.9
               out(i)=5;              end;end;
for i=251 : 300
            if outputs(i) <= 0.9
               out(i)=0;
```

```
        elseif outputs(i) >= 0.9
                out(i)=6;            end;end;
      out1=single(out');
 % CSA Final Accuracy
      psomse=mse(out1,targets);
      MSEError=abs(mse(targets)-mse(out1));
      cnt=0;
      for i=1:sizenet
          if out1(i)~= targets(i)
              cnt=cnt+1;
          end;
      end;
     fin=cnt*100/ sizenet;
     psoacc=(100-fin)-psomse;

%% Step 5, Display the classification result

figure
set(gcf, 'Position',  [50, 100, 1300, 300])
cmpso = confusionchart(out1,targets);
cmpso.Title = (['CSA NN Classification =  ' num2str(psoacc) '%']);

%%%%%% Functions description %%%%%%%%%%

%% Crow Search Algorithm NN training

function [Network2  BestCost] = NBCSA(Network,Xtr,Ytr)

IW = Network.IW{1,1}; IW_Num = numel(IW);
LW = Network.LW{2,1}; LW_Num = numel(LW);
b1 = Network.b{1,1}; b1_Num = numel(b1);
b2 = Network.b{2,1}; b2_Num = numel(b2);
TotalNum = IW_Num + LW_Num + b1_Num + b2_Num;
NPar = TotalNum;

% Problem, and CSA parameters declaration
pd=NPar;
N=20;
AP=0.1;
fl=1.5;

% Randomly initialization of the particles (crows) between lower and
% upper bounds
l= -1;
u= 1;
for i=1:N
    for j=1:pd
```

```
        x(i,j)=l-(l-u)*rand;
    end
end

% Evaluation of the population using the cost function

xn=x';
ft = fitness(xn,Xtr,Ytr,Network, N);

% Save the population and they fitness in memory
mem=x;
fit_mem=ft;

% The CSA generates new solutions where crows chase other crows and
% lying randomly through the search space
tmax=100;
for t=1:tmax
    num=ceil(N*rand(1,N));
    for i=1:N
        if rand>AP
            xnew(i,:)= x(i,:)+fl*rand*(mem(num(i),:)-x(i,:));
        else
            for j=1:pd
                xnew(i,j)=l-(l-u)*rand;
            end
        end
    end
% Evaluation of the new population using the cost function
xn=xnew';
ft = fitness(xn,Xtr,Ytr,Network, N);

% Update position and memory
    for i=1:N
        if xnew(i,:)>=l & xnew(i,:)<=u
            x(i,:)=xnew(i,:);
            if ft(i)<fit_mem(i)
                mem(i,:)=xnew(i,:);
                fit_mem(i)=ft(i);
            end
        end
    end
end

% Display the best particle and its fitness value
[a, b] = min(fit_mem); respf = ['Best fitness:'];
respp = ['Best particle (crow):'];
disp (respf); min(fit_mem)
```

```
disp (respp); resp = mem(b,:);
% best = resp(ind_me2m(:,b))
Network2 = NetConstruct(Network,mem(b,:));
BestCost = min(fit_mem);

end

%% fitness function
function ft = fitness(xn,Xtr,Ytr,Network, N)
    ft = zeros(N,1);
        for ii = 1:N
            X = xn(:,ii);
            Network = NetConstruct(Network,X);
            YtrNet = sim(Network,Xtr')';
            C = mse(YtrNet - Ytr);
            ft(ii,1) = C;
        end
end

%% Network construction
function Network2 = NetConstruct(Network,X)
    IW = Network.IW{1,1}; IW_Num = numel(IW);
    LW = Network.LW{2,1}; LW_Num = numel(LW);
    b1 = Network.b{1,1}; b1_Num = numel(b1);
    b2 = Network.b{2,1}; b2_Num = numel(b2);
    IWs = X(1:IW_Num); IW = reshape(IWs,size(IW,1),size(IW,2));
    LWs = X(IW_Num+1:IW_Num+LW_Num);
    LW = reshape(LWs,size(LW,1),size(LW,2));
    b1s = X(IW_Num+LW_Num+1:IW_Num+LW_Num+b1_Num);
    b1 = reshape(b1s,size(b1,1),size(b1,2));
    b2s = X(IW_Num+LW_Num+b1_Num+1:IW_Num+LW_Num+b1_Num+b2_Num);
    b2 = reshape(b2s,size(b2,1),size(b2,2));
    Network2 = Network;
    Network2.IW{1,1} = IW;
    Network2.LW{2,1} = LW;
    Network2.b{1,1} = b1;
    Network2.b{2,1} = b2;
end
```

When the network is generated, the CSA is employed to improve the internal parameters of the NN to perform a better classification of the data. In this case, the optimization technique (CSA) is called a function which is described in the section of functions description, in this section the CSA employs its search strategy for determining the best solution considering the classification data as is shown in Step 3. Once the result of the CSA is performed the parameters are used for generating the final NN trained for the specific task. Step 4 determines the error and the mislabeled data to show the classification result using a confusion matrix. Finally, in Step 5 the result is displayed showing the right and worn classification as is shown in Figure 9.10.

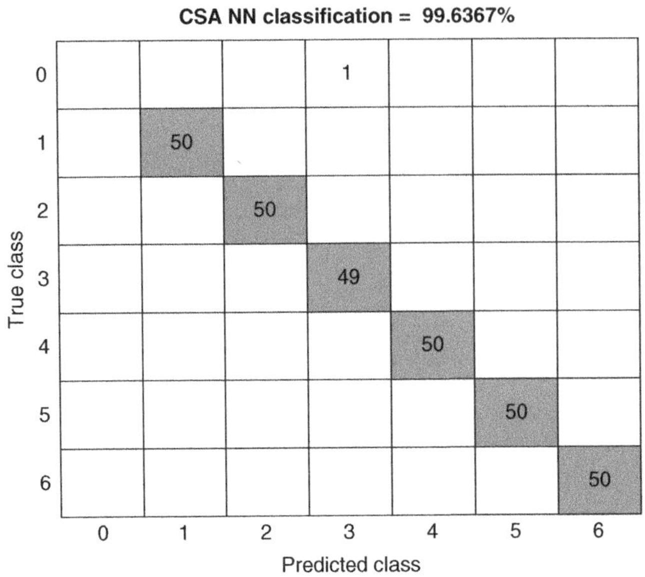

Figure 9.10 Result of classification using the CSA_NN and the percentage of accuracy.

References

Askarzadeh, A. (2016). A novel metaheuristic method for solving constrained engineering optimization problems: Crow search algorithm. *Computers and Structures* 169: 1–12. https://doi.org/10.1016/j.compstruc.2016.03.001.

Biau, G. and Devroye, L. (2015). *Lectures on the Nearest Neighbor Method*. Retrieved 27 August 2023, from http://www.springer.com/series/13852.

Buniyaadi, A., Taufique, S.K.T., and Kumar, V. (2020). Self-recognition in corvids: evidence from the mirror-mark test in Indian house crows (*Corvus splendens*). *Journal of Ornithology* 161 (2): 341–350. https://doi.org/10.1007/s10336-019-01730-2.

Farhat, N.H. (1992). Photonit neural networks and learning mathines the role of electron-trapping materials. *IEEE Expert-Intelligent Systems and Their Applications* 7 (5): 63–72. https://doi.org/10.1109/64.163674.

Hosmer, D.W., Lemeshow, S., and Sturdivant, R.X. (1989). *Applied Logistic Regression*, 3e. Wiley. https://www.wiley.com/en-us/Applied+Logistic+Regression%2C+3rd+Edition-p-9780470582473.

Meraihi, Y., Gabis, A.B., Ramdane-Cherif, A. et al. (2021). A comprehensive survey of Crow Search Algorithm and its applications. *Artificial Intelligence Review* 54 (4): 2669–2716. https://doi.org/10.1007/s10462-020-09911-9.

Mousavi, S.M.H., MiriNezhad, S.Y., Mosleh, M.S. et al. (2017). A PSO fuzzy-expert system: as an assistant for specifying the acceptance by NOET measures, at PH.D level. In: *2017 Artificial Intelligence and Signal Processing Conference (AISP)*, 11–18. https://doi.org/10.1109/AISP.2017.8324116.

dos Santos Coelho, L., Klein, C.E., Mariani, V.C. et al. (2018). Electromagnetic optimization based on gaussian crow search approach. In: *2018 International Symposium on Power Electronics, Electrical Drives, Automation and Motion (SPEEDAM)*, 1107–1112. https://doi.org/10.1109/SPEEDAM.2018.8445209.

Shalev-Shwartz, S. and Ben-David, S. (2013). Understanding machine learning: from theory to algorithms. In: *Understanding Machine Learning: From Theory to Algorithms*, vol. 9781107057. https://doi.org/10.1017/CBO9781107298019 Cambridge University Press.

Shalev-Shwartz, S. and Srebro, N. (2008). SVM optimization: inverse dependence on training set size. *Proceedings of the 25th International Conference on Machine Learning*, 928–935.

Wickramasinghe, I. and Kalutarage, H. (2021). Naive Bayes: applications, variations and vulnerabilities: a review of literature with code snippets for implementation. *Soft Computing* 25 (3): 2277–2293. https://doi.org/10.1007/s00500-020-05297-6.

10

Metaheuristic Methods for Clustering

10.1 Introduction

Clustering is one of the most important tasks in machine learning projects. Clustering is a set of techniques which aim to create homogeneous groups of objects or entities called clusters. Each group of objects share similarities among their elements. Different clusters yield to different categorization or classes among data. In most of the data science projects, after the data cleaning process and preparation, clustering methods are often carried out before any analytical modeling.

Clustering falls under the category of unsupervised learning (Ezugwu et al. 2022). That means there is no labeled class for a given dataset. The objective of each clustering algorithm is to form groups of elements without prior knowledge of each input data vector. Each clustering algorithm assigns membership values to all data linked to each cluster center. However, even when clustering algorithms are essential techniques for data analysis process, they contain some limitation such as initialization, false positive response, and sensitivity to data outliers.

On the other hand, metaheuristic methods have been widely used in several disciplines since they employ different search mechanisms to determine optimal solutions in complex optimization tasks. Recently, metaheuristic approaches have been applied to overcome some difficulties of clustering. The flexibility of metaheuristics can reformulate the clustering task by improving the performance of the clustered outcomes (Dhaenens and Jourdan 2022).

In the year 2009, Xin-She Yang and Suash Deb proposed an evolutionary algorithm based on the phenomenon of nest parasitism which is present in some kind of birds, fish, or insects. Within nature, there is a kind of bird called a cuckoo bird, which represents a species that uses the phenomenon of parasitism to lay eggs in the nests of other species. The Cuckoo Search Method (CSM) has been proposed as a model that mimics the natural behavior of cuckoo birds that computationally solves optimization problems.

This chapter describes the CSM as a metaheuristic optimization algorithm for improving the clustering process of K-Means (KM) clustering algorithm widely used in several applications (Wilkin and Huang 2008). Throughout the chapter, MATLAB will be used to implement CSM to reformulate some widely used clustering algorithms. This hands-on approach will enable readers to gain practical experience and become proficient in using metaheuristic methods to improve the clustering process.

Machine Learning and Metaheuristic Computation, First Edition.
Erik Cuevas, Jorge Galvez, Omar Avalos, and Fernando Wario.

10.2 Cuckoo Search Method (CSM)

In the year 2005, Robert Payne describes in his book entitled, "The Cuckoos" the bird class of cuckoos (Payne and Sorenson 2005). In his work, Payne describes that this class of organisms promotes what is known as nest parasitism. This consists of the female depositing her eggs in the nests of other species, where the host parents feed and raise the cuckoos. This natural mechanism of selection of nests foreign to the biological parents of a cuckoo bird generates a controversy, since when the cuckoo egg opens, the new individual will do its best to throw the other eggs, so that this is the only one that can receive food from the host parents.

The phenomenon of nest parasitism consists of the female cuckoo depositing her eggs in nests belonging to other bird species, because the female cuckoo is not in charge of caring for and feeding her young. However, the controversy begins when the hatchling breaks her egg and begins to throw the other eggs or hatchlings out of the nest. This mechanism promotes the criterion of natural selection, which indicates that only the strongest individual is able to survive.

In 2009, Yang and Deb (2009) proposed an evolutionary algorithm based on the nest parasitism behavior of some bird, fish, and insect species. The CSM algorithm uses nest parasitism behavior as a search operator and at the same time uses Lévy flights (Pavlyukevich 2007) to mimic the flight of the cuckoo bird. The combination of these two operators makes the CSM algorithm an interesting proposal since, thanks to the combination of its operators, the optimal solution of an optimization problem is obtained in an efficient way.

In the CSM, the metaphor of nest parasitism behavior in cuckoo birds is used to formulate a search operator, where the candidate solution (cuckoo egg) is the particle that explores in a certain search space (nest). Likewise, the flight performed by these birds to deposit eggs in host nests can be emulated based on what is known as a Lévy flight. The Lévy flight describes a random behavior, which shares similarities with the trajectories commonly used by birds, insects, and other animals to move in their habitat.

Additionally, the CSM has an iterative structure. That is, it presents similarities with other metaheuristic techniques. The iterative nature of CSM lies in using a set of candidate solutions, operated under a context of exploration (Lévy flight) and exploitation (nest parasitism), which together achieve optimal solutions for solving optimization problems. It should be noted that, in the same way, the CSM algorithm also uses the concept of survival of the best individual, since, as can be observed, the behavior of nest parasitism indicates that each cuckoo brood throws the remaining broods out of the nest, so that only this one is left and can survive and develop.

10.3 Search Strategy for CSM

The CSM is based on the natural interaction of cuckoo birds with their environment. That is, female cuckoo birds make a journey from one nest to another of different bird species, leaving behind an egg in each of the nests she visits. This causes the host bird of a certain nest to take care of all the eggs in its nest, including those of a cuckoo bird. Naturally, when a cuckoo bird leaves an egg in a certain nest, the egg it leaves will have to have a certain color similar to the eggs found in that nest, this to avoid suspicion from the host birds. The purpose of leaving eggs in nests is for the host bird to take care of the offspring. That is, the host bird is in charge of feeding and protecting the cuckoo brood.

When the cuckoo hatchling breaks its egg, it begins to get stronger day by day, which means that if there are other eggs or hatchlings in its nest, the cuckoo hatchling pushes the rest out of the nest until it is left alone in the nest. The objective of this action is that the host bird feeds and protects only the cuckoo brood, since following the paradigm of natural selection, the cuckoo bird proved to be the strongest individual in the nest.

This survival mechanism of the cuckoo hatchlings can be translated into a search strategy for an optimization algorithm, since, as can be analyzed, at the moment that the cuckoo hatchling breaks its egg, it will try to be the best individual in that population, which means that this individual will seek to have the best position in the nest.

Because cuckoo birds present a complex mechanism of selection and reproduction, abstracting all these natural situations to obtain an algorithmic structure capable of solving optimization problems is a complicated process. In order to simplify the natural process involved in the nest parasitism behavior of cuckoo birds and to obtain a computational representation, it is necessary to propose certain rules that, in general terms, mimic these concepts. Three rules that abstract the interaction mechanisms of cuckoo birds are described below.

- Each cuckoo bird carries one egg at a time, and deposits it in a random nest from a possible set of nests.
- The nest containing the eggs that represent the best solution will be taken into account for subsequent generations.
- The host bird will be able to discover whether or not an egg belongs to its nest. That is, each host bird when it arrives at its nest, it can either attend to the cuckoo egg or get rid of it, or else the host bird can leave the nest, since it could be understood that the nest does not belong to it.

Another of the fundamental aspects to be reviewed when discussing this algorithm is the way in which it can mimic the flight that cuckoo birds make to deposit eggs in host nests. Traditionally, evolutionary computational algorithms use random values in their operators to simulate a stochastic process abstracted from nature, social aspects, and even physical aspects. It is well known that an evolutionary computation algorithm without a random part will tend to fail to obtain the solution of an optimization problem. For this reason, metaheuristic algorithms use *Random Walk* to produce new solutions in the search space. However, random walk presents some problems when used in multidimensional spaces, as it can produce duplicate values across iterations. Faced with such a circumstance, the need to model more complex behaviors of nature, Lévy flights offer an interesting and powerful alternative without incurring the problems of random walk. The main advantage of Lévy flight is that they can mimic the natural flight of birds, insects, and other animals in a computationally efficient way (Chawla and Duhan 2018).

In response to this discussion, the CSM uses Lévy flights to mimic the flight of the cuckoo bird when depositing eggs in host nests. This causes the CSM to better explore the entire search space involved in the optimization process.

Finally, the CSM, like most metaheuristic algorithms, uses a population of individuals, where each one of them is considered as a candidate solution to a given optimization problem. Computationally speaking, each of the members of the population are elements that make up a multidimensional space.

In order to develop the ideas of the biological process of the cuckoo birds for the formulation of the CSM, the CSM can be described in several stages. The first one consists of the initialization of a population that randomly generates solutions (eggs) where these solutions are interpreted as positions in the search space. The second computational procedure involves the calculation of the random movement within the search space. For this stage, the Lévy flight is used to imitate the flight of the cuckoo bird to deposit its eggs in host nests. The third operation replaces the current solutions following a random principle. Finally, the last stage of this algorithm consists in selecting in an elite way the best solution in each of the generations of the algorithm.

In the following subsections, we describe the population structure in the CSM as well as each of the steps mentioned above in order to formulate an algorithmic structure.

10.3.1 Initialization

Within the optimization process of the CSM, it is required to have a set of N solution vectors (individuals) that will evolve through the generations. For this, in CSM, a population of individuals (eggs) $\mathbf{X}$, will be composed by a set of parameter vectors $\{\mathbf{x}_1^k, \mathbf{x}_2^k, \dots, \mathbf{x}_N^k\}$ where each parameter vector $\mathbf{x}_i^k$, represents a position in a d-dimensional vector space $\{x_1, x_2, \dots, x_d\}$ that defines the search space of the problem to be solved.

Like most evolutionary algorithms, the CSM begins by generating an initial population of individuals (solutions) uniformly distributed and spread over the entire domain of the search space. Each individual in the population will act as a d-dimensional vector to solve an optimization problem.

At this stage, the limits under which the population will operate by means of the search operators must be indicated. These limits are defined as lower limit $\mathbf{lb} = [lb_1, lb_2, \dots, lb_d]$ and upper limit $\mathbf{ub} = [ub_1, ub_2, \dots, ub_d]$. Once these bounds have been specified, each of the individuals will be generated as follows:

$$\mathbf{X} = \mathbf{lb} + \mathbf{r}(0, 1) \cdot (\mathbf{ub} - \mathbf{lb}) \tag{10.1}$$

where $\mathbf{lb}$ and $\mathbf{ub}$ represent the lower and upper bound vectors respectively, while $\mathbf{r}(0, 1)$ denotes a vector of random numbers within the uniformly distributed interval (0,1).

10.3.2 Lévy Flight

In metaheuristics, randomness is considered one of the pillars under which evolutionary algorithms are defined. Without randomness, many evolutionary algorithms could not work when trying to find an optimal solution to an optimization problem with multimodality. Since a multimodal function contains multiple convexities (minima or maxima) which make it more complicated to solve. Under this circumstance, an evolutionary algorithm without randomness presents stagnation in its performance as well as an algorithm based on derivative.

To solve the problem presented by classical optimization techniques, evolutionary algorithms use randomness as an operating mechanism that allows them to escape from the local minima or maxima of a function so that the search strategy focuses on finding the global optimal solutions (global minimum or maximum).

The technique most used by evolutionary algorithms is the so-called *Random Walk*. What this technique does is to perturb in a very small proportion the neighborhood of an individual, so that it escapes from a local minimum or maximum or, failing that, helps in the intensification of the search process. The latter significantly improves the exploitation stage of any evolutionary algorithm. However, random walk presents some drawbacks that make it prone to fail in situations when the dimensionality of a certain optimization problem increases.

To overcome these drawbacks, some random mechanisms have been proposed in the literature. Among them, the one that has been shown to perform better than random walking is the well-known Lévy flight. Lévy flight generates random movements using a Gamma distribution to mimic most of the biological processes found in nature, such as the flight of birds, the trajectories performed by a school of fish, etc.

Under this procedure, and following the analogy of cuckoo birds, the cuckoo bird flies through an environment locating possible nests of birds of different kinds in order to deposit its eggs in those nests. This is done by the cuckoo bird so that another bird will be in charge of raising; feeding and protecting the cuckoo egg that was deposited. Since the flight of the cuckoo bird is a complex behavior, the way in which it could be computationally abstracted is by means of the mechanism offered by Lévy's flight.

The effect of calculating a Lévy flight causes that, during the optimization process, the search strategy for the optimal solution is gradually refined in each generation. Above all, it is important in the exploitation stage of the CS algorithm, remembering that the exploitation stage refers to the way in which search agents use the information of their environment to be able to position themselves in strategic zones of the search space. Thus, increasing the probabilities of finding the global solution to the optimization problem. In order to calculate the Lévy flight, the initialization stage of the algorithm had to be previously executed.

Once the initialization process described in the previous section has been executed, the CS algorithm will use the information provided by the current population and this will be used to calculate the Lévy flight of each of the individuals in the population. It is here that the CS algorithm will aim to relocate the solutions to other areas of the search space to increase the chance of finding the optimal solution. Thanks to the calculation of the Lévy flight for each individual, the CS algorithm has gained popularity in recent years, since, as will be seen later, the calculation of the Lévy flight is not highly complex.

Within the specifications of the CS algorithm, the Lévy flight is used to improve the global search stage. Lévy flights are produced by a Gamma distribution, which significantly improves the exploration stage of the evolutionary algorithm, in contrast to the random movements produced by techniques based on random walk. Lévy flights represent one of the most powerful operators in evolutionary algorithms since they mimic complex behaviors such as bird flight. The calculation of a Lévy flight can be mathematically defined as follows:

$$L \sim \frac{\lambda \Gamma(\lambda) \sin(\pi \lambda / 2)}{\pi s^{1+\lambda}}, \quad s \gg s_0 > 0 \tag{10.2}$$

where $\Gamma(\lambda)$ represents the Gamma distribution and s represents the step size. To perform an efficient implementation of the Lévy flights described in Eq. 10.2, the Mantegna algorithm is used (Mantegna 1994). For the implementation of Mantegna's algorithm, some computations are required, for which the following is assumed:

$$s_i = \frac{\boldsymbol{u}}{|\boldsymbol{v}|^{\frac{1}{\beta}}} \tag{10.3}$$

where vectors $\boldsymbol{u} = \{u_1, \ldots, u_d\}$ and $\boldsymbol{v} = \{v_1, \ldots, v_d\}$ are d-dimensional vectors and $\beta = \frac{3}{2}$. For each element of the vectors $\mathbf{u}$ and $\mathbf{v}$, the way to obtain is described below:

$$u \sim N\left(0, \sigma_u^2\right), \qquad v \sim N\left(0, \sigma_v^2\right)$$

$$\sigma_u = \left(\frac{\Gamma(1+\beta) \cdot \mathrm{sen}\left(\pi \cdot \frac{\beta}{2}\right)}{\Gamma((1+\beta)/2) \cdot \beta \cdot 2^{(\beta-1)/2}} \right)^{1/\beta}, \qquad \sigma_v = 1 \tag{10.4}$$

Finally, Lévy's flight is obtained, as described below:

$$L_i = 0.01 \cdot s_i \left(\boldsymbol{x}_i^k - \mathbf{x}_{\text{best}}^k\right) \tag{10.5}$$

where $\boldsymbol{x}_i^k$ is the current (individual) solution at the k-th iteration and $\mathbf{x}_{\text{best}}^k$ is considered as the best global solution so far. Under this circumstance, the new solution produced using the described Lévy flight calculation $\boldsymbol{x}_i^{k+1}$ is calculated as:

$$\boldsymbol{x}_i^{k+1} = \boldsymbol{x}_i^k + L_i \tag{10.6}$$

10.3.3 Solution Replacement

In the CS algorithm, once the Lévy flight value for an individual is calculated, it has to be decided whether the solution obtained by Eq. 10.6 will replace the current individual $\boldsymbol{x}_i^k$. Within the bioinspired analogy of the cuckoo bird, once the cuckoo bird flies into its environment and deposits its egg in the host nest, it is now that the host bird discovers the cuckoo egg. When the host bird discovers that it has an extra egg in its nest, it has three possible actions, one is to abandon the nest, another possible action is for the host bird to drop the cuckoo egg, and the third is for the host bird to adopt the cuckoo egg. If the host bird succeeds in adopting the cuckoo egg, as soon as it hatches and begins to grow stronger day by day, it will do everything possible to throw the other eggs that share the nest.

The cuckoo brood performs this procedure to obtain all the food and care that the host bird provides. This mechanism is based on the idea of survival of the principle of natural selection, which implies that only those individuals that manage to adapt better to their environment will be able to survive in subsequent generations.

The computational way to abstract the bioinspired behavior that takes place between the cuckoo egg with its host nest lies directly in the exploitation stage of the CS algorithm. Recalling that the exploitation stage of any evolutionary algorithm aims to refine the search strategy in promising areas within the search space. In the CS algorithm, the operation of replacing the solutions aims at perturbing the positions of the individuals by considering the information of the neighboring solutions. This mechanism efficiently reflects the cuckoo egg metaphor, increasing the possibility of finding the global optimal solution.

Under this operation, a set of solutions is selected in a random way to be replaced by a new value. Each individual $\boldsymbol{x}_i^k$ can be selected by a probability $p_a \epsilon [0, 1]$. For implementation, a random number r_1 is generated within the interval $[0, 1]$. If r_1 is smaller than p_a, the solution $\boldsymbol{x}_i^k$ is selected and modified by Eq. 10.7, otherwise, the solution $\boldsymbol{x}_i^k$ remains unchanged. This procedure can be summarized by the following model.

$$\boldsymbol{x}_i^{k+1} = \begin{cases} \boldsymbol{x}_i^k + \mathbf{r}(\mathbf{0}, \mathbf{1}) \cdot \left(\boldsymbol{x}_j^k - \boldsymbol{x}_h^k\right), & \text{if } r_1 < p_a \\ \boldsymbol{x}_i^k, & \text{otherwise} \end{cases} \tag{10.7}$$

where $\mathbf{r}(\mathbf{0}, \mathbf{1})$ is a normally distributed random number, and the subscripts j and h correspond to integer random numbers in the interval $[1, N]$.

10.3.4 Elitist Selection

Another fundamental pillar of evolutionary algorithms lies in the principle of survival described in the process of natural selection. That is, only the strongest individuals will survive, while the weakest individuals will die. Making the analogy of this fact in an evolutionary methodology, in each iteration of the CS algorithm the best solution (global minimum/global maximum) obtained up to that moment will be maintained. This is an illusion to the natural selection process since, during the optimization process, individuals may represent a very good solution, but if the elitist principle is not considered, in the following iterations, it may diverge from the optimal solution. Thus, the algorithm may not be able to solve the optimization problem in question.

The elitist mechanism used in the CS algorithm is an easy procedure to implement, since it is only necessary to check the quality of the solutions and keep the individual (solution) that presents the best value in its evaluation of the objective function.

In the CS algorithm the elitist criterion is based on the following rule. If the value resulting from the evaluation of the produced solution Eq. 10.7, is better than the value resulting from the evaluation of the current solution $\boldsymbol{x}_i^k$, then the solution $\boldsymbol{x}_i^{k+1}$ replaces the current solution $\boldsymbol{x}_i^k$, otherwise, the solution $\boldsymbol{x}_i^k$ will remain in the next iteration. This mechanism can be summarized as shown below:

$$\boldsymbol{x}_i^{k+1} = \begin{Bmatrix} \boldsymbol{x}_i^{k+1}, & \text{if } J\left(\boldsymbol{x}_i^{k+1}\right) < J\left(\boldsymbol{x}_i^{k}\right) \\ \boldsymbol{x}_i^{k}, & \text{otherwise} \end{Bmatrix} \tag{10.8}$$

10.4 Computational Procedure

As described in the previous section, the CS algorithm drives the search strategy toward the global optimum value using four operations that define the bioinspired behavior of the cuckoo bird. The first operation is the so-called initialization. At this stage, a set of individuals is created and initialized. This set represents the solution vectors that will act as search agents in an optimization problem.

The next operation is the calculation of the Lévy flight. Lévy flights represent one of the most powerful and efficient mechanisms to mimic complex behaviors found in nature, such as the flight of birds, some insects, and some schools of fish, among others. This mechanism directly promotes the exploration stage of the CS algorithm, since the type of motion obtained causes the solution vectors to spread throughout the search space. The third operation is the replacement of the solutions, this is where the search process is refined in such a way that each of the solution vectors has a higher probability of finding the global optimal solution in promising zones of the search space that are smaller than the zones explored by the Lévy flights. Within the stages of an evolutionary algorithm, exploitation refines the search process, thus improving the approximation of the optimal solution. Due to this fact, the better the performance of an exploitation operator the better the solution obtained. For this purpose, the CS algorithm is based on a simple rule, the current solution will be replaced by a particle that is randomly generated using information from other solutions. This makes the refined search process start to converge gradually to the global optimal solution. Finally, the fourth operation is based on the elitist selection process, which considers that in each generation of the CS algorithm the best solution obtained so far will be kept on record. The final effect of this selection is that the global optimum solution will be maintained, whether it is a minimum or a maximum, depending on the problem statement.

10.4.1 Metaheuristic Operators for CSM

For each of the stages of the CS algorithm seen in the previous section, a set of specific steps is necessary in order to implement the operators required for the CS algorithm. Each of these steps

Table 10.1 Typical parameter configuration for the CSM.

Parameter
p_a
0.25

represents a characteristic behavior of the solution vectors in each of the iterations. Since most evolutionary algorithms have configuration parameters, the CS algorithm is no exception. However, the CS algorithm requires only one parameter: p_a, which is referred to as the discovery probability. Table 10.1 shows the typical setting of the single parameter of the CS algorithm.

The generic algorithm used by the search process of the CSM can be summarized in the Pseudo-code 10.1:

Pseudo-code 10.1 ***General Procedure to Implement the CSM***

Input: *N*, *Max_gen*, $k = 0$.
$\mathbf{X}^k \leftarrow$ **Initialize**(N); **Step 1**
while $k<=Maxgen$ **do**
$\mathbf{X}^{k+1} \leftarrow$ **LévyFlight**($\mathbf{X}^k$) **Step 2**
$x_i^{k+1} \leftarrow$ **SolutionReplacement**($\mathbf{X}^{k+1}$) **Step 3**
$\mathbf{g} \leftarrow$ **ElitistSelection**($\mathbf{X}^{k+1}$); **Step 4**
$K \leftarrow k+1$
end **while**
Output: $\mathbf{g}$

In general, for each of the individuals in the population, Steps 2–4 described in Pseudo-code 10.1 are executed generation after generation in order to obtain a global optimal solution. The initialization of the solution vectors is executed only once, which is when the CS algorithm starts, once the evolution process is initiated, the Lévy flight is calculated for each of the solution vectors and in the same way this movement is refined by applying the replacement operation of the solutions so that, finally, the optimal solution of a certain optimization problem is obtained by means of an elitist criterion.

Figure 10.1 illustrates the flowchart describing the complete process carried out by the search strategy of the CS algorithm. As illustrated in the diagram, the CS algorithm initializes a set of initial solution vectors $\mathbf{X}^0 = \{\mathbf{x}_1^0, \mathbf{x}_2^0, \dots, \mathbf{x}_N^0\}$, randomly generated within the bounds of the search space. Subsequently, the algorithm executes the Lévy flight operators, replacement of the solutions and elitist selection criterion as shown in Pseudo-code 10.1 considering the parameter settings described in Table 10.1. Finally, when the total number of generations that make up the whole optimization process of the problem to be solved has elapsed, the algorithm returns the best solution found by this process.

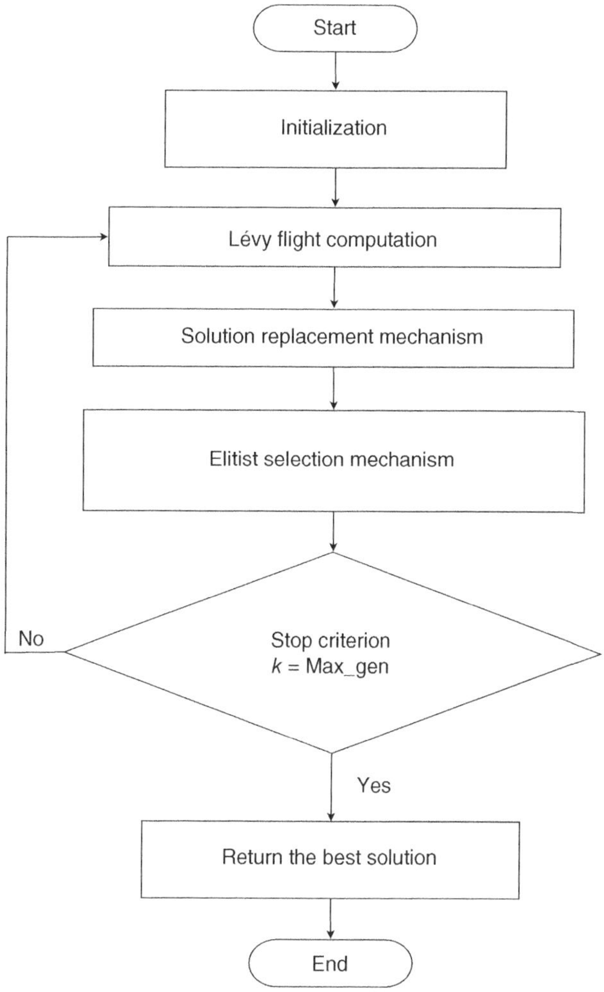

Figure 10.1 Flowchart of the computational process for the CSM.

10.5 Implementation of the CSM in MATLAB

In Algorithm 10.1, it is described the MATLAB code for the CSM. To observe the functionality of the algorithm, the code encodes a benchmark function commonly used in performance testing related to the optimization of continuous functions. In this example, the Schwefel function is implemented, so that the reader can observe the functionality of the CSM considering a minimization process.

The Schwefel function exhibits a non-convex unimodal surface in a two-dimensional space and contains single global minima and multiple local minima. The non-convex feature is used to test the scaling of the search strategy of the CSM method when it operates over surfaces with many local optima. On the other hand, the Schwefel function is continuous and non-convex, which indicates that not any optimization technique either classical or metaheuristic can reach the global optimum. The mathematical model of the Schwefel function is as follows:

$$f(x) = 418.9829 \cdot d - \sum_{i=1}^{d} x_i \cdot \sin(\sqrt{|x_i|})$$
$$-500 \leq x_i \leq 500, \quad i = 1, 2, \ldots, d \tag{10.9}$$

Finally, so that the reader can see the behavior of the datapoints on the Schwefel function surface, at each iteration the movement of the solutions (datapoints) on the Schwefel surface is plotted.

```
%Algorithm 10.1
%% INITIAL CONFIGURATION FOR THE OPTIMIZATION PROCESS
%Clear memory and Close Matlab windows
clear all;
close all;

%% Step 1 INITIALIZATION
%The size of the population is established
n = 50;
%The maximum number of iterations is established
N_IterTotal = 1000;
%The number of decision variables is established
dim = 2;
%The limits of the search space are defined
lb = -500;
ub = 500;
%Parameter initialization of the CSM
pa=0.25;
%Iteration counter
iter = 0;
%Initialization of the initial population
if size(ub,2)==1
    nest=rand(n,dim).*(ub-lb)+lb;
end
if size(ub,2)>1
    for i=1:dim
        high=ub(i);down=lb(i);
        nest(:,i)=rand(n,1).*(high-down)+down;
    end
end
%The fitness values of the initial population are obtained
for j=1:size(nest,1)
    fitness(j) = ObjectiveFunction(nest(j,:),dim);
end
```

```
%The best solution is obtained from the initial population
[fitnessXbest,K]=min(fitness) ;
xBest=nest(K,:);
%The plot the function to be optimized is computed
 if dim<=2
    rangeUpLb=ub-lb;
    figure(1)
    x=[lb:rangeUpLb/100:ub];
    y=x;
    [xg,yg]=meshgrid(x,y);
    [row,col]=size(xg);
    for l=1:col
        for h=1:row
            z(h,l)=ObjectiveFunction([xg(h,l),yg(h,l)],dim);
        end
    end
 end
%Iterative process of the algorithm
while iter <= N_IterTotal

    %% Step 2 LÉVY FLIGHT
    beta=3/2;
    sigma=(gamma(1+beta)*sin(pi*beta/2)/(gamma((1+beta)/2)*beta*
2^((beta-1)/2)))^(1/beta);

    for j=1:n
        s=nest(j,:);
        %Mantegna's Algorithm
        u=randn(size(s))*sigma;
        v=randn(size(s));
        step=u./abs(v).^(1/beta);
        stepsize=0.01*step.*(s-xBest);
        s=s+stepsize.*randn(size(s));
        if size(ub,2)==1
                for i = 1:dim
                    if (s(1,i) < lb)
                        s(1,i) = rand(1,1).*(ub-lb)+lb;
                    end
                    if (s(1,i) > ub)
                        s(1,i) = rand(1,1).*(ub-lb)+lb;
                    end
                end
        end
        if size(ub,2) > 1
                 for i = 1:dim
                    high=ub(i);down2=lb(i);
                    if (s(1,i) < down2)
```

```
                    s(1,i) = rand(1,1).*(high-down2)+down2;
                end
                if (s(1,i) > high)
                    s(1,i) = rand(1,1).*(high-down2)+down2;
                end
            end
        end
        nest(j,:)=s;
    end
    for j=1:size(nest,1)
        fnew = ObjectiveFunction(nest(j,:),dim);
        fitness(j)=fnew;
    end
    [fitnessXbest,K]=min(fitness);
    xBest = nest(K,:);

    %% Step 3 Solution Replacement
    K=rand(size(nest))>pa;
    stepsize=rand*(nest(randperm(n),:)-nest(randperm(n),:));
    new_nest=nest+stepsize.*K;
    if size(ub,2)==1
        for j = 1 : size(new_nest,1)
            for i = 1:dim
                if (new_nest(j,i) < lb)
                    new_nest(j,i) = rand(1,1).*(ub-lb)+lb;
                end
                if (new_nest(j,i) > ub)
                    new_nest(j,i) = rand(1,1).*(ub-lb)+lb;
                end
            end
        end
    end
    if size(ub,2) > 1
        for j = 1 :  size(new_nest,1)
            for i = 1:dim
                high=ub(i);down2=lb(i);
                if (new_nest(j,i) < down2)
                    new_nest(j,i) = rand(1,1).*(high-down2)+down2;
                end
                if (new_nest(j,i) > high)
                    new_nest(j,i) = rand(1,1).*(high-down2)+down2;
                end
            end
        end
    end
    for j=1:size(nest,1)
        fnew = ObjectiveFunction(new_nest(j,:),dim);
```

```
            if fnew<=fitness(j)
               fitness(j)=fnew;
               nest(j,:)=new_nest(j,:);
            end
        end

        %% Step 4 Elitist Selection
        [fitnessXbest,K]=min(fitness) ;
        xBest=nest(K,:);
        %The plot the population is generated
        if dim<=2
            surf(xg,yg,z);
            title('Schwefel function')
            hold on
            plot3(nest(:,1),nest(:,2),fitness(1,:),'o','markersize',6,
'markerfacecolor','r');
            plot3(xBest(1),xBest(2),fitnessXbest,'o','markersize',10,
'markerfacecolor','g');
            drawnow;
            hold off
        end
        %Iteration counters
        iter = iter + 1;
        fprintf('Iteration: %d\n',iter);
        fprintf('Best solution: (%d,%d)\n',xBest(1),xBest(2));
        fprintf('Best fitness: %d\n',fitnessXbest);
end

%%OBJECTIVE FUNCTION
%Schwefel function implementation
function fit = ObjectiveFunction(L,dim)
    [N,~]=size(L);
    for i=1:N
        fit(i) = (418.9829*dim)-(sum(L(i,:).*sin(sqrt(abs(L)))));
    end
end
```

The Algorithm 10.1 graphically shows the evolution of the population using the iterative structure of the CSM. The plotted graph is shown in Figure 10.2.

In Algorithm 10.1, the Step 1 configures the initial parameters required by the optimization process. Such configuration relies on setting the maximum number of iterations, the population size, the number of decision variables involved in the optimization process, and the definition of the limits of the search space. The Step 2 defines the computation scheme for the Lévy flight calculation based on the Mantegna's Algorithm. Then, in Step 3 the solution replacement mechanism is employed. Step 4 defines the elitist selection procedure. In the algorithm, the objective function to be optimized is implemented after the definition of the main loop. The objective function considered in this chapter is the well-known Schwefel function.

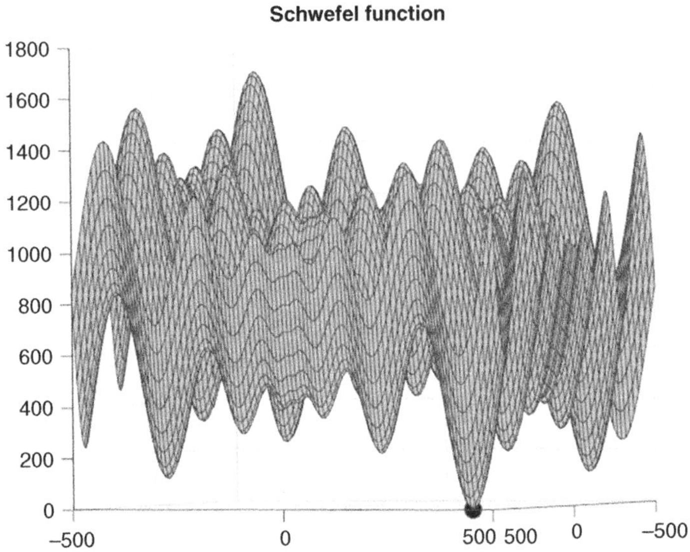

Figure 10.2 The graph of the Schwefel function produced by CSM.

10.6 Cuckoo Search Method for K-Means

K-Means (KM) algorithm is one of the most widely used partitional clustering algorithm. Partitional clustering methods aim to group data vector by optimizing a specific objective function by an iterative process.

KM is considered as an unsupervised learning method which classifies unlabeled data by grouping them by inherent features of the data vectors rather than predefined (supervised) categories. The objective of KM is to separate data vectors into K different clusters while the position of the centroids for each cluster is adjusted at each iteration based of the minimization of the distance among data vectors to their respective centroids.

KM starts by selecting K representative points as initial centroids. Then, each data vector is assigned to its closest centroid. To measure closeness relationship between data vectors and centroids, distance metrics are commonly employed as spatial relationships to measure similarity among two data vectors. Once the initial assignment of data vectors, the position of each centroid is updated. The position adjustment in this step, is computed as the mean values of each coordinate position. Finally, this process repeats until a stop criterion is achieved. The learning process of the KM is based on the iterative process of these two steps. KM is also considered as a greedy algorithm which guarantees to converge into a local minimum. However, the optimization process (minimum distance) is considered as NP-Hard problem (Maronna 2015).

The basic idea behind the KM algorithm is that attributes of an object can be efficiently represented as vectors in a vector space. Within this framework, the primary objective is to minimize the cumulative intra-cluster variance or, equivalently, the standard deviation. To accomplish this process, KM organizes data vectors into clusters, with each cluster characterized by a central point called centroid. Through iterative structure, each centroid is updated according to continuous data assignation to nearest centroids. KM creates clusters that exhibit minimal variance within themselves while maximizing the separation between clusters. This process produces distinct clusters within the dataset, making KM a representative technique to data-driven applications (Ikotun et al. 2023).

The KM method unfolds through a systematic and iterative procedure that can be summarized as follows:

Step 1: Determine the Number of Clusters (K):
As the initial stage, this step involves deciding how many clusters the dataset should be divided into. In KM, the number of clusters is represented by the K. Then, the position of each K cluster is determined. Commonly, the initial positions are random within the data space. As can be concluded, the initial position of each cluster, is the most crucial decision and can significantly impact the quality of the clustering process.

Step 2: Initial Partitioning:
After determining the K number of classes, each data vector is assigned to one of these classes. This assignment can be done in terms of distance relationship among each data vector and each cluster centroid. Data vectors will be assigned to their closest centroids.

Step 3: Centroid Computation:
After the initial assignment, KM updated each cluster centroid. The centroid for each cluster represents the geometric center of all the data vectors within a cluster.

Step 4: Distance Computation:
In this step, KM computes the distance between each data vector and the updated centroids from the previous step for all K clusters.

Step 5: Partition Refinement:
In this step, KM constructs new partitions based on the new distance values from previous step. Each data vector is associated to its closest cluster centroid.

Step 6: Recalculation of Centroids:
After the new partitions are formed, the centroid for each cluster is updated. These updated positions for each centroid represent the new geometric centers of their respective clusters.

Step 7: Iterative Process:
Steps 4 through 6 are iteratively repeated until the stop criterion is achieved. The stop criteria occurs when data assignation does not change or may be any other alternative convergence criterion, such as a predefined number of iterations is met, etc.

As it can be discussed, KM is an iterative procedure which learns how the centroids must be located through the dataset. This iterative procedure allows KM to iteratively refine the clustering solution, seeking to minimize the variance within clusters while maximizing the separation between them. The final outcome is a set of well-defined clusters that effectively group similar data vectors.

The main objective of the KM is to determine the optimal positions of K cluster centroids. This strategy is considered as the learning mechanism of the KM. The positioning of these centroids can significantly influence the clustering solution.

The KM method is a partitional clustering algorithm since it operates by the influence of minimizing the distance between each data vector to each cluster centroid. Mathematically, KM divides a set of n vectors $\mathbf{x}_1, \mathbf{x}_2, \ldots, \mathbf{x}_n$ into m groups $G_1, G_2, \ldots, G_m$. Each group is characterized by its centroid $\mathbf{c}_{1, 2, \ldots, m}$ which is computed by an objective function. Commonly, the cost function in the KM process, is defined in terms of Euclidean distance as follows:

$$J = \sum_{l=1}^{m} J_i = \sum_{l=1}^{m} \sum_{(k,\, \mathbf{x}_k \in G_i)} \|\mathbf{x}_k - \mathbf{c}_i\|^2, \tag{10.10}$$

where J_i represents the cost attributed to i-th cluster. The value of J_i depends on the spatial distribution of the vectors belonging to G_i and the position of its centroid $\mathbf{c}_i$.

The division of the elements in each group is defined by an element u_{ij}. This binary factor determines the correspondence of a vector to a group. Under these circumstances u_{ij} is 1 if the data $\mathbf{x}_j$ belongs to the group G_i and zero in case of nonmembership. Thus considering u_{ij} Eq. 10.9 can be reformulated as follows:

$$J = \sum_{i=1}^{m} \sum_{j=1}^{n} u_{ij} \cdot \|\mathbf{x}_j - \mathbf{c}_i\|^2 \tag{10.11}$$

which represents the sum of the squared distances of each data $\mathbf{x}_j$ assigned to the group G_i. According to the objective function from Eq. 10.11. Finding the values of u_{ij} and $\mathbf{c}_i$ that minimize J, solve the clustering association problem.

The KM method minimizes the objective function J through an iterative procedure that is based on two steps. In the first step, the positions of the centroids are fixed respect to u_{ij} in the minimization of the objective function J. In the second step, the objective function J is minimized respect to each centroid $\mathbf{c}_i$ while the values u_{ij} are fixed. These two steps repeat until stop criterion is achieved.

In the first step of the process, the values of u_{ij} are first determined. Due to the inherent nature of the objective function J is linear with respect to u_{ij}, a closed form of computing the values of u_{ij} can then be obtained. Each term u_{ij} involves a different and independent group G_i, so it is possible to find each term u_{ij} separately. Under such circumstances, the value of one is chosen for u_{ij}whenever the centroid represents the minimum distance relation $\|\mathbf{x}_j - \mathbf{c}_i\|^2$. This can be mathematically formulated as:

$$u_{ij} = \begin{cases} 1 & \text{if } i = \arg\min_{l} \|\mathbf{x}_j - \mathbf{c}_i\|^2 \\ 0 & \text{otherwise} \end{cases} \tag{10.12}$$

In the second step of the process, the values of $\mathbf{c}_i$ are determined by holding fixed the values of previously u_{ij} calculated in the first step. Due to the inherent nature of the objective function J is quadratic in terms of $\mathbf{c}_i$, J can be minimized respect to $\mathbf{c}_i$. This can be mathematically expressed by:

$$2 \cdot \sum_{j=1}^{n} u_{ij} \cdot (\mathbf{x}_j - \mathbf{c}_i) = 0 \tag{10.13}$$

Finally, the values the centroid $\mathbf{c}_i$ can be computed as:

$$\mathbf{c}_i = \frac{\sum_{j=1}^{n} u_{ij} \cdot \mathbf{x}_j}{\sum_{j=1}^{n} u_{ij}} \tag{10.14}$$

where the denominator of Eq. 10.14 represents the total number of elements assigned to the group G_i. As a result, it is evident that the point $\mathbf{c}_i$ represents the average position of all the data vectors assigned to group G_i.

10.6.1 Implementation of KM algorithm in MATLAB

In this section, an example of the implementation of the KM method is exhibited. The MATLAB code in Algorithm 10.2 is presented by using the built-in functions of MATLAB to implement the cluster analysis of the KM method with synthetic data.

```
%Algorithm 10.2
%% INITIAL CONFIGURATION
%Clear memory and Close Matlab windows
clear all
close all

%% Step 1 Set a default random sequence generator to produce
standard random values
rng('default');

%% Step 2: Set 100 datapoints, this will be the dataset
X = [(randn(50,2)*0.75)+1;
     (randn(50,2)*0.25)-1];

%%Step 3: Compute K-Means algorithm over the dataset from Step 2
[idx,C] = kmeans(X,2);
D1 = find(idx==1);
D2 = find(idx==2);

%% Step 4: Plot the clustered data
figure(1)
title('Data in 2 clusters by K-Means')
plot(X(D1,1),X(D1,2),'xk','DisplayName','Cluster 1');
hold on
plot(X(D2,1),X(D2,2),'ok','DisplayName','Cluster 2');
plot(C(:,1),C(:,2),'.k','MarkerSize',30,'DisplayName','Centroids');
legend({'Cluster 1', 'Cluster 2','Centroids'})
fprintf('Centroid 1: (%d,%d)\n',C(1,1),C(1,2));
fprintf('Centroid 2: (%d,%d)\n',C(2,1),C(2,2));
```

In Algorithm 10.2, Step 1 indicates which random number generator will be used. The `'default'` instruction from `rng` function uses a random generator whose output will be the same at each execution of the code. This scheme is used for reproducibility purpose, so the reader can follow a generic output from the clustering process. Step 2, generates 100 datapoints in a random fashion. This datapoints will be the dataset used for clustering process by the KM. In Step 3, the built- in function `kmeans` is used considering two clusters. Finally, in Step 4, the data and the cluster centroids are plotted. The output of the Algorithm 10.2 can be seen in Figure 10.3.

In Figure 10.3, the produced output from KM for the test dataset of Step 2 in the Algorithm 10.2 is shown. As it can be shown, each datapoint from the dataset is associated into one of the two possible clusters.

The KM clustering process is simple to implement but a powerful technique since the user can define the number of classes according to a specific data project. Different cluster division of groups will produce different cluster groups.

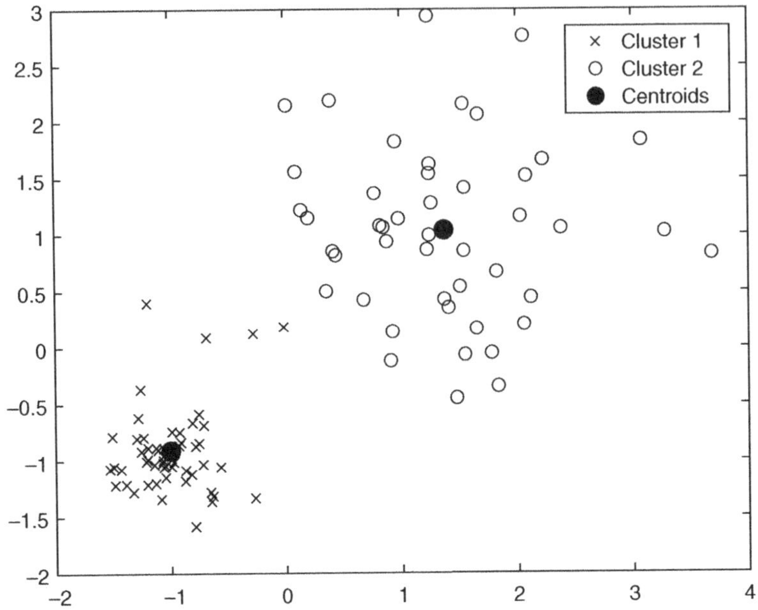

Figure 10.3 Data separated by two clusters by the K-Means algorithm.

10.6.2 Cuckoo Search Method for K-Means

K-means method is one of the most popular unsupervised classification methods. KM starts with an arbitrary number of K cluster centers then; an iterative procedure is applied to update the initial cluster centers. This mechanism is achieved by a minimization criterion, where the algorithm reduces the Euclidean distance among cluster centers and datapoints. However, the inherent nature of the algorithmic structure of the KM allows to reformulate the minimization criterion by considering different optimization approaches.

In this section, the CSM is employed as an optimization technique to assist the clustering process of the KM algorithm. This section allows readers to understand the KM algorithm as an optimization approach, where different implementations of the objective functions allow different cluster outcomes. Under such circumstances, this section considers the use of a metaheuristic algorithm to group data.

The basic idea behind the synergy of CSM and the KM is that the reader can realize that metaheuristics are universal optimization methods and how they can be applied to solve clustering problems. The presented framework has the advantage of both KM and CSM to improve some of the limitations of traditional KM. Within this framework, the primary objective is to minimize the dispersion of clusters among data.

One important aspect to discuss is that traditional KM method can be improved in different ways through applying several optimization approaches. Each of these approaches can reformulate in different fashion each step of the KM method. For example, the selection of the K cluster centroids can be reformulated as an optimization problem prior to the next steps of the KM. Another approach can substitute the spatial relationship among data by considering different aspects such as information entropy, and so on. In this section, the computation of the cluster centers will be formulated as an optimization scheme. This mechanism is one of the most common adaptations of traditional KM.

To accomplish this process, the original structure of the CSM must be adapted to incorporate the required functionality to update the cluster centers. For that, the CSM-KM methodology begins by producing a set of N_p population members, each population member will represent a set of K cluster centroids. Then, the evolutionary strategy of the CSM will update the clusters centroids by each individual in the population based on the information retrieved by the objective function to minimize the dispersion of clusters. Finally, when a stop criterion is achieved the final cluster centroids will be obtained.

The CSM-KM method unfolds through a systematic and iterative procedure that can be summarized as follows:

Step 1: Determine the Number of Clusters (K):
As well as the original KM method, the CSM-KM method requires the decision of how many clusters the dataset should be divided into. Since the same synthetic dataset generated in Algorithm 10.2 will be used for comparison purposes, in the proposed method $K = 2$ is defined.

Step 2: Population Initialization:
Within the optimization process of the CSM-KM method, requires a set of N solution vectors (individuals) that will evolve through the generations. For this, in CSM-KM, a population of individuals (eggs) $\mathbf{X}$, will be composed by a set of parameter vectors $\{\mathbf{z}_1^k, \mathbf{z}_2^k, \ldots, \mathbf{z}_N^k\}$ where each parameter vector $\mathbf{z}_i^k$, represents a set of cluster centroids $\mathbf{z}_i^k = \left\{\left(x_{i,1}^j, x_{i,2}^j\right), \left(x_{i,1}^j, x_{i,2}^j\right)\right\}, j = 1, \ldots, K$. The initial centroid values for each population member are generated by random values considering the lower limit **lb** and the **ub** in the dataset to be used.

Then, the fitness for each individual will be computed. Since the main difference of KM and CSM-KM is the way, the data is grouped in this chapter the following objective function will be defined in the entire optimization process:

$$J(i) = \frac{\sum_{j=1}^{K} \sum_{\forall \mathbf{x}_j \in G_{ij}} \|\mathbf{x}_j - \mathbf{z}_{ij}\|^2}{N} \tag{10.15}$$

where K is the number of clusters (Step 1, in this case each population member is composed by two pair of values, each pair corresponds to the two-dimensional coordinates), j corresponds to the j-th cluster. $\mathbf{x}_j$ represents the datapoint belonging to the j-th cluster. $\mathbf{z}_{ij}$ corresponds to the centroid values for the j-th cluster, and N represents the number of elements of the dataset.

Step 3: Lévy Flight:
Traditional KM iteratively updates the centroids values based on the assigned datapoints to each cluster. In CSM-KM, the centroid values are computed based on the Lévy flight structure of the CSM. This mechanism improves the search capabilities by exploring over the entire search space. Since each parameter vector $\mathbf{z}_i^k$ is composed by a set of centroid values, each centroid component will be adjusted by using Lévy flight computation.

Step 4: Solution Replacement:
As well as the original CSM, the CSM-KM will use the straightforward steps described in Section 10.3.3 for replacement of the best solutions been so far.

Step 5: Elitist Selection:
Within the elitist criterion, the same scheme is applied by the CSM-KM for updating the best set of centroids been so far (Section 10.3.4).

In the following sub-section, the implementation of the CSM-KM will be presented.

10.6.2.1 Implementation of CSM to KM Clustering in MATLAB

An example of the implementation of the KM method as an optimization problem is presented in this section. The MATLAB code in Algorithm 10.3 considers the search strategy of CSM as an optimization algorithm, and the fitness function from Eq. 10.15. To make a fair distinction between Algorithms 10.2 and 10.3, the same synthetic data is used as the input dataset.

```
%Algorithm 10.3
%% INITIAL CONFIGURATION FOR THE OPTIMIZATION PROCESS
%Clear memory and Close Matlab windows
clear all;
close all;

%% Step 1 DETERMINE THE NUMBER OF CLUSTERS K
%Definition of the number of K clusters
Kclusters = 2;

%% Step 2 POPULATION INITIALIZATION
%Set a default random sequence generator to produce standard
random values
rng('default');
%Set 100 datapoints, this will be the dataset
Dataset = [(randn(50,2)*0.75)+1; (randn(50,2)*0.25)-1];
%The size of the population is established
n = 10;
%The maximum number of iterations is established
N_IterTotal = 50;
%The limits of the search space are defined
lb = [min(Dataset(:,1)) min(Dataset(:,2))];
ub = [max(Dataset(:,1)) max(Dataset(:,2))];
%Parameter initialization of the CSM
pa=0.25;
%Iteration counter
iter = 0;
%Initialization of the initial population
for i = 1 : n
    nest(i,1) = rand * (ub(1)-lb(1))+lb(1);
    nest(i,3) = rand * (ub(1)-lb(1))+lb(1);
    nest(i,2) = rand * (ub(2)-lb(2))+lb(2);
    nest(i,4) = rand * (ub(2)-lb(2))+lb(2);
end
%The fitness values of the initial population are obtained
for j = 1 : size(nest,1)
    fitness(j) = ObjectiveFunction(nest(j,:),Dataset);
```

```
end
%The best solution is obtained from the initial population
[fitnessXbest,K]=min(fitness) ;
xBest=nest(K,:);
%Iterative process of the algorithm
while iter <= N_IterTotal

    %% Step 3 LÉVY FLIGHT
    beta=3/2;
    sigma=(gamma(1+beta)*sin(pi*beta/2)/...
(gamma((1+beta)/2)*beta*2^...
((beta-1)/2)))^(1/beta);

    for j=1:n
        s=nest(j,:);
        %Mantegna's Algorithm
        u=randn(size(s))*sigma;
        v=randn(size(s));
        step=u./abs(v).^(1/beta);
        stepsize=0.01*step.*(s-xBest);
        s=s+stepsize.*randn(size(s));
        if (s(1) < lb(1) || s(1) > ub(1))
            s(1) = rand * (ub(1) - lb(1)) + lb(1);
        end
        if (s(3) < lb(1) || s(3) > ub(1))
            s(3) = rand * (ub(1) - lb(1)) + lb(1);
        end
        if (s(2) < lb(2) || s(2) > ub(2))
            s(2) = rand * (ub(2) - lb(2)) + lb(2);
        end
        if (s(4) < lb(2) || s(4) > ub(2))
            s(4) = rand * (ub(2) - lb(2)) + lb(2);
        end
        nest(j,:)=s;
    end
    for j=1:size(nest,1)
        fnew = ObjectiveFunction(nest(j,:),Dataset);
        fitness(j)=fnew;
    end
    [fitnessXbest,K]=min(fitness);
    xBest = nest(K,:);

    %% Step 4 SOLUTION REPLACEMENT
    K=rand(size(nest))>pa;
    stepsize=rand*(nest(randperm(n),:)-nest(randperm(n),:));
    new_nest=nest+stepsize.*K;
    for j = 1 : size(new_nest,1)
```

```
        if (new_nest(j,1) < lb(1) || new_nest(j,1) > ub(1))
            new_nest(j,1) = rand * (ub(1) - lb(1)) + lb(1);
        end
        if (new_nest(j,3) < lb(1) || new_nest(j,3) > ub(1))
            new_nest(j,3) = rand * (ub(1) - lb(1)) + lb(1);
        end
        if (new_nest(j,2) < lb(2) || new_nest(j,2) > ub(2))
            new_nest(j,2) = rand * (ub(2) - lb(2)) + lb(2);
        end
        if (new_nest(j,4) < lb(2) || new_nest(j,4) > ub(2))
            new_nest(j,4) = rand * (ub(2) - lb(2)) + lb(2);
        end
    end

    for j=1:size(nest,1)
        fnew = ObjectiveFunction(new_nest(j,:),Dataset);
        if fnew<=fitness(j)
           fitness(j)=fnew;
           nest(j,:)=new_nest(j,:);
        end
    end

    %% Step 5 ELITIST SELECTION
    [fitnessXbest,K]=min(fitness) ;
    xBest=nest(K,:);
    %Iteration counters
    iter = iter + 1;
    fprintf('Iteration: %d\n',iter);
end
fprintf('Best solution: Centroid 1: (%d,%d) Centroid 2: ...
(%d,%d)\n', xBest(1,1),xBest(1,2),...
xBest(1,3),xBest(1,4));
fprintf('Best fitness: %d\n',fitnessXbest);
%Plot the dataset and final centroids
figure(1)
plot(Dataset(:,1),Dataset(:,2),'xk','DisplayName','Original Data');
hold on
plot(xBest(:,1),xBest(:,2),'.k','MarkerSize',...
30,'DisplayName','Centroid 1');
plot(xBest(:,3),xBest(:,4),'.k','MarkerSize',...
30,'DisplayName','Centroid 2');
legend({'Original Data', 'Centroid 1','Centroid 2'});
title('Original Dataset and Final Cluster Centroids');
hold off

for dataIndex = 1 : 100
    dTemp1 = pdist2(Dataset(dataIndex,:),xBest(1,1:2));
```

```
    dTemp2 = pdist2(Dataset(dataIndex,:),xBest(1,3:4));
    if dTemp1 < dTemp2
        dataClass(dataIndex,1) = 1;
    else
        dataClass(dataIndex,1) = 2;
    end
end
    tempIndex1 = find(dataClass(:,1) == 1);
    tempIndex2 = find(dataClass(:,1) == 2);

%Plot the dataset clustered by the final centroids
figure(2)
plot(Dataset(tempIndex1(:,1),1),...
Dataset(tempIndex1(:,1),2),'xk', 'DisplayName',...
'Cluster 1');
hold on
plot(Dataset(tempIndex2(:,1),1),...
Dataset(tempIndex2(:,1),2),'ok', 'DisplayName',...
'Cluster 2');
plot(xBest(:,1),xBest(:,2),'.k','MarkerSize',...
30,'DisplayName','Centroid 1');
plot(xBest(:,3),xBest(:,4),'.k','MarkerSize',...
30,'DisplayName','Centroid 2');
legend({'Cluster 1', 'Cluster 2', 'Centroid 1','Centroid 2'});
title('Clustered datapoints by Final Cluster Centroids');
hold off

%%OBJECTIVE FUNCTION
%Objective function implementation for clustering
function fit = ObjectiveFunction(L,Dataset)
   [N,~]=size(L);
   for i = 1:N %Se obtiene el fitness de cada par de clusters
       for dataIndex = 1 : 100
           dTemp1 = pdist2(Dataset(dataIndex,:),L(i,1:2));
           dTemp2 = pdist2(Dataset(dataIndex,:),L(i,3:4));
           if dTemp1 < dTemp2
               dataClass(dataIndex,1) = 1;
           else
               dataClass(dataIndex,1) = 2;
           end
       end
       tempIndex1 = find(dataClass(:,1) == 1);
       tempIndex2 = find(dataClass(:,1) == 2);
       sum1 = sum(pdist2(Dataset(tempIndex1,:),L(i,1:2)));
       sum2 = sum(pdist2(Dataset(tempIndex2,:),L(i,3:4)));
       fit(i) = (sum1 + sum2) / 100;
   end
end
```

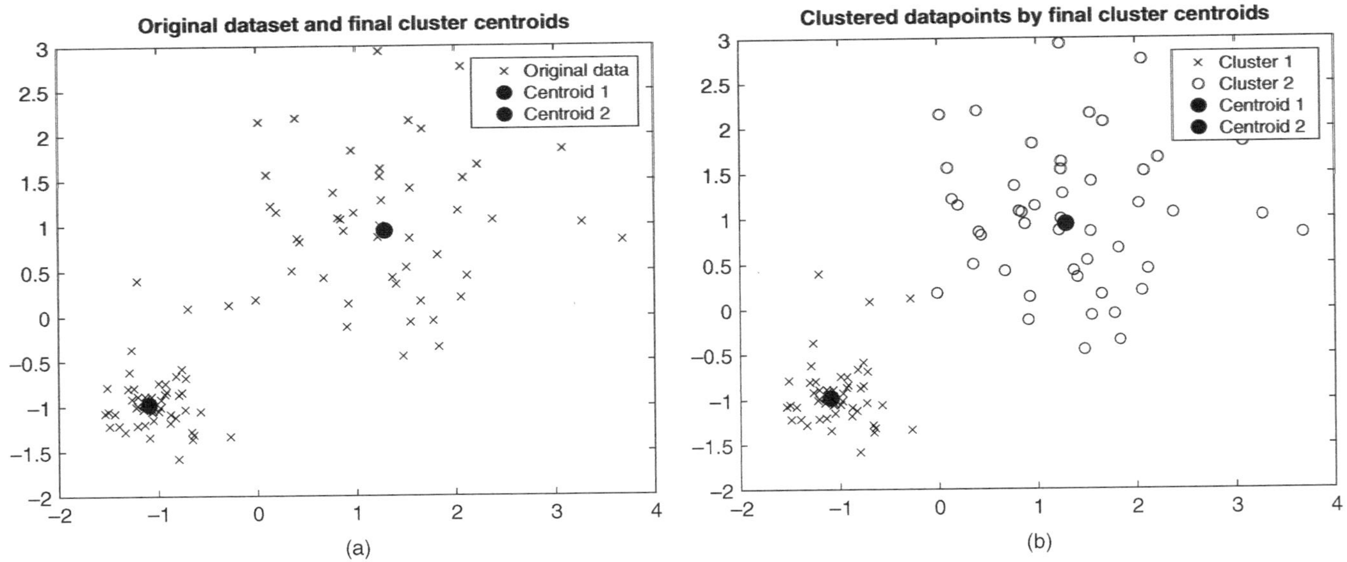

Figure 10.4 Data separated by two clusters by the CSM-KM algorithm. In Figure 10.4(a) the original data and the centroids produced by the CSM-KM is presented. In Figure 10.4(b) the original data is assigned to each cluster defined by the centroids produced by the CSM-KM.

In Algorithm 10.3, Step 1 indicates the number of desired clusters. Step 2 indicates which random number generator will be used. The `'default'` instruction from `rng` function uses a random generator whose output will be the same at each execution of the code. This scheme is used for reproducibility purpose, so the reader can follow a generic output from the dataset. Step 3 generates 100 datapoints in a random fashion. These datapoints will be the dataset used for clustering process by the CSM-KM. In Step 3, the Lévy flight method is implemented to update the position of each set of centroid values. In Step 4, the solution replacement mechanism is implemented. Finally, in Step 5 the elitist selection scheme is described. The output of the Algorithm 10.3 can be seen in Figure 10.4.

In Figure 10.4a, the produced output from CSM-KM for the test dataset of Step 2 in the Algorithm 10.3 is shown. As it can be shown, each centroid is represented by a filled circle. Each cluster centroids was produced by the optimization process of the CSM-KM method. In Figure 10.4b, the data generated in Step 2 is also exhibited. However, in this case the data is assigned to its corresponding cluster based on the cluster centers obtained by the optimization process.

As it can be shown, the KM method is a powerful and flexible clustering process that can be improved by considering different stages as an optimization formulation. Different optimization formulations may produce different cluster divisions.

References

Chawla, M. and Duhan, M. (2018). Levy flights in metaheuristics optimization algorithms – a review. *Applied Artificial Intelligence* 32 (9–10): 802–821. https://doi.org/10.1080/08839514.2018.1508807.

Dhaenens, C. and Jourdan, L. (2022). Metaheuristics for data mining: survey and opportunities for big data. *Annals of Operations Research* 314 (1): 117–140. https://doi.org/10.1007/S10479-021-04496-0.

Ezugwu, A.E., Ikotun, A.M., Oyelade, O.O. et al. (2022). A comprehensive survey of clustering algorithms: state-of-the-art machine learning applications, taxonomy, challenges, and future research prospects. *Engineering Applications of Artificial Intelligence* 110: 104743. https://doi.org/10.1016/J.ENGAPPAI.2022.104743.

Ikotun, A.M., Ezugwu, A.E., Abualigah, L. et al. (2023). K-means clustering algorithms: a comprehensive review, variants analysis, and advances in the era of big data. *Information Sciences* 622: 178–210. https://doi.org/10.1016/J.INS.2022.11.139.

Mantegna, R.N. (1994). Fast, accurate algorithm for numerical simulation of Lévy stable stochastic processes. *Physical Review E* 49 (5): 4677. https://doi.org/10.1103/PhysRevE.49.4677.

Maronna, R. (2015). Charu C. Aggarwal and Chandan K. Reddy (eds.): Data clustering: algorithms and applications. *Statistical Papers* 57 (2): 565–566. https://doi.org/10.1007/S00362-015-0661-7.

Pavlyukevich, I. (2007). Lévy flights, non-local search and simulated annealing. *Journal of Computational Physics* 226 (2): 1830–1844. https://doi.org/10.1016/J.JCP.2007.06.008.

Payne, R.B. and Sorenson, M.D. (2005). *The Cuckoos. Bird Families of the World*, vol. 15, 618. Oxford: Oxford University Press.

Wilkin, G.A. and Huang, X. (2008). K-means clustering algorithms: implementation and comparison. In: *2nd International Multi-Symposiums on Computer and Computational Sciences (IMSCCS 2007)*, 133–136. https://doi.org/10.1109/IMSCCS.2007.51.

Yang, X.S. and Deb, S. (2009). Cuckoo search via Lévy flights. In: *2009 World Congress on Nature and Biologically Inspired Computing, NABIC 2009 – Proceedings*, 210–214. https://doi.org/10.1109/NABIC.2009.5393690.

11

Metaheuristic Methods for Dimensional Reduction

11.1 Introduction

Dimensionality reduction, which refers to reducing the number of dimensions in a dataset, has increasingly gained the attention of data analysts as the volume of available data in any field keeps growing at a fast rate. In general, datasets with high dimensionality are undesirable since the volume of the feature space can be so big that the available data is too sparse for data analysis techniques to deliver reliable results. One way to overcome this limitation is to increase the amount of data considered for the analysis, which is not always possible and can, in turn, lead to higher computing power demands. A different approach is reducing the number of dimensions in the dataset, removing redundant and irrelevant features to transform the data to a lower-dimensional space in which it retains some meaningful properties of the original data, ideally close to its intrinsic dimension.

Dimensionality reduction techniques are usually divided into feature selection and feature extraction. While feature selection techniques search for a subset of the input features, the latter group transforms the data to a latent space of fewer dimensions. Different metaheuristic algorithms, such as ant colony optimization (ACO), firefly algorithm, flower pollination algorithm, and genetic algorithm, among others, have proved to be useful for feature selection and extraction, mainly in the field of medicine. This chapter focuses on applications of the ACO algorithm to dimensionality reduction techniques. We begin by presenting the ACO algorithm itself; then, we show the generalities of ACO to dimensionality for feature selection and feature extraction.

11.2 Ant Colony Optimization (ACO)

The ant colony optimization (ACO) is a swarm intelligence algorithm inspired by the foraging behavior of ant colonies introduced in the early 1990s by M. Dorigo and colleagues (Dorigo et al. 1996). The ACO, like other metaheuristic algorithms for the solution of combinatorial optimization problems (Blum and Roli 2003), does not aim to find the best solution but a good enough approximation within a reasonable window of time.

As it occurs in other social insects, such as bees, termites, and wasps, the highly structured organization of ant colonies allows the emergence of complex behaviors that greatly surpass the individual capabilities of their members. For the development of the ACO algorithm, Dorigo et al. (1996) considered a prime example of complex behavior observed in ant colonies, their collective

Machine Learning and Metaheuristic Computation, First Edition.
Erik Cuevas, Jorge Galvez, Omar Avalos, and Fernando Wario.

foraging. When foraging, ants begin by randomly exploring the nest's surroundings. Once a food source has been located, they analyze essential characteristics such as quantity and quality of the food available and bring some samples with them back to the nest. On their way back to the nest, ants leave a trail of pheromones that other ants later use to find the food source. The strength of pheromones deposited by food-carrying ants directly correlates with the food site's properties; hence, highly profitable food sources have the best chances of being revisited. As the profitability of food sources decreases, their paths are less transited, with pheromone density decreasing as well. Additionally, since pheromones evaporate, paths leading to lesser-quality food sources fade quickly enough for scout ants to search for other food sources. This dynamic is perceived as a type of communication mediated by pheromones and has been thoroughly studied through various experimental setups (Deneubourg et al. 1990).

To understand the ACO computational procedure, it is essential to remember that it was initially conceived to solve discrete optimization problems, like the traveling salesman problem (TSP). The core idea behind the ACO approach to optimization problems is the incremental construction of solutions. In the same way, ants find their way to a particular food source by following existing pheromone traces and choosing between paths when coming across intersections. Candidate solutions in the ACO are built by a series of probabilistic choices made by artificial ants. The inner process of the ACO algorithm can be divided into three parts: pheromone representation, ant-based solution construction, and pheromone update.

11.2.1 Pheromone Representation

The pheromone representation refers to an array of k different n-dimensional solutions, each accompanied by its function value and an associated weight w. Hence, the pheromone representation consists of a $k \times n$ matrix and two k-length vectors (see Figure 11.1).

The solutions matrix is first initialized at random within the limits of the search space. Then, the function values $f(S_l)$ are computed using the problem's cost function for all k solutions and ranked accordingly. Lastly, the associated weight values w are calculated following the Gaussian function defined in Eq. 11.1, where k is the number of solutions, l is the solution's position in the rank, and q is a modulation parameter known as selection pressure. Small q values result in weight vectors strongly biased toward the best solution, while large q values result in more balanced vectors.

$$w_l = \frac{1}{qk\sqrt{2\pi}} e^{-\frac{(l-1)^2}{2q^2k^2}} \tag{11.1}$$

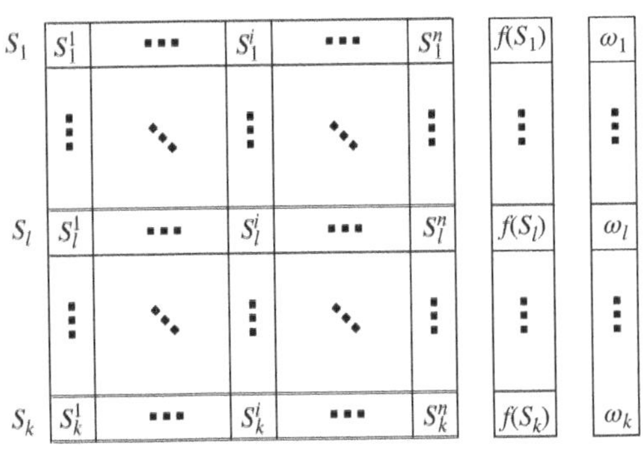

Figure 11.1 The ACO pheromone representation consisting of k n-dimensional solutions, along with their associated function-value and weight vectors.

11.2.2 Ant-Based Solution Construction

To create a new solution, ACO performs two iterative steps. First, a solution element S_l^j is selected for each of the n dimensions based on the selection probability of each solution (see Eq. 11.2).

$$p_l = \frac{w_l}{\sum_{r=1}^{k} w_r} \tag{11.2}$$

Then, a Gaussian sampling is performed for each of the selected elements using Eq. 11.3:

$$g(x, \mu, \sigma) = \frac{1}{\sigma\sqrt{2\pi}} e^{-\frac{(x-\mu)^2}{2\sigma^2}} \tag{11.3}$$

where the mean μ is the selected element S_l^j and the standard deviation $\sigma = \xi D$. The parameter $\xi > 0$ is the learning rate, also known as the pheromone evaporation rate in ACO, and D is the average distance between the selected element and all elements of the same dimension of the remaining $k - 1$ solutions (see Eq. 11.4).

$$D = \sum_{r=1}^{k} \frac{\left|S_r^j - S_l^j\right|}{k-1} \tag{11.4}$$

11.2.3 Pheromone Update

At each iteration of the ACO algorithm, a set of m new solutions is created. Once the set is complete, the function values $f(S_l)$ for all m new solutions are computed using the problem's cost function.

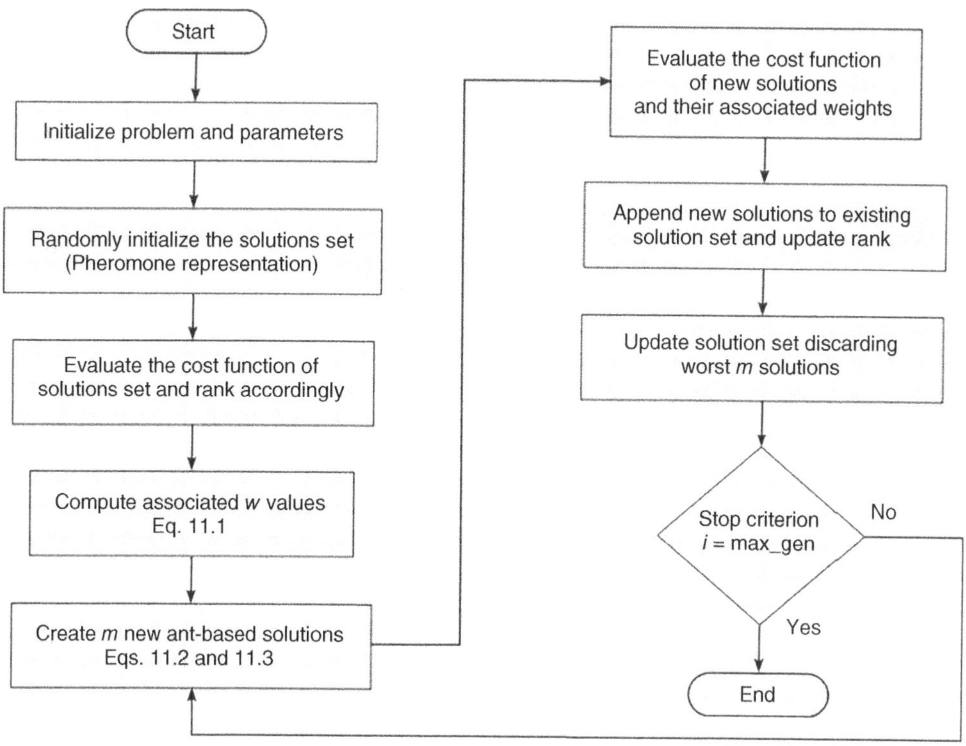

Figure 11.2 Ant colony optimization (ACO) flowchart.

Finally, the m new solutions are appended to the existing solution set and ranked according to their function value. To keep the number of elements in the solution set constant, only the first k solutions are passed by to the next iteration. New ant-based solutions are generated, and the pheromone representation is updated at each iteration till a stop criterion is met. The overall functioning of the ACO algorithm is shown in the flowchart in Figure 11.2.

The implementation in MATLAB of the ACO algorithm to find the minimum of the Rastrigin test function is presented in Algorithm 11.1. To ease its understanding, the code is divided into 6 steps that can also be found in the ACO flowchart (see Figure 11.2).

```
%Algorithm  11.1
%Clean data
close all
clear all

% Step 1, problem, and ACO parameters declaration
% problem parameters
l_bound = -5.12;          % lower boundary
u_bound = 5.12;           % upper boundary
dim = 2;                  % dimensionality

% ACO parameters
max_it = 300;             % Maximum number of iterations
K = 40;                   % Number of original solutions
M = 10;                   % Number of ant-based solutions
q = 0.1;                  % Selection pressure
zeta = 0.1;               % Evaporation rate

% Create aux structure
aux_ant.Position = [];
aux_ant.Cost = [];

% Create Pheromone representation matrix
ANT = repmat(aux_ant, K, 1);

% Step 2, randomly initialization of the candidate solutions
% (pheromones) within the search space bounds

for j=1:K
    % Random solution
    Ant(j).Position = unifrnd(l_bound, u_bound, [1,dim]);
    % Evaluation
    Ant(j).Cost = fitness_function(Ant(j).Position);
end
```

```
% Step 3, sort solutions according to fitness
[~, SortOrder]= sort([ANT.Cost]);
ANT = ANT(SortOrder);

% Init fitness history
fitness_history = zeros(max_it,1);

% Step 4, compute the weights associated to the candidate solutions
w_vector = 1/(sqrt(2*pi)*q*K)*exp(-0.5*(((1:K)-1)/(q*K)).^2);
% Selection probabilities
p = w_vector/sum(w_vector);

% ACO main loop
% Step 5, generate new solutions through ant-based solution
% construction
for it=1:tmax
    % Means matrix
    means = zeros(K, dim);
    for j = 1:dim
        means(j,:) = ANT(j).Position;
    end
    % Standard deviations matrix
    sigma = zeros(K, dim);
    for j = 1:dim
        D = 0;
        for r = 1:K
            D = D+abs(sigma(j,:)-sigma(r,:));
        end
        sigma(j,:) = zeta*D/(K-1);
    end
    % New solutions set
    new_pop = repmat(aux_ant, M, 1);
    for t = 1:M
        % Init solutions matrix
        Newpop(t).Position = zeros([1,dim]);
        % Solution construction
        for i=1:dim
            % Select Gaussian kernel
            l = RouletteWheelSelection(p);
            % Gaussian random variable
            new_pop(t).Position(i) = means(l,i)+sigma(l,i)*randn;
            % Check that solution is within boundaries
            new_pop(t).Position(i) =...
min(new_pop(t).Position(i),u_bound);

            new_pop(t).Position(i) =...
max(new_pop(t).Position(i),l_bound);
```

```
            end
            % Cost function evaluation
            new_pop(t).Cost = fitness_function(new_pop(t).Position);
        end

% Step 6, update population
    % Append new solutions to existing population
    ANT = [ANT
           new_pop];
    % Sort according to fitness
    [~, SortOrder]= sort([ANT.Cost]);
    ANT = ANT(SortOrder);
    % Keeping only best solutions
    ANT = ANT(1:K);
    % Update fitness history
    fitness_history(it) = ANT(1).Cost;
end

%*******************************************************************
% PLOT COST FUNCTION AND BEST SOLUTION
%*******************************************************************
% Graphic representation Rastrigin
range=u_bound - l_bound;
figure(1)
x1=[l_bound:range/100:u_bound];
y1=x1;
[X1,Y1]=meshgrid(x1,y1);
[row1,col1]=size(X1);
for q=1:col1
    for hh=1:row1
        vector = [X1(hh,q),Y1(hh,q)];
        zz(hh,q)= A*n+sum(vector.^2-A*cos(2*pi*vector));
    end
end
mesh(X1,Y1,zz, 'edgecolor', [0.5,0.5,0.5]);
hold on

% Add best solution
plot(ANT(1).Position(1), ANT(1).Position(2),'o', . . .
     'markersize',6,'markerfacecolor','r');

%*******************************************************************
% FUNCTIONS
%*******************************************************************

%*******************************************************************
% Rastrigin cost function
%*******************************************************************
```

```
function ft = fitness_function(xn)
    A = 10;
    n = size(xn);
    cal = xn.^2-A*cos(2*pi*xn);
    ft = A*n+sum(cal);
end
```

In Step 1 of the algorithm are defined the parameters of the problem and the ACO algorithm itself, namely, the dimensionality of the problem, lower and upper boundaries, maximum number of iterations, number of solutions (population size), number of ant-based created solutions, selection pressure (q), and pheromone evaporation rate (zeta - ξ). In Step 2, the first set of solutions is randomly initiated, considering a uniform probability distribution across the entire search space. In Step 3, the solutions are ranked according to their fitness values, and their associated weights are computed in Step 4. The main loop takes place in Steps 5 and 6. First, new solutions are created through the ant-based solution construction method in Steps 5. Then, in Step 6, the new solutions are appended to the existing ones to create an extended set from which only the best k solutions will be kept. Finally, the algorithm iterates over Step 5 and 6 till the stop criteria is met. Figure 11.3 shows the function and the best solution found by the ACO optimization.

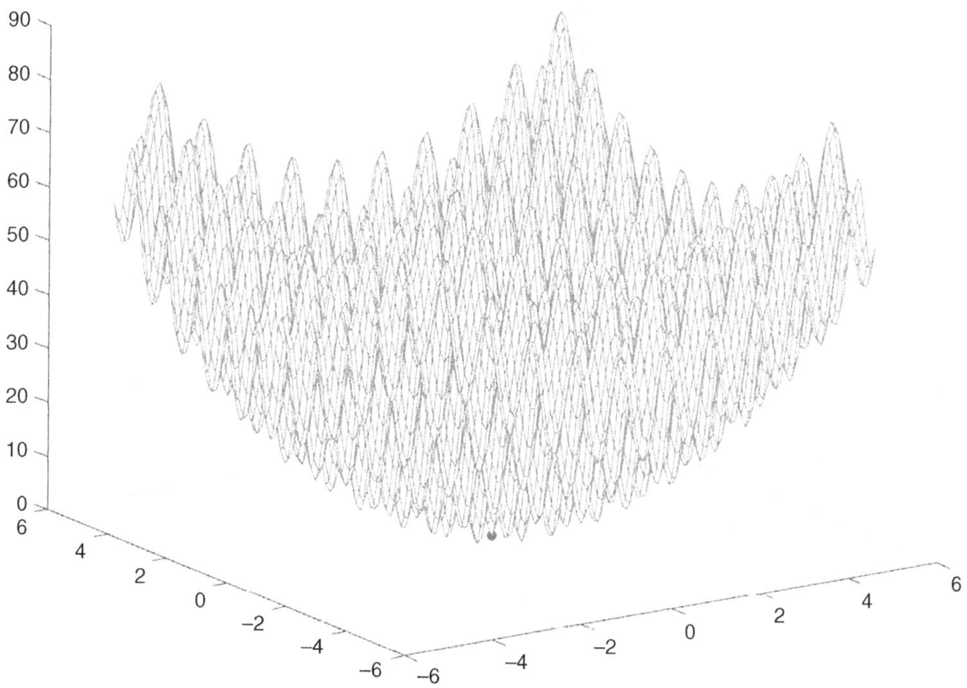

Figure 11.3 The Rastrigin fitness function employed for the optimization process and the best solution found by ACO.

Note

Metaheuristic methods can always be modified to work with different types of problems. However, each method is conceived with a particular kind of problem in mind. In the case of ACO, it is best suited to combinatorial problems that meet the following criteria:

- **Problem Representation**: The problem must be representable in the form of a graph with a set of nodes and edges.
- **Cost Function**: There must be an effective cost function that measures the "goodness" of node to the next for each possible path in the solution space.
- **Construction of New Solutions**: A mechanism to create new solutions must be established.
- **Pheromone Updating Rule**: A suitable rule to update pheromone levels at each iteration must be defined.

11.3 Dimensionality Reduction

The amount of data generated daily is constantly increasing, not only in the number of instances but also in its dimensionality. Although ideally, more and better-described data allows for more comprehensive analysis, it also poses a challenge in finding the proper methodology capable of processing such a vast amount of data while being cost-effective regarding computational power requirements. One way to deal with this issue is to reduce the dimensionality of the data to analyze. Dimensionality reduction removes irrelevant or redundant data, improving, in turn, the performance of the analysis.

Dimensionality reduction techniques can be classified into two broad groups: feature extraction and feature selection. Feature extraction techniques transform the data from its original representation space into a new latent space in which the complexity of the data is reduced. Among the most popular methods for feature extraction are the principal component analysis algorithm (PCA) and latent semantic analysis (LSA). In recent years, convolutional neural networks (CNN) have also gained popularity as an alternative to traditional approaches to feature extraction. On the other hand, feature selection techniques, as its name suggests, aim to find a subset of features that retains all meaningful properties of the original data set. The feature selection classification encompasses three kinds of methods: filter, wrapper, and embedded methods. The firsts are based on a statistical analysis of the features. Wrapper methods explore the feature space in search of the best subset of features. Meanwhile, embedded methods integrate feature selection and data classification into one single algorithm.

Metaheuristic algorithms, as one of the best approaches to solving combinatorial problems (Blum and Roli 2003), have proven to be successful in solving the feature selection problem following a wrapper-based approach. Among the metaheuristic algorithms that have already been applied to feature selection are the Ant Lion Optimizer (ALO) (Emary et al. 2016a), Grey Wolf Optimization algorithm (GWO) (Emary et al. 2016b), Artificial Bee Colony (ABC) (Hancer et al. 2018), Grasshopper Optimization Algorithm (GOA) (Mafarja et al. 2019), Whale Optimization Algorithm (WOA) (Hajihashemi et al. 2019; Mafarja and Mirjalili 2018), and the ACO (Ke et al. 2008; Li et al. 2013).

The use of ACO has been particularly prolific for feature selection tasks. In Kanan et al. (2007), an ACO-based feature selection method is tested with the ORL (Olivetti Research Laboratory) faces database, outperforming a GA-based method with fewer features and execution time. Patil et al. (2009) proposed an ACO/random forest-based hybrid filter-wrapper search technique whose performance, when tested with a database of biological active molecules used during the CoEPrA competition, compares well with the available competition results. Robbins et al. (2007) presented a modified ACO to work on high-dimensional gene expression datasets, able to identify small subsets of highly predictive and biologically relevant genes. Yu et al. (2009) introduced an ACO/SVM classifier capable of selecting tumor-related marker genes.

Note

There are several benefits of applying dimensionality reduction to datasets, among the most relevant:

- It removes redundant and noisy data.
- Reducing dimensions may allow for visualization.
- Improves the classification process.
- Data storage space is reduced.

11.4 ACO for Feature Selection

To solve the feature selection problem with ACO it is first necessary to reformulate it in a graph-like problem. If each one of the features in the dataset are seen as nodes and the edges connect consecutively chosen features, effectively forming a path graph. This way, the search for the optimal features in the context of ACO can be interpreted as the ants traveling between *n* different nodes, where these are selected one at a time based on a transition rule. This scenario is illustrated in Figure 11.4, where the ants look for feature subsets within an 8-feature space. As examples of how the ant-based solution construction occurs, consider the following: the first ant starts its path at node **a** and can choose among any of the remaining 7 nodes to add to its path; after choosing node **c** based on a selection rule, it repeats the process adding nodes **d**, **g**, and **b**, to end with the feature subset *{a, c, d, g, b}*. Following the same procedure, the second ant arrives at the feature subset *{h, g, f, e, d}*.

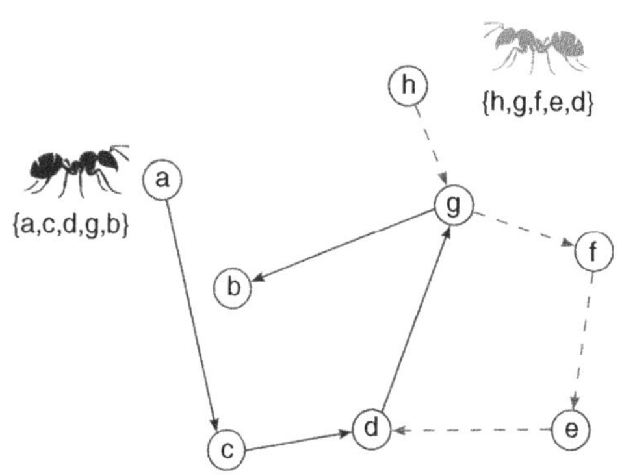

Figure 11.4 Graph-like approach of ACO to the feature selection problem.

Since ACO was initially conceived to solve the TSP, when solving a feature selection problem all candidate solutions would consist of a fixed number of elements. Hence, maybe the most straightforward way that comes to mind for solving feature selection with ACO is to set the algorithm for a fixed number of features right from the beginning.

Nevertheless, it is still possible to generate subsets with a different number of features using the original ACO. One valid approach would be to allow features to be included multiple times within the candidate solutions but to consider only one instance when computing their fitness. A different approach is used by Kanan et al. (2007), whose overall process is illustrated in Figure 11.5. First, the solutions population is initiated by randomly selecting k features. Each of the features chosen represents the first node from which each ant starts its path construction. Ants add new features from their initial positions, one at a time, following a probabilistic transition rule until a stopping criterion is satisfied. Once all solutions have been built, their fitness is computed to update the pheromone. Then, new solutions are created to renew the solutions population. The process is executed iteratively until the performance goal is achieved or the maximum number of iterations has been completed.

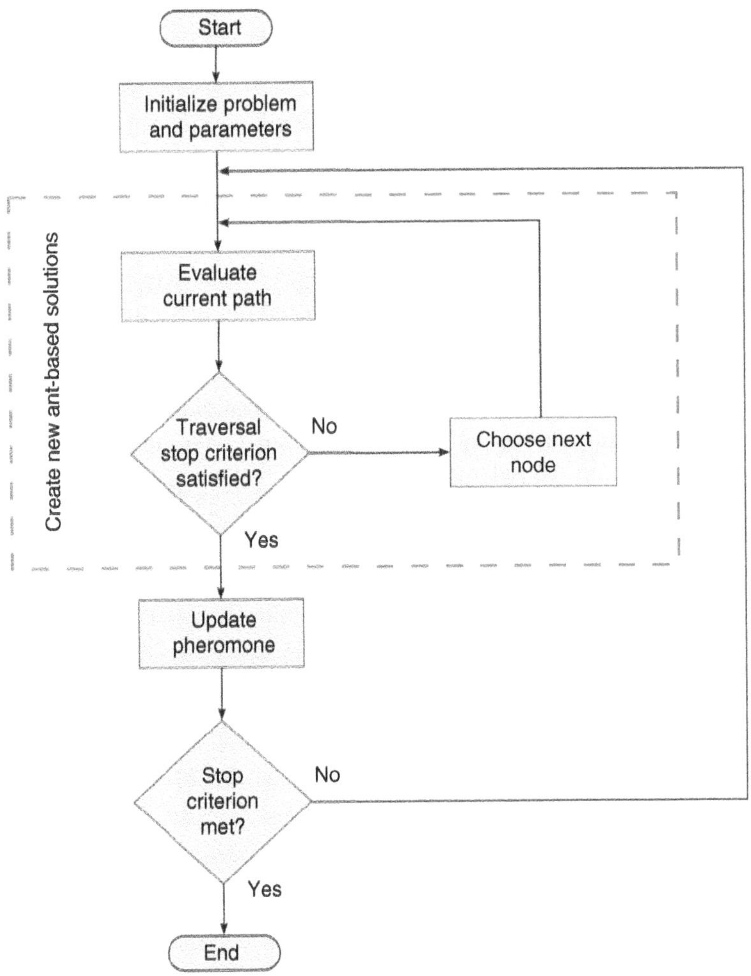

Figure 11.5 Flowchart for the ACO-based feature selection method.

The probabilistic transition rule proposed by Kanan et al. (2007) is represented by Eq. 11.5.

$$p_{ij}^k(t) = \begin{cases} \dfrac{[\tau_{ij}(t)]^\alpha \cdot [n_{ij}]^\beta}{\sum_{l \in J_i^k} [\tau_{il}(t)]^\alpha \cdot [n_{il}]^\beta}, & \text{if } j \in J_i^k \\ 0, & \text{otherwise} \end{cases} \tag{11.5}$$

where k is the number of ants (solutions), n_{ij} is the heuristic desirability of adding feature j to the solution when at feature i, J_i^k is the set of nodes next to node i that have not yet been added to solution k. $\alpha > 0$, $\beta > 0$ adjust the relative importance of the pheromone value and heuristic information and $\tau_{ij}(t)$ is the amount of pheromone on edge (i, j).

Note

Nowadays, it is not uncommon to find applications of metaheuristic techniques in the field of medicine. In particular, they have been widely used in healthcare data to diagnose, yielding better results than traditional methods. A study conducted by Kaur et al. (2023) on "metaheuristic optimization techniques for feature selection in disease diagnosis" found that between 2011 and 2022 over 150 impactful papers with these characteristics were published. The metaheuristic techniques found in these papers include spider monkey, cuckoo search algorithm, lion optimization technique, moth flame technique, bat-inspired algorithm, grey wolf algorithm, whale optimization, and dragonfly optimization technique. Regarding their applications, they were used to select and optimize the features to predict diseases such as diabetes, liver disease, Alzheimer's disease, brain disorder, heart disease, and COVID-19. As the amount of available healthcare data increases, metaheuristic techniques will gain terrain in the field of medicine, not only in the last step of diagnosis but also as part of data preprocessing before feeding the data to other machine learning algorithms.

References

Blum, C. and Roli, A. (2003). Metaheuristics in combinatorial optimization: overview and conceptual comparison. *ACM Computing Surveys* 35 (3): 268–308. https://doi.org/10.1145/937503.937505.

Deneubourg, J.L., Aron, S., Goss, S. et al. (1990). The self-organizing exploratory pattern of the argentine ant. *Journal of Insect Behavior* 3 (2): 159–168. https://doi.org/10.1007/BF01417909.

Dorigo, M., Maniezzo, V., and Colorni, A. (1996). Ant system: optimization by a colony of cooperating agents. *IEEE Transactions on Systems, Man, and Cybernetics, Part B: Cybernetics* 26 (1): 29–41. https://doi.org/10.1109/3477.484436.

Emary, E., Zawbaa, H.M., and Hassanien, A.E. (2016a). Binary ant lion approaches for feature selection. *Neurocomputing* 213: 54–65. https://doi.org/10.1016/J.NEUCOM.2016.03.101.

Emary, E., Zawbaa, H.M., and Hassanien, A.E. (2016b). Binary grey wolf optimization approaches for feature selection. *Neurocomputing* 172: 371–381. https://doi.org/10.1016/J.NEUCOM.2015.06.083.

Hajihashemi, V., Hassani, Z., Dehmajnoonie, I. et al. (2019). Hybrid algorithms of whale optimization algorithm and k-nearest neighbor to Predict the liver disease. *EAI Endorsed Transactions on Context-Aware Systems and Applications* 6 (16): 156838. https://doi.org/10.4108/eai.13-7-2018.156838.

Hancer, E., Xue, B., Zhang, M. et al. (2018). Pareto front feature selection based on artificial bee colony optimization. *Information Sciences* 422: 462–479. https://doi.org/10.1016/J.INS.2017.09.028.

Kanan, H. R., Faez, K., and Taheri, S. M. (2007). Feature selection using ant colony optimization (ACO): a new method and comparative study in the application of face recognition system. 63–76.

Kaur, S., Kumar, Y., Koul, A. et al. (2023). A systematic review on metaheuristic optimization techniques for feature selections in disease diagnosis: open issues and challenges. *Archives of Computational Methods in Engineering* 30 (3): 1863–1895. https://doi.org/10.1007/s11831-022-09853-1.

Ke, L., Feng, Z., and Ren, Z. (2008). An efficient ant colony optimization approach to attribute reduction in rough set theory. *Pattern Recognition Letters* 29 (9): 1351–1357. https://doi.org/10.1016/J.PATREC.2008.02.006.

Li, Y., Wang, G., Chen, H. et al. (2013). An ant colony optimization based dimension reduction method for high-dimensional datasets. *Journal of Bionic Engineering* 10 (2): 231–241. https://doi.org/10.1016/S1672-6529(13)60219-X.

Mafarja, M., Aljarah, I., Faris, H. et al. (2019). Binary grasshopper optimization algorithm approaches for feature selection problems. *Expert Systems with Applications* 117: 267–286. https://doi.org/10.1016/J.ESWA.2018.09.015.

Mafarja, M. and Mirjalili, S. (2018). Whale optimization approaches for wrapper feature selection. *Applied Soft Computing* 62: 441–453. https://doi.org/10.1016/J.ASOC.2017.11.006.

Patil, D., Raj, R., Shingade, P. et al. (2009). Feature selection and classification employing hybrid ant colony optimization/random forest methodology. *Combinatorial Chemistry & High Throughput Screening* 12 (5): 507–513. https://doi.org/10.2174/138620709788488993.

Robbins, K.R., Zhang, W., Bertrand, J.K. et al. (2007). The ant colony algorithm for feature selection in high-dimension gene expression data for disease classification. *Mathematical Medicine and Biology* 24 (4): 413–426. https://doi.org/10.1093/imammb/dqn001.

Yu, H., Gu, G., Liu, H. et al. (2009). A modified ant colony optimization algorithm for tumor marker gene selection. *Genomics, Proteomics and Bioinformatics* 7 (4): 200–208. https://doi.org/10.1016/S1672-0229(08)60050-9.

12

Metaheuristic Methods for Regression

12.1 Introduction

Regression analysis is a statistical procedure in which the main objective is to investigate the relation between two or more variables in order to predict the value of one of them through the knowledge of the value of the others. Regression is one of the most employed supervised learning that builds a model using a well-known dataset. The dataset contains the training data of N elements, where $\mathbf{x} = (x_1, x_2, \dots, x_N)^T$ is the input vector or independent variable, and $\mathbf{y} = (y_1, y_2, \dots, y_N)^T$ the output vector or dependent variable. The main objective of the regression is to generate a model that better fits the training data such as the real function where the data is obtained as possible without having any explicit knowledge. Once the model is trained, it can be able to relate the unknown input values x to a certain output y.

Under this consideration, training the model that better characterizes the relation of the input data is necessary to determine the parameters that shape such a model. Several methods are employed for this task, but most of them are based on deterministic techniques that in some cases determine suboptimal solutions due to the complexity, high dimensionality, and nonlinear nature of many applications. In this chapter, the most known and used optimization approach is presented. The Genetic Algorithm (GA) is a bioinspired technique proposed by John Henry Holland (1992). It is based on the behavior of the genes and their interaction, and it is described in detail below.

12.2 Genetic Algorithm (GA)

GA was presented in 1992 by Holland inspired by the gene combination of the chromosomes of the living beings where parents procreate chromosome children that heredity their information. GA employs crossover, mutation, and selection to extract the chromosome's combination and perform a search strategy. GA employs the principles of natural selection to determine the feasible solutions (chromosomes), under such circumstances, the chromosomes that have better qualities have better chances to survive. A cost function is necessary to measure each chromosome regarding the problem to be treated to determine which chromosome has a certain quality associated with it.

Machine Learning and Metaheuristic Computation, First Edition.
Erik Cuevas, Jorge Galvez, Omar Avalos, and Fernando Wario.

12.2.1 Computational Structure

From the computational implementation point of view, the GA optimization process considers a set of N candidate solutions (chromosomes) that evolve through generations in the search strategy. Under such an approach, GA generates a population of chromosomes (individuals) defined as $\mathbf{X}$ composed of a set of parameters $\left\{\mathbf{x}_1^k, \mathbf{x}_2^k, \ldots, \mathbf{x}_N^k\right\}$ where each vector $\mathbf{x}_i^k$ represents the position in a d-dimensional vector space $\{x_1, x_2, \ldots, x_d\}$ which defines the search space of the problem to be solved and sometimes known as set of decision variables. Each vector (chromosome) is modified by the operators of the GA; crossover, mutation, and selection which are used in the optimization process.

After the population is generated through the search space, each element is evaluated using the objective or cost function required by the problem to be solved. This implies that for each chromosome $\mathbf{x}_i^k$ a fitness value $f\left(\mathbf{x}_i^k\right)$ is associated with it. It is worth noting that the fitness value gives us valuable information about the search space by the decision variables. The initialization process and the operator employed in the GA optimization process are described below.

12.2.2 Initialization

As most of the optimization techniques for the initialization process, a set of individuals are randomly generated using a normal distribution. In this stage, the upper and lower bounds are determined by the user according to the problem to be solved, these bounds are defined as $\mathbf{ub} = [ub_1, ub_2, \ldots, ub_d]$ and $\mathbf{lb} = [lb_1, lb_2, \ldots, lb_d]$ respectively. These bounds are the domain of the decision variables of the problem, once the bound are set each chromosome is generated as below:

$$\mathbf{X} = \mathbf{lb} + \mathbf{r}(0, 1) \cdot (\mathbf{ub} - \mathbf{lb}) \tag{12.1}$$

where $\mathbf{ub}$ and $\mathbf{lb}$ are the upper and lower bounds, and $\mathbf{r}(0, 1)$ is a vector of normally distributed random numbers within the interval $[0, 1]$.

12.2.3 Selection Method

To select the elements of the population that continue with the optimization process, a selection method must be considered. Proportional approaches are the most used selection procedures in the optimization tasks which are based on certain information such as the fitness value of each chromosome. Within this category, there are the roulette wheel and stochastic reminder which are described below.

12.2.3.1 Roulette Wheel Selection

This selection method was proposed by De Jong (1975), and is the most used selection approach due to it employing the information on the fitness value of each chromosome to generate a probabilistic model that assigns the chances of the chromosomes to be selected as the parents to the crossover process. To visualize this selection method graphically, Figure 12.1 represents the probability distribution of five solutions where the element with more probability of being selected for the crossover is p1 with 30% and the less probability is p5 with 5%.

For determining the probabilistic value associated with each chromosome, Eqs. 12.2–12.4 are performed respectively. Then, a uniformly distributed random number r is generated and compared with the individual, if the probability is higher than the random number ($q_i > r$), it is selected to

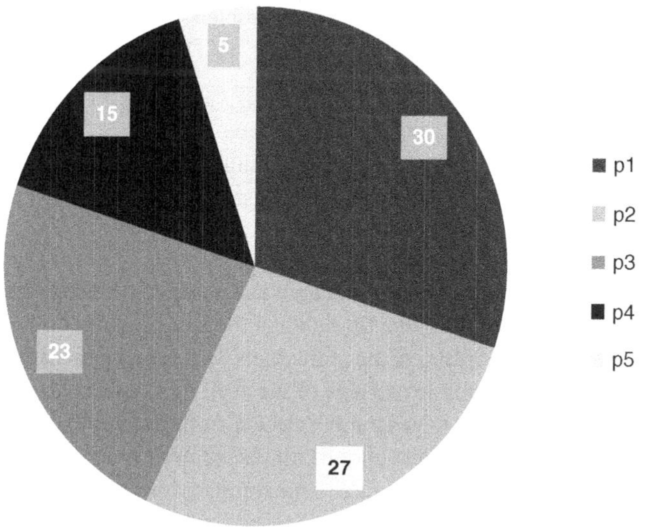

Figure 12.1 Roulette wheel selection based on fitness value information.

continue with the iterative process. This process is computed for each element of the population and repeated throughout the complete optimization procedure.

$$E = \sum_{i}^{N} f(x_i) \tag{12.2}$$

$$p_i = \frac{f(x_i)}{E} \tag{12.3}$$

$$q_i = \sum_{j}^{i} p_j \tag{12.4}$$

12.2.3.2 Stochastic Reminder Selection

This approach has shown a better performance regarding roulette wheel selection due to it employing a generation of parents to a later crossover which considerably increases the diversity of the generated solution. Nevertheless, this method presents some flaws such as premature convergence. For computing this method, it is necessary to determine the expected value for each element of the population as described below:

$$v_i = \frac{f(x_i)}{E/N} \tag{12.5}$$

Under this approach, the number of parents is indicated for assigning an identification number and computing the expected value of the selected parents. The integer part (e_i) of the expected value v_i represents the times of copies that the chromosomes previously selected are generated, and the roulette method is used to determine the number of previously selected parents.

12.2.3.3 Rank-Based Selection

This selection method is mainly based on the stochastic reminder in which hierarchies or ranks are assigned to each chromosome regarding the fitness value of each individual. The main purpose of this method is to rank each solution in the interval of [0, 1] where 1 is the better element.

This approach sorts the individuals regarding the fitness function of the problem to be treated and the expected value is computed as follows:

$$v_i = m + (M - m)\left(\frac{rank_i - 1}{N - 1}\right) \tag{12.6}$$

where M and m are 1.1 and 0.9 respectively. Such values are experimentally defined for solving several engineering problems, these parameters can be considered as adjustment values.

12.2.3.4 Tournament Selection

Most selection methods are based on the expected value of each candidate solution. In contrast, tournament selection employs a more direct technique using the value of the cost function or the population. This approach focuses on the selection nature of the individuals, which means a direct competition between chromosomes, stronger elements are capable of survival.

To perform this selection procedure, N elements are randomly selected from the population, and then an individual is selected considering two possible options: the best rank element based on its fitness value is selected, or a random number is generated and compared with a number previously preset by the user. If the last condition is fulfilled, the best element of the population is considered, otherwise, the worst individual is selected. As can be seen, different selection methods can be performed to determine the elements that are considered to continue with the iterative process, and the best selection approach depends on the application to be treated.

12.2.4 Crossover

Crossover is a biological abstraction of the genetic material recombination in nature, in which the individuals' information is shared to generate a new population with better capabilities to survive than the last one. Under this consideration, following the biological metaphor, the children are generated using the information of both parents. Still, at the same time, the children must have their own characteristics which means that such chromosomes must be modified in a later step. To perform the crossover approach, two particles (chromosomes) p_1 and p_2 are selected considering a previously described selection method. For this example, a chromosome of eight decision variables is contemplated as below:

p_1							
0	0	0	0	0	0	0	0
		↑					

p_2							
1	1	1	1	1	1	1	1
		↑					

If we consider that the cross point is the third position of each parents p_1 and p_2 as the arrows indicate, and continuing the simplest crossover approach to generate two new chromosomes (children) h_1 and h_2 as shown as follows:

h_1							
0	0	0	1	1	1	1	1
		↑					

h_2							
1	1	1	0	0	0	0	0
		↑					

The complete crossover can be summarized in three main steps; the cut point, which means the position of the variable decision vector. Then, a copy of the selected cut point is generated in a new chromosome, and finally the chromosome with the values corresponding to the decision variables of the parents.

12.2.5 Mutation

As mentioned before, this operator is employed to generate new chromosomes based on some individuals previously selected. As in nature, children are born by the combination of parents' genes but certain mutation in the descendant is performed which implies that each individual is unique, this metaphor is extrapolated to the main process of GA. Computationally, this process is carried out to produce a new population with particular characteristics; for a better understanding of this process the following example is described.

h_1							
0	0	0	1	1	1	1	1

h_2							
1	1	1	0	0	0	0	0

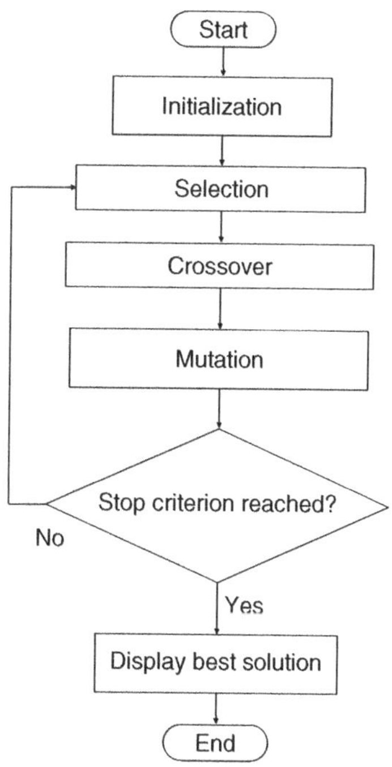

Figure 12.2 Genetic algorithm (GA) flowchart.

Considering that h_1 and h_2 are individuals generated by the crossover from two parents, the mutant operator modifies some of the chromosome's variables. The mutant operator is controlled by a mutation rate r_m, and the process can be summarized in the following steps. A uniformly distributed random number is generated in the interval [0, 1] for each element of the population and compared regarding the mutation rate, if $r_m \leq$ rand no action is performed, but if the condition $r_m >$ rand is fulfilled the change of a variable of the chromosome is conducted. To illustrate the complete functioning of the GA can be shown in the flowchart of Figure 12.2, and the complete computational implementation is reported in Algorithm 12.1.

```
%Algorithm 12.1
%Clean data
close all
clear all

%%Step 1, problem, and GA parameters declaration
dim=2;
lb = -2*pi;
ub = 2*pi;
Popusize=50;

%Crossover rate, number of childs, mutants, and mutation rate
cr=0.7;
nch=2;
nm=round(0.3*Popusize);
mr=0.1;

%Selection parameter
beta=8;

%% Stet 2, randomly initialization of the particles and first cost
function evaluation
temporal.Position=[];
temporal.Fitness=[];
pob=repmat(temporal,Popusize,1);

for i=1:Popusize
    pob(i).Posicion=unifrnd(lb,ub,[1 dim]);
    pob(i).Fitness=sin(pob(i).Posicion(1))*...
exp((1-cos(pob(i).Posicion(2)))^2) +...
cos(pob(i).Posicion(2))*...
exp((1-sin(pob(i).Posicion(1)))^2) +...
(pob(i).Posicion(1)-pob(i).Posicion(2))^2;
end
```

```
%% Sorting population
Costs = [pob.Fitness];
[Costs, SortOrder] = sort(Costs);
pob=pob(SortOrder);

%% Storage best and worst solution
xbest=pob(1);
xworst = pob(end).Fitness;

%% Step 3, Main iterative process
iter=100;
for it=1:iter

    %% Compute the probability of the selection method by the
roulette approach
    P=exp(-beta*Costs/xworst);
    P=P/sum(P);

    popc=repmat(temporal,nch/2,2);
        for k=1:nch/2
        r=rand;
        c=cumsum(P);
        i1=find(r<=c,1,'first');

        r=rand;
        c=cumsum(P);
        i2=find(r<=c,1,'first');

        i1=randi([1 Popusize]);
        i2=randi([1 Popusize]);

        p1=pob(i1);
        p2=pob(i2);

        %% Step 4, Crossover procedure
        x1 = p1.Posicion;
        x2 = p2.Posicion;
        alpha=unifrnd(-cr,1+cr,size(x1));

        popc(k,1).Posicion=alpha.*x1+(1-alpha).*x2;
        popc(k,2).Posicion=alpha.*x2+(1-alpha).*x1;

        popc(k,1).Posicion=max(popc(k,1).Posicion,lb);
        popc(k,1).Posicion=min(popc(k,1).Posicion,ub);

        popc(k,2).Posicion=max(popc(k,2).Posicion,lb);
        popc(k,2).Posicion=min(popc(k,2).Posicion,ub);
```

```
        % Fitness function evaluation of new solutions
        vector = popc(k,1).Posicion;
        popc(k,1).Fitness=sin(vector(1))*...
exp((1-cos(vector(2)))^2) +...
cos(vector(2))*exp((1-sin(vector(1)))^2) +...
(vector(1)-vector(2))^2;
        vector = popc(k,2).Posicion;
        popc(k,2).Fitness=sin(vector(1))*...
exp((1-cos(vector(2)))^2) +...
cos(vector(2))*exp((1-sin(vector(1)))^2) +...
(vector(1)-vector(2))^2;
    end
    popc=popc(:);

    %% Step 5, Mutation approach
    popm=repmat(temporal,nm,1);
    for k=1:nm

        i=randi([1 Popusize]);
        p=pob(i);
        x = p.Posicion;
        dim=numel(x);

        nmu=ceil(mr*dim);

        j=randsample(dim,nmu);

        sigma=0.1*(ub-lb);

        popm(k).Posicion=x;
        popm(k).Posicion(j)=x(j)+sigma*randn(size(j));

        popm(k).Posicion=max( popm(k).Posicion,lb);
        popm(k).Posicion=min( popm(k).Posicion,ub);
        vector = popm(k).Posicion;
        popm(k).Fitness=sin(vector(1))*...
exp((1-cos(vector(2)))^2) +...
cos(vector(2))*exp((1-sin(vector(1)))^2) +...
(vector(1)-vector(2))^2;
    end

    pob=[pob
        popc
        popm];

    %%Sort population
    Costs=[pob.Fitness];
```

```
    [Costs, SortOrder]=sort(Costs);
    pob = pob(SortOrder);


    pob=pob(1:Popusize);
    Costs=Costs(1:Popusize);

    %% Storage best solution at iteration it
    xbest=pob(1);
    xworst = pob(end).Fitness;

    %% Graphic representation at each iteration
    if dim<=2
        rango=ub-lb;
        figure(1)
        x1=[lb:rango/100:ub];
        y1=x1;
        [X1,Y1]=meshgrid(x1,y1);
        [row1,col1]=size(X1);
        for q=1:col1
            for hh=1:row1
                vector = [X1(hh,q),Y1(hh,q)];
                zz(hh,q)=sin(vector(1))*...
exp((1-cos(vector(2)))^2) +...
cos(vector(2))*exp((1-sin(vector(1)))^2) +...
(vector(1)-vector(2))^2;

            end
        end
        mesh(X1,Y1,zz);
        hold on
         for j = 1: Popusize

           plot(pob(j).Posicion(1), pob(j).Posicion(2),...
'o', 'markersize', 6, 'markerfacecolor', 'r');
         end
        drawnow;
        hold off
    end

    %% Step 6, Display best solution at each iteration
    fprintf('Iteracion: %d\n',it);
    fprintf('Best individual: (%d,%d)\n',...
xbest.Posicion(1), xbest.Posicion(2));
    fprintf('Best fitness: %d\n',xbest.Fitness);
end
```

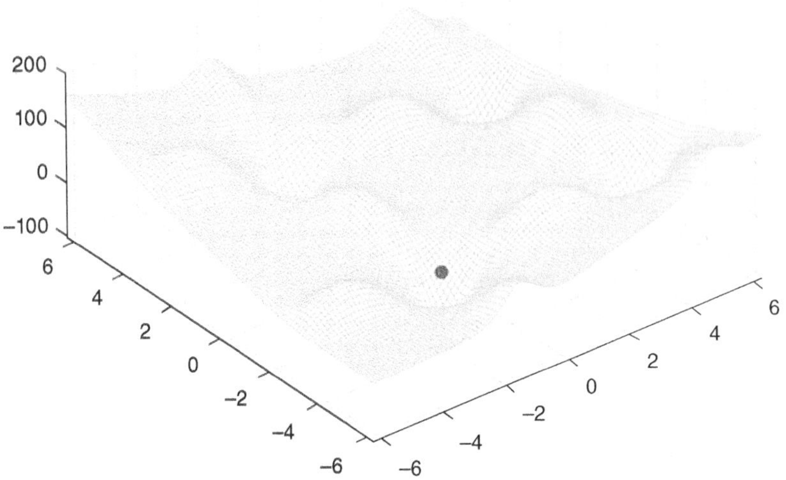

Figure 12.3 Fitness function employed for the optimization process, and best solution determined by GA.

Algorithm 12.1 shows the computational scheme of the GA approach where Step 1 performs the GA and problem variables initialization. Then in Step 2, the GA initializes the population through the search space considering the lower and upper bounds by a normal distribution, after that each chromosome is evaluated by the cost function (quality measure), and the population is sorted to order the solutions. In Step 3, the main iterative process starts where the probability of the selection method is computed. Then the crossover of the elements that fulfill the condition of crossover rate is carried out. Once the mutation of some elements of the population is performed, the cost function is employed to determine the quality of the new population. When the iterative process reaches the stop criterion, the best solution is finally displayed with its respective cost function value. Figure 12.3 shows the function and the best solution that the GA performs.

12.3 Neural Network Regression with Artificial Genetic

To perform an example where the GA is employed for improving the regression, a case of study of marriage-divorce data set is employed. In this example, different variables are considered such as education, age, and mental health, just to mention a few are considered. Under such considerations, the GA improves the rate learning of a neural network (NN) to perform the analysis of marriage-divorce regression (Muhammad et al. 2017). Algorithm 12.2 presents the complete functioning of the regression employing NN-GA. First, the marriage-divorce data is loaded and separated into Targets and Inputs, and then the number n of neurons is defined by the user (in this example the number of neurons is set at 9). Once the NN is generated, in Step 3 an error function is defined to determine the quality of the solutions employed through the complete optimization process. Step 4 performs the GA as in Algorithm 12.1, the main difference is the cost function to be optimized and the dimension of the problem. GA searches the parameters of the NN that better fit the regression response regarding the data. Finally, the result of the optimization process is used

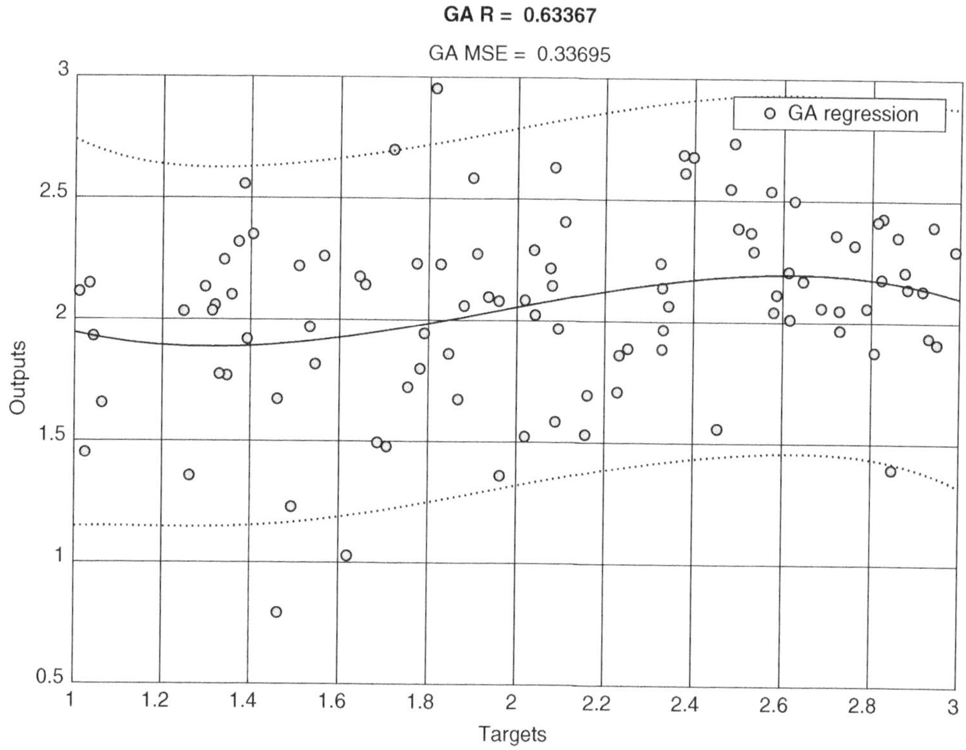

Figure 12.4 Graphical representation of the regression using a NN optimized with GA.

to perform the NN in its final form, and the error metrics are computed to measure the quality of the solution determined by the GA. The graphical representation of the regression is calculated in Step 5 and Figure 12.4 shows the result. In the section of functions, the cost function and the complete GA are declared which are employed in the complete application process.

```
%Algorithm 12.2
%Clean data
close all
clear all

%Step1, Loading the data and divide into Target and Inputs
Data=load('Marriage_Divorce_DB.mat');
Inputs=Data.Marriage_Divorce_DB(:,1:end-1);
Targets=Data.Marriage_Divorce_DB(:,end);

%Step 2, Defining the number of neurons and perform the first model
n = 9; %Neurons
net = feedforwardnet(n,'trainoss'); %NN
```

```
[net, tr]= train(net,Inputs', Targets');

%Step 3, evaluation of error
h = @(x) NMSE(x, net, Inputs', Targets');
sizenn=size(Inputs);sizenn=sizenn(1,1);

%Step 4, iterative process of the optimization process
[x, cost] = GA (h, sizenn*n+n+n+1);

%Final NN optimized by GA
getwb(net);

%Outputs and errors are obtained.
Outputs2=net(Inputs');
Outputs2=Outputs2';
Err_MSE2=mse(Targets,Outputs2);
CC= corrcoef(Targets,Outputs2);
CC= CC(1,2);

%Step 5, Graphical representation of the regression is displayed
[population3,gof3] = fit(Targets,Outputs2,'poly3');
plot(Targets,Outputs2,'o',...
'LineWidth',0.7,...
'MarkerSize',5,...
'MarkerEdgeColor','g',...
'MarkerFaceColor',[0.9,0.3,0.1]);
title(['GA R =  ' num2str(1-gof3.rmse)],...
['GA MSE =' num2str(Err_MSE2)]);
hold on
plot(population3,'b-','predobs');
xlabel('Targets');ylabel('Outputs');   grid on;
ax = gca;
ax.FontSize = 12; ax.LineWidth=2;
legend({'GA Regression'},'FontSize', 8,'TextColor','blue');hold off


%% Functions
function NMSE_calc = NMSE( wb, net, input, target)
 net = setwb(net, wb');
 error = target - net(input);
 NMSE_calc = mean(error.^2)/mean(var(target',1));
end


%% GA
function [xbest, y]= GA (fit, dim)
lb = -5;
```

```
ub = 5;
Popusize=10;

% Crossover rate, number of childs, mutants, and mutation rate
cr=0.7;
nch=2;
nm=round(0.3*Popusize);
mr=0.1;

% Selection parameter
beta=8;

%% Randomly initialization of the particles and first cost
%% function evaluation
temporal.Position=[];
temporal.Fitness=[];
pob=repmat(temporal,Popusize,1);

for i=1:Popusize
    pob(i).Posicion=unifrnd(lb,ub,[1 dim]);
    pob(i).Fitness= fit (pob(i).Posicion);
end

%% Sorting population
Costs = [pob.Fitness];
[Costs, SortOrder] = sort(Costs);
pob=pob(SortOrder);

%% Storage best and worst solution
xbest=pob(1);
xworst = pob(end).Fitness;

%% Main iterative process
iter=100;
for it=1:iter

    %% Compute the probability of the selection method by the
roulette approach
    P=exp(-beta*Costs/xworst);
    P=P/sum(P);

    popc=repmat(temporal,nch/2,2);
        for k-1:nch/2
        r=rand;
        c=cumsum(P);
        i1=find(r<=c,1,'first');
```

```
        r=rand;
        c=cumsum(P);
        i2=find(r<=c,1,'first');

        i1=randi([1 Popusize]);
        i2=randi([1 Popusize]);

        p1=pob(i1);
        p2=pob(i2);

        %% Crossover procedure
        x1 = p1.Posicion;
        x2 = p2.Posicion;
        alpha=unifrnd(-cr,1+cr,size(x1));

        popc(k,1).Posicion=alpha.*x1+(1-alpha).*x2;
        popc(k,2).Posicion=alpha.*x2+(1-alpha).*x1;

        popc(k,1).Posicion=max(popc(k,1).Posicion,lb);
        popc(k,1).Posicion=min(popc(k,1).Posicion,ub);

        popc(k,2).Posicion=max(popc(k,2).Posicion,lb);
        popc(k,2).Posicion=min(popc(k,2).Posicion,ub);

        % Fitness function evaluation of new solutions
        vector = popc(k,1).Posicion;
        popc(k,1).Fitness=fit (vector);
        vector = popc(k,2).Posicion;
        popc(k,2).Fitness=fit (vector);
    end
    popc=popc(:);

    %% Mutation approach
    popm=repmat(temporal,nm,1);
    for k=1:nm

        i=randi([1 Popusize]);
        p=pob(i);
        x = p.Posicion;
        dim=numel(x);

        nmu=ceil(mr*dim);

        j=randsample(dim,nmu);

        sigma=0.1*(ub-lb);
```

```
        popm(k).Posicion=x;
        popm(k).Posicion(j)=x(j)+sigma*randn(size(j))';

        popm(k).Posicion=max( popm(k).Posicion,lb);
        popm(k).Posicion=min( popm(k).Posicion,ub);
        vector = popm(k).Posicion;
        popm(k).Fitness=fit (vector);
    end

    pob=[pob
         popc
         popm];

    %%Sort population
    Costs=[pob.Fitness];
    [Costs, SortOrder]=sort(Costs);
    pob = pob(SortOrder);


    pob=pob(1:Popusize);
    Costs=Costs(1:Popusize);

    %% Storage besto solution at iteration it
    xbest=pob(1);
    xworst = pob(end).Fitness;
    y = xbest.Fitness;
end
end
```

12.4 Linear Regression Employing an Artificial Genetic

A linear regression problem employing the GA is performed as a final example of regression. For this task, a set of data randomly generated is used to determine the better model that fits the training data to generalize new input data to the model. As was previously explained, linear regression consists of generating a line that minimizes the distance between all data and the linear model. Under such circumstances, the slope and the y-intercept of the line must be determined by the optimization approach (GA).

Algorithm 12.3 shows the complete optimization process for determining the best linear model that fits the random training model. As in previous examples, the code is explained using steps, which are just three simple steps. In Step 1, the training data is generated using uniformly distributed random numbers, which implies that every time the algorithm is performed different training data is generated.

In Step 2, the GA is called as a function previously defined in the Functions section of Algorithm 12.3. After the iterative process reaches its stop criterion, the GA returns the best element which is used to determine the best line for the training data (Step 3). Finally, Figure 12.5 shows the best result determined by the GA in order to a better understanding of the optimization process.

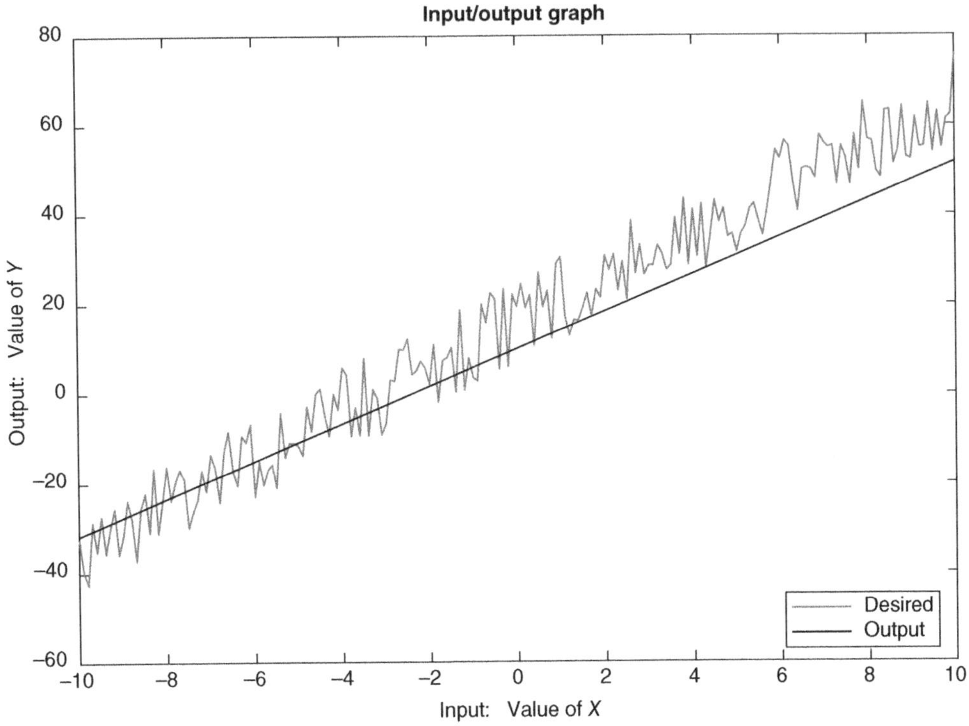

Figure 12.5 Graphical representation of the linear regression using the GA.

```
%Algorithm 12.3
%Clean data
% Step 1, Training Data
xt=-10:0.1:10;
yt=5 * xt + 6 + 20*rand(1,length(xt));

%Step 2, GA perform
[xbest, yout]= GA (xt, yt);

%Step 3, Visual representation of regression
% The best solution is used to determine the line that
% better fits the data
y=xbest.Posicion(1,1)*xt+xbest.Posicion(1,2);

% The line determined by GA is plotted regarding the data
% for visualization
plot(xt,yt);
hold on
```

```
plot(xt,y,'r');
legend('Desired','Output','Location','Best');
xlabel('Input ');
ylabel('Output ');
title('Input/Output Graph');


%% Functions

function [xbest, yout]= GA (xt, yt)
lb = 0;
ub = 10;
Popusize=100;
dim = 2;

% Crossover rate, number of childs, mutants, and mutation rate
cr=0.7;
nch=2;
nm=round(0.3*Popusize);
mr=0.1;

% Selection parameter
beta=8;

%% Stet 2, randomly initialization of the particles and first
%% cost function evaluation
temporal.Position=[];
temporal.Fitness=[];
pob=repmat(temporal,Popusize,1);

for i=1:Popusize
    pob(i).Posicion=unifrnd(lb,ub,[1 dim]);
    y = pob(i).Posicion(1,1) * xt + pob(i).Posicion(1,2);
    e = sum (y - yt);
    pob(i).Fitness= e;
end

%% Sorting population
Costs = [pob.Fitness];
[Costs, SortOrder] = sort(Costs);
pob=pob(SortOrder);

%% Storage best and worst solution
xbest=pob(end);
xworst = pob(1).Fitness;

%% Main iterative process
iter=3000;
```

```
for it=1:iter

    %% Compute the probability of the selection
%% method by the roulette approach
    P=exp(-beta*Costs/xworst);
    P=P/sum(P);

    popc=repmat(temporal,nch/2,2);
        for k=1:nch/2
        r=rand;
        c=cumsum(P);
        i1=find(r<=c,1,'first');

        r=rand;
        c=cumsum(P);
        i2=find(r<=c,1,'first');

        i1=randi([1 Popusize]);
        i2=randi([1 Popusize]);

        p1=pob(i1);
        p2=pob(i2);

        %% Crossover procedure
        x1 = p1.Posicion;
        x2 = p2.Posicion;
        alpha=unifrnd(-cr,1+cr,size(x1));

        popc(k,1).Posicion=alpha.*x1+(1-alpha).*x2;
        popc(k,2).Posicion=alpha.*x2+(1-alpha).*x1;

        popc(k,1).Posicion=max(popc(k,1).Posicion,lb);
        popc(k,1).Posicion=min(popc(k,1).Posicion,ub);

        popc(k,2).Posicion=max(popc(k,2).Posicion,lb);
        popc(k,2).Posicion=min(popc(k,2).Posicion,ub);

        % Fitness function evaluation of new solutions
        vector = popc(k,1).Posicion;
        y = vector(1) * xt + vector(2);
        e = sum (y - yt)^2;
        popc(k,1).Fitness=e;
        vector = popc(k,2).Posicion;
        y = vector(1) * xt + vector(2);
        e = sum (y - yt)^2;
        popc(k,2).Fitness=e;
    end
```

```
        popc=popc(:);

        %% Mutation approach
        popm=repmat(temporal,nm,1);
        for k=1:nm

            i=randi([1 Popusize]);
            p=pob(i);
            x = p.Posicion;
            dim=numel(x);

            nmu=ceil(mr*dim);

            j=randsample(dim,nmu);

            sigma=0.1*(ub-lb);

            popm(k).Posicion=x;
            popm(k).Posicion(j)=x(j)+sigma*randn(size(j))';

            popm(k).Posicion=max( popm(k).Posicion,lb);
            popm(k).Posicion=min( popm(k).Posicion,ub);
            vector = popm(k).Posicion;
            y = vector(1) * xt + vector(2);
            e = sum (y - yt).^2;
            popm(k).Fitness=e;
        end

        pob=[pob
             popc
             popm];

        %%Sort population
        Costs=[pob.Fitness];
        [Costs, SortOrder]=sort(Costs);
        pob = pob(SortOrder);


        pob=pob(1:Popusize);
        Costs=Costs(1:Popusize);

        %% Storage besto solution at iteration it
        xbest=pob(end);
        xworst = pob(1).Fitness;
        yout = xbest.Fitness;

    end
    end
```

References

De Jong, K.A. (1975). Analysis of the behavior of a class of genetic adaptive systems. http://deepblue.lib.umich.edu/handle/2027.42/4507.

Holland, J.H. (1992). Genetic algorithms – computer programs that "evolve" in ways that resemble natural selection can solve complex problems even their creators do not fully understand. *Scientific American* 267: 66–72.

Muhammad, S., Mousavi, H., Younes Mirinezhad, S et al. (2017). An evolutionary-based adaptive Nnuro-fuzzy expert system as a family counselor before marriage with the aim of divorce rate reduction. http://openarchive.nure.ua/handle/document/11745.

Index

Note: *Italicized* and **bold** page numbers refer to figures and tables, respectively.

Machine Learning and Metaheuristic Computation, First Edition.
Erik Cuevas, Jorge Galvez, Omar Avalos, and Fernando Wario.

n

Printed and bound by CPI Group (UK) Ltd, Croydon, CR0 4YY
17/09/2026
14964315-0005